A POWER STRONGER THAN ITSELF

A POWER STRONGER THAN ITSELF

GEORGE E. LEWIS

The AACM and American Experimental Music

The University of Chicago Press : : Chicago and London

The University of Chicago Press, Chicago 60637
The University of Chicago Press, Ltd., London
© 2008 by George E. Lewis
All rights reserved. Published 2008
Paperback edition 2009
Printed in the United States of America

18 17 16 15 14 13 12 11 10 09   2 3 4 5 6

ISBN-13: 978-0-226-47695-7   (cloth)
ISBN-13: 978-0-226-47696-4   (paper)
ISBN-10: 0-226-47695-2   (cloth)
ISBN-10: 0-226-47696-0   (paper)

Library of Congress Cataloging-in-Publication Data

Lewis, George, 1952–
    A power stronger than itself : the AACM and American experimental music /
George E. Lewis.
        p. cm.
    Includes bibliographical references (p.   ), discography (p.   ), and index.
    ISBN-13: 978-0-226-47695-7 (cloth : alk. paper)
    ISBN-10: 0-226-47695-2 (cloth : alk. paper)
    1. Association for the Advancement of Creative Musicians—History. 2. African
American jazz musicians—Illinois—Chicago. 3. Avant-garde (Music)—United States—
History—20th century. 4. Jazz—History and criticism. I. Title.
    ML3508.8.C5L48   2007
    781.6506′077311—dc22

                                                                2007044600

♾ The paper used in this publication meets the minimum requirements of the American
National Standard for Information Sciences—Permanence of Paper for Printed Library
Materials, ANSI Z39.48-1992.

contents

preface

THE AACM AND AMERICAN EXPERIMENTALISM

Since its founding on the virtually all-black South Side of Chicago in 1965, the African American musicians' collective known as the Association for the Advancement of Creative Musicians (AACM) has played an unusually prominent role in the development of American experimental music. Over more than forty years of work, the composite output of AACM members has explored a wide range of methodologies, processes, and media. AACM musicians developed new and influential ideas about timbre, sound, collectivity, extended technique and instrumentation, performance practice, intermedia, the relationship of improvisation to composition, form, scores, computer music technologies, invented acoustic instruments, installations, and kinetic sculptures.

In addition to these already ambitious achievements, the collective developed strategies for individual and collective self-production and promotion that both reframed the artist/business relationship and challenged racialized limitations on venues and infrastructure. In a 1973 article, two early AACM members, trumpeter John Shenoy Jackson and cofounder and pianist/composer Muhal Richard Abrams, asserted that "the AACM intends to show how the disadvantaged and the disenfranchised can come together and determine their own strategies for political and economic freedom, thereby determining their own destinies."[1] This optimistic declaration, based on notions of self-help as fundamental to racial uplift, cultural memory, and spiritual rebirth, was in accord with many other challenges to traditional notions of order and authority that emerged in the wake of the Black Power movement. The AACM is part of a long tradition of organizational efforts in which African American musicians took leadership roles, including the early-twentieth-century Clef Club, the short-lived Jazz Composers Guild, the Collective Black Artists, and the Los Angeles-based Union of God's Musicians and Artists Ascension, or Underground Musicians Association (UGMAA/UGMA). The AACM, however, became the most well known and influential of the post-1960 organizations, achieving lasting international significance as a crucial part of the history of world musical experimentalism.

The corporate-approved celluloid description of the AACM in the Ken Burns blockbuster film on jazz contrasts markedly with the situation in the real world, where the AACM's international impact has gone far beyond "white college students—in France."[2] Musicologist Ekkehard Jost called attention to both the economic and the aesthetic in summarizing the AACM's influence. "The significance and the international reputation of the AACM," Jost maintained, "resulted not only from their effectiveness in organizing, but also, above all, from their musical output, which made the designation AACM something like a guarantee of quality for a creative music of the first rank."[3]

While most studies that extensively reference the AACM appear to be confined to an examination of the group's influence within an entity putatively identified as the "world of jazz," the musical influence of the AACM has extended across borders of genre, race, geography, and musical practice, and must be confronted in any nonracialized account of experimental music. To the extent that "world of jazz" discourses cordon off musicians from interpenetration with other musical art worlds, they cannot account for either the breakdown of genre definitions or the mobility of practice and method that informs the present-day musical landscape. Moreover, accounts of the development of black musical forms most often draw upon the trope of the singular heroic figure, leaving out the dynamics of networks in articulating notions of cultural and aesthetic formation. While individual musicians are certainly discussed at length in this volume, the focus is on the music, ideas, and experiences emanating from the collective. On this view, the AACM provides a successful example of collective working-class self-help and self-determination; encouragement of difference in viewpoint, aesthetics, ideology, spirituality, and methodologies; and the promulgation of new cooperative, rather than competitive, relationships between artists.

In that regard, I am reminded of how, a few years ago, my former student Jason Stanyek (at this writing a professor of music at New York University) called my attention to a very vital aspect of U.S. slave communities that proved fundamental to my conception of the questions that this project could address. In an important revisionist work, anthropologists Sidney W. Mintz and Richard Price ask how, in the face of their radical ethnic, linguistic, and cultural diversity, "such heterogeneous aggregates of men and women could compose a social order for themselves, within the boundaries of maneuver defined by the masters' monopoly of power."[4] The philosopher of music Lydia Goehr poses a related question in expressing her "sense of wonder at how human practices come to be, succeed in being, and continue to be regulated by one set of ideals rather than another."[5] Speaking of the birth of African American culture, Mintz and Price seem to answer both Goehr's question and their own, in probing the ways in which slave communities promulgated "certain simple but significant *cooperative* efforts," that is, communitarian institution-building that was undertaken in order "to inform their condition with coherence, meaning, and some measure of autonomy."[6]

As if in illustration of this point, Famoudou Don Moye, the longtime percussionist and member of the AACM collective, the Art Ensemble of Chicago, has affirmed the necessity of acting in concert in order to move beyond simple strategies of resistance. "Along with defiance you have organization," Moye declared. "There have been moments of defiance throughout the history of the music, but the strength of the effort and the strength of the cooperation between the musicians and their unity of effort is what enables us to survive. Anytime the musicians are not strong in their unity, the control factor goes over to the *other* side."[7]

The anthropologist John Szwed, who has written extensively on jazz in recent years, maintains that

> The esthetics of jazz demand that a musician play with complete originality, with an assertion of his own musical individuality. . . . At the same time jazz requires that musicians be able to merge their unique voices in the totalizing, collective improvisations of polyphony and heterophony. The implications of this esthetic are profound and more than vaguely

threatening, for no political system has yet been devised with social principles which reward maximal individualism within the framework of spontaneous egalitarian interaction.[8]

In fact, the pursuit of individualism within an egalitarian frame has been central not only to the jazz moment, but also to African American music before and since that moment. For example, Samuel Floyd has spoken of the ring shout as featuring "individuality within the aggregate."[9] Indeed, it seems fitting that in the wake of the radical physical and even mental silencing of slavery (as distinct from, say, an aestheticized silence of four minutes or so), African Americans developed an array of musical practices that encouraged all to speak. As a socially constituted scene, the AACM embodied the trope of individuality within the aggregate, both at the level of music-making, and at the level of the political organization of the collective, thereby providing a potential symbol for the new, utopian kind of sociopolitical system that Szwed describes.

To the extent that AACM musicians challenged racialized hierarchies of aesthetics, method, place, infrastructure, and economics, the organization's work epitomizes the early questioning of borders by artists of color that is only beginning to be explored in serious scholarship on music. The late Harvard musicologist Eileen Southern, who single-handedly placed African American musical history on the academic map with her important general account, *The Music of Black Americans,* was invested in an instrumental view of historical research as fostering social change. As Southern saw it in a 1973 article in *Black World,* "Conventional histories of music and style-analysis texts generally ignored the Black man's contribution to music. . . . White-oriented histories, the white-oriented dictionaries, bibliographies . . . were amazingly silent about the activities of Black musicians."[10]

Echoing the critiques of countless jazz musicians, Southern goes on to assert that regarding African American music, "the quality of much of the writing is extremely poor, done by amateurs with little knowledge about the folkways and traditions of Black people." This was harsh criticism indeed—from which, moreover, black writers were not spared. "The output of a pitifully few Black writers has helped somewhat to fill the abyss," she wrote. "However, a half-dozen or so books hardly constitute a bibliography of respectable proportions."[11] Southern's call to action was certainly not aimed only at academics: "If we Black folk are serious about our commitment to the rediscovery and the redefining of our heritage in the fine arts, our scholars must take upon themselves the responsibility for developing an appropriate and exemplary literature. . . . Unless there is documentation, the names of Ulysses Kay, Duke Ellington, Isaac Hayes, Leontyne Price, Sarah Vaughan, B. B. King—to cite a few—may mean nothing to readers in the 21st century."[12]

As people who have read my article on post-1950 improvised and indeterminate musics know, I have a central interest in the issues that Southern identified—in particular, the failure of many journals and histories devoted to experimental music to publish articles in which African American experimentalists discuss their processes, ideas, and forms.[13] Even when the subject under discussion is improvisation, the discourse consistently (and sometimes militantly) erases African American artists and cultural tropes.[14] Thus, a major interest for me in writing this book was documenting, through both historical and ethnographic work, the fact that experimentalism in music can have many different histories. Following a far different path to experimental practice than most members of the white American avant-garde, the influence wielded by AACM musicians overflowed the banks of the jazz river, confronting whiteness-based new music histories with their self-imposed, race-based conundrums. At the same time, histories of post-1960 African American experimental music, which developed in the midst of one of the most turbulent and unstable periods in U.S. history, also tend to confound standard narratives, which may account for why so few of these stories have actually been told to date.[15]

The development of a notion of "experimental" and "American" that excludes the so-called bebop and free jazz movements, perhaps the most influential American experimentalist musics of the latter part of the twentieth century, is highly problematic, to say the least. The continuing development of this discursive phenomenon in the music-historical literature can be partly accounted for in terms of the general absence of discourses on issues of race and ethnicity in criticism on American experimentalism.

Thus, for some time, historians of experimentalism in music have stood at a crossroads, facing a stark choice: to grow up and recognize a multicultural, multiethnic base for experimentalism in music, with a variety of perspectives, histories, traditions, and methods, or to remain the chroniclers of an ethnically bound and ultimately limited tradition that appropriates freely, yet furtively, from other ethnic traditions, yet cannot recognize any histories as its own other than those based in whiteness. Thus, following Southern, I see my work on the AACM, as well as my work on experimental music more broadly, as an interventionist project, an activity aimed at encouraging the production of new histories of experimentalism in music.

acknowledgments

This book presents a close reading of a particular, highly diversified, and widely influential musical network/movement, rather than an overview of a received genre, or of the life and work of an individual. I want to express my thanks to the University of Chicago Press, and in particular, my editor, Douglas Mitchell, for seeing the need for this kind of detailed research on post-1965 African American musical experimentalism. Since the turn of the new century, the study of post-1965 improvised music has slowly been gathering critical mass in anglophone scholarship, as with the work of Fred Moten, and there is Eric Porter's analysis of the writings of African American experimental musicians such as Anthony Braxton, Leo Smith, and Marion Brown, Canadian literary theorist Ajay Heble's set of critical essays, *Landing on the Wrong Note,* and ethnomusicologist Mike Heffley's book on post-1965 European improvisation, *Northern Sun, Southern Moon: Europe's Reinvention of Jazz.*[1] Sociologist Herman Gray's work has focused on Steve Coleman and other younger-generation experimentalists, while ethnomusicologist Deborah Wong has extensively documented histories and practices in Asian American jazz and improvisation movements.[2]

Other recent and important studies are published in two notable anthologies: *Uptown Conversation: The New Jazz Studies,* edited by Robert G. O'Meally, Brent Hayes Edwards, and Farah Jasmine

Griffin; and Daniel Fischlin and Ajay Heble's *The Other Side of Nowhere*.[3] Heble's tireless efforts have led directly to the recent emergence of a peer-reviewed, bilingual, Web-based journal devoted to improvisation studies, *Critical Studies in Improvisation/Études Critiques en Improvisation,* which is providing a forum for new critical work by a new crop of younger scholars, some of whom are represented in these anthologies. Jason Robinson, Julie Dawn Smith, Michael Dessen, Dana Reason Myers, Stephen Lehman, Salim Washington, David Borgo, Daniel Widener, Tamar Barzel, Kevin McNeilly, Ellen Waterman, Vijay Iyer, and Jason Stanyek explore experimental improvisation by combining ethnographic and historical practice. To many of us, the work of Sherrie Tucker, while not directly concerned with experimental music, has nonetheless been important for its theorizing of the place of gender analysis as a necessary component of our work. As my UCSD colleague, the psychoacoustician Gerald Balzano, pointed out to me at the outset of my academic career, the teaching of improvisation as an academic discipline requires an exemplary source literature, and my aim is for this book to take its place among the growing body of new studies on improvisation.

Finally, my interest in anglophone work should not be taken as undermining my interest in work on improvised music by nonanglophone writers, whose work I draw upon extensively in this book. In a globalized environment, the lack of attention paid in the United States to the very well-developed nonanglophone writing on improvisation by people like Ekkehard Jost, Wolfram Knauer, Bert Noglik, Franco Bolelli, Hans Kumpf, Davide Sparti, Christian Broecking, Jean Jamin, Patrick Williams, Francisco Martinelli, Alexandre Pierrepont, and the late Peter Niklas Wilson (one of the few whose writings have been rendered in English) can be seen as a serious lacuna that impoverishes Stateside scholarship. Here, as in the anglophone case, some of the most intriguing texts have been written by practicing musicians, such as vibraphonist Christopher Dell's *Prinzip Improvisation.*

I'd also like to thank all the people who have been asking me about when this book would finally be finished and available. It has been very gratifying to receive the moral support and encouragement of so many people, including both colleagues and members of the concertgoing public. After my 2005 interactive computer performance with the drummer Louis Moholo-Moholo at Johannesburg's UNYAZI festival—the first computer music festival held on the African continent—I found that even in South Africa, a country I had never visited, people were anticipating the book's arrival, even to the point of creating rumors to the effect that it had been published and asking me where they could obtain it.

I should probably explain to those readers why it took so long to bring this book to fruition. For one thing, the work on the book coincided with a number of dramatic changes in my life. To summarize, I got married, changed jobs, and moved house, and in the meantime, my wife and I had a baby. All the while, I continued to pursue other academic writing, performances, composition, and teaching. Here, I thank my family—my father, George T. Lewis, my sister Cheryl, and her new nephew (my father's new grandson), Tadashi George Masaoka Lewis, whose amazing attention at eight months of age allowed us both to sit with each other quietly, each beavering away on his own project. My amazing wife, Miya Masaoka, was patient enough to let it all happen in the midst of her work as a sound artist and composer.

Not all of the interviews found their way into a book that could easily have been (and at the midpoint of the work, really was) three times as long as the present version. To incorporate all of the many observations from the ninety-plus people I did interview was a practical impossibility, and I regret not being able to use all the insights I gained from that work. For similar reasons, including a detailed discography was beyond the scope of this book. In the interests of partial redress of this absence, I have included an appendix in which more recent recordings by AACM artists are listed. A full discography, of course, would be a book in itself, and I am hoping that some enterprising person takes on that task. A final regret concerns the lack of detailed musical analyses in this volume. Because of the scope of the book, however, focusing on particular musical approaches ran the risk of inappropriately exemplifying the work of particular individuals as emblematic of the AACM as a whole. Perhaps there are other milieus in which I (or others) can pursue the analytic project. Overall, there is certainly much more work to be done on the AACM, and my hope is that this published research can help future scholars to go further.

A project of this magnitude cannot be realized without the support of an entire community, of whom only a few could ever be acknowledged in a limited space. I apologize for my fallibilities and poor recollection in possibly not acknowledging each and every one of the many people who helped this project along. I am indebted to the Academic Senate of the University of California, San Diego, including the Critical Studies / Experimental Practices area of the Department of Music, under whose auspices I began the research for the book, and to Columbia University, where the work was completed. The support of my colleagues in both institutions, as well as the resources of the Edwin H. Case Chair in American Music at Columbia, was critical in allowing me to complete the project.

I'd like to thank Wolfram Knauer, Arndt Weidler, and the Jazz-Institut Darmstadt for their tremendous support in allowing me to create an extensive photocopy library of contemporaneous reviews from German and French journals; Mary Lui, for access to the Larayne Black Archive at the Chicago Historical Society; and Deborah Gillaspie, the curator of the Chicago Jazz Archive at the University of Chicago, for access to the Jamil B. Figi Collection. Special thanks are also due to Columbia's Jazz Study Group at the Center for Jazz Studies, to whom many of these ideas were exposed as they crystallized, and particularly to Farah Jasmine Griffin, Robert O'Meally, and Brent Hayes Edwards for supporting my efforts; and to Mark Burford, then editor of *Current Musicology,* and Quincy Troupe, then editor of *Black Renaissance Noire,* who published early versions of some chapters. I thank the Center for Black Music Research for their ongoing support of my efforts, as well as the scholars associated with the École des Hautes Études en Sciences Sociales (EHESS) in Paris—in particular, Patrick Williams, Jean Jamin, and their many fine students, such as Alexandre Pierrepont, whose set of AACM interviews in the journal *Improjazz* constitutes an important source for future work.

I completed the initial transcriptions and overall structure of the project at a residency at the Civitella Ranieri Foundation in Umbria, Italy, and I am grateful to the foundation, and to Chinary Ung for placing me in touch with them. The University of California Humanities Research Institute, and its director, David Theo Goldberg, provided important research support during my 2002 residency there, and the members of the residency were invaluable in allowing me to bounce ideas off them: Renee Coulombe, Susan Leigh Foster, Anthea Kraut, Jason Stanyek, Eric Porter, Simon Penny, Georgina Born, Adriene Jenik, and Antoinette LaFarge. I owe immeasurable debts to three people whose early encouragement and support were crucial in forging my career as a scholar: my former colleagues, Jann Pasler of UCSD's program in Critical Studies/Experimental Practices, and Peter Gena, chair of the Time Arts Program at the School of the Art Institute of Chicago; and Samuel Floyd, founder of the Center for Black Music Research.

Substantial portions of two earlier articles of mine appear in this book. Text from my "Experimental Music in Black and White: The AACM in New York, 1970–1985," from *Current Musicology* 71–73 (Spring 2001–Spring 2002), 100–157 was apportioned across chapters 4, 9, and 11; and chapter 7 is an expanded version of "The AACM in Paris," from *Black Renaissance Noire 5*, no. 3 (Spring/Summer 2004). I would like to thank those journals for allowing me to include that work here.

Thanks to John Litweiler and Bernard Gendron, who read early drafts of the manuscript and provided many important suggestions; to good friends Bonnie Wright and Lisle Ellis for crucial emotional support; to Maggi Payne, Neil Leonard, and Harumi Makino for various kinds of help and general insight; to Ted Panken, for making his archive of interviews available to me well before their appearance on the Web; and to Sharon Friedman Castlewitz, for her multiyear efforts in sending me clippings of virtually everything written about the AACM in the Chicago press, making me aware of the tremendous respect and overall cachet the collective's younger members have earned and maintained to the present day. Special thanks are due to Tracy McMullen, Robert Freeberg, and my North Park neighbor Dan Ashworth, who saved crucial materials from damage due to a sudden water problem in my San Diego home; and among my current Columbia graduate students, I'd like to thank in particular Benjamin Piekut and Rebecca Kim. Kim provided me with important perspectives and references on the history of John Cage in Chicago; Piekut pointed out relevant perspectives from research he performed on the letters of Henry Cowell at the New York Public Library, and shared references on African American perspectives on New York's downtown art and music scenes of the 1950s and 1960s. Among those who provided needed help with my French translations were Chadwick Jenkins, Jean-Jacques Avenel, and Julianna Vamos.

A number of musicians and scholars provided access to their personal archives, including George Lipsitz, Douglas Ewart, Reggie Nicholson, Joseph Jarman, Leo Smith, King Mock, John Stubblefield, Amina Claudine Myers, Famoudou Don Moye, J. D. Parran, Oliver Lake, and the late Evod Magek. In particular, the photographs of Nancy Carter-Hill, Robert Sengstacke, Terry Martin, Scott Pollard, and AACM bassist Leonard Jones, some of which appear in this volume, provided invaluable insight into the early activities of the organization. Ernest Dawkins and Mwata Bowden of the Chicago Chapter of the AACM were particularly instrumental in making the AACM archives available to me, and I thank the many musicians who opened their homes, donated their time to our interviews, and provided me with memorabilia, photographs, articles, scores, and other important reference materials. Others, such as Ewart, Iqua and Adegoke Colson, Leroy Jenkins, Nicole Mitchell, and Maia, read the manuscript carefully, correcting errors and adding ameliorations.

Special thanks are due to the staff of the University of Chicago Press, including senior editor Carol Fisher Saller, whose sharp eye and ear for language nudged the text toward greater readability; Tim McGovern for his excellent work with the images; and Rob Hunt, whose marketing acumen worked to ensure that the book would be known as far and wide as possible.

I was particularly grateful when, in September 2001, I was notified that I was to join my AACM colleague and friend Anthony Braxton as a MacArthur Fellow. At the same time, the truly extraordinary resources—half a million dollars over a five-year period (not to mention the moniker of "genius," which pleased my father and sister greatly) came with a set of implications for my creative life that I am still working out at this writing. Paradoxically, rather than speeding up the work, the fellowship slowed down the pace, as I felt empowered to dig more deeply into areas that I had previously thought were beyond the scope of the book. Those readers who would be quick to insist that in the case of jazz or jazz-related practices, many major innovations took place with nothing like the level of infrastructure I used to write this book, might want to ask themselves the question that so many musicians ask—namely, what those innovations might have looked like given additional support. Even if we lend particular credence to the old African American saying "We've done so much with so little, now we can do anything with nothing," at the very least, one wonders what, for example, Charlie Parker's orchestral music might have sounded like had he managed to live long enough to pursue his plans to study and collaborate with Edgard Varese:

> CP: Well, seriously speaking I mean I'm going to try to go to Europe to study. I had the pleasure to meet one Edgar Varese in New York City. He's a classical composer from Europe. He's a Frenchman, very nice fellow and he wants to teach me. In fact he wants to write for me because he thinks I'm more for . . . more or less on a serious basis you know, and if he takes me over . . . I mean after he's finished with me I might have the chance to go to the Academy of Musicalle [*sic*] out in Paris itself and study, you know. My prime interest still is learning to play music, you know.
>
> PD: Would you study playing or composition?
>
> CP: I would study both. I never want to lose my horn.
>
> PD: No, you never should. That would be a catastrophy [*sic*].
>
> CP: I don't want to do that. That wouldn't work.[4]

Where some might see self-denial in Parker's responses to the inter-viewer, I detect an antiessentialist project at work. Clearly, Parker and Varese are simply seeking to expand their musical horizons, challenging the preconceptions of U.S. society regarding the identity and possibilities of American music along the way. After all, if Charlie Parker was not an "American maverick" (in Michael Broyles's phrase),[5] the concept has no meaning beyond simplistic ethnic cheerleading. If Parker saw both compos-ing and improvising as part of his "prime interest in learning to play music," do we take him at his word, or do we scoff at his supposed delusions and/or pretensions, imposing a romantic discourse that, even posthumously, de-nies Bird both agency and mobility?

In the end, these were the kinds of issues that animated the creation of the AACM. As Muhal Richard Abrams told me in one of our many interviews, "Don't give me a name. I'm not taking it. I'm Muhal Richard Abrams, and I'm playing music."[6] In the end, I see this book as a tribute to the four founders of the AACM—Muhal Richard Abrams, Jodie Christian, Steve McCall, and Phil Cohran—for their extraordinary achievement. Mu-hal Richard Abrams, Peggy Abrams, and Richarda Abrams have been there for me throughout, and their familial support over the course of my life has been crucial. I thank Muhal for his support and that of the New York Chap-ter of the AACM throughout the project; for being the most critical reader that one could possibly imagine; for unstinting access to his materials, his ideas, and his amazing memory; and for daring to be "a man with an idea."

introduction

AN AACM BOOK:
ORIGINS, ANTECEDENTS, OBJECTIVES, METHODS

Around the fall of 1996, I had been promoted to full professor in the department of music at the University of California, San Diego. I was sitting in the office of my colleague, F. Richard Moore, who probably doesn't realize his role in the creation of this book. Dick had just finished his landmark book, *Elements of Computer Music*,[1] and was busy extending cmusic, his set of software tools for musical experimentation. Dick saw cmusic as an example of a research project blending creativity and science, and pointed out to me that this was the very sort of project that might not receive support outside of the academic environment, even if the underlying ideas were arguably fundamental to the field of music technology. That was an argument I understood, because as an itinerant artist, I had tried to write on planes and trains, in the manner that one imagined Duke Ellington doing during the writing of his memoir, *Music Is My Mistress*. Now, I began to wonder about the kinds of projects I could initiate that would best utilize the strengths of the academic infrastructure in ways that complemented or exceeded my already established career as an itinerant artist. I began to think seriously about writing a biography of Muhal Richard Abrams.

As it happened, that year, 1996, Wadada Leo Smith had invited Muhal for a residency and concert in his program in African American improvisational music at the California Institute of the Arts. Muhal had invited me to participate in the concert, and so I drove up to Valencia from San Diego with the intention of sounding him out about the project. We went on a long walking excursion in the desert warmth, ostensibly searching for an espresso bar, although Muhal doesn't drink coffee. When I broached my idea, he quickly shook his head—but then said that he would rather be part of a book project on the history of the AACM. That possibility had also crossed my mind, of course, and it seemed completely appropriate, since so many of our dreams as members of the collective had focused on creating a book about that history.

In 1981, Joseph Jarman and Leo Smith interviewed each other with a view toward constructing a general history of the AACM.[2] The project was never completed. In the end, realizing such a work requires considerable infrastructure, by which I mean a network of people who are willing to engage the work—read it, comment on it, publish it, distribute it, and provide the time and funds for the kinds of ethnographic and historical research that the life of an itinerant artist makes difficult, even given the amazing achievements of the early twentieth-century African American historians that the late Jacob Carruthers called "the old scrappers," including J. A. Rogers and John G. Jackson, among others.

I had already begun to realize that the AACM membership would never trust an outsider to construct its history. As AACM cofounder Jodie Christian told me in 1998, "Muhal said that it should be somebody in the AACM, and pretty soon, somebody will write a book; this was four or five years ago. One time I thought he would write one, but he ain't got time to write no book."[3] So Muhal and I began talking about what the book could be, and I came away from the project with a determination to begin writing. At the behest of Samuel Floyd, then the dynamic director of the Center for Black Music Research, I had just completed my first published article for *Black Music Research Journal,* and was ready to proceed with a new project. During a visit to the Midwest in December 1997, I began interviewing musicians, starting (naturally) with Muhal. It quickly became evident that our conversations would range far beyond the biographical orientation that one might expect. Naturally, Muhal was vitally concerned with how the organization would be represented in the narrative.

> If it's going to be a musicology thing, or a thing that includes the AACM and talks about all this other stuff, I'm not going to participate. I'll just cut right out right now. We've waited too long to put out a document. I don't want to be part of that. . . . I didn't spend all these years to be put in

a situation that didn't have nothing to do with what I did. This book gives an opportunity to do what the musicians say happened.[4]

It became clear, however, that a book that did justice to the work of the AACM would have to move beyond a project of vindication, and would have to include more than just the voices of musicians. My working method necessarily juxtaposed oral histories of AACM members with written accounts of the period, a process that combines the ethnographic with the archival. I performed more than ninety-two interviews with members and supporters, ranging anywhere from two to six hours in duration, and for the older members, two or three such interviews were sometimes necessary. These interviews provided me with important insights, reminded me of things I had forgotten, and destabilized comfortable assumptions I had made. In many, perhaps most, cases, the remembrances I recorded of Chicago, New York, Paris, and other geographical/historical locations were powerfully corroborative of the written histories of these same places and eras. As a complex, multigenre, intergenerational network of people, places, and musical and cultural references began to emerge in my notes, I saw a responsibility to be inclusive, rather than to concentrate on those AACM members with more prominent public profiles. Even so, certain members have achieved more notoriety than others, and I felt that this would naturally come out in the course of the work. In any event, I do regret not being able to interview everyone I would have liked to.

The worldwide impact of the AACM has been amply documented in many countries—in print, on recordings, and in popular and specialty magazines, academic treatises, and books. As a scholar, it would be irresponsible of me to simply ignore this level of paper trail, or to dismiss these additional narratives out of hand. Thus, the book features a very conscious effort to problematize the "creator vs. critic" binary that both inflects and infects critical work in jazz, while at the same time providing unique and personal insights that only orature can provide.

"I was glad that somebody did come on the scene that was in the AACM and knew some of our members and had a little idea about the group itself," Jodie Christian observed in our 1998 interview. "Being in the organization, you had a chance to see some things yourself. You could make those kinds of judgments from that period of time. You can do that because you were there. It wouldn't be something that you surmised, but something that actually happened, and when you say it, it's authentic." As a scholar, however, I want to handle the idea of "authenticity" with extreme care. In fact, I was not there when the AACM began, though I am always flattered by those of my forebears who, when memories fail, somehow place me at the scene. My construction of the AACM is but one of many possible versions, and my hope is that other scholars will take up aspects of the AACM's work for which a more detailed discussion eluded the scope of this already rather long book.

Truth be told, however, the "real" story, if there is one, will not be captured in a set of recordings or an archive of texts. Here, I take my cue from an unnamed AACM musician's answer to a query from writer Whitney Balliett about "the" AACM sound: "If you take all the sounds of all the A.A.C.M. musicians and put them together, that's the A.A.C.M. sound, but I don't think anyone's heard that yet."[5] Nonetheless, what I am hoping for is that a useful story might be realized out of the many voices heard in this book, the maelstrom of heteroglossia in which we nervously tread water.

Autobiography—factual, fictional, and virtually every variation thereof—has constituted a crucially important African American literary form, both in the scholarly literature, such as Charles Davis and Henry Louis Gates's classic work, *The Slave's Narrative,* and in popular works, from James Weldon Johnson's *Autobiography of an Ex-Colored Man* to the *Autobiography of Malcolm X,* Alex Haley's *Roots,* and the Delany Sisters' *Having Our Say.*[6] The insistence on autobiography, as Jon Michael Spencer maintains in his book on Harlem Renaissance composers, *The New Negroes and Their Music,* became a weapon in the battle over the historicity of the African diaspora, where issues of credit and vindication were of prime importance.[7] In the 1960s, both people of letters and people in the street were vitally invested in this struggle for history.

It should therefore be not surprising that the historiography of jazz is similarly dominated by autobiography, most often in the form of transcribed and published interviews, as well as the frequent "as told to" ghost-written efforts. For instance, as historian Burton Peretti has noted, the interviewers for the National Endowment for the Arts Oral History projects of the 1970s were largely drawn from the ranks of "veteran jazz writers." Certainly, historians owe a debt to these writers, who pursued their enthusiasms for their subjects in the face of considerable disapprobation concerning the utility of documenting black music. Nonetheless, for Peretti, "the interviewers tend not to ask the questions that would be of most interest to scholars. They are strong on straight biography, who played with whom, discographies—and anecdotes, anecdotes, and more anecdotes. They tend to avoid addressing issues of intellectual development, social context, racial conditions, or the subjects' views of culture, history and philosophy."[8]

The effect of these serious omissions is to decontextualize the music, to frame it as outside the purview of both general social history and the history of music. This experience indicated the need for viable alternatives to the journalistic paradigm that, according to Peretti, still dominates the historiographical process regarding black music. My musician colleagues had been looking for these alternatives for many years. In pianist Jodie Christian's experience, "There were a lot of hits and misses with people trying to figure out in their minds what this was about and what that was about. Even though they were interviewing people, they would come up with their own idea about what the AACM was about." On one view, this was certainly understandable; in my experience, the people who were trying to figure out what the AACM was about included, most crucially, AACM people themselves. Thus, my collegial interview/conversations seemed automatically to turn to the very issues that Peretti found lacking in many of the NEA interviews: intellectual development, issues of race, class, and gender, musical form and aesthetics, and the interpretation of history. I began to notice a distinct lack of funny stories and anecdotes, even from people such as the late Lester Bowie, whom we all knew to be given to pointedly ironic jocularity. I imagine that for some readers, these preoccupations could seem unnecessarily dour at times in comparison with other kinds of musicianly texts that rely in large measure on interviews.

Perhaps this serious mien was an inevitable artifact of an interview process that often felt like a kind of collaborative mode of writing history, after the fashion that James Clifford has proposed,[9] even if the adoption of this collaborative ethos seemed to develop spontaneously, rather than as a conscious and studied attempt to address the issues Clifford identified regarding the authority of the interviewer. People felt free to explicitly express their love for the AACM, an organization that in many cases had given them creative birth and nurturing. Interviews served as a form of generational reconnection for some of my subjects, who frequently asked about what had been happening over the years to the people with whom they had been so intensely involved, and about where the organization was headed now. In this way, the book became an autobiography indeed—the autobiography of a collective, a history of an organization that developed into an ongoing social and aesthetic movement. Perhaps at least part of that movement's dynamism was derived from the clarity with which its members realized that the project could not really be completed; its unfinished nature became its crucial strength.

Historical, autobiographical, and ethnographic processes necessarily cast the historian-ethnographer in the role of intermediary between the subject and the public. The construction of this role during the process of engaging the oral narrative is obviously of prime importance, since the process involves not only transcription, but also interpretation and editorial choices. To pretend that race and gender do not mediate these proceedings is needlessly naïve; at the same time, to claim special advantages based solely on these factors is equally untenable. Thus, a signal factor in the historicization of black music concerns the fact that in the vast majority of cases prior to the late 1960s, as Amiri Baraka pointed out in an important essay from 1963, "Jazz and the White Critic," those doing interviews with black jazz musicians were most often white, male, and of a different class background than the person being interviewed.[10]

In the 1970s, this began to change. For me, and for many musicians, the watershed work of this generation was the drummer Arthur Taylor's book of interviews with his musical colleagues, *Notes and Tones*.[11] Taylor's initially self-published book demonstrated forcefully that the questions that Burton Peretti felt were of most interest to scholars were also of great interest to the important musicians of the period, such as Betty Carter, Max Roach, Miles Davis, Ornette Coleman, and many others. While Peretti's critique of oral histories does not directly connect the failure of scholars to review these seemingly fairly obvious areas of interest to institutionalized systems of ethnic and class domination, articulated as a form of historical denial, to Taylor and to many of his subjects, this was precisely what was at stake. Thus, Taylor's book functioned as perhaps the sharpest musician-centered critique then available of the racialization of media access, which both for Taylor and his subjects, amounted to a form of censorship. In a self-conscious act of intervention, Taylor used his insider status as a canonically important drummer to allow his subjects wide latitude to critique the discourses and economic and social conditions surrounding their métier, including possible distinctions between being interviewed by white critics and by black colleagues.

Even as so much African American literature, from the slave narratives forward, favored the autobiographical in some way, it was becoming clear to me that what was needed was not only a compendium of personal reminiscences and observations, but also a framing of the AACM in dialogue with the history of music and the history of ideas. In fact, AACM members who published critical work in the 1970s and 1980s tended to take this approach. Leo Smith's writings, notably his 1973 *Notes (8 pieces) source a new world music: creative music,* and his 1974 "(M1) American Music,"[12] were closely followed by Anthony Braxton's massive three-volume *Tri-Axium Writings,* a work that, while clearly in dialogue with John Cage's 1961 manifesto *Silence,* Amiri Baraka's 1963 *Blues People,* and Karlheinz Stockhausen's 1963 *Texte zur Musik,* extends considerably beyond each of these texts, both in length and in range of inquiry. For me, the works of these AACM members constituted sources of inspiration and instruction for my own research, as did Derek Bailey's influential book, *Improvisation: Its Nature and Practice in Music.*[13]

With these texts as antecedents, I felt that my goals could be better accomplished by deploying methodologies associated with academic historical inquiry, rather than with journalistic models. Of course, this issue is connected with the writerly voice of the book. Early on, several good friends and colleagues were concerned that the book avoid "academese," or the arcane jargon that these well-meaning people associated with scholarly books. These associates felt that using more accessible language would produce a friendly and nonthreatening introduction to the AACM and its work that would appeal to a wide audience. The jazz writer Stanley Dance was evidently a devotee of this approach, judging from his critique of two jazz studies anthologies published in the 1990s by film scholar Krin Gabbard, *Representing Jazz* and *Jazz among the Discourses:*

> There is original thought here, but the reader is immediately confronted by the language academics apparently use to communicate with one another. Sometimes it reads like a translation from the German, at others that they are merely trying to impress or indulging in a verbal cutting contest. Here are a few of the words you should be prepared to encounter: hermeneutics, commodified, contextualizing, conceptualize, hyperanimacy, taxonomic, metacritical, rhizome, perspectivizing, nomadology, indexical, polysemy, auratic, reification, metonymic, synecdoche, biodegradability, interstitial, valorize, diegetic, allegoresis, grammatology, oracy, centripetality, and esemplastic.[14]

Dance felt that these kinds of words "obviously impose considerable restraint on the transfer of knowledge."[15] Girding against what he saw (correctly) as an attack on his métier, the writer grumbled that "the academics tend to be critical and rather patronizing about the accepted journalistic standards of jazz writing, which, to judge from their back notes, they have investigated haphazardly." Finally, Dance ventured that instead of drawing from writers such as Gunther Schuller, "Gabbard's people seem more attached to Theodor Adorno and Roland Barthes, of whom the average unscholarly jazz fan has probably never heard." For me, however, the interdisciplinary approaches to black music and improvisation in the Gabbard texts—the work of Nathaniel Mackey, Robert Walser, Lorenzo Turner, John Corbett, and Scott DeVeaux, among others (as well as the references to Adorno and Barthes) were inspiring, announcing a new generation of writers on improvised music who were, first, declining to conflate oversimplification with accessibility; second, asserting common cause with intellectuals in other fields concerning the ways in which music could announce social and cultural change; and finally, seeking liberation from the Sisyphean repetition of ersatz populist prolegomena that seemed endemic to the field.

Another important book that came out around this time was Ronald Radano's *New Musical Figurations,* an account of the career of Anthony Braxton that included a chapter on the AACM that was much closer to my own experience than anything I had read before, and which introduced a new character to the heretofore white-coded historiography of American experimentalism: the "black experimentalist."[16] These texts helped me to realize that in looking for ways to theorize the music I had been trying for so many years to compose, improvise, and perform, I needed to involve myself with the tools, methods, and discourses that had been developed in a range of fields of inquiry. Doing so would not only allow readers less invested in music but familiar with those discourses and debates to find commonalities with the histories surrounding new music, but could also provide musically oriented readers unfamiliar with those discourses with an opportunity to engage them on familiar ground. As I began to publish, I discovered a rapidly developing, questing new literature, a group of wonderful new colleagues, an exciting crop of graduate students, and an international reading public, including many musicians, who were eager for a new kind of writing about music that did not patronize the reader or assume his or her ignorance of the matters under review. Perhaps most gratifying of all, in these new texts, complex ideas were worked out at sufficient length and in detail in a manner that seemed compatible with my experience as an artist.

Thus, as I told an interviewer/friend in 2002 regarding the progress of this book, "I've made some concessions to narrativity. Someone else can write the Cliffs Notes later." Indeed, in the nine years since I began this project, a new generation of progressive musicians has come out of Chicago, whom I can mention only in passing, such as cellist Tomeka Reid, guitarist Jeff Parker, trombonist Steve Berry, and rapper Khari B; trumpeters Robert Griffin and Corey Wilkes; singers Dee Alexander and Taalib'Din Ziyad; drummers Chad Taylor, Mike Reed, and Vincent Davis; saxophonists Matana Roberts, Aaron Getsug, and David Boykin; bassists Darius Savage, Josh Abrams, Cecile Savage, and Harrison Bankhead; and many others. Perhaps one or more of those people will create a sequel, after one fashion or another. For now, one of the aims of this book is to help those younger artists in dealing with the richness of the legacy that they carry, as well as in understanding what has been achieved, what was shown to be possible, and what remains to be realized.

The stakes are quite high in this endeavor, as I realized when a friend alerted me to a letter in the British magazine *Wire* from the African American experimental musician Morgan Craft, living in Italy at this writing. I found his remarks both poignant and terribly telling:

> So here we are in the year 2005 and I actually agree to sit down and write about being black, American and experimental in music. The genesis springs from looking at a magazine devoted to challenging, progressive musics from around the world, and seeing their top 50 list for last year (*The Wire* 251) and the only black Americans were rappers (three) and old jazz era men (one living, one dead). So I bring up this observation about the lack of a black American presence on the avant garde scene under the age of 50 just to see if maybe I'm not paying attention. I'm constantly fed this steady stream of future thinking folks from Germany, Japan, UK, Norway, etc, but when it comes to America all I hear about is the genius that is free folk or if it's black it must be hiphop, jazz, or long dead. How many more articles on Albert Ayler do we really need?[17]

In fact, black artists on both sides of the age-fifty divide shared Craft's dilemma, and the analysis of this issue is central to this book. Literary critic Fred Moten has expressed this issue so well and so succinctly that I want to preview his remarks here before redeploying them in another chapter:

> The idea of a black avant-garde exists, as it were, oxymoronically—as if black, on the one hand, and avant-garde, on the other hand, each depends

for its coherence on the exclusion of the other. Now this is probably an overstatement of the case. Yet it's all but justified by a vast interdisciplinary text representative not only of a problematically positivist conclusion that the avant-garde has been exclusively Euro-American, but of a deeper, perhaps unconscious, formulation of the avant-garde as necessarily not black.[18]

Part of my task in this book, as I see it, is to bring to the surface the strategies that have been developed to discursively disconnect African American artists from any notion of experimentalism or the avant-garde. This effort, as Craft seems to have noticed, has now moved into the international arena. If Craft—and Ayler, for that matter—exist simply as oxymorons in an international consensus based on the presumption of pan-European intellectual dominance (a dynamic extending beyond the individual phenotypical to the collective institutional), the histories and analyses that I recount here are meant to shepherd young African American artists such as Craft through the convolutions and contortions that were needed to construct this ethnically cleansed discourse; to encourage younger African American artists to see themselves as being able to claim multiple histories of experimentalism despite the histories of erasure, both willful and unwitting; and to reassure young black artists that if you find yourself written out of history, you can feel free to write yourself back in, to provide an antidote to the nervous pan-European fictionalizations that populate so much scholarship on new music.

The set of issues Craft identifies was also rather well symbolized in a lecture I attended by a scholar who insisted that if academics hoped to have any real effect on the culture, the only music worth studying and writing about was music that "everybody" listened to. As an example, this well-known speaker referred to an even better-known rapper who, despite his misogynistic lyrics, was someone who needed to be "dialogued" with so that scholars could reach young African Americans in particular with more "enlightened" ideas. I was struck by the superficiality of this understanding of the many ways in which music exercises cultural impact. First of all, in my experience, young African Americans are generally particularly pleased to discover the depth and breadth of the cultural artifacts created by their forebears. I write these words directly to those young people who, along with those ancestors, are participating in the development of a most influential panoply of expressive voices, not all of which will be heard by majoritarian culture. Nonetheless, it should be pointed out that much of the most influential music of the twentieth century—music that will probably never appear on any major U.S. television network—was nonetheless being avidly attended to by the heroes of rock, the early rappers, and techno's originators—or was it purely coincidental that so many early Mothers of Invention fans absorbed Edgard Varese's manifesto, strategically placed on the back of the albums: "The present-day composer refuses to die!"

On that view, it should come as no surprise that the impact of music on culture cannot be meaningfully investigated simply by reviewing Sound-scan figures or tuning in to *Dancing with the Stars*. Moreover, advocating the neglect of "unpopular" sonic constituencies in favor of yet another safe valorization of corporate-approved cultural production—this time disguised as "critique" or "dialogue"—seemed to revoke local musical agency, even as the term "local" moves beyond its original, geographically centralized meaning toward a technologically mediated articulation of diaspora. As scholars, we ignore at our peril the networks that carry the flows of new musical ideas, since it's so easy to miss nascent musical phenomena while they are still growing—in other words, the trajectory of hip-hop culture itself, not to mention its heir apparent, reggaeton, a phenomenon that like its predecessor from the Bronx, flows across borders of class, race, geography, and language.

This is not a version of the standard, hopeless rejoinder to those who point out the obvious lack of mass audience for some kinds of new music—that "one day," this music will be vindicated by ending up in everyone's ear. Rather, I wish to point out that naturalizing this kind of vindicationism as a goal may be misdirected. African American culture has produced a vast array of musical practices, which have been taken up to varying degrees by a diverse array of constituencies. Some of these practices, however, remained indigestible to powerful players such as modern media corporations, whose products, in economist Jacques Attali's 1977 formulation, were recursively reinscribed through a powerful "economy of repetition" that drowned out alternative voices. For Attali, "Free jazz created *locally* the conditions for a different model of musical production, a new music. But since this noise was not inscribed on the same level as the messages circulating in the network of repetition, it could not make itself heard."[19]

This observation seems to evoke a special need for vigilance on the part of music scholars. As Attali wrote, "Conceptualizing the coming order on the basis of the designation of the fundamental noise should be the central work of today's researchers. Of the only worthwhile researchers: undisciplined ones. The ones who refuse to answer new questions using only pre-given tools."[20] Thus, if we wish to avoid the appearance of positioning not only the musical production of entire cultures, but also our own research, as wholly owned subsidiaries of corporate megamedia, we will be obliged to tune our discourses to the resonant frequencies of insurgent musical forms around the world, to make sure that we can hear Attali's "new noise."

chapter summaries

This study of the AACM is intended to illustrate some of the strategies black musicians used in negotiating the complex, diverse, and unstable environment of contemporary musical experimentalism. The book documents both the ongoing relevance of 1960s changes in power relations, and the effort to erase the importance of those changes via corporate-backed canon formation efforts that often seem deliberately distanced from notions of musical value and influence collectively developed by communities of artists. This book is not only a personal product, but also the result of consultations with a diverse, internationally articulated community of artists, listeners and viewers, supporters, critics, and even detractors. It is a reconstructive project, performed to help me recover my roots, uncover retentions, and discover my own musical foreparents.

I do not pretend to speak for the AACM, and this book does not represent the "official AACM point of view." I try to let the members' own experiences and words tell the story, but at the same time, affirming my own interpretive function is the only truthful standpoint I can assume. In the course of my research, I needed to keep in mind that this is the documentation of a community of which I am a member, and thus, even while maintaining a critical orientation, the most important responsibility of researchers to the communities they document is to "do no harm." In that light, I cannot recuse myself from the sense that the book's primary constituency is the AACM membership itself. Hearing the stories of the first-generation AACM musicians with whom I had worked for so many years, I became even more admiring of their perspicacity, their resourcefulness, their perseverance in the face of adversity, and above all, their sheer optimism. As an ethnographer and historian, I write in the hope that this work will help the AACM and the communities it has touched to realize just what they have accomplished, as well as all that they might accomplish in the future.

Chapter 1: Foundations and Prehistory

It is striking to encounter the differences in background, upbringing, experiences, and social and economic networks between the working-class histories that informed black experimentalism and the white, middle- and upper-class sensibilities, expectations—and frankly, entitlements—that conditioned the rise to prominence of its white counterpart. As multireed performer Joseph Jarman, an AACM original member, told me in 1998, "All of these people that we are talking about came from very, very struggling environments. Every one of them started out at the bottom—maybe not the flat bottom, but pretty close. But there was no class thing at all, I'm sorry. We don't have any upper class."[1]

This chapter takes the Great Migration as its primary informing trope. The first-generation AACM founders were all children of the first wave of migrants to venture north. Here, literary theorist Farah Jasmine Griffin's analyses of texts around the migration constituted an important influence on my own reflections on the first-generation AACM musicians.[2] Like many migrants' recollections, the stories of the South told by the early AACM founders tended to coalesce around the theme of loss: in particular, the loss of land, and the fall from a state of independence that such losses produced. Another Southern theme concerned the social and physical violence to which these communities were constantly subjected; usually, some watershed threat obliged the former Southerners to become refugees. Following Griffin, I observe that the migrants' twin assertions of mobility and agency set the stage for how these musicians looked at artistic practice later in their lives. Following the trajectory of these families into the urban world of Chicago, sociological data on the economic state of the black community dovetails with personal narrative as I try to give a sense of how these young musicians grew up during the Depression years—not only their musical backgrounds, but their interests in sports, art, and literature; their educational and religious backgrounds, which varied widely; their lives at home, and their relationships with their parents—in particular, the black mothers who supported their early musical educations through social clubs and second jobs.

Despite growing up in the presence of legendary high-school band directors, the musical beginnings of many of the early AACM founders drew most crucially upon a tradition of autodidacticism that dominated jazz performance learning until the 1960s and 1970s, when the rise of secondary and postsecondary jazz education began, all but overwhelming the earlier pedagogical model by the early twenty-first century. I try to show how this ostensibly individualized autodidact practice of jazz learning was in most cases self-consciously collective, and moreover, hardly as socially Darwinist as some rather famous observers, including Ralph Ellison, have suggested. Here, I connect Scott DeVeaux's account of the economic advantages of jazz standardization with the accounts I collected of black Chicago's bebop "main scene" of the 1950s, a poorly documented scene for which the usual New York–centric historical tropes provide at best a rather too Procrustean fit. In later chapters, I try to trace how and why this autodidactic impulse gradually became institutionalized by this generation of Chicago musicians, as they moved to establish a new, critical practice of postjazz collective education as an alternative to the evident inadequacies of the education they had been receiving. I follow this earliest generation to the point where they are just beginning to explore their art, either through touring with bands, as most did, or through intense personal exploration, like saxophonist Fred Anderson, who is not known to have toured with any bands other than his own.

Chapter 2: New Music, New York

This chapter draws upon the work of historian Daniel Belgrad, whose notion of an "aesthetic of spontaneity" in the 1950s is useful in theorizing the explorations of chance, choice, and mobility that were taking place in both American musical production and the new European music of the time. The chapter takes pains to critically examine several rather starkly divergent accounts of the Greenwich Village art scene of the late 1950s, a precursor of the multimodal New York art scene into which the AACM would later emerge. Here, I place pressure on those histories that seem to arbitrarily disconnect transgressive art practices pursued by African Americans from the notion of the historical avant-garde.[3] Amplifying the observations of Fred Moten, I argue that this dominant, largely unquestioned narrative in performance studies tends to naturalize what is in fact a form of pan-Euroethnic propaganda.

This expanded context is required for two reasons: first, to establish a framework for later chapters that position the work of AACM musicians in the late 1970s as exposing major inconsistencies in this internationally promulgated story; and second, to encourage future historians of this crucial period in American musical history to pay more serious attention to the dynamics of race and class than has been the case to date. Near the end of the chapter, I return to Chicago, drawing upon the narrative of local writer J. B. Figi to point out that a historiography of the period dominated by New York–centered portrayals of integrated subcultures cannot account for the development of an experimentalism that, like the AACM (and Sun Ra), emerged largely in the context of hypersegregation. At the very least, a second model of the emergence of new music is strongly suggested here.

Chapter 3: The Development of the Experimental Band

This chapter follows the progress of the young Richard Abrams, whose rapid development as a composer and improvisor at this time included encounters with the ideas of Joseph Schillinger on the one hand, and the tutelage of bandleaders King Fleming and Will Jackson on the other. By the 1960s, autodidact practices of the kind Abrams, trumpeter Philip Cohran, and many others were following were important not only to learning music, but also to emerging explorations of alternative lifestyles, diet, and histories. These explorations became a form of resistance to dominant narratives that were felt to be complicit in reducing rather than expanding the health of the black community.

I introduce a younger generation of musicians, including Joseph Jarman and saxophonists Roscoe Mitchell and Henry Threadgill, as a prelude to the account of the origins and practices of the Experimental Band, widely viewed as the major precursor of the AACM itself. At the same time, I also critique accounts of the origins of AACM musical practices (including those of some musicians) that assume, often without close listening or historical analysis, an overly simplified notion of an evolutionary relationship with the work of Sun Ra. I imagine that for some Sun Ra partisans in particular, the conclusions I come to in this chapter may seem difficult, but I am hoping that paying closer attention to timelines and musical examples will help in establishing a firmer basis for those zones of influence and confluence that do exist; for disestablishing assumptions for which the evidence has proven shaky, tendentious, or really nonexistent; and for reminding readers of the many areas of divergence, along the lines of method, aesthetics, and artistic and political goals and strategies, that existed between the two musical organizations.

Chapter 4: Founding the Collective

The centerpiece of this crucial chapter is drawn from audio recordings of the very first AACM meetings, which were held in May 1965. The recordings do much to dampen speculation regarding the motivations of the musicians in forming the organization. For example, the taped evidence seriously undermines the idea/rumor that the AACM was conceived by its founders and original members as a kind of alternative musicians' union. Nonetheless, communitarianism as a means to control one's resources is a major theme of this chapter, and I cite a number of twentieth-century attempts by African American artists to pursue this strategy, including the work of theater artist Bob Cole, the Clef Club, and musicians Gigi Gryce, Max Roach, and Charles Mingus; the UGMAA in Los Angeles; and the attempt by John Coltrane, Yusef Lateef, and the Nigerian drummer Babatunde Olatunji to create a performance space in Harlem in 1965.[4] The case of the Jazz Composers Guild is reviewed at some length, and I also review both the published critical opposition to these musician-led efforts to control the conditions of their work, and the internal debates and dislocations surrounding those efforts.

The chapter's account of the decline of South Side jazz clubs in the 1960s situates musical practice as a species of cultural and economic production which suffered as part of an overall descent into crisis, not only in Chicago's black community, but in black communities around the country—a fact of obviously crucial significance that cannot be gleaned from cursory scans of sales figures. Musicians of the period routinely compared this decline with the music's apparent recrudescence on the largely white North Side, as part of an overall drain of cultural resources from the black community, and I maintain that it was this consciousness, as well as the desire for work, that animated the formation of the AACM. On this view, the first concerts of the AACM were established not merely as an alternative to jazz clubs, but as a wholly new type of presentation of a new music that was not really well received in the few remaining clubs anyway.

The last, long section recounts the work of the four AACM founders—Richard Abrams, Philip Cohran, pianist Jodie Christian, and drummer Steve McCall[5]—in conceiving the idea of a musicians' organization, recruiting participants for the first meetings, and setting the agenda for the wide-ranging discussions that ensued. The taped discussions, which I present in narrative form, demonstrate the diversity of musical direction (and gender) exhibited in the first meetings. Moreover, there is every indication that the musicians were moving to organize themselves in a relatively formal way. Rather than a band, these musicians were realizing a cultural organization. I examine the role of race in the discussions, situating the meetings in a space analogous to that inhabited by other grassroots black organizations that were started during the early Black Power period, in which a younger generation of black activists were sharply critical of what they saw as the failure of biracial coalition politics to improve social and economic conditions for African Americans.

The meanings of the terms "creative music" and "creative musician" are discussed by the meeting participants at a level of detail that casts doubt upon accounts that portray these terms as eponymous for "jazz" and "jazz musician." Clearly, had they wished to do so, the founders and original members could easily have included "jazz" in the name of the collective. That they did not, as well as the fact that the word "jazz" rarely appears in hours and hours of meetings, leads to the conclusion that the AACM's nascent discursive strategy was not a simple renaming enterprise designed to preserve genre boundaries and practices. Taking the musicians' words and discussions at face value, I conclude that their strategies of self-naming and self-fashioning were performed as a means toward transforming not only their livelihoods, but also their very lives and musical selves. Being a "creative musician" in this sense is an act of perpetual becoming, an assertion of mobility that can take one anywhere at all, beyond the purview of genre or method.

I draw upon first-wave AACM trumpeter Leo Smith's short book from 1973, *Notes (8 pieces) source a new world music: creative music,*[6] in concluding that a major aspiration of the theory that "jazz" and "creative music" are synonyms is the reification of the very borders that the musicians were trying to erase through their revised discourse. This concretization also comes bundled with an attempt to discursively revoke the mobility of the musicians themselves. To shore up this concretion, an ad hominem–based essentialism is deployed in asserting that the creative musicians were "really" jazz musicians after all. That this framing was in serious question can be gleaned from an exchange in a later chapter in which Muhal Richard Abrams counters another member's use of the term "jazz" with the rejoinder, "We're not really jazz musicians." The usual rejoinder to this expression of self-determination draws heavily upon a vulgar version of the institutional theory of art—that is, whatever they may call themselves, these musicians were part of an economic and social art world of jazz—or, as Eddie Murphy's gruff barber character in the film *Coming to America* spat out in dismissing Muhammad Ali's declared change of name, "I'm gonna call him Clay. That's what his momma called him."

These "world-of-jazz" discourses frame the music and the culture as wholly autonomous, even in the face of massive historical evidence to the contrary. In contrast, in these early proto-AACM discussions, the sense of becoming and the intimations of transition and openness are particularly strong. Who is "really" a jazz musician at a time when so many artists in the world of white American experimentalism, for example, were able to describe themselves without opposition as "former" jazz musicians? The example highlights how what I whimsically call the "one-drop rule of jazz" is effectively applied only to black musicians; as later chapters show, musicians of other ethnicities have historically been free to migrate conceptually and artistically without suffering charges of rejecting their culture and history.

Chapter 5: First Fruits

This section, again drawn in largest measure from the meeting tapes, chronicles the growing pains and identity crises experienced by the new organization. I discuss the first attempts at self-governance, self-promotion, and self-production by itinerant musicians without access to major resources. As the membership expanded, drawing younger members who were distanced from the bebop practice that marked the experiences of most of the older early members, the focus of the collective's activities began increasingly to center around new musical forms. I trace the early debates in the AACM that led to a split over issues of aesthetics, populism versus elitism, canon promulgation and historical reference, and the overall relevance of experimental music to the black community.

The rest of the chapter is given over to accounts of musical method and practice, as described by the musicians themselves, and as chronicled in press accounts of intermedia-oriented events given by Jarman, Mitchell, and other AACM artists. I trace the growing response of local and national press to the music, culminating in the first commercially produced AACM recordings, as well as the first concerts at the University of Chicago, organized by a group of faculty and graduate students that included Douglas Mitchell, now my editor for this book. One important event was a collaborative performance between Fred Anderson, Joseph Jarman, and John Cage, in which Doug himself performed on drums.

Chapter 6: The AACM Takes Off

A centerpiece of this chapter concerns the role of the arts in the rise of black consciousness in Chicago, as two short-lived but well-remembered and highly influential community initiatives, the Organization of Black American Culture (OBAC) and Philip Cohran's Affro-Arts Theater, became major forces in the cultural and political awakening of the area. The AACM School, with its communitarian alternative and supplement to traditional music education, was also begun during this period. Using narratives produced during the period, I examine the impact of the politics of gender and sexuality in the black community on the perception of the AACM in particular. I also recount the ambivalence of black intellectuals regarding the vanguardist sounds emerging from black experimental music scenes, as a militant African American cultural nationalism conditioned the Black Arts Movement's search for authenticity. Here, I examine the roots of Amiri Baraka's mid-1960s analysis of the black middle class, both in his 1963 *Blues People* and his highly influential 1966 essay, "The Changing Same (R&B and New Black Music)" in sociologist E. Franklin Frazier's scathing 1957 portrait of the black middle class, *Black Bourgeoisie,*[7] an account that drew substantially upon "sociology of deviance" ideas that were highly influential during the 1950s.

Music histories have been loath to come to terms with the interaction between cultural nationalism and anticorporate notions of self-determination, except where these have been articulated by Europeans or European Americans. In that light, I also discuss bell hooks's observation that even while many black musicians adopted nationalist positions, many others resisted nationalist-inspired restrictions upon their work. In fact, some musicians adopted both positions simultaneously, a stance that was certainly not limited to African Americans. For example, a manifesto such as John Cage's *Silence,* with its articulation of a pan-European intellectual history that became naturalized as constitutive of an overall American musical identity, is as starkly culturally nationalist as anything published during the heyday of the Black Arts Movement.

The creation of the long-lived and still-controversial AACM-identified slogan, "Great Black Music," arose during this period. The term became part of the AACM's politically inflected approach to media analysis and intervention, which in turn was an artifact of an overall questioning of received wisdom and authority that African Americans, as well as other groups in U.S. society and abroad, were promulgating. At times, both musicians and audiences found themselves precariously situated atop the horns of a class-inflected populist-versus-elitist dilemma, grappling along the way with knotty issues of control and appropriation of a "cultural property," black music, that was simultaneously the most commodified and the most closely policed music in history.

Chapter 7: Americans in Paris

This chapter chronicles the encounter with the European music scene by the eight AACM members who first ventured across the Atlantic in 1969. Here, I also discuss the rise of the critically important first generation of European musicians who eschewed European jazz's former, self-confessed derivative nature in favor of a specifically pan-European musical identity. I identify the 1969 Baden-Baden Free Jazz Treffen [Meeting], at which the AACM and the new Europeans met, as emblematic of a form of identity politics articulated both through sound and via critical reception.[8]

The trip to Europe was the major catalyst in bringing the music and ideas of the AACM to worldwide prominence, and I describe the varied motivations of the members of the collective toward making the trek as partly influenced by the apparently distanced view that AACM musicians held toward the conceptions of free music then being promulgated in New York. Using sociologist Bennetta Jules-Rosette's work on black Paris, I contrast the ongoing impact of these musicians and their free jazz colleagues on French cultural history with their near-complete absence from U.S.-produced histories of black culture in France. A review of the media reception to these first AACM forays in Europe is complemented by the recollections of the musicians themselves in constructing my account of the AACM musicians' European experiences, and in particular, their Paris experiences. I explore French views on the relation of free jazz to the 1968 student upheavals in Europe, and on American black nationalism, including the fascination in the French jazz press with the ideas of Amiri Baraka, easily one of the most influential African American intellectuals of the time in Europe.[9]

I describe the uneasy encounter between the musicians' ideas of themselves as cosmopolitan border crossers and the demands upon them to accede to received notions of jazz and the naturalized role of the black musician, even as those notions were being challenged across the board at this time. To make sense of this seeming contradiction, it may be fruitful—in this situation as in so many others—to view "jazz" not as a set of musicologically codifiable (however vaguely so) characteristics such as "swing," but as a race-, gender-, and class-inflected social location within which sound and musical practice take on additional meanings. In this light, it becomes easier to understand the task undertaken by the AACM musicians (as well as artists such as Ornette Coleman) to articulate a mobility of practice that in relatively nonracialized circumstances would be seen as operating outside the frame of jazz. Clearly, for these black working-class musicians, sound and musical method were not enough to accomplish that feat; in fact, the socially determined frame of jazz definition continually transformed its topography to accommodate virtually any direction these and other black musicians might take.

Chapter 8: The AACM's Next Wave

The chapter is largely concerned with the situation in Chicago for the AACM collective during and after the Paris sojourn. Despite considerable instability in venues and governance during this time, the collective continued to hold regular meetings and concerts, and also took on several new and younger members whose backgrounds were far different than those of the oldest AACM generation. The interaction between the generations prepared the ground for expansion, renewal, and challenge, as the AACM entered its tenth year of existence in 1975. The backgrounds of these newer members, which I probe in some detail, provide personal perspectives on the social upheavals taking place in the United States, such as the civil rights movement, the many student protests and campus takeovers, and draft resistance around the U.S.–Vietnam War.

I describe the ways in which AACM members financially negotiated the contrast between the continued rise of the AACM's visibility in U.S. jazz journals, and its strong support in the Chicago press, with the relative paucity of work in Chicago itself. This local lack of work was eventually balanced by growing opportunities for performance in Europe and even, for some members, by "major label" support from the U.S. record industry, prompting a number of these musicians—most prominently, the former Parisian expatriates—to give up on Chicago almost entirely. A kind of AACM diaspora (as writer Francis Davis once put it) emerged, as musicians, seemingly influenced by the example of their Europe-based colleagues, tried living in the rural Midwest, on the West Coast, and the eastern seaboard, and New York City. The AACM members' music was growing and maturing at this time as well, and I touch upon the changes in compositional and improvisative method being articulated by some AACM composers during this important transitional period.

Benjamin Looker's book on the Black Artists Group, the historically important midwestern artists collective whose emergence was influenced by the AACM, was sufficiently thorough to preempt my own work on the group, so in the interests of bringing to publication a project that was already rather late, the section on BAG in this chapter has been reduced to a size that would nonetheless respect the historical contiguity that binds BAG to the AACM.[10] I would like to thank Oliver Lake, Hamiet Bluiett, Marty Ehrlich, James Jabbo Ware, Baikida Carroll, the late Emilio Cruz, and in particular, J. D. Parran, for making themselves, their photographs, and BAG documents available to me.

Chapter 9: The AACM in New York

One important aspect of my work has been to follow the example of the AACM musicians themselves in challenging the assumed centrality of New York City to every jazz narrative. In the place of this romantic ideal I have outlined a distributed, internationalist vision that recognizes the prominent place of both European and midwestern American metropoles in nurturing the AACM's development and mediating its later notoriety. At the same time, recounting the struggles and successes of the large group of AACM musicians who invaded New York City en masse in the mid-1970s—a phenomenon reminiscent of the Great Migration itself—allows me to extend the actor-network model of "jazz" that I pursue throughout the book.

In particular, I draw upon that model in showing that AACM musicians were recognized at the time as playing a critically important role in fostering the breakdown of traditional barriers separating jazz and classical music, or low and high musical cultures, in ways that moved far beyond the miscegenationist model of early Third Stream thinking. In this respect, AACM musicians updated and revised a model pursued by black classical composers, an important group of creative music-makers who, I maintain, have been all but ignored by the major black cultural critics and public intellectuals who have come to prominence since 1960.

I observe that AACM musicians working in New York pursued membership in a variety of music scenes, including New York's "downtown" sociomusical networks, which had rarely included African American musicians since the Greenwich Village split between black and white vanguardist intellectuals in the early 1960s that I discuss in chapter 2. Powerful social, cultural, and economic forces were arrayed in opposition to the mobility-oriented standpoint taken by those AACM musicians who opted for a multiple-network practice. I refer here not only to my research, but also to my experience as music curator of a major New York experimental art venue of the period. I note that the loft jazz of the 1970s, seemingly a re-crudescence of its 1960s counterpart,[11] was in essence similar in infrastructural focus and motivation to other experimental arts activity taking place in alternative spaces around New York, as artists banded together to present new work in noncommercial venues.

Finally, I confront at some length the seeming inability of much contemporaneous media reportage devoted to music (jazz and classical) to either account for or support this early border crossing by a largely black musical community. Tied to outdated, racialized musical categories, many music reviewers and their editors seemed nonplussed at first by the musicians' genre refusals, and this confusion gradually transformed itself into an open hostility that had little to do with the race of the reviewer.

Chapter 10: The New Regime in Chicago

Chapter 10 returns to a Chicago-based AACM scene that was both transformed and partially transfixed by the goings-on in New York. A major generational shift was coming to the organization, as younger musicians who had not gone to New York with those predominantly older members began to exercise important influence in Chicago. Most of this latest wave of AACM members came of age in the wake of the 1968 assassination of Martin Luther King, and the apparent abandonment of working-class black neighborhoods in Chicago to the ministrations of powerful street gangs, such as the Disciples and the Black P. Stone Nation. White-coded rock music was a fact of life for this generation, many of whom listened to it (and played it) in equal measure with blues, jazz, and R&B. Unlike the earlier generation of AACM musicians, most of this group attended college, and grew up in arguably somewhat more affluent circumstances (sometimes considerably so) than their older colleagues.

By this time, few first-wave AACM members still lived in Chicago. Many younger members of the collective had never worked with the older musicians, and in a number of cases, had not even met them. The reminiscences of those who joined the AACM in Chicago during this time often point to this development as symptomatic of a kind of leadership vacuum. Perhaps inevitably, tensions between the Chicago and New York groups developed, in which generational difference sometimes became mapped onto perceived or real differences in aesthetics and musical direction. I recount the attempts by New York and Chicago members to ameliorate what was rapidly becoming a serious geographic, experiential, and generational divide through "national conferences" and "anniversary concerts," where collective solutions were sought for the AACM's organizational issues as it expanded its geographical purview, and for issues related to work and infrastructural support for music-making.

I review how the mobility-oriented artistic stances of the AACM and similar organizations challenged cryptically race-based distribution policies that marked U.S. government and private funding for the arts. I also draw upon the work of my former student, ethnomusicologist Ellen Weller, in exploring the effect of U.S. government funding on the development of a nonprofit arts industry in which bureaucrats worked to remodel grassroots arts organizations in the image of the heavily corporatized, hierarchical forms of governance that they themselves deemed most workable. I then use this model to examine the particular case of the AACM.

Chapter 11: Into the Third Decade

The central thesis of chapter 11 concerns the role played by a group of enterprising, talented, and visionary women in transforming the AACM, challenging its view of itself at its very core. This group of mostly younger women grew up with the strictures and barriers to which black women who aspired to become artists and musicians were subject. This chapter, more than any other in the book, allows me to explore the intersection of gender, class, and race in depth, including the constructions of masculinity that some AACM musicians apparently took to be essentially constitutive of the collective's identity in the wake of the dynamics of black cultural nationalism in the United States.

This chapter also looks critically at the promulgation of powerful, corporate-backed canon formation initiatives in the jazz world of the 1980s. AACM musicians, to the extent that they bore membership in jazz-identified worlds, found themselves in the thick of the debates over tradition and innovation that marked this period. At the same time, as I note, the movement to promote a unitary jazz canon that excluded experimental music never gained sufficient traction in Chicago to overshadow what the city, along with much of the rest of the world beyond the borders of the United States and the limitations of its corporate media, felt was the AACM's creation of a homegrown movement of historical importance.

In fact, the Chicago mediascape began to treat the AACM—meaning not only its founders, but also its youngest exponents in Chicago—with a level of support sometimes bordering on reverence. In the meantime, the level of local black community support and respect for the AACM strongly contradicted the argument that the "new music," which by now was decades old, had no significant black audience. At the same time that the AACM's local profile was rising, however, the international profile of many of its youngest members was somewhat less prominent than that of the older members. The "new music" of the AACM of the 1990s was much different from its 1960s and 1970s counterpart, a fact remarked upon both domestically and by commentators in Europe.

Chapter 12 (Transition and Reflections), and Afterword

The final chapter was conceived as an opportunity for me to contribute personal reflections about some of the AACM members who have, as many of us delicately put it, made their transitions. The afterword is conceived as a combination of Bakhtinian heteroglossia, Gatesian signifying, and the venerable antebellum practice of collective improvisation known as the ring shout. This conclusion is constructed more or less as a virtual AACM meeting, where the words of my AACM colleagues, as told to me in interviews, comprise just one of the many discussions of issues around the organization's past, present, and future that continually arise whenever members of the collective come together.

1

FOUNDATIONS AND PREHISTORY

Coming North: From Great Migration to Great Depression

In terms of both personal histories and historical resonance, the roots of AACM discourses of mobility and atmosphere can be traced to the decades-long movement known as the Great Migration. From around 1915 to the early 1960s, working-class black migrants, hoping to better their condition in the classic fashion of the American Dream, streamed out of the Old Confederacy in one of the largest internal relocations in U.S. history. The oldest members of the AACM's first wave, including pianist and composer Richard Abrams, saxophonist Fred Anderson, pianist Jodie Christian, drummer Jerol Donavon, trumpeter Phil Cohran, drummer Steve McCall, and violinist Leroy Jenkins, were all born between 1927 and 1932, the children of migrants who settled in Chicago and St. Louis.

The migration narrative inevitably turns upon the question of loss—in particular, the loss of land. African Americans in the South were subjected to economic warfare, including land seizures and various forms of terrorism, whether state-sponsored, privatized, or formulated through private-public partnerships.[1] The practice of "whitecapping," whereby whites physically drove blacks from their land and confiscated it, compounded the difficulties blacks already faced in buying and owning land, ultimately contributing greatly to the urgency of plans to leave the South.[2] The fiercely independent Cohran family, whose history dates to the Revolutionary War, was living in an area near Oxford, Mississippi, dubbed "Coontown," where Philip Cohran was born in 1927. The family owned land and farm equipment, but as Cohran tells it,

> They had killed my grand-uncle Floyd, and Derry, the one that got all the property, told them that we have the land, and ain't nobody gonna get that. They took his money, he said, but you can't get the land because I got documents and we're holding this land. At that period of time black people did not issue ultimatums to white folks in Mississippi. So all of the Cohran name had a bad thing on it, so I'm sure that my mother was working all the time on getting me out of there before I got to my teens.[3]

Thus, when Cohran was about nine years old, his parents made their way to Missouri. His father got a job as a cook at restaurant in Troy, while the family lived with friends in St. Louis.

Jerol Donavon's family knew that the South could be a very dangerous place for black people who dared to display evidence of successful, independent entrepreneurship. The second of eleven children, Donavon was born in 1927 in a small Arkansas town founded by his grandfather, who had come from Memphis to buy land and farming equipment in an area close by Little Rock. The family built a general store, a sawmill, and a small farm with crops that included cotton, rice, and sorghum. One very late evening, whites with shotguns ambushed his father, grandfather, and uncles. Donavon's father was badly wounded, but survived.[4] The incident prompted Donavon's family, as with so many other black migrants, to abandon the area. Arriving in Chicago in the early 1930s, Donavon's family stayed at their grandfather's South Side home, a six-room apartment on 43rd Street and St. Lawrence Avenue, where one of Donavon's uncles was also living.

Leroy Jenkins's great-uncle Buck had come to Chicago under very different conditions from the fabled train ride of Louis Armstrong from New Orleans that has become the stuff of nostalgia. Like many migrants, Buck Jenkins lacked train fare, so one day in the 1920s he simply hopped a freight train from the little town of Prospect, Tennessee. After securing employment and housing, Uncle Buck earned enough money to send for Leroy's father Henry, who found steady work at the Spot, a tavern at 43rd Street and Cottage Grove Avenue on Chicago's South Side. Henry Jenkins, who, as it happens, became acquainted with Richard Abrams's father at the Spot, eventually married the boss's Mississippi-born niece, and in 1932, Leroy was born in Chicago's Cook County Hospital, the public hospital that was the birthplace of countless black Chicagoans.[5] The marriage ended in divorce, however, and Jenkins's mother moved to 45th and Champlain.

If migrants to Chicago were hoping to escape from segregation, their disappointment had to be profound, as the 1920s and 1930s saw the developing stages of Chicago's effective confinement of African Americans to designated areas on the city's South Side and West Side. The 1930 census revealed that two-thirds of all black Chicagoans lived in hypersegregated tracts that were at least 90 percent black.[6] By 1940, more than 330,000 black citizens were "packed solidly . . . on a narrow tongue of land, seven miles in length and one and one-half miles in width,"[7] from 22nd Street to the north to 67th Street at the southern end, and from Cottage Grove Avenue and Lake Michigan on the east to the Rock Island Railroad tracks around Wentworth Avenue on the west.[8] Cordoned off from "white" areas of the city by restrictive covenants, political machinations, and violence, large numbers of black newcomers from the South, almost regardless of income level, competed with earlier waves of migrants for a limited supply of available and affordable space.

As a result, this area, which an enterprising editor of a local black newspaper dubbed "Bronzeville,"[9] was far more diverse than most other Chicago communities in terms of demographic parameters other than race, such as social class, economic status, and occupation. As sociologists St. Clair Drake and Horace Cayton observed, "If you're trying to find a certain Negro in Chicago, stand on the corner of 47th and South Park long enough and you're bound to see him."[10] Clustered around this center of the "Black Belt" were its major commercial, financial, service, and religious institutions, such as the Hotel Grand, and Provident Hospital, founded by black physician Daniel Hale Williams, the first doctor to successfully perform open-heart surgery. Right at 47th and South Park was the Regal Theater, a major symbol of black entertainment in pre-1960s Chicago, where virtually anyone who was anyone in black popular music performed. Hard by the Regal were many other important centers for live music, such as the Savoy Ballroom, the Club De Lisa, the Sutherland Lounge, and literally hundreds of smaller, more intimate nightspots.

After a brief dalliance with the fast, exciting life on 47th Street, migrants to Chicago discovered that working-class black life in the North bore little resemblance to the Zion of economic freedom that they had envisioned. Jodie Christian's father was born in Little Rock, Arkansas, into a sharecropper's family. Realizing the futility of that life, Christian's grandfather sold his livestock and sent his family to Chicago, where Christian was born in 1932 on 44th Street and Prairie Avenue. As a young boy, Christian heard from his parents about how when people would come South, "they would have rings on, they looked good" as they exhorted others to join them in the North. But when families like Christian's finally arrived from the South, they found to their horror that "some people lived in basements, with rats and stuff. They couldn't believe that it was the same people. Because where they were living, at least they had their own house—they weren't crowded up in one room." Indeed, Depression-era Bronzeville's once-spacious apartments and houses were now being radically subdivided to gather in the burgeoning black population. Dwellings that had previously housed single families were converted to hold two or three times that number, and the dynamic of extended families often featured two or three generations living in minuscule apartments that the real estate industry euphemistically dubbed "kitchenettes."[11] The young Leroy Jenkins, along with his sister, his mother, his grandmother, two aunts, and the occasional boarder, all lived in the same three-bedroom apartment.[12]

Moreover, much of the housing stock available in black areas of the city lacked hot running water; often, there was only one toilet per floor.[13] The frequent absence of central heating was a major issue, given the city's long, bitterly cold winters. Instead of repairing decaying housing infrastructure or encouraging black outmigration, however, governmental authorities built enormous "projects" within the existing Black Belt to warehouse the black population. This massive "urban renewal" (later dubbed "Negro removal" by wags) effectively destroyed as many housing units as it replaced.[14] When the first of these projects, the Ida B. Wells Homes on East 39th Street, opened in 1941, over seventeen thousand applications were received for just sixteen hundred units.

Among the successful applicants was the future Willa McCall, who had come to Chicago as a toddler from North Carolina in 1916. Stephen McCall IV, the oldest of her three children, was born in the city in 1932. Beating the drum in a 1940s edition of Chicago's Bud Billiken Parade, the annual black youth event sponsored by the black newspaper of record, the *Chicago Defender*, young Stephen experienced a musical epiphany. As his mother tells it, "He saw this big drum in there and he just wanted to beat that drum, but somebody was going to have to help him, because he was a little guy with little skinny legs. He just got a chance to beat this drum. Oh, he was so happy. They gave him the desire of his heart, playing that drum on the Bud Billiken Parade."[15]

Richard Abrams's paternal grandparents brought the family to Chicago, where Abrams was born in 1930 as the second of nine children. A self-employed handyman, Abrams's father was born in Alabama, and found work maintaining and cleaning stores on the mostly white North Side. Abrams remembers his father as "well-educated, very smart, but . . . there's this phenomenon that happened because of racism to keep black people out of certain kinds of situations—so I guess he elected to say, well, I'll just make my own stuff,"[16] an assertion of self-determination that Abrams explicitly connects with the goals of the AACM. Abrams's mother, born in Memphis, worked at home as a housewife. Her militancy about excellence and independence through education made a strong impression on all of her children. She would take young Richard to the YMCA on 40th and Indiana, warning him to stay close by and behave himself while she took her weekly piano lesson.

Born in 1927,[17] Malachi Favors lived across the street from Jodie Christian; the bassist and future Thelonious Monk collaborator Wilbur Ware lived just around the corner. One Favors family dwelling, with two bedrooms, a dining room, and a living room, was home to eight children—plus a roomer. Each winter evening, Favors's mother heated irons in the fireplace, then wrapped them in towels and placed them under the children's blankets to keep them warm. In the morning, the family would dress themselves in front of the fire.[18] During the cold winters, the widespread use of kerosene lamps, coal stoves, and gas ovens for cooking and heating resulted in an epidemic of fires. Favors's childhood memories include stories about the nearly two hundred people (sixty of whom were children) who died in thousands of South Side fires between 1947 and 1953, an epidemic that the *Chicago Defender* called "another Chicago Fire, except that it has been on a three-month installment basis."[19] Some fires were deliberately set by landlords, often with fatal results, and in many cases, the surviving tenants simply moved back into the burned-out buildings. Among Favors's many vivid childhood memories of summer, the spectacle of dead rats in the street as roadkill stands out. Favors's memory here substantiates historical accounts of the lax approach taken by Chicago's city government to trash pickup in the black community, where pest infestations, culminating in sometimes-fatal rat attacks on children in kitchenettes, were endemic.[20]

Naturally, everyone was trying to bring in money. During World War II, the ubiquitous "victory gardens," established as support for the American troops abroad, also provided needed food for those at home. Donavon's father held down two or three jobs at once—carpentry work, cab driving, and later a stint as a Pullman porter, while Donavon did paper routes and set pins in bowling alleys to bring money home. In the Abrams family apartment, hot water for bathing and cooking had to be heated on a coal stove in the living room, which also provided heat in the winter. Abrams earned small change hauling coal from the basement, or carrying sizable cakes of ice for the icebox. Abrams's paternal grandfather was "what you call a junk man," selling the fruits of neighborhood foraging. Abrams and his brother would pull the cart around the neighborhood, eventually arriving at a junkyard on State Street, where the items would be sold.

Black people believed fervently in the American Dream and strove to realize the classic American paradox of pulling themselves up by their bootstraps. However, the Depression hit black Chicagoans especially hard, and almost half of Chicago's 1930s black population was receiving some form of public relief.[21] After his parents' divorce, as Leroy Jenkins recalls, "We were on welfare for a little while. We used to get free milk. They had a place where you could go and get your milk and butter and cheese."[22] Nonetheless, members of this earliest AACM generation did not consider themselves deprived. Jerol Donavon remembers that "we were very fortunate—we never went hungry. We went to the relief station and got food and clothing, and my father worked on the WPA.[23] You didn't want your friends to see you going to the relief station, but man, I had my wagon right there. I found out later on, after we all grew up and everything, that just about all my friends had been doing the same thing."

Despite the fact that Jerol Donavon described his 43rd Street area as "one of the roughest in the city," he remembered the neighborhood as "like one big family. Everybody knew each other." Abrams, whose family lived nearby on Evans Avenue, also remembered the area as a rather congenial place to live. Talk to a long-time or former resident like Favors and you will hear about those who came out of the area and made good, like Lorraine Hansberry, Sam Greenlee, and many others.

The oldest of the AACM musicians were grade-schoolers between the height of the Depression and the onset of World War II. Like most black children, they attended all-black grammar schools. Abrams and Donavon met at Forrestville School, a couple of blocks from their homes. Other Forrestville pupils included Leroy Jenkins, saxophonist Johnny Griffin and trumpeter and record producer Paul Serrano. Of course, as Abrams recalled, "Forrestville was a standard public school, based on white history. There was no mention of black people in history at all, not even George Washington Carver. You studied about Columbus, Amerigo Vespucci. They had the music of Glück and people like that." Despite these limitations, however, the teachers were committed to their pedagogical mission. "They educated you in the stuff that they had," remembers Abrams. "If you didn't learn, they called your parents."

When the kids weren't at school or working, they might be playing ball in the many vacant lots that sprang up in the wake of the demolition of old housing. Later, Sparrow's Pool Room, right below the 43rd Street elevated train station, was one of a number of alternative community institutions where information was exchanged and virtuosity was on display. Abrams remembered Sparrow's as "the Carnegie Hall of the poolrooms." A young man could obtain much practical knowledge hanging out there, and a good pool player could make enough money to become an important community personage. The poolroom proprietor, because "he was street-wise, he was making money, and he owned something," as Abrams put it, might surpass a schoolteacher in community respect. "We were impressed with education," he emphasized, "but we weren't so much impressed with going to college. We could see it, and the teachers who were educated and highly trained would tell us. But they were in the neighborhood with us. We didn't see that going further, but we could see Duke Ellington and them going further, and Jackie Robinson, Louis Armstrong."

Philip Cohran observed, "My father went to college, but he became a Pullman porter, because they made much more money. A college degree wasn't worth ten cents in Mississippi for a black man." As Abrams observed, the Pullman porter was "the star of the neighborhood. He was sharp, and made all kinds of money off those tips, serving rich people and stuff." Other crucially important educational experiences were gained just by hanging out on the corner, where individual talent and ability could manifest themselves in myriad ways. "These people were individuals—in their ways," said Abrams. "Some were expert pickpockets. Their thing was getting on the bus every morning like they were going to work, and picking pockets. That was how they made their living. Basically, they were self-employed. This is Chicago." Leroy Jenkins's father worked for a notorious local gangster whose business was "policy," a popular, private, and illegal lottery that was "a socially accepted form of gambling that had a semblance of legitimacy within the African American community . . . managed by individuals who represented a cross-section of the population."[24] As Leroy Jenkins recalled, "My dad played, everybody played."

Abrams recalls that "the people who made the most money in the neighborhood were the hustlers—the gamblers, the pimps. Real heroes, like 'Baby' Bell, who was the Art Tatum of the pimps." Jodie Christian remembers that many young people in the community not only emulated the sharp dress of the local hustlers, but also followed other, more distressing pursuits. "They had shotguns; they drove these old Packard cars," he marveled. "I don't know where their parents got money to buy them a car. None of our parents had a car. It was almost like watching a movie to see these young people act like that. And they were serious. I know a lot of people got killed in gang fights, just like they do now." Malachi Favors admitted that as a preteenager on 41st and Langley, "I was sort of a little gangbanger, but gangbanging was different from what it is now. You got your reputation by dealing with your fists. I wasn't all that good at first, but I got ran home from school a couple of times, and one time a little short guy came to my rescue. He was pretty bad, so I started running with him. Then he quit, and I took over."

Abrams also knew the gang turf well. "The strong areas were 43rd Street, 39th Street, and 35th Street. There were gangs, but there was no shooting. Cats would have fights and—very seldom—somebody would get stabbed or something like that." Eventually, fighting and general truancy led Abrams to the feared Moseley School, a predominantly black reform school for boys near 16th Street and Michigan Avenue. Moseley combined vocational education with corporal punishment, administered via what Abrams remembers as "an oak-wood stick about that long and about that thick." Wrong answers on tests would inevitably draw a sharp whack on the backside. "You'd put your hands on the desk and bend over, and he'd hit you like he meant it," Abrams remembered. "You miss five, you get five hard ones back." Recess at Moseley was "full of hoodlums, the worst you could get. You had to be a strong individual, and you had to know some strong individuals that had a group." On the other hand, Moseley's black teachers included black histories in their teaching. Abrams felt that "I learned more at Moseley about who I might be as a black person in this country than I did in the public school." The teachers "insisted on your learning about your black self. . . . In Forrestville they weren't doing that."

Early Musical Experiences

At the age of five, Philip Cohran won first prize in a citywide talent contest in St. Louis, singing and dancing up a storm. After a period of piano study, Cohran joined an elementary school band in Troy, Missouri, playing a trumpet bought for him by his mother for twelve dollars. "It came in a cloth bag with a drawstring, packed in straw," Cohran laughed. "They gave me the mouthpiece and showed me how to make the sound. I had six or seven blocks to walk home, and I played all the way home—*baaaahhh, buuuhhh.* By the time I got home I couldn't play a note. The teacher was the football coach and a trumpet player. He was stopping at all the houses to demonstrate to the parents what they had paid for. So he said, 'Show me how it sounds, Phil.' I was like, *pffffftt!*"

Talent shows were an important black community tradition, but Wilmot Fraser's description of musical enculturation also identifies a different kind of mentoring relationship.[25] While in Fraser's narrative, mentoring was largely a male province, the role of black women as musical nurturers for the young AACM musicians was crucial. Throughout the Great Migration, as Darlene Clark Hine points out, black women "played a critical role in the establishment of an array of black institutions." While Hine was speaking in particular of churches and mutual aid societies, she also identifies black music, notably the blues, as part of "the resiliency of cultural transference that black women brought to the North."[26] Many classical music events were also organized by black women's clubs such as the Ritzy Matrons, of which Leroy Jenkins's mother was a member in the 1940s.[27] Paralleling the ways in which wealthy white women such as Claire Raphael Reis and Alma Wertheim served as patrons of classical composers, performers, and institutions in the 1920s and 1930s,[28] black mothers, grandmothers, sisters, and aunts of far more modest means bought instruments and paid for lessons. Mothers taught their young offspring and performed with them in churches.

Even if this kind of female-directed, often church-based support system did not directly extend to jazz-identified environments such as nightclubs, it was nonetheless critical, not only to the emergence of the AACM, but to the careers of black musicians across the United States. However, like the work of the white female arts patrons, black women's clubs were widely disparaged, particularly for their supposed aspirations to what were later called "bourgeois" lifestyles. Nonetheless, these institutions became major sources of early and ongoing support for classical performers such as pianist and composer Philippa Duke Schuyler, who had become something of a "role model" playing in black churches throughout the United States."[29]

In 1939 or 1940, Leroy Jenkins's aunt, barely four years older than he was, brought home a boyfriend named Riley, who had brought a curious musical instrument with him. "He played the violin for me, a piece called "Czardas," the Hungarian dance by Victor Monti. It's a standard violin piece at recitals [sings difficult, finger-busting passage]. I had never heard anything like that before. All I was hearing was Eckstine, Louis Jordan, Billie Holiday, the Ink Spots, the Mills Brothers." Young Leroy pleaded with his mother to get him a violin. Jenkins's first instrument, a half-size, red-colored violin, came from Montgomery Ward, and cost twenty-five dollars, which his mother paid for on credit. Jenkins thought that his new instrument had "an awful sound. I almost gave it up, but Riley was around, and he was the star pupil. I could hear him and say, oh, it was me and not the violin. I figured I'd keep doing it and I'd sound like Riley."

Jenkins's mother, a devout churchgoer, regularly brought her son to St. Luke's Baptist Church, where the pianist was Ruth Jones, later known as Dinah Washington. Miss Jones accompanied the young boy in performances of Bach and Gounod, while herself being tutored by the great gospel singers Sallie and Roberta Martin. Soon, Jenkins joined the church orchestra and the choir at Ebenezer Baptist Church, under the direction of O. W. Frederick, Riley's teacher. "Fess," as Frederick was known, became Jenkins's first formal music teacher. Jenkins grew up under the baton of Frederick, with his spouse, Miss Rita Love, at the piano, performing on the violin at church socials, teas, and banquets, and often playing the music of black composers such as William Grant Still, Clarence Cameron White, and Will Marion Cook.[30]

Jodie Christian's aunt was both a devout churchgoer and a pianist. She taught music to Christian's mother, who eventually became a church pianist in her own right. Christian's mother became her son's primary musical mentor. Christian learned the basics of boogie-woogie from his mother, who frequently took him to performances at the Savoy, the Regal, and the Chicago Theater in the downtown area. She was eventually tapped to direct the church choir, but as Christian noted, "she couldn't direct it and play the piano. So she taught me everything about a song so she could stand in front of that choir. And I was eager . . . when you're eager to do something you learn fast." The church had an organ, so mother and son would play piano-organ duets at services. Christian's father also sang and played the blues on piano in speakeasies and rent parties, but ultimately stopped performing and followed his wife into the church, prompted in part by their mutual desire to short-circuit any possible entrance into a life of hard drinking. Christian notes that between his mother and his father, "it was obvious what I was going to do. . . . Between the two, I guess that spells jazz."

Radio and recordings were a critically important form of mentoring for this first generation of the AACM. Christian's father's brother-in-law "had a collection of records in the 'thirties of all the blues players, which would be a collector's item now. They honored those records just like they were gold or silver or something. They cherished them, kept them in a folder, never let them get scratched. He never let us handle them. When I'd come to the house, *he* always played them." Jerol Donavon would listen to jazz with his uncle, who would identify the musicians for him. An average radio listener could learn to recognize individual musicians by ear, since unlike late twentieth-century jazz radio, live shows were frequent, the pieces were short, and the names of the artists were usually announced right after the piece was played. Donavon's family, reflecting an aspect of Southern heritage common to the transplanted African Americans, also listened to country and western music, which they called "folk music."

Along the lines suggested by bell hooks in her essay on African American communal performance,[31] in Jodie Christian's family, Friday evenings were often reserved for performance parties. "We entertained each other," Christian remembered. "My mother played, my father played, my aunt played. We didn't cook. We ate at Miss Merritt's, who was a lady who owned a barbecue and chicken place right down the street." Back down South, Jerol Donavon's family would get together at neighborhood jamborees, picnics, and church events to sing and play music on guitar, violin, and piano. Virtually everyone was self-taught, and played by ear—or "by air," as people said. Up North, the performances mostly stopped, but the memory remained, symbolized by a piano in their home. In any event, other stages were still available. As a child during the Depression, Donavon would get together with other young children, performing on 47th Street on pots, buckets, or whatever was available. They sang, danced, and passed the hat until the police would come and shoo them away.

Just three public high schools on the South Side educated nearly all of Chicago's black teenagers in the 1940s and 1950s. Jodie Christian and Malachi Favors went to Wendell Phillips High, named for the nineteenth-century abolitionist orator. DuSable High, where Abrams went to school, opened its doors in the mid-1930s, named for the Creole founder of the late eighteenth-century trading post that later became Chicago. Later, a third high school, Englewood, became available to serve the rapidly growing black population, including Steve McCall and Jerol Donavon, whose first instruction in music was in Englewood High's ROTC drum and bugle corps.

Many of the musicians who extended the discoveries of bebop in Chicago learned important musical skills under the tenacious batons of two legendary band directors: Major N. Clark Smith at Phillips, and Captain Walter Dyett, first at Phillips and later at DuSable High.[32] Smith had guided the musical education of Lionel Hampton, Milt Hinton, and Ray Nance. Dyett, a multi-instrumentalist who played violin, banjo, and piano, was celebrated far and wide for the pupils he had nurtured to success in the music world. Pianists Martha Davis and John Young, singers Dinah Washington and Nat "King" Cole, bassists Milt Hinton and Richard Davis, organist Dorothy Donegan, saxophonists Gene Ammons, Clifford Jordan, and John Gilmore—all of these and more studied under Dyett. The Captain frequently played at the well-known Warwick Hall on East 47th Street for dances like the "Peps," which attracted Richard Abrams and other neighborhood teenagers. Dyett's students performed at the annual "Hi Jinks" musical, playing both big-band jazz and "light classical" fare with the school's concert band. Famous musicians performed with the students in Dyett's high-school assemblies; Lionel Hampton hired the young phenom, saxophonist Johnny Griffin, right out of Dyett's high-school band. Dyett hired the better students, like Young, Griffin, Donegan, and the Freeman brothers—saxophonist Von, guitarist George and drummer Bruz—for outside gigs, such as ballroom dances, church socials, and teas, where the students became integrated at an early age into the professional world.

As befitting their military titles, Major Smith and Captain Dyett headed relatively autocratic pedagogical regimes. In particular, "Cap" was well known for his extreme irascibility. "I remember one time I fell asleep," said saxophonist Eddie Harris. "He kicked the chair out from under me, and I got up off the floor with my clarinet all sprawled everywhere!" For Harris, Cap's methods, though seemingly a bit extreme, were necessary to instill discipline in young African Americans as a means of training them to cope with a hostile world. "He had to be rough," Harris explained, "because the guys who came to that school were extremely rough. And he didn't tolerate that. He would either go upside your head, [or] have you bring your parents up to school."[33]

The intensely committed Dyett would do just about anything to get the students to realize their potential. "I guess everybody has a Walter Dyett story," said Leroy Jenkins. "I even saw him cry one time. 'Aw man [quavery voice], you're messing up the music, all you have to do is this . . ,'" Jenkins chuckled. "When we saw Captain Dyett cry, we said, oh, we gotta do something about this, because we were used to this man cussing us out and carrying on." According to Richard Davis, Dyett would hold "mind power" sessions where students would discuss their life goals and were exhorted to realize their dreams. Later, Dyett would follow these students' careers, even visiting them in New York.[34]

Like many young people, Abrams and Favors were more interested in sports than in music, so they never took part in Dyett's classes.[35] The awareness of music, however, was not completely blocked out. "I was playing sports, but I knew all the guys," said Abrams. "I would go and peep in on 'em, but they'd be sitting there practicing all the time. I wanted to play [sports], but I would always check the music out." At DuSable, Abrams knew Gilmore, Griffin, and Davis, as well as bassist Betty Dupree, trombonist Julian Priester, and saxophonists Freeman, Charles Davis, and Laurdine "Pat" Patrick. Christian did study music at Phillips, where Maurice McGee headed a choir known as the Sharps and Flats that sang "everything from opera to the blues—all the standard songs, like "All the Things You Are." Seeing that the twelve-year-old pianist lacked formal training, McGee advised Christian to use the written music as a graphic score, relying on his ear to create parts for himself: "When the notes go up, you go up. When the notes go down, you go down. He knew that I could anticipate the harmony; that's how I learned to read the music."

Throughout the 1940s and 1950s, the formal musical education of most black students ended after high school, so band teachers like Dyett and Smith, and their counterparts around the country (including the father of Lester, Byron, and Joseph Bowie in St. Louis), were effectively responsible for most of their musical training. It was by no means lost on these young people that universities or colleges other than historically black institutions rarely hired even the most extensively educated African Americans as faculty members. Certainly, a career as a classical composer or performer was simply not a realistic option, even at a time when the cold war was creating demand for academic centers of "contemporary music" as a riposte to Communism.[36] Among those who persisted in training for such a career in spite of these daunting odds, many hearts were undoubtedly broken. Prudently, black students like Leroy Jenkins pursued postsecondary education to obtain teaching credentials that qualified them for work as a grade-school or high-school music teacher. As Richard Abrams observed, this was "one of the *real* options" for black musicians seeking steady, reliable employment. Jenkins went from DuSable High to the historically black Florida A&M University in Tallahassee on a bassoon scholarship, but soon switched back to violin. "I was studying from two great black violinists, Bruce Hayden, and Elwin Adams. Both probably, deep down in their hearts, disappointment killed them. These were bona fide players. The only reason why they weren't accepted was purely because of their color."

Black institutions were widely recognized in African American communities around the United States for their strict standards of excellence. At Lincoln University's Laboratory High School in Missouri, Philip Cohran's teachers included O. Anderson Fuller, reputed to be the first African American to earn a PhD in music in the United States, and Ruby Harris Gill, a specialist in the study of spirituals. Cohran was also mentored by F. Nathaniel Gatlin, who later moved to Virginia, founded the Petersburg Symphony, and pursued a successful career as chair of the music department at Virginia State University.[37] Despite this record of excellence, however, many black families saw music study as an impractical waste of scarce dollars. "When I graduated from high school," Philip Cohran remembers, "my mother told me she wasn't going to finance any music education." Cohran went to Lincoln University as a chemistry major, and performed with Lincoln's band, the Collegians, along with bassist Wendell Marshall, who became a member of the Duke Ellington Orchestra. After just one year, however, Cohran's parents separated, and he was forced to break off his studies.[38] Cohran was deeply disappointed at not being able to finish college, but his friend Alphonso Hilliard, who later headed St. Louis's black hospital, Homer G. Phillips, reoriented his friend, pointing out that "man, Lincoln University ain't the world. Hell, most people ain't never heard of it."

Improvisation and Autodidacticism in 1950s Chicago

As a child, Richard Abrams had been fascinated by music, film, sculpture, and painting. As he tells it, one day in 1946, "It hit me. I don't want to go to these schools no more; I want to go to music school." He dropped out of DuSable and began piano study with a classically trained pianist, a woman who was a member of his church. Later, he enrolled at the Metropolitan School of Music downtown, which eventually merged with Roosevelt University. Supporting his studies in counterpoint, keyboard harmony, theory, and composition with a day job at a downtown printing company, Abrams eventually bought a second-hand piano.

Around the age of fifteen, Malachi Favors met a slightly older associate who took him to listen to some new music. "I heard Charlie Parker and Dizzy Gillespie, and aw, man, it took me *away,*" Favors recalled. "I started going to the Regal, and that's when I began to hear all the bands, like Duke Ellington and Earl Fatha Hines. I became connected to the bass—somehow I was fascinated by the bass." Hearing Oscar Pettiford play a solo on "C Jam Blues" with Ellington further stoked his desire: "He was the one that really made me want to play bass."

Of course, jazz was not taught in the schools at all, not even in Southern black colleges, most of which strongly resisted this ostensibly déclassé "devil's music." Musicians learned through a combination of private teachers, high-school music classes, and most crucially, autodidact methods and practices.[39] Aspiring improvisors worked with recordings, sought out more knowledgeable musicians as mentors, and practiced with others who were on their level, or a bit more advanced. In this kind of pedagogy, control of the pace, approach, and nature of learning was up to the learner, in dialogue with whatever communities, traditions, histories, or genres he or she felt to be important or attractive. This freedom could also shield the learner from the often quite directed insults and discouragements that were a normal part of African American participation in white-dominated, Eurocentric pedagogical processes.

Favors learned about chord changes, time, and form in an autodidactic, yet community-mediated fashion. "I went down and paid on a bass," recalls Favors, "but I didn't know anything about music at all. I was almost in tears, but I struggled along, struggled along." Studying with downtown classical bassists proved financially daunting for the young Favors, but through a stroke of good fortune, Favors met Wilbur Ware and Israel Crosby, his major early influences. Even with Ware as a mentor, however, autodidacticism continued to be the rule. "Wilbur really couldn't teach anything, because he didn't know how to explain," said Favors. "Even though he was one of the great bass players, he played, I guess, strictly by ear. But whatever he does, it was something else, so I just picked it up."

In the 1940s and 1950s, Bronzeville's main drags—63rd and Cottage, 55th Street, 47th Street, 43rd Street, 39th Street, and South Parkway—were alive and throbbing. Favors described the South Side of Chicago during this era as "the greatest entertainment section in the world."[40] You could hear the cream of the Chicago and national musical crop, as well as standup comics, chorus lines of "female impersonators" and male and female "shake dancers." Weekend editions of the *Defender* featured several pages of entertainment ads, and famous musicians like Billie Holiday and Lester Young attracted sizable audiences on their regular stops in Bronzeville, alongside up-and-coming local artists like saxophonist Tom Archia and drummer Wilbur Campbell. To insiders like saxophonist Von Freeman, "it was just a singing, swinging era. And of course, I was running around there trying to get all of it I could get, get it together and try to piece it together."[41]

After three years in Frankfurt, Germany, Martin Alexander was discharged from the army and came to Chicago in 1954. Known by his childhood moniker, "Sparx," Alexander was born in Columbus, Ohio, and started playing trombone around 1947, at the age of twelve. He had once visited Chicago with the local Elks Band, a marching outfit that also included the young Roland Kirk. Now, returning to Chicago as an independent young man of nineteen, Sparx was stunned and elated at the music he encountered on the South Side. The novelist Ralph Ellison, writing in 1948, had complained that "the lyrical ritual elements of folk jazz have given way to the near-themeless technical virtuosity of bebop, a further triumph of technology over humanism."[42] For Sparx, however, standing on the corner of 63rd and Cottage Grove, "It was like stepping into paradise. Any direction you went from there would be joints on both sides of the street where the music was going on. You didn't have to go in a joint. You could just walk up and down the street. All the cats would be around."[43] Surrounding Sparx on 63rd Street were venues such as the Kitty Kat Lounge at 63rd between Champlain and St. Lawrence, where pianists Ahmad Jamal and John Young held court; the Crown Propellor, the Stage Lounge, the Pershing Lounge, and Nixon's Show Lounge; and in the 1960s, McKie's Disk Jockey Show Lounge. There were entrepreneur Joe Segal's sessions at Budland, and the Monday night sessions on 47th Street at the Sutherland Lounge and the Trocadero.[44]

The young drummer Alvin Fielder came to town during this high point of the South Side bebop scene. Fielder was born in 1935 in Meridian, Mississippi, a regular stop for artists such as Duke Ellington, Count Basie, Ray Charles, Dizzy Gillespie, Buddy Johnson, Lionel Hampton and B. B. King. Fielder had been inspired to start playing drums as a young teenager after hearing a neighbor's record of Max Roach with Don Byas. Within a year, Fielder began working in dance bands, rhythm-and-blues bands, and blues clubs.

Fielder's father was a practicing pharmacist, and in 1951, young Alvin decided to follow in his father's footsteps, taking pharmacy courses at New Orleans's Xavier College. At the same time, he began studying with drummer Ed Blackwell, and met Ellis Marsalis, a tenor saxophonist at the time who later became well known as a pianist. Fielder notes that Blackwell and Marsalis were "part of the first of the bebop movement down in New Orleans," along with clarinetist Alvin Batiste and drummers Wilbert Hogan, Tom Moore, and Harry Nance.[45] Transferring to Houston's Texas Southern University in 1953, Fielder studied pharmacy in the morning, worked with local drummers in the afternoon, and performed at night.

After graduation, Fielder attended graduate school in manufacturing pharmacy at the University of Illinois at Chicago. After registering for classes, the young student headed over to the South Side to catch some music. His first night on the scene went something like this:

> This first club I went in was on Stony Island between 62nd and 63rd . . .
> it was Lester Young, Johnny Griffin, Norman Simmons, Victor Sproles,
> and a drummer by the name of Jump Jackson. Then we drove to a club
> named Swingland. . . . I hear this BAD music, unbelievably terrible. Johnny
> Griffin, John Gilmore, [bassist] Bill Lee, Wilbur Campbell, and Jodie
> Christian. They're playing "Cherokee," Wilbur Campbell asleep on the
> drums, but I mean, BURNING. Oh, man! I couldn't believe my ears. I had
> never heard anything that bad in all of my life. I sat there and I listened,
> man, and I got nervous. I had to leave the club.[46]

Meanwhile, Richard Abrams was playing all kinds of gigs—blues, jazz, stage shows, rhythm and blues, and church socials. At a certain point, the contradictions between what he was experiencing in school and what was going on in the street became too glaring to ignore:

> I was in class one day and the teacher who was doing keyboard harmony
> asked me, "Do you know *April in Paris?*" I said, "Sure," because I was out
> in the street playing; I knew all the songs. I was part of the scene, and to
> be part of the scene you had to know what you were doing. "Well," he
> says, "a friend of mine was on a job last night and they called it, and he
> didn't know the changes. How do *you* play it?" I said, "Oh . . . he's talking
> about himself." So I said, OK, I'm not coming back to this school. So I fin-
> ished the class and I left and never went back there.

Abrams's formal piano study was replaced by a lifelong dedication to autodidactic research and exploration. "I was determined to teach myself because that way I could go directly at what I wanted."

For young black South Side musicians coming of age in the 1950s, the nightly (and daily) jam sessions at the Cotton Club on 63rd and Cottage Grove were an important site for that kind of training. Von Freeman, Johnny Griffin, or another top gun might be running sessions after hours in what Richard Abrams called "the main scene." A visitor on the scene might well encounter people like saxophonists Clifford Jordan, Eddie Harris, Nicky Hill, John Gilmore, and Gene Ammons; bassists Wilbur Ware and Rafael Garrett; drummers Ike Day and Marshall Thompson; and pianists such as John Young, Andrew Hill, Willie Pickens, and the young Jodie Christian.

By the mid-1950s, childhood classmates Abrams and Jerol Donavon had reconnected as Cotton Club regulars. According to Donavon,

> They'd be playing up there seven nights a week, all day, all night. It would close up at four o'clock in the morning, and we would go to the restaurant on the corner, and stay in there until seven o'clock, and then come in to clean the place up. You'd open back up at seven, and go right back in there and start playing again. You'd hate to go home. You'd stay there till you couldn't stay no longer, then fall asleep in the booth, or get up and go home and go to sleep and come back.

This explicitly experimental atmosphere featured a group of musicians who, night after night, explored the contours, borders, and possibilities of the bebop language. In contrast to the academic music scene, at the Cotton Club, "It was not how much you know, but how much you can show," said Abrams, "whether you can stay with the pace . . . it was full combat. They played anything—at any speed. The first few tries [at breaking in] didn't work." At these times, Abrams observed, the solution was clear. "You had to go back to the drawing board. But nobody rejected you. It just was obvious that you weren't making it. Nobody had to show you anything. Maybe you'd ask a cat about some changes." The recordings that emerged from this period, such as Wilbur Ware's *The Chicago Sound* with Griffin, Campbell, and saxophonist John Jenkins,[47] evince an attitude of self-assurance and optimism. Secure in the knowledge that the music they were creating was theoretically sophisticated, exciting, and above all, *new,* the musicians displayed an easy, ludic confidence in extending the harmonic practices of their bebop forebears in new and challenging directions.

Many commentators have described the late 1930s swing orchestras in Fordist terms. As Ekkehard Jost described the situation in swing bands, "Space for solo improvisation was reduced to a minimum, individualism was not in demand, the arrangements predictable, the musicians interchangeable. 'King of Swing' Benny Goodman remarked that it was difficult for him to remember the names of his musicians."[48] Bebop's smaller ensembles offered a more personal form of expression, and gradually a "jam session" model of performance became highly influential. Historian Scott DeVeaux's analysis summarizes "jamming" both as model and medium: "The repertory is reduced to a handful of structures: the blues, Gershwin's 'I Got Rhythm,' and other pop song 'standards.' The only fixed personnel is a rhythm section of piano, bass, guitar, drums (although one can make do with less: in hotel rooms, drummers often spread a newspaper on a briefcase and played it with brushes."[49]

Operating in this reduced environment, the musicians nonetheless created original works incorporating an astonishing variety of innovative chord sequences, all developed from the intense experimentation of the bebop and hard bop years. The sequences themselves, however, were almost invariably drawn from a small set of basic harmonic cadences, primary forms such as twelve- and sixteen-bar blues, and AABA "rhythm changes" and ABAB song forms drawn from Tin Pan Alley sources. Finally, there was the Tin Pan Alley repertoire itself, performed at medium to fast tempi, or as slow, rubato-leaning "ballads."[50] These basic forms were more or less well known to musicians who came up as young improvisors in sessions like those at the Cotton Club in Chicago. Knowledge of these building blocks enabled musicians to improvise proficiently on almost any tune that was called. Even less familiar tunes were usually based on more-or-less standard sequences, and could be negotiated by ear if necessary; at the most, a brief demonstration prior to performance might be all that was needed. Alternatively, a musician might simply wait his or her solo turn and glean the necessary information aurally.

Of course, these late-night sessions taught the musicians about more than just music. Young musicians, local heroes, and nationally known artists would network and exchange information informally, rubbing elbows and shoulders with each other. As DeVeaux observes,

> The jam session was an integral part of the "art world" that constituted their professional life. It was both recreational and vocational. The element of escape and recreation is obvious: the jam session was a part of nightlife, a window onto the varied entertainments of the city for young and energetic men with some money to burn. But it was also a kind of work. Musicians counted on having this time to practice, to work out new

ideas and techniques, to exchange information, to network with their colleagues, to establish a rough-and-ready hierarchy of competence—all useful and necessary activities that could not practically be carried out on the bandstand.[51]

Jerol Donavon recalled that musicians from out of town would come to the Cotton Club and other after-hours clubs to play with the local luminaries. In this way the young drummer was able to meet and play with some of the best musicians in the world, including the Montgomery Brothers (Wes and Monk), the Jones Brothers (Elvin, Hank and Thad), Clifford Brown, Max Roach, Roy Haynes, Ben Webster, Art Blakey, John Coltrane, and Sonny Rollins. Certainly, the fact that men would constitute a dominant supermajority in this world was taken for granted by most musicians (and writers) of this generation; the observation of writer Ralph Ellison that success in the jam session involved the "recognition of manhood"[52] lends credence to historian Eric Porter's observation that jazz was "a site of male artistic accomplishment during and after the war."[53]

One is not sure whether to take Ellison's remark as an ethnographic observation or a behavior prescription for the (male) musician, but in any event, as Porter points out, "only a handful of women participated as musical equals in the bebop community, whose self-conception also tended to be masculine in orientation."[54] Some went so far as to claim that this state of affairs was somehow ordained by a higher power, as one well-known Chicago musician who was active in this era later declared to a researcher: "Very few women can play Jazz—black women—or any color. But you get the average black man—he is Jazz. . . . Whereas other people have other things—the ability to make money or whatever—we have this unique ability—the black male—to make Jazz. Something that the Creator gave us."[55]

In addition to his interest in the putative maleness of jazz performance, Ellison was clear and celebratory regarding the jam session as social Darwinist site:

> The health of jazz and the unceasing attraction which it holds for the musicians themselves lies in the ceaseless warfare for mastery and recognition—not among the general public, though commercial success is not spurned, but among their artistic peers. And even the greatest can never rest on past accomplishments, for, as with the fast guns of the Old West, there is always someone waiting in a jam session to blow him literally, not only down, but into shame and discouragement.[56]

On the surface, Ellison's observation appears congruent with the experiences of people like vibraphonist Emanuel Cranshaw, a contemporary of Abrams on the South Side bebop scene, who remembers that high standards of musicianship were strictly, if informally, enforced.

> If you got up there and were messing a cat would say, get off the stand. Oh, cats used to get kicked off right and left. Eddie Harris got kicked off, Muhal got kicked off. Then, they were very tempo-oriented. You had to learn how to play fast in a hurry. They would just step like [beats loudly on the table at an impossible tempo]. The most famous sessions, one was at the Cotton Club, which was at 63rd and Cottage. Johnny Griffin had the house band. Johnny Griffin could play as fast as the wind.[57]

In talking with the musicians, however, one also realizes that bebop-based jam sessions on the South Side went far beyond the romantically macho "cutting session" model so attractive to American literature and folklore. While the jam session was indeed a competitively based system of authority and virtuosity, Ellison's protocapitalist, social Darwinist framing of the jam session system seems undercut by accounts that speak of communal generosity rather than shaming. Jodie Christian remembers the atmosphere of gruff, laconic learning that permeated the late-night sessions:

> Now and then you might ask a question, or they might tell you something without you asking a question: "Go home and practice, man, because you need to know your scales, you need to know your chord changes." So you went home and worked on it. Next time you'd come out, you'd be *halfway* ready. . . . I don't think that they thought in terms of teaching or imparting knowledge, the ones who were advanced in playing. Of course they were, but I don't think you can think in terms of that. When you are in a community, you *do*.

For those who *did*, their eventual breakthrough would never be forgotten. "I'd be wanting to play so bad," Donavon remembered. "I'd go and get up on the bandstand and everybody would walk off." He recalls John Gilmore telling him, "Man, just keep on practicing. Just don't let the cats get you down. When they walk off the stage, just be more determined." Eventually, his persistence and hard work paid off, when saxophonists Frank Foster and Johnny Griffin called him up to play a superfast version of "Cherokee." "I knew he wasn't talking to *me*," Donavon said, "but I looked around and I was the only drummer sitting there. I sat down and played, and I don't know where it came from, but it came, brother. After that, as soon as I hit the door, 'Hey man, you gon' play some tonight?'"

Nightclubs and high schools were by no means the only opportunities for musical learning in the lives of Chicago musicians. The black musicians' union of Chicago, Local 208 of the American Federation of Musicians, was the first black AFM local, founded in 1901 in the wake of implacable opposition from white musicians to the admission of "colored" military band musicians to Chicago's AFM Local 10, which had been founded just one year earlier. Eventually, more than fifty race-identified dual-local systems were established, in Philadelphia, Pittsburgh, Boston, Los Angeles, Cincinnati, and a host of smaller cities across the United States.[58] New York's Local 802, which admitted blacks and whites on an equal basis, was a major exception to this rule.

A signal figure in the development of Local 208 was the violinist William Everett Samuels, who joined the union in 1918,[59] the year that the local bought its first building,[60] and who eventually became an important figure in the black local's development. Samuels's oral narrative, published posthumously in 1984, saw the black union as a species of independent black business, providing both employment and professional training for African American musicians, while protecting them from the exploitation that was endemic to the music business as Samuels and many others saw it:

> Ma Rainey, Bessie Smith, Huddie Ledbetter, Blind Lemon Jefferson, Jelly Roll Morton and them didn't make no money. . . . I knew Joe Oliver. He used to go and record and they would go in there and stay five or six hours and if they made sixty-five or seventy dollars for the whole group for all day, they were happy. Then when it came time for selling the records, there was no rule to give them no royalties. So all they got out of it was the fifty or sixty dollars. The industry made all the money. The White manager made money.[61]

At Local 208's building at 39th and State Street in Bronzeville, older union musicians served as role models, teachers, and oracles for younger aspirants like Richard Abrams, who recalls,

> It was incredible just to be in an all-black union. The white union was downtown; never the twain should meet. The black musicians' union was on 39th and State. They had a union hall where you could go and

rehearse, with a nice grand piano. Somebody was always rehearsing up there. You could hear some of the best musicians you'd ever want to hear, and you'd be standing there with your mouth open. . . . They had all these guys that were around when Louis Armstrong came from New Orleans. You had all those guys that played in different kinds of orchestras, who had been prominent black musicians on the scene. They could read music *real good,* and could play jazz and classical music. A lot of them were good composers who never got a chance to display their wares.

Union membership was mandatory as a practical matter, and Jodie Christian's aunt helped him gather the $47.50 union initiation fee. Malachi Favors had a job during the day, which enabled him to save up the funds to join. "I didn't know one note from another, but the cats would call if you were in the union," Favors chuckled. "When they couldn't get Wilbur Ware, or all these other good bass players, they'd call and get anybody: 'Are you working, man?'" Even for those who had more or less steady work, other aspects of the musician's life could be daunting. By 1946, Philip Cohran paid a visit to Chicago. He was already an up-and-coming young trumpeter, playing around St. Louis with Chuck Terry's band, which included saxophonist Fred Washington, Jr., an important early influence on the younger generation of St. Louis experimentalists, such as Oliver Lake and Julius Hemphill. Cohran noticed immediately that drugs, particularly marijuana and heroin, were easily obtained at Chicago's black clubs. "The pot man used to come around and turn everybody on at intermission," said Cohran. "In those days the police didn't even know what pot was. You could fire up a joint while you were talking to 'em." Leroy Jenkins recalled that at DuSable High,

> It was like Dopeville USA. Dope was sold in the hallways. I was copping in the hallways. Heroin was like a disease in the community. . . . Everybody was experimenting with it, all my friends. They had it on the block. On 47th Street where we used to go to hear entertainment, now you'd see guys on the corner dealing. It was like a plague. They'd say, "Leroy's doing it? A church boy, plays the violin?"

Music historian Ekkehard Jost cites a statistic revealing that around 16 percent of African American boys with birthdates between 1931 and 1951—the period in which most first-wave AACM musicians were born—had been arrested at least once on drug charges.[62] Leroy Jenkins's ironically humorous remembrance corroborates this. "We'd go see Charlie Parker at the Pershing. You'd go in the bathroom, it would smell like a weed house. Everybody'd go in the bathroom, smoke their little joints. The police would be busting people left and right in the bathroom. It was like comedy if you think about it now. They'd open up the stalls: "Awright, come out! [Laughs.]" More seriously, drug dependency, with its ever-present danger of overdosing on contraband substances of unknown provenance and potency, arguably led to the premature demise of a number of important artists, such as the young Chicago saxophonist Nicky Hill, dead at the age of twenty-eight in 1963.[63] In addition, many musicians ended up not in health-care facilities, as with Charlie Parker's well-known stay at the sanatorium in Camarillo, California, but in federal prison. Leading Chicago musicians, such as saxophonist Gene Ammons, were jailed for heroin use in the 1960s. Ultimately, drug use became yet another means by which young African Americans of the period were introduced to the criminal justice system.

In the end, Cohran's brief sojourn in Chicago proved daunting and discouraging: "It was too fast here for me." He returned to St. Louis with the intention of giving up music entirely, but decided instead to take over the leadership of a band at a local club, transforming the ensemble into the Rajahs of Swing in 1948.[64] "We selected the name "Rajahs," coming off of Duke and Count, Earl Hines, you know. Our costumes were maroon corduroy jackets, gray flannel slacks, and blue suede shoes—with turbans! But we couldn't find nobody who could tie a turban. I had to get a silk scarf, and I got my landlady to sew it together. They called us, 'them boys with the rags on their heads'—but they didn't forget us."

In 1950, Cohran went on the road with Jay McShann, a major exponent of the Kansas City blues style that, as Johnny Griffin told an interviewer in 1990, was the dominant influence on musicians working out of Chicago in the 1950s. "The Chicago musicians, we played the music not of New Orleans, but we played the music that was emanating from Kansas City. That was the style. . . . Kansas City was like the center of that Basie-type music, that Jay McShann type, Walter Brown Blues singing type, Jimmy Rushing, Joe Turner Blues singing type, you know."[65] Touring around the country with McShann introduced the young Cohran to a wider world, jumpstarting his practice as a composer. Cohran realized that, in order to advance as a composer, he would have to resist many of the blandishments that were endemic to the road musician's life:

When I was with McShann we had whole sheets of time. I always was a loner, and when we'd go to other cities, I'd go to the libraries. I couldn't get nobody to go to no library, man. Cats thought I was crazy. We were playing joints, and none of the cats would get up till about 1 or 2 o'clock in the afternoon, man. I couldn't live like that. I'm an early riser. Even though we'd go to bed at 4 am, I'd have to get up by 10. I couldn't stay in bed.

Cohran was drafted in 1951, but avoided being sent to Korea. Instead, he was tapped for music study at the U.S. Naval School of Music, which was then part of the Anacostia Naval Station in Washington D.C. "I was at the Naval School of Music, and we only operated from 8 to 4," recalls Cohran, "so I had all the evenings."

Historian Darlene Clark Hine notes that "black women faced greater economic discrimination and had fewer employment opportunities than black men. Their work was the most undesirable and least remunerative of all northern migrants."[66] Even so, "a maid earning $7 a week in Cleveland perceived herself to be much better off than a counterpart receiving $2.50 a week in Mobile."[67] Thus, around 1940, Fred Anderson, born in Monroe, Louisiana, in 1929, was brought by his mother to the Near North Chicago suburb of Evanston. Living with her son and her sister in a one-room apartment, and lacking much formal education, Anderson's mother found a job making ten dollars a week, while taking care of her son and studying for and obtaining her beautician's license. Anderson's family eventually moved into a larger place where young Fred had his own room—all without help from his father, who had split from the family before the move north.

The saxophonist describes himself as "a quiet guy, like an introvert, but I do a lot of thinking about what I want to do, and about being my own person, not being influenced. I never followed anybody."[68] Although his mother discouraged him from participating in Evanston's poolroom life, Anderson, like Abrams, recalls his days spent there as highly motivational. "By me not having a father, I used to always be around older guys, and they would talk to me and I would be listening," said Anderson. "That was one of the things that gave me an idea that I had to be doing something, instead of just standing around." Growing up on the predominantly black west side of Evanston in the early 1950s, Anderson was listening to Lester Young, Jay McShann, Duke Ellington, Johnny Hodges, and Illinois Jacquet on the radio and the jukeboxes, and attending performances by Lester Young and Wardell Gray. Most crucially, he heard Charlie Parker live at the Savoy Ballroom, the Pershing Ballroom, and the Beehive. Sometime after World War II, Anderson decided that music would be centered in his life:

> A guy named Lester Watts, I went over to his house. The first record I ever heard of Charlie Parker, he played it for me. He had an alto saxophone, and he was trying to play it on his saxophone. He couldn't play it, but at least it gave me an idea. . . . My aunt bought my cousin a saxophone. He didn't play it, so it laid around the house. We were all living together, and I picked it up and started playing it. But she sold it; I guess she wanted to get her money back. So that's when I bought my own saxophone. I had a little job, and I saved up the money—my last $45.

Anderson began an aesthetic trajectory that represented perhaps the purest articulation of the autodidact's path. He was one of the first of the early AACM musicians to establish a kind of private exploration outside the club system. "I never played in any dance bands," he emphasized, and having dropped out of high school, Anderson never played in school ensembles either. "I was always an independent cat. Me being an only child, maybe that was it. I sort of, like, taught myself music. I was trying to find something that I wanted to do, and music was the thing where I could be by myself. The AACM was the only thing I've ever been a part of. I was never in a club, I was never in a gang. I was always a lone cat."

Instead of touring with working groups, Anderson was taking private lessons, teaching himself, and listening carefully to more experienced musicians who lived in North Chicago and the South Side,

> There was a lot of musicians out in Evanston, so I had a lot of music around me. A guy named Martin Baugh taught me a lot of stuff. He gave me some theory books. I took these theory books and studied on my own. I knew Junior Mance, and Buzz MacDonald, who played [saxophone] with Gene Ammons. Bucky Taylor [drums] was around, and Billy Wright [saxophone] used to take me around on his gigs. They had a little place called the Subway Lounge, where I met Ira Sullivan.

By the late 1950s, Anderson was studying theory at Roy Knapp's music school on Wabash Avenue in downtown Chicago, and working as a waiter to support his family. In 1957 he met trumpeter and fellow Evanstonian

Bill Brimfield, when Brimfield was eighteen, nine years Anderson's junior. Brimfield was born in Chicago in 1938, and grew up in Evanston. He studied piano at age six, and violin at age nine. In an unpublished short biography, he was quoted as saying, "I had seen *Young Man with a Horn* with Kirk Douglas four times and I knew I had to be a trumpet player." He played in marching and concert bands in high school, and later studied with a former member of the Chicago Symphony.[69] "Me and Brimfield used to get together and play a little bit, just to woodshed," Anderson said. "We used to go to the practice rooms at Northwestern [University]. I was learning all the tunes, and I taught Brimfield his first Charlie Parker tune. He was in the high-school band, and he was hooked up on Louis Armstrong, then he got introduced to Miles later on." Brimfield agreed, saying in his biography, "Fred used to take me in the basement and make me play 'bop' tunes all day. . . . I originally wanted to play like Louis Armstrong, my first idol, and later Harry James who I still admire, but while in high school somebody gave me a Miles Davis record to listen to and that was it. I could play some of his solos note for note."[70]

The End of an Era

Certainly, for many musicians, critics, and listeners who came to maturity during the 1950s, nothing that came after could really compare. At the time, it must have seemed as though all that excitement would last forever. But changes were already looming, changes that would prove more rapid and thoroughgoing than anyone could imagine. As the 1960s emerged, the relative informality and flexibility that marked the development of jazz performance practice during the 1940s and 1950s was slowly, almost imperceptibly beginning to harden, conditioned by the stark economic pressures that accompanied the endemic undercapitalization of the field. Following Scott DeVeaux's account makes it easier to see that a performance practice that began as a combination of relaxed social networking and musical learning was eventually transformed into a performance model from which few deviations were tolerated. As DeVeaux points out, the economic success of such jam session–based productions as the Jazz at the Philharmonic concerts produced by Norman Granz lay in the understanding by musicians and promoters that "the music would have to be deliberately transformed. The repertory would have to be converted into clearly defined economic units, preferably original compositions, for which authorship could be precisely established. The often chaotic atmosphere of the jam session would need to be streamlined and subtly redirected toward paying audiences."[71]

Economic forces could well have conditioned the progress of jamming-as-performance in crowding out large-ensemble and other performance modes. First, the jamming model obviated the need to rehearse or learn difficult written music, thereby avoiding costs for arrangers' fees, rehearsal time and space, and music copying. Second, the standardization of the small-group model provided little incentive for producers and venue owners to present larger ensembles when cheaper and arguably similarly lucrative alternatives were available. Like its industrial counterpart, a standard musical repertoire needing relatively little infrastructure to operate would incur fewer expenses in attracting customers. On the one hand, this enhancement of the possibilities for generating profits could lead to more work for musicians. On the other, that work would inevitably be filtered through the machinery of capitalist mass production, and nonstandard modes of performance would be discouraged on economic grounds. Since, for the most part, individual musicians and bandleaders could rarely afford independent productions requiring more extensive instrumental forces and rehearsals, the small size of most ensembles—piano, organ or guitar, bass, and drums as a foundation, and various horns comprising a "front line"—became fairly ubiquitous.

For a relative handful of musicians, what was most crucial about the Cotton Club period was the feeling that something different from all that was in the air, seemingly just around the corner. Around 1951 or so, Abrams had met bassist Donald Rafael Garrett, whom he credits with being a major influence on the future directions that Chicago music would take. "He was a phenomenal musician," said Abrams. "His intuitive understanding of music was incredible." Speaking of himself and his friend Garrett, who was "brilliant, also in social thinking," with a "nomad, Bohemian personality," Abrams declared that "we were headed outside. We were deliberately breaking some rules. To us, Bird and them were like people who broke ground. We copied them religiously, but that was not the end; we didn't sacrifice our individualism to do it. There were some on the scene who did, but we didn't. We started to draw and paint, because we felt like that—doing things differently."

2

NEW MUSIC, NEW YORK

Cultures of Spontaneity: Integrationism and the Two Avant-Gardes

By 1950, what historian Daniel Belgrad has called an "aesthetic of spontaneity," promulgated among "a loose coherence of individually unique artists, writers, and musicians,"[1] was at the heart of much of the most daring American expressive culture. Many of these artists were based in New York City, arguably the cultural center of the United States, and an environment that nurtured bebop, free jazz and free improvisation, indeterminacy, the musical New York School, the Black Mountain and Beat poets, the Abstract Expressionist painters, and later, early minimalism, the Judson Church dance experiments, and the Living Theater and its offshoots.

Poet Ronald Sukenick's 1987 memoir of the Greenwich Village art scene of the era attests that "the uniquely native American art form, jazz, became, through the fifties, more central than ever for underground artists of all kinds."[2] The Beat poets, for example, were well known for their spontaneously generated "bop prosody."[3] In Abstract Expressionist circles, jazz was widely admired by people as diverse as Franz Kline, Jack Tworkov, Willem de Kooning, Joan Mitchell, Grace Hartigan, and Larry Rivers, who introduced his tenor saxophone improvisations as part of his work. The painter Lee Krasner observed that her husband, the painter Jackson Pollock, "would get into grooves of listening to his jazz records—not just for days—day and night, day and night for three days running. . . . He thought it was the only other really creative thing happening in this country."[4]

The love that these writers and visual artists had for jazz was unquestionably ardent. At the same time, one notices that in many narratives of the period, including Sukenick's, jazz is discussed, observed—and above all, consumed—but the musicians rarely appear as participants in any aesthetic or political discussions. Even if, as Sukenick remembered, "Digging Bop is one of the main ways subterraneans can express their cultural radicalism,"[5] bebop appears as a source to be drawn from, rather than a site for intellectual exchange between white and black artists and intellectuals. As historian Eric Lott observed, "In the postwar cultural formation, beboppers were a black intelligentsia—the other New York intellectuals—only dimly perceived by a myopic left."[6] Fred Moten, in his audacious foray into black radical aesthetics, *In the Break,* traces the same outlines as Lott's regarding the historiography of the avant-garde:

> What I've been specifically interested in here is how the idea of a black avant-garde exists, as it were, oxymoronically—as if black, on the one hand, and avant-garde, on the other hand, each depends for its coherence on the exclusion of the other. Now this is probably an overstatement of the case. Yet it's all but justified by a vast interdisciplinary text representative not only of a problematically positivist conclusion that the avant-garde has been exclusively Euro-American, but of a deeper, perhaps unconscious, formulation of the avant-garde as necessarily not black.[7]

There is little question of the essential trenchancy of Moten's observation. At the onset of the 1960s, the New York music scene was fairly diverse in terms of ethnicity. In addition to its dominant white component, Asian-born artists, such as Yoko Ono, Nam June Paik, and Toshi Ichiyanagi, a student of John Cage, played central roles. Work by European composers such as Sylvano Bussotti, Karlheinz Stockhausen, Giuseppe Chiari, and Stefan Wolpe, as well as that of Japanese composers such as Toshiro Mayuzumi, was regularly performed alongside the work of Americans John Cage, Earle Brown, Christian Wolff, La Monte Young, Richard Maxfield, Morton Feldman, David Behrman, Frederic Rzewski, Alison Knowles, James Tenney, Philip Corner, Max Neuhaus, Malcolm Goldstein, Charlotte Moorman, Gordon Mumma, Robert Ashley, Alvin Lucier, and others.

In his 1963 book, *Blues People,* the young LeRoi Jones brought out the fact that that "the young Negro intellectuals and artists in most cases are fleeing the same 'classic' bourgeois situations as their white counterparts."[8] Accounts of the early 1960s New York avant-garde, however, seem unable to assimilate Jones's point, preferring to exceptionalize the black artists and their concerns. Indeed, in the majority of these accounts, the marginality of African Americans in particular is assumed, even as the transgressive new black music of Cecil Taylor, Ornette Coleman, John Coltrane, and others was influencing artists around the world.

Performance historian Sally Banes goes to some length to mitigate the racialized dislocations of power in the 1960s Greenwich Village scene. "Although blacks and whites generally did occupy separate aesthetic domains, as they always had in the segregated history of American arts," she writes, "at this particular moment those arenas briefly overlapped. Greenwich Village was already a place where blacks and whites could mingle socially."[9] However, even as Banes points out that white artists "danced black social dances and listened to black popular music,"[10] her centering of personalized integrationist subcultures ignores structures of institutional and social power that underlay the career strategies available for deployment by white artists in what was, after all, a competition for resources. As cultural theorist Jon Panish writes, this kind of appeal to a noninstitutional mode of analysis "misses (or at least minimizes) the important power struggle that is bound up in the sort of cultural contest where different meanings are attributed by members of different groups to the same material."[11]

In Banes's account, African American culture appears once again as consumable exotica, always and already available to the "mainstream." At the same time, her account seems to celebrate the ways in which "white writers and other hipsters appropriated elements of black cultural style, from marijuana to sexual freedom to jazz prosody."[12] One might want to bracket the question of whether the identification of marijuana and sexual freedom as part of "black cultural style" advances racial stereotypes, but in any event, one can concur with Panish that, for whatever black-derived resources white artists felt comfortable in using, "it was precisely because these Euro-Americans stood in a superior social and political position vis-à-vis African American culture that they could appropriate or exploit these resources."[13]

The presence of poets Ted Joans and LeRoi Jones, perhaps among the few African Americans active and relatively accepted on the downtown scene of the 1950s and early 1960s, is alluded to in first-person narratives by Sukenick and Hettie Jones, LeRoi Jones's first, Jewish American spouse.[14] In both accounts, however, as in Banes's history, the two poets stand out in a sea of white faces. Jones himself recognized the issue in his 1962 essay, "Tokenism: 300 Years for Five Cents," which in the light of his Greenwich Village experience, could be said to articulate the autobiographical.[15] For Joans, whose phrase "Bird Lives" took on an enduring life of its own in the wake of Charlie Parker's death,[16] this status was not without its opportunities for an ironically resistive humor. Hettie Jones recalled that Joans and photographer Fred McDarrah sometimes "rented themselves to parties as 'genuine beatniks,' dressed appropriately and carrying a set of bongos, an instant symbol for Negro culture."[17] Here, Joans was undoubtedly pointing up the fact that the white Beats, as Daniel Belgrad noted, "seem to have remained willfully innocent of the racial power dynamics structuring their reception of the music—dynamics that allowed them to move more freely between African American and white social spaces than many black jazz musicians themselves."[18]

An incident involving LeRoi Jones, recounted in Ronald Sukenick's memoir, demonstrates this well.

> Years later Gregory Corso would remind Allen Ginsberg about an incident involving LeRoi Jones/Baraka. "Remember how we went to read in Washington, D.C.? He crawled underneath the backseat. I never saw a man in my life do that, and I said, 'Hey, LeRoi, what're you doing there?'
>
> "He says, 'Don't you understand, I'm in Washington, D.C., I'm in a place where they don't like Blacks.'
>
> "I said, 'What, the capital of the United States?' So he woke me up to the ball game on that. Right. This class guy."
>
> "He wouldn't get out of the car to go into a drive-in," says Ginsberg. "And he was right at the time, I didn't realize."
>
> "Me neither. I figure, all right, I'm Italian but at least I'm white so they can't fuck with me too much."[19]

Baraka's 1984 *Autobiography of LeRoi Jones* presents a markedly different image of the Village from Banes's retrospective assumption of the inevitability of art-world segregation. Baraka describes an integrated art world that included such black painters as Vincent Smith, Sam Middleton, Virginia Cox, and Arthur Hardie. Nonetheless, Baraka recalls that "there was no doubt that for many black intellectuals, like their white counterparts, white intellectual Europe was the source and site of the really serious intellectual pursuits. . . . The intellectual worship of Europe is in one sense only the remnants of colonialism, still pushed by the rulers through their 'English

Departments' and concert halls!"[20] In this regard, Baraka gradually came to understand his white mentors' influences as sympathetic, but also "merely a continuation of the other 'whitening' influences I had been submitting to enthusiastically under the guise of information, education."[21] Following a watershed 1959 trip to Cuba in which he met artists from all over the African diaspora, Baraka remembers that "I began to feel, even though I was definitely still a member of the downtown set, somewhat alienated from my old buddies. Perhaps alienated is too strong a word, but I peeped some distance had sprung up between us."[22] Shortly thereafter, Baraka left the Village arts scene for Harlem. His departure, according to Banes, "drastically shrank the African American representation in the downtown avant-garde, leaving the Village bereft of its leading black voice."[23]

The reasons for Baraka's departure, however, seem opaque to Banes, who describes the incident as "paradigmatic of the shift by African Americans to political and aesthetic separatism."[24] The trope of voluntary black separatism seems designed to preempt any possibility that actions by white-dominated institutional, social, and political frameworks could be invoked either to explain Baraka's move, or to illuminate the reasons why, in her words, "very few African Americans or other people of color systematically played a part" in the early sixties avant-garde.[25] Of course, this mode of theorizing, as Fred Moten noted, naturalizes the implicit racing as white of the notion of a "sixties avant-garde" itself—a curious framing, to be sure, in a period where John Coltrane, Albert Ayler, Ornette Coleman, Cecil Taylor, Sun Ra, and countless other radical black artists were based in New York. Here, black artists faced an especially frustrating conundrum. Even as a strong investment was being made in the positional and referential freedom of white artists, for black artists there was a concomitant assumption that either total Europeanization or a narrowly conceived, romanticized "Africanization" were the only options. In this discursive environment, engagement with African American culture could not serve as one element among many. Rather, race itself was assumed to overdetermine the identity of the black creative artist.

Thus, Banes's observation that "white and black artists could not help but have different artistic and political agendas"[26] need not be accompanied by the notion that a simplistic and unreflective urge to separatism on the part of black artists lay at the root of the matter. Rather, we may read her remark against its grain, in recognizing that a race-mediated asymmetry of experience between white and black artists and intellectuals contributed to an eventual dislocation between them as the 1960s commenced. One possible source of this distancing, exemplified by Baraka's trip to Cuba, was that black artists were expanding the domestic agenda of "civil rights" toward a focus on a protopostcolonial consciousness that sought common political and social ground with an international black diaspora. In contrast, as Banes acknowledges, "for this predominantly white avant-garde of the early sixties, the notion of equality was a generalized one and did not particularly focus on racial equality."[27] Rather, "equality of opportunity to show one's art was one of the purposes for founding the alternative institutions" such as Film-Makers' Showcase, Judson Dance Theater, Caffe Cino, and Flux-hall.[28]

On Banes's view, "The white avant-garde's preoccupation with egalitarianism reflected many of these artists' own experience of entering the hitherto upper-class world of high art en masse. . . . Their own forms of symbolic leveling were first and foremost expressions of their own situation—that is, their aim was the democratization of the avant-garde in terms of class, and sometimes gender, but not race or ethnicity."[29] For Baraka and other black artists, however, the immense political, social, and cultural changes that were unfolding meant that "life had to be more than a mere camaraderie of smugness and elitist hedonism."[30] The white avant-garde movement was seen by black artists such as Baraka as overly invested in a kind of bourgeois individualism that black artists could not really afford to pursue. Moreover, the movement failed to articulate a critique of bourgeois culture that could interrogate both its own implication in that culture and its racialized power base.[31]

Indeed, a dominant sentiment among members of the white musical avant-garde drew upon modernist notions of music as politically disinterested, even disempowered. One extended foray into the subject, published in 1969 in the musician-centered journal *Source: Music of the Avant Garde,* consisted of telephone interviews—rather like a poll—with white experimentalists such as Charlotte Moorman, John Cage, David Tudor, Morton Feldman, Roger Reynolds, David Behrman, Harold Budd, Robert Ashley, Robert Moran, Daniel Lentz, Jerry Hunt, Barney Childs, Dick Higgins, Terry Riley, Steve Reich, James Tenney, Lukas Foss, and Frederic Rzewski. There was a surprising unanimity among this diverse group of artists in answering the question "Have you, or has anyone ever used your music for political or social ends?"[32] The article's preface acknowledged that "much of today's mass-culture music is being used for these ends," a fact that was obvious enough at a time when artists and genres from around the world— Bob Marley, Peter Tosh, Bunny Wailer, Bob Dylan, Country Joe, Curtis

Mayfield, Sly Stone, Jimi Hendrix, new Latin American song, calypso, and many others—articulated overt opposition to racism, poverty, and war in their music.

During this turbulent period, however, references to issues that were burning throughout the United States, from civil rights to the war in Vietnam, were rarely to be found in the pages of journals documenting the products of American musical experimentalism. Of the new-music artists polled for the *Source* article, only cellist and performance artist Charlotte Moorman, the only woman interviewed, unabashedly embraced the idea that music's purview might involve the direct transmission of political messages: "I've used my own interpretations for political and social ends on various occasions, because I've wanted to reach people. . . . All the pieces I do, I hope, have social elements to them, and many, I hope, have political elements. . . . Just about every piece that I do, especially the pieces of Nam June Paik, have political or social overtones."[33]

For the most part, however, a clear majority of the artists polled were relatively confident in asserting variants of two central beliefs. The first notion, heavily influenced by Theodor Adorno's notion of the heroic function of new music as oppositional to mass culture, held that contemporary musical composition constituted a political and social force that, as Lukas Foss asserted, "will inevitably end by contributing towards a new social and political climate."[34] This frankly vanguardist self-image was complemented by another, seemingly contradictory belief, again succinctly put by Foss: "Our work should not, and probably cannot be used for ulterior ends of any kind."[35] What emerged from this bipolar belief system was a notion of music as creating an atmosphere for contemplating change, while eschewing what Terry Riley called "the big politics in the sky."[36] Generalized notions of democracy, egalitarianism, or anarchy might properly be embedded in specific works, as with Riley's signature work from 1964, *In C*, which the composer described as "very democratic, no one had a lead part, everyone supposedly contributing an equal part. . . . In that sense, I guess it's social."[37]

At the same time, Banes avows that "white artists adopted, perhaps not always consciously, elements of African American art and performance. These included improvisation and the fusion of the arts usually considered separate in the Euro-American tradition."[38] One should be reminded that the practices of improvisation and fusion of the arts, quickly and casually glossed over here, are hardly minor issues. Indeed, Banes's suggestion that "the African American tradition of musical improvisation was translated into theater, dance, and other artistic practices of the white avant-garde"[39] places black culture (if not black artists) at the core of crucial paradigm shifts in American experimentalism. Banes, however, is at pains to limit her understanding of the "Africanization of American culture"[40] to mainstream mass entertainment, and cryptic allusions to it on the part of the white avant-garde.

Moreover, at least in musical circles, whatever separation was developing was accentuated by the fact that black and white avant-garde musicians tended to perform in separate spaces, often with vast asymmetries in infrastructure. Banes notes that "in spite of their own attacks on the bourgeois values of Euro-American high art, the concerns and the practices of the white avant-garde still grew inexorably out of that high art tradition,"[41] which was being buttressed by private foundations and donors and university residencies designed to protect its artists from commercial Darwinism. The sums expended were often breathtaking. For instance, between 1979 and 1983, the Dia Foundation "poured $4 million" into composer La Monte Young's conceptual work, "Dream House."[42] In contrast, the "natural" home of the black musical avant-garde was presumed to be the jazz club and the commercial sector.[43]

In the end, the love of jazz articulated by the 1950s Beats and Abstract Expressionists was not reinscribed by their downtown New York descendants of the 1960s. Sukenick's narrative describes the scene at an early-sixties New York party, where painter Andy Warhol, who was just coming to prominence in the early 1960s, "had his own scene in the back room that represented a sharp break with the past and its values. Down with 'painterly' qualities in art, with the aesthetic purity of artists. Down with the 'tyranny of jazz,' in Danny Fields's phrase, as the standard for pop music, and up with extramusical values like noise, volume, performance, dance, politics, sex."[44]

In the meantime, the experience of many black artists was summarized in a passage from Baraka's autobiography: "Europe as intellectual center was yet another stone to the weight of 'alienation' from black (if that is not too strong a word) that was building up in me. Exiting from one world and entering another."[45] Fashions were changing, and jazz's links with Abstract Expressionism meant that when Ab Ex gave way to Pop, the putatively white art world's romance with black culture also came to an end. Attention turned to the emerging form known as rock, a music that was spearheading the massive capitalization of media corporations, in part because its black origins were quickly being pushed down a formless memory hole.[46]

Beyond a Bebop Boundary: The Challenge of New Music

By the late 1950s, in the midst of the emerging standardization of the bebop revolution, it had become clear to many musicians that reports regarding the death of formulaic modes of expression had been greatly exaggerated. As Cecil Taylor observed in 1961, "Now the young Negro musician *can* play it safe. . . . They're playing exactly the same way; even the same tunes."[47] Gradually, a group of new musicians emerged who were critical of the new Fordism that had seemingly defined the directions for black musicians along rigidly commodified lines. The implications of bebop's cultural stance and its construction of the autonomous, modernist black artist were now being taken up by a new generation, intent upon radically revising the previous generation's methodological premises. One such movement, the emergence of the "free jazz" of Ornette Coleman, Cecil Taylor, John Coltrane, and many others, was part of an explosion of new and radical musical ideas in the 1960s that also included minimalism, and most publicly, the rise of rock.

No single musician could be credited with promulgating the wide-ranging challenges to the conventions of improvisation that appeared at the onset of the 1960s. Rather than a single notion of "freedom," various freedoms were being asserted across a wide spectrum of musical possibilities. Musicians as diverse as Abbey Lincoln, Max Roach, Charles Mingus, Sonny Rollins, Miles Davis, Herbie Hancock, McCoy Tyner, Joe Henderson, Tony Williams, Eric Dolphy, and many others, all created new music with novel formal schemes and instrumental techniques.[48] Increasingly, no sound was seen as alien to the investigations of improvising musicians, with the possible exception of electronically synthesized and modified sound, which met with widespread resistance despite early experiments by Eddie Harris, and the later adoption of keyboard synthesizers by Miles Davis, Chick Corea, and Herbie Hancock.

The oboe, bass clarinet, fluegelhorn, and soprano saxophone reentered the instrumentarium, along with percussion, reeds, and flutes from around the world. Moreover, extensive experimentation was transforming the characteristic sounds of the standard instruments. Trombonists such as Roswell Rudd recontextualized the timbres of the early New Orleans musicians, and the sound of the saxophone proved able to traverse a range from Coleman Hawkins to Albert Ayler, both of whom were alive and active during this period. Multiphonics and other extended instrumental and vocal techniques were to be found in the work of people like Abbey Lincoln, Jeanne Lee, Leon Thomas, and Pharoah Sanders. Reflecting the increasing globalization of sound, composer-improvisors such as Yusef Lateef were listening to music from Africa, Asia, South and Central America, and Oceania, as well as Native America and the products of European and American high-culture experimentalism. Musicians such as Wayne Shorter pursued intercultural collaborations with the creators of these forms and sounds.[49]

The notion of drummers as primary timekeepers had already broken down with the work of Kenny Clarke, who pithily suggested to a colleague in the 1940s that rather than relying on the drummer, each musician should be personally responsible for the articulation of tempo and meter. Then, with the advent of Sunny Murray, Milford Graves, Andrew Cyrille, and Beaver Harris, the implications of the nonhierarchical approach to time became evident, as tempos were irregular, constantly changing, or even completely absent—challenging the centrality of "swing" to the identity of jazz, or (on some views) redefining the nature of swing itself. Gradually, relationships between ensemble players became more fluid, and as collective free improvisations advanced mutable notions of foreground and background, distinctions between soloists and "rhythm sections" began to blur. Instruments that formerly assumed background roles, such as the bass, came to the front with the work of virtuosi such as Charles Mingus, and later, Scott LaFaro and Henry Grimes. Drummers such as Tony Williams and Dannie Richmond, not usually referenced in standard accounts of so-called free jazz, drew upon the work of their predecessors, notably Max Roach, in developing a "melodic" conception that situated percussion timbres and rhythms at the foreground of musical texture.

The rhythmic complexity of melodic lines and harmonic rhythm increased markedly, as Charlie Parker's smooth, stepwise melodies were expanded into the wide intervallic leaps of Eric Dolphy. Motivic improvisations became more frequent, whether in a harmonically open context, as with Ornette Coleman, or in a more determined context, as with Sonny Rollins.[50] As the recycling and subversion of melodies, harmonic sequences, and forms from Tin Pan Alley became less of an issue, harmonic and modal schemes became more fluid. Harmonic practices ranged through quartal, serial, polytonal, pantonal, microtonal, and atonal techniques, eschewing the late Romantic notions of teleological tonality that bebop practice had revised. One classic early example is Bill Evans's "Flamenco Sketches" from Miles Davis's *Kind of Blue* recording, where a sequence of five modes recurs, with the duration of each mode being chosen interactively by the ensemble and soloist in real time.[51]

Improvised dialogues between poetry, theater, and music, explored by the beat generation in the 1950s, became a recurring feature in the 1960s, notably in the work of Archie Shepp, as well as the recording of Amiri Baraka's audacious poem "Black Dada Nihilismus" with the New York Art Quartet.[52] Improvised music became part of a multimedia environment that treated sound, visuals, text, and stage dress as integral features, and moreover (particularly among radical black artists) did not shy away from the inclusion of either the frankly political or the overtly spiritual. The durations of recorded pieces, once limited to the memory capacity of shellac-based media and the imperatives of radio airplay, expanded greatly. The long-playing vinyl record, which could hold up to twenty minutes per side, provided musicians with the means of experimenting with extended forms. Pieces of thirty to forty minutes in length, often in several movements, became more frequent, reflecting a revised situation in concerts and clubs, where, as John Coltrane put it in an interview, "we don't play the set forty-minute kind of thing anymore."[53]

As a result, improvisors began to think in terms of structural integrity on a larger scale. For instance, Coltrane evidently regarded his *Love Supreme* suite as an integrated work. At its 1965 Paris performance, the important producer and head of the jazz section of Radio France, Andre Francis, used standard "world of jazz" qualifiers to define the purview of Coltrane's sphere of influence, introducing Coltrane and his associates as "four musicians who are among the most important in the contemporary world *in the field of jazz*."[54] Francis went on to announce, "John Coltrane will play a tune—in fact, a *composition* in several movements."[55] Here, the producer audibly catches himself during his speech, as he suddenly appears to reflect upon the difference between a tune and a composition, and upon the difference between what Coltrane was doing and the standardized jazz that his discourse seemed to favor. At the end of the four-movement performance, which had lasted barely thirty minutes, Francis informs the audience that the concert was over. To disappointed groans and boos, the producer explains, "Comprenez, chers amis, que la musique ne se mesure pas au chronometre" (Understand, dear friends, that music is not measured with a stopwatch). Leaving the stage after the performance, Coltrane's implicit statement that there really was no point in following the extended suite with another piece could be said to express a notion of the organic wholeness and integrity of the work.[56]

Ultimately, it was the notion of "original music" itself as a key to self-determination for artists that seemed most attractive. Much of the "freedom" of the new musical approaches of the early 1960s grew out of the reliance by younger musicians—including many not generally associated with the "free" movements—on their own compositional talents. Ornette Coleman, for instance, played his own work almost exclusively—to the consternation of many critics and musicians. During this same period, rock music was also moving decisively away from cover tunes toward original composition. However, rock's discursive environment lacked the classicizing, canonizing impulse that had become active in the jazz field. Thus, in the minds of some critics, the move away from prefabricated forms became conflated with the notion of simply throwing away form as such,[57] a debate that returned in spades in the 1980s with the advent of neoclassicist revival in the jazz-identified art world. In both cases, many critics read this presumed rejection of form—correctly—as a symbolic challenge to traditional authority.

Certainly, the earliest development of free improvisation as an important practice in jazz, as well as allied traditions in American music and its offshoots, was a multiregional, multigenre, multiracial, and international affair. The composer Charles Ives privately recorded a short series of free improvisations between 1938 and 1943, as well as some highly personal versions of movements of his *Concord* Sonata that featured spontaneously conceived sections that apparently do not correspond to the printed score. The 1949 recordings of Lennie Tristano, *Intuition* and *Digression*, constituted an early, if not widely discussed, public irruption of jazz-identified free improvisation in the United States.[58] Ornette Coleman, Don Cherry, Charles Mingus, and Eric Dolphy all developed their work in Los Angeles during the late 1950s, and brought their new music, as it were, to the metropole, where they found Cecil Taylor and others already creating a different version of it. In 1959, a group of Afro-Caribbean immigrants to Britain, including saxophonist Joe Harriott, trumpeter Shake Keane, and bassist Coleridge Goode, joined with pianist Pat Smythe and the influential British drummer Phil Seamen to create what Harriott christened "free music." Totally independently of their American counterparts, the work of these Londoners favored collective, fragmented improvisation with frequent dynamic contrasts.[59]

Nonetheless, as German musicologist Ekkehard Jost points out, "it is plain that the early forms of free jazz and the innovations that marked its path came for the most part from black musicians. Furthermore, its most significant emotional components are not those of a diffuse 'world music,' but clearly derive from a music that is Afro-American in the broadest sense."[60]

Scott DeVeaux, among many others, has observed that "free jazz is often associated with the black nationalist politics of the 1960s." DeVeaux adds, "but it hardly needed the militant rhetoric of ethnicity to be controversial."[61] Jost, among others, has pointed out the nature of the musical risk: "Without question, free jazz, with its retreat from the laws of functional harmony and tonality, the fundamental rhythm that went throughout, and the break with traditional form schemes, posed the most radical break in the stylistic development of jazz."[62]

Of course, these challenges to conventional notions of sound, time, form, personality, tradition, and genre were new not only to jazz, but to music more broadly, since many of these ideas and practices were subsequently taken up in other genres, including contemporary classical music and the emerging experiments in rock. As with Andre Francis's sudden, onstage reconsideration of Coltrane's musical intent, the needless limitation of purview in Jost's observation may have its origins in "world of jazz" discourses that tend to close down the kinds of border-crossings that had been in evidence all along, unintentionally working to provincialize a musical tradition where exchange of sonic narratives has long been in evidence.

Particularly unsettling to many was the musicians' realization, completely congruent and coterminous with the situation in white experimental music, that "no sound, no device need be alien to their music."[63] Trombonist Grachan Moncur III declared that "if I have to bang on a dishpan with a stick, I'll do that too" in order to get meaning across.[64] In the same article, saxophonist James Moody, a member of the earlier generation now invoked as an icon of jazz conservatism, agreed with Moncur's assessment. "Any sound makes sense to me. Any sound at all. You fall on the floor—it makes sense. You fell, didn't you? Music is supposed to represent a feeling."[65]

This widespread notion that music is inherently representational of emotional states could be viewed as a crossover from late Romanticism. This new music, however, was being formed in a historical period in which so much art and music made by white artists, particularly Abstract Expressionism, was framed as progressive due to its nonrepresentational quality. In that light, the insistence by blacks that music has to be "saying something"[66] becomes part of a long history of resistance to the silencing of the black voice. Indeed, as might be expected from a people whose genetic, historical, and cultural legacies were interrupted through sustained, systematized violence, every effort was made by the musicians to recover rather than disrupt historical consciousness. Rather than an ordering of sounds for which the composer alternately claims parenthood and disclaims moment-to-moment responsibility, the new black musicians felt that music could effectuate the recovery of history itself.

Concomitantly with the rise of the new music, a kind of parallel salon scene was developing in Harlem and the East Village that included musicians such as Cecil Taylor, saxophonists Archie Shepp and Marion Brown, drummer Sunny Murray, painters Bob Thompson and Joe Overstreet, and writer A. B. Spellman.[67] For Hettie Jones, writing in 1990 of her life as the first wife of Amiri Baraka, "the racial balance in our house shifted, as a black avant-garde—writers, musicians, painters, dancers—became part of the new East Village, just coming into that name."[68] As Baraka remembers, his "new, blacker circle" of associates[69] felt that a major revolution in music was once again being spearheaded by African American musicians in jazz clubs like the Five Spot, the Half Note, and the Village Gate, in smaller coffeehouses such as the White Whale, and in private lofts. As Baraka remembers, "I especially liked Morton Feldman's music, Cage's audacity and some of the other things. But we were mostly into the new black music."[70]

In these circles, an explicitly asserted relationship between art and life was the rule rather than the exception. As Albert Ayler said to interviewer Nat Hentoff in 1966, "I've lived more than I can express in bop terms. Why should I hold back the feeling of my life, of being raised in the ghetto of America?"[71] Similarly, pianist McCoy Tyner gave Valerie Wilmer the title of her influential 1977 account of black experimental musicians, declaring that their music was "as serious as your life."[72] Nonetheless, for many commentators and musicians, the roots of the new musicians' assertion of criticality lay in the bebop musicians' political awareness, as saxophonist Jimmy Lyons noted: "Bebop was in a certain sense very romantic. It talked about heroic actions, about things that had to be done both politically *and* musically, but they didn't *do* them. Basically, in bebop it was about the *idea* of what had to be done, instead of actually doing something. We're doing it now."[73]

For DeVeaux, this new music "simply carried the model of modernist experimentation (but without an explicit Eurocentric focus) to its logical, if unsettling, conclusion."[74] Musically risky, unstable, emotional, often unabashedly political and even confrontational, the music was sharpening the already glaring contradictions between the twin roles of entertainer and experimentalist assigned to black artists to the point where the contradiction could no longer be sustained. Thus, the new musicians felt great pride in creating a new music that was "part of a rising black consciousness among young Negroes in all kinds of milieus."[75] In the new black music, for Baraka, "there was a newness and a defiance, a demand for freedom, politically and creatively, it was all connected.[76] We knew the music was hip and new and out beyond anything anyone downtown was doing, in music, painting, poetry, dance, or whatever the fuck. And we felt, I know I did, that we were linked to that music that Trane and Ornette and C. T., Shepp and Dolphy and the others, were making, so the old white arrogance and elitism of Europe as Center Art was stupid on its face."[77]

Critical Responses: Anger, Noise, Failure

Certainly, as Scott DeVeaux notes, in this period, "freedom from musical convention becomes conflated with freedom from oppressive political structures."[78] The music's protagonists repeatedly go on record with the understanding that their work represented a personal response to social and political conditions, as well as the economic conditions under which they regularly worked. According to Shepp, for example, the musicians' shared condition of apparent economic servitude was a prime factor in their dissatisfaction. Speaking of the white-dominated structures of the jazz music industry in terms that clearly recalled slavery, Shepp declared that "you own the music, we make it. By definition, then you own the people who make the music. You own in us whole chunks of flesh."[79]

Undoubtedly, the new black musicians' pointed, politically charged critiques of dominant American values encouraged a 1966 *New York Times* magazine article by Hentoff to summarize the new music in a headline as "Black, Angry and Hard to Understand." Indeed, the highly charismatic, photogenic, and highly quotable Archie Shepp was not shy about proclaiming that "we're not simply angry young men—we are enraged. And I think it's damn well time."[80] For many listeners, particularly whites, the trope of anger seemed new to the encounter with black music, which had up to this point been culturally marked as nonthreatening and generally good-humored. A scene from Amiri Baraka's 1964 play, *Dutchman,* suggests that such views now represented a kind of whistling in the dark:

> Charlie Parker? Charlie Parker. All the hip white boys scream for Bird. And Bird saying, "Up your ass, feeble-minded ofay! Up your ass." And they sit there talking about the tortured genius of Charlie Parker. Bird would've played not a note of music if he'd just walked up East Sixty-seventh Street and killed the first ten white people he saw.[81]

The criticism of the new music as "just noise" can be seen as a hold-over from antebellum days, when the music of black slaves, as historian Jon Cruz notes, "appears to have been heard by captors and overseers primarily as noise—that is, as strange, unfathomable, and incomprehensible."[82] As Cruz points out, for slave owners to hear only noise is "tantamount to being oblivious to the structures of meaning that anchored sounding to the hermeneutic world of the slaves." To hear only noise is to "remain removed from how slave soundings probed their circumstances and cultivated histories and memories."[83] Similarly, the noisy anger of the new musicians seemed strange, surprising, and unfathomable to many critics, along with the idea that blacks might actually have something to be angry about.

In this regard, Coltrane's rejoinder to characterizations of his music as "angry" could function as a sort of double entendre. The saxophonist's avowed goal of trying to show "the many wonderful things he knows of and senses in the universe"[84] was an apt way of reminding the critical fraternity of the power and purpose of music. However, Coltrane's universalist rhetoric could also be read as a masked statement of resistance, similar to many that subalterns have issued. The composer of "Alabama," dedicated to the children murdered in the infamous bombing of Birmingham's 16th Street Baptist Church, could only have been angry at a heinous act whose symbolism directly threatened not only the lives of all black people, but the humanity of all.

One can imagine a number of reasons for musicians to articulate this kind of indirect resistance. Certainly, fear of economic reprisal could have played a role. For instance, one critic, writing in 1966, perhaps inadvertently issued a kind of threat to Coltrane in a performance review. The writer speculated on the harm that Coltrane, a champion of younger artists, could be inflicting upon himself by continuing to support members of "the extremist faction" of new musicians, mentioning in particular saxophonists Shepp, Ayler, and Carlos Ward: "If Coltrane has an obligation, real or imagined, to these people whom he insists on carrying on his coattails, does he not also have an obligation to his audience? They come to hear him, not those others. They don't hear him. Will they come back? Coltrane is playing a dangerous game in which the risks are all his. The others, the have-nots, have nothing to lose. He does."[85]

An early essay by Ronald Radano maintains that the initial reception of the new music by critics was largely favorable. However, this optimistic claim appears to be undermined by even a casual review of Leonard Feather's monthly "Blindfold Test" columns in *Down Beat* during this period. The Blindfold Test was a journalistic appropriation of a widespread listening practice in which more experienced listeners played recordings for novices, asking them to identify the musicians. This social practice of acculturation taught musicians and listeners to identify styles, eras, and other aspects of improvisation. In the published tests, however, professional musicians advanced public critiques of their colleagues. While the fun for readers lay in realizing that even professional musicians were not unerringly perfect in their judgments of style, as music historian Ekkehard Jost saw it, the tests served to accentuate generational divides and destabilize collegial solidarity:

> What was extraordinarily convenient for the large conservative element of 1960s jazz criticism was that with the dawn of free jazz, the solidarity of silence among jazz musicians found its end. If earlier, the musicians had scrupulously avoided expressing something negative before a man of the press, or even an outsider, free jazz had now opened the sluice-gates of discretion. Older musicians described younger ones as charlatans who didn't understand their craft, who were wantonly destroying jazz, and who would not swing.[86]

A number of musicians from earlier generations or representing other styles of music were asked by Feather to comment on the new music, often with depressingly predictable results. Rarely did Feather subject the new musicians to the test, allowing them to comment on the work of their forebears. Trumpeter Ruby Braff had "never heard anything as disjointed and mixed-up in my life."[87] In a well-known comment on a Cecil Taylor recording, Miles Davis accuses the critics of manufacturing consent and hyping the new sounds. "Is that what the critics are digging? Them critics better stop having coffee. . . . Just to take something like this and say it's great, because there ain't nothing to listen to, that's like going out and getting a prostitute."[88] Feather prods Davis by informing him that "this man said he was influenced by Duke Ellington." The trumpeter replies, "I don't give a ——! It must be Cecil Taylor, right? I don't care who he's inspired by. That —— ain't nothing."[89] Other musicians, such as arranger and multi-instrumentalist Benny Carter, were simply nonplussed. "When people like Gunther Schuller and John Lewis, whose musicianship I respect, back and support this so openly and so fervently, I don't know what to think."[90]

One of the few established musicians interviewed for Feather's Blindfold

Tests who dissented from the cavalcade of negativity was Sonny Rollins, who had hired Ornette Coleman's associate, trumpeter Don Cherry, for the recording *Our Man in Jazz*.[91] Furthermore, Rollins was reported to have played "free, new-thing collective jazz" with Prince Lasha, Sonny Simmons, Henry Grimes, and Charles Moffett at a 1963 benefit event for a Greenwich Village social service center.[92] At the outset of the interview, Rollins pointedly and preemptively reminded the critic that "as you know, Leonard, I'm in favor of Ornette and many of the things he has done." The saxophonist went on to identify in Coleman "qualities you can find in everybody since Louis Armstrong—all the good guys."[93]

During his test, Charles Mingus noticed that no recordings of new music had been played for him. Perhaps realizing Feather's strategy of letting others speak for him, the bassist volunteered a comment on Coleman's music that still ranks with the most insightful views of the saxophonist's early work. "You didn't play anything by Ornette Coleman," Mingus told Feather, prepared to assert agency in the interview. "I'll comment on him anyway. . . . One night Symphony Sid was playing a whole lot of stuff, and then he put on an Ornette Coleman record. . . . It made everything else he was playing, even my own record that he played, sound terrible. . . . I'm not saying everybody's going to have to play like Coleman," the bassist and composer concluded, "but they're going to have to stop copying Bird."[94]

Even so, it is doubtful that any music, anywhere, has received such harsh criticism as did this new music in its formative years. The Radano article blamed the musicians' "hard-edged radicalism" and "superior and self-righteous attitudes" for the vehemence of the negative critical response.[95] According to this view, "the jazz avant-garde, bent on the recognition of its art, began an ambitious, hard-line campaign against all who opposed its music, a campaign that split the community into two hostile camps."[96] Had the new musicians not manifested these attitudes, the author claims, they could have presented their unusual music without any resistance from the mainstream. The pure embodiment of this hard line was saxophonist Shepp, most prominent among the musicians who "preached their extremist doctrines in issue after issue of the major publications of the jazz community."[97] As the article frames it, Shepp, Amiri Baraka, and writer Frank Kofsky, among others, often deployed race as a battering ram. Kofsky, who in 1970 published an important text linking the new music with radical black nationalism,[98] comes in for particular criticism for his charge that the editorial staff of *Down Beat* was "thoroughly ingrained with the precepts of white supremacy."[99] Kofsky's comment seemed to confirm Radano's suggestion that regardless of the topic, avant-garde spokesmen who appeared in print in jazz magazines inevitably seemed to base their arguments on racial oppression by a dominant white society. "Racism" became the collective cry, the watchword for the avant-garde jazz community. Any type of opposition, whether directed towards a group or an individual, met with the wrath of the jazz avant-garde, who branded as "racist" the entire jazz establishment.[100]

The negative critical response to the new music, however, preceded by a number of years the most intense period of political controversy over race in the jazz field. Coleman and other new musicians had been receiving sometimes quite vitriolic press reviews as early as 1961.[101] What is more, critics often made sharp distinctions among the new musicians, playing them against each other in print, as in a 1962 article in which prominent critic Martin Williams made it clear that "my opinion of John Coltrane's current work in no way reflects my opinion of Ornette Coleman's." Williams was a major supporter of Coleman, whose "atonal" playing Williams contrasted with Coltrane's "conventional and traditional" music.[102] Moreover, the severity of the critiques bore scant correlation with the degree of political militancy of an individual musician. For instance, John Coltrane, known for gentle, expansive statements of aesthetics and purpose, was subjected to an intense campaign of critical vituperation. One particularly egregious example was a 1961 *Down Beat* article by critic John Tynan, who referred to a Coltrane-Dolphy performance as "anarchistic," "gobbledygook," and, most infamously, as "a horrifying demonstration of what appears to be a growing anti-jazz trend."[103]

By 1962, Leonard Feather, emboldened by this and other critical commentary, felt sufficiently secure to stop hiding behind Blindfolded musicians, calling Tynan's "anti-jazz" comments "as acute as they were timely."[104] Rather than remaining passive in the face of the violence of the critiques, Coltrane and Eric Dolphy (who had attracted negative notice despite his strong connections with Third Stream composer Gunther Schuller) replied directly to the most extreme framings of their work in a 1962 *Down Beat* cover story, "John Coltrane and Eric Dolphy Answer the Jazz Critics." Rather than offering anecdotes about life on the road and lists of colleagues who were all "fine musicians," Dolphy and Coltrane, in a rather prosaic tone, foregrounded issues of infrastructure, aesthetics, technique, content, and form in their work.

Along the way, in this early form of talking back to the media, the two men quietly expose the cultural insularity that had guided much of the criticism. Perhaps not knowing of French composer Olivier Messiaen's 1940s work with translating bird calls into instrumental sounds, the interviewer skeptically questions Dolphy's use of bird sounds: "Are bird imitations valid in jazz?" Affirming his own artistic agency, Dolphy graciously responded, "I don't know if it's valid in jazz, but I enjoy it."[105] The saxophonist went on to directly address the issue of the power and authority of critics, calling both for dialogue and for responsible journalism. "If something new has happened, something nobody knows that the musician is doing," Dolphy offered, "[the critic] should ask the musician about it. Because somebody may like it; they might want to know something about it. Sometimes it really hurts, because a musician not only loves his work but depends on it for a living. If somebody writes something bad about musicians, people stay away."[106] Coltrane agreed. "I have even seen favorable criticism which revealed a lack of profound analysis, causing it to be little more than superficial." Asserting the agency of the artist while at the same time framing musical reception in terms of a social network in which many positions were possible, Coltrane concluded that "understanding is what is needed."[107]

Ultimately, Radano's early article was obliged to admit the highly problematic nature of the many harsh critiques. Nonetheless, the historian saw a "more judicious perspective" emerging at mid-decade.[108] However, the record easily supports an alternative reading, where, if anything, critical commentary became even more shrill as the decade progressed. According to the reviewer of Coleman's 1960 recording *This Is Our Music,* Coleman had been prematurely "declared a genius and the prophet of the jazz to come." Perhaps seeking to debunk this kind of "hype," the reviewer had this to say:

> The technical abominations of his playing aside—and his lack of technical control is abominable—Coleman's music, to me, has only two shades: a maudlin, pleading lyricism and a wild ferocity bordering on bedlam. His is not musical freedom; disdain for principles and boundaries is synonymous not with freedom, but with anarchy. . . . If Coleman's work is to be the standard of excellence, then the work of Lester Young, Louis Armstrong, Charlie Parker, Duke Ellington, and all the other jazzmen who have been accepted as important artists must be thrown on the trash heap.[109]

In 1962, Coleman's *Free Jazz* was simultaneously applauded and viciously attacked in a double *Down Beat* review. John Tynan's pithy, sarcastic second review asks, "Where does neurosis end and psychosis begin?" The narrative features a rhetorical plea for the restoration of order and authority. "If nothing else," he wrote, "this witch's brew is the logical end product of a bankrupt philosophy of ultraindividualism in music. 'Collective improvisation?' Nonsense. The only semblance of collectivity lies in the fact that these eight nihilists were collected together in one studio at one time and with one common cause: to destroy the music that gave them birth."[110] Another infamous quote cast Coltrane as an apostate who had defiled the temple of the mainstream. The critic reacted with evident horror to a concert featuring Coltrane's late group, with Pharoah Sanders, Alice Coltrane, and Rashied Ali: "One wonders what has happened to Coltrane. Is he the prisoner of a band of hypnotists? Has he lost all musical judgment? Or is he putting on his audience? Whatever the answer, it was saddening to contemplate this spectacle, unworthy of a great musician."[111]

Ultimately, the intensity of the anti–new music journalism only corroborated the musicians' frequent public pronouncements that the reception and distribution of black music suffered from a kind of overseer mentality on the part of the critical community, and the commercial community that stood behind it. Historian Ekkehard Jost, operating from a European perspective, offers a scathing critical indictment of the U.S. journalism of the period, which for him, "brought to light nothing other than the ignorance and—perhaps unconscious—infamy of large segments of American jazz criticism, and its carelessness in terms of the most elementary rules of its craft. Of course, there were also a number of critics who approached the new jazz with sympathy, whether for inherently musical reasons, or only ideological ones. However, they were in the minority and seldom published in the standard journals."[112] Moreover, for many critics, the nature of the music itself militated against any hope of audience success. "Avant-garde jazz," claimed Radano, "is not music for the masses—black or white,"[113] and on this view, the musicians' attacks on the establishment provided "an excuse" for their "lack of recognition by both the black and the jazz communities." In this account, supportive offerings from "non-musician" supporters such as Frank Kofsky and LeRoi Jones were based in "blind-faith" rather than "objective analysis."[114]

Undoubtedly, the contemporaneous critical atmosphere of *Besserwissen* influenced the production of one response in particular, in the form of one of the most hotly contested essays of the period, LeRoi Jones's 1963 "Jazz and the White Critic."[115] Writing in *Down Beat*, Jones asserts that it was the critics, and white critics in particular, who had failed, rather than the musicians. Jones begins with a provocation: "Most jazz critics have been white

Americans, but most important jazz musicians have not been."[116] The writer is unafraid of a generalized ad hominem approach to the field, maintaining that

> because the majority of jazz critics are white middle-brows, most jazz criticism tends to enforce white middle-brow standards of excellence as some criterion for performance of a music that in its most profound manifestations is completely antithetical to such standards—in fact, quite often is in direct reaction against them. (As an analogy suppose the great majority of the critics of Western formal music were poor, uneducated Negroes?)[117]

Jones's review of the European origins of American jazz criticism makes the point, unremarkable in our own day but seriously controversial in the 1960s era of New Criticism, that the work of critics, as members of a given society, would inevitably "reflect, at least, some of the attitudes and thinking of that society, even if such attitudes were not directly related to the subject they were writing about, i.e., Negro music."[118] Jones argues that black music was treated by musicologists in a very different way from Western music, where the relevance of historical and cultural factors to criticism was supposedly a given.[119] Jones ends with a prediction that "criticism of Negro music will move closer to developing as consistent and valid an esthetic as criticism in other fields of Western art."[120] For Jones, this development would inevitably be based in American tropes, an assertion that (perhaps surprisingly in this case) recapitulates the project of Alain Locke for the vindication of black music as standing at the center of the very notion of American culture.

> In jazz criticism, no reliance on European tradition or theory will help at all. Negro music, like the Negro himself, is strictly a phenomenon of this country, and we have got to set up standards of judgment and aesthetic excellence that depend on our native knowledge and understanding of the underlying philosophies and local cultural references that produced blues and jazz in order to produce valid critical writing or commentary about it.[121]

A Far Cry from New York: Segregation and Chicago Music
By the late 1950s, Chicago's Black Belt Bantustan, teeming with two generations of black migrants, was poised to burst its bounds. In the wake of

the demise of the legal basis for restrictive covenants following the 1948 Supreme Court decision in *Shelley v. Kramer*,[122] Bronzeville families began to cross the established borders, encountering staunch resistance from white communities. Real estate speculators encouraged the not-so-great migration known as "white flight," obtaining property at bargain rates from white homeowners desperate to flee, and reselling them to black families at much higher prices and interest rates. Once blacks seeking housing on the South Side were able to cross Cottage Grove Avenue, the traditional barrier separating Hyde Park from the Black Belt to the west, the University of Chicago, working with the city administration, moved decisively to restrict the black presence in its Hyde Park neighborhood via a strategy of "managed integration."[123]

Another common form of white resistance to integration deployed both random and coordinated violence. Black families moving into previously white areas faced danger from white residents, and furious civil disturbances, such as the Fernwood riot of 1947, the 1949 Englewood riot, the Cicero riot of 1951, and the Trumbull Park riot of 1953, involved thousands of people and often took days or even years to fully contain. Historian Arnold Hirsch describes the situation in a number of Chicago neighborhoods as exhibiting a "pattern of chronic urban guerrilla warfare,"[124] as local beaches, schools, playgrounds, and parks, as well as commercial and cultural establishments, such as stores, dance halls, and movie theaters, became sites for skirmishes between newer black residents and visitors and ad hoc gangs of working-class whites.

The integrationist subcultures active in 1950s and 1960s New York have long formed the model for more generalized assumptions in jazz historiography concerning attitudes toward race in jazz art worlds. In contrast to the somewhat integrated Bohemia of 1950s and 1960s New York, however, the atmosphere that nurtured the AACM was solidly rooted in a geographically and socially overdetermined black community. Though white musicians and patrons did appear on the South Side of Chicago, the few narratives documenting the music of 1950s black Chicago do not support the presence of any kind of sustained integrationist subculture. Writer J. B. Figi, one of the early supporters of the AACM, explained that at the turn of the 1960s, passage across the North-South divide constituted something of a border experience for musicians.

> Black musicians were welcome on the North Side, generally, once they
> got where they were going. But there was heavy segregation here. Blacks

were not welcome outside of the Black community. They didn't go to the Loop to eat, except maybe a few places. It was just a very kind of segregated situation. So, there wasn't . . . there was a lot more white musicians going to play in the Black community than there was the other way around, primarily because there was so much prejudice and it was so difficult for Black people to move around the city without incurring all kinds of nasty things, that it just didn't happen that much.[125]

Figi further remembers that the mobility of white listeners was also being discouraged: "There weren't really a lot of . . . a lot of white people going to the South Side, and there were a whole lot of white people telling you, "You're crazy. You can't go down there, you'll get killed."[126] According to Figi, the general atmosphere of segregation extended to employment opportunities and collegial relationships among musicians:

> There was also a Jim Crow thing working amongst which musicians played the North Side and which played the South Side. The Kenton and Herman Bands and so on would be playing the North Side, primarily, and a lot of white Be-Boppers would be playing the North Side. And some of them would play the South Side as well. Most of the Black Be-Boppers would be playing the South Side. A few of them might venture to the North Side, but primarily there was a split there. Charlie Parker played the Argyle Lounge, but more than . . . more often than not, it was white players playing in those areas . . . I mentioned it because it was . . . it was considered somewhat of a landmark, he played the North Side and, you know, played that club.[127]

Multi-instrumentalist Ira Sullivan (tenor saxophone, alto saxophone, and trumpet) was one of the few whites who performed extensively on the South Side. In February 1961, a Sullivan group featured Richard Abrams and his close associate, bassist Donald Rafael Garrett, along with Wilbur Campbell and Nicky Hill, who died of "unknown causes"—in all probability, a heroin overdose—just two years later. Roland Kirk was also living and working in Chicago, and the Ira Sullivan–Roland Kirk Quintet performed at the Sutherland in September 1960, with Abrams and Garrett.[128] Comparing the South Side to the North Side in terms of creative atmosphere, Sullivan used the familiar black slang word for "white person" to declare in a 1960 *Down Beat* profile that "most ofays didn't understand me. . . . They'd argue for an hour about who was to play what. But on the south side, we only wanted to play. We'd play with tenor and drums if that's all that was there. It was an entirely different attitude."[129]

Down Beat was a Chicago-based publication, but its exploration of issues of segregation in its own backyard was assigned to Canadian writer Gene Lees, who had moved to the city in 1959 to take a position at the magazine.[130] In a 1960 "Report on Chicago," Lees accurately described the contemporaneous situation. "To see what is happening in jazz in Chicago today," the writer noted, "you can divide the subject into two parts: north side jazz and south side jazz." Lees, who later authored a book touting the importance of integrationist subcultures in jazz,[131] was clearly nonplussed by the absence of such subcultures in Chicago music. Despite these appearances, Lees worked hard at finding ways to describe the cultural and economic differences between the North Side and the South Side music scenes without using the words "Negro" and "white." This was done by drawing upon the West Coast jazz stereotype of the "cool" to describe the work of a set of mostly white (though unmarked as such) North Side musicians, such as violinist John Frigo, trumpeter Cy Touff, and pianist Dick Marx. The writer described their work as "polite, subtle, and generally, out of the main vigorous stream of contemporary jazz."[132]

As Lees saw it, the North Siders benefited from a work environment that offered a range of jazz and commercial work, as well as club-based sinecures. In contrast, the writer's selection of Lurlean Hunter to represent the South Side offers the revelation that the African American singer "saw her career wither on the vine, and for a while had no work at all—not even in Chicago."[133] In any event, Lees contrasts Hunter's femininity with the "big-toned and virile-sounding" Johnny Griffin, as well as Ira Sullivan and Eddie Harris, as best representing "the typical Chicago jazz of today."[134] The writer was clearly impressed by South Side jam sessions, and makes special mention of those that were being booked by the young jazz entrepreneur Joe Segal.[135] Lees portrays a lively South Side club and theater scene, as well as the Near North Side club, the French Poodle, where the Richard Abrams Trio happened to be holding forth regularly at the amazing hour of 7:30 a.m.[136]

The article cites statistics from an unnamed source asserting that Chicago accounted for 8 percent of U.S. jazz record sales—nearly twice as high a percentage per capita as New York. Nonetheless, as Johnny Griffin rather acidly put it, "The difference between Chicago and New York is that a musician who comes from New York can get work in his home town."[137] At the time, both Griffin and Sullivan, according to the article, were dividing their time between Chicago and New York. Eddie Harris, soon to have a hit recording, *Exodus to Jazz*,[138] told Lees that part of the difficulty with being based in Chicago was a culture of diffidence regarding matters of promotion. "Everyone is inclined to do nothing—both club owners and record companies," said Harris. "They ignore you unless you go elsewhere . . . the club owners wait to see what New York does and says."[139]

3

THE DEVELOPMENT OF
THE EXPERIMENTAL BAND

Alternative Pedagogies of Experimental Music

For many musicians, the space race began not in 1957 with the So-
viet Union's launch of the satellite Sputnik, but in 1946, when the
pianist Herman Blount came up on the train from Birmingham to
Bronzeville. Soon after his arrival, Sonny (as he was called) landed
a job with Fletcher Henderson's orchestra at the Club De Lisa on
55th and State, a gig that he held down until mid-1947, when the
Red Saunders Band succeeded Henderson. Sonny stayed on, rehearsing the band and refashioning Saunders's backup arrangements for
singers like Laverne Baker, Dakota Staton, Joe Williams, and Sarah
Vaughan. Blount founded his own band in 1950, with people like
saxophonists Harold Ousley, Von Freeman, Earl Ezell (later Ahmad
Salaheldeen), and John Jenkins, bassist Wilbur Ware, and drummer
Vernel Fournier.

Sometime in 1952, Blount announced that the Creator had ordered
him to change his name. He went downtown to the Circuit Court
of Cook County and legally became "Le Sony'r Ra." In addition, he
registered a business under the name of "Sun Ra."[1] Most musicians
in Chicago, however, still knew him as Sonny, one of the qualified
musicians of the South Side's musical community. As Jodie Christian
remembers,

> My first encounter with him, he was playing stride piano, working at the It Club on 55th and Michigan. He was a good pianist, playing conventional piano, stride. We were playing, and Sun Ra was playing as a single pianist, a cocktail piano player opposite us. He hadn't become "Sun Ra" then. I never heard anybody say that they remember when he started to organize this type of band, the space band. All of a sudden, it was there.

In 1952 Sonny began to seek out younger musicians from Captain Dyett's DuSable regime, including drummer Robert Barry and saxophonist Laurdine "Pat" Patrick, to form a group called the Space Trio. Eventually, Sun Ra's band began to grow, with exciting young musicians such as trombonist Julian Priester; percussionist Jim Herndon; bassist Victor Sproles; trumpeters Art Hoyle, Hobart Dotson, and Dave Young; and saxophonists James Spaulding, John Gilmore, Charles Davis, and Marshall Allen. Sonny's charisma, erudition, and creativity inspired the musicians, who regarded him as their mentor. As Marshall Allen observed, "Sun Ra taught me to translate spirit into music."[2]

Around this time, as Sonny's compositional palette became richer, he coined the term "Arkestra" for his band. "That's the way black people say 'orchestra,'" he observed laconically.[3] At the Arkestra's daily rehearsals, Sonny began to explicitly connect his music with projects of identity, philosophy, historical recovery, and mysticism. He explored the role of black people in the creation of civilization, and maintained that music could both change individual moral values and affect the fate of the world. The titles of his pieces began to connect two major themes—the infinite, Ethiopianist Zion of outer space, and the African mothership of Egypt, Ethiopia, and Nubia.

As anthropologist and Ra biographer John Szwed has noted, with Sun Ra, "music often seemed to be the subtext for some grander plan, one not always clear to the musicians."[4] Whatever the plan, Jodie Christian saw at first hand that Sonny's disciplined domination of the Arkestra was absolute.

> One day he was playing at Budland and the whole band was there, but Sun Ra wasn't there. So I told John [Gilmore] and them, why don't y'all hit and Sun Ra can come in later? "Naw, we don't hit till Sonny comes in." Sonny comes in an hour later. He ran in, sat down at the piano, and the band took their seats. You know what he said? "Let that be a lesson." So at the end of the set I asked John, what was the lesson? He said, I don't know, but Sonny said it was.

Alvin Fielder met Ra while working a dance gig on the West Side in 1959. "He asked me where I was from, and I told him I was from Mississippi. So he said, 'Look, man, I bet you can play some shuffles.'" Sonny invited Fielder to an Arkestra rehearsal. "I was way above my head. I thought I was playing well, but as I look back, I'm sure that I wasn't. Anyway, Sunny invited me to join the band. So I did." Fielder played with Ra in 1959 and 1960. "Of course, the money wasn't that great. But then again, as I look back, I should have been paying him."[5] Late in 1960, Sun Ra's spaceship, with John Gilmore, Marshall Allen, and Pat Patrick on board, blasted off from Chicago for points east, eventually landing in New York City in January 1961.[6] By 1962, the composer and pianist was preparing for an important New York concert with his Cosmic Jazz Space Group.[7]

Philip Cohran had been working with the Arkestra since John Gilmore had brought him to a rehearsal in 1958.[8] For Cohran, Ra's example "opened my world up as a composer. I had written a few songs of merit before I got with him, but he taught me the one thing that really made a difference in my life, and that is: whatever you want to do, do it all the time. Once I learned that, there was no looking back."[9]

All the same, Cohran decided not to climb aboard for the Arkestra's New York foray. "When I left 'The Society,'" Cohran remembered, "everybody thought I was crazy. When I told Sun Ra that I was going to deal with my own thing, and I quit the band, I started studying on my own. I said, I don't need nobody else to tell me what to do, I'll just go ahead and do it myself. So I started studying every day." In fact, during this time, the possibility of challenging the societal status quo drew many African Americans toward independent research into historical and spiritual knowledge. Richard Abrams says that "I always had a keen interest for looking into the so-called 'occult arts.' Around '59 or '60 I really started getting into that. One of the first books I read was *Autobiography of a Yogi* by Paramahansa Yogananda. It awakened something in me that needed awakening. I bought literature and bought literature, and ended up finding out about the Rosicrucians. I got in touch with them and hooked up with the Rosicrucians."[10]

As Abrams became known as one of Chicago's up-and-coming pianist-composers, two musicians exercised a profound impact upon his musical direction. The composer, arranger, and trumpeter William E. "Will" Jackson, who had played with Jimmie Lunceford, lived down the street from Abrams, and began to informally teach the young pianist the craft of arranging and orchestration. Around 1955, Jackson introduced the young composer to pianist Walter "King" Fleming, perhaps the most important early local influence on Abrams's piano improvisations.[11] Abrams began to compose, arrange, and play for Fleming's band. "Every so often," Abrams remembers, "they would let me sit in at the piano, until I would make a mistake and they would tell me to get up. But they would put me back down there until I learned how to do it." Attracting the attention of radio personality Daddy-O Daylie, Abrams, saxophonist Nicky Hill, bassist Bob Cranshaw, drummer Walter Perkins, and trumpeter Paul Serrano formed a band called the MJT+3. In 1957, the group's first recording, *Daddy-O Presents MJT+3*,[12] featured a number of Abrams compositions, including "No Name," which was actually composed collaboratively by Abrams and Fleming.[13]

Abrams was also moving further along the autodidact path that had led him away from the conservatory. "I could always make up music," Abrams remembered, "but it was plain stubbornness. I wanted to do it my own way. Even as a kid, when I didn't even know how to do it, I would rebel against the mainstream situation." The search for a way of teaching himself led him to the pianist, composer, and arranger Charles Stepney, who introduced Abrams to Joseph Schillinger's unusual system of musical composition. Stepney, a house arranger for Chess Records, was soon to apply Schillinger-related principles, along with ideas from composer Henry Cowell's early text, *New Musical Resources*[14] and the work of György Ligeti, to his landmark work for Ramsey Lewis, the Dells, the Rotary Connection and Minnie Riperton, Phil Upchurch, Muddy Waters, and Earth, Wind, and Fire.[15] Stepney introduced Schillinger's books to Abrams, who ended up buying his own copies.[16] Everywhere he went over the next four years, Abrams kept these two massive tomes at the ready, teaching himself the complete system and developing new ideas under its guidance.

Schillinger was a pianist, composer, and theorist who came to the United States from Russia in 1928. Something of a polymath, Schillinger collaborated on experimental electronic instrument design with fellow Russian expatriate Leon Theremin and Cowell, who wrote the foreword to Schillinger's signal work, the 1,600-page *Schillinger System of Musical Composition*, first published in the mid-1940s. The elusive Schillinger Society published and distributed the system as two large, expensive books containing many detailed musical examples, and in 1945, former Schillinger student Lawrence Berk founded the Schillinger House of Music to carry on the master's teachings. In 1954, the school changed its name to the Berklee School of

Music, as its curriculum expanded to include genres outside the canon of pan-European classical music, most notably jazz.[17]

Schillinger taught that a wide variety of expressive forms, including both tonal and post-tonal harmony, could be both generated and analyzed algorithmically using mathematical formulae. His system emerged alongside other mathematics-oriented formal methods that emerged in the mid-to-late 1940s, such as French composer Olivier Messiaen's 1944 *Technique de mon langage musical,*[18] and later, the integral serialism that developed in America, with the work of Milton Babbitt, and in Europe, in the work of Karlheinz Stockhausen and Messiaen's former student, Pierre Boulez. Schillinger's work with graphic elements, which anticipated by more than a decade the stochasticism of Iannis Xenakis,[19] seemed to be justified by the premise of Cowell's "overture" to the first volume of the Schillinger system, which held out the promise of using the system to move beyond well-established musical methods that were appearing stiflingly hegemonic in some circles: "The currently taught rules of harmony, counterpoint, and orchestration certainly do not suggest to the student materials adapted from his own expressive desires," Cowell wrote. "Instead he is given a small and circumscribed set of materials, already much used, together with a set of prohibitions to apply to them, and then he is asked to express himself only within these limitations."[20]

While serialism based its rule sets firmly on the chromatic scale, and bebop harmony revised Wagnerian chromaticism, the Schillinger system made few presumptions concerning materials. Rather, whatever materials were identified by the composer as salient—rhythmic, harmonic, timbral, melodic, dynamic—became the basis for further generation and transformation. Thus, as Cowell noted, "the Schillinger System offers possibilities, not limitations; it is a positive, not a negative approach to the choice of musical materials." As such, the system was equally suited "to old and new styles in music, and to 'popular' and 'serious' composition."[21] For this reason, the Schillinger system soon attracted composers from Earle Brown to B. B. King. The explicit organicism of Schillinger's *Mathematical Basis of the Arts* connected musical invention with forms active in the natural environment, advancing the basically synaesthetic proposition that gestures active in one art form could find explicit, ordered, primordial analogues in another.[22]

Positing an explicit role for the religious and spiritual aspects of music, Schillinger's ideas ran counter to modernism's secularist ideal. As a budding painter who had already explored the synaesthetics of Kandinsky, Abrams was excited about Schillinger's construction of a necessary, ordered connection between sound, sense, science, emotion, reason, and the natural world. These ideas resounded with Abrams's own explorations of the connection between music and spirituality. "I was really educated now, in a big way," Abrams exulted, "because I was impressed with a method for analyzing just about anything I see, by approaching it from its basic premise. The Schillinger stuff taught me to break things back down into raw material—where it came from—and then, on to the whole idea of a personal or individual approach to composition."

While Abrams was beginning to get a foothold in the Chicago musical scene, Steve McCall left the city to join the U.S. Air Force. Eventually, his orders took him to Bangor, Maine, where he ran the service club. "The service being what it was, it was a typically bad experience," his sister Rochelle recalled. "Somebody put a note on the door, 'All Niggers, Coons and Nightfighters Be Off The Street By Midnight.'"[23] McCall returned to Chicago in 1954, and found a job in the airline industry.[24] During that time, he bought his first set of drums, and used free air travel passes to visit New York and Philadelphia, where he took drum lessons from Charles "Specs" Wright, who had animated the big bands of Dizzy Gillespie and Earl Bostic.[25] Watching the styles of Marshall Thompson, Wilbur Campbell, James Pettis, and Vernel Fournier, among others, by 1960 McCall had become one of the most sought-after young drummers in Chicago.[26]

Around that same time, Abrams was looking for an outlet for his new ideas, and an opportunity emerged to do just that in 1961, when "there was a group of mainstream guys that formed a band for cats to write charts and things. We were rehearsing at the C&C Lounge on Cottage Grove and 63rd. A cat named Chuck ran it. It was a great big old long place, with a stage up front. They had floor shows in there. Eddie Harris was a part of it, Marshall Thompson." By 1960, the ad hoc, informal educational system of jazz, combining high-school band training, informal jam sessions, home schooling, and autodidacticism, had already produced some of the world's most influential music. Even so, many experienced Chicago musicians were seeking ways to address the limitations of this model of learning. For instance, neither high-school ensemble classes nor jam sessions taught theory in a consistent way. Vibraphonist Emanuel Cranshaw describes one of the alternatives that some musicians pursued in the mid-1950s:

> Cats like Chris Anderson used to have classes in this basement on 39th and Lake Park, the way Barry Harris used to do. He was playing with a guitar player, a cat named Leo Blevins. Leo wouldn't do much teaching,

it was mostly Chris. Cats would come by with notebooks and he'd get up and talk. All the cats that you know—Herbie [Hancock] would go down there, and [pianist] Harold Mabern. Muhal was probably down there too.

Jam sessions, as historian Scott DeVeaux observes, "did not test such crucial professional skills or specializations as sight-reading, leading a section, or the endurance required to be the high-note man in a trumpet section."[27] Moreover, competition-based models of music-making tended to relegate collectivity and solidarity among musicians to the background at a time when more collaborative notions of the relationship of community to individuality were being pursued in many segments of the African American community. Thus, there were practical reasons for creating an environment in which musicians could rehearse, teach, and exchange knowledge across generations, as Eddie Harris told an interviewer in 1994. "Trying to play around Chicago," Harris explained, "you figured there are guys that never played first chair, there are guys that never played on a big band, and there are other guys that never had an opportunity to write for a large number of people, and there are people that wanted to sing, and sing in front of a band—so let's form a workshop."[28]

Harris credits trumpeter Johnny Hines as cofounder of the workshop, which at first attracted over one hundred musicians: "You start meeting guys, like the late Charles Stepney . . . There became a group of us. Muhal Richard Abrams, Raphael [Rafael] Garrett, James Slaughter, [drummer] Walter Perkins, Bill Lee. There was a small group of us who were on the same wavelength in trying things . . . not just sit down and play an Ellis Larkins run or a Duke Ellington run . . . we all wanted to try some different things."[29] The C&C Lounge provided a minimal but absolutely vital initial infrastructure for the musicians. Chicago trumpeter William Fielder, the brother of Alvin Fielder, recalls that "the C&C Lounge was a school for young musicians. Chuck and Claudia, his wife (C&C), offered the musicians a wonderful musical opportunity. The club would be empty and Chuck would say, 'Play for me.'"[30]

Eyes on the Sparrow: The First New Chicagoans

The C&C-based ensemble gradually developed a largely generational divide between musicians who wanted to develop the band in a more commercial direction, and others who wished to continue the radical explorations for which the group had been formed. As Eddie Harris recalled, "Johnny Hines tried to take the musicians more our age; he wanted to go into the Regal Theater so he could have a band to really accompany all the stars that come in there. Muhal had taken the younger musicians and let them learn in reading on scales and playing with each other."[31] After Harris left to pursue his fortunes from *Exodus to Jazz,* the rehearsal ensemble soon dissipated, but a new ensemble, consisting largely of the younger players who were gathering around Abrams, started regular rehearsals at the C&C. The ensemble, which gradually came to be known as the Experimental Band, became a forum for Abrams to test his new, Schillinger-influenced compositional palette. Abrams recalls simply, "I just gathered together some people around me, some younger guys, and started to keep things going." Two of these "younger guys," saxophonists Roscoe Mitchell and Joseph Jarman, played critically important roles in what was later to become the AACM. Mitchell and Jarman had not participated in the fast life of the 63rd Street jam sessions that had animated the young adult experiences of Abrams, Donavon, Favors, and Christian. For these two younger musicians, adulthood and musical maturity would come in the 1960s, a very different decade indeed.

Born in Chicago in 1940, Roscoe Mitchell grew up in the western part of Bronzeville. Like Favors's, Mitchell's parents were religious, and his uncle was the minister of a spiritualist church. "I used to really enjoy the music in the church," Mitchell recalled. "At the time I wasn't that interested in the sermons."[32] Since the 1930s, Washington Park had been a center of black South Side life, with tennis, softball, swimming, and horseback riding.[33] As a young person, Mitchell often spent an entire day in the park, talking to older musicians and watching them as they practiced.

Jarman was born in 1937 in Pine Bluff, Arkansas. His father left the family just as Joseph was born, and within a year his seventeen-year-old mother joined the Great Migration to Chicago, finding a job in the defense industry. Unlike virtually all of the early AACM musicians, Jarman lived on the largely white North Side, and attended an integrated school, Schiller Elementary, just down the street from his home. The family's eventual move to Bronzeville, near 48th and St. Lawrence, was the occasion for considerable turbulence in Jarman's new life at school. "I had a lot of trouble and a lot of fights," Jarman explained, "because it was a completely different society, a different moral and ethical standard. Then we moved back to the North Side and I went back to Schiller. This is all in that puberty range, ten to fourteen years of age. When I went back to Schiller, I got in trouble because I had been so influenced by the other school. I became a 'bad boy.'"[34]

Jarman and Mitchell were thoroughly steeped in Hollywood-style popular culture. It cost nine cents to go to the movies, and Mitchell and his young friends would walk about two miles from 59th and State, crossing over the Bronzeville border to the white movie theater, the Southtown, on 63rd and Halsted. Mitchell and his family listened avidly to Chicago radio's Al Benson and McKie Fitzhugh, as well as Symphony Sid's New York–based shows. And then there was television, an important, even revolutionary force that had not been part of the growing-up process for Jodie Christian's generation. Locally, Chicago's Old Swingmaster, Al Benson, featured singers such as Joe Williams on his 1951 TV show, and the *Mahalia Jackson Show* appeared in 1955. At the national level, black performers, including the Ink Spots, the Mills Brothers, Bill "Bojangles" Robinson, Nat King Cole, Martha Davis, Cab Calloway, Louis Armstrong, Carmen McRae, Lionel Hampton, and Duke Ellington all appeared. In 1950, Hazel Scott had her own fifteen-minute TV show in New York, and in 1952, singer Billy Daniels became the first African American to have his own nationally sponsored television show.[35]

However, as commercial television grew, so did the racism of its corporate leaders. By the late 1950s, the medium had resolved "to keep blacks off national television as much as possible."[36] Instead, television portrayed marvelous white people, living in sumptuous, yet not too ostentatious homes, driving new cars that never broke down (at least not for long), playing with their kids and friendly dogs, and tending crisply manicured lawns. Although for the 1950s black working class, TV was a prime portal through which white middle-class values and ideologies entered their lives, as George Lipsitz has observed, the exclusion of African Americans from full participation in white society meant that their culture was not completely permeated by the values and images of the dominant culture.[37] In fact, very few blacks in Mitchell's neighborhood owned or had access to a television set, and in "real life," as Mitchell remembers, "We didn't really have to look on TV for role models because they were all in our neighborhood." African Americans of Mitchell's generation regularly encountered blacks who did not conform to media stereotypes, allowing neighborhood residents to more easily detect and critique the social and political agendas embedded in the medium.

Through his aunt Mary and his uncle Preston, "the family renegades in Chicago," Joseph Jarman was introduced to the Regal Theater, and to local nightclubs.

I would go there to play with my cousins, and I began to learn the names of these people—Lester Young, Charlie Parker, James Moody, Nat "King" Cole, Miles Davis. They would be playing this music every time I went there, but I didn't know the name of the music; it was just pretty music. I knew all the singers—the popular music, but I was more drawn to this other music because you just listened, and what you heard was inside rather than words and rhythms that they would suggest through the popular forms.

In the mid-1950s, Mitchell's family moved briefly to Milwaukee, where he started high school and began playing the clarinet. His brother Norman came to live with the family, bringing along a collection of 78 rpm jazz recordings—"'killers,' they used to call them. Louis Armstrong, J. J. Johnson. Billy Taylor was very popular back then. Lester Young, Coleman Hawkins." As with Jarman, this strange new music exercised a peculiar power over Mitchell. "For me that was a weird time," Mitchell recalled, "because after I started listening to jazz I didn't want to listen to anything else any more. There was a certain coolness that went along with that—you understood jazz, that made you cooler. After a while I went back to include all those other musics I had grown up with."

Entering DuSable High School, Jarman was drawn to Captain Dyett's band. His parents could not afford to buy him a trumpet, Jarman's preferred instrument, so he joined the band as a snare drummer. "All you needed was a drum pad and drumsticks, which cost about six dollars. The drum I played belonged to the school, and I couldn't take it home." Another future AACM member living nearby, James Johnson, played bassoon in the Dyett band. Johnson and Jarman would practice together, eventually developing a unique daily schooltime lunch ritual: "We would go across the street every day, usually without very much lunch money, maybe fifty cents a day. We refused to eat in the lunchroom. We would go across the street and put a nickel apiece in the jukebox. We could hear three songs for a dime. We would always play this one song by James Moody, 'Last Train from Overbrook.' We would play that every day." In addition to performance classes, the school's version of music history recalled Abrams's 1940s grammar school experiences:

They'd show these films of white operas and white orchestras, like Mozart's music—Mozart was real big—Beethoven's music, and Brahms. That would be a part of our musical education. The teacher would show it, then talk about it, and you'd write a little paper on it. This was music history, but it was never really appealing. It was nice, but it was so much nicer to be in the band room hearing that live stuff.

Mitchell characterizes those who went to DuSable during the Dyett era as "fortunate," but even Englewood, where he went to high school, had its advantages. He began playing baritone saxophone in the high-school band, and borrowed an alto saxophone from another student. Jazz was not taught at Englewood, but getting to know the precocious saxophonist Donald "Hippmo" Myrick, who later became associated with both Philip Cohran and Earth, Wind, and Fire, made up for that lack. "He kind of took me under his wing, because he already knew the stuff," said Mitchell. "He was a fully accomplished musician in high school."

The historian Robin D. G. Kelley has raised the possibility that some future AACM members were radicalized in part by the challenges of military life—not only combat, but also the racism that was endemic to service in the U.S. armed forces.[38] In 1955, in his junior year in high school, Jarman dropped out and joined the army. "I went into the Airborne school, and the Ranger school, because you could make extra money. I made it through basic training and jump school as number two, because they wouldn't accept a black as number one." The army was where Jarman started to play the alto saxophone: "I got out of 'the line'—the death zone—by transferring to the band. The first saxophone I had was a plastic one, like Ornette Coleman. The bandmaster gave me thirty days to get my act together or he would kick me back into the line. In that band were a lot of people who helped me to get my act together."

Mitchell joined the army in 1958. Army musicians had plenty of time to practice and exchange information, and Mitchell met a number of saxophonists, such as Nathaniel Davis, as well as fellow Chicagoans Ruben Cooper and Lucious White, Jarman's neighbor as a young person. Mitchell also came into contact with Palmer Jenkins, Sergeant Mitchell, William Romero, and Joseph Stevenson, "who was incredible on the saxophone. He was a great influence on Anthony [Braxton] when Anthony was in the army." Mitchell was eventually transferred to Heidelberg, Germany, where he frequented local jam sessions at places like the well-known Cave 54, where pianist Karl Berger, trombonist Albert Mangelsdorff, saxophonist Bent Jaedig and other European and American musicians met and performed together. Hard bop was the coin of that realm, although Ornette Coleman's music was beginning to make an impression. During this time, Mitchell met saxophonist Albert Ayler, who was in a different army band, stationed in France. After duty hours, Mitchell would go to sessions and listen to Ayler:

> I didn't really know what he was doing, but I did know, because I was a saxophonist, that he had an enormous sound on the instrument. They would have these sessions, and everybody was, you know, talking about him behind his back, but one time they played a blues. Albert played the blues about three choruses straight. After that he started stretching, and something went off in my head—"Oh, I see what he's doing now." It made an impression on me.

In August 1958, Jarman was discharged. "It was not something I wanted to continue," Jarman said, "because it was very anti-human, this attitude they were making people into."[39] After a brief visit home to Chicago, he experienced a kind of odyssey: "I went wandering around the United States. I went to Arizona. My aunt was there. I stayed there for eight months or so. I couldn't talk during this period; I was mute. I went to the Milwaukee Institute of Psychiatric Research in Wisconsin, as an outpatient, and enrolled in the Milwaukee Institute of Technology. They got me to be able to talk again, and I haven't shut my mouth since."[40]

After his discharge from the army, Mitchell felt that "it was pretty much set that I was going to be a musician." With the support of his father, who offered to provide him with a place to stay, he decided to use his GI Bill funds to go to Chicago's Woodrow Wilson Junior College in 1961, where he met Jarman for the first time. "Jarman was already into a contemporary-type bag when I met him. He was always a little bit out there, all the time." The two musicians studied with Richard Wang, who was, according to Jarman, "very adventurous as far as 'jazz' music was concerned, as well as 'classical' music." According to Wang himself, who has to be credited along with the redoubtable Walter Dyett in any history of the early AACM members, in addition to the standard lessons in theory, counterpoint, and keyboard harmony, the young musicians were exposed to the music of the Second Viennese School, as well as John Coltrane and Ornette Coleman.[41] The standard texts included Paul Hindemith's classic 1946 *Elementary Training for Musicians,* which later became an aspect of AACM autodidacticism. Other texts included Hindemith's 1945 *The Craft of Musical Composition* and composer Arnold Schoenberg's 1951 *Style and Idea.*

Wang's students, who performed in jazz and classical ensembles, included Malachi Favors and saxophonists John Powell, Anthony Braxton, and Henry Threadgill, as well as Richard Brown, who was playing piano and clarinet, rather than the saxophone for which he became known years later under his adopted name of Ari. Friday afternoons were devoted to rehearsals that brought Wilson students together with the cream of Chicago's musicians. Present at these events were people like Eddie Harris, Charles Stepney, drummers Steve McCall and Jack DeJohnette, bassists Betty Dupree and Jimmy Willis, pianist Andrew Hill, and several musicians who had been part of the Sun Ra Arkestra, including trumpeter Hobart Dotson and percussionists Richard Evans and Jim Herndon. In the meantime, Jarman, Favors, Threadgill, pianist Louis Hall, and drummer Richard Smith (now Drahseer Khalid) had formed their own group, playing hard bop.

One day in 1963, Roscoe Mitchell turned up at a rehearsal of the Experimental Band at the C&C Lounge, and met Richard Abrams, who had been introduced to the saxophonist by pianist-drummer Jack DeJohnette.[42] Malachi Favors, an early member of the rehearsal band, remarked to Abrams how impressed he was by Mitchell's playing. "Muhal kind of took me in," Mitchell recalled. "I'd go to school, and I'd go straight from school to Muhal's, when he was living in that little place off Cottage Grove, down in the basement. I remember he had painted everything that velvet purple color. Sometimes I'd be down over to Muhal's at ten, eleven, twelve at night, playing or working on music."

Soon, Mitchell and Favors began rehearsing together and developing new compositions, often with two other young experimentalists, trumpeter Fred Berry and drummer Alvin Fielder. Fielder was becoming aware that "there comes a point where you go from a notion of swinging and keeping a pulse to a notion of time being something different. . . . Sun Ra had always told me, 'Al, loosen up,' I didn't know what he meant, really."[43] Looking for something different, Fielder visited New York for nearly a year in 1962, but somehow, the music being played by what he remembered as a "clique" of musicians from Boston, Detroit, and Chicago was not satisfying his growing urge to find another path. "I first started to loosen up after meeting Muhal," Fielder said. Abrams was performing in a trio with Rafael Garrett and Steve McCall. Fielder replaced the peripatetic McCall, and began to meet musicians from a younger circle of experimentalists. "The first time I played in a so-called free group was with Roscoe," Fielder noted.[44] As he told writer Ted Panken, "Roscoe Mitchell came to a rehearsal I was doing with Muhal, Kalaparusha [Maurice McIntyre] and [trombonist and bassist] Lester Lashley. He just sat and listened, and asked me could I play free [laughs]. I said, 'Yeah, I play free,' So he invited me to a rehearsal with Freddie Berry and Malachi Favors. That's how the original Roscoe Mitchell Quartet started."[45]

"The first compositions we played in Roscoe's group were very much like Ornette's music," Fielder recalled. "I developed a philosophy there that I wanted to play my bebop as loose as possible and I wanted to play my free music as tight as possible."[46] Up to that point, Fielder had been playing around town with musicians like saxophonists Cozy Eggleston and Earl Ezell (later Ahmad Salaheldeen), and pianist Danny Riperton, the brother of singer Minnie Riperton. Now, he was in the process of crossing a personal, conceptual, and professional Rubicon, with a very different kind of music. Discovering at first hand the social dynamics of the "Inside/Outside" binary, Fielder noticed that "None of the bebop cats would call me any more, once I started working with Muhal and Roscoe."[47] Meanwhile, Mitchell was trying to get his friend Joseph Jarman to come down and play with the Experimental Band. As Jarman tells it,

> Roscoe said, you oughta come, there's this guy who's got a rehearsal band down here. He's a nice guy and he knows a lot about music. So I went down there and there was this guy, and he greets you like you were his brother or something. He said, welcome, and there were all these people in there, and I had to step back, because some of them were like famous people—local Chicago musicians, Jack DeJohnette, Scotty Holt, Steve McCall. And then this guy gave me an invitation whenever I felt like it to come by his house and get music lessons. He'd offer you herb tea and it would be so *good*," Jarman recalled. "He was into herbology, astrology, painting, all this mystical stuff that I had dreamed of. It was like I had found a teacher.

After daily classes with the dedicated, expansive Wang, the young musicians would join the nightly throng at Peggy and Richard Abrams's tiny basement apartment on South Evans, where they would explore musical, cultural, political, social, and spiritual ideas. Abrams's range of experiences and interests deeply affected the young musicians. "Muhal's place would always stay packed with people," said Mitchell. "He'd have all this time for all these people, and still at the end of the week he'd come to the band with a big-band chart."

Abrams's leadership of the Experimental Band extended and revised the alternative pedagogical direction begun in 1961 at the C&C, with the ensemble functioning as a site for exchange, learning, and experimentation across generations: "The Experimental Band gave me a place to play this music I was writing, but the younger musicians couldn't read the music, because it was too advanced for them. So I had to make up ways for them to play it, all these improvised ways for them to do stuff. I would have them learn a passage, do hand signals for them to play different things." The collective-oriented atmosphere of the Experimental Band became a regular forum that recalled the spirit of Will Jackson and King Fleming. As Abrams affirmed, "The attention that they gave me and the help that they gave me awakened something in me that needed to extend out to other people. Whenever someone newer in the music scene would come along, I would always be willing to help if they sought my help, and I would always reflect back on the fact that those gentlemen helped me."

With the Experimental Band, Abrams moved to create cooperative situations where musicians could both learn new ideas and techniques from others, and bring in their own music and hear it performed. Mitchell and Jarman soon started composing music under Abrams's guidance. Jarman's recollection was of an open situation where exploration would be encouraged:

> He said, "Write whatever you want, and we'll look at it." There was no judgment thing. We might say thumbs down or thumbs up individually or personally, but no one would ever say that publicly. I might bring a piece in and they'll play it. They won't say whether they like it or not but they'll do their darnedest to play it as best as they could. Underneath they might have been saying, "What does this guy think he's doing?" Or, "Wow, thumbs up." But still they would do it.

Mitchell's narrative points up how the composer-centered aspect of the AACM can be seen to emerge directly from Abrams's encouragement. "I was getting my writing chops together," said Mitchell, "and he [Abrams] always encouraged people to write, write, write. He was showing us all of these different compositional methods. He always had a deep appreciation for all kinds of music, and studied all kinds of music. He had a lot to draw on, and he passed it on freely to the people that wanted to learn that." The new musical resources that were being explored were by no means limited to composition. New ideas and ways of thinking about structure in improvisation were also being hammered out. As Jarman told an interviewer in 1967, Abrams would say, "Don't just think about what you're playing when you're playing a solo—think about what came before and what's going to come after."[48]

Typically, however, Abrams minimizes the extent of the contact between himself and the younger musicians to a single crucial encounter. Abrams remembers that his initial advice to Mitchell concerning composition was to "write down what you're playing on your horn. He proceeded to do that—that's where 'Nonaah'[49] and stuff like that comes from—and he's never looked back since, and we never discussed composition any more."

"That's not really true," said Mitchell. "He would always be turning people on to books, and talking about scores. Maybe he just doesn't realize the effect that he had on people's lives." In fact, the young musicians were in constant, almost daily contact with Abrams. Saxophonist Gene Dinwiddie, an original AACM member, remembers that "Everybody was following him around like little puppies."[50]

Charles Eugene Dinwiddie's father was an evangelist who traveled throughout the South, but the family eventually settled in Cairo in southern Illinois. Dinwiddie had "dabbled around with my brother's clarinet in grade school." But later, as it had for Abrams and Malachi Favors, the lure of music seemed to pale besides the glamour of high-school sports. Even so, his childhood sweetheart, Flo, remembers Gene "from when he first started sneaking into the 13th Street Tavern to play his horn, in Cairo. Thirteenth Street was where the bad people hung out—a rough tavern. His daddy was a minister and he had no business down there. I would walk by there and he'd be up on stage trying to play."[51]

After high school, Dinwiddie attended Southern Illinois University for two years, then joined the Marine Corps. Discharged in 1958, he moved to Chicago to be with his brother. Two years later, Dinwiddie married Flo, starting more than "thirty-eight glorious years" that ended only with his passing in 2002. Dinwiddie had started playing the saxophone after his discharge from the marines, but in an interview, Flo reminded Gene of a story that speaks to a very different model of the origins of experimentalism:

> The turning point in your life, when you got really serious about playing music, was when you were driving the bus at Christmastime and the guy put the knife to your throat. You got off the bus and he came home and

said, I'm never driving the bus again. He was trying to drive the bus and do the music, because he had a family. You went directly to music, because this is what you loved and this is what you wanted to do.

Dinwiddie began attending rehearsals of the Experimental Band. As he and many other former participants attested, the unswerving emphasis in the Experimental Band was on "original music."

> One guy brought in an arrangement of "Shiny Stockings." They wanted to hear something that was trendy, on the radio. Muhal said, "Naw." Muhal didn't allow any licks to be played. No licks. Coming through the bebop era, you heard a lot of clichéd solos, little places where you sound like another artist, something that you had heard before, something that had been played before. He didn't want any licks played. You were supposed to be a "creative musician." It's hard to create—to just come out of nowhere. I think it was spiritual.

Peggy Abrams and Flo became fast friends in the wake of their commonalities surrounding the love of music. They were carrying their first children at the same time, as they surveyed the South Side club scene of the early 1960s. "You didn't have to worry. Two women could go there. You wouldn't sit at the bar, but if Peggy and I wanted to go, we could go. You were treated well, and it was safe. After it was over you'd come out and get a jitney cab."

According to Joseph Jarman, saxophonist Troy Robinson, an original AACM member, was "probably the most prolific writer among us. He played clarinet but every week he would bring in two pieces, and they would be like an hour long. We used to get bugged with him because he was so fluent." Robinson was born in Chicago in 1935. His father worked in Chicago's now-defunct slaughterhouses, and his mother stayed at home, caring for Robinson and his two siblings. Robinson went to DuSable High School, but like several other future AACM members, he didn't take music instruction there. Around 1961, when he was about twenty-six years old, Robinson became fascinated by his saxophone-playing cousin, who "was playing all of the standards, like Stella by Starlight, Cherokee. Then he would stop and he would tap-dance. He was just awesome."[52]

Robinson found a saxophone in a pawnshop and started taking lessons at the Chicago Conservatory of Music. Meanwhile, like Dinwiddie, Robinson drove a Chicago Transit Authority bus to ensure a living.[53] Around 1963 or 1964, Gene Dinwiddie took Robinson to the Experimental Band. As Robinson tells it,

> We were reading charts. I liked that. We were just rehearsing, we weren't playing anywhere. I think it was every Monday or Tuesday evening, just reading Richard's charts, or you could bring some charts in yourself. He started giving me some ideas for writing some charts. Me and about three other people came down with charts, and he liked mine. He said, "Troy, you need to come over." I went over to his house, and that's when I started learning different methods of composition, and started writing more. Then Richard started playing a lot of my stuff when we were having rehearsal. I used to go over to his house at least twice a week, studying. He didn't charge me. I guess he saw that I had something. Everybody liked to be with Richard because he was so warm.

Henry Threadgill remembers meeting Richard Abrams at an Experimental Band rehearsal "somewhere in '63 or '64."[54] Despite his being somewhat younger than Mitchell and Jarman, the open atmosphere helped him to fit in. Threadgill was born in 1944 in Bronzeville, right at 33rd and Cottage Grove. As with Leroy Jenkins, Threadgill's family migration story differs markedly from the romantic standard exemplified by Louis Armstrong's fabled trek:

> My grandfather, Henry, he brought my grandmother and my father up to Chicago. He drove liquor for the Mob, all the way to Canada. My father would jump in the car with him all the time. He wouldn't go to school, and my grandmother would be very upset. He kind of picked his stuff up from the kind of life he got involved in from my grandfather, in a sense. They would travel all over America with a couple of .45s on the seat, running liquor all the way to Canada from Alabama, Georgia. He made enough money that he brought the family to Chicago.

"My father? My father was a gambler," Threadgill chuckled.

> When I was a kid, up to third grade, he ran gambling houses, because I remember him taking us there. He wasn't in numbers, the policy wheels. He did cards, craps. They had tables, the croupiers and stuff. All kinds of people came to these gambling places, because he used to

have a lot of money. A new Cadillac every year, new clothes, fabulous clothes. These were just gamblers, they didn't really deal in violent crime or extortion.

During these highly singular field trips, music served as a kind of baby-sitter. "He would give us money to put in the jukebox," recalled Threadgill. "It would be all jazz on the jukebox, because my father loved jazz, and he knew all those people, Basie and all of them. He would go to Mexico and Spain with them on vacation and stuff." Threadgill's father also had records at home: "I used to go to my father's house and just stay for the weekend, and just play records. Duke, Gene Ammons, Count Basie, Modern Jazz Quartet."

Threadgill's parents split up when he was about three years old. Suddenly, in a small dwelling, "We were up with my grandmother, grandfather, my mother's brothers and sisters," said Threadgill. "All of us lived together." The family moved to Englewood when Threadgill was in the fourth grade. To make ends meet, his mother "did all kinds of things, making lampshades, accounting, working in banks." The now-defunct Maxwell Street market area on Chicago's West Side was known to many as "Jewtown" because of its historical demographics, even though during Threadgill's time, the area's immigrant Jewish population was largely vestigial. Like many black families, Threadgill's people visited the market on weekends to buy staples and clothing, and to hear Muddy Waters, Howlin' Wolf, and the other bluesmen who performed regularly on the market's outdoor stages.

Threadgill started playing piano at the age of four, taking lessons as finances permitted. "My aunt was going to school to be an opera singer," he recalled. "That's how we got the piano in the first place. I learned how to play boogie-woogie. I would practice Meade Lux Lewis and Albert Ammons. I kept that on the radio. I could figure out harmony because I could play the piano." In his early teens, Threadgill began playing saxophone and clarinet at Englewood High School, where he placed second in the citywide championship on tenor, performing light-classical works. Even so, high-school music was less attractive than the 63rd Street nightlife scene. "I've been going in joints since I was fourteen," Threadgill told me in our interview. "I used to *live* at McKie's. I saw everybody. All you would do is take your horn. They would say, just sit over there, young blood, and don't you even *think* about no drink. They'd see you with your horn, and they would say, just sit over there and get you a Coca-Cola or something."

Threadgill began playing jam sessions on tenor around 1961, during what turned out to be the 63rd Street area's final period of vitality. Threadgill admits that "I wasn't doing nothing major. I had to play the head, and then get out of the way." He garnered still more experience playing in polka bands, Dixieland ensembles, and rehearsal big bands. Doing parade gigs with the old-timers in Veterans of Foreign Wars bands, the young saxophonist performed critical functions for the musicians, who ranged upward of seventy-five years of age. With no chance to relieve themselves while on the march, "Cats had to wear bladders. We'd be on the bus. Everybody said, 'Hold it,' Cats would whip out their bladders and attach them to their johnsons. They'd say, 'Get over here, boy,' and then I'd tape it up under the bottom of the shoe."

Threadgill came to Wilson Junior College in 1963, right after high school. One day, he came into Wilson's student cafeteria, and fellow student Milton Chapman pointed out "somebody you gotta meet."

> I looked in this crowd of people and I saw this guy sitting by himself at a table up against the wall with a black charcoal jacket, dark trousers, a pair of old comfort shoes, and a bald head and a navy turtleneck sweater, with a brown briefcase on the floor. He didn't have much money, and he was having just a roll, a bowl of soup, and a cup of tea. I said, that's the guy, right? I knew that this was not a regular guy here.

Threadgill remembers "the guy," Joseph Jarman, as "the first way-out guy I met" at Wilson. Under the tutelage of Richard Wang, Threadgill became excited about his courses in harmony and analysis, and developed a study group with Mitchell and Jarman. "I used to turn in anywhere from five to fifteen versions of any harmony assignment," Threadgill recalled. "You could ask Richard Wang. I would stay up all night, because you could see all these possibilities. We had these blackboards, and we'd be drinking tea and taking NoDoz." At the study group sessions, Mitchell introduced Threadgill and Jarman to the Art Blakey and Horace Silver charts that he had transcribed during his army days.

Threadgill also counts his attendance at concerts of the University of Chicago Contemporary Chamber Players, directed by composers Easley Blackwood and Ralph Shapey, among the important formative experiences that marked his early years.

> I met Hindemith and Varese in person. With Hindemith I had just kind of validated something that I had already learned, but the Varese was some-

thing I couldn't touch. I didn't know what the hell was going on, and I didn't know why I liked it. I positioned myself and grabbed his hand and told him how many pieces of his that I liked. He just looked at me for a long time, very earnestly. You gotta remember that I knew that he was the one who taught William Grant Still, so I knew that he was okay.[55]

Muhal Richard Abrams recalls that "Roscoe brought Joseph around, and both of them brought Henry later," but Threadgill remembers that he was at the Experimental Band slightly before the others. The music students at Wilson had a jazz interest club, and used some of the club's funding to engage Abrams to perform. Shortly thereafter, Mitchell, Jarman, and Threadgill all found themselves sitting in rehearsals of the Experimental Band, alongside Donald Myrick, Eddie Harris, and bassist Louis Satterfield. But by early 1965, Threadgill had dropped out of both the Experimental Band and Wilson Junior College. A call to spiritual arms was the primary motivation, with the saxophone the weapon of choice. Threadgill began playing his tenor saxophone for the Lord, with all his heart and soul, but something was missing: "The minister told me he wanted me to come up and play 'His Eye Is on the Sparrow,' I played it, and all them old sisters, what they called the 'pillars of faith,' they just kind of sat back and some of them fell asleep. When I finished, it was like a grunt. I knew I hadn't done nothing." Then, the pastor made a suggestion regarding instrumentation that Threadgill hadn't considered before. "The minister said, Henry, I got a saxophone up under the pulpit. It's smaller than yours. I want you to take it to the shop and get it fixed. I'll pay for it. I reached up under there and it was an alto. I took it to the repairman, and they fixed it up in a couple of days. The minister said, I want you to play that same song on Sunday. It got house."

As Threadgill discovered, in the church environment, "The tenor saxophone don't translate. You can play the blues, but for those people, it doesn't work." A Church of God evangelist from Philadelphia, Horace Shepherd, happened to be at services that day. "I had known about Horace Shepherd from the time I was five or six years old. He was called 'The Child Wonder,' My grandmother and them used to go to the tents. Black people kept newspaper clippings." Alto saxophone in hand, Threadgill went to Philadelphia with Shepherd's evangelism troupe, which included musicians and singers. "I was playing in camp meetings, speaking in tongues, pulling snakes out of people's mouths. Vernard Johnson was my only competition, and I could beat his ass. I bet he was glad I got out of there, because he couldn't compete with me at that time [laughs]."

There was much to be learned from Shepherd's approach to evangelism-as-theater. As Threadgill observed, Shepherd's sermons "were compositions—they were structured."

> It's all done in stages. I'd walk from the back of the tent [sings], *Doooh-Oooooh-Weee,* and by the time I got to the front, I better have them people on their feet. By the time I got right in front of the bandstand, the organ and the piano kicked in behind me [sings]. The people were like, Oww! Then the choir jumped up and they go to screamin'. Then the soloists come out, and I'm playing behind them, free—that's right, just free. I'd be gone by then, *Aaaahhh! Wooo! Waaah!* By the time we'd get the crowd to a certain level, Shepherd would come out there and leap over the pulpit into the audience and do a split. The people would be hysterical by that time.

"You didn't know what Shepherd was gonna do," marveled Threadgill. "He was so crazy he might swing in on a rope."

Leonard Jones came to the Experimental Band around 1964. Jones was born in Cook County Hospital in 1943. His mother, who was born in Chicago, and his father, who came to the city as a child from Alabama, grew up in the Chicago of the 1920s and 1930s. Jones saw his father, a Chicago policeman, only sporadically during his childhood. Jones's mother worked various jobs as a waitress and cashier, and eventually became a dietary supervisor. Jones's parents divorced when he was four, and he, his mother and two siblings moved into a severely subdivided West Side apartment at 14th and Ashland. Jones's grandparents occupied one room, and his uncle slept in the living room on a foldaway bed. The room occupied by Jones and his family was directly above the stage at Harry and Vi's, a local blues bar that competed with the famous Zanzibar, just a block away. Literally living with the blues, Jones heard "all the blues cats, you name 'em. I mean everybody played in Harry and Vi's Lounge, Muddy Waters, Howlin' Wolf, Otis Spann, Willie Dixon, and a lot of people I just don't remember. You always went to bed late because you couldn't get no sleep. The music was always coming upstairs."[56]

When Jones was thirteen, his family moved into one of the most notorious Chicago housing projects, the Stateway Gardens at 35th and State on the South Side. "We moved into a building that was brand spanking new, but it didn't stay that way long," said Jones. "At first it wasn't too bad, the youth were just breaking out the light bulbs. At first they were fixing things real quick. Then they were defecating and peeing in the halls. I don't know what made people do things like that." Practicing a form of avoidance behavior, Jones began to spend much of his time indoors listening to records. From his mother, he picked up a taste for Billie Holiday, Duke Ellington, Count Basie, Coleman Hawkins, and Ben Webster. His father loved the big bands, and had a record player with "an astronomical sound." Joining a mail-order record club, the first records Jones ever owned, "like a lot of cats in my age group," were Dave Brubeck's "Take Five," and guitarist Johnny Smith's classic version of "Moonlight in Vermont."

Giving up on the vocational high-school education that he initially thought useful, Jones joined the army at seventeen, going first to Fort Leonard Wood in Missouri for basic training, then to Fort Gordon, near Augusta, Georgia. Jones was used to garden-variety Chicago racism, but his upbringing had not prepared him for being physically removed from the USO building in Augusta:

> I mean, out in the street, in my nice green American uniform with my
> little brass buttons and my little brass things on my cap. Soaking wet in
> the rain, they put me out in the street—very politely, but I had to go. If I
> didn't go politely, they would have made sure that I went some other way.
> I mean, I had never experienced anything like—this is already February
> 1961. Civil rights stuff had been going on for years, but in the bus station
> in Augusta, Georgia, they had water fountains, white and colored, just
> like I had been reading about.

Jones's interest in music performance began in earnest when he was shipped off to Bad Kreuznach in Germany, one of many bases maintained by American forces facing the Warsaw Pact. Jones was surprised to find that American-style racism had already been imported into Germany:

> Everything was just like it was in America—segregated. There were black
> bars, because you didn't go into the bars where the white cats were be-
> cause there were always fights. . . . About two or three seconds after you
> got in the door, somebody'd be saying, "There's some niggers in here!"
> The stories the white soldiers would tell about you! They used to tell all
> the little German kids that we had tails that came out at midnight.

Listening to the Eighth Division Army Band, Jones was fascinated by "this thumping sound that old cats got, this basic, walking bass," and began to dream of playing the bass himself. Under the influence of a bass-playing fellow soldier, Melvin Lane, Jones discovered Thelonious Monk, Sonny Rollins, and Jackie McLean. "It was like coming out of a dark room and having the light turned on. . . . Those were the things that said, now this is what music should sound like." Soon after, another soldier brought another light. "He had that blue and yellow record called "Ornette." I didn't know who it was, or what kind of music it was. I just knew I liked it—and he didn't. So I bought the record from him. When I put it on, a whole 'nother world opened up."

By early 1962, Jones began to have trouble submitting to everyday life in this man's army. "I hated the army, and I wasn't a very good soldier. I balked at the kind of authority that these people were trying to exercise over me. I got myself in trouble, and they gave me what they call a summary court-martial, which is at the lower end of the court-martial scale." Upon his conviction, his U.S. Savings Bond allotment was canceled, but what was meant as a sanction became an opportunity. The black bars were located at a considerable distance from the Bad Kreuznach base, and each time he visited them, Jones would pass a music store with an old plywood bass prominently displayed in the window. 'What they wanted was the money so I could pay the fine," said Jones. "So I had to go cash the bonds, but when I cashed the bonds I went directly to that music store and bought that bass. There was $300 in bonds, but they got $175. The other $125 I bought the bass with, and that's how I got started playing the bass."

Jones was discharged in November 1963, and proceeded directly to 125th Street in Harlem, where the rush of teeming humanity nearly overwhelmed him. Jones was ecstatic. "This was like life, man. I had been in the army for three years. I had been dead! I went in a record store, and pulled out every Jackie McLean record this cat had. I took them back to catch the train, Erie Lackawanna, New Jersey, to Chicago, back to 35th and State. I was going to be a musician. I was going to learn how to play just like them old cats on those records." Jones took music courses at the Chicago Conservatory of Music, and at Loop Junior College. He also began classical bass studies with Rudolf Fahsbender, who was also teaching Stafford James, Malachi Favors, and the young and very precocious Charles Clark.

Born in 1945, Clark had studied with Wilbur Ware, and had begun playing professionally in 1963.[57] According to Joseph Jarman, "Charles was still expanding, growing, developing. He was vital and outgoing, always with a smile, and ready to go. Also he was interested in rehearsing twenty-four hours a day. He was studying down at Roosevelt or somewhere. He would go to school and come over to my house and we would rehearse forever and then he'd go home for a minute and come back." Clark brought Jones to a rehearsal of the Experimental Band sometime in 1964. The band was rehearsing at the Abraham Lincoln Center, a Frank Lloyd Wright building that then housed a social services center. "It didn't take too long before Muhal and I hit it off," said Jones. "He lived in the basement, on Evans. That place was so crowded. It was crammed full of stuff. Muhal and I used to sit and drink all this horehound tea and go over music. I'd study the Schillinger, and he'd show me things at the piano. He would do astrological stuff, lay out the tarot cards. I had no idea what was going on."

In addition to his music studies, Jones was going through what he called "a spiritual transition" in which he, like Abrams, joined the Rosicrucians. As a result of these studies, Jones became aware of an antinomy that had to be resolved. "I wanted to study the bass, but I also wanted to be hip and slick," he reflected. "I was in between living that black lounge life and going over to that music. Maybe it might have worked out and I would have just been a cat that hung out in clubs and played changes, but I never did fit into that world, and I gave up wanting to live in the taverns and the lounges." With Jones's rededication to music, he and Clark became fast friends. Jones described Clark as "an enthusiastic cat, a dynamo. Anytime Charles came into the room, the whole atmosphere in the room changed. It was like something happy had happened." Clark introduced Jones to the financially marginal life of the struggling young experimentalist, South Side version, circa 1964:

> All the cats stayed at the Dorchester on 62nd and Dorchester. It was a
> place that must have had about five or six stories. Roscoe used to live right
> across the street. M'Chaka Uba was Allen Joyner at that time, and he lived
> in there. Abshalom [Ben Shlomo],[58] you had to have special signals to go
> visit him, because he never had no money to pay his rent. I used to come
> and visit Charles all the time, and Charles too, you had to have signals.
> You'd call Charles and he'd say, knock three times and twice. Then he'd
> know who it was and you could get in.

At the Dorchester, Jones met Wilbur Ware, who took Jones with him to jam sessions and literally pushed him onstage. "Usually what would happen is that Wilbur would introduce a 'young, up-and-coming bass player'—that didn't know no tunes," Jones laughed. "I'd have to go up and play after Wilbur played, on somebody else's gig."

M'Chaka Uba was born Allen Joyner on the South Side in 1943, the child of migrants from Mississippi, and the cousin of athlete Jackie Joyner-Kersee. Though he considers himself African American, he accounts for his Asian features by noting that his mother was the product of a relationship with a member of the Mississippi Delta's Chinese community that had actively intermarried with African Americans before the 1950s.[59] Uba grew up in Englewood, around 59th and State. His father, who drove a Chicago Transit Authority bus for thirty years, fought in World War II. His mother "lived in the church," which happened to be an outpost of the Church of God in Christ, where Malachi Favors's uncle was the pastor. "When my mother got to rolling all out on the floor, I started crying because I didn't know what was wrong with her. All the men had to get around her and hold her hands. She's got the Holy Ghost now."[60]

When he was six years old, Uba started taking violin lessons at the now-defunct downtown Chicago music store, Lyon and Healy's. Uba continued the lessons for six years, but "when I got twelve, all the kids in the neighborhood started calling me a sissy. I became disinterested in playing Boy Paganini." Eager to prove his bona fides as a tough guy, Uba was expelled from the Catholic School he attended, and eventually ended up in the fearsome Moseley School, the same reform school that had received Richard Abrams in the 1940s. Upon "graduating" from Moseley, Uba entered Englewood High School around the same time as Henry Threadgill. Uba switched to trumpet, and he and Threadgill were chosen for the All-City Band.

Uba served in the army between 1962 and 1964, and was stationed in Kaiserslautern, Germany, where he met Mal Waldron and Duke Jordan. He decided to learn the bass, and an unexpected accident kept him on course. "I didn't even know about Vietnam. If I hadn't broken my leg, I'd be dead." Upon discharge, Uba began to focus intensely on music. He met Joseph Jarman, and began rooming with him—"nine people and a Great Dane dog in one room"—and began studying bass with Rafael Garrett. "I never ever paid him one penny, because he would not accept it," said Uba. "And you didn't have an hour lesson with Rafael Garrett. It was eight hours."

Eventually, Uba moved into an apartment at the Dorchester, becoming part of a scene that was alternately exciting and baffling to the sixteen-year-old drummer Thurman Barker. "This was my first experience with what they would call beatniks," Barker recalled. "It was kind of like a little community, with all these musicians in this one building. I had never been around musicians like these, and I found them to be interesting, you know?" Barker was born in 1948 at 60th and Indiana on the South Side. His parents met in the small, all-black town of Boley, Oklahoma, where they found employment with the Civilian Conservation Corps during the Depression, coming to Chicago between 1937 and 1941. Neither had finished high school at the time, but both eventually found employment in the steel mills. By 1955, this relatively secure employment allowed the Barkers to buy a two-flat building on 80th and Langley. The upper floor housed Barker's Aunt Louise and her children, and the Barkers rented an extra bedroom to a roomer.

Mesmerized by a drummer's performance in his eighth-grade classroom, Barker asked his parents for music lessons. His mother sent him to the American Conservatory, on South Michigan Avenue in downtown Chicago, where he studied first with James Dutton, and later with Harold Jones, who had played with Count Basie and was one of the most respected percussionists in the area. To pay for the lessons, Mrs. Barker took a second, extremely dangerous job, selling Avon cosmetics in the notorious Robert Taylor Homes, the largest public housing project in the world, and a federally financed breeding ground for despair whose architectural aesthetics brought to mind nothing so much as a giant penitentiary. The combination of the weekly lessons and listening to classical music on a record player he received for his fourteenth birthday kept Barker away from the growing gang activity in his neighborhood. At the same time, Barker was hardly isolated from street culture.

> My routine was that I would come in, practice my music, and listen to
> classical music. Then, maybe I would go and hang out with the guys on
> the corner and sing doo-wops. I hung out with a lot of the rough guys
> in the neighborhood, guys who were in and out of jail all the time. But
> somehow, I knew when it was time to hang and when it was time to leave.
> I get the feeling that they kind of respected me for that.

Barker played in the concert band at the now all-black Hirsch High School, but generally found high-school music uninteresting compared to the scene outside. In 1962, Jones had recorded *Exodus* with Eddie Harris, and was rehearsing and jamming on Mondays with a group of bus drivers who were also musicians. Jones brought the fourteen-year-old Barker to a rehearsal, introducing him to playing jazz. Soon Barker began to get paying work at weddings, and even in nightclubs, which, technically speaking, he was too young to even enter. His parents were convinced of their son's maturity, however, and welcomed the fact that the music lessons were bearing real fruit.

At Hirsch, Barker had been hanging out with Richard Abrams's son, "Little Richard," who (quite understandably) had another nickname, "Bucks." Barker knew that Bucks's father was a musician, and one day in 1964, Bucks and Barker ran into Troy Robinson, who was driving his usual bus route. The young drummer knew Robinson as an alto saxophonist, one of the bus drivers who played on Mondays, and Bucks knew Robinson as a regular at the Experimental Band rehearsals. Soon after, Robinson brought Barker to the Experimental Band. "I think I sat in, and I remember that I was received well. They put some music there, and I sat there and I read the music. I felt warmly appreciated." An Experimental Band rehearsal, in Barker's reminiscence,

> was run very orderly. Whoever had their composition up would direct it; of course, they would explain it first. Because we're talking about people who had really gotten up into their music, man. In fact, they had changed the music notation. They used different music notation. . . . I had played all these other gigs with people, and there was no music. I would just go up and play. But here I come down to the Experimental Band, and these guys not only have music for the brass and woodwinds; they've got a chart for me. So that was in itself different.[61]

King Mock was on drums that day, and the older drummer took young Thurman under his wing. "He was a very warm person," said Barker. "I was always expressing at these rehearsals that the music we were doing was new to me, and that I really didn't know what to play. I remember King Mock saying, just play. Mock was very influential in terms of helping me to feel comfortable. . . . You gotta remember, me being young, and not knowing these guys, the one thing that drew me in is that they would talk to me. They would treat me like I was in their generation."

Mitchell, among others, remembers of the Experimental Band that "I don't think we did that many concerts." In fact, Abrams and others have maintained that the Experimental Band never performed publicly. Although Abrams retains a number of scores from the period, there are no known recordings of the ensemble from this pre-AACM period. According to Abrams, recordings were made purely for work and study purposes, and so there seemed at the time to be no real reason not to record new rehearsals right over the old. Financial pressures were undoubtedly also a factor in the reuse of old tapes to record the rehearsals. Despite the lack of public performance, however, the band managed to garner small notices. In May

1963, *Down Beat*'s Ad Lib section announced that Abrams had been leading a rehearsal band on Tuesdays at a South Side social service institution, the Abraham Lincoln Center on Oakwood and Langley, since the summer of 1962. According to the tiny blurb, the aim of the rehearsals was "eventually to present the workshop in concert, the purpose being to draw attention to the talents of Chicago jazzmen." Writer J. B. Figi even remembers a concert by Abrams in the summer of 1964—"a proud display of his rehearsal groups, orchestra and quintet (Mitchell, Dinwiddie, Garrett, McCall)."[62]

In the end, Abrams encouraged the musicians to regard the Experimental Band as their tool for personal growth:

> In the final analysis, I impressed them with the fact that they should do their own thing. We got this group here, and when you do your own thing, we'll play your thing. It's not in the sense that I took any one aspect of what I was doing to drape it on anybody else. The best I've always been is an example, but not because I wanted to be an example. I would just go my own way, and whoever wanted to go with me had to go their own way. I was older and more experienced, but they weren't relinquishing or sacrificing their individualism.

"Muhal was more than a teacher of music," concludes Mitchell. "He was a teacher of life. He was too big to be pushed into one corner."

4

FOUNDING THE COLLECTIVE

Urban Decline and the Turn to Communitarianism

During the last phase of the Great Migration, from 1950 to 1965, Chicago's black population doubled from 14 to 28 percent of the total; in 1965, Chicago's African American population topped one million for the first time. In the heyday of the Cotton Club, Bronzeville's musical center was 63rd Street, previously a border zone between the black and white communities.[1] That heyday was all too brief, however, as the advent of the 1960s saw the sudden decline and near-disappearance of the area's music venues. Like a canary sounding the alarm in a mineshaft, the Cotton Club was one of the first to go, closing for good in the late 1950s. The musical action shifted temporarily to another Cottage Grove club, McKie's Disk Jockey Show Lounge, run by entrepreneur and radio personality McKie Fitzhugh, one of the few black club owners in the city. McKie's was one of the last South Side venues to feature, along with the best and brightest of Chicago's musicians, nationally known improvisors such as John Coltrane. Leslie Rout, a cultural historian who also had experience as a saxophonist in Chicago, noted that by 1967, "there did not exist on the South Side of Chicago a single club that booked nationally established jazz talent on a consistent basis."[2]

The disappearance of the South Side club scene has never been adequately explained, though anecdotal speculations and academic generalizations abound. Most popular music theorists connect the demise of jazz club scenes in black urban areas with a decline in popularity of "abstract" jazz in favor of more dance-oriented musics. This conventional wisdom is certainly buttressed by national sales figures, but at the local level in Chicago, the thesis is complicated by a number of factors. Many musicians ascribe the decline of Chicago's South Side clubs to deliberate city government action. Roscoe Mitchell blamed the situation on licensing laws that were introduced in the late 1950s, where clubs were taxed according to the number of musicians on the bandstand.[3] On this view, discriminatory enforcement and harassment of both club owners and patrons were designed to prevent clubs from thriving, as a means of encouraging neighborhood gentrification and a concomitant rise in real estate values; the added expenses would force many clubs to abandon live music altogether in favor of recorded music.

In any event, taking into account the widespread economic deterioration in black urban areas across the United States problematizes explanations based largely on jazz sales figures. Reflecting the situation for blacks nationally, in 1966, "a peak prosperity year" for most residents of the Chicago area,[4] 20 percent of the black labor force in Chicago was employed at incomes below the official poverty line. Desperately poor people were stockpiled in ever more imposing modernist "projects" like the Robert Taylor Homes. Just three years after the opening of the Taylor Homes in 1962, fully half of its twenty-eight thousand tenants were on welfare, and, as Arna Bontemps and Frank Conroy noted in 1966, "as usual, upkeep and maintenance were neglected and repairs rarely made."[5]

Schools in black areas, housed in dangerously decaying buildings, were becoming desperately overcrowded as well. Sensibly, Bontemps and Conroy connected the declining school infrastructure with an "appalling increase in juvenile delinquency." Many black children (including me) attended school in half-day shifts, with no compensation at all for the instructional time lost. Released prematurely from instruction, these children often had nowhere to go but the streets, which seemed preferable to "the small, dark rooms they called home."[6] These children, now the majority of the public-school population in Chicago, were herded into cold, drafty, trailers, called "Willis Wagons" in sardonic reference to the widely disliked school superintendent, Benjamin F. Willis. The trailers, touted as an "innovative" response to overcrowding, were often built over limited playground space, forcing children into the street at recess.[7] Resources from U.S. president Lyndon Baines Johnson's "Great Society" antipoverty programs, perhaps the last twentieth-century attempt at a domestic American Marshall Plan, trickled down to Bronzeville, sometimes in bizarre fashion. The vacuum asserted by the lack of educational infrastructure was filled by "youth gangs," such as the East Side Disciples and the Blackstone Rangers. The Rangers, later known as the "Black P. Stone Nation," received a $1 million grant from the Office of Economic Opportunity.[8]

In this rapidly decaying environment, not only jazz clubs, but rhythm-and-blues joints were also disappearing, along with Bronzeville's movie houses, banks, clothing stores, bookstores, doctors' offices, and quality restaurants. These establishments were quickly replaced by fast-food chicken shacks and endless variations on the corner liquor store. By 1967, 63rd Street was a musical ghost town, except perhaps for bluesman Arvella Gray's frequent appearances with his steel guitar under the El station at 63rd and Cottage Grove. Concomitantly, music clubs were opening up in nonblack areas of the city, notably the white North Side and western suburbs, further complicating the standard explanation. Musicians began to connect this musical outmigration from the South Side with notions of exile and stolen legacies of culture. Speaking to AACM cofounder Philip Cohran, trombonist Martin "Sparx" Alexander put the situation plainly: "Phil, you mentioned about us being 'robbed,' about the music being taken away from us. When I first came to Chicago in the Fifties—around 63rd and Cottage—that was a kind of Mecca. The music was all over. You could walk up and down the street and hear brothers playing everywhere. You didn't need to go in no joint. . . . They were localized in terms of *our* community. But something happened."[9]

For the most part, contemporaneous accounts of the local Chicago music scene in *Down Beat* describe little of the musical ferment then active in Chicago's black community, even though the magazine itself was based in Chicago. In a 1966 article in the Canadian journal *Coda,* one Chicago-based writer remarked rather dryly that *Down Beat*'s "reticence on local developments is thought-provoking, to say the least."[10] The Chicago-based experimental musicians most frequently mentioned were the three white members of the Joe Daley Trio, with saxophonist Daley, bassist Russell Thorne, and drummer Hal Russell. The group, according to a *Down Beat* review, comprised "the city's foremost 'new thing' group," playing both their own music and pieces like Ornette Coleman's *Rambling.*[11]

An article by J. B. Figi in a small, independent publication based in Detroit gives a completely different picture of Chicago's new music scene, one in which black musicians were far more prominent. Playing on the etymology of Chicago's name, which comes from an Algonquin word meaning "onion swamp," Figi noted that there was indeed a great deal of new music activity, but that "listeners saw only the tops of the onions."[12] Figi mentions Richard Abrams, Rafael Garrett, Steve McCall, Gene Dinwiddie, Fred Anderson, Roscoe Mitchell, Bill Brimfield, and Robert Barry, among others, declaring that "summer 1964 made it clear that there were musicians committed to the new music, and that some of them spoke it as a native tongue, not something picked up from phrase-books. . . . But, as commitment grew, so did evidence that acceptance would not be forthcoming from the existing order."[13]

In 1910, the classically trained composer-performers Will Marion Cook and James Reese Europe drew upon communalist models in founding the Clef Club as a site for bringing together black musicians of diverse backgrounds to develop both the music and the business of music. The "Clefies," as they were known, managed to purchase their own clubhouse in Harlem, as well as a branch in Chicago.[14] The Clef Club's vindicationist strategy included the formation of a symphony orchestra, in the belief that providing opportunities for black musicians to learn the craft of symphonic performance would counter the notion that blacks were incapable of interpreting Western classical music at the highest level. The hope was that greater opportunities for African Americans in such ensembles would emerge, both for performers and composers. At the same time, Clef Club members took full advantage of their familiarity with a diversity of styles to become well known as leaders of various popular and classical ensembles. Among the most notable of these ensembles was army Lt. Europe's all-black Hell Fighters military band, which became a sensation in World War I France for its ability to effortlessly code-switch between black protojazz styles and classical music. The Negro String Quartet, founded in 1919, was active on the East Coast, performing both standard works of European composers and compositions by contemporary black composers such as Edward Margetson and Clarence Cameron White.[15]

The Clef Club's strategy of control of their products had long been pursued by black artists, notably including theater artists and composers Bob Cole, James Weldon Johnson, and J. Rosamond Johnson, who sought to maintain both creative and financial control of their productions in the face of legal chicanery, boycotts, and blacklisting. Cole and the Johnsons, according to Paula Seniors, "presented Black men and women as college students, soldiers, patriotic heroes, and romantic characters for the first time on the

American stage."[16] Their work resisted both the racialized channeling of black artists into particular genres or venues, and the dominant blackface minstrelsy and coon song genres that dominated the American theater. The massive commodification of black imagery was still in relative infancy at the beginning of the twentieth century, but Cole and the Johnsons were already fighting white producers' attempts to assert spurious claims to authorship of their original work. For Cole, whose 1906 *Shoo-Fly Regiment* was the first theater production completely conceived, created, and run by African Americans, "uplifting the race" meant "full ownership and control of the theatrical product,"[17] as his 1898 "Colored Actor's Declaration of Independence" affirmed: "We are going to have our own shows. . . . We are going to write them ourselves, we are going to have our own stage manager, our own orchestra leader and our own manager out front to count up."[18]

By the mid-1940s, however, this first wave of twentieth-century formal collective activism among black musicians had seemingly faded, though individual attempts by musicians to challenge systems of domination persisted. In 1952, Charles Mingus and Max Roach had started their own firm, Debut Records.[19] In 1955, saxophonist Gigi Gryce, along with Benny Golson, founded their own publishing companies, Melotone Music and Totem Music, to handle rights and royalties for their own works and those of other composers. African American lawyer (and later New York Supreme Court justice) Bruce Wright, who helped set up the companies, told an interviewer that "one of the reasons [Gryce] was setting up Melotone and Totem with Benny was that he felt that black jazz musicians were being cheated by record companies, by producers. . . . He established these publishing companies to become an honest broker in a field where musicians believed they were being cheated in large part."[20]

It made sense for musicians to control their own publishing, as Horace Silver observed, "because we could not only control our music 100%, own the copyright 100%, but also get 100% of the money rather than 50% of the money."[21] However, complicating the situation further, according to Silver and others, was the fact that record companies such as Blue Note and Prestige had formed their own music publishing companies, and were coercing musicians who wanted to record to place their compositions with the company. This would allow the record company to obtain part of the royalties for a given composition. In addition, the companies often demanded the copyright for the works. As Bruce Wright explained, "For years, if jazz musicians wanted their music recorded by established labels, the record companies would often insist that some stranger's name be added as co-

composer. In that way, royalties would have to be split with someone unknown to them, usually a relative of an executive. If there was resistance,
there would be no record date."[22] According to Wright, Gryce's companies
were essentially blackballed by the industry. "Black musicians were being
told that if they placed their music with Melotone or Totem, they need
not expect any record dates in New York."[23] Desperate to record, musicians
pulled their music from Gryce's companies. In 1963, Gryce released to their
original owners the publishing rights to over two hundred compositions
by people such as Marcus Belgrave, Clifford Brown, Ray Bryant, Lou Donaldson, Bob Dorough, Art Farmer, Benny Golson, Hank Jones, Duke Jordan, Booker Little, Howard McGhee, Blue Mitchell, Thelonious Monk, Lee
Morgan, Julian Priester, Hale Smith, and Randy Weston.

By the mid-1960s, many musicians were reconceptualizing the discursive,
physical, and economic infrastructures in which their music took place. In a
1966 interview, John Coltrane made it clear that "I don't care too much for
playing clubs, particularly." Elaborating, the saxophonist explained that "the
music, changing as it is, there are a lot of times when it doesn't make sense,
man, to have somebody drop a glass, or somebody ask for some money
right in the middle of Jimmy Garrison's solo. . . . I think the music is rising, in my estimation, it's rising into something else, and so we'll have to
find this kind of place to be played in."[24] In the same interview, Coltrane
presented his notion of what artists needed to do in order to improve their
situation. "There has to be a lot of self-help, I believe," Coltrane said. "They
have to work out their own problems in this area."[25] In fact, sporadic attempts toward independence had been going on for some time. Charles
Mingus and Max Roach organized a musician-run festival of "Newport
Rebels" on the fringes of the 1960 Newport Jazz Festival to provide an alternative to what they saw as the commercialization, racism, and economic
exploitation that the mainstream festival displayed. The alternative event,
which took place alongside a riot that caused the cancellation of several
concerts, featured young radicals Randy Weston and Ornette Coleman.
The event was also supported by elder statesmen Coleman Hawkins, Roy
Eldridge, and Jo Jones, who commented that "the big festival forgot about
music, but these little kiddies have got to have a chance to be heard. That's
one reason why we did this."[26]

This attempt by musicians to take charge of their own concert production was denigrated at length in a *Down Beat* article by writer Gene Lees,
who ignored the cross-generational aspect of the event in turning his reportage into an ill-tempered, ad hominem assault on Mingus himself. Ac-

cording to Lees, the musicians' festival was "unorganized," although on one night five hundred people reportedly attended. Lees sarcastically described the musicians' public meeting announcing the formation of a "Jazz Artists Guild": "They were going to fight the wicked forces conspiring against the jazz artist. They were going to book concerts and other events. They would oppose Birdland, another symbol to them of the forces of evil."²⁷ Indeed, the message that "acceptance would not be forthcoming from the existing order" could not have been lost on the musicians.

To support the view that the Jazz Artists Guild project was a quixotic one, the writer used a quote from Horace Silver, who wished the guild well, while observing that "jazz musicians aren't very good businessmen, as a rule."²⁸ By 1965, however, John Coltrane was proving quite a good businessman, sufficiently successful as an artist to control his own publishing, his own recording studio, and his own record company. According to the Nigerian musician Babatunde Olatunji, Coltrane and Yusef Lateef were working with him on plans to organize an independent performance space and booking agency. Olatunji portrays the saxophonist as declaring in their conversation that "we need to sponsor our own concerts, promote them and perform in them. This way we will not only learn how to take a risk but will not have to accept the dictates of anybody about how long you should play, what to play and what you get."²⁹ The three musicians drafted a tripartite mission statement:

1. To regard each other as equal partners in all categories.
2. Not to allow any booking agent or promoter to present one group without the other two members of the Triumvirate.
3. To explore the possibility of teaching the music of our people in conservatories, colleges and universities where only European musical experience dominates and is being perpetuated.³⁰

One of Coltrane's last performances, titled "The Roots of Africa," was produced by the new organization in April 1967 at Olatunji's Center of African Culture in Harlem. While Coltrane's subsequent passing apparently ended this collaboration,³¹ the need for change was evident to many musicians, and the efficacy of highly individualistic strategies for accomplishing their goals was very much in question. Academic and musician Leslie Rout, Jr., identifying a "craving for individualism" by musicians as the source of their economic problems, leavened his version of the standard call for black unity with this observation that "jazzmen have almost no control over the business end of their vocation. . . . Tightly-knit associations of jazz artists, allied on either a regional or local basis and led predominantly by black Americans, must gain significant control over the production, cost, and presentation of their art, or face the perpetuation of the intolerable conditions so often criticized."[32]

One of the first collectively organized 1960s responses to the dire situation for black musicians took place in Los Angeles. An outgrowth of pianist Horace Tapscott's Pan Afrikan Peoples' Arkestra, the UGMA (Underground Musicians' Association, later the Union of God's Musicians and Artists Ascension), was formed in 1964, just before the massive rebellion in the Watts area of the city.[33] The New York–based Jazz Composers Guild, also founded in 1964, was perhaps the most widely publicized effort at collective self-determination of the early 1960s. Two determined iconoclasts, trumpeter and composer Bill Dixon and pianist Cecil Taylor, were widely credited with the idea of bringing into multiracial coalition the most committed new musicians in the New York area, including pianist Paul Bley, saxophonist Archie Shepp, composer Carla Bley, trumpeter Mike Mantler, trombonist Roswell Rudd—and Sun Ra, who was by this time well established in the city.

In 1965, Dixon clearly stated the prime rationale for organizing musicians: "Those of us whose work is not acceptable to the Establishment are not going to be financially acknowledged. As a result, it is very clear that musicians, in order to survive—create their music and maintain some semblance of sanity—will have to 'do it themselves' in the future."[34] According to Dixon, the guild's purposes were "to establish the music to its rightful place in the society; to awaken the musical conscience of the masses of people to that music which is essential to their lives; to protect the musicians and composers from the existing forces of exploitation; to provide an opportunity for the audience to hear the music; to provide facilities for the proper creation, rehearsal, performance, and dissemination of the music."[35] In practice, as economist Jacques Attali noted, the guild's members "directed their efforts toward becoming more independent of capital."[36] The organization's economic strategy aimed at creating a musician-controlled infrastructure for recording session production, product distribution, concert promotion, and event presentation.

A *Down Beat* review of the 1964 "October Revolution in Jazz" event that sparked the formation of the guild was grudging in its admission that the musicians had succeeded in organizing a successful production.[37] A second event at New York's Judson Hall in December of that year featured the Cecil

Taylor Unit, the Bill Dixon Quintet, Paul Bley, the Sun Ra Arkestra, and the Jazz Composers Guild Orchestra. Performing were the cream of New York's avant-garde of the period, including trombonist Roswell Rudd, trumpeter Charles Tolliver, saxophonists Jimmy Lyons, Marshall Allen, Marion Brown, John Tchicai, Steve Lacy, and Archie Shepp, drummers Andrew Cyrille, Rashied Ali, and Milford Graves, pianist Burton Greene, bassists Alan Silva and Buell Neidlinger, and many others.[38]

Guild concerts were held weekly at a loft on Seventh Avenue in Manhattan, located two floors above the Village Vanguard jazz club.[39] At guild-produced symposia, musicians and critics debated topics such as "The Jazz Economy" and "Jim Crow and Crow Jim."[40] The group's plans also included ownership of its own concert space, and incorporation as a nonprofit, tax-exempt organization for the purposes of applying for grants. However, in the end the guild lasted little more than a year, as the clash of strong-willed personalities, operating in the intensely competitive atmosphere of New York and the highly charged racial atmosphere of the United States, rendered its activities and goals untenable.

Retrospective accounts by Paul Bley and Bill Dixon as to the reasons for the guild's demise provide a glimpse into the extreme divergence of views within the guild. In his 1999 autobiography, Bley was skeptical of the viability of collectives in general: "All collectives, regardless of size, are usually run by a handful of key people who come to all the meetings and do all the work. . . . Every time I had been through one of these situations, I vowed never to waste my time doing it again."[41] Bley was particularly skeptical of the ability of collectives to produce music of high quality. "People choose to play with one another on the basis of their ability," Bley declared. "A collective would most probably encourage over-socialisation, over-fraternalisation, over-democracy. . . . You have the poorest players playing with the best players. It's not the best way to get the music along quickly."[42] The pianist described guild meetings as something akin to psychodrama: "What a bunch of wounded souls there were at these meetings. Talk about group therapy. It was nothing for someone to stand up at a meeting and talk for two or three hours about the pain that they felt, the struggle—intergroup, inter-race, inter-class, inter-family, inter-musical, *inter-everything*. The next night, the working nucleus of the Guild would get together and do all the work."[43]

Bley saw Dixon as manifesting an autocratic style that posed particular problems. "Bill saw [the guild] as a family of his friends," Bley recalled. "And if he wasn't friendly with anyone at a particular time it was ruled by

dictate."[44] Certainly, Dixon's frank and public contemporaneous observations concerning internal conflicts in the multiracial Guild could conceiv-
ably have been disconcerting, even to guild members: "Even in the guild,
which is comprised of some very intelligent people, there has been a subtle,
but apparent, indignation on the part of the white members (and this is
something I think nearly all white men have in them) that a black man . . .
myself, Cecil . . . could conceive and execute an idea that would be intelligent and beneficial to all."[45]

For Dixon, white musicians were treated "significantly better, but not
much better—that's why they're in the guild—than are black musicians,
and that is simply because they play jazz, which is looked upon as something 'primitive.'"[46] Dixon further asserted that white artists "are not bound
by an enforced social tradition that relegates them to one area of musical
expression. The Negro plays jazz because that music is close to him—it's
his way of life—and because, qualified or not, the other areas of musical
expression are closed to him."[47] In contrast, Bley was relatively unsympa-
thetic to the possibility that there might be a need to work through class
and race dynamics that may have affected white and black musicians in different ways. This did not mean, however, that the pianist was unmindful
of being in a white minority in the guild. Echoing the views of many 1960s
whites, both in the North and in the South, for Bley, the racial situation
had been relatively harmonious up to the 1960s until "social consciousness"
intervened:

> Unfortunately, being one of the 4 White people in the group it was dif-
> ficult for me to live with the pain with my friends who were in pain be-
> cause the Black players I knew prior to that didn't regard themselves as
> being in a painful situation, they regarded themselves as being in a joyous
> situation. It was when the musicians began to adopt a social consciousness
> that they had their own workloads to pursue over and above the greater
> financial reward of a group of musicians.[48]

For Dixon, race also played a central role in the organization's demise,
but along a very different axis from what Bley saw:

> Of course this is America you're talking about and racism in America is
> such that the parent society which has robbed and pillaged everything—
> they would rather lose some things rather than have the people that they

have oppressed come up with a solution. And in the JCG it was finally
like that. The white ones wanted to . . . try and let everyone else participate even though they can't or don't want to. And that was the reason
for its failure.[49]

Bley felt that one important reason for the failure of the guild was the
unworkability of one of its central policies—that individual members must
refuse work offered from outside the guild unless the guild as a whole approved the engagement.[50] Abandoning the organization's collectivist policy,
Archie Shepp decided to sign with Impulse, the same company that published John Coltrane's work. According to Bley, Dixon received Shepp's decision poorly. "Archie had a family to support," Bley observed, "and he sure
wasn't going to turn down *any* money, certainly not a lump of money like
an Impulse contract. That was it for Bill. He got up and left the meeting.
He didn't return until months later. That was a problem because he was
the founder. After that, Roswell Rudd and I ran the Guild for over a year."[51]
According to Bley's account, Dixon returned, months later, and demanded
that the next meeting be held at his house, but "when the meeting time
came, the following Thursday at the appointed hour, nobody showed up. I
didn't show up, nobody showed up, for reasons no one knows. There were
no phone calls, there was no decision in advance."[52]

Commenting on the downfall of the guild, Cecil Taylor had this to say:

> The musicians don't just have something to do with art in society. They
> are themselves the society, even if they only find themselves on the pe-
> riphery. Either actively or unconsciously they revolt against a bizarre soci-
> ety. I believe that the Guild did not survive because the people who were
> dealing with it did not raise enough social consciousness; they neglected
> everything that has to do with what a person who lives in New York today,
> who not only wants to earn his living but also to honestly express himself,
> experiences in everyday life.[53]

"We bungled an opportunity," Taylor reflected. "But at least we tried
something. . . . In spite of it all, it was not in vain. We came out of it a bit
with a bit more cunning.[54] Referring approvingly to the goals of the guild,
John Coltrane told an interviewer in 1966 that "I don't think it's dead. It
was just something that couldn't be born at that time, but I still think it's
a good idea."[55]

Born on the Kitchen Table: Conceiving the Association

> My mother was playing whist and that's when the labor pains began. That's
> where I was born, right there at that table.
> —Jodie Christian

The earliest histories of the Great Migration framed the movement as animated by a kind of spontaneous, leaderless combustion. These accounts
claimed that the movement resulted not so much from conscious agency
on the part of migrants, but from a kind of "historical imperative" conditioned largely by external factors such as economic pressures and climactic
conditions.[56] One notices the similarity of this trope to the conventional
wisdom that casts improvisation in general, and the products of black music in particular, as both lacking in structure and insensitive to historical or
formal concerns. As a consequence, the historiography of jazz has rarely
been able to find a place for tropes of deliberation, planning, and organization on the part of musicians. Rather, the image of the creative process
for black musicians has favored clichéd images of spontaneity, along with
portrayals of musicians as irresponsible, cryptically cliquish, and desirous
of instant gratification.

In contrast, Steve McCall's mother Willa remembers a series of rather
sober, intensely reflective meetings. "The AACM was born at my kitchen
table," she declared in our interview. "You had four of them, I think, at the
beginning. Richard Abrams, Phil Cohran and Steve . . ."

"And Jodie, Mom," added Willa McCall's daughter, Rochelle Toyozumi.
"Malachi came in later."

"That's right, Jodie Christian," Willa McCall agreed. The meetings could
well have taken place in early 1965, in the South Side housing project where
the McCall family lived and where young Stephen McCall IV grew up.
Toyozumi remembers the optimism that marked these encounters:

> They sat there at the table and they went on about what they could
> do, and how strong they would be. They were trying to get a plan, some-
> thing that would be good for black musicians, those that were starting
> out, those that were struggling, people that had no way of bringing this
> music before the public. They were just sick of what was going on, and
> they talked about what could we do for our selves. They had the cour-
> age of their convictions, and they would step out on that. They were not
> afraid to do it. That's the kind of people it took to make the AACM.

Jacques Attali sees a particular quote from Malcolm X as foreshadowing the kind of organization that was fervently desired by these artists. The quote, which valorizes improvisation as a way to create conditions for change, points up something of the mindset that was emerging in important segments of the black community at mid-decade, shortly before Malcolm's murder in 1965:

> The white musician can jam if he's got some sheet music in front of him. He can jam on something he's heard jammed before. But that black musician, he picks up his horn and starts blowing some sounds that he never thought of before. He improvises, he creates, it comes from within. It's his soul; it's that soul music. . . . He will improvise; he'll bring it from within himself. And this is what you and I want. You and I want to create an organization that will give us so much power we can sit and do as we please.[57]

In Phil Cohran's hoodoo-tinged origin story, the AACM was conceived in the shadow of Dinah Washington's final resting place:

> I can remember Steve McCall and Muhal walking along by Oakwood Cemetery. . . . We hadn't seen each other in a long time. We were all part of the same generation. You see, we were musicians who had come up under Bird and Dizzy and all of these guys, and then we looked up one day, and all that was snatched away. . . . There was a general feeling that we had been robbed of our culture. So we stopped and we started talking about how tough times are. . . . We wanted to do something about it.[58]

Abrams, Christian, Cohran, and McCall sent postcards to the cream of Chicago's African American musicians, announcing a meeting to be held on May 8, 1965, at Cohran's South Side home on East 75th Street near Cottage Grove Avenue. Abrams recorded this and subsequent meetings on his Sony portable reel-to-reel recorder, and the discussions on the tape made it clear that the aim of the meeting was the formation of a new organization for musicians. The postcard that participants received presented a fourteen-point agenda. The first point to be addressed concerned "original music" and "creative music," indicating that among Chicago musicians, a notion as to what these terms might signify may already have been developing. The other talking points listed on the postcard covered logistical matters, financial issues, the projected organization's form and day-to-day operation, the nature of its legal standing, and its future plans and possible expansion. The points, apparently in this order, were: (2) size of groups, (3) concerts, (4) salaries, (5) places to play, (6) guests of performers, (7) promotion, (8) dues, (9) order and discipline, (10) charter, (11) name, (12) membership, (13) broadening scope of operation, and (14) collaboration.[59]

This first meeting was conducted using more or less standard parliamentary procedure. The rules for the meeting required each participant to state his or her name to the chair before speaking, so that the tape itself could augment, or perhaps eventually replace, conventional written minutes. As a result, some sense of who was there at the early meetings can be gained from the people who spoke.[60] The wide-ranging discussions in these early meetings, in which musicians are speaking frankly among themselves, rather than to any outside media, evince nothing so much as an awakening of subalterns to the power of speech. Moreover, in direct contradiction to the overwhelming majority of critical commentary on the AACM, terms such as "new jazz," "the avant-garde," or "free jazz" were seldom, if ever, used in the discussions. Even "black music" was not directly mentioned, although it was obvious that many meeting participants directly connected the new organization's aims with those of black people as a group.

Abrams, as the presiding chair, called the meeting to order at around 2 p.m., calling for discussion on the first agenda item. "First of all, number one, there's original music, *only*," Abrams began. "This will have to be voted and decided upon. I think it was agreed with Steve and Phil that what we meant is original music coming from the members in the organization."[61] As might be expected from a group of strong-willed, relatively experienced artists, competing notions as to the nature and purpose of "original music" were in play throughout, and Cohran, Abrams, Christian, and McCall were adamant in their understanding that the eventual success of the process of organizing depended on hearing all voices. "I want it understood," emphasized Abrams, "that we by no means meant to dictate any laws or any standing rules as to this group. We only made suggestions as to a start. We don't want to stifle nobody, because we wouldn't have anything if we cut you off from what you might want to do for the sake of a few." Steve McCall agreed. "We've all been talking about it among ourselves for a long time in general terms. We'll embellish as much as we can, and get to what you really feel because we're laying a foundation for something that will be permanent."

As with the Great Migration, precedents for meetings such as these may be sought not only in the immediate circumstances facing these artists, but also in deeper historical and cultural tropes. For musicologist Samuel Floyd, an imperative for letting all voices be heard emerges most centrally in the ring shout, a postslavery form of "participation performance" (to adopt Fluxus artist Allan Kaprow's term) in which the people form a circle, moving, singing, and shouting rhythmically, while individual actors take impromptu solos as the spirit may move. In addition to Floyd's notion of the centrality of a "metaphor of the ring" to African American musical culture,[62] a more proximate motive force was the influence of bebop, one of the "standard musics" that constituted the immediate background of most of these musicians. Here, one can find further precedent via Daniel Belgrad's observation that bebop's notion of intersubjectivity "implies that participatory democracy is the form of political economy with the greatest vitality and the most potential power."[63] Indeed, it is entirely understandable that a people who were silenced by slavery would develop a music, jazz, in which everyone would have their say, and the ring shout–like, performative nature of the May 8 meeting was evident from the first moments.

The rationale for forming an organization for the support of new, original music recalls such earlier efforts as the Society for Private Music Performance (Verein für musikalische Privataufführungen), founded by composer Arnold Schoenberg in 1918. As Schoenberg wrote, the society's purpose was "to present contemporary music in circumstances conducive to its proper appreciation."[64] According to music historian Robert Morgan, the society "furnished an early reflection of the isolation of new music from 'official' concert institutions, and thus of the need to find a more specialized forum for its presentation."[65] Speaking in the meeting, trumpeter Fred Berry, who had been developing new music with Roscoe Mitchell, Malachi Favors, and Alvin Fielder, saw a similar need: "For original music to be presented, it needs some help. It needs help, from us. This is why we're doing this. The standard music needs no help to be presented. If you want to play standards, or standard music, there are places to do this. You're working your gigs, you're playing the standard music there. But this is for something new and something different that has no other medium."

"What were your basic ideas that you had in mind, you and these three people?" asked bassist Melvin Jackson. "Maybe we can all build on the original idea."

"We spoke in terms of discussing the furthering of creative music," Abrams replied. "We had thought about, you know, giving our own concerts, you see, as a start, and then expand into other things that would enhance the project in general."

"All of us are creative musicians," said Cohran, "and that's why we were invited together to form an association or a group, so that we can play our music, or the music that's in our hearts, and the music of our experience and training, and desires, because we can't do this any more."

"The whole idea," explained McCall, "is basically to organize to better the whole situation of work, as far as performing-wise, the writing, and giving concerts, and whatever, to encompass as much as we can."

"I think the reason original music was put there first," Cohran continued, "was because of all of our purposes of being here, this is the primary one. Because why else would we form an association? Because we're all denied the privilege of expressing what is in us. I would like to suggest that if we have a motto or a purpose, that it be connected with promoting and playing and exchange of original music."

"I don't think you can talk about original music without including concerts and promotion," Jodie Christian said, to general assent from the very experienced musicians present at the meeting. "The only jobs that we're gonna have where we can really perform original music are concerts that *we* promote, because the type of jobs that we're gonna get won't call for original music."

These musicians could not have hoped for support similar to that offered to university-based white American experimentalists in the wake of the cold war. Nor could they have imagined the kind of European social-democratic cultural support—again, a product of post–World War II political arrangements—that fueled the work of the early European free jazz musicians, whose rise to prominence paralleled that of the AACM. As Philip Cohran observed, the new organization was on its own. "By us forming an association and promoting and taking over playing our own music," he warned, "it's going to involve a great deal of sacrifice on each and every one of us. And I personally don't want to sacrifice, make any sacrifice for any standard music."

"I think that for the most part all of us would play original music anyway," said pianist Ken Chaney. "But do we want to really put a barrier out and say that that's all that's going to be allowed? Because we're still not free then either. We're just bound to original music."

"I prefer to play music from the past, present *and* the future," said bassist Betty Dupree. "Let's play all of it."

"The only thing that I'm concerned with personally is good music," Melvin Jackson opined. "Just to say, 'original music,' that's not my mood all the time, it might not be your mood all the time."

The comments by Dupree, Chaney, and Jackson connected music performance with issues of personal freedom, mobility, and individuality. In contrast, for Abrams, the assertion of personal freedom, while clearly an advance on the situation at standard gigs, was no longer sufficient at a time when "self-determination" formed a prominent aspect of the radical black political agenda. "All music is good, and I'm sure that this group will not be a source of cutting anyone off from doing most of the things that they want to do," Abrams said reassuringly. "But at least we would have something that would definitely and directly push us at all times, personally, because this is what we need. We need to be remembered as representing ourselves."

"The standard music, we've all played it," said McCall. "But for *this* organization, you know, for the promoting of having cats to write original compositions, for getting together and presenting, in concert, and as a means of a livelihood, you dig, like making some money, getting out of *your* things, the things that we all create among ourselves. Being at a concert just for standard music, you know, there doesn't have to be this kind of a group for that kind of thing."

"This is a long range project, you see," Jodie Christian explained optimistically. "You can't look at what's happening now, or what was happening behind you, because we don't expect this organization just to be put in a spot over here while we play our other gigs over here. We expect this to branch out so we won't have to go on those other gigs and play things that we don't want to play."

About forty-five minutes into the meeting, saxophonist Gene Easton summarized the differences of understanding in the meeting regarding the notion of originality. For Easton, the salient questions concerned the viability of systems old and new, the relationship to tradition, the expanding horizons of thought and opportunity, and an increasing awareness among artists of a wider world of music. Easton expressed the urgency of the aesthetic crisis that was at the core of the musicians' decision to emancipate themselves through reliance on their own creative resources.

"I think we're getting closer to an explanation of this term, 'original music,'" Easton said. "'Original,' in one sense, means something you write in the particular system that we're locked up with now in this society. We express ourselves in this system because it's what we learned. As we learn more of other systems of music around the world, we're getting closer to the music that our ancestors played and which we are denied the right to really stretch out in.

"I feel that the authors of this business structure here," Easton continued, "had in mind sound-conscious musicians, if necessary finding a complete new system that expresses *us*. We're locked up in a system, and if you don't express in the system that is known, you're ostracized. And there are many, many, far too many good musicians put in that position because they don't, uh . . ."

"Conform," said a voice.

"But there are far better systems," Easton declared. "As we tried to progress in jazz, we find that there's expression on a much higher level than we had been led to believe. And presently, we will be locked up for the rest of our days in this system unless we can get out of it through some means such as this."

The long and thoughtful silence that followed Easton's remarks was broken by Roscoe Mitchell. "I move that we take a vote on it so we can go on to the next one."

"Is there a second?" Abrams asked the meeting.

"I second it," said Cohran.

"It has been moved and seconded," Abrams intoned, "that we take a vote on number one, titled 'Original Music,' Are we ready for questions?"

"Before we vote on whether or not we're going to play original music," Fred Berry ventured, "there has to be a clear-cut definition in everyone's mind of what original music is."

"We're not going to agree on what exactly original music means to us," Abrams observed. "We'll have to limit—now—the word 'original' to promotion of ourselves and our own material to benefit ourselves."

Berry was persistent. "Give it a definition."

"The cards originally said 'creative music,'" said Easton, "and creative music can only be original anyway, in a true creative sense."

"When we say 'originality of the music,'" ventured Jackson, seeking further assurances, "I want to know, now this 'original thing,' like we say 'original music'—this is original personal preference."

Abrams tried to meet Jackson's concerns halfway. "I think what we mean by 'original,'" Abrams eventually answered, "is direct output from your system, your personal system.

"Your personal preference," Abrams added, "but original as far as you writing the music yourself."

"Wait now, this is where you're taking on a dictator part," Jackson objected. "Maybe I don't care to write, but I still care to play good music."

Jackson's observation gave Abrams pause. "You made something come to mind that I hadn't thought about," said Abrams. "I'd like to think that to participate in a group like this it wouldn't stifle anybody whether you wrote a tune or not. We are in need of not only composers, we have to have musicians to play it."

One should not mistake this comment for an attempt to reproduce the division of labor between "composer" and "performer" that characterized Western classical music. Rather, to these musicians, being "a musician" meant working out of a hybridized model of creative practice that negotiated between individuality and collective membership, and which assumed primary creative agency for each artist. "It is clear that we have performers and composers, you know," Abrams continued. "But basically, musicians are performers, composers and all, at the same time. You write music when you stand up and practice your instrument." Here, Abrams draws upon a tradition that regarded "composition," or the creation of music, as a cooperative, collective practice, responsive to the conditions and histories from which the individual musicians sprang.

Abrams and McCall felt strongly that the imperative of original music went beyond narrow strategies of self-promotion. "When we speak of ourselves," Abrams declared, "we not only speak of the group as registered members, we speak of ourselves as a whole, as a people."

"That covers a lot of territory," Jerol Donavon mused.

"As we begin to give concerts and maybe concerts with cats in other groups in other cities and things," Steve McCall predicted, "by saying the promotion of ourselves, that might mean playing Lee Morgan, 'Sidewinder,' to promote *me* on the concert stage." McCall's conclusion expressed a certain finality. "So now we got to say, original music—of *us*. Our original music."

Without objection, Abrams called the question. "We're gonna take a vote right now. All in favor of promoting ourselves, in the form of presenting our own music, within the scope of this organization, signify by saying 'Aye.'" In quick response came a unified shout of "Aye."

Even though the meeting had already been in session for more than two hours, no one was ready to adjourn. The meeting continued, point by point, through the postcard agenda. Philip Cohran began by suggesting that the group present a concert each week, with a rotating order of groups to ensure that all members had a chance to perform. Reggie Willis suggested that it might be possible to present more than one group per week. At the same time, however, Willis brought up an important issue regarding salaries. "This is just an assumption on my part," said Willis, "but it seems to me salaries are pretty set in accordance with union rules."

A 1968 *Down Beat* article about the AACM noted that "one of the musicians' primary concerns was to avoid coming into conflict with the bylaws of the musicians' union."[66] In the 1960s, the power of the union effectively controlled the musicians' very livelihoods, and Chicago's Local 208, the black musicians' local, exercised very tight control of clubs and theaters on its circuit, sending officials to spot-check ensembles for union membership. A leader who featured nonunion members could be fined or even suspended from the union, effectively foreclosing future work. Union musicians performing with nonunion musicians could be similarly sanctioned. Venues that employed nonunion musicians would be branded as "unfair," and union musicians would be barred from performing there. The musicians in the meeting worried about how to present concerts with more than one group if a union wage could not be provided for every musician. Featuring more musicians at a concert than were specified in the union contract constituted an infraction with potentially serious consequences.

Melvin Jackson suggested pursuing a variance with the union to waive the normal contract process. "I know personally that these things can be gotten around," said Jackson. "By this being a new organization, you can do these things with the sanction of the union, man. All you got to do is just go down there and talk with them."

Jodie Christian disagreed strongly. "I don't care for this 'sanction of the union.' The only dealings I want to have with the union is, I make up my contract and pay my dues. That's the only way I want to become affiliated with them. If we would have wanted to make this a union thing, we would have gone down there and had their permission and formed right there. But we decided this was our own thing, so we handle it our own way."

"This is sort of like self-employment, right here, what we got going," Christian reminded the meeting. "If we feel that we need a second group to be featured with that first group, we can do that without going to the union to do it—at all."

"See, we're dealing with concerts," Abrams agreed. "We're not dealing with these joints. They got that. They got all of that. We are dealing with concerts, and we are privileged to eliminate any middleman that we are pleased to. You can walk up to a man and say, I want to rent this hall and here's the money. Now he can either rent his hall or not. But if you walk up and say, look, I'll call you tomorrow, I'm gonna see if I can get the money from these cats, what you got?"

Up to this point, most of these musicians had been working for other people on a fee-for-service basis. Now that they were proposing to set themselves up as producers, they suddenly found themselves on both sides of the negotiating table, wondering how to pay themselves. It was becoming obvious that the musicians themselves would have to contribute to the group's welfare via payment of dues, just as they were contributing a union-stipulated percentage of their salaries to Local 208 as "work dues." As Abrams reminded the meeting, "This is a self-supporting organization," a fact that was underscored when Philip Cohran took the floor as the meeting stretched out past five in the afternoon. Cohran's remarks offer some idea of the extreme undercapitalization that marked the origins of the AACM. "It takes money to send out cards and all, the tape costs money," announced Cohran, "So we are in need of a collection from the people gathered, whatever you can afford."

"I suggest twenty-five cents, all around," Abrams said. "All in favor of the suggestion, signify by saying Aye." After a murmured general assent, Abrams declared that "the ayes have it. There will be a twenty-five-cent collection for those who can afford it."

"I got eleven cents," one member announced with some alarm. "Others, don't worry about it," said Abrams. After the collection was taken, a date for the next meeting was arranged. "The first thing that we should do," suggested bassist Charles Clark, "is try to elect officers, provided there's enough people."

"Alright," said Abrams. "All in favor of adjournment, signify by saying Aye." The room roared "Aye."

"This meeting now stands adjourned. Signed, Chairman Richard Abrams."

"Alright, baby," someone shouted.

Naming Ceremony: Black Power and Black Institutions

The second meeting took place a week later, on Saturday, May 15, 1965. Some of those who attended the first meeting did not return for the second, but others came with the expectation that officers were to be elected. Trombonist Julian Priester, who had been a regular member of Sun Ra's Arkestra and was now performing with Art Blakey, was visiting Chicago and was present at the meeting.[67] "I'd like you to tell myself and anyone else in the room," Priester asked the meeting chair, "what is the exact purpose, or purposes, of this organization?"

"Well, it was voted on and passed by everyone present," Abrams replied, "that we in this organization will play only our own music—original compositions or material originating from the members within the group, in the sense of concerts, exploitation around music that we write."

"But it would seem," Priester ventured, "that if you put too many restrictions on the activities, at this point of just getting organized, you're going to put a lot of obstacles in your way. For instance, to me, everyone in here is not a composer. Everyone in here is not writing music, and so right there you exclude them."

"No, no one's excluded," Abrams insisted. "We have to have performers *and* composers. We realized at the time that everyone is not gifted to a great deal of writing. But now, I feel this way, that you may not be Duke Ellington, but you got some kind of ideas, and now is the time to put 'em in. Wake yourself up. This is an awakening we're trying to bring about."

"But taking into consideration economic factors involved," Priester continued, "as musicians we're going to be working in front of the public, and different people, club owners or promoters . . ."

"No, no, we're not working for club owners, no clubs," Abrams interrupted quickly. "This is strictly concerts. As far as this organization is concerned, we're not working taverns, because we believe we can create enough work in concert. See, there's another thing about us functioning as full artistic musicians. We're not afforded that liberty in taverns. Everybody here knows that."

"When you say 'us,'" Priester asked, "are you speaking strictly of the physical members of the organization . . . excluding race or anything, anybody who is, uh . . ."

"Well, the members of the organization, whoever happens to be a member of the organization," Abrams replied.

"And how do you become a member?" Priester asked.

"Well, we're here now becoming members, since it was voted on and agreed upon that we elect officers today," Abrams said. "Now after the election of officers, I would say, then we have the start of an organization. After that, I'm sure we will decide on how we will accept other people in, after we've organized—whether they'll be screened in some way or whatnot like that."

"Before we get to the election of officers and some of the other points," Ken Chaney suggested, "we should think about exactly what we're going to be—if we're going to be, say, a society, something, for the advancement of creative music, or something like that."

Gene Easton agreed. "If we had a stated philosophy, and we knew whether we were a nonprofit organization, just how we plan to operate," Easton observed, "it would help to clear the thinking on some of the points that we are going into more or less cold."

The discussion began to wander around these points until the singer Floradine Geemes stepped in. In an impromptu yet confident and deliberate manner, the structure that the AACM was still using in the twenty-first century seemed to spring forth fully formed from her head. Geemes was able to directly identify, perhaps in a way that the overwhelmingly male membership was unable to countenance, the major issue evinced by the meeting's lack of focus. "Seems like most of the people here have fear," Geemes noted quietly, going on to present a lesson in basic organizational structure and function to the assembled artists. "When you say 'elect officers,'" Geemes began, "they have fear of president, vice president, secretary, chairman. But with basic parliamentary law, there shouldn't be any fear of a chairman."

Perhaps referring indirectly to the previous discussion, in which the union was depicted as an autocratic force vis-à-vis the musicians, Geemes was reassuring. "That doesn't mean that the officers have control of it and you have no say-so. 'Officers' only means that as president you have control over the meetings. "'Vice president' only means that if the president is not there, you got someone to carry on," Geemes continued. "'Recording secretary' is now recording whatever we have to discuss now, taking down the most important points. 'Financial secretary,' once we're organized, will eventually come into the picture.

"And that's all basic parliamentary is," the singer concluded. "It's the order of this group, and from there you've got your organization started. You can go into anything you want from there."

Perhaps stating the obvious, Easton observed gravely that "I think that the young lady spoke more clearly and evidently understands more about parliamentary procedure than the rest of us." Shortly thereafter, the task of nominating and electing a board was completed, and Abrams called out the names of the newly elected officers. "Richard Abrams is president; Jodie Christian is vice president; Flora Geemes is secretary, Phil Cohran, financial secretary; Sandra Lashley, recording secretary; Ken Chaney, business manager; Jerol Donavon, sergeant-at-arms; and Steve McCall, treasurer."[68]

The officers convened their first meeting a few days later at Philip

Cohran's 75th Street apartment, on Thursday, May 20, 1965 at around 7 p.m. Bassist Malachi Favors also took part in the discussion, as this first "executive board" developed policy suggestions to place before the organization as a whole for approval. The very first issue taken up, however, was not strictly organizational, but spiritual. At the May 15 meeting, bassist Nevin Wilson had remarked, "I'm concerned with what happened when we started this meeting—facing the East, and all that. What's the faith in this? Is it Islamic?"

"Well, that was for prayer purposes," Abrams explained.

"You could be any faith you wanted?"

"Any faith you wanted."

Now, Jodie Christian, a Jehovah's Witness, brought the issue up again, and Malachi Favors explained that "the planet rotates to the East. When you face the East you're standing proudly. Somebody might think that facing the East has something to do with the Muslims, or Islam, or something like that."[69]

"I picked the East simply because life feeds out of the East into the West," Abrams said. "And it returns to the East. It returns home. It's man's written role, it's an example, each day, of what he is here to do . . . among many other explanations, and I'm sure there could be quite a few."[70] The meeting turned to questions of fund-raising. "Let's take number eight first, which is dues," Abrams began, referring to the original postcard agenda from May 8. "Now I had thought of, say, a dollar a week for each member, which could give us a pretty fair cushion for promoting the first concert, maybe the first two concerts."[71]

"When Sandra [Lashley] was trying to collect," Floradine Geemes remembered of the May 15 general meeting, "someone said, 'I wasn't there last week,' or 'I can't afford it this week.'" A dollar a week may not seem like very much to those familiar with other, better-funded experimental music subcultures. The dues issue, however, underscores the point that the AACM's grass-roots community activism started literally from nothing— with all of the stresses that this implies. "All of us are in a strain at times," Abrams ventured, "and we may tend to get behind in our dues, not because we're lax, but simply because we're not able to pay 'em. Sometimes we're not working and sometimes we are. There are days when we don't have a dollar—at all. All the money goes right out of your pocket into . . . your responsibilities."

"I think the strictest rule that we can have on this, man," said Jerol

Donavon, "is that everybody has to be paid up when their time comes to playing the concert. And if their dues are not paid up, then they make arrangements to come before the executive board to explain why, and the executive board determines whether they can play or not."

The next agenda item was to work out the basics of becoming a nonprofit organization. "You have to state your purposes and everything," Cohran explained, "and then draw up a set of rules and by-laws, with a lawyer, and then you put it before the state."

"But a gig is for profit," Christian wondered aloud. "Isn't this a profit organization?"

"No, not really," Abrams replied. "We are promoting creative music as an art—culture." Talk of culture, in turn, brought questions regarding the new organization's relationship to traditional philanthropy. "Once we get our name and our charter and everything," said Cohran, "I think we should approach some businessmen, like Fuller, some of these people that's got some money. They might not do anything, but I think we should approach them on the basis of what we're trying to do culturally."[72]

"I disagree," McCall responded sharply, perhaps fearing that deviating from a strategy of full self-reliance could compromise the organization's independence.

"It's just to subscribe to what we're doing with no strings attached," Cohran ventured, "merely to run an ad on the program that says that he supports what we're doing."[73] No final agreement on this point was reached, and the meeting moved on to discuss promotion.

"To open up strongly," suggested Steve McCall, "means to open up with a plan in mind for more than just one concert. Instead of running more or less random concerts or what have you, we should have a series of concerts, so we have a program."

"It's going to take more than two weeks to promote an event," said Donavon. "Will we have placards and things made up?"

"We had these little things we passed out, and they were all over the city, just everywhere," said Abrams. "They were just as good as placards, 'cause a lot of people got 'em."

In the meeting's final moments, the question of who would give the first concert was approached whimsically by Cohran. "I think that the following Saturday, we should have all of the musicians to bring their instruments to the meeting. Everybody would get up and play for so many minutes," Cohran jokingly suggested," and then the whole body will vote on who they want to represent them in the first concert." To general laughter, the trumpeter evoked the spirit of the cutting contest, now clearly viewed as an artifact of a bygone age.

On Thursday, May 27, 1965, the second meeting of the executive board of the as yet unnamed organization took place at Philip Cohran's home. Answering the roll call were Richard Abrams, Steve McCall, Jerol Donavon, Ken Chaney, Philip Cohran, Sandra Lashley and Floradine Geemes. The first order of business was point eleven on the postcard agenda, a name for the organization. A name was necessary, not only to focus public attention on the new organization itself for purposes of advertising and promotion, but also to obtain a state charter, and to help consolidate the organization's membership behind a suitable image. "I have a name, but I'm not satisfied with it," ventured Cohran. "The name that I've finally come up with is 'Association of Dedicated Creative Artists,' It says everything I want to say, but it seems like it could be put in another way."[74]

"What you had on the card," Ken Chaney reminded everyone, "was 'a meeting for the advancement of creative music.'"

"That sounded good," Cohran mused. "'Association for the Advancement of Creative Music,' That was what got everybody there." The ensuing discussion demonstrates that the AACM, as with most African American organizations, did not eschew the spiritual as part of its organizational philosophy. "What initials would that give?" Abrams asked. "'A.A.C.M,' That would put a Nine on us, initial-wise."

"Really?" McCall responded, "That's good."

"Sandra wanted to know how I arrived at the number nine for the letters in the name," Cohran said to Abrams, "and I told her that this was your conversation, not mine."

"Numerology," Abrams replied. "'A' represents '1,' 'M' represents '4,' 'C' represents '3,' M and C would be 7, and the two A's are one apiece. That's nine. All the letters in the words might present something else," he warned, "but what you are called, a nickname or whatever it is, that's the vibration they put on you in numbers, regardless of what your name is.

"So we'll be referred to as the A.A.C.M most of the time, which would signify that this is a Number Nine organization," Abrams observed.

"That's as high as you can go," someone responded.

"True," Abrams replied, "but that's a high vibration to live up to. It could cause as many low things as high things if you don't live up to it. We think and feel in a spiritual manner about what we're doing."

Jacques Attali has asserted that the advent of "free jazz" was provoked by "the organized and often consensual theft of black American music."[75] Certainly, this understanding extended right into the naming of the new organization. "What are we calling it?" asked Sandra Lashley, who was taking notes. "'The Association for the Advancement of Creative . . . 'Music,' or 'Musicians?'"

Cohran's thoughtful response evinced a keen awareness of that long history of exploitation. "If the association is to advance the creative musicians, they are the ones who need advancing," Cohran declared. "We can all create music and somebody else can take it and use it. The musicians are the ones who need the help."

"We've been advancing creative music all along," declared Donavon, and McCall finished his sentence: "but nobody has been advancing us." That seemed to settle the matter. The name, "Association for the Advancement of Creative Musicians" and its acronym, "A.A.C.M.," were adopted unanimously by the board.

On Saturday, May 29, 1965, at 2 p.m., the next general meeting of the organization took place at the Abraham Lincoln Center, a local community-assistance institution located at 700 East Oakwood Boulevard, in a building designed and built in 1905 by Frank Lloyd Wright and Dwight Heald Perkins that now lay in the heart of Bronzeville. Steve McCall persuaded the center staff to make its facilities freely available to the musicians,[76] and as the tape was rolling, the sounds of musicians practicing could clearly be heard.[77] The first order of business was the membership roll call, which is given on the tape.[78] After the meeting was "called to order with prayer," Sandra Lashley read the minutes of the May 27 executive board meeting. The two name choices, "Association of Dedicated Creative Artists," or "A.C.D.A," and the board-recommended name, "Association for the Advancement of Creative Musicians," or "A.A.C.M," were presented to the general body. A clear preference for the name "A.A.C.M." quickly emerged, and with little further comment, the name Association for the Advancement of Creative Musicians was unanimously adopted. Gene Easton asked that the new organization be referred to henceforth as "the association" instead of "the club," reflecting a shift in self-image toward a more solid basis for imagining community.[79]

A number of housekeeping matters were pursued, moving toward the final agenda item, the election of a four-person board of directors, along the lines that Julian Priester had suggested in the May 15 meeting. Elected were Roscoe Mitchell, Malachi Favors, Fred Berry, and Gene Easton. A seemingly innocent question by pianist Bob Dogan led the group into a heated debate about race. "I got two members of my band who are not in the group and they are interested in getting into the group," Dogan ventured. "I'd like to know if I can take it upon myself to invite them into the next meeting so they can become members."

"Well, we're open for membership, aren't we?" Abrams asked.

"You know, they're not on the mailing list now," Dogan hesitated. This observation that the musicians "were not on the mailing list" seemed to be a tacit message that the musicians in question were white. On the other hand, Dogan himself was white, and by all indications, he was "on the list," as one of those specifically invited to the meeting by the original call. Thus, embodied within the issue brought to the table by Dogan was a complex dynamic of personal and professional interaction, crucially mediated by race and culture, where mappings of whiteness and blackness to insider-outsider binaries were defined not so much by phenotype as by issues of trust, collegiality—and power.

"We have a consideration to make too, in reference to what we're doing," Abrams began tentatively. "Actually, we haven't said it, but the membership is confined to a certain area or group of musicians.

"This is not in reference to whether a person's group can perform," he added. "As it stands now, the members in your group will perform with your group. We're going to have to make a consideration as to whether we're going to have an interracial organization, or have it as it stands now in reference to membership."

"You mean that if someone is a certain race then they can't come into the group," Dogan queried.

"I mean that we are going to have to decide whether we will have an interracial group or not," Abrams replied. "Being frank about it, when we started we didn't intend to have an interracial group. Not as opposed to another race, but we made it on the premise that each has his own, up to a certain height. Then, the collaboration and contact with the other races or body takes place."

"Yeah, but that would throw some low blows to a lot of cats that might really be interested," said Dogan.

This discussion mirrored developments taking place in the larger context of black political positions that were developing in the 1960s. A younger generation of black activists was sharply critical of what they saw as the failure of biracial coalition politics to advocate radical change. As Stokely Carmichael and Charles Hamilton wrote in 1967, "The concept of Black Power rests on a fundamental premise: *Before a group can enter the open so-*

ciety, it must first close ranks. By this we mean that group solidarity is necessary before a group can operate effectively from a bargaining position
of strength in a pluralistic society."[80] Many of Chicago's newer black cultural organizations were moving in a similar direction. For Carmichael and
Hamilton, "The point is obvious: black people must lead and run their own
organizations."[81] This point was articulated in greater detail by the Student
Non-Violent Coordinating Committee (SNCC) in 1966, and by the Congress of Racial Equality (CORE) in 1968, when these organizations removed
whites from their ranks.[82] Many activists also noted that black-white coalitions were frequently subject to fracture, due to unequal expectations of
power between whites and blacks.

Operating in the midst of a social system that routinely invests heavily
in white privilege, even the most committed organizations could be fatally
compromised from without. In Will Menter's account of the Jazz Composers Guild, Bill Dixon resented the apparent fact that after the demise of the
guild, Carla Bley and Mike Mantler managed to receive the grants that the
JCG had been trying for. Dixon attributed this to the fact that the JCG was
known for having black leadership. "When I was trying to get money, no
one had any," Dixon observed. "The minute I left them these people gave
them money to do things that they wouldn't give me to do. It's incredible. I
can almost say that in America you don't want a Black man showing people
anything if you can avoid it. And the same thing can be advanced by a white
person and it's good—it's valuable and should be subsidised."[83]

At the same time, Dixon recalled that many black musicians, in this era
of heightened black cultural nationalism, questioned the reasons for creating a multiracial, rather than an all-black organization. "People said why did
you have a mixed group? But I thought even the White musicians weren't
doing that well and I thought we had more chance if we made it mixed."[84]

Perhaps with this history in mind, Abrams argued that "an interracial
organization has to be awfully strong, brother, because it can be torn apart.
We see evidence of it in the Composer's Guild in New York. People are
trying to contribute things to the white members and withhold it from the
colored members—in the same group.

"This was stated by one of the originators of the organization, if you
read the account in *Down Beat* magazine," Abrams continued, probably referring to the Robert Levin article on Bill Dixon that had been published in
Down Beat just weeks before.[85] "He as much as said that he feared the organization was gonna crack because of it.

"This is not opposed to white musicians," Abrams declared. "We know that we clearly have economic, social and other obligations to ourselves because of our position as black musicians. We've been lacking a lot of things, and we have to bring up ourselves. We know what is going on with ourselves personally, as musicians at large, as participants in this organization, and as participants in this country, period." The remark indicated an implicit understanding of the difference between a notion of "racism" as the individualized practice of "prejudice" and the institutionalized exclusion to which they and their forebears had long been subjected. On this view, forming a black organization as a primary strategy of empowerment constituted a challenge to white-controlled economic, social, and discursive networks. At the same time, clearly present was the hope that with the eventual empowerment of black people, the need for race-specific political and economic strategies might be diminished. As Abrams explained to Dogan, "We're not fighting a racial fight. We're promoting ourselves and helping ourselves up to the point where we can participate in the universal aspect of things, which includes all people."[86]

Philip Cohran, perhaps as a way of fostering more careful consideration of the issue, put forth a motion that "the racial aspect of the membership" be the first order of business at the next general meeting. Cohran's attempt to table the topic was swept away by Abrams, again articulating an institutional rather than an individualist analysis. "There are good musicians on the North Side too, I mean white musicians," Abrams insisted. "It's not their fault the way these people manipulate things. The musicians don't do it. It's the people that control the thing." The rising tone of Abrams's soliloquy began to take on the tone of a revivalist preacher. To a rising chorus of murmuring assent, prior to the adjournment of the meeting, Abrams declared, "Our ticket is to get ourselves together as a body. They got the thing set up in a certain way, but they can't control us, because we have the music, and this is what they're after. Now, if that's not a good reason for organizing, I don't know what is. Don't think in terms of, 'Aw man, I ain't prejudiced,' That's not the point. We're talking about getting an alliance."

5

FIRST FRUITS

The First Year: Concerts, Critics, and Issues

> The AACM means a *new order;* possibility of order in the middle of
> the musical, catch-as-catch-can world.
> —J. B. Figi, "Jazz"

On August 5, 1965, the Association for the Advancement of Creative
Musicians was chartered by the State of Illinois as a nonprofit, tax-
exempt organization. The incorporators, or signatories to the charter,
were Philip Cohran, Stephen McCall, Jodie Christian, Sandra Lashley,
and Richard Abrams. The board of directors listed on this first official AACM document included Eugene Easton, Lester H. Lashley,
Malachi Favors, Jodie Christian, and flutist Robert R. Green. The official address of the corporation was listed as 511 East 87th Place, the
address of Lester and Sandra Lashley.[1] Legally, the organization was
obliged to state its purposes to be chartered. Rather than cobbling
together a set of vague phrases in the interests of flexibility, the organization took this obligation with the utmost seriousness. Particularly
for a "Number Nine" organization, the resulting set of nine purposes
reflected serious engagement with social, cultural, and spiritual issues
affecting black musicians and their community.

Historian Eric Porter points out that despite many bebop musicians' attempts to foster an image of respectability, the music was

never quite able to escape its association with social deviance.[2] For instance, in 1960, anthropologist Alan Merriam, one of the founders of modern ethnomusicology, collaborated with his colleague Raymond Mack in publishing a sociological survey of the "jazz community." The two academics presented an image of the "jazz musician" as a childlike idiot-savant who exhibited "anti-social behavior."[3] The researchers quoted prominent jazz critics, such as Barry Ulanov, in support of the thesis that the musicians' supposed lack of training in moral philosophy and the liberal arts contributed to their "immaturity and disorganization."[4] Moreover, displaying extreme naïveté concerning black musicians' access to white media, the two scholars maintain that the jazz musician was "relatively illiterate in respect to the verbal expression of his own art . . . the musician has remained silent and allowed others to do the talking for him,"[5] thereby colluding in his own isolation from the world.

The nine purposes of the AACM, as outlined in the charter and printed in subsequent brochures and publications produced by the organization, may be easily read as an attempt to counter these and other widespread stereotypes about black musicians that had infected not only the academic world, but the dominant culture generally:

- To cultivate young musicians and to create music of a high artistic level for the general public through the presentation of programs designed to magnify the importance of creative music.
- To create an atmosphere conducive to artistic endeavors for the artistically inclined by maintaining a workshop for the express purpose of bringing talented musicians together.
- To conduct a free training program for young aspirant musicians.
- To contribute financially to the programs of the Abraham Lincoln Center, 700 E. Oakwood Blvd., Chicago, Ill., and other charitable organizations.
- To provide a source of employment for worthy creative musicians.
- To set an example of high moral standards for musicians and to uplift the public image of creative musicians.
- To increase mutual respect between creative artists and musical tradesmen (booking agents, managers, promoters and instrument manufacturers, etc.).
- To uphold the tradition of cultured musicians handed down from the past.
- To stimulate spiritual growth in creative artists through recitals, concerts, etc., through participation in programs.[6]

New AACM members were provided with an "Informational Memorandum of Requirements and Expectations" that listed the organization's
rules and regulations. According to this memo, the membership fee for the
AACM was three dollars, with weekly dues of one dollar. The document
outlined procedures governing the weekly meetings, the organization's
governance structure and procedures, the rights of members to challenge
existing regulations and create new ones, concert production, salaries and
deportment, and order and discipline:

> When an AACM member wishes to submit the name of a potential new
> member, the following information must be submitted to the General
> Body: name, address, phone number & instrument.
>
> Any member wishing to leave a meeting must request permission from the
> Chair.
>
> Any law passed by the Board of Directors may be challenged by any member
> in a General Meeting by a motion to amend.
>
> The device of individual balloting will be utilized for the election of officers.
>
> Any member who abstains from voting must explain the abstention.
>
> The majority personnel of any performing group on an AACM concert must
> be AACM members in good standing.
>
> AACM members must be at the site of the concert one hour ahead of time.
> All concerts will start at the stated time. In the event the leader of a per-
> forming group finds it necessary to start late, a 15 minutes grace period
> will be given.
>
> Union scale salary will be paid all performing members depending upon
> the locality in which concerts are held. All vocalists must be covered by
> A.G.V.A. and will be paid as performing musicians during concerts.
>
> Any member who has knowledge of any person or persons or acts that tend
> to undermine the AACM is obligated to report same to the Chairman
> without delay. [7]

By early August, the organization was preparing for its first concerts,
which were held on the South Side at the now-defunct South Shore Ballroom on 79th Street near Stony Island Avenue. To advertise the events,
Richard Abrams and Ken Chaney authored a press release that was printed
more or less verbatim (though without byline) in the Chicago *Defender.*
This "open letter to the public" gave the organization's purpose as providing "a concert showcase for original contemporary music." The next
paragraph proclaimed that "our ultimate goal is to provide an atmosphere

that is conducive to serious music and performing new unrecorded compositions. We hope to create a spontaneous atmosphere that is unique to our heritage and to the performing artist. Our aim is universal in its appeal and is necessary for the advancement, development and understanding of new music."[8]

The language of the announcement, which uses terms that recall high-culture, pan-European "classical music" culture—"contemporary music," "serious music"—already distances the organization from jazz-oriented signifiers. At the same time, despite the fact that the organization later became known for the slogan "Great Black Music," neither this press release nor the nine purposes make any reference to race, or to the cultural nationalism that was burgeoning among African Americans. This points to the possibility that the ultimate goal of the group was indeed, as Abrams said at the conclusion of the May 29 general meeting, "helping ourselves up to the point where we can participate in the universal aspect of things, which includes all people."

The first AACM event featured the Joseph Jarman Quintet with bassist Charles Clark, drummer Arthur Reed, and the two original members of the AACM living in Evanston, saxophonist Fred Anderson and trumpeter Bill Brimfield. The concert took place on August 16, 1965,[9] and the AACM produced a printed program whose cover page featured an early version of the "treble clef" AACM logo, designed by Jerol Donavon. The second page lists the AACM purposes, and the third page lists the compositions and the musicians' names. The concert featured pieces by Jarman, Brimfield, and Anderson, including the latter's "Saxoon," "Dark Day" and "Something Like Sonny."[10] The second event on August 23 featured Philip Cohran's Artistic Heritage Ensemble, including Gene Easton and pianist and singer Claudine Myers.[11]

The concerts took place at 8, the standard time for concert music events. Production values for the early events were guided by the goal of creating "an atmosphere conducive to serious music," including concert-style seating, the printing and distribution of advertising, attempts to obtain appearances on radio, securing venues for advance ticket sales, and overall stage and venue management. The musicians themselves handled most of these activities; Flo Dinwiddie remembers that her friend Peggy Abrams, an AACM member as well, "did the secretary and paperwork stuff." Leonard Jones, who joined the AACM shortly after its formation, recalled the experience of AACM-style self-promotion and organization:

They'd organize the series, who was going to be playing. The concerts would be printed on these little postcard-sized flyers. You'd come to the meeting and everybody would take a stack. Then you'd just hit the streets. Some cats might be seen at 63rd and Cottage, waiting for people to get off from work at El stops and bus stops. You just gave them to people on the street, in the schools, wherever people were at, in the black community.

Eric Porter writes that during the bebop period, "musicians' ability to make their ideas known was restricted by the extent to which they agreed with or could successfully influence writers."[12] Fortuitously, these first AACM concerts attracted immediate notice in *Down Beat* magazine. A biweekly at the time, the magazine's "Strictly Ad Lib" section presented (without bylines) short notices and announcements for concerts in urban areas around the United States. Shortly after the August 16 concert, the Ad Lib section presented a notice about that concert and the formation of the AACM, as well as an announcement for the upcoming August 23 event. This short notice, stating that the organization's goal was "to provide a concert showcase for original music," was perhaps the first AACM notice to appear in a national publication.[13] An October *Down Beat* blurb reported that the new AACM series, held on Monday nights at the St. John Grand Lodge on 74th and Ingleside on the South Side ("a nice little place, about 200 or 300 seats, a regular type of stage," was how Troy Robinson remembered it), was "attracting a good deal of attention from musicians and listeners interested in the avant-garde," with concerts by Roscoe Mitchell with Fred Berry, Alvin Fielder and Malachi Favors; and the Joseph Jarman group with Lester Lashley on trombone.[14]

Just this small amount of publicity, appearing regularly throughout the AACM's first year of existence, undoubtedly played an important role in bringing early notice of the fledgling organization and the Chicago new music scene to a large readership located both in the United States and abroad. The timely placement of these notices came from the efforts of a small coterie of new music adherents who had gained a foothold in the magazine's editorial section, including Larry Kart, Terry Martin, J. B. Figi, John Litweiler, and Pete Welding. Their conviction (along with that of the producer Charles "Chuck" Nessa) that the work of the AACM constituted the most groundbreaking music of the period led them to proselytize for what they called "the Chicago avant-garde" at seemingly every opportunity. It is these first supporters of the AACM to whom more recent researchers, as well as the AACM musicians themselves, owe a debt of gratitude, not only for their excellent descriptions of the music itself, but also for their tenacity in championing this strange new music.[15]

The AACM held more or less weekly general body meetings at Abraham Lincoln Center throughout the summer of its first year. Meetings were usually followed by Experimental Band rehearsals. The minutes to the meeting of October 2, 1965, as read aloud by Sandra Lashley, revealed that barely two months after the organization had received its state charter, a shakeup in governance was in progress. This early turbulence in leadership and governance reflects the difficulty itinerant artists necessarily have in maintaining stable organizational leadership. The irregular nature of freelance professional life militated against regular performance of AACM duties, for which the members were not paid, of course. In the complete absence of government or private subsidy, virtually the only sources of funds were concert ticket sales (for which each member had a quota) and the membership dues of a dollar per week, which as we have already seen, were irregularly paid. At one point in the meeting, Cohran noted that regarding dues, "a good percentage of the membership is going to be in arrears."[16] A number of the musicians also had demanding day jobs, such as driving buses or teaching school; few, if any, were employed in academic institutions devoted to music. An extended period on tour could make it impossible for a member to perform such necessary organizational functions as weekly meeting attendance, record-keeping, business and legal meetings, or other regular duties. As a result, making sure that such work assignments as ticket sales and advertising would be carried out was a continual struggle.

Even more pressing issues loomed on the horizon. Although saxophonist Jimmy Ellis, an early AACM member, told an interviewer in 1998 that "there was no dissension among us,"[17] the October 2 meeting revealed serious differences in outlook regarding the organization's musical purposes and aesthetic direction. A number of members had serious doubts as to the commercial viability of the new music being presented under the AACM's aegis. "Once I heard what the cats were doing, I said, we can't present this nowhere," recalled Cohran.

> It was hard enough on a Chicago audience. The first concert where Joseph [Jarman] and them played was beautiful, but it must have been their audience, you know, who could handle it. After I performed my concert, fans who had come to hear me came back to hear the next group perform. When my fans attended the concert, they said, man, this ain't what

I thought it was going to be. They couldn't deal with the dissonances. In Chicago you could get away with that, but you couldn't go to Evanston with that, man. You couldn't go to Gary with that. People wanted to see some boogaloo or something.

The October 2 meeting's confrontation with issues of aesthetics and tradition exposed differences concerning the direction of the AACM that separated even the founding members from each other, and which went right to the heart of what the AACM would eventually become. Noting that the purpose of the AACM was understood to involve the presentation of original music, Ellis nonetheless felt that "maybe I hear the sound of another drummer. Maybe I might want to play 'The Harlem Blues' by W. C. Handy. If I couldn't perform what I feel, to me this is a limitation, and I couldn't see myself being involved."[18] Abrams responded that "We didn't figure it as a limitation because we didn't restrict members from doing what they wanted to do outside of the organization. So there's no limitation on it, unless you consider the main motive or purpose of the organization as limited."

Philip Cohran noted that "We had this hassle when I explained about playing the spirituals. There are a lot of different types of music all around the world, but the music of our essence, or of our roots, could be set aside as something special, and could be performed. I feel that very strongly."

"If we accept any compositions other than original compositions, then we may as well accept all compositions, period," said Steve McCall, "If I decide to play a classical piece on a musical program, and I would try to explain the integral part that it plays, say, in the development of New Orleans music, it wouldn't be out of place, to show the heritage of the music as it is now.

"But . . ." McCall paused for emphasis. "The thing that this organization was gotten together to do was to promote and to advance and to afford an opportunity for the musician to put forth his own personal compositions— compositions that probably would never be heard otherwise. If we were going to cover the whole entire spectrum, we would have to revamp and redo the entire organization. It would have to be an entirely different type of operation altogether."

"My own personal belief," McCall concluded, "is that we don't even need an organization to do that."

Jerol Donavon raised the ante and the temperature of the debate by throwing down a gauntlet. "The basic reason for this Association to get together, to start in the first place, was to play original music," Donavon declared. "Everyone who came into the Association was told this in the beginning. I think that those people who do not want to go along with the Association, we're not asking you to stay." Donavon's blunt challenge prompted considerable tumult, after which Roscoe Mitchell seconded Donavon's remarks. "Our purposes are made clear," Mitchell said. "The people are not expecting to hear anything familiar when they come—at least they shouldn't be."

As with so many AACM meetings, this watershed meeting was moving beyond the logistical toward the frankly philosophical. Philip Cohran mused that "To me the most important thing about a composer is his purpose . . . My purpose is to awaken in my people their heritage—their music—which they are running from." Richard Abrams presented his own version of the "awakening" motif. "This organization is set out to awaken the psyche, through originality, not only feelings," Abrams spoke passionately. "We are dealing with something that is intuitive *and* scientific. This takes it out of the realm of pure emotion or pure science. It's a combination of both."

"Now there's only one thing to do," Abrams declared, throwing down the gauntlet once more. "Our purpose is to play original music. If it's not going to be original music, then I as president and as a member will have to step out." Abrams paused, then pulled back. "Are there any other comments?" The membership's momentary hush seemed to last for a very long time. Jimmy Ellis broke the silence. "What we are doing today is not so great," he observed gravely. "There are musicians who came before us who had minds that are just as fresh today as your mind. And this music is something that has been going since the beginning. It is almost impossible for a young jazz musician . . ."

"We're not really jazz musicians," Abrams interrupted.

Ellis went on, incorporating the correction. "It is almost impossible for a young musician to play this music if you have no knowledge of the history. The music that we have created is a music that people all over the world are trying to imitate. There are people who are in the history of this music, who had composed compositions that it is necessary for a musician to know, because a tree without roots has no foundation."

"It's a sad thing for me that we are talking about this today," Ellis continued. "I don't think that there is anyone who is more interested in original music than me. But when I sit down and listen to Billie Holiday, and listen to some of the old records, maybe by someone you never heard of, this is a music that we should learn something about. The Japanese take more interest, and we should be ashamed that this is so. We talk about playing original music—beautiful. But can't you see how important it is to know what has preceded you?"

"We are getting ready to start classes," Jerol Donavon countered, "and I'm sure that we have someone, such as Mr. Cohran, who is well versed in the history of the Negro musician. If anyone wants to learn these things, come to class and learn.

"We are not playing to musicians alone," Donavon said. "We are playing to the public, you dig, and it's time for some new music. You say that the Japanese know more about our music than we do? That's cool—but *we made it.* Everyone else is trying to learn about our music so they can play it.

"If I wanted to play standard tunes, I don't have to come to this Association," Donavon continued. "I come to this Association so I can play music that we compose ourselves, that I compose, that any member of this Association composes."

"We are in the midst of a revolution—when I say 'we,' I mean black people," Malachi Favors said. "When I came into the organization, I didn't know that it was this way, but now that I've found out, I've accepted it. I'm going down with the ship, or however you want to take it," Favors joked, providing needed comic relief to a very tense moment as laughter went around the room.

"I would like to read Purpose Number Nine," Abrams ventured, reading from the AACM purposes, "which stipulates 'spiritual growth in creative artists through participation in programs, concerts and recitals.'" Abrams continued to read. "Number Three: To conduct a free training program for young aspiring musicians . . . To cultivate young musicians and to create music of a high artistic level for the general public through presentation of programs designed to magnify the importance of creative music.'"

"Now how can we do that in any other way," Abrams demanded, "but presenting creative, original music?"

"What is 'original music'?" asked Alden Lee. "Everything that you do has been influenced by something else. You're going to present original music, be it good or bad? You don't care about that part. You just want to present original music. The audience you play for, they have to accept this music.

"They might come once," continued Lee, "but when they find things not to their liking, what's going to happen to the organization?"

"We have an audience—as big an audience as the universe," Abrams exclaimed. "All of this music has a lot to do with disrupting any status quo or system, but I'm not saying that this is our purpose. As I said before, our purpose is to awaken the psyche."

"Are you interested in awakening the psyche of the performing musician," the poet David Moore asked, "or are you interested in awakening the psyche of the audience?"

"The musicians," responded Abrams without hesitation. Moore was incredulous. "You're not interested in awakening the psyche of the audience?"

"Ever since we started playing music, each and every one of us in this room, the music that we've been playing has been strictly for the audience," said Jerol Donavon. "We have never been able to play music that we wanted to play ourselves. That was another reason for forming this Association, so that we could play what *we* wanted to play for a change, instead of playing 'Night Train,' and 'Shotgun' and all that stuff that people constantly press you to play when you're on your job."

"All the compositions that are being written in the Association," Donavon reminded the meeting, "came from our musical heritage. All this music that has been played in the past leads us up to this point where we can create new sounds and new compositions. Our musical heritage is with us all the time, so I don't see why we have to be worrying about that.

"So, Mr. Chairman," Donavon suggested, "I make a motion that the meeting be adjourned." Numerous seconds to the motion arrived with alacrity.

Inevitably, with such strong personalities around the meeting table, disagreements over aesthetics were taken personally. Philip Cohran began to feel that "Lester Lashley and Muhal, they were vociferous against any idea I put on the table. They would all jump on my ideas as wrong."[19] Within six months of the October 1965 meeting, a number of members departed, including some who had been present at the organization's inception. As the AACM became better known, these private disagreements became public. Cohran told writer Bill Quinn in 1968 that "Under the structure of the AACM, the achievement of my longtime purposes was too limited for me to remain a member."[20] In an interview published in 2001, Cohran framed his differences with the AACM in terms of the role of tradition in the organization:

> My studies put me in the vein of studying the ancient music, and I became one who submits to his ancestors. In that way, I embrace their concepts of sound and thought, and I hope that someday I will be eligible to receive some of the knowledge they had and was lost. But most of the

guys that came into the AACM wanted to take the music that Sun Ra was playing when they would play "out." They want to play "out" all the time because it didn't require any discipline. That was my opinion. Later on, they developed tremendous discipline, but at that time it was just playing notes, That didn't do it for me.[21]

Cohran's final AACM concert took place at the St. John Grand Lodge on December 27, 1965. The event featured compositions by Gene Easton as well as Cohran's compositions.[22] As Cohran put it in our interview, "I said, I may as well just get out of here and go ahead and do what I'm doing. I don't need nobody to tell me what I already know. I started producing my own thing, and a whole lot of guys left, mostly the traditional musicians, who were already accomplished. Ken Chaney, I think he left before I did, and Jimmy Ellis left."

Jimmy Ellis left the AACM in 1966. In 1968, the saxophonist told Quinn about the misgivings he had expressed in AACM meetings regarding the exclusive emphasis on new music: "What the musicians have forgotten is the tradition of this music: W. C. Handy, for instance. If a musician can only play bop, he isn't making it, is he? Without a knowledge of the past, there is no future. How can I know where I'm going if I don't know where I've been? Billie Holiday, Sidney Bechet, we can't forget them."[23] In 1998, Ellis told the African American scholar Arthur Cromwell, "I didn't stay in the AACM because to me it was created for the advancement of nothing but new music. To me, it's the whole circle. You've got to advance, but I didn't want to be locked into one phase of nothing. It wasn't a falling out with me."[24]

New Arrivals and the University of Chicago

Regarding the AACM's focus on new music, Jodie Christian explained to writer Quinn that "the music played by the association is the choice of the members. We chose to play original music. Original means rock or bop or anything, as long as it is the musician's own composition. The fact that much of the music is new is merely the result of the number of young players in the association."[25] One of these young players, Claudine Myers, was born in 1942 in Blackwell, Arkansas, a small rural village about fifty miles northwest of Little Rock. Myers was brought up largely by her great-aunt, a schoolteacher, and her great-uncle, a carpenter by trade who played the clarinet, piano, and flute, and had attended Tuskegee Institute in the first decade of the twentieth century.

Myers fondly remembers the environment of her childhood, even given the segregation that was constitutive of everyday life. "In Arkansas we never felt inferior to white people," she remembered. "We wanted equality, but we were happy in our world, except that you knew that you automatically accepted the white fountain and the black fountain."[26] The house in which Myers spent her earliest years had a well and an outdoor toilet, as well as a garden where fruits were grown for canning. The family kept chickens and pigs in the yard. "As kids we weren't allowed to see the hog killing," said Myers, "but we used to run around with the hog bladder and blow it up like a balloon. You never heard of that?"

Myers's great-aunt taught first through fifth grade in the two-room school Myers attended; the other teacher taught sixth through eighth grade. Unlike the public schools in Chicago that Abrams, Donavon, Favors, and Christian attended, this small schoolhouse taught black history and culture and had hot lunches for the pupils. Of course, the welfare of female students was very strictly monitored. "If you had to go to the bathroom, they would always send somebody with you. As a girl, you didn't go by yourself." Myers was raised in the local Methodist church, where, as with the area's Baptist church, the music was at a very high and intense level. "The whole congregation was all in rhythm," Myers said. "You'd be laying on your grandmother's lap and your head would be going." Gospel quartet singing was the rage, and Myers's great-aunt took her to hear the choirs. "People would come from everywhere to hear these quartets," Myers recalled. "The white people would come to our churches for quartet singing."

Favorites on the record player included Sister Rosetta Tharpe and the Highway QCs, as well as Myers's particular love, the Davis Sisters from Chicago. Along with Sunday radio services direct from Little Rock, another Myers favorite was country and western great Hank Williams. "He had this song where the little boy helped his mother make up the bed, and she gave him some money to buy him a chocolate ice cream cone. And on his way back home [pause for effect] *he dropped his chocolate ice cream cone.* I think that's why I like chocolate now. Country and western music was so visual."

Myers started taking piano lessons around the age of four, and when she was seven, her family moved to Roosevelt, a black community outside Dallas. Myers took piano and violin lessons, but eventually, partly for financial reasons, settled on the piano, taking weekly lessons of fifteen minutes each. The women of Myers's church organized the young girls into a singing group that imitated the styles (including the thigh-slapping rhythms) of groups such as the Swan Silvertones, the Five Blind Boys of Alabama, and the Mighty Clouds of Joy. By the sixth grade, Myers had become proficient enough to serve as the pianist for the vacation Bible school, and she was soon active as one of the main pianists and vocalists in her church. In high school, a new teacher started Myers on Chopin études and other European classical music, but just as Myers was starting to garner paying work as a pianist in local Sunday church services, she was dismayed when her family decided to return to tiny Blackwell. Nonetheless, Myers was soon leading both rhythm-and-blues and gospel groups.

At all-black Philander Smith College, a Methodist school in Little Rock with an enrollment of around seven hundred students at the time, Myers lived in the dormitory, where female students had to be chaperoned to attend Monday evening movies. She learned music for pipe organ, and was practicing the piano intensely. "I was studying Beethoven, because I had to give a concert when I graduated. I thought I was going to be a teacher and be a concert pianist on the side [chuckles]." As with most black students of the period, however, she became aware of the practical possibilities open to people of color in the world of pan-European concert music. "My aunt said, be a teacher. That was security, you know. So I majored in music education." Unusually for a postsecondary institution in the 1950s, Philander Smith taught both European music and jazz, including a healthy dose of Euro-American modernism. "The head of the music department taught us Carter, Copland, Virgil Thomson, and Stockhausen," Myers remembered, "but he had a little jazz band that played for the high-school proms. He found out I could play the piano, and he gave me a gig. I made $200. That's when I learned to play the blues on the piano."

In her second year, Myers moved to an apartment in Little Rock, where she was approached with an offer of club work by a young woman who was known locally as "the black Elizabeth Taylor." The Safari Room, located in Memphis, Tennessee, about an hour's drive from Little Rock, was located in a hotel where she met many of the black musicians of Memphis, including Ike Turner. "He was practicing every day down at the hotel, so I went down there," said Myers. "I really wanted to see Tina. They said she was upstairs asleep. We never would see her at rehearsal. I sat in and played, and Ike said, Oh, you play good." However, the Safari Room gig ended in failure. "I played about two nights and the man had to let me go because my repertoire was too small. I knew Bach's two-part inventions, 'Misty,' and 'Greensleeves,' I copied Ella Fitzgerald and Nina Simone, Dakota Staton."

Licking her wounds, Myers was mentored by Art Porter, Sr., a major musician in the area. Living in Little Rock, Porter taught high-school music, led his own choir, and played at the local white country clubs. He taught Myers the practicalities of jazz piano harmony, and she began to play solo piano and organ gigs. At times, the contrast between Saturday night and Sunday morning led to some embarrassing moments. "I would be playing nightclubs on weekends, and wake up and go to church and play the organ," Myers laughed. "I'd fall asleep during the minister's sermon."

After graduating from college, Myers moved to Chicago in 1963, and eventually landed a part-time substitute teacher position at a public elementary school on the South Side. At a local club she met a young man who was an aspiring conga drummer and photographer. With a teaching job offering some measure of security, Myers hadn't thought much about trying to play professionally in Chicago, but at one of the many places where the drummer-photographer tried to sit in, the bandleader somehow discovered that Myers played the organ. She sat in, and the bandleader fired his organ player and hired her. Soon after, Myers caught the attention of bandleader Cozy Eggleston. On one gig with Eggleston in 1964, Myers met Jerol Donavon, who formed an organ trio with Myers and the formidable saxophonist Don "Skip" James, brother of classical and jazz bassist and orchestral composer Stafford James.

In the declining days of the South Side club scene, Donavon was running his own jam sessions at McKie's on 63rd Street, starting at ten o'clock at night and going until four in the morning. After the gig, Myers would head for home, and then to her teaching job. Around 1964, Jerol Donavon introduced Myers to Richard Abrams. She became a close friend of the Abrams family, and Donavon brought Myers into the AACM, where she performed with Philip Cohran on the second AACM concert. Eventually, Myers and Donavon became close, but learned to compartmentalize the various facets of their relationship. "We were going together, and I'd be mad about some stuff," Myers recalled. "I learned that it's about music, and to keep your personal business off the stage."

In late 1965, through the efforts of students and faculty at the University of Chicago, a "Contemporary Music Society" began organizing concerts with AACM musicians in university concert halls and other campus spaces, including the Reynolds Club, the university's student union, which offered space for student events free of charge.[27] Joseph Jarman was helping the society to organize the concerts, as well as Friday-night jam sessions with people like Andrew Hill, Jack DeJohnette, Richard Abrams, and Rafael Garrett.[28] By this time, as Leonard Jones said in an interview, "a lot of black people lived in Hyde Park." "That was who we were trying to attract." In addition, the university connection led to larger audiences that were more diverse in terms of race, class, age, and other demographic factors.

At the Harper Theater in Hyde Park on November 26 and 27, 1965, the society organized a midnight concert collaboration between Joseph Jarman, several of the university students, and composer-performer John Cage. The concert was controversial, to say the least, judging from *Down Beat* reviewer Pete Welding's review of the event—the first major review of an AACM musician to appear in a national publication. "Cage did a concert at Mandel Hall," Jarman recalled, "and [the students] asked if he would be interested to collaborate with me, to do a concert at Harper Theater. I had read 'Silence' and I had collected his music. I liked it. So I felt really honored to do that." As the concert program announced, "To our knowledge, this is the first time that Mr. Cage has performed a work with a group of jazz musicians." The program affirmed Jarman's "great artistic and conceptual indebtedness" to Cage, and recounted a meeting between Jarman and Cage at a festival of contemporary music at which Jarman asked the composer if he would perform with the Jarman group.[29]

At the concert, the Jarman Quintet performed first, with Fred Anderson, Bill Brimfield, Charles Clark, and Arthur Reed, followed by the Cage-Jarman collaboration, titled "Imperfections in a Given Space," which featured Cage himself performing electronic sounds, Ellis Bishop on trumpet, Bob Hodge on bass, and a young University of Chicago graduate student, Doug Mitchell, on percussion. According to the *Down Beat* reviewer, "Cage sent a variety of electronic stimuli through a complex of electronic amplification equipment (the sound of an eraser on paper, or of water being swallowed, when amplified a thousand times, makes for an eerie listening experience indeed!), to which the Jarman group was to respond musically."[30]

In our interview, Jarman's account of Cage's demeanor was congruent with other contemporaneous descriptions of the composer's gentle way of interacting. "He just said [imitates], 'I'm setting up this . . . [pause] . . . Do as you feel.' [Laughs.] And he just started playing. And because of my experience with the AACM concerts, I just started playing, and moved all over and blended horns." Cage's own account of the encounter, published years later in an interview with frequent interlocutor Richard Kostelanetz, was considerably different from Jarman's. There, Cage framed himself as something of a teacher for a group of unnamed "black musicians." Moreover, despite his professed lack of interest in improvisation (reiterated later in the interview), Cage somehow managed to find ways to critique the musicians' performance practice—at their request. "And I said to them that one of the troubles was that when they got loud, they all got loud. And they said, 'How could we change that?' They were willing to change."[31]

While one could well imagine that the AACM musicians were open to learning from Cage, the notion that these musicians would have learned about space and silence from him is at variance with the recorded evidence of AACM improvisations from the period.[32] Moreover, as Cage scholar Rebecca Y. Kim has noted in an unpublished paper, the program notes for the Cage-Jarman event employed "a language of historical synchronicity, identifying two parallel movements in new music"—hardly an attitude that one might attribute to a mentor-student relationship.[33] In any event, the *Down Beat* review, which had no particular criticism of Cage's work per se, criticized Jarman and his musicians for their supposed failure to respond to Cage's sounds. The reviewer found that the group created "little in the way of actual interaction with what Cage was generating; it was as though the group were merely sending into the air its own unrelated signals at the same time as the electronic ones were being generated, with little or no regard to ordering or organizing the combined sounds into something meaningful."[34] Most of the rest of the review was given over to musings on how collective improvisation, while requiring true group empathy, was unfortunately attracting "more than its share of outright charlatans."[35] These evaluations aside, assuming that the reviewer's descriptions reflected something of the reality of the event, the approach of the Jarman group as it is described here seemed to represent well the Cageian practice and aesthetic of indeterminacy.

For Jarman, "it was really beautiful, and I wish we had recorded it. It was awesome." The reviewer's take was considerably less sanguine. Punning on the collective work's title, he found that the concert's "manifest imperfections and inconclusive nature led to boredom and sterility," producing "aridity and lifelessness."[36] Jarman recalls that at least one other very experienced listener shared the reviewer's opinion to some extent. "*Down Beat* didn't like it, and my mother didn't like it either. She said [imitates]: 'Joseph, if you *ever* play with that man again, don't tell me, please. I love you, I love your concerts, I come to all of them, but if you're going to play with him, don't tell me,' 'Yes, ma'am.'

Leonard Jones came to the performance with something of the Zen beginner's mind:

At the time I had no idea of the musical importance of John Cage. His name kept cropping up at that time in this area of avant-garde or experimental music. But Joseph has always been exotic, and Cage was exotic just like the Japanese dancer that Joseph would have performances with in the '60s. I remember that Cage sat on the stage next to a table, and he had a microphone attached to his throat. He sat there and he gargled water, and Joseph played the saxophone. That's the one and only time that I've seen John Cage live. I remember Charles [Clark] being there, but other than that I don't remember anybody else. At the time, it seemed to me that a lot of it was conceptual, and I was pretty new to music; I didn't start playing the bass until I was twenty years old.

"Nobody liked it, and that made it even better," Jarman recalled. "Right after that, they actually invited me to go up to Ann Arbor to the ONCE Festival. That was a beautiful experience.[37]

In May 1966, a second major *Down Beat* review of an AACM composer appeared. Roscoe Mitchell's concert at the University of Chicago's major concert venue, Mandel Hall, presented two works that later became Art Ensemble of Chicago classics, *People in Sorrow* and *Old*.[38] Besides Mitchell, the musicians included Richard Abrams, Gene Dinwiddie, Lester Lashley, Charles Clark, and Alvin Fielder. The same reviewer who found the Jarman-Cage collaboration difficult called Mitchell's group "the most completely successful, and among the most promising, of Chicago groups working the avant-garde vineyards."[39] For this reviewer, Mitchell's work featured a "gentle, sardonic slyness" and a "burlesquing of jazz tradition." One Mitchell piece presented a "parody of the military mind," perhaps a timely intervention at a time that the Vietnam War was raging.[40]

Philip Cohran's recollection that AACM concerts in the black community "died" seems at variance with the apparent continuation of the weekly concerts at St. John's Grand Lodge, each billed as "a cultural event for all ages." Well into 1966, presentations of new music by Roscoe Mitchell, Claudine Myers, Troy Robinson, Jodie Christian, Joseph Jarman, and Charles Clark, among others, were featured.[41] Other AACM events, as well as non-AACM events featuring AACM members, took place in galleries, churches, and, indeed, in lounges and taverns, whose atmosphere the music tended to transform toward a concert orientation. Jerol Donavon and Claudine Myers, in particular, took the new music into Chicago clubs, such as the Hungry I in Old Town, and the Robins' Nest on 71st and Stony Island.[42]

In July 1966, perhaps the first multicolumn article on the AACM in an arguably major music publication appeared (without byline) in *Down Beat's* "News" section, in the magazine's first few pages. Jodie Christian, Philip Cohran, Richard Abrams, and Steve McCall were named in the article as "the driving forces behind the group at its inception." According to the article, "Abrams, a nonsmoker and nondrinker, was anxious about the stigmas many laymen attach to the private lives of jazz performers." Thus, one goal of the AACM was to "set an example of high moral standards for musicians and to return the public image of creative musicians to the level of esteem which was handed down from past cultures." The article mentioned Cohran's Artistic Heritage Ensemble, the groups of Jarman and Mitchell, and the Experimental Band, as well as people like Maurice McIntyre, Lester Lashley, Sandra Lashley, Charles Clark, Leonard Jones, Thurman Barker, and a new face, trumpeter John Shenoy Jackson, who was now serving as an AACM spokesperson.[43]

The oldest of the early AACM members, Jackson (known universally by his last name) was born in 1923 and raised in Hot Springs, Arkansas. According to Will Menter, who interviewed Jackson as part of his late 1970s doctoral fieldwork on the AACM, Jackson's father was a restaurant owner and "no-nonsense type cat" who liked music, but discouraged his children from becoming musicians. In Menter's view, the fact that Jackson's father was a committed follower of Marcus Garvey deeply affected the young Jackson in terms of "feelings of obligation towards his own two children and the future of the Race."[44] "I suppose I knew about the South African situation when I was about 4 or 5 years old," said Jackson. "My father didn't wear diamonds because he knew if he wore a diamond some Black family was suffering in Cape Town."[45] Jackson came to Chicago in the 1950s to study at Roosevelt University, following a stint in the U.S. armed forces during World War II. According to Menter, Jackson's World War II career was a model of creative finagling. Seeing no reason to get killed, "he manoeuvred himself into a position where he had control of his own records, so that whenever any training came up he simply entered on his card that he had had it already. He only fired a gun once during his 5 years in the army."[46] Later, Jackson's administrative virtuosity allowed him to work his way up to a position of considerable supervisory influence in Chicago's massive welfare bureaucracy.

Just as the AACM was being formed, a friend from college referred Jackson to Richard Abrams. Jackson purchased musical instruments for his sons, hoping that they could get started via the AACM. Discovering that the new organization was meant for experienced musicians, "out of the instruments that I had purchased for my sons I just picked up the trumpet and tried to get a sound out of it and started playing and was doing quite well." Jackson soon realized that "when I bought an instrument for my kids it was a sort of unconscious transference I was making, wanting them to play when I really wanted to play." At the time, Jackson was forty years old, but reflecting the atmosphere of extreme optimism and confidence that the AACM tended to encourage, Jackson declared to Menter, "I firmly believe if I'd started when I was a child I'd be one of the giants in the field."[47] Despite the seriousness with which he was pursuing his music, however, Jackson had no interest in becoming a full-time musician. Rather, as he observed, "The way I became involved was that I had certain administrative talents of being able to channel certain efforts in certain directions. A way of getting along with people to get them to do what had to be done. I think maybe that is why they took me into the organization."[48]

Jackson quickly became the public face and critically important administrative wizard of the AACM. His inimitable style, with its understated modesty and wry, pointed humor, could be found on grant applications, answers to fan and business inquiries, and even published articles. Moreover, Jackson's connections with the public aid bureaucracy helped some of the struggling AACM artists to survive. As Joseph Jarman recalls, "He actually cared for me and many others through the City of Chicago finance department, though many would not admit it. We were all poor and he put us on the assistance rolls so we would be able to make it. It was because of him that I was able to pay my rent. I know he helped many others, and those who feel free can mention it."

In June 1966 the now defunct music magazine *Sounds and Fury* published John Litweiler's three-column piece on the AACM, describing a number of AACM concerts that had recently taken place at St. John's Grand Lodge and the University of Chicago's Mandel Hall. For one concert, Troy Robinson had transformed his daytime occupation into art, with "a clever, hectic number inspired by the Cottage Grove bus." Litweiler suggested that the work of the AACM musicians evinced "a common turn toward formal thinking" and "a strong sense of design," and that the organization's "relative success suggests the direction jazz is likely to take in future years." At the same time, noting the demise of clubs around the United States, the reviewer poses a stark question: 'Will the new jazz be strictly a concert music?' "[49]

The concerts at St. John's Grand Lodge continued sporadically throughout 1966, but by early July of that year, the Abraham Lincoln Center became the main site for the regular AACM concert series, as well as the Saturday morning general body meeting. AACM concert flyers billed each concert as "a cultural event of contemporary music," and concerts by Roscoe Mitchell, Charles Clark, Richard Abrams, and Joseph Jarman, among others, were presented.[50] In the meantime, AACM musicians were taking part in local jam sessions—with mixed results, as Thurman Barker recalled:

> After Experimental Band rehearsals on Mondays, we would all get together and say, hey, let's go to a jam session. There were some on the North Side, on Wells Street, and some on the South Side. We were not well liked outside of our Oakwood Lincoln Center community, and there was always this talk about, well, you know they're not going to let us play, so we need to go up as a group. And that's what we literally did. We would go and crash these sessions. The musicians and the people who ran the establishment were never very happy when we got there. There was always a problem getting in, and it was always sort of a scene, but we always managed to get in and play, as a group. This could be six or seven people, and nobody would play with us. The musicians that were already there wouldn't play, but whenever we played we got tremendous applause. It was great.

At least one of entrepreneur Joe Segal's jam sessions, held in early July at the well-known North Side club Mother Blues, featured a potpourri of AACM members, including two new figures, trumpeter Lester Bowie from St. Louis, and violinist Leroy Jenkins, who had returned to his hometown after nearly fifteen years in the South.[51] Back in 1950, Jenkins had obtained a scholarship to Florida A&M University in the city of Tallahassee, playing in both the concert band (on saxophone and clarinet) and the high-stepping football band. He quickly found himself immersed in the social and musical life of the area, however: "Actually I wasn't doing anything but drinking and carousing, studying the violin and playing in blues bands." Moreover, Tallahassee was hardly a hotbed of musical experimentation. Jenkins found Miami a bit more hospitable, playing sessions on saxophone in Frenchtown and visiting area clubs and juke joints.

After receiving his advanced degree in 1961, Jenkins spent four years as a roving violin and viola instructor in Mobile, Alabama. He returned to Chicago around the summer of 1965, taking a job in the public schools. He had given up his other instruments to concentrate on the violin, and was developing a more or less conventional jazz violin repertoire when a set of chance occurrences sent him in a different direction. "My former violin instructor, Bruce Hayden, had come to Chicago," recalled Jenkins in our interview. "He stayed at my house until he got his stuff together. He started seeking out work, and he got a gig playing with Muhal, somewhere. He came back and told me about it. He told me about a concert that night, and told me I should come, an organization called the AACM or something. So we went, Bruce and I."

The concert, one of the earliest regular AACM events, presented Roscoe Mitchell's music at St. John's Grand Lodge, and featured Maurice McIntyre, Charles Clark, Malachi Favors, Alvin Fielder, and Thurman Barker. "Roscoe was way ahead, you know," said Jenkins. "It wasn't anything about changes or bar lines, or even musical notes. After intermission, Bruce and I went out, because we felt so ignorant. For the first time, he asked *me* [whispering], man, what are they doing? Bruce was highly steeped in bebop. He couldn't understand it, so he didn't want anything to do with it. I was fascinated by it." Jenkins, who knew Richard Abrams slightly, soon found himself taking part in an AACM rehearsal at Abraham Lincoln Center.

> There was Kalaparusha [Maurice McIntyre], [Christopher] Gaddy, Charles Clark, Thurman Barker, Roscoe, Lester Lashley. Muhal was conducting, bringing us in, bringing us out. I thought it was Muhal's band, but really it was just Muhal's night to experiment with his ideas. He was doing a form of conduction, actually.[52] At first I didn't dig it, but I kept coming down there. I was curious. I thought to myself, these motherfuckers are crazy, and they were dead serious.

Jenkins slowly found himself drawn into this new music: "The atmosphere was free enough for you to do your thing, and nobody was putting it down. I didn't have to copy off Roscoe or Joseph or Muhal or anybody. I could just do my thing. It was different from what I had associated with jazz before. So I joined up, and after a while I changed my whole style on the violin."

William Lester Bowie, Jr. was born in 1941 in Frederick, Maryland, where his father was also born. Bowie's background exemplifies the notion of the "musical family." Saxophonist Byron is three years Lester's junior, and trombonist Joseph is twelve years younger. His mother, a college graduate, was a federal employee, and Bowie Sr. was, according to his son, "a Captain Dyett type" who had earned a master's degree in music education with a specialization in trumpet, and brought up several generations of musicians over a thirty-year career as a high-school band director at St. Louis's Booker T. Washington Technical High School. "We were some of the most fortunate blacks," said Lester Bowie, "because we got to see real blacks who were great teachers. They could never hope to have careers in symphony orchestras, so they ended up being our high-school instructors."

Bowie studied trumpet with his father first, performing in school and in church. By the age of fifteen, attending Sumner High School, Bowie became a member of the musicians' union, doing gigs with Chuck Berry, and fronting his own band, the Continentals, with fellow St. Louisans John Hicks on piano, and Floyd LeFlore on trumpet. Other high-school classmates included drummer Phillip Wilson and saxophonist Oliver Lake. The St. Louis of Bowie's era, the late 1950s, was just as segregated as in Philip Cohran's period. As Bowie recalls, "I was about fifteen before I knew any white people."[53] Nonetheless, the Continentals were able to play in white areas by augmenting their rock-and-roll repertoire with the odd polka number.

Believing that "college was square," Bowie joined the army in 1959, right after graduating from high school, motivated by a desire "to go out there and be fucking and shit, smoking reefer and buying pussy, gambling, drinking—all that shit I'd been reading about."[54] Joining the army to see the world, Bowie was disappointed to spend his entire army career, "three years, my whole time, in Texas—Texas!" Told that there were "no openings" in the local army band in Amarillo, Bowie was given the choice of being in the bugle corps or the military police. "I said, I'll take the police. It sounds like fun," he laughed. "We could beat up on white boys, because we were the police. I did town patrol, but mostly it was patrolling the base itself. Me and another brother, we always had patrol together, and we had these hip trucks, Ford pickups."[55]

Robin D. G. Kelley's speculation that future AACM members could have been radicalized in part by the challenges of military service[56] was once again borne out in Bowie's case, but the "fun" of exercising coercive payback-power under color of law quickly paled next to Bowie's sense of the larger picture. "I was gung ho," said Bowie. "I believed in the shit. I was a good soldier until I realized what was happening, that weren't no blacks getting promoted, nothing happening. It was Southern racism. Here I was, I had a couple of years in, and I still hadn't gotten past that first stripe. That's when I turned crook."[57] In a tale reminiscent of the adventures of Yossarian, the central protagonist of Joseph Heller's wartime black humor novel, *Catch-22,* Bowie was said to be running whisky bootlegging and gambling concessions on the base, perhaps with the tacit connivance of local authorities.

One transgression, however, could not be overlooked. "One day we were watching TV in a day room in the barracks. I had to do something and I said I'd be right back. When I came back it was a white boy sitting in my seat. I said, you know, you're in my seat. In his Southern drawl, he was like [imitating], well, if you move, you lose."[58] As Bowie remembered, "I ain't never been afraid of white folks. A lot of people got that fear built in, but I don't."[59] "I whipped out my motherfucking heat and started popping caps right around his head. That motherfucker fell to his knees, 'Lester, Lester, please don't . . .' 'Motherfucker, if you ever . . . I'll blow your motherfucking head off. Who the fuck you think you talking to?'"[60]

Bowie soon found himself court-martialed, receiving six months in prison, including a period in solitary confinement. As with Malcolm X, the seemingly endless stretches of time in prison allowed Bowie to seriously consider his future, perhaps for the first time as an adult. "I decided to get serious and be a full time pro in music," Bowie said. "But I knew I didn't really play that well to be a pro."[61] Leaving the service with a general discharge, Bowie enrolled in music courses at the historically black Lincoln University. Finding one great teacher, Mr. Penn, Bowie nonetheless found himself largely at odds with what he saw as the provincial and contradictory (if far from atypical) attitudes of a black institution regarding black music.

> The head of the music department called me in one day about me playing with this Blues band. He says to me that as a student of Lincoln University's Music Department, he didn't feel that it was appropriate for me to be playing in a Blues band. I told him to kiss my motherfucking ass. I told him to get the fuck out my face cause I make my living playing this damn horn. And that I ain't no seventeen year old motherfucker just coming out of high school, don't tell me what the fuck I should be playing.[62]

Bowie's subsequent experience at North Texas State University, where he was part of the earliest crop of jazz students in the first degree-granting program in jazz in the United States, proved first enlightening, then daunting. Given the presence in the community of such amazing musicians as saxophonists Billy Harper, James Clay, and David "Fathead" Newman, Bowie found the atmosphere at the school itself incongruous, to say the least. "I'm trying to figure out, how can these motherfuckers be up here studying black art, and got the audacity to be racist? I went there one year, then dropped out."[63] When Bowie decided to abandon academia, his real education began, as he toured midwestern and Southern blues joints with the great St. Louis musicians, Albert King and Little Milton. Sometime in 1963 or 1964, working with another of St. Louis's leading musicians, Oliver Sain, Bowie met his future spouse, the singer Fontella Bass, who was also part of the band. Recording for Chess Records in Chicago, Bass created tunes such as "Don't Mess Up a Good Thing," and her classic hit, "Rescue Me."[64] Bowie and Bass were married just as her career was taking off. "Naturally, we followed the money, and moved to Chicago," Bowie noted.[65] He began doing jingles sessions at Chess, and soon became Bass's musical director, working with the groups of singers Jackie Wilson and Jerry Butler. "I had a '51 classic Bentley, a motorcycle, a hip apartment in Chicago," Bowie recalled. "I was plenty happy."[66]

At the same time, "I had gone through all the bands around Chicago and I was just bored."[67] One day, an associate, Delbert Hill, took Bowie to a rehearsal of the Experimental Band. "He said I wouldn't be bored," Bowie recalled to bluesman and author Lincoln T. Beauchamp, Jr. (also known as Chicago Beau). "Muhal Richard Abrams was having the rehearsal, man, I had never seen so many weird motherfuckers in my life . . . in one place. I said this is home here. As a musician there's always a couple of dudes you hang with. But here was thirty or forty crazy motherfuckers all in one spot. So I made that rehearsal and Muhal had me play a solo. Before I got home good the phone was ringing . . . Cats calling up asking me to be in their band."[68] Bowie later explained, "That was what I had been looking for, an opportunity to really deal into the music, and to make some sort of statement where cats were trying to do something for real. The statement was that we can do this ourselves. You can't hire us, we can hire ourselves, we can produce ourselves, we can create this music on a high level. Wasn't no bullshit. I was staunch AACM after that."[69]

In the spring of 1936, Maurice Benford McIntyre's mother made a visit to her hometown of Clarksville, Arkansas, where baby Maurice was born later that year. His mother soon returned to Chicago, where McIntyre grew up. McIntyre's parents were well-to-do by South Side standards; his father was a pharmacist, and his mother was a seamstress. At first, the family lived at 58th and Calumet on the South Side, across from the elevated train station, in the same building as future drummer Warren Smith and filmmaker-to-be Melvin Van Peebles. In 1951, with the fall of restrictive covenants, the McIntyres moved to 54th and Greenwood Avenue in Hyde

Park, in the shadow of the University of Chicago. McIntyre's mother played piano, and her young son took saxophone lessons for two years, starting at age nine. McIntyre's father took him to see Duke Ellington, but McIntyre was more interested in the emerging hard bop. "I remember when Warren and them put a Charlie Parker record on, I ran out of their house. It scared the shit out of me. I liked Monk. I was into the doo-wop groups, the Orioles, the Ravens. I was listening to Chet Baker and Gerry Mulligan a lot. Those were my first influences. Then I progressed from them to the black artists, the hard bop people—Jackie McLean, the Jazz Messengers, Clifford Brown, Sonny Rollins."[70]

McIntyre remembers that he was one of "only seven black people" who attended the virtually all black Hyde Park High School in 1950. He soon dropped music and instead lettered in football, dreaming of going professional, perhaps like South Sider Buddy Young, one of the first African Americans to do so. Becoming a father at seventeen, however, obliged McIntyre to combine high-school study with a full-time job at the Schwinn Bicycle Company. Eventually becoming bored with bikes, McIntyre decided to try music once again, enrolling at Chicago Musical College at Roosevelt University. After less than two semesters, however, McIntyre developed a serious drug habit, losing his job in the process. Improbably, around 1957, he decided to go to New York.

> I had a brand-new horn, but I couldn't even blow my nose. I got in a
> cab and told the cabdriver to take me to 125th and Seventh Avenue. He
> did, and I heard all this rumbling coming out of Small's Paradise. Them
> cats was burnin', man. I walked right up on Hank Mobley. This cat was
> burnin', I was standing there with a cigarette in my hand, and some kind
> of way I started burning my pants. This cat next to me said, hey man,
> your pants are on fire. I said, shut up! Hank was playin', tearing it down.
> I burned a hole in my pants listening to Hank Mobley.

McIntyre's funds soon ran out, and his new saxophone ended up in pawn. His parents sent him a twenty-five-dollar bus ticket home. Warren Smith was already making a living working Broadway shows, and helped his childhood friend to retrieve his horn. Back in Chicago, however, his drug predilections caught up with him once more. "I got arrested in 1959, and I got six years for cashing people's checks. I asked the judge to send me to Lexington, Kentucky, to do my time. Sam Rivers was down there, and Tadd Dameron. Wilbur Ware. A lot of people came through there." Even so, McIntyre's first musical experiences at the "Lexington Conservatory of Music" were humbling. "When I first got there people used to pack up. I couldn't play at all, I couldn't even tune up. They would hurt my feelings—aw, man, here this guy comes. They used to call me 'Freight Train.' I finally realized that I didn't know what I was doing. I did two years and nine months, and all that time I stayed in the practice room all day long."

"When I got out of there on August the twentieth of 1962," said McIntyre, "I was a professional musician, and I ain't been back to jail since." He started to work and tour with blues and jazz bands, playing hard bop with well-respected Chicago musicians such as pianist and arranger Tom Washington. Sometime between 1964 and early 1965, McIntyre met Richard Abrams, Fred Anderson, and Roscoe Mitchell at the jam sessions at the club Fifth Jacks on the West Side. This was a time of transition, when jam sessions often became sites for uneasy confrontations between new music and traditional forms. "Sometimes Roscoe and Fred Anderson would be there, and they'd break up the session," McIntyre laughed. "Everybody would be standing around, talking about, what the hell are those guys doing? Fred Anderson would be, *Wahhgggh!!* Roscoe would get up there and join him—*Ahhgggh!!*"

"I was going over to the West Side, playing—*trying* to play—with all them guys," McIntyre recalled.

> They made me feel like I wasn't really making it. I was getting ready to quit. I remember Muhal saying one night, Man, don't quit playing, man, you can play. I said, man, them guys are treating me like a stepchild. He said, don't let that bother you. Come down to my band rehearsal, Monday night, down at Lincoln Center. I went down to the band rehearsal, and he kept encouraging me. I stayed in the Experimental Band. Muhal kept me from giving up.

Abrams and Mitchell introduced McIntyre to the work of newer musicians, such as Ornette Coleman. Eventually, McIntyre, Mitchell, and Malachi Favors began rooming together in an apartment on 87th and Prairie. Both Mitchell and McIntyre were working at the Victor Comptometer Company, and when they weren't working, they were practicing and debating the future of music.

> I would be trying to learn how to play Hank Mobley licks and stuff, right? Roscoe would say, what are you trying to play that shit for? Man, why

don't you play your own music? He would get mad. He'd say, man, they done played that stuff, over and over, and they played it better than you can play it. That was just a whole new frame of reference. It wiped the whole shit clean—Bird is *over.* Roscoe was instrumental in me trying to find out who *I* was.

Travel, Recording, and Intermedia

The association between McIntyre, Mitchell, and Favors led to McIntyre's being asked to perform on the first commercially released recording of the music of AACM composers, Roscoe Mitchell's *Sound.*[71] The impetus for the release of *Sound* and several subsequent AACM recordings came largely from a young music enthusiast, Charles "Chuck" Nessa, who was working at the Jazz Record Mart in 1965. Located on Chicago's North Side, the mart was owned by Robert Koester, who had also created his own independent record label, Delmark, already well known for album releases in the areas of Chicago blues and New Orleans–style jazz. Nessa's continual prodding led Koester to sign Roscoe Mitchell, Joseph Jarman, and Richard Abrams, identified by Nessa in a 1966 *Coda* article as "the most interesting" among the AACM musicians, to recording contracts.[72]

In the late summer of 1966, Roscoe Mitchell took a group into a North Michigan Avenue studio for a session supervised by Nessa himself.[73] Three Mitchell pieces— "Sound," "Ornette," and "The Little Suite"—were recorded in two sessions, one on August 11 and a second on September 18. On October 20, Joseph Jarman recorded "Non-Cognitive Aspects of the City," a work combining music with an extended poem by Jarman himself, and Fred Anderson's "Little Fox Run."[74] Delmark released *Sound* in late 1966, and the Jarman pieces were released in 1967 as part of Jarman's album *Song For.*[75]

A 1999 article in the recording-technology magazine *Tape Op* detailed the difficulties faced by the engineers during these AACM recording sessions. While the article understandably frames the problems largely in terms of recording techniques, the techniques themselves had become mediated by the dominant culture's vernacular notion of "jazz." Given the standardized culture of "jamming-as-performance," the engineers generally knew what to expect in producing a standard jazz recording of the era—a relatively compact dynamic range, turn-taking in a clearly defined and often pre-selected order of solos, fairly constant backing of piano, bass, and drums, and the odd unaccompanied bass or drum solo. Even much of the so-called free jazz of the period, including the work of Coleman, Shepp, Coltrane, Taylor, and Ayler, often closely followed this model.

At the time of the AACM recording sessions, this limited-infrastructure, restricted-form model of music-making was well within the capabilities of journeyman jazz recording engineers and analog tape–based recording equipment. While the recording studio used for the Mitchell session had a variety of microphones, as well as a mixing console designed by Rupert Neve, widely considered one of the best manufacturers in the industry, only three audio tracks could be used for the master recording itself. As the *Tape Op* article notes, "without an obvious market for these records, no one invested huge resources in recording them."[76]

Even so, the music of Mitchell, Jarman, and Abrams proved "drastically different from what had been recorded before."[77] Chuck Nessa recalled that, for the engineer, "this was the strangest stuff he'd ever encountered."[78] First of all, the range of instrumental color did not conform to the Fordist jazz model. All of the musicians on "Sound" performed on more than one instrument, and bassoons, oboes, and cellos competed with the "main instruments" played by the musicians. Various kinds of "little instruments" took the soundstage, including large arrays of harmonicas, tambourines, whistles, bells, homemade and found instruments, gongs, washboards, and other miscellaneous percussion that jostled for attention with both sung and spoken word. The extended performance techniques employed by the players, even on the traditional instruments, often favored extremes of volume and timbre, from soft textures that required close-in miking to "the harsh overtones used by the reed players."[79] The wide dynamic range of the music, from ultra-pianissimo to intense fortissimo, required the engineers to record at a level high enough to minimize tape noise, while making sure to avoid distortion. On the other hand, the performance techniques themselves could have made it difficult for the engineer to know exactly what constituted "distortion." As drummer Alvin Fielder recalled simply, "They had problems miking us."[80]

Listening to the final recording of "Sound," the untrained or distracted ear would be hard-pressed to identify soloistic turn-taking, although that is in fact what occurs at times. At other moments, collective improvisations with shifting textures posed suspenseful challenges. The nonsymmetrical compositional forms exhibited in these AACM recordings, the frequent interjections and intercutting of unusual material, the sudden and drastic shifts in texture and color, made it difficult to predict what would happen next. The *Tape Op* article reported that "Nessa was concerned about the music's ability to communicate with listeners, and felt that achieving this goal was one of his tasks as producer."[81] For Nessa, this concern translated into the assertion of sonic analogues between this new music and traditional models of jazz music-making.

> I realized that this was the first AACM music to appear and it was the first Roscoe Mitchell record. We'd recorded "Sound" and we'd recorded "Ornette," and there was no place that you heard Roscoe Mitchell playing with drums behind him. Afterwards, I said to Roscoe, "We're going to be giving this to a lot of people who don't know anything cold about this; they're going to be coming to it blankly. To have the leader of the group, who is the saxophone player, never playing when there are any drums playing is kind of bizarre." I said, "Maybe on "Ornette" you could do it with drums behind you." On the first take that we did the first day, it's a cello behind him, playing pizzicato like crazy, and it's wonderful. But I said, "Maybe we could do that with drums behind you." So the next date when we came back, he did it again with drums behind him. And that's what came out.[82]

In our interview, Alvin Fielder matter-of-factly recalled that "we rehearsed that music for three or four months, and we had played it several times. He actually had it written out."[83] Two takes of "Sound" were recorded. Analog vinyl technology of the period could not accommodate a piece whose duration exceeded about twenty minutes, and as it happened, the preferred studio take was too long to be used. Nessa and Mitchell decided to edit the two takes into the single performance that was released on the original vinyl.[84] The compact disc reissue of *Sound* includes the second take of the piece, and comparative listening between the two takes appears to support Fielder's recollection. The high degree of similarity between parts of the two takes reveals much about the mix of composed and improvised structures in the work.

For Jarman's *Song For,* Jarman's regular quintet, with Fred Anderson, Thurman Barker, Charles Clark, and Bill Brimfield was augmented by Steve McCall, and a new figure, pianist Christopher Gaddy, who had just returned from army service. Jarman recalls his "discovery" of Gaddy and Clark in Hyde Park. "I found Christopher and Charles on the street at 53rd. Charles was an extraordinary bass player. He started to develop. He would practice diligently and he was totally committed to the thing. It was like triplets. We were that close. It was like one unit. We would play every day. Christopher was more of a gentleman, more stylish, and intellectual. Charles was like, hey, what's up." Gaddy's father, Christopher Gaddy, Sr., came to Chicago from Arkansas in the 1930s. According to an article in the Chicago *Defender,* the elder Gaddy, who worked for more than thirty years at the Illinois State Department of Labor, was "a beloved man of music to hundreds of Chicagoans."[85] Mamie Gaddy and her husband were proud of their son's membership in the AACM, and did a great deal to assist the collective in its formative years.

By all accounts, their only child was a studious, but frail young man. Leonard Jones remembered Gaddy this way: "Round glasses, beard, close-cropped hair. He was a highly intelligent, gentle person. I mean, Gaddy wasn't no *normal* piano player. Andrew Hill's playing was real abstract. Gaddy's piano playing was like that." According to a published report in *Down Beat* in 1968, Gaddy had sustained internal disorders during his U.S. Army service, for which he spent a year in Walter Reed Army Hospital in Washington, D.C.[86] Despite Gaddy's recurring illnesses, Jarman recalled that "he would still work and practice diligently, and we were a very powerful unit."

The Detroit area had also become a hotbed of musical ferment, with trumpeter Charles Moore and the Detroit Contemporary 5, tenor saxophonist Davis Squires, drummer Danny Spencer, and pianist Stanley Cowell among the new Detroit adventurers. Concerts at Wayne State University featured Cowell, Moore, Paul Bley, and Marion Brown.[87] The independent Artists Workshop, which frequently featured musical events, was coordinated by activists John and Magdalena "Leni" Sinclair. John Sinclair, a drummer and critic, later became the manager of the rock band MC5, as well as the "Minister of Information" of the White Panther Party, an activist group whose 1968 "10-Point Program" recalled Abbie Hoffman's "Youth International Party," the "Yippies." Joseph Jarman was a frequent visitor to the Detroit new music scene, as both musician and writer. In 1967, Jarman performed with poet Diane DiPrima in a benefit event for the Artists' Workshop.[88] Jarman, Ron Welburn, and J. B. Figi were contributors to a small independent journal, *Change,* edited by John and Leni Sinclair with Charles Moore. *Change* featured extensive coverage of experimental improvised music and jazz events in Chicago, Detroit, and New York. The writing ranged from more or less formal reviews to personal letters. Announcements about the latest free jazz recordings from Europe appeared, citing musicians such as clarinetist Michel Portal and pianist François Tusques.

The spring/summer 1966 issue of *Change* included a letter from Jarman about his recent travel experiences. In Newark, Jarman encountered the music of Noah Howard, and in Toronto, he went to hear Marion Brown. In New York, Jarman heard Cecil Taylor and Archie Shepp, writing that Shepp's music "sings across the dead landscape of that city." At the same time, Jarman also advanced a sharp critique of the New York club scene: "By the way in New York i went to Slug's. The musicians playing there at the time were 'very important' yet the music was, as they say in New York, *very tired;* of this i only wonder why?"[89] Roscoe Mitchell also went on this trip,[90] and his retrospective comments regarding the difference in aesthetics between New York and the new Chicago music complement those of Jarman. "When we went to New York to sit in at Slug's, the way the New York musicians were playing was totally different from us. They never really played anything that was soft or anything like that. We were going around with these kelp horns and whistles. The Chicago people got intense, but they also got soft, and they also were incorporating other sounds into their music."

A Litweiler piece on alto saxophonists in the Canadian magazine *Coda* highlighted Mitchell, Jarman, and another new face, the young Anthony Braxton, who had begun performing in Chicago in the autumn of 1966 after returning from army duty. Braxton, according to the review, was "offering a heavy, original music," and even "an awkward, difficult music . . . changing almost from week to week."[91] By 1967, Braxton's own group, with Leroy Jenkins, Charles Clark, and Thurman Barker, was playing at the Phamous Lounge on 71st street near Jeffery Avenue, on the South Side.[92] Braxton was born in 1945, and grew up around 61st and Michigan Avenue on the South Side. His father and mother were divorced when he was four, and he and his brothers were raised by his mother and stepfather. Both father and stepfather came to Chicago from Mississippi in the 1940s. Braxton's stepfather found a job at Ford Motor Company, and later learned to repair television sets. His mother, a homemaker, descended from Creek Indians, grew up in Tulsa, Oklahoma, and was just six years old at the time of the 1921 Tulsa race riot, one of the worst in the history of the United States.[93]

"I grew up in a very musical household," said Braxton, "in the sense that there was a great appreciation for music, but mostly for popular music, the doo-wops, and the blues. My mother loved gospel music and church music, Dinah Washington. My brother Juno had his own vocal groups, and they rehearsed in the house, so eventually I would get my own vocal doo-wop group in grammar school."[94] Braxton also experienced music in the church, from "some of the farthest reaches of the Baptist scene with the screamers, to a calmer Reverend Clay Evans and his church, with the very beautiful choirs."[95] At a certain point, however, he began to explore other spiritual options, including a brief dalliance with Catholicism, before realizing that "more and more, I would move away from organized religion, and in the sixties, discover Zen, Scientology, and go through the various viewpoints—at least the ones I could handle."

At Betsy Ross Grammar School, as Braxton relates, "we were told we could change the world. We were told we were as good as anybody, and we really believed it." This sense of equality was sorely tested when Braxton left his home community to attend Chicago Vocational High School (CVS) on 87th near Jeffery Avenue. Braxton remembers a Polish American majority at CVS, with Russian Americans, and Jewish Americans also prominent; he estimates the school's black population as about one-eighth of the student body when he entered in 1960. The neighborhood surrounding CVS was on the front lines of racial integration, and Braxton remembers that "there was a race war at the end of every school year. It was all nice and neatly arranged, so if you wanted to avoid the race riot, you didn't come to school on the last day."[96] For Braxton, both blacks and whites had some adjusting to do in the new environment of integration.

> I was curious and interested in meeting these guys on the one hand. On the other hand, I came to the encounter with my own racist viewpoints—We're better than they are, every white guy hated me because I was black, that every white guy didn't have the problems that I had, that a white guy, just by virtue of being white, had a better life. If you were able to get past some of that, I was able to have some very nice friendships.

Braxton began his musical studies at CVS, studying saxophone and clarinet, playing in the marching band and the jazz band, and eventually taking private lessons with Jack Gell, with whom Henry Threadgill also studied. Also in attendance at CVS was the prodigious saxophonist Claude Lawrence, widely viewed as one of the most promising young musicians of the period. Inspired by saxophonist Paul Desmond and (as with Leonard Jones) the music of Dave Brubeck, Braxton eventually got his own saxophone. He practically lived at the now-defunct Met Music Shop, a record store near his house that was considered one of Chicago's finest.

By the time Braxton left high school, "I had everything I needed on the South Side of Chicago—being in front of my record player, playing Brubeck, a little Jackie McLean, a lot of Warne Marsh. Practicing the saxophone, being in the Melody Makers in high school. . . . It was becoming apparent to me that more and more, music was the thing I was most interested in, even though I never thought about being a professional musician." Braxton entered Wilson Junior College in 1963, where he met Roscoe Mitchell, Henry Threadgill, and many others. It was "the first opportunity for me to be in an African American musicians' environment with guys who were serious to the point of death." In addition to bebop, newer worlds of music were unfolding for Braxton. "I had been dealing with Ornette Coleman's music, buying the records. I had already discovered that there was much more to life than Paul Desmond and Warne Marsh, including African-American musicians I didn't even know about. It was much more than I even realized. I thought I knew something, but the guys I met there were about twenty miles ahead of me."

By this time, in addition to attending college and holding down a part-time job, Braxton was the father of a young daughter. "I was almost at the point of being kicked out of my family's house—a young man who wanted to be with his woman, and didn't want anybody to tell him what to do. In fact, I should not have been there, and that's what my stepfather told me." Suddenly, sometime in 1964, Braxton joined the army, after passing the Fifth Army Band test. "It was the best thing that ever happened to me," he said. "I met musicians, I played in wonderful orchestras, and I received a lot of encouragement." Studying hard bop, he met the virtuoso graduate of Englewood High, saxophonist Donald Myrick, as well as the highly accomplished saxophonist Sonny Seals, who gave Braxton a "crash course in bebop." At the same time, Braxton recalls, "There was a period where I was the only African American man. Lockers turned upside down, nigger go home, all kinds of sabotage. I used to cry a lot in that period. I couldn't believe how cruel people could be to one another." Stationed in Seoul, Korea, with the Eighth Army Band, Braxton studied with Joseph Stevenson, who presented him with a reminder of home. "He told me after being in Korea for a month or two, Braxton, you're one of the hardest workers I've ever seen. There's only one guy that you remind me of, a guy I taught a long time ago. His name was Roscoe Mitchell. I said, what? He said, he was in the Army with me in Germany. He played strange music as well, and I tried to help him out."

"About three months before I was about to get out, I started hearing about Vietnam," said Braxton. "Fifty percent of the 113th Army Band was sent to Vietnam. I got out just in time." Discharged in 1966, Braxton went to see his cousin Rafiki. "He said, you've come at the right time. There's a group of guys you've got to check out. You'll like these guys. They're totally out." The two men went to a concert, "and who was selling the tickets? Monsieur Mitchell! I see the Muhal Richard Abrams Sextet, and the Kalaparusha Quintet. Incredible evening. Two weeks later, I was in the Experimental Band. I was in the AACM, playing with people who could relate to the kinds of things I liked. . . . One rehearsal with the Experimental Band and I was in heaven."

Braxton's description of an Experimental Band rehearsal suggests something of the excitement he felt: "We play 'NN-1' [an Abrams composition]. I say, I'm going to show these motherfuckers what it's all about—thirty-second notes, Coltrane, Cecil Taylor. I finished my solo, and Jarman stood up and said [sings] *Bwaaaah!* [silence], *Oom* [silence], *Pfffft!* I said this motherfucker is totally out of his motherfucking mind, and this is the baddest shit I've ever heard in my life."

Braxton, Leroy Jenkins, and Leonard Jones all made their recording debuts on the Richard Abrams Delmark session that was released in 1967 as *Levels and Degrees of Light.*[97] For both the Abrams recording sessions and Jarman's *Song For,* there had been a slight upgrade of equipment, to a four-track recorder with 1/2" tape. Also, one of the Abrams sessions was recorded at the Chess Records studio. One other major change in the Abrams recording was the use of electronic processing. Each of the three pieces on the recording—"Levels and Degrees of Light," "My Thoughts Are My Future: Now and Forever," and "The Bird Song"—was awash in dense studio reverberation. Around this time, Eddie Harris's use of electronics was among the most extended among musicians working in the African American tradition. Anticipating Miles Davis by at least two years, Harris used the newly invented electric pianos, and recorded pieces with real-time electronic sound processors such as the Varitone, an "octave divider" that synthesized parallel octaves above or below the pitch of a horn, and the Echoplex, an early tape-based delay line noted for its portability.[98]

The use of electronics by Abrams and Harris proved controversial and widely misunderstood in a world of jazz in which acoustic instruments became conflated with musical, and eventually, cultural and even racial authenticity. For critic Ron Welburn, apparently referring to Eddie Harris in Addison Gayle, Jr.,'s volume of essays, *The Black Aesthetic,* "The varitone gimmick for saxophone muddles the feeling and sound. . . . Black musicians should re-evaluate the technological intrusions now threatening our music; times may come when that technology will be useless. Our music is our key to survival."[99] Rock recordings taking place at this same time, however—most notably, the Beatles' 1967 *Sgt. Pepper's Lonely Hearts Club Band,* produced by the visionary George Martin—dispensed with this notion of authenticity in favor of the use of studio techniques influenced by European composers such as Karlheinz Stockhausen on the one hand, and by rock 'n' roll producer Phil Spector on the other. Legendary Chicago producer Charles Stepney, who had worked with Abrams and Harris in the earliest incarnations of the Experimental Band, introduced similarly innovative uses of electronics in the work of the Rotary Connection and Minnie Riperton.[100] For Welburn, however, rock musicians were "in a technological lineage extending through John Cage, Stockhausen, Edgard Varese, all the way back to Marconi and the wireless. White rock is a technology, not a real music."[101] Thus, Miles Davis, who took a similar postrepresentation approach to the electronic manipulation of improvisation in a studio context with his innovative album *Bitches Brew,*[102] was similarly criticized by Welburn and many others. "Electronic music," Welburn wrote, "can make the black man blind from the sight of money and the white man rich on his deathbed, laughing absurdly at having fooled the niggers this last go-round."[103]

In furthering the notion that technology was inevitably raced as "white," many of these critiques found common cause with canonically important literary figures who ostensibly celebrated this supposed gulf separating blacks from technology. A crucial passage from poet Aimé Césaire's 1938 *Cahier d'un retour au pays natal* [*Notebook of a Return to the Native Land*] appears to base the purity of black subjectivity in nonengagement with technology:

> o friendly light
> o fresh source of light
> those who invented neither powder nor compass
> those who could harness neither steam nor electricity
> those who explored neither the seas nor the sky
> but those without whom the earth would not be the earth[104]

Critic Abiola Irele contends that this passage "derives quite evidently from a partisan rejection of the scientific and technological culture of the West," but also, "beyond its polemical intent, the passage is also a poetic statement of an alternative path to knowledge—that of an intuitive grasp of a living universe in intimate relation to human consciousness and sensibility." Indeed, Irele contends that the passage uses the technical nonproficiency of

African civilizations as support for a "vibrant affirmation of racial pride."[105] Of course, the views of many producers and critics, both within and beyond the music industry, were hardly as nuanced as Césaire's, advancing often enough an oversimplified, essentializing view of black music as best served by a minimum of technological mediation. Norman Mailer, writing in 1973, went so far as to say that "Since the Negro has never been able to absorb a technological culture with success, even reacting against it with instinctive pain and distrust, he is now in this oncoming epoch of automation going to be removed from the technological society anyway."[106]

Silverstein notes Delmark owner Robert Koester's opinion that the reverberation on the Abrams recording was "a little bit corny."[107] John Litweiler found it "unpleasant and distorting," while a British reviewer, complaining that the words spoken by poet David Moore could not be understood, felt that the reverb "obscured a wide range of textural development," perhaps not noticing that, in fact, the electronics were part of the texture itself.[108] Many reviews of *Levels and Degrees of Light* assumed a quality deficit in the recording itself, which could have been perceived as a slap at both the studio engineer and the recording company. In a 1969 *Ebony* article, A. B. Spellman called David Moore's collaboration with Abrams "totally empathetic, though the engineer's sensitivity was not."[109]

The first major feature article on an AACM member, Roscoe Mitchell, was published in April 1967. In the summer of 1966, Terence "Terry" Martin, the article's author, had just come to the United States for the first time, as a new University of Chicago faculty member in biology. A music enthusiast and accomplished photographer who wrote and published articles on music in British journals, the young scientist found himself wondering what his new home, so far from the presumed centers of U.S. cultural production, would offer in the way of music. "I would not be hearing the major figures of the new jazz: Coleman, Taylor, Ayler, Shepp, et al.," Martin wrote, "though I could anticipate some fine city blues, and there were hints that there was a Chicago avant-garde movement, presumed by the outsider (at least by me) to be largely derivative if sincere."[110]

Martin's initial disappointment turned to excitement as he began to feel that the AACM musicians "may be said to constitute a third wave of innovators in the new music, following, but largely uninfluenced by, Shepp, Ayler, et al." Martin describes Mitchell's path by observing that "it was the music of Coltrane and Eric Dolphy that would lead to the understanding of Coleman and the concept of free jazz."[111] Martin's article summarized some of Mitchell's musical ideas, including those that could be regarded as a challenge to New York–based free jazz orthodoxy. The emphasis on silence and space that was developing among AACM composers and improvisors was emphasized by Mitchell himself, who was quoted by Martin as observing, "A lot of musicians play so loud all the time that you can't really hear the true value of the notes. Each note has a direction, and if you play loud, you cover up its direction, and you never really get anything established."[112] Advancing a notion of composition as the creation of an environment, Mitchell noted that in order to perform his new music, "you deal with whatever atmosphere the composition sets up, and pretty soon I don't think I'll have compositions at all. That would be what I consider to be playing really free music—where no one has any certain one thing they *have to* do. If everybody is building something constructive, it's okay. . . . Definitely everybody stimulates each other in our music."[113]

Mitchell went on to describe the compositional philosophy that produced his first album, *Sound: "Sound* is a composition that deals, like I say, with sound, and the musicians are free to make any sound they think will do, any sound that they hear at a particular time. That could be like somebody who felt like stomping on the floor . . . well, he would stomp on the floor."[114] Indeed, AACM musicians asserted similar kinds of new freedoms across the board. At one Jarman performance, "a motorcycle came across the stage to represent the possibility of rapid movement. Careful, don't drive too fast."[115] At a Roscoe Mitchell Art Ensemble event in December 1966, Lester Bowie opened the event by stalking across the stage wielding a shotgun. Later, drummer Leonard Smith danced with an oversized Raggedy Ann doll, accompanied by Malachi Favors's banjo. Another performance saw Favors wearing bells on his ankles and stripes painted on his face, while Phillip Wilson appeared in "a massive blond wig."[116] In an academic journal, musician and historian Leslie Rout described an AACM concert by Mitchell, Joseph Jarman, Thurman Barker, Malachi Favors, and Phillip Wilson at Washington University in St. Louis. In this performance, two skits were presented:

> In the first, while the musicians played "Hail to the Chief," a figure
> dressed in enlisted man's uniform, Fifth Army arm patch, four stars on
> each shoulder, and a rubber mask of Lyndon Johnson, strode about the
> stage waving wildly. When the pseudo-LBJ mounted the platform to
> speak, one of the musicians hurled a cream pie in his face (wild applause
> and laughter from the audience). In a second skit, Joe Jarman read the
> Gettysburg Address with musical accompaniment. When he entoned the

words ". . . that all men were created equal" he disgustedly threw away the script. (Again shouts, wild applause). It was imaginative but predictable political slap stick.[117]

The two evenings of Joseph Jarman's large-scale *Bridge Piece,* described by Jarman as "the biggest thing I ever did" up to that point,[118] took place at the University of Chicago's Ida Noyes Hall on February 9 and 13, 1968. The piece simulated a discotheque with slide and film projections on the walls and ceiling. The audience was seated while the musicians moved around the space; a woman hung aluminum wrapping paper on audience members while a Top 40 station blared on a portable radio.[119] Jarman described the methods used in the first night's performance in a conversation with Leo Smith in 1981.

> The first night consisted of a live band and a tape of that band, playing simultaneously the same composition. The variation came in the mistakes that the musicians made playing the composition. After the notated parts, those spaces where improvisation occurred were different. It sounded like two of the same person playing a solo, for example. . . . The audience was given a sack that they would have to put over their heads. They were directed into areas where they would have to sit down or stand up. There were two people walking through the audience with portable radios. There was a juggler in the audience, and a tumbler who had to tumble over people. The place was super-packed, crowded with strobe lights, smoke, all kinds of stuff happening.[120]

On the first night, those wearing ties were not admitted. On the second evening, matters were reversed:

> The following night was complete formal attire. The band was in complete tuxes, and you could not get in if you were not formally dressed, and a lot of people were turned away. That turning away was as much a part of the performance as attendance. Most of the people enjoyed performing in the first environment because that was a part of their immediate culture that they could dig—a big wild party. But the demand for formal conformity in the sense of attire turned a lot of people off. Women could not get in unless they had skirts and dresses on. Some people actually went home and changed in order to participate.[121]

The *Coda* reviewer was somewhat nonplussed by the work, which "was apparently intended to engage all the audience's senses continually and more or less equally, a physical impossibility." The critic felt that the work indicated a "crisis" in Jarman's work, and his claim that "the aesthetic premise of carefully structured, deliberately spectacular 'chaos' is shaky at best, and in this case it quickly became tedious"[122] inadvertently demonstrated a certain distancing from contemporaneous practices of intermedia and performance art. A similar distancing was evident in critical reception of an earlier Jarman performance at the Abraham Lincoln Center in early 1967. The concert featured Jarman's regular group with Fred Anderson, Bill Brimfield, Charles Clark, Thurman Barker, and Christopher Gaddy. The review by Bill Quinn described the setting as "giant pop-poster canvases of Ku Klux Klansmen and Alabama sheriffs hung high at stage rear. . . . A couple strolled onstage, drinking from paper cups. . . . There was a murder, and the body, fallen amid the junk on the floor, was hauled away."[123]

Quinn objected to this "social commentary," claiming that "it is artistically more difficult and braver to reflect beauty (not cuteness) than only the ugly scene that some of us have to exist in. The call here is for a balance between the two—reality has both."[124] The reviewer's prescription for improvement, however, completely ignored the premises and intentions of the work he had seen, in favor of a more or less traditional jazz notion of dues-paying patrilinealism. "At this point, for purposes of technique, they would benefit from playing with jazzmen from various periods and in various contexts, in night clubs as well as concert halls, with boppers as well as free players. Jackson Pollack [*sic*] once painted murals like Diego Rivera, as Coltrane once blew like Dexter Gordon—it made both of them stronger."[125]

How a deeper involvement with bebop jamming and nightclubs might have made the theatrical elements of the work more effective seems difficult to discern; in any event, as Roscoe Mitchell pointed out to Quinn in 1968, "This is a period when musicians are getting more into exhibition along with the music, as well as incorporating everything that has come to pass—classical European, Indian, African—everything." Jarman told the same interviewer that "African musicians were also actors, dancers, etc. What we're doing just reestablishes an old tradition. . . . What we are trying to do is present a total expression that an audience has to approach with greater involvement than merely listening."[126] In this context, Amina Claudine Myers's recollection of Mitchell should come as no surprise:

He just had periods when he'd go through these creative, artistic happenings—events. In his painting he'd put a button or a safety pin or something on the painting, for "Dementia." He had this big top hat that he was wearing for a time, and then he was going around with a cigar box. He'd come up to you and open it up. One time he was giving you things from out of the box. He gave me a little skeleton that I still have. Then a couple of months later he was asking for stuff to put in the box.

In October 1967, the second major feature on an AACM musician appeared in *Down Beat* under John Litweiler's byline. According to the article's title, Richard Abrams was "A Man with an Idea," namely, the idea of creating the AACM itself. "Without composer-pianist-clarinetist-Abrams," Litweiler maintained, "there might be some kind of avant-garde underground in Chicago today, but few will [argue] that Abrams's personality and point of view have largely shaped what does now exist."[127] In the article, Abrams described music as valuable not only for its own sake, but as a means to transformation of consciousness—echoing the discussion on "awakening the psyche" that animated the contentious AACM meeting of October 2, 1965:

> The new musicians have a need for mind expansion. . . . Environment and experience determine the need—but the *need* for expansion is what we all have in common. There are people who've been fed up with the lies they've been told, and they want to break out of it. So it can get way past the intellect, into what I call the spiritual plane. Intuition takes what it needs from the intellect when they meet; emotion is used to develop beauty once it gets to this plane.[128]

Of his compositional process, Abrams noted that "I always had composing music to tell a story in mind. I wasn't always able to do it, didn't have the musicians to carry it out. I plot a story, and the music is just furthering the symbolism."[129] Nonetheless, for Abrams, written music was only one aspect of the overall performance: "You don't need much to get off the ground when your musicians are spontaneous enough—just rehearse and let things happen. Donald Garrett used to tell me that someday there wouldn't have to be written compositions—he saw it before I did. I had to write quite a bit until I had musicians who could *create* a part, and then I wrote less and less. Now I can take eight measures and play a concert."[130]

In a Canadian piece from May 1967, Litweiler went even further, venturing the idea that the AACM musicians "seem to be suggesting the next revolution in jazz."[131] Whether or not the music of the AACM constituted a revolution, in an era when the word "revolution" was being tossed about with a certain insouciance, there was no question that the collective conception that dominated the AACM, both institutionally and artistically, challenged the commodification of individuality itself—the "star system," with its sharp distinctions between "leader" and "sideman" that had been authoritatively written into the discursive canon of jazz. In an environment where, as musicologist Marcia Citron notes, "the concept of multiple creators, whether specific individuals or community effort, contrasts with the ideology of the individuated composer so valued in the West,"[132] the challenges posed to critical reception by the AACM's collective creativity necessitated changes in the way that music was reviewed. So much of jazz reviewing, then as now, depends upon the thumbnail sketch that compares the individuality of musician A to his or her canonical forebears. Does the work remind one of Hawk, Pres, Trane or Newk? Papa Jo or Philly Joe? Duke or Count? Kid, Jay, or Kai? Miles or Pops?

Such descriptions were seen to lose their power in performances in which the predominance of personal virtuosity as the measure of musicality is removed, and where individual style is radically devalued in favor of a collective conception that foregrounds form, space, and sonic multiplicity. For many among the reviewers who sought to understand the new music, the dynamics of the AACM's collective environment foreclosed the comparative thumbnail sketch in favor of direct, phenomenological descriptions of how the music sounded. This change in critical consciousness placed writers closer to the experience of music-making itself, and was of far more value, both to contemporaneous readers and to historical accounts.

As Ekkehard Jost has observed, "That this [collective] form of organization, completely atypical given the star-syndrome of American jazz, was discovered in 1960s Chicago, and took on particular importance in the milieu of the AACM, was of course no accident, but rather an expression of the social consciousness of the AACM people."[133] Following Jost, the collective articulation of musical form that had become an AACM commonplace reflected the institutional and even political conceptions that animated the organization itself. Describing a concert billed as a benefit for the politically oriented Artists Workshop in Detroit, writer John Litweiler remarked that of seven musicians (Jarman, Gaddy, Clark, Barker, Bowie, Wilson, and Favors), "only Favors played a solo as such."[134] If this was to be a revolution, it would be a revolution without stars, individual heroes, or Great Men. As

Joseph Jarman told Bill Quinn in 1968, "The concept of leader separates man from himself."[135]

Memories of the Sun: The AACM and Sun Ra

Although comparisons of this kind were rare in contemporaneous commentary, for many later commentators, the "theatrical" aspect of these early AACM performances seemed inevitably to recall the work of Sun Ra, who became well known for his incorporation of visual elements. As jazz historian Allan Chase has noted, "Many writers have speculated that the organization and its members' music reflected Sun Ra's influence."[136] Indeed, from the mid-1950s until his departure from Chicago in 1960, Sun Ra's work was a major aspect of Chicago's experimental musical atmosphere, and it would be reasonable to assume that his influence would have carried over to the younger generation. Sun Ra biographer John Szwed, for example, maintains that by 1959, Ra's audiences included "future members of the Associated Artists of Creative Music [*sic*] like Muhal Richard Abrams and Joseph Jarman"[137] Szwed's contention is supported by a 1968 article by Terry Martin in which Jarman describes his encounter with Sun Ra's music: "His band used to work at the Wonder Inn, and I would go out there to hear them (and many of the other young musicians would be there). We would listen to the band and hear him talk."[138]

Anthony Braxton, who was fifteen and negotiating Chicago Vocational High School at the time of Sun Ra's departure, expressed his view of the matter in a 1988 interview with Graham Lock:

> L: Although he left Chicago before the AACM came into being, do you think Sun Ra had a particular influence on the Chicago music of the mid-sixties?
>
> B: His use of theatre was very important. The Art Ensemble can be looked on as an extension of what Sun Ra had established in that context.[139]

Critic John Corbett's expansive liner notes to a Sun Ra reissue that included some of the last work Ra recorded in Chicago (in late 1960) make even more extended claims which are worth quoting at length:

> Finally, with percussive "little-instruments" and formal restructuration on the front burner, these recordings point in the direction that future Chicagoans—including Phil Cohran and Malachi Favors, both of whom

played with the Arkestra—would forge with the Association for the Advancement of Creative Musicians (AACM). . . . The influence is probably quite direct; for instance, on the day he left for Montreal never to live in Chicago again, John Gilmore called fellow tenor saxophonist Fred Anderson—who four years later could help charter the AACM—and asked him to sub on a gig he was going to miss.[140]

In this light, critic Terry Martin's contemporaneous 1968 observation that "despite some similarities, for example, the widespread use of bells, gongs etc., which has been further extended, particularly by Roscoe Mitchell, Sun Ra and his soloists exert surprisingly little direct influence on the present generation of jazz innovators in Chicago"[141] might seem somewhat curious, even needlessly contrarian, and certainly far less frequently referenced than the standard narrative of linear evolution. However, there exists considerable contention on this very point, which is worth exploring at some length. For instance, Roscoe Mitchell barely experienced the final moments of Sun Ra's tenure in Chicago, while the slightly older Jarman had somewhat closer encounters with the older master and his cohort. As Jarman recalls,

> You could just go down on Cottage Grove and hear Sun Ra. When I got out of the army in 1958 I lived in a basement on 55th and Calumet, and Sun Ra lived on the top floor in a little room. He would have thirteen, fourteen guys in there rehearsing every night. A friend of mine took me to John Gilmore's house, which was on 63rd Street. We went up the back stairs, and Gilmore was standing in his kitchen practicing. His kitchen was sky blue with birds flying all over it.

Mitchell remembers a more tenuous connection:

> When I got back from the army, Sun Ra was on his last leg in Chicago, but they were still around. On the West Side they had this place called the 5th Jacks, where they used to have these sessions every Wednesday night. Ruben Cooper [saxophonist] would go, and a lot of Sun Ra's people would go to those, like Pat Patrick. John Gilmore wasn't around there that much.

Henry Threadgill and saxophonist Virgil Pumphrey, who later became known as Abshalom Ben Shlomo, lived in the same neighborhood and grew up playing together. In our interview, Threadgill, who is about a year older than Braxton, recalled a first-hand experience. "Sun Ra rehearsed in the neighborhood at 63rd and Morgan, in the back of the meat market, Gilmore and them. There were stacks of music. They would pull up fifteen, twenty charts. We were sitting up there under them, looking at the music and listening to them and trying to figure out stuff." Trombonist Martin "Sparx" Alexander, born a decade earlier than Braxton and Threadgill, saw Sun Ra as something of a catalyst for communal experimentation: "I used to follow Sun Ra around. He used to play in Calumet City over at the strip joints. There was a certain attraction, even though what he was doing, some of the cats didn't, uh . . . [chuckles]. In my head, he was kind of the forerunner before Muhal, in terms of bringing musicians together in a kind of commonality of producing the musical art forms."

Gene Dinwiddie, born in 1936, also recognized the anteriority of Sun Ra's work to that of his own generation in the Experimental Band. "Sun Ra was a catalyst for the new music," Dinwiddie said in our interview. "He was before Muhal, as a matter of fact. I'm not saying that Muhal was copying anybody, but this new music, Sun Ra was playing it when Muhal was playing with the MJT+3. When Muhal was with MJT+3, Sun Ra was in the cosmos." At the same time, in response to my question as to whether the AACM's work was similar to Sun Ra's, Dinwiddie said flatly, "Naw. We had Roscoe's band, played one thing. We had Phil Cohran's band, more of an African thing. We had Fred Anderson, he played different. There were different sounds, different styles, different people, different individuals."

In any event, much, if not most, of the case for Sun Ra's influence on later Chicago new music rests not upon substantiations of "direct," that is, face-to-face, *influences,* but upon direct *comparisons* between Ra and Richard Abrams. As Chase observed, "Like Sun Ra, Abrams . . . was a versatile pianist and arranger with a background in earlier jazz piano styles who gained considerable experience as an accompanist to visiting and local artists beginning in his teens."[142] Thus, we have two black pianist-composers working in Chicago who investigated "occult philosophies," jazz, theatricality, and large ensemble performance. In this case, does correlation imply causality? Corbett's answer seems strongly affirmative: "Despite many great black artists' claim that Ornette Coleman was their developmental link, these recordings make clear that the connection we've always suspected went beyond costumes and rhetoric; that is, that the musical spirit embodied by Muhal Richard Abrams, The Art Ensemble of Chicago, Kalaparusha Maurice McIntyre, and Anthony Braxton blew into the Windy City from the planet Saturn via Birmingham, Alabama. Sun's torch was passed and the Chicago underground was ready to burn."[143]

In this context, the work and history of the AACM primarily serves as a means of supporting claims of prescience with regard to "avant-garde" practice that are routinely made for Sun Ra's music. Inconveniently for this thesis, however, few first-generation AACM musicians other than Philip Cohran have named Sun Ra as a major influence on their work. In the 1968 Martin article, Jarman makes it clear that regarding Sun Ra, "there was not the dominant influence you might look for, but certainly an influence in the spirit of reaching out."[144] Instead, as Corbett acknowledges, there is Mitchell's 1967 account of a personal breakthrough in the wake of hearing Coltrane and Coleman,[145] as well as Abrams's later understanding in 1978 that "Ornette Coleman is the one who was really a forerunner and an inspiration for the whole field."[146]

Certainly, like most Chicago musicians of his generation, Abrams knew and respected Sun Ra and his work. On the other hand, as Abrams told an interviewer in 1967, "Whenever Sun Ra and I met, we never talked about music."[147] In part this could have reflected a generational divide, since it was certain that younger members of the emerging new music community spent time together listening and discussing ideas. Abrams remembers a conversation with Rafael Garrett and Pat Patrick. "Pat Patrick brought us this Ornette Coleman record," said Abrams in one of our discussions. "We were just knocked out by that. We had never heard anything like that. We [Rafael Garrett and I] were impressed by Ornette Coleman, but we were already out into what we were doing."[148]

Corbett's ready, preemptive response in the Ra recording's liner notes amounts in effect to an assertion that the musicians' references to Coleman constitute a simple (however cryptic) denial regarding their "true" influences that should perhaps be viewed skeptically, if not disregarded outright. Such a denial would cry out for explanation—perhaps in this case, a version of Harold Bloom's thesis of the "anxiety of influence,"[149] in which an ambivalent Oedipal conflict is seen to lie at the root of an artist's struggle to realize his or her own voice. Inevitably, according to Bloom, this ambivalence is expressed via a "misreading" of the older artist's work. In this case, the promulgation of the "little instruments" that populated the early AACM recordings, generally attributed to Malachi Favors, can be read as a willful "poetic misprision" of Sun Ra, with whom Favors played in the late 1950s.[150] However, Favors traced his use of the concept not to Sun Ra, but

to his encounter with an African ballet performance he attended in Chicago
in the 1950s:

> TP: When did the little instruments start getting incorporated into the ar-
> senal of the Art Ensemble?
>
> FAVORS: Well, I think I started from an African influence. As I told you, I
> saw this African ballet, and I just felt that this music belonged in jazz,
> in so-called jazz. I remember once I came in, we were going to have a
> concert or a rehearsal or something, and I came with these little instru-
> ments, and Roscoe asked me, "What are you going to do with that,
> man?" I said, "I'm going to play them in the concert!" And from then
> on, after that, we just started elaborating on little instruments. Pretty
> soon Roscoe and Joseph and Moye, they were little instrument kings![151]

Finally, one would expect the evidence supporting a dominant Sun Ra
influence to be a bit more convincing than an account of a telephone call
from John Gilmore to Fred Anderson, who, as we have seen, was not a
signatory to the original AACM charter despite Corbett's claim. If we take
at face value the writer's suggestion that recorded musical evidence can
help to settle the matter, Sun Ra biographer John Szwed pointed out that
the vast majority of Sun Ra's recorded music prior to his departure from
Chicago was decidedly tonal in nature,[152] relying heavily on the same AABA
formulas and bebop harmonies that animated the work of such hard-bop
composers as Benny Golson. This fact could not have been lost on any
listener or musician having even a passing familiarity with the harmonic
practices of the period, and for younger musicians who were never a part
of the Arkestra's inner sanctum, such as Jodie Christian, the irony of the
contrast between the futuristic titles, such as "Brainville," and the conventional structures in the music might well have stood out. In that regard,
Jodie Christian's remarks on the matter might be more unsurprising that
one might expect. "To my way of thinking," said Christian in our discussion
of this issue, "Sun Ra's band did not influence the new music in Chicago. I
think he had something entirely, altogether different. Sun Ra was around,
but he was an older person. Sun Ra was a more conventional player. That's
all we ever heard when we first met him."

Certainly Ra's version of these hard-bop forms operated in very personalized ways; at the same time, the apparent lack of connection between the
methodologies in Ra's work at this time and the new music coming out of
New York and California is particularly striking. However, the Chicago re-

cordings Corbett discusses do evince a widening range of methods. For example, African-inspired improvised modal vamps appear on several pieces, around the same time that Miles Davis, Charles Mingus, and John Coltrane were exploring that ground. Unusual extended percussion improvisations appear, some of which recall the work of the ostensibly eccentric composer Moondog, whose recordings on homemade percussion instruments such as the "oo" and "trimbas," often classified as a species of exotica, were released on a 1953 recording.[153] Strange combinations of instruments, such as microtonally tuned strings, began to compete with Sun Ra's versions of AABA "rhythm" chord changes, and the performative and theatrical elements in the work became more intense, reflecting the influence of the stage shows and "shake dancers" that practically all South Side musicians had known throughout the 1950s.

As Chase has noted, Sun Ra's New York music of 1961 to 1964, a period during which his music turned definitively away from standard forms, was probably not heard by many in Chicago. "Judging by the recordings," Chase observes, "it was in Sun Ra's early 1960s New York music that the similarities to the AACM's music were most profound."[154] Moreover, according to Chase,

> The Art Ensemble of Chicago's theatrical presentation resembled Sun Ra's on the surface, but seen in the context of 1960s experimental arts (happenings, jazz and poetry events, and avant-garde theater, for example) and new expressions of respect for African-American culture and history, a variety of possible sources are apparent. These similarities of background go farther to explain the parallels between Sun Ra's and the AACM's music in the 1960s than do assertions that the AACM's music is simply an evolution of Sun Ra's music.[155]

Certainly, Sun Ra became aware of the AACM as it was developing. Chase cites the composer-pianist's apocryphal account of a meeting between himself and Abrams in 1964 in New York, in which Ra asserts his own supposed centrality to the AACM's origins, in the same way that John Cage retrospectively positioned himself as a teacher of the unnamed "black musicians" he met on his 1966 visit to Chicago.

> Sun Ra suggested that they go to the World's Fair, but (according to Sun Ra) Abrams said he had come to apologize for being one of those ridiculing Sun Ra in Chicago, and that he had come to realize that he had

to "follow in my [Sun Ra's] footsteps" and organize something to help musicians, and to rehearse with them every day (Sun Ra interview). If the story is accurate, it implies that the Arkestra provided a model of discipline and dedication for Chicago musicians, although aspects of the philosophy and presentation that helped motivate their dedication had also brought the Arkestra ridicule from some quarters.[156]

Along the lines suggested by Vijay Iyer, however, a major distinction between the Arkestra paradigm and that of the Experimental Band (and later, the AACM) concerns the issue of "the centrality of the bandleader figure."[157] Ultimately, it is the assumption that both organizations featured highly centralized leadership, animated by powerful father figures, that seems to account for the apparent power of the comparisons between Sun Ra and the AACM. As Joseph Jarman remembered, however, the crucial difference between the two rested upon the conception of collectivity. "I also went to audition for Sun Ra's band, and I could have been accepted, but I just got a feeling that I probably shouldn't. [Sun Ra and the Experimental Band] were similar in many ways, except the philosophical approach and concept was different. In Sun Ra's organization he had everything to say and do. In Muhal's organization everybody could say and do. That was the big difference."

6

THE AACM TAKES OFF

The Black Arts Movement in Chicago

The early AACM features and reviews rarely explored the complex relationship between the new Chicago music, radical politics, and the issues of race that were raging during the 1960s, instead focusing on an art-for-art's sake philosophy that seemed at variance with the larger purposes of many musicians. A 1967 Philip Cohran concert paid special tribute to John Coltrane, who had passed away in September of that year at the age of forty. For some reason, the reviewer felt that the music of Cohran's Artistic Heritage Ensemble was "inappropriate" to the spirit of such a tribute, asserting that "his selling gimmick is to lecture audiences on some detail from *Every Boy's Book of Negro History* and then play a ditty 'based' on that detail."[1] Another critic of a Cohran event felt that "it is depressing to sit with the Negro bourgeoisie, who support these groups and listen to mild musical admonitions about hair-straightening etc. The liberal Negro audience, of course, now lets its hair grow curled, but out in the ghettos hair-straightening, poverty and violence still prevail."[2]

Of course, Cohran's work expressly sought to combat "hair-straightening, poverty and violence" through the power of music, declaring that "the musician has a great responsibility to elevate his people as he entertains."[3] The program notes for Cohran's final

AACM concert in December 1965 had already eloquently expressed his vision of the context, purposes, and possibilities of original music:

> Having a knowledge of the strength and function of music in ancient cultures and tracing its development up to the present culture of which we are a part, it is unmistakably clear that the use of music has digressed rather than progressed. Our aim in presenting original music to the public is to restore that basic strength and function through adherence to natural laws and spiritual applications. We hope to present this heirloom, left to us by the great black scientists of our ancient heritage, to the blind, mentally affected, shut-ins, the very old and very young and to the general public.[4]

In the summer of 1967, the Artistic Heritage Ensemble pursued a community music performance project at an unusual venue—the 63rd Street Beach on the South Side of Chicago. Cohran's regular lakefront performances conveyed ideology as well as sound:

> We'd be over there jammin', see. . . . And I was breakin' down history to 'em, . . . you know, different things I was dealin' with. Like I had a song on the wigs, you know, "The Talking Drum." I'd sing that and the "sisters" would take their wigs off and hold it up and say, "I ain't going to wear it no more," you know. And then people started wearing dashikis and "sisters" started wearing robes and things. . . . It really was the beginning of Blackness in Chicago.[5]

"Because this was a searching period, there was really a lot of controversy going on, a lot of turmoil," said Leonard Jones. "The focus was on black people doing for themselves, taking hold and being in control of their destinies." This new black consciousness inevitably affected the presentation of AACM events. At the first AACM concerts, "Everybody played this wild, chaotic music in these little suits and these little old skinny ties," Jones laughed. Soon enough, however, the Western-styled suits, dresses, and hairstyles started to disappear. Among others, Claudine Myers began to rethink the connection between clothing, hair, and identity.

> At first I was doing permanents, and that took all my hair. Then I went to wigs. If somebody came to my house I'd put my wig on. I had false eye-

lashes, and I had a dress made low-cut, with a push-up bra. Muhal got on me about my hair, about the wig, and I got tired of the wig too. I called the assistant principal and said I was coming to school with a natural. At that time I said, if I lose my job over my hair, then I lose my job.

For many, the new black consciousness involved modifying or entirely dropping "slave names," the European names inherited by blacks from putative slave masters. Allen Joyner, who had joined the AACM around this same time at the behest of Charles Clark, remembers that "my second wife, Yemaya, named me M'Chaka Uba. I had to go for it because this was during the black movement." Whether motivated by this ideology or by other factors, Richard Abrams adopted the name Muhal sometime in 1967. Claudine Myers added the name Amina at the urging of Jerol Donavon, who became Jerol Ajay, and eventually Ajaramu. "His name, he made up," recalled Myers. "He said it meant, 'a drummer.'"

"We all got off into our names right around the time that Muhal chose his name," Ajaramu told me in our interview.

> A guy told me, you musicians should start using black names. He said, a hundred years from now, people will think Duke Ellington was a white man, because he has a white name. People identify you by your name, and since you're black, you should have a black name, a name from Africa. I chose one name, because I felt that was enough. It was an identity thing. I was so proud to be a black man, and I wanted the whole world to know that I am black. Not that I have anything against white people. I'm just proud to be what I am and who I am.

After his departure from the AACM, Philip Cohran was moving decisively to found his own performance and community meeting space. He took over an old movie house at 39th and Drexel in Bronzeville, renaming it the Affro-Arts Theater. In an interview, Cohran explained the unusual spelling of the name: "'Af'" for Africa and 'Fro' for 'from out of.'" Cohran's fund-raising methods were highly ingenious. Drawing upon the community consciousness that his 63rd Street Beach performances had engendered, at the final beach event he announced his intention to found a theater. He challenged those who were ready to support him to come to a meeting at the St. John Grand Lodge (the same location where AACM concerts were taking place) the following evening. "About eighty people showed up. And

I was pretty encouraged by that. . . . I ran off copies of statements [which said] 'I authorize this person to solicit money to build a Black theater in my name—Phil Cohran.' I signed it. They took it around and raised $1,300 just asking, walking up and down the street. . . . We got the $1,300 plus my record money, and other things that we had done."⁶

The Affro-Arts Theater opened its doors at 8 p.m. on December 2, 1967. According to historian Clovis E. Semmes, over seven hundred people attended the opening, which featured Cohran's Artistic Heritage Ensemble. "The colorful wall murals, Eastern/African garb, and unique musical sounds that drew heavily from the root tones and rhythms of Black music around the world portended a different mode of life for African Americans. The theater projected a warmth and sense of spirituality. One could find support for a new identity that extended unbroken from the present into a rich ancient past."⁷

As Semmes notes, the Affro-Arts Theater "became a focal point for a growing Black consciousness among African Americans in Chicago."⁸ The theater provided a forum for radical political figures, such as Rev. Albert Cleage and Amiri Baraka, as well as important artists such as singer-activist Oscar Brown, Jr., Pulitzer Prize–winning poet Gwendolyn Brooks, and Nigerian drummer Babatunde Olatunji. Choreographer Darlene Blackburn, a close colleague of Cohran, and Chicago poet, activist, and educator Haki Madhubuti (known at the time under the bebop-recalling but parent-given name of Don L. Lee), were also frequent participants in Affro-Arts programs. Reflecting Cohran's love of spirituals, Rev. Spencer Jackson's family of gospel musicians also took part in a number of events at the theater.⁹ Of course, performances by the Artistic Heritage Ensemble often took center stage. In these performances, as Semmes notes, "Health, love of self, spiritual reality, and historical connections were common themes."¹⁰ As Cohran remembers, "We had music classes. We had dance classes. And we had a womanhood and a manhood class to teach the people health and to teach them order and civilization."¹¹

Cohran's work, as well as that of the AACM, was an important part of a complex network of forces operating around black cultural consciousness in Chicago. These forces also included the Organization of Black American Culture, formed in June 1967. OBAC (pronounced in quasi-African fashion, oh-BAH-see) was a collective of African American artists and writers, including painter Jeff Donaldson, later to become a leading figure in the Africobra art movement of the 1970s. According to Donaldson, OBAC was formed "to organize and coordinate an artistic cadre in support of the 1960s bare-bones struggle for freedom, justice and equality of opportunity for African Americans in the United States."[12] Participants at OBAC's initial meeting "viewed cultural expression as a useful weapon in the struggle for black liberation. The group agreed that the essential function of 'a people's art' was to build self-esteem and to stimulate revolutionary action."[13] OBAC worked closely with a number of Chicago's black cultural organizations, including the Affro-Arts Theater and the Kuumba Theatre, as well as what Donaldson called "a close relationship with the Association for the Advancement of Creative Musicians."[14] This relationship was no doubt founded upon the close personal collaborations between Donaldson and Richard Abrams, which extended back to the early 1960s, when Donaldson and Abrams collaborated on community arts projects. In fact, Donaldson's large-scale painting, "JamPact/JelliTite (for Jamila)" depicts Abrams, Charles Clark, and James Brown in full improvisative effect.[15]

With the famous "Wall of Respect," OBAC's work audaciously revitalized American mural painting. This twenty-by-sixty-foot collectively created painting reclaimed the seedy tavern at 43rd and Langley whose outer wall served as the site for the work. The mural depicted heroic black figures in a fashion inspired in part by the revolutionary Mexican muralists Diego Rivera, David Alfaro Siqueiros, and Jose Clemente Orozco, as well as African American heroic muralists such as Elizabeth Catlett, Hale Woodruff, Samella Sanders Lewis and John Biggers, who had been active since the 1940s.[16] Moreover, the frank media intervention confronted the fact that, as Donaldson observed, "blacks were rarely seen on billboards, in print or other public media before 1967."[17] For Donaldson, the process by which the wall was created "called into question the validity of art for art's sake."[18] The painter's recollection of the public scene around the wall as it was going up further emphasizes the impact of this kind of art-making on the community.

> Curiosity seekers, uneasy tourists, art lovers and political activists of every stripe congregated daily and in ever increasing numbers. Musicians played as the work proceeded. Writers recited their works. Don L. Lee (Haki Madhubuti) and Gwendolyn Brooks composed special poems in tribute to the Wall. Dancers danced, singers sang, and the air was charged with camaraderie and pioneering confidence. Before the Wall was finished on August 24, 1967, it already had become a shrine to black creativity, dubbed

the "Great Wall of Respect" by writer John Oliver Killens, a rallying point for revolutionary rhetoric and calls to action, and a national symbol of the heroic black struggle for liberation.[19]

As an institution, OBAC did not long survive the creation of the wall. The group fell prey to internal disputes, which Donaldson saw as having been exacerbated by the Federal Bureau of Investigation's infamous COINTELPRO program, an initiative of the law enforcement agency's notoriously racist director, J. Edgar Hoover. Years later, declassified FBI memos from August 1967 showed that the COINTELPRO program explicitly aimed at infiltrating and destabilizing activist movements across the United States.[20] The program's special targets included both radical black movements, such as the Black Panthers, and the more conservative civil rights activities of Martin Luther King.[21]

There is little question that the Affro-Arts Theater was subjected to similar scrutiny. John Litweiler, writing in the Canadian journal *Coda* in 1968, attributed the theater's momentary closing in 1968 to the undercover machinations of the Chicago Police Department. Public lectures given at the theater by LeRoi Jones and Stokely Carmichael served as the pretext for finding sudden "entertainment license" violations, harassing Cohran into closing the theater. By 1970, the theater had succumbed to "internal dissension, financial problems, and political harassment."[22] Moreover, the original Artistic Heritage Ensemble was itself in the process of dissolution. After the group disbanded, some of its original members, as well as newcomers Donald Myrick, trombonist Willie Woods, and percussionist Derf Reklaw-Raheem, formed a new group called the Pharaohs that asserted a Cohran-influenced Afrocentric funk.[23] Others worked with drummer Maurice White in forming the supergroup Earth, Wind, and Fire. According to Semmes, White visited a number of AHE rehearsals and concerts, and eventually adopted the amplified mbira, which Cohran had christened the "frankiphone" in honor of his mother Frankie.[24]

Critical attention to the work of the AACM was beginning to mushroom. In October 1967, a long article in the *Chicago Sun-Times* presented names that had rarely, if ever, seen the light of day in a mainstream, that is, white, daily newspaper, including Lester Lashley, Jerol Donavon, and the trumpeter Frank Gordon. Also mentioned was saxophonist Virgil Pumphrey, who, as a member of Ben-Ammi Carter's Hebrew Israelite sect, had become Abshalom Ben Shlomo sometime in 1966 or 1967. Ben Shlomo had performed in the Experimental Band, and his ensemble presented concerts

on the AACM's series at the Hyde Park Art Center, and the White Elephant
Pub on the West Side.[25]

New Arrivals and New Ideas

An important bellwether of jazz fashion and commercial impact are the
two annual *Down Beat* magazine popularity polls—one a compilation of
the opinions of "recognized" critics, published in the summer, the other a
mail-in poll for readers and subscribers, appearing just before the December
holidays. Within the Critics' Poll, two categories, "Established Talent" and
the somewhat wordy "Talent Deserving of Wider Recognition" (TDWR),
were established. In 1967's Critics Poll, even as the same issue announced
the passing of John Coltrane, an AACM musician, Roscoe Mitchell, was
recognized for the first time, in the category of alto saxophone TDWR.
Mitchell found himself in the company of Charles McPherson, who placed
first that year, as well as Marion Brown, James Spaulding, Frank Strozier,
and Lee Konitz.[26] That was also the crucial year in which the AACM's focus
on new music began to crystallize. New ideas began to flow into Chicago,
brought by a range of younger musicians. Some of these musicians, such
as Leo Smith and John Stubblefield, were part of the last major wave of the
migration that had nurtured the founding AACM musicians.

Smith was born in 1941 in the Mississippi Delta town of Leland. He was
brought up by his mother, a talented cook with her own catering business,
and his stepfather, blues guitarist and singer Alec "Little Bill" Wallace. The
atmosphere in his home was suffused with the blues:

> On Sunday night, nobody's playing a gig. There's Milton Campbell, three
> or four other musicians, all guitar players, in my house. They're sitting
> around telling long stories, and most long stories by blues guys are about
> women. And they're drinking. They got one or two of their buddies
> there, who are buying. I'm sitting in the doorway, eleven or twelve years
> old. I sat and watched that scene, and I said to myself, whoa, I'd like to be
> a musician.[27]

After a brief dalliance with the mellophone at the start of his high-school
years, Smith began playing the trumpet. Soon he was playing area juke
joints with his own blues band, sometimes four nights a week. During the
day, the young trumpeter was becoming known statewide as a schooled
musician of great promise, under the tutelage of high-school band director
Henderson Howard. The band director entered Smith in contests and tal-

ent shows around the state, and Smith's first experience with improvisation on the trumpet came after seeing the feat performed by a trumpeter with the well-known local band, the Red Tops. Smith soon developed his own reputation for improvisation. "The band director would fix spaces for me to improvise on the football field and in the bleachers," Smith related. "I had arranged 'Fever' for me as a showcase, and the parts were put together communally. When we played those pieces, the whole damn stadium went crazy."

Smith was particularly interested in becoming a composer, and his teachers nicknamed him "Schubert" in recognition of his diligent and studious nature. They arranged his schedule so that he could spend extra time in the library.

> One of the things I did in the library was look for composers. And the thing I did inside of looking for composers was to look for black composers. At the age of thirteen, I knew about Scott Joplin, Blind Tom, James Reese Europe, guys that you didn't hear about in those days. The thing I figured out at thirteen was that a composer wrote music. That meant I was a composer right away, instantly. If you write your piece today, you're already a composer.

Possessed of a sterling high-school resume, Smith received scholarships to Mississippi State College and Alcorn A&M University. However, he had his heart set on attending Jackson State, and when a scholarship to that school did not materialize, Smith joined a touring band and went to Los Angeles. From there, around 1964, he went into the army. Almost immediately, at auditions for the local army band, he encountered the situations that would eventually radicalize him and other black soldiers. "I went to this band training school in Fort Leonard Wood, Missouri. Most of the black guys were being washed out at auditions. . . . The black guy who was teaching trumpet, who they wouldn't let me study with, didn't have a problem. But the other guys, the white guys, would always make erroneous reports on my progress."

In this and other situations, Smith generally refused to back down, and matters came to a head during his posting to Paris, where his band was asked to play an ambassador's ball. "We played Ornette Coleman pieces, or things like 'All Blues,' but all free. The military band played, and my band played. We played 'Three Blind Mice,' but it was free. The people stopped dancing, of course. The Ambassador's Ball *stopped dancing*. One woman came up to the bandstand and said that she was a lady, but not a tramp, or something like that. They stopped us from playing after they saw the reaction."

Smith was called on the carpet by the bandmaster, and was even threatened with court-martial. "He considered me as being arrogant and disrespectful, so he says, what you played, people didn't want to hear. People like what Dave Brubeck plays, but you're not going to hear them liking the kind of music you play. I said to him, well, Dave Brubeck's not important for me. It just got confrontational. But I knew my rights. He couldn't court-martial me for that."

However, Smith had not reckoned with the retributive culture of the army. One day, he was caught out of uniform while on guard duty, and with predictable results for someone who was perceived as being "uppity," was sentenced to fifteen days of labor after duty. "I dug a ditch, I cleaned out ditches, two or three hours every day after work, because of that music." Smith was discharged in 1967, and was married shortly thereafter. Both he and his wife had relatives in Chicago, and while in the army, Smith had been reading the *Down Beat* reports by Litweiler and Martin on Chicago's burgeoning new music scene. He also met a fellow soldier who gave him Anthony Braxton's telephone number, and as soon as Smith got to Chicago, he called Braxton. "He was excited to hear from somebody that knew him. Two or three days later I got together with Braxton, and I had that book of Ornette Coleman's compositions. So we played compositions out of there, and worked on that. We worked on some of his stuff, and worked on a piece of mine. That was our first meeting, in January of '67." Smith was soon introduced to other AACM members, and he formed a study group with Braxton and Joseph Jarman.

> Joseph, Braxton and I got together and looked at ideas about music. We would meet at Braxton's house because it was kind of central. At the first meeting we looked at the people we liked, our influences. That was very enlightening. We looked at other countries' music. I was very interested in the music of Debussy, for example, and so was Joseph. Braxton was talking about Stockhausen. It was kind of formalized.

The family of John Stubblefield IV, who was born in 1945, migrated to Arkansas during his father's Depression-era work in the CC Camps.[28] The family lived on Little Rock's South Side, which, as Stubblefield notes, "was sho' nuff the ghetto. Black and white did not live together. You went to all-black grade school, all-black high schools, and all-black colleges, pretty much."[29] While neither of Stubblefield's parents finished high school, his father, an inventor, found work as a machinist, while his mother worked as a domestic, and served as secretary of a Holiness, or "Sanctified" church in Little Rock. Stubblefield's parents explicitly related their church experiences to African roots. Thus, the young Stubblefield grew up with the awareness of being related to Africa, and in grade school he was an NAACP junior member. Both parents loved music, particularly the music of Ellington and Andy Kirk, and Stubblefield's father was a personal friend of pianist and composer Mary Lou Williams. In the fourth grade, Stubblefield began studying piano at the behest of his father, who had bought a piano in 1955, outfitting the instrument with a mechanical interface that allowed it to perform independently of human control.

Stubblefield began playing the saxophone at twelve years of age, around the same time as the 1957 desegregation battles in Little Rock's Central High School were heating up. In addition to learning the usual concert band pieces, marches and light-classical repertoire, he wisely spent time with more popular pursuits, and by the tenth grade, he was being sought after as a working professional, earning upward of $200 per week as part of the house band at the Flamingo Club, one of the largest black clubs on Little Rock's Ninth Street central entertainment district. North Texas State turned down his application for admission to their fledgling jazz program, so in 1963, Stubblefield entered Arkansas AM&N College,[30] whose alumni included bassist Jamil Nasser and trombonist Garnett Brown. Once again, Stubblefield was directed and prudent, earning a bachelor's degree in music education with a major in saxophone and clarinet. After graduation, he was eager to test his mettle in New York, but along the way, he stopped in Chicago, where he had relatives. "I got there in July of 1967. Pharoah Sanders had called me, and I was going to catch him and John Coltrane at the Plugged Nickel. I'll never forget reading the Sun-Times on the bus: 'Jazz Star John Coltrane Dies,' It just wiped me out. I got off the bus with tears in my eyes and walked all the way from the West Side to the South Side."[31]

The Vietnam War was raging, and Stubblefield decided to stay in Chicago, earning exemption from military service by taking a job in a federal program as a public school music teacher. Meanwhile, the small notices in *Down Beat* about the AACM had not escaped Stubblefield's notice, and sometime after arriving in Chicago, he got in touch with Claudine Myers, whom he knew from working on Little Rock's Ninth Street. The stories about their first meeting back in Little Rock differ in interesting ways. As Stubblefield recalls, Myers was a member of the prestigious African American sorority, Delta Sigma Theta.[32] "She was a Delta, and I brought a band to her college to play at her sorority's ball. As the bandleader, I've got this eight-piece band. She comes up to me and asked can I sit in. I said, no, you can't. On the break she came up and played with her trio and wiped us out."

According to Myers, "We had a sorority ball, and I had hired Arthur Porter to play for us. He come sending John Stubblefield and them over there. That's how I met Stub, in Little Rock. They let me sit in and I played 'Misty.' They were good, too, but I didn't see him no more after that, until Chicago." When he wasn't teaching, Stubblefield was working in rhythm-and-blues touring bands. At a Chess Records date, he met Lester Bowie, who invited him to an AACM concert. In November 1967, with the recommendation of Claudine Myers, Stubblefield became an AACM member, inducted on the same day as Lester Bowie's brother, saxophonist Byron Bowie.

Another new face, saxophonist Wallace McMillan, began to make his presence felt around this time. LaRoy Roosevelt McMillan was born in St. Louis in 1941. His mother had come to St. Louis from Mississippi, and like Stubblefield's mother, grew up in the Sanctified church, which had strong and originary roots in Mississippi. The family lived in the black community of St. Louis, where McMillan, who was given the alternative name of Wallace at an early age, was raised by his mother and grandmother. McMillan's father, who did not live with the family, owned a shoeshine and shoe repair parlor around Laclede and Ewing Avenues where young Wallace learned to shine shoes. In addition, the elder McMillan was a saxophonist, and loved to listen to music. Most days in the shop, the sounds of Gene Ammons could be heard above the hum of the machines.[33] Early on, the younger McMillan's favored instrument was drums, and from the age of eight or nine he performed in talent shows where the master of ceremonies was the well-known St. Louis radio personality, Spider Burke. McMillan was strongly attracted to Latin jazz, particularly Mongo Santamaria and Cal Tjader. At Sumner High, Lester Bowie, Byron Bowie, and trumpeter Floyd LeFlore were among McMillan's classmates. Initially, McMillan played drums and bongos, but picked up the flute in response to his love of Latin music, studying with a member of the St. Louis Symphony.

McMillan had been very active as a high-school athlete, and entered Lincoln University in 1959 on a track and field scholarship. At the same time, he was majoring in music, where he met saxophonist Julius Hemphill. After just one year, McMillan crashed out of school as a result of overcommitment among athletics, music, and academic study. In the age of compulsory military service, leaving school meant getting a letter from the army, and since McMillan had joined the navy reserves while in college, he entered the navy instead. Going on active duty in 1960, he learned both the techniques of antisubmarine warfare and the musical techniques on offer at the Navy School of Music at Anacostia.

McMillan left the navy in 1967, his service time having been extended a year due to personnel needs for the Vietnam War. By the time he returned to St. Louis, he was proficient on baritone saxophone as well as congas and flute, but something seemed to be missing, as a conversation with the influential St. Louis saxophonist Freddie Washington, Jr., made clear.

> When I got back to St. Louis I was told by Freddie Washington, you got a day job? I said, yeah. He says, where are your horns? I said, under the bed. He said, you're going to get to be like a whole lot of cats. One day you'll come home from the job and you'll want to get your horn out and practice, but you're gonna be too tired and you're not gonna do it. You're gonna go and eat and go to bed. After a while it'll be one or two weeks before you remembered the last time you took your horn out. After a while you will not be playing any more. That is what St. Louis is all about.[34]

"I got up one day, threw all my instruments in a Volkswagen and hit out for Chicago. I had to hit Chicago the tail end of '67, going into '68." Like many St. Louisans, McMillan had family in the area, who helped him to find work. He sat in with different bands, and eventually reconnected with Lester and Byron Bowie, who told him about the AACM.

> I think I was invited to the Jackson Park Fieldhouse about '68 to hear the AACM Big Band. Lester was there, Byron played, Leo Smith, Lester Lashley, Joel [Brandon], Paul Ramsey, M'Chaka and Charles, maybe Clifton Heywood. He was one of the flute players. You know that record "On the Beach"?[35] That's where they played. John Jackson came up to me. Between Lester and Byron, they had told John Jackson that I played saxophone. Byron was getting ready to do something and they needed someone to play baritone in the band. That's when I was asked.

The AACM School

In less than a decade, a dichotomy had developed between the new music, which had come to call itself "outside"—meaning outside the frame of traditional method—and the earlier, bebop-based music, which was dubbed "inside" in response.[36] Of course, the polarizing discourse of "inside" and "outside" also referred to the jazz economy, where, at least in 1960s Chicago, those with access to club gigs and other work could be seen as literal insiders. The outsiders were the insurgents who, being unattractive for a variety of reasons to the supporters of the economy of traditional music, were organizing their own events outside that framework. Moreover, many musicians felt that a notion of linear evolution obtained between inside and outside playing, such that only those who had mastered the earlier forms were truly "qualified to go out." Saxophonist Von Freeman, universally revered among Chicago musicians, was sympathetic to the new music and later incorporated some of its methods into his own work. At the same time, as a card-carrying bebopper even before the Cotton Club period, Freeman felt that "nobody wants to hear anybody go Out if he hasn't learned In. You see, if you haven't learned your basics and you didn't come up through all these saxophone players and trumpet players and piano players and drummers, the people who were fundamental in creating this music, if you didn't pay your dues in that, well, nobody wants to hear you play Outside, because you don't know In."[37]

The perception that younger musicians had not paid their dues was reflected in the advice given to them by musicians such as Eddie Harris. The saxophonist and electronic musician, who was always sympathetic to the methods of the AACM, nonetheless observed that the AACM musicians' practice of playing among themselves could serve to limit their exposure to other forms. Speaking with *Down Beat* writer Bill Quinn, Harris counseled the AACM musicians to "gain experience everywhere they can . . . especially the younger cats in the group."[38] At the same time, for many inside Chicago musicians, the presence in the experimental scene of a peer such as Richard Abrams validated the music itself, just as the support of John Coltrane had done for the work of Marion Brown, Archie Shepp, Pharoah Sanders, and the New York avant-garde in general. As Jodie Christian said, "Even me, I didn't know that much about free-form music or the avant-garde. But because I knew Muhal, and I knew that Muhal could play straight ahead, I knew there must have been something there. He wouldn't be doing this for nothing. So that made me say, let me find out what it is."

Christian accurately gauged the desire of at least some of the younger players: "I figured that most of the guys who were playing free form want to play conventional things, but some of them really just don't know how yet." Leonard Jones, Charles Clark, and Malachi Favors, as well as another Chicago bassist, Stafford James, were all studying classical bass with people such as David Bethe, Rudolf Fahsbender, and Joseph Guastafeste, then the principal of the Chicago Symphony. In addition, as Jones recalls, "At the same time that we were all doing the more experimental things, the more creative things, as bass players we were all struggling to learn how to play some chord changes." Despite his ongoing conservatory percussion studies, Thurman Barker, recalling a conversation with Charles Clark, also expressed a desire to become a more complete musician:

> I would say, Charles, I really love the music, it feels good, but I just don't know what the hell I'm doing. I don't know what to play. Charles would say, yeah, I know what you mean. I feel the same way. I would like to try to play more swing. So we decided that we would ask Muhal if we could do some trios. Muhal was open to it, and we found ourselves rehearsing a few days a week over at Muhal's place. Me, Charles and Muhal, playing tunes. Muhal was demonstrating changes. Charles didn't know much about changes and neither did I. That's what was bothering us. I began to get to know Muhal a lot better, and I began to be a little bit more reassured musically about what was going on.

Until the 1980s, with the recrudescence of bebop methods among younger musicians, questions of the location and substance of virtuosity had generational implications. As Emanuel Cranshaw noted, "I think Muhal felt that there was a lack of foundation. You can't keep having cats coming up here playing who don't know anything."[39] This understanding conditioned the beginnings of the AACM School of Music, the "free training program for young musicians" that had already been promised years earlier in the AACM charter. At a general AACM meeting in October 1965, Abrams announced that "we have made a first slight step toward our training program."

"Before we can train, as our purposes say, 'young, aspiring musicians,'" Abrams observed, "we have to have an internal training program in order to raise up some teachers. We know that we have to strengthen this organization, through helping to bring each other up musically." The best way to do this, in Abrams's view, was through "the teaching of theory, as thorough as it can be," as well as sight-singing and ear training. In pursuit of this goal, Abrams, Ken Chaney, and Jodie Christian started Wednesday afternoon theory classes for AACM members. Abrams saw the training as "collaborations between so-called teachers and so-called students . . . the word 'student' is not what I mean, I'm using it for communication."[40] Statements like these emphasized the egalitarian, nonhierarchical vision of pedagogy that exemplified Abrams's own private practice with people like Clark and Barker.

Despite a lack of money and materials, the AACM School opened in the fall of 1967 in the basement of Abraham Lincoln Center, moving in 1968 to the Parkway Community House.[41] The work of the school, which was highlighted in a 1968 *Down Beat* article,[42] was an idea born in the crucible of the Black Arts Movement—an alternative institution operating in the black community, facing issues of creativity and innovation through the development of pedagogical methods that combined literature with orature. Classes were run by AACM members, and were held each Saturday morning at the center, starting promptly at 10 o'clock. As Mitchell remembers it, each class usually ran about an hour long. "Anthony Braxton was teaching harmony. Lester [Bowie] was teaching a brass class. Ajaramu was teaching the drummers. I was teaching a woodwind class. Muhal had a class in composition. He'd start off with people who didn't know anything about music, and gradually take them through it, explain to them how scales and intervals worked."[43]

In one of our many interviews, Abrams presented a summary of what a first-time student in his class would encounter in the first few lessons:

> We learn how to develop things from the raw materials. First of all, before we write any melody, I deal with the scales and derivatives of scales, which brings us across modes—Ionian, Dorian, Phrygian. We're listening to stuff that's around us, and then we can transcend. We're not captive to the usage of things around us, the empirical part.
>
> I take a tetrachord 2 + 2 + 1, C + D + E + F. We have to have a note to start from. That's the first four notes of the major scale. If we proceed with the major scale, from the F we get another 2, to G. From the G we get another 2, to A. And then, from A to B another 2, and from B to C, a 1. So you have 2, 2, 1, with a 2 in the middle, then 2, 2, 1. That's the major scale, and you can start it on any note of the major scale.
>
> They have music paper by now, and they take this scheme and transfer it back to notation, so that they can see it. We're heading towards composing, personal composing. We're collecting these components,

so we won't be puzzled by how to manipulate them. First, we organize ourselves rhythmically, so that we have some idea of how to move things around in a variety of ways. We learn all the major and minor scales, and related scales, like the double harmonic scale, stuff that we hear around us.

We haven't started talking psychologically yet, and we haven't talked about how the Chinese or the Indians have different tunings. That's left to personal investigation, which is strongly encouraged.

Then I make an impression upon the students by playing it. All the time they're getting an appreciation of what they hear around them, all over television, the symphony orchestra, everywhere. When you hear something a little more abstract, then you go investigate to find out how it was developed. This is giving you the basis for looking into it. If it uses notes, rhythms and harmony, you can find out what it is.

Next I give rules for generating melodies. First, write an uneven amount of notes; end on the same note you start on; never make two skips in a row, because we're trying to separate out chordal melodies. There are six or seven rules, then we start to construct melodies. Then we bring rhythms over, and we write a rhythm for the melodies. So in about the third session, we're composing melodies. Here's a person who didn't know anything in the first session, and they're creating with full confidence in knowing what they're doing. They know the materials they're using. I encourage people to be forthcoming to teach other people, and assisting them.

The AACM School was developed out of this.

Roscoe Mitchell, who served as the school's first dean, noted that at first. "maybe there were 10 to 15 students," some of whom were also studying music in the public schools. However, the school quickly became popular through word of mouth, because of the evident progress that students were making. "The younger kids didn't have musical training at all," recalled Leo Smith, "and their parents saw them a couple of weeks later, able to hold their horns and make a few sounds, and engage in blowing."

"In that school, we were the students," M'Chaka Uba recalled. "Muhal taught us, then we finished up, we taught the community. I still have Muhal's notes to this day." Amina Claudine Myers, who taught vocalists along with Sherri Scott, remembers that "Muhal had this graph paper, the Schillinger—Oh, God! [Laughs.] We had to do stuff with graph paper. I was hanging in there, but I didn't know nothing." John Stubblefield studied the Schillinger system with Abrams in the school for over a year, and by all accounts, was an enthusiastic instructor as well. Among the early students who were taught from scratch by Stubblefield, Braxton, Mitchell, and Jarman, the saxophone-playing Cooper twins, Michael and Phillip (later Michael Cosmic and Phillip Musra, stood out, as well as multi-instrumentalist and artist Douglas Ewart, who eventually became a member of the AACM, and later its president.

For John Shenoy Jackson, the AACM School was about "what we owe our foreparents, because we wouldn't be where we are if it weren't for them."[44] Seeing the AACM as "50% music and 50% 'social uplift.'"[45] Jackson declared that "in the AACM we're into more than just the music, so our basic thing is to protect our race, protect our Black children, protect our Black boys and girls and to raise them up to be strong and broad-shouldered and proud. This is the undercurrent behind the AACM, this is why we have the school, this is why we go and play free in schools sometimes, go out into the community."[46]

"You could probably imagine that, with teaching school through the week, I didn't want to throw down on the weekends in that way," said Stubblefield, "but I found myself involved with it, the service that it was to the community. I respected that." Lester Bowie observed that "when you go to an AACM school, you don't have any particular dogma forced on you, where you gotta play free or you gotta play this way or that way. . . . The thing that was really taught was individualism."[47] For Mitchell, the school exemplifies the ideals of mobility and individuality that animated the AACM itself: "The AACM's philosophy was to learn, along with your instrument, how music functions. You were learning many things—art, philosophies. Certainly there are a lot of valid concepts. The problem comes when you get too fixated on one concept as being the only concept. You don't have to throw away one concept in order to try out another. . . . The AACM was more aimed at creating an individual than an assembly line."

Performing Self-Determination
The first academic notice of the AACM's activity as an organization came in a 1967 article in the *Journal of Popular Culture* by an African American academic historian, Leslie B. Rout, an accomplished saxophonist who had worked briefly with Roscoe Mitchell and Muhal Richard Abrams. The article's sources included interviews done in early June 1967 with Muhal Richard Abrams, Roscoe Mitchell, Lester Lashley, and writer Bill Quinn, among others. Rout's searching critical history and appraisal of the AACM's early

years may not have had as much public impact as the *Down Beat* articles, but the work is nonetheless one of the most detailed contemporaneous African American perspectives on the AACM. For Rout, the AACM was "an excellent specimen for a more scientific examination. Hopefully, such a study would provide new perception into the racial convulsions that have and will continue to sweep the country."[48]

The historian sets the scene at the University of Chicago's Mandel Hall, using a far more skeptical tone than the *Down Beat* writers. "After the first tune lasted one hour, I became bored and left the room," Rout reported. Rout seemed surprised to discover that much of the audience did not share his disinterest, and honestly wondered how he, as a putative insider, could find himself somehow out in the cold. "As a musician, I wondered: Most of these people are probably not musically trained, and some of them have had no prior grounding in any form of jazz. How much of this, the most complex form of jazz yet attempted, could they understand?"[49] For Rout, the question of the race and youth demographics of the audience for the University of Chicago concerts meant that "the association's productions are more dependent upon the support of the beard-and-sandal set than its members care to admit."[50] With hindsight, however, it seems curious that Rout did not present reports from any of the black community venues at which AACM members performed—in particular, the weekly Abraham Lincoln Center events that were going on at this same time.

At AACM concerts, according to Rout, "No tunes were announced, there were no programs and aside from an intermission announcement, verbal communication between performers and the audience was kept to an absolute minimum."[51] This very different notion of what Rout saw as jazz performance called into question the enjoyment that jazz was supposed to present: "After studying the grim looks on the assembled faces, it occurred to me that smiling or showing teeth was also frowned upon. Whatever happened to all the joy that used to be in jazz?"[52] Rout was struck by the fact that there was no smoking or drinking by the audience during AACM performances. Rout interviewed jazz writer and *Down Beat* associate editor Bill Quinn, who complained that "*AACM* will hold a concert at a place where you can't smoke or drink. You can carry the integrity bag too far. If they (i.e., *AACM* members) want to be abstainers, fine, but . . ."[53]

In the end, Rout felt (as did Quinn) that the future of the AACM could be assured by moving closer to the conventional jazz model—"playing a few sessions with yesterday's rebels" from the bebop period, as well as announcing the tunes and introducing the performers.[54] On the other hand, somewhat later, Rout points out something that, in his view, made the AACM unique:

> It represents the only successful attempt in the U.S.A. thus far to form an avant-garde jazz cooperative which allows the individual artist to present his music in the manner he deems favorable, have it performed by empathetic cohorts, and receive a payday in the process. Most intriguing is the fact that young Chicago jazzmen have done the impossible without the assistance of the national establishment or the local tastemakers. Psychologically, the gradual emergence of *AACM* again gives the lie to the suspicion still prevalent among many blackmen, that the Negro can never effectively operate anything on his own.[55]

On the other hand, Rout wondered how the faithful weekly tithe of a dollar per week by thirty to thirty-five members could possibly produce economic viability. During the initial AACM organizational meetings, Steve McCall and Philip Cohran had been at odds over interfacing the AACM with corporate funding. Two years later, the skepticism about this course of action, in an era of black self-determination and "do-for-self" thinking, was even greater. Speaking with Lashley, Rout suggested "(a) a loan, or (b) a grant from some federal program or private foundation. Lashley smiled and shook his head. Suggestions along this line had already been vetoed. The bulk of *AACM* members wanted no part of 'Whitey's' dirty money because then they might be beholden to or dependent upon either the Caucasian interests or the despised black bourgeois."[56]

According to Rout, "a clear majority of members felt it necessary to oppose the acceptance of any assistance from the established sources of beneficence . . . success was not enough. *AACM* has to succeed without the aid of the white-controlled power structure."[57] Rout saw this as flying in the face of reality: "Such an attitude may be popular in Negro nationalist circles, but it does not pay the freight. Unless new sources of income are tapped, growth and activity must continue at a relatively low level . . . many *AACM* members will have to exchange some of their ideological biases for some stiff doses of pragmatism if they hope to make relatively rapid progress."[58]

On its own terms, however, the organization began to develop a pragmatic structure for sharing work among its members, as Leo Smith recalled.

From time to time a few gigs would get called in. Somebody would say, we have this gig at so-and-so college, and we need a trio or a quartet or a large ensemble. If a gig like that came to the office on the telephone, it was an AACM gig, and it had to be put on the table. If one person's ensemble had it the last time, it was supposed to go to somebody else the next time. Of course, sometimes people would ask for special people, like the Art Ensemble, Joseph, Muhal, and occasionally Braxton. If it wasn't their time, they would arrange for somebody else to put it together. It worked, because Muhal don't compromise too much. "I'm sending you an AACM band. What do you want? Everybody is just as good as everybody else."

An unpublished, fictional journal/narrative by pianist Claudine Myers, written around this time, depicts some of the dreams and aspirations that this sense of the collective produced. The narrative's dramatic setting is a Saturday afternoon at the Abraham Lincoln Center, where AACM members are going about their creative business in an optimistic, hopeful spirit. "I was writing it as it was happening," Myers recalled. Musicians such as Maurice McIntyre, Leo Smith, and Anthony Braxton appear among the playfully drawn characters, and nicknames are used for others, such as Malachi Favors ("Mal"), John Stubblefield ("Stub"), Fontella Bass ("Fonnie"), and Roscoe Mitchell ("The Rock"). Since the narrative carried the eponymous byline of one "Ariae," a certain "Claudine" herself appears as a character.

A Day in the Life . . . .

By Ariae

Ajaramu and Claudine went to the Center to rehearse; saw Mal and Lester on their way downtown. Mal: "Downtown?" "Yeh." "Bring me a sandwich." "O.K."

Walked in the auditorium. Stub was playing the piano; Anthony Braxton sweeping. Leo was cleaning the office. Claudine proceeded to The Rock's desk. She told Leo that she was going to study with Anthony to learn his theories on notation, sounds . . . Leo said, "Get your own thing. You don't need someone else's. No one can say I'm playing someone else's thing. I went to the library, read books etc. to see what was happening. When some motherfucker (excuse the expression) asks me, I'll tell them where."

Stub walks in. "You people are really cleaning up. How does that bridge go on Jeanne?" "I don't know," replied Claudine. Braxton enters and checks with Leo about cleaning up. Sits down, crosses his legs, coat in lap, looks around, always looks innocent. Of what?

Fontella walks in. "CHECK THOSE BOOTS OUT!!" states Anthony. "I AIN'T SEEN NO BOOTS LIKE THOSE!! Ohhhhhhhhh," he screams to show his boot appreciation. Claudine and Fonnie continue to talk.

Ten minutes passed. The Rock is still working on changing his papers. In walks Maurice looking in drawers. Claudine: "Roscoe, you've been looking and doing that for 15 minutes." "So . . . might do it for 10 more." Maurice is sipping honey.

While Maurice's group is rehearsing, Rock, Braxton and Leo enter. "We're stealing your song, Rock. You've got a hit!" (They were speaking of Rock's composition, "Rock Suite"). Rock replied, "When we get our own record company, we'll put it on a 45." They proceed to the office.

After the first rehearsal, Larry Bowie is playing Straight, No Chaser with Braxton. "Can you play tempos?" "Uh-uh." "Like this? 1–2–3–4?" "Yeh." They proceed to play. After the tune, Claudine hugs Larry. "Beautiful!" "Thanks!" Larry is only 9 yrs old.

Anthony came down with his contrabass clarinet, "The Rock" had his bass sax. Later Fonnie and Claudine sang and played the piano. Fonnie and Claudine threw in a little 500 Rummy to make the day complete (smile).

"BRAXTON, YOUR HAIR IS NAPPIER THAN MINE! Where's that big horn you got?" Muhal had come on the scene.

Joseph promised to use Claudine in the second part of his "symphony." "Oh Good." Jarman, Bowie, Maurice continued to discuss music. "Louis Armstrong is making more money then he ever did." "That's what he supposed to do."

Joseph from toilet: "Bowie!" "Yeh!" "We're going to have a Charlie Parker festival and play the music of John Coltrane too." "We should have a Charlie Parker festival the same day as Coltrane's."

Joseph: "I've been happy all day. The music. . . ." Everybody's drinking herb tea.

(Signed) Ariae[59]

This dramatization of daily life in the AACM seems to demonstrate the foreshortening of the gulf between art and life that was being pursued by its members. Another similarly directed event, one that formed an important watershed moment in the development of organizational solidarity, was the performance of *The Dream,* a two-act play with music, written by

Abrams and performed sometime in 1968. By turns intensely dramatic and broadly humorous, the performance process for the piece involved both musical and theatrical improvisation. "Before the play started," Myers recalled, "Muhal would be backstage, saying, "No dialogue, nothing written. We'd sit back there for a few minutes, and he'd give us the synopsis. And that stuff *worked!* It ran for a month, on the weekends. We had to make up stuff for a whole month. It's amazing. I guess there were a few white people in there, but the audience was mostly black. It was crowded."

A 1977 narrative by Joseph Jarman, published in a book of his writings, provides an overview of each scene, as well as the overall performance process:

> METHOD
> reach down deep inside of what you are
> and bring up the reality of
> the "part"—you don't need the
> "training" of the "actor"; you need the training
> of yourself, what you are already—that is enough.
> how to act in each "scene";
> don't "act" at all become *yourself* out
> of your life and do the scene, the reality
> of it, as it is the facts of your life
> are the only theatre needed. [60]

The central characters of *The Dream* were "Note" (Jarman) a struggling musician, and "Blues & Accidental" (Myers), a woman he meets at a local nightclub jam session. Note plays in a band led by a tough but compassionate singer, "B Natural" (Fontella Bass). Besides the lead actors, the "AACM Players"—Henry Threadgill, Anthony Braxton, Leo Smith, Lester Bowie, M'Chaka Uba, Ajaramu, Wallace McMillan, Thurman Barker, Byron Bowie, and others—served as stage extras, as well as performing both free improvisations and standard jam session tunes as part of the depiction of party scenes, love scenes, and fights.[61]

The play examined many of the same social and cultural tropes explored by Philip Cohran and many other black artists of the period. In the climactic moment, the sensitive artist Note leaves Accidental after realizing the folly of their adoption of ruinous, materialistic white middle-class values (symbolized by Accidental's blonde wig):

NOTE: Every time I look around, here you come . . . yellow wigs, red wigs, green wigs, blue wigs—

ACCIDENTAL: That's right. I was wearin' em when you met me. You ain't shit! You ain't done nothin', You ain't a man. You ain't nothin'.

Note starts to leave.

ACCIDENTAL: You know what? You should take a course on the responsibilities of a man, baby, because you don't have it. You don't know what it is to be a man. If you leave, baby, you can forget about coming back.

NOTE: That's exactly what I'm gonna do.

ACCIDENTAL: You want eat here and screw your whore, you know? Go to some of your friends' house. They don't ever have no money for nothing. Go on with the rest of them people that's nothin', You ain't nothin'.

NOTE (*shouts*): You can take this house, you can take the color TV, you can take that car . . . you can take it all, and stick it up your black ass, you understand?

Note leaves.

ACCIDENTAL (shouts behind him): You ain't nothin'! You ain't nothin'! Shit-ass nigger!

The door slams.

ACCIDENTAL: I should have married me somebody who had a college education.

The audience guffaws and bursts into applause. [62]

"The play got so real that it scared me, we got so into character," said Myers. "Joseph was reading *Down Beat* looking for places to play. I snatched the magazine out of his hands: 'You need to be reading the want ads and looking for a damn job!' Joseph had a look on his face that killed me."

Before his performance in *The Dream,* Henry Threadgill was following developments in Chicago as best he could from Southeast Asia, where he was stationed as an army infantryman in 1967. Threadgill had been with the Horace Shepherd evangelism troupe for nearly two years. His musical colleagues made overtures to him to join the AACM, but he was firmly attached to the religious life. Now and then a friend would encounter Threadgill on a Chicago street corner. "I was with the radical people, them people out on the street trying to get you," Threadgill remembered. With the draft and the Vietnam War in full and murderous effect, Threadgill thought that there might be a way to do what earlier generations of musicians had done—engage military service while avoiding actual fighting in favor of musical performance. He joined the army in 1966 with what he believed was an explicit contractual understanding that he would be pursuing his profession, that is, music. At the time, Threadgill saw the army as a traditional site "where you could go and practice, and get paid. That's why cats went in there, like Trane, Wayne Shorter, Clark Terry."

At first, Threadgill secured a rather cushy assignment as an arranger. "I didn't even have to get out of bed in the morning," he recalled. "I didn't have to make reveille. I didn't even have to put on army clothes unless it was necessary." Stationed in St. Louis and Kansas City, Threadgill had plenty of time to hang out with Oliver Lake and other St. Louis experimentalists. He even met an army colleague who had served with Anthony Braxton in Korea. "They were telling stories about Braxton in the army after he left," Threadgill laughed. "Everybody wanted to kill him. He would have Coltrane and Cecil Taylor blasting up to the top, and he would be playing all day and all night when cats were trying to get some sleep."

Things were going rather well until Threadgill was asked to write an arrangement for a medley of patriotic American songs, as part of a ceremony including the state governor, the local Catholic archbishop, the head of the Fifth Army, the mayor of Kansas City, and other notables. Somehow, Threadgill used the occasion to present a coded challenge to traditional authority. "I wrote this music, but I wrote it the way I write music, and the harmony I was using at the time was very way out, twentieth-century harmony, Cecil Taylor, Sun Ra and all that. It premiered in Kansas City. They said some general jumped up and the guy from the church said it was blasphemous. They cut it off." The next morning at band rehearsal, an officer rushed in and the band members came to attention:

> Announcement from such-and-such army headquarters, so-and-so-and-so, the transfer of Private Henry Threadgill to Pleiku . . ." I said, who? The cat kept on reading. "Private Threadgill will be attached to the fourth infantry. . . . He has thirty days to get his papers in order and report to . . . the upland section of South Vietnam." I jumped up straight out of my seat and said, "Ain't this a bitch!" I was way out of order, but I didn't even give a fuck.

Threadgill went on active duty during the murderous Tet Offensive of 1968, widely regarded as a turning point in the way that the U.S. public perceived the war. "You can do your profession," he rued, "but when they want you to be a foot soldier, you're a foot soldier."

On March 12, 1968, the celebratory and optimistic mood that permeated the AACM was severely tested when Christopher Gaddy, the pianist in Jarman's quintet, passed away, less than a month before his twenty-fifth birthday. Jarman's recently released *Song For* became his only recorded performance. Leonard Jones's remembrance of Gaddy's passing was all the more poignant for its directness and simplicity:

> I met Gaddy when he came out of the Army. Christopher lived in the basement of his parents' building. I took Christopher to the hospital to have his dialysis. Christopher had developed kidney disease in the Army. Christopher was also a Rosicrucian and we were always talking about spiritual things. Young cats searching, trying to find themselves. The day before Christopher died, I'm the one that took him to the hospital. I asked him when did he want me to pick him up. He said, don't worry about it, that he didn't think he would be coming home. He died about 5 o'clock that morning.

Wadada Leo Smith's story gave some inkling of the closeness between Gaddy and Charles Clark:

> The first time I knew anybody that wasn't afraid to die, it was Christopher Gaddy. He talked about it, openly. The doctors had told him that if he didn't have a kidney transplant, he would die. He said, OK, I'm not afraid of that. Gaddy was saying that when he passed he was going to India to study with his teacher. The night he passed, him and Charles smoked some herb in the hospital together. He told Charles that he was going to take off. When they came to get him to clean his blood, he took off. When his mother called Muhal, she told Muhal that Gaddy had gone to India.

At the memorial service, AACM members Abrams, Jarman, Clark, and Barker performed. Jarman composed the piece "Song for Christopher" for his second Delmark recording, *As If It Were the Seasons.*[63] In a sense, the entire album seemed to constitute a memorial to Gaddy.

For many in the AACM, Christopher Gaddy's passing intensified their understanding that life was fleeting, and that as much should be made of the time one has as possible. This meant that it was time to utilize the upsurge of interest in their music to take their sounds beyond Chicago's borders. Gene Dinwiddie, an early member of the pre-AACM Experimental Band, was one of the first to test his wings. At this time, as Dinwiddie saw it, creative differences were quietly surfacing within the AACM. "Roscoe and Joseph Jarman, they were a little too hip for me. I made an effort, I played with Roscoe, but that just wasn't something I wanted to do. In the band we had with Alvin Fielder and Malachi Favors, I always wanted to play straight ahead. Roscoe would play his part, and it would be totally different."

In 1966, Steve McCall played on sessions with blues guitarist Paul Butterfield.[64] McCall introduced Dinwiddie to Butterfield, and "a year or so later," recalled Dinwiddie, "I was playing at Big John's in Chicago with Otis Rush and Mighty Joe Young. Paul and Elvin Bishop came by. Paul approached me and that's how I got that job." In 1967, in the wake of the legendary, record-setting snowstorm that shut Chicago down, Dinwiddie joined the Paul Butterfield Blues Band. His family moved to New York in 1969, where they lived until the late 1970s, when they eventually settled in La Puente, east of Los Angeles.

Troy Robinson had opened his own storefront performance space at 76th and Cottage Grove. The space had a piano, and Robinson built the stage himself. "We had dancers and we'd do plays," Robinson recalls, "but about fifteen or twenty people would show up, so I couldn't keep up the place. Michael Davis was there, Malachi Thompson, Richard Brown, Joey [Joel] Brandon." Robinson described the audience as mixed. "Most of the whites were into the new music, but it was mostly blacks, with their dashikis." Gradually, Robinson began to feel a sense of disillusionment with a certain intolerance that he detected among some members.

> I'd get a chance to play once every month, or every two months, and no money was coming in, so naturally I was doing some other stuff too. I was playing with Operation Breadbasket, and they were like, I'm playing some cheap music. It was like, I had sold out. Some people got upset about it. They were saying that I wasn't really a true creative musician, a true AACM member. I was hurt by that. I was at a rehearsal, and this was said to me, and I was asked to leave.

Soon after, Robinson decided to leave Chicago for California to become involved in writing movie scores, but he "found out that there was a line from here to San Diego" of people trying to break into that business. "I started writing music for children's plays and teaching at a children's center."

Not long after Christopher Gaddy's passing, Mitchell, Favors, and Bowie presented a "Farewell Concert" announcing their extended trip to California,[65] where Mitchell met a future close collaborator, the multi-instrumentalist Gerald Oshita. A pioneer of the Bay Area's Asian American improvisation movement, Oshita was performing in a trio with Rafael Garrett, the eternal nomad from Chicago, and Oakland-born drummer Oliver Johnson.[66] Anthony Braxton, Leroy Jenkins, and Leo Smith, who had become active as a collective ensemble, also sought out musical possibilities there.[67] In November 1968, Steve McCall was touring Germany with a group led by Marion Brown, with Gunter Hampel, trumpeter Ambrose Jackson, and bassist Barre Phillips.[68] Alvin Fielder moved back to Mississippi to take over the family business in pharmacy.

In Leo Smith's retrospective view, "it was a very touchy moment for the AACM around 1968."

> In an organization there are always power plays, no matter if everybody loves everybody, because somebody thinks they can do the job better, or do it differently, or make a different kind of impact. A lot of issues were going on about how to run the AACM. The Art Ensemble had gotten a little bit of power, and so they were making the essential challenges. It was obvious that somebody from the Art Ensemble needed to, wanted to, or should be, leader of the AACM.

Lester Bowie became the second president of the AACM in September 1968[69] with Leo Smith as vice president. It was during this year that the AACM moved its base of operations for both concerts and the school to the Parkway Community House at 500 East 67th Street on the South Side. "The Parkway House gave us a whole theater in the round, which held about a hundred people in there," Bowie recalled. "We had office space, we had a phone number. We had our own space, and we could represent cats so they could rent cars, get cribs, rent apartments."

One public face of Bowie's tenure as president was a short-lived AACM newsletter, the *New Regime*. Similar in style to an underground literary magazine, and published in multiple colors on ordinary grade-school construction paper, the *New Regime* featured personal histories, pictures of members, commentary, photographs, artwork, fiction, and poetry. Also prominent were advertisements for the newly released AACM recordings, and biographies of associated artists, such as choreographer Darlene Blackburn. Upon opening the first issue, one is drawn to Maurice McIntyre's ringing manifesto:

> The Association for The Advancement of Creative Musicians is an organization of staunch individuals, determined to further the art of being of service to themselves, their families and their communities. . . . We are like the stranded particle, the isolated island of the whole, which refuses to expire in the midst of the normal confused plane which must exist—in order that we may, but with which we are constantly at war. We are trying to balance an unbalanced situation that is prevalent in this society.[70]

Bowie offered a trenchant analysis of the situation facing not just black artists, but colonized and subaltern people around the world. For Bowie, "our music . . . is the tool with which the burden of oppression can be lifted from the backs of our people."[71] Bowie advocated the study of communication itself as an essential part of the creative musician's struggle, recognizing that this study would inevitably have larger implications for subalterns generally: "In order for any one people to dominate, suppress or otherwise control another people, they must first cut off (or at least control) the other peoples lines of communication between themselves. In other words, the oppressed people must not only have a complete lack of knowledge of themselves or anything else, but must be denied the means by which to find communication."[72]

Bowie observed that artists must recognize their roles as part of a highly contested and politicized communications network:

> Somehow, someway, the oppressed people must be convinced to perpetuate their own oppression. They must be convinced that they don't want to communicate between themselves; That they don't want to know anything about themselves or anything else. Most of all, they must be convinced that there is nothing to know about. They must be led to believe that they have no music, art, cultural sense or anything else. In order to do this, there can be no communication between the people and their Artist's and in order to do that all lines of communication between the Artist must be eliminated, controlled or otherwise dominated by the oppressor.[73]

Bowie's analysis of the commodification of musicality is singularly insightful, and appears uncommonly prescient to boot:

> The musicians must be convinced to fight, hassle and undermine each other. They must be led to believe that success (Artistic or otherwise) can only be: by being negative. They must believe, that the only way to be is negative toward their fellow musicians. They must be made to discourage rather than encourage their fellow musicians' needs, desires and right to play. This is accomplished by several means; By far, the most effective means is to take the few (very few) negative cats and make them big STARS. Setting them up as examples for the other musicians to follow.[74]

In the *New Regime,* Henry Threadgill took the opportunity to talk back to the media by critiquing the state of music criticism.

> The question has been tossed about many times in recent years primarily by Black artists, that the term JAZZ had taken on too many false and bad connotations, stigmas, etc., and in what is basically a commercial-materialistic-capitalistically oriented country taken on a too limited conception in terms of art. Thereby setting the stage for a foreseeable dead end in terms of progressive creativity . . . derived from within what has become a preconceived Music-concept-thought-mode.[75]

As a solution, Threadgill advocates precisely what the *New Regime* was trying to accomplish: musicians taking responsibility for historicizing and theorizing their own practice.

> When we look at western Music History, some of the best critics and writers were themselves first musicians and composers. Why? Because they knew where the music was "at" that time—they were talking about. Not leaving the task of writing and reviewing to the "out-of-time-of-tune reviewers of society." . . . Who else in this Aquarian Age would be better suited to speak about this product than the instrument through which it appears? Surely, if such highly creative music can come from such minds, the same minds can give some insight about it and themselves in relationship . . . not just by being its creators and performers.[76]

Anthony Braxton's writings in the *New Regime*'s first edition included both poetry and aesthetic musings, often with a whimsical edge. Parodying one of jazz journalism's most clichéd questions, Braxton listed his musical influences as "Desmond, Trane, Ornette, Earl [*sic*] Brown, Muddy Waters, Stockhausen, the Mack Truck Corporation, the streets of Chicago, General Motors and Snooky Lanson."[77] At this early stage, Braxton had not yet developed the extended conceptual vocabulary for which his later *Tri-Axium Writings* and his post-1974 album liner notes became known, but the passion in his writerly voice was evident:

> The acceptance and understanding of all music is necessary, if the total destruction of the idea of art in all its forms is to be brought about in our lifetime. That the West is in the eleventh hour is now undebatable. We must redefine every aspect of what we now call art. . . . We must bring spiritual awareness (not as a "thing"—a way to cash in on the cosmics) to the center of the stage. . . . Steps must be taken to show that all art is one.[78]

Although the magazine was projected to appear monthly, only two undated issues were ever published, both in 1968. In the second and final edition, Joseph Jarman adopted a confessional mode, and perhaps could be forgiven for portraying the AACM and the Experimental Band as something of a Synanon-like cult:

> until i had the first meeting with Richard Abrams, I was "like all the rest" of the "hip" ghetto niggers; i was cool, i took dope, i smoked pot, etc. i did not CARE for the life that i had been given. in having the chance to work in the Experimental band with Richard and the other musicians there, i found the first something with meaning/reason for doing—that band and the people there was the MOST important thing that ever happened to me . . . i could go on and on about Richard and Roscoe, but i'd like to keep it short.[79]

The release of the Mitchell, Abrams, and Jarman recordings, as well a session led by Lester Bowie, prompted considerable critical commentary, both in the United States and abroad, about the "Chicago school" of improvised music.[80] In March 1968, the AACM received major notice in Europe with an extended article by Martin in the British journal *Jazz Monthly*. Richard Abrams, Roscoe Mitchell, and Joseph Jarman were featured on the magazine's cover. The article begins with the context in which the music known as free jazz emerged, noting that the music "was not the creation of a single genius."[81] For Martin, the importance of this music lay in its articulation of collective form:

> It is the role of the ensemble as a source of extended improvisation that seems to me to be particularly significant to the development of the new music, i.e. of jazz itself. The individual and ensemble qualities of this quartet will be the subject of a future essay, but I should perhaps mention that the tremendous tone palette available to the quartet is put to the service of a self-generating ensemble style based on individual creativity and group memory. The result is a wide ranging music, which wanders freely into all musical forms, subjecting them to its own encompassing structures, and they are empirical and organic in nature.[82]

It is at this point that the panoply of approaches favored by the AACM begins to exhibit a postmodern sensibility, even if Martin himself did not necessarily recognize this at the time. "Their familiarity with various musical systems," Martin observed, "has convinced them that no one has all the answers to their expressive needs; the best musicians can call any of these to service as the occasion demands. Their concept includes the freedom to accept as well as reject traditional values."[83] With regard to the modernist/postmodernist divide, musicologist Ronald Radano's critical biography of Anthony Braxton tried to draw a bright line by exceptionalizing Braxton's work relative to the AACM as a whole:

> Whereas most of his AACM colleagues remained committed to free-jazz practice in the mid-1960s, Braxton had already begun to express the liberties of the postmodern, ranging across genres and exploring high-modernist concert music and experimentalism. Soon he would transcend the jazz category altogether, actively participating in experimental-music circles, most notably in New York, where he collaborated with the composer-performers Philip Glass, David Behrman, and Frederick [*sic*] Rzewski.[84]

As we have seen above, however, the range of issues engaged by the contemporaneous critical reception of the AACM places enormous pressure on this reading. First of all, "experimentalism" as a practice (as distinct from a genre) was not limited to white composers or histories, but was part and parcel of the AACM's direction. Secondly, the foreshortening of historical perspective and the multiplicity of voices, emblematic of the "liberties of the postmodern," were being worked out by many AACM composers. Indeed, the AACM itself, as an organization, could be viewed as a postmodern articulation of multiperspectivalism that, as Martin noticed, would confound attempts to ground either its genesis or its apotheosis in the work of any single AACM individual. Lawrence Kart's review of Mitchell's *Congliptious* for example, was typical in its observation that "the entire range of jazz, and other musics, too, is seen as a musical language, an historical present, which these musicians draw upon with unparalleled freedom."[85] *Congliptious* included three unaccompanied solos by Mitchell, Malachi Favors, and Lester Bowie. British critic Max Harrison noticed that the unaccompanied pieces avoided constructing long lines, while "the ensemble performances are completely episodic; the moods shift and flicker but their implications are never followed through."[86] Thus, the reviewer was unable to find any form that was "detectable to sustained, concentrated listening."[87]

At least part of the issue here could have involved this reviewer's evident investment in the ongoing competition between "jazz" and "serious music"—in this case, the work of John Cage, to which, in Harrison's view, the Mitchell work was said to be related, if only in a relation of epigonality. Invoking the standard trope of competition between Afrological and Eurological worlds of music that had been active since the 1920s, Harrison, also noted as a reviewer of "classical" music, found this epigonality to be an issue, not only with Mitchell's work, but also with "jazz" itself. Thus, Mitchell's music was said to be "elementary" in its explorations, and "in too much of a hurry."[88]

In contrast to this dour view was Will Smith's Stateside review of the same work in the August 1969 issue of *Jazz & Pop*. Smith saw *Congliptious* as "a totality of joy—all-seeing, fun-mad dance of bursting, bristling complexity and energy . . . a wriggling mass of glad happenings—the lightning sound of mad sanity contained."[89] Even more to the point, the Smith review confronts directly what Harrison's review omitted: Lester Bowie's witty, explicit challenge to the authority of the critical community itself, in the spoken dialogue to his unaccompanied solo: "Excuse me, uh, Mr. Bowie! I'm Dave, uh, Flexingbergstein of, uh, *Jism* Magazine. Is jazz—as we know it—dead . . . yet?"[90] After a solo of extraordinary ludic caprice, Bowie answers his own question, observing, "Well, I guess that all depends on what you know," clearly implying that the critical community's knowledge might need some revision in the face of the new realities that this music was presenting. Roll over, Beethoven, indeed.

A further case in point concerns Chuck Nessa's first release on his own label, Lester Bowie's *Numbers 1&2*,[91] with Roscoe Mitchell, Joseph Jarman, and Malachi Favors, which was reviewed by Michael James in a 1968 edition of the British *Jazz Monthly*.[92] The reviewer's seemingly unfavorable description of the album could be seen as pointing up the difficulties with critical reception of the AACM's incipient postmodernist fragmentation and collage strategies. James found the recording "intransigently episodic, rejecting not only the traditional jazz values of a swinging beat and a basic harmonic framework, but also the notion of delineating or developing a dominant mood." The music exhibited "a quickfire succession of emotional vignettes, jarring from one to the other over the album's 46 minutes with utter disdain for any logic of development, other than that at times concealed in the musical substance itself." Curiously, for James, the playful, quiet, gentle music on the recording somehow represented "the fears and frustrations of the Negro in American society today. The kaleidoscopic juxtaposition of emotions it offers is the more easily understood when one reflects on the quality of life in the Negro ghettos of the U.S.A.; and likewise, the motivation behind these men's rejection of traditional European values."[93]

Given the reviewer's valorization of traditional jazz song forms, as found in the work of the great musicians of the past—"Armstrong, Hawkins, Parker, Davis, yes, and Ornette Coleman too"—the review's objection to the absence of such forms in the Bowie recording was understandable. Rather than taking the opportunity of "marshalling their inventiveness into significant form," the musicians had reached "unthankful ground," where only "a paltry crop" could be raised. In the end, the reviewer's reference to philosopher Susanne Langer's ideas (albeit in an unusual interpretation) found Bowie and his associates wanting.[94]

This review was balanced by a later, highly favorable review of the same album that appeared in the same journal. The critic, Jack Cooke, noted that due to the large number of instruments on the recording, including glockenspiel, cowbell, chimes, voices, "it's not possible to say precisely who plays what."[95] The reviewer realized that the standard thumbnail sketch approach to reviewing musical style lacked utility in this context. Because "the cohesion and versatility of the group makes it impossible to impose quick comparisons or snap judgments. . . . In these circumstances, 'reconciles the approaches of both Ornette and Albert Ayler' is not only a little thin as a description but could be positively misleading."[96] In a later piece, the same reviewer listened to Abrams's *Levels and Degrees of Light* and Jarman's *Song For,* finding the work of the AACM musicians to comprise "a synthesis of existing techniques and methods rather than any substantially new outlook"—a common early trope in critiques of the postmodern. At the same time, despite his lack of sympathy for Abrams's use of reverberation techniques, the reviewer noted that "the range of techniques they are using is very wide indeed."[97]

One important marker of the organization's growing visibility in its home town was a lengthy 1968 feature article in the *Chicago Tribune*'s Sunday magazine section, which devoted fourteen pages of descriptive text and vivid photography to "The Association."[98] Then, at the end of 1968, the first piece in the U.S. trade press analyzing the work and influence of the AACM as an organization appeared in *Down Beat*'s 1968 yearbook. Bill Quinn, an African American writer, presented a capsule history of the collective, calling it the "most prolific group of its type" in the United States. This after less than three years of existence."[99] The Quinn piece starts with a question posed at a conference on the humanities that had taken place that year: "Does the AACM have anything to do with Black Power?" the young man asked Richard Abrams. "Yes," replied Abrams. "It does in the sense that we intend to take over our own destinies, to be our own agents, and to play our own music."[100] Indeed, for Quinn, the most important aspect of the AACM was that "these black jazz musicians are organized . . . not from without by virtue of agents, THE UNION, or promoters, but from within, through mutual respect and sheer rigid-middle-finger determination to master their destinies. This is one promise of Black Power."[101] Quinn saw a diversity of musical and political viewpoint within the AACM as an important aspect of the organization's character: "A generation may separate one member from the next; one wears beads, a beard, and shirts of psychedelic hues, while another is in a dark suit, white shirt, and a highly introverted tie. Privately, a member may be an antiwarblacknationalmilitantsocialist or fairly unconcerned about anything outside the sphere of his musical involvement."[102]

Cultural Nationalism in Postmodern Transition

One issue that the 1968 Quinn article identified as salient, in this era of focused attention to issues of black empowerment, was the purpose and effect of having white members in the group. The article treated race as just one more element of diversity within the AACM. For Quinn, an AACM member

> does not even have to be black—Gordon Emmanuel [*sic*], vibist and for-
> mer case worker with the Cook County Department of Public Aid, is the
> group's lone white member. Emmanuel, who lives hard by the former
> jugular vein of the South Side's black ghetto, in an apartment once oc-
> cupied by bassist Wilbur Ware, works in the same matter-of-fact harmony
> with association members as the others do. Everyone who opposed his
> entry seemingly has either left the group or come to terms with him as a
> member.[103]

Emanuel, who later became known as Emanuel Cranshaw in honor of his adopted brother, bassist Bob Cranshaw, started playing vibraphone in his late teens. As he noted in a biography accompanying an Abrams concert program, he was proudest of having graduated from the "University of the Cotton Club."[104] Cranshaw had performed on Richard Abrams's *Levels and Degrees of Light,* and, at the recommendation of Fred Anderson and Abrams, became an AACM member in 1967.

Bill Quinn wrote that Cranshaw's membership was "usually made more of outside the organization than within it, though a few members caused a ripple or two on the sea of brotherhood at the time of his entry."[105] In fact, his membership developed into a highly contentious issue, as Cranshaw himself remembers. "I used to get things from people in generalities, like, I'm not doing any work on any concerts involving white cats." Leslie Rout had observed that "on the question of race, Mitchell thought the inclusion of one white member advantageous, but stated flatly that black nationalists among AACM members had drawn contrary conclusions."[106] Indeed, in the context of the burgeoning influence of a newer kind of African American cultural and political nationalism, one could well imagine the AACM coming under considerable pressure regarding its bona fides as a truly "black" organization as long as Cranshaw remained a member. As Leonard Jones observed, "We just happened to have this white cat. He was the only one that was there. He just seemed like the one person in this organization that could somehow bring destruction, or whatever cats were feeling at the time. There were a lot of pressures building up, and the organization was young and just starting to develop."

One of the members who was opposed to Cranshaw's membership, according to Rout, was Lester Lashley, a signatory to the original AACM charter. In this account, for Lashley,

> the central purpose of AACM is the maintenance of the Negro's historical heritage, and as he puts it, this goal is "always in the back of our minds." Since jazz is seen as the Negro's gift to America, or "our thing" as some prefer to call it, Gordon Emmanuel's [sic] election precipitated a major crisis. Lashley observed that once Emmanuel was voted in, a number of AACM members opted out. He further remarked that despite Emmanuel's good record, numerous association members remained markedly hostile.[107]

By early 1969, the pressures had become too strong to ignore. As Cranshaw remembers, "The day it happened, Peggy [Abrams] called me and said, are you OK? I said, yeah. I didn't completely know what she was talking about. I guess Muhal was at the meeting, and Muhal called later on and he told me what had happened, about me being voted out, and Jodie called me. Alvin Fielder told me that it was brought up and cats voted on it, and that was that."

The vibraphonist apparently had no idea that forces were moving against him, or that the situation could change so quickly. "Jodie [Christian] called me up and said that he wanted to explain," said Cranshaw. "He said that he voted against me because he didn't want me to go through all those kind of changes, like arguing with the cats, you know." As Christian himself recalled, "Because of the people in the organization, we thought it would be best for it to be black, and we told them. There were certain movements, social movements, and we thought that it would create a problem. So it was best for now that we start out with just blacks, and we wouldn't have no problems with prejudice and stuff like that."

Leonard Jones said in an interview at his home near Düsseldorf in 1998, "there were only three people that I remember that voted to keep Gordon in—Joseph, Charles and myself." Abrams, as chair, abstained, but in 1998, he reiterated his opposition to the vote. "When it came to Emanuel Cranshaw, the reason I was not for that vote was because I felt he was an exception to that. Although he was of white parentage, he was of black upbringing." Indeed, Cranshaw's view of his own racial background differed from that of his erstwhile colleagues. In our interview, he explicitly stated that he did not think of himself as "white," eventually underscoring that understanding in establishing his relationship with bassist Bob Cranshaw.

Moreover, by all accounts, the vibraphonist had functioned as well as any other member, attending and performing at concerts, putting up posters and distributing advertising, working on concert production, and attending meetings. Abrams, speaking in 1998, observed that

> It was felt by some that we needed to have a black organization and not
> have white people in it, because we needed something that was uniquely
> our own. This is still dealing with people's perceptions of what happened
> with slavery and all the infiltration of black people's organizations. But he
> was by no stretch of the imagination any kind of infiltrator. Gordon was
> a person who had been around us and on the South Side with us just like
> everybody else.

At the same time, Cranshaw remembers now that "I wasn't as much into that music as Muhal and Joseph and all those cats, and neither was Jodie. The main thing—not the only thing, but the main thing about joining the AACM was the fact that they had control over their product, which is something you should have. It wasn't so much that I was a dedicated avant-gardist."[108]

It was unlikely, wrote Leslie Rout in 1967, "that *AACM* will accept any more whites in the near future."[109] Rout framed the issue as one of tolerance and reverse racism, ignoring the complexities of power that made interracial coalitions difficult to sustain in the 1960s: "Initially, it was conceivable that the association's members might be more tolerant of those whites whose views on socioeconomic matters were sympathetic, but further observation tended to negate such a contention. One might have a friend in the sense that 'some of my best friends are Negroes,' but in the final analysis all white men are enemies."[110] Surely, this last judgment has proven far too categorical, since for a number of members, ambivalence about the affair persists to this day. "These people did not hate him, but they didn't want that mixed image," noted Abrams. "The image was just as important as a real fact. The image was elevated to a reason." For Leonard Jones,

> It hurt me that he was voted out because Gordon was a pretty hard
> worker. Gordon was dedicated to the cause of the AACM, and the
> cats voted him out. On any level you look at it, it was wrong. Now,
> thirty-something years later you could look at it in retrospect and say, it
> was wrong but maybe it was the right thing to do at that particular time.

I'll never say that this was the right thing because I voted against it—but in retrospect, with all the things that were happening at that time, it might have been the most beneficial thing to do, so that the organization could continue to prosper inside the black community.

In our interview, Amina Claudine Myers admitted that

I was one of the ones that was against having somebody white in the organization. Whites were always having something. They always run everything, come in and take over our stuff, but this was something black that we had created, something of our own, and we should keep it black. It was that kind of mentality that I had at the time. Today I have a different feeling. Music is open, and that's what I look at now. There's got to be a spiritual quality, regardless of what the color is.

After his departure from the organization, Emanuel Cranshaw continued to work with various AACM members, performing on Abrams's third Delmark recording, *Things to Come from Those Now Gone*.[111] "Naturally, I was closer to Muhal than anyone," Cranshaw said. "I was never that close with, like Roscoe, and all those cats. We didn't do much running together." Despite Cranshaw's expulsion, the AACM's issues regarding authentic blackness continued. One long-time AACM observer felt that part of the reason why the AACM never appealed to "the masses" was because of the presence of so many whites at concerts.[112] Members of the powerful Chicago youth gang, the Blackstone Rangers, sometimes attended AACM and Affro-Arts events. Even the gang's notorious leader, Jeff Fort, was sometimes in attendance, and as M'Chaka Uba related, the issue of the audience's racial composition came up among gang members.

I always tried to get away from Jeff Fort, but I wound up in his house. When these guys would come to the concerts [at Lincoln Center], I would tell them to go up there and sit your ass down and listen to the music. They'd come in there saying, what are all these brothers doing with these white folks. This is our hood. And I'd explain to 'em. Let 'em know what's happening. Ajaramu did that too.

Moreover, in the closely knit, almost small-town atmosphere that persisted in the African American community during the waning days of high American apartheid, the sexual politics of cultural nationalism also affected the reception of the AACM, as personal relationships inevitably took on political significance. In the 1960s, in the midst of changing sexual and social patterns, black women articulated pointed critiques of black man–white woman relationships in particular. Michele Wallace's 1978 summary of the issue was complex, multifaceted, and controversial. For Wallace, the black male/white female issue constituted a primary symptom of a gendered dislocation between black men and black women, where unequal power relationships, black male macho and sexism, and the exploitation of both by the dominant culture, played primary roles.

Black man/white woman relationships, according to Wallace, engendered feelings of resentment and rejection among some black women, who "made no effort to disguise their anger and disgust, to the point of verbal, if not physical, assaults in the streets—on the white women or the black man or on both."[113] Many black women took these relationships as a sign of the rejection of black female beauty and desirability—this time by the black male, rather than the dominant white culture. Farah Jasmine Griffin credited Abbey Lincoln with being one of the first to publicly acknowledge "the pain and disappointment many black women experience when black men prefer white women aesthetically and sexually."[114] For Griffin, "While many ethnic groups experience these kinds of tensions, the legacy of white supremacy makes it especially painful for some black women. More than any other group of women, black women have been deemed unfeminine and the furthest from the white supremacist ideal of beauty."[115]

Griffin noted anecdotally that "anyone who has frequented clubs where jazz musicians jam has noted that often among the women who frequent clubs in search of black musicians, many are white."[116] Griffin presented Lincoln's view that "white female rejects and social misfits are flagrantly flaunted in our faces as the ultimate in feminine pulchritude. Our women are encouraged by our own men to strive to look like the white female image as much as possible."[117] In such an atmosphere, what seemed to be a particularly glaring hypocrisy in the midst of so much routine talk glorifying, say, "our Nubian queens," also presented the spectre of the large numbers of black women who, according to Wallace, never find mates.[118]

Poet, activist, publisher, and educator Haki Madhubuti was perhaps one of the more influential Chicago-based authors of the period who were examining critical social and political issues in the African American community from this standpoint. One of Madhubuti's early books, 1973's *From Plan to Planet*, is subtitled *The Need for Afrikan Minds and Institutions*. His views on the political significance of black-white relationships reflected a widespread perspective that was active during this early period of the AACM, one that placed the personal and the political in close association:

> Many of our Afrikan diplomats are married to Europeans. Yet, we don't see any Rockefeller, Ford, DuPont or Mellon, etc., married to any blacks. Yet, we feel that we can obtain our freedom by marrying our enemies. That is nonsense. Talking black and sleeping white. We should know by now that the European-American will use any means in his power to maintain his domination over the world; and if it means using their women, they will be used.[119]

A panoply of Afrocentric literature, well known in Chicago, took similar or related stances on this issue, and black popular magazines, such as the Chicago-based *Ebony* and *Jet,* made it clear that interracial dating, particularly between black men and white women, was beyond the pale of proper black conduct. In such a complex atmosphere, it is fully understandable that those who believed, as Wallace suggested, that black men dated white women as a means of asserting social equality and "manhood,"[120] would look askance upon the presumed inauthenticity of such relationships. Some AACM performances reflected this position, as Amina Claudine Myers recalled. Trombonist Lester Lashley, an accomplished and academically trained painter, combined image and music in a particularly provocative performance in St. Louis: "Lester had this big painting and it had some kind of lice around it, of a black man with a white woman standing behind him with long blonde hair, who was holding his privates. It was covered up, and then during the concert the cover was snatched off. It was strong stuff. Maybe one or two people walked out."[121]

Many musicians felt that love was a personal matter, and that society should not intrude, but even if pianist Hampton Hawes could declare regarding a potential mate, "I wouldn't care if she was green and had red breath . . . if she's for real, solid,"[122] the simple fact was that society did intrude. "People wouldn't talk to me for a long time because of the black thing, because I was living with a white woman," said Leonard Jones. "I could understand it, but I had a woman that was on my side, I don't care what color she was. The rest of it don't mean nothing to me." For Madhubuti, this attitude constituted sheer denial:

> The brother generally defends his position with white women by saying that, well she is an individual—she is not like the rest—she is not the en-

emy. If the sister used the same logic and said of the white boy, he's an individual, he's not the enemy, we wouldn't have any enemies. But that kind
of crazy logic comes from association with crazy people. You don't see
any Jews marrying Arabs, do you? They are serious about their survival.
Are we?[123]

At the same time, as Wallace pointed out, popular black literature of the
period rejected feminism, claiming that black women were "already liber-
ated." In Wallace's view, this left black women in particular with no discursive atmosphere in which to collectively analyze or confront issues of empowerment affecting black women. Complicating this picture still further
were the ways in which many black cultural nationalists conceived black
women's roles. Ironically, as historian Patricia Hill Collins points out, in the
absence of a black feminist movement, attempts to reconstruct "authentic"
black culture and identity drew heavily on white middle-class notions of the
nuclear family,

> in which benevolent male authority ruled, with women assuming their
> proper, natural roles as wives and mothers. Within this interpretive frame-
> work, strong African-American women in Black families and in Black
> civil society were labeled deviant. . . . Although Black cultural national-
> ism staunchly opposed racial oppression, it ironically incorporated
> dominant ideologies about White and Black gender roles into its domain
> assumptions.[124]

In 1998, Jarman admitted that similar assumptions were an issue in the
AACM during the period of his most intense involvement with the organization. "If you'll notice," he observed in our interview, "all of the women
who became members were somehow connected with already active male
members. I think that had something to do with, you know, the woman is
supposed to walk behind you on the left-hand side, rather than right alongside you." At one early point, reflecting this gendered attitude, the AACM
membership even voted to seat men and women on opposite sides of the
concert space. The arrangement was short-lived, however. "I went to a concert one time," Joseph Jarman recalled, "and they had all the women sitting
on one side and all the men sitting on one side. Aah, that ain't happening.
It didn't last. It wasn't true to our cause. It had been voted in, but it got
voted out." "I think some thing about heritage, nationalism was in the air,"
said Thurman Barker. "There were a few people who were for it and some

people thought it was, you know, a lot of bullshit." Jarman felt strongly that this incident spoke to larger issues.

> Subconsciously that aspect of blackness was being manifested in the orga-
> nization. This is something that feeds into black culture, and is condoned
> by the general American society. I don't think any of us ever thought of
> that, but it was a part of the collective consciousness that we didn't really
> view. . . . Because of the male egotistical bullshit in identity, the females
> were just not permitted the same opportunities as the males who made
> application to join.

In March 1969, foot soldier Henry Threadgill returned to the United States, landing briefly in Washington State before returning to St. Louis, where he renewed his association with the St. Louis music and art scene. By this time, the Black Artists Group, an energetic, interdisciplinary collective of experimental writers, theater artists, filmmakers, visual artists, and musicians, was in full effect, with its own building right in the center of Laclede Town. It was in St. Louis that Threadgill finally finished his military service. "[M'Chaka] Uba got Muhal and them to send papers for me to get discharged early because I had a teaching position in Chicago with the AACM. Then I started playing with the AACM on a permanent basis."

The afternoon of April 15, 1969, saw a potentially devastating blow come to the AACM with the unexpected death of Charles Clark, an original member of the organization, and at twenty-four, its youngest. Along with Thurman Barker, Clark had been a mainstay in many AACM groups, and had taken part in three recording sessions, Abrams's *Levels and Degrees of Light,* and Jarman's *Song For* and *As If It Were the Seasons.* Clark was stricken on his way home from a rehearsal with the Chicago Civic Orchestra, of which he had recently become a member as a result of his classical bass studies. Leonard Jones, who studied with some of the same classical teachers as Clark, remembers that

> The day before Charles died, we talked on the telephone. The Civic
> Orchestra was opening up a whole other thing for Charles. They had
> accepted him, he was there. Joseph Guastafeste was tutoring him, and I
> said, Charles is finally doing what he wanted to do because he wanted to
> do other things besides the stuff that we were doing. The very next day,
> Marabia [Clark, his spouse] called me and said Charles had died. He had

a cerebral hemorrhage in the IC [Illinois Central train] station down on Randolph Street.

With the passing of Clark, the split between the AACM and Philip Cohran was momentarily forgotten. A memorial service was held on April 18, 1969, at the Affro-Arts Theater, with musical tributes by Jarman, Lester Bowie, Wallace McMillan, Anthony Braxton, John Stubblefield, Roscoe Mitchell, M'Chaka Uba, Ajaramu, and a choir of percussionists. As the crowd filed out, Richard Abrams enjoined them to "keep close to the contribution made by this great brother." After his death, the Civic Orchestra established a scholarship in his name, to be given each year to a young, talented, African American musician.[125]

The deaths of Christopher Gaddy and Charles Clark deeply affected the younger AACM members in particular. Two members of their own generation had died suddenly; any of them could be next. Even today, those who were closest to the two men have difficulty talking about that time. Leonard Jones mused that "I can accept death now. It's not something that destroys me, but at that time, it was a little bit difficult. These were my friends, these were my peers, these were cats that were in my age group, the cats that I hung out with and liked to talk with, and both of them died within the year."

"I was devastated, absolutely devastated," recalled Jarman, "at losing both of them because they were a very powerful influence on me. They had the energy and the power. We were doing all kinds of research together, you know. It wasn't just the music, but other things we would discuss—numerology, food. They had contributed a great deal of support to my work, and therefore to my life. It was at this time of being emotionally shattered that Roscoe and Lester and Malachi invited me to play music with them."

This was the budding partnership that ultimately led to the emergence of the Art Ensemble of Chicago.[126] In an interview with musician, activist, and writer Lincoln "Chicago Beau" Beauchamp, Jarman recalled his belief that the three fellow AACM colleagues had reached out to him in his crisis:

> I believe to this day they called me to help me, because they sure didn't need me. . . . Lester invited me to play on his *Numbers 1&2*. We had a good time doing that, then they invited me to play a concert with them. And then very rapidly, if I did a concert I would ask them to play. If Lester did a concert, he would ask me to play. The same with Roscoe, if he did a concert, he'd ask us to play.[127]

After Charles and Christopher died," said Leonard Jones, "I didn't want to play any more. After Charles died, there was an exodus." Indeed, the possibility of leaving Chicago was again being discussed among the musicians. Steve McCall had been dividing his time between Europe and America as early as 1967.[128] Sandra Lashley left the AACM to try her hand in New York, appearing on a 1970 McCoy Tyner album as "Songai," a reference to the fifteenth-century West African empire known as Songhay.[129] Sherri Scott eventually left to join Maurice White in the newly formed singing group, Earth, Wind, and Fire. Abshalom Ben Shlomo was soon to leave for Dimona, Israel, in the Negev Desert. with Ben-Ammi Carter's Hebrew Israelite sect. A polygamous community dubbed "Black Hebrews" in the popular press, the sect promulgated strict laws proscribing premarital sex, homosexuality, tobacco, and alcohol.[130] In a January 1969 article in *Jazz and Pop,* Anthony Braxton was talking of "getting away to Europe or somewhere. . . . What I'm doing needs freedom, man, and the closer I get to what I feel it is I'm getting to I realize the pressure of the city, whatever its contribution to my own personal inspiration, is liable to cut me down."[131]

In the early 1960s, both black and white intellectuals had enlisted the new black music as perhaps the purest exemplar of what Andrew Ross calls the "Golden Fleece of the intellectuals' century-long search for a democratic people's art that was both organic and post-agrarian."[132] By mid-decade, however, it was becoming obvious to leading black cultural nationalists that the music of Sun Ra and Albert Ayler was not leading "the masses" to a higher consciousness. Another new black music, based solidly in R&B, the blues, and the emerging "soul music," was clearly topping the black charts, and was exercising a growing influence in the black community. To avoid being tarred with the brush of elitism, those who wished to lead were obliged to run quickly to catch up with their presumed followers.

The socialist realism–tinged pronouncements of cultural nationalists regarding the need for black music to reflect vox populi had resulted in many of the music's most ardent adherents expressing a deep ambivalence over the directions being taken by the "new black music." Nowhere was this ambivalence more eloquently expressed than in Amiri Baraka's influential 1966 essay, "The Changing Same (R&B and New Black Music)." As Baraka notes, "The form content of much of what is called New Thing or Avant-Garde or New Music differs (or seems to differ) from Rhythm and Blues, R&B oriented jazz, or what the cat on the block digs."[133] At the same time, by reminding readers that "I'm talking about what is essentially *Black Music*," Baraka seeks to bring together two musics, both black, which were widely perceived to have separate concerns and audiences. Indeed, the essay collapses a large, complex, even contradictory body of signs onto a notion of two opposing cultures within black America, expressed as a binary ambivalence between the metaphors "blues" and "jazz." As Baraka says, "The differences between rhythm and blues and the so-called new music or art jazz, the different places, are artificial, or they are merely indicative of the different placements of spirit."[134] In the next breath, the writer asserts a seemingly contrasting thesis, claiming that "any analysis of the content of R&B, the lyrics, or the total musical will and direction, will give a placement in contrast to analysis of new jazz content."[135]

The black middle class was once again enlisted as the beast of this piece. Invoking eugenicist tropes redolent of the jazz debates of the 1920s, Baraka declares that "jazz seeks another place as it weakens, a middle-class place."[136] Here, Baraka extends the binary asserted in his earlier work between the "middle-class Negro" and "the blues people." As Baraka writes, "The middle-class Negro wants a different content (image) from James Brown, because he has come from a different place, and wants a different thing (he thinks)."[137] These characterizations received powerful academic backing from sociologist E. Franklin Frazier's scathing analysis of the "self-hatred" of the black middle class. Besides conclusions drawn from his own ethnographic work, Frazier's thesis relied heavily on a 1951 book by psychiatrists Abram Kardiner and Lionel Ovesey, *The Mark of Oppression: Explorations in the Personality of the American Negro.*[138] Like Alan Merriam's article on jazz musicians and Howard Becker's early work on club date musicians and marijuana smokers (two groups among which there may have been some overlap), Kardiner and Ovesey's work on "the Negro" was part of a body of research regarding "deviance" that was in vogue in the anthropology, sociology, and psychology of the period.[139]

For Frazier, black self-hatred was the result of "the frustrations which they experience in attempting to obtain acceptance and recognition by whites."[140] More recent evidence, in the form of sociological surveys regarding relative rates of black and white participation in the arts, seems to undercut Frazier's view. For example, a 1995 report by the National Endowment for the Arts showed that black audiences attend jazz-related and other historically Afro-American art events at a much higher rate relative to population than whites.[141] Concomitantly, as shown by research from 1990 by two respected arts sociologists, Paul DiMaggio and Francie Ostrower, blacks participate in "Euro-American high culture" events at somewhat lower rates than whites, particularly in public events.

This dynamic, the researchers conclude, cannot be accounted for by theories predicting acculturation by blacks and a concomitant convergence of tastes—in other words, Frazier's thesis as well as that of Baraka's "changing same" article. Nor does the data suggest a dynamic where greater economic competition between blacks and whites results in greater divergence of taste. Instead, the research suggests a dynamic that conventional black cultural nationalism finds paradoxical: namely, that arts participation of the black middle class both converges with that of whites with regard to Euro-American forms, *and* remains distinctively committed to Afro-American forms. As the researchers maintain, blacks exhibit patterns of "dual engagement, based on occupancy of multiple roles that provide incentives for involvement with both elite Euro-American and historically Afro-American art forms."[142]

For DiMaggio and Ostrower, this reflects "the need of upwardly mobile minorities to maintain credible membership claims in both dominant and minority cultures."[143] Compatible with this view is theorist Kobena Mercer's identification of a "diasporan aesthetic" that features "a powerfully *syncretic* dynamic, which critically appropriates elements from the master-codes of the dominant culture and *creolizes* them, disarticulating given signs and rearticulating their symbolic meaning otherwise."[144] Mercer sees this tendency as a kind of "critical dialogism": "Critical dialogism has the potential to overturn the binaristic relations of hegemonic boundary maintenance by multiplying critical dialogues *within* particular communities and *between* the various constituencies which make up the 'imagined community' of the nation. . . . Such dialogism shows that our 'other' is already inside each of us, that black identities are plural and heterogeneous."[145]

What Mercer describes as "dialogism" is, for DiMaggio and Ostrower, a sign that black Americans must exhibit "a bicultural competence that Americans with more limited role sets need not achieve."[146] In other words, the old saw about having to be "twice as good" seems to hold sway here. In explaining these findings, moreover, the researchers explicitly cite W. E. B. DuBois, one of the greatest sociologists America has produced, in ascribing a dynamic of "double consciousness" to black Americans' arts participation.[147]

Thus, black audiences appear to be able to assimilate both Beethoven and the blues, a fact that should not have discomfited writers such as Baraka, who were well educated by their mentors, such as Sterling Brown, in the classic literature and music of both cultures. In fact, it should have been obvious at the time that the black middle class, far from abandoning its roots, had enlisted the Miracles, Little Johnny Taylor, and James Brown into its conservative, deeply religious vision of black society.

Ultimately, in this essay Baraka was seeking a merged consciousness in which the power of black unity is asserted through recognition of how the two cultures, middle-class and working-class, can come together in "the meeting of the tones, of the moods, of the knowledge, the different musics and the emergence of the new music, the really new music, the all-inclusive whole. The emergence also of the new people, the Black people conscious of all their strength, in a unified portrait of strength, beauty and contemplation."[148] On the other hand, unlike the actualized visions of generations of African American musicians, who had insisted that no tradition was alien to their purview, Baraka's writerly prescription sought to mandate exclusively black sources for black creativity as the foundation for this unity. On this view, to be avoided at all costs was any debilitating contact with the Other, the European, the white. Those who continued to insist upon a more mobile creative vision would pay the price for their apostasy, in terms that usually took the form of charges of elitism and epigonal European imitation, as Baraka makes clear: "Although, to be sure, too often the 'unswinging-ness' of much of the 'new' is because of its association, derivation and even straight-out imitation of certain aspects of contemporary European and white Euro-American music . . . whether they are making believe they are Bach or Webern."[149]

In a sense, Baraka seeks to justify the seeming alienation of the new black music from familiar forms by reminding potential listeners of its essential blackness. With increased black mobility, however, a fragmentation of the previously unified black American subject of the popular imagination was already in progress. A revised articulation of diaspora, with new positions along lines of geography, class, gender, national origin, language, education levels, and economic status, was preparing the ground for the realization that many different ways to be black were emerging. In the words of Sly Stone's "Everyday People," there were now "different strokes for different folks," problematizing and often completely frustrating calls for "black unity." In this sense, Baraka's division of black culture into "blues" and "jazz" elements itself announces a rupture in the unified notion of a "blues people" that he had so confidently borrowed from Ralph Ellison just a few years before.

Other critics, less connected with the new music, expressed far less ambivalence than Baraka. In 1971, Ron Karenga, who as Maulana Karenga conceived the now-canonical African American holiday of Kwanzaa, issued a ringing assertion, in the strongest possible terms, of the necessity of what he called "social criteria for judging art." For Karenga, "all art must reflect and support the Black Revolution, and any art that does not discuss and contribute to the revolution is invalid, no matter how many lines and spaces are produced in proportion and symmetry and no matter how many sounds are boxed in or blown out and called music."[150] Drawing on Leopold Senghor's and Aimé Césaire's conception of Négritude, Karenga goes on to insist that "Black art, irregardless of any technical requirements, must have three basic characteristics which make it revolutionary. In brief, it must be functional, collective and committing. . . . So what, then, is the use of art— our art, Black art? Black art must expose the enemy, praise the people and support the revolution."[151]

Thus, as Leonard Jones noted of the period, the new consciousness of African heritage "went into a thing about musical concepts too. Some cats' music was just not black enough." As critic bell hooks points out, however, these kinds of prescriptive judgments "did not allow for recognition of multiple black experience or the complexity of black life."[152] As hooks suggests, Black Arts Movement critiques played a leading role in challenging and ultimately de-authorizing the primacy of pan-European expression in the creative arts in ways that furthered the project of black mental decolonization.[153] Moreover, the movement's insistence on recognizing the social, economic, and political implications of cultural production included sharp ripostes to notions of art's autonomy. At the same time, however, the movement's insistence on mass culture as the primary locus of black musical authenticity, as hooks saw it,

> reinscribed prevailing notions about the relationship between art and mass culture. The assumption that naturalism or realism was more accessible to a mass audience than abstraction was certainly not a revolutionary position. Indeed the paradigms for artistic creation offered by the Black Arts Movement were most often restrictive and disempowering. They stripped many artists of creative agency by dismissing and devaluing their work because it was either too abstract or did not overtly address a radical politic.[154]

Hooks's assertion of aesthetic mobility seems to counter the notion, still advanced routinely by many popular culture theorists in the face of considerable contrary historical evidence, from Blind Tom to Derrick May, of a necessary racial homology between black cultural production and its eventual audience. As hooks asserts, "African-Americans are empowered to break with old ways of seeing reality that suggest there is only one audience for our work and only one aesthetic measure of its value. Moving away from narrow cultural nationalism, one leaves behind as well racist assumptions that cultural productions by black people can only have 'authentic' significance and meaning for a black audience."[155]

For hooks, it was important to recognize that "avant-garde jazz musicians, grappling with artistic expressivity that demanded experimentation, resisted restrictive mandates about their work, whether they were imposed by a white public saying their work was not really music or a black public which wanted to see more overt links between that work and political struggle."[156] Thus, for this new generation of musicians—as with previous ones—music became a way to push and challenge the economic, geographic, and informational boundaries of the "ghetto," even as that ghetto was now being heavily romanticized as the natural home for a New Africa. In a 1997 interview, Abrams summarized the dilemma:

> In educating yourself to an extent that gives you a wider appreciation for total music, you naturally will come up with situations that will not be just things that you can identify as "black," or as "what black people ought to be doing." We're musicians. I'm a musician. I like a lot of things, so why should I deny that I like a Beethoven symphony because somebody might say that ain't black? Or somebody white might say, "He has no right to do that, he's a black musician."

Deeply embedded in the stances of many Black Arts Movement critics, as hooks suggests, is "a deep fear that the power of art resides in its potential to transgress boundaries."[157] As a result, black music, heavily commodified on the one hand, was heavily policed on the other, as Joseph Jarman implied:

> Some of my peers would never admit that they were into the hippie culture—the flower children, free living, the awareness of LSD and what it did to people's consciousness. That's not a part of the illusionary black history orientation that they want to be identified with. I knew all the Beatles songs at that time. The Art Ensemble in Europe would perform opposite very famous rock stars from that era. We used to go to the

Detroit Artists Workshop, which was the home of the MC5. We used to rehearse in the same place in Chicago as Mike Bloomfield. We had the Black Panther Party, the hippies had the White Panther Party.

Jarman's performances, among many others in the AACM, seemed to deliberately provoke those who sought such conventionalized images of race.

I got in trouble at an AACM performance—of course I was supported by the AACM but I was questioned by some of the other people. I had a black dancer and a white dancer. The white dancer was doing ballet across the stage, clear and beautiful ballet. The black dancer was doing wild spirals, running up and down the aisles, screaming and hollering. Their view was, "You mean the blacks are crazy, or what?" Actually, what they were doing was expressing the external view of things.[158]

In considering this period, in which cultural nationalism held considerable force, Anthony Braxton points to some possible grumblings within the AACM itself as to the directions that some of his music, as well as that of Leo Smith, was taking. "Later, my work and Leo's would be viewed as not as 'black' as some of the musics that were reaching into Africa," Braxton recalled." It was in this period that that controversy began to ensnarl me, even in the AACM; because I was not interested only in Africa, I was interested in Africa *and* in Europe *and* in Asia."[159] Of course, as we have already seen, the same could be said of any number of AACM musicians of the period. In that light, the extreme divergence of views within the AACM casts doubt upon Ronald Radano's contention in his important Braxton biography that "an African-inspired cultural nationalism became the official position of the AACM."[160]

Certainly, for some members, Africa provided essential inspiration. For John Shenoy Jackson, the organizational structure and folkways of the AACM was "set up on the same basis, more or less, as the African culture's set up where elders really—a lot of the youngsters won't even say anything around the elders in the AACM until they're asked to speak. Most of the older cats, if we see one of the younger cats getting round wrong, I mean we question them about it. And he will give us a civil answer, there won't be any friction at all."[161] For others, such as Jarman, both Europe and Asia were obviously important sources of inspiration. To complicate matters still further, when Maurice McIntyre became "Kalaparusha Ahrah Difda" in 1969, he did so as much in response to spiritual and even sonic concerns as to cultural nationalism.

> Someone told me that "Kalaparusha" basically means "spirit conscious-ness." It has a lot of meanings. "Kala" means black, because there's this tribe of people in Africa called the Kala. "Parusha" is Indian, and it means "never-ending spirit." It's Sanskrit, from the Bhagavad Gita. "Ahrah" is just a sound. "Difda" is a planet that comes through the solar system around the 20th of March. I saw it on a chart.[162]

Roscoe Mitchell, responding to interviewer Art Cromwell, who read Ra-dano's quote to him, said,

> Cats read a lot of stuff, and so what? Jimmy Ellis was a Rosicrucian. Mala-chi (Favors) was interested in Africa, particularly ancient Egypt. I read some Dr. Ben, just like you probably did . . . along with Stockhausen, Richard Wright, Paul Robeson. Braxton read science fiction and books on chess. There was a tradition here in Washington Park where speakers from the whole spectrum spoke. It was the times. We were all curious. And so what? What is this cat *really* trying to say?[163]

Even as Jerol Donavon became Ajaramu in response to the tenor of the times, he nonetheless could view the issue of nationalist naming as histori-cally transitional.

> I was playing with Jug, and George Freeman said, Ajaramu? That's kind of a hard name to remember. I told him that it don't make no difference what kind of name you have. If people want you, they'll remember it, you dig? Hey man, when I cut out of here, a thousand years from today, people look and see the name Ajaramu, they ain't gonna give a damn who it was in the first place—"aw, that was a dude used to play drums." By that time, no telling what kind of people'll be walking around here—if there are any people here at all. They ain't gonna be saying, is he white or black?

Rather, according to Joseph Jarman, "We were able to participate in a whole universal kind of world, rather than just be motivated by an isolated one."

It was not only the black community that had influence on me and several others, but it was also the parallel hippie community that had developed during that time. So there was the black awareness movement and the hippie awareness movement. And some of us were equally involved in each. . . . A lot of those things were important—I think—to the development of the consciousness of these AACM people, because it was a very exciting time on all fronts. It was the hippies who gave me my first gig at the University of Chicago, with Steve McCall and Charles Clark and Fred Anderson. If it hadn't been for them, we wouldn't have ever been there.

Anthony Braxton was clear in his contention that

part of the significance of the AACM was that we were not tied to any one ideology. We come to a meeting. First things first: We face the East. Then the meeting would start. At no time during my whole involvement with the AACM did anyone ever try to tell someone else what to think—or what to think about the East, or what aspect of the Eastern philosophy you should relate to, or any of this kind of axiomatic syllogisms that you had to pass before you could be in the AACM. We did face the East as a way of symbolically and spiritually connecting with the forces from Africa.

Muhal Richard Abrams would later insist upon a mobile, heterophonic notion of the possibilities for unity, saying that "there are different types of black life, and therefore we know that there are different kinds of black music. Because black music comes forth from black life."[164]

7

AMERICANS IN PARIS

Conceiving the World Audience

One important cultural nationalist trope involved analyses of who would "control" African American cultural production. Clovis E. Semmes, writing about Philip Cohran, notes that "the expropriation of African American culture by European American institutions of ideation is a well-established fact and cultural dilemma facing African American creative artists and intellectuals. . . . Cultural products, particularly music, language, dance, and stylistic norms are absorbed into the broader White-controlled commodity system, redefined, and used to advance the economic dominance of mainstream institutions."[1] Semmes identifies three stages that mediate that production:

> First, the African American community spawns and shapes its
> creative agents who in turn express and advance the cultural ethos
> and aspirations of that community. The market for these creative
> agents is first an internal one. Second, as others (outside of the
> community) recognize and perceive social and economic benefits
> from these cultural products, a new external market develops. The
> artist begins to service this market but remains focused on his or
> her root, internal, or home market. Third, as the external market
> becomes dominant, the artist tends not to focus on the home mar-

ket and begins to alter his or her cultural products to accommodate the perspectives, expectations, economic potential, and legitimating power of the external market. At this point, external or mainstream markets begin to imitate, co-opt, and expropriate African American cultural products.[2]

For Semmes, this third stage must be avoided, "for fear of distortion, absorption, and negation."[3] To counter this bowdlerization, African Americans must "look within their midst and select, support, and legitimate their progressive artists, teachers, and leaders who have rejected commercial co-optation in behalf of community development."[4]

There is little question that the intensity of market forces can indeed lead to profound changes in any music or art. All too often, however, careful analyses of the sort Semmes makes were oversimplified in support of the notion that black music, in order to remain pure and avoid "cultural theft," must somehow be made inaccessible to people from outside the black community. In most cases, this was to be accomplished by having the musicians simply stay at home. From inside the hypersegregated Chicago black community of the 1960s, such a strategy seemed to some to be relatively simple to implement. The strategy, however, ignores the fact that despite all the barriers, the music inevitably manages to emerge. Moreover, as an economic strategy in a world based on trade across borders, the confinement of music within limits that, after all, were enforced not by blacks, but by white-controlled structures of dominance, appears at variance with the lived experiences of most artists.

In this respect, Lester Bowie, in an interview with Chicago Beau, stated an obvious fact about life as a musician that counters the romantic provincialism of those who insist that true musical authenticity, as well as control over one's art, consists in remaining in one's home community.

> Part of the job of a musician is that of a messenger. If you ain't ready to be a messenger, forget it. You need to get a job in the post office or somewhere. If you ain't ready to travel, pack up your family, or pack up yourself and hit the road, you're in the wrong business. Because that's what music is about. It's about spreading knowledge and education, and re-education. It's about spreading. You have got to travel with it to spread the word. Like all the people in the past that have had to travel to spread the music.[5]

The MJT+3 in performance, late 1950s. *Left to right:* Richard
Abrams, piano; Paul Serrano, trumpet; Bob Cranshaw, bass;
George Coleman, tenor saxophone; Walter Perkins, drums.
Collection of Muhal Richard Abrams.

The classic organ trio, ca. 1964: Claudine Myers, organ;
Skip James, tenor saxophone; Jerol Donavon, drums.

Steve McCall, early 1960s.
Collection of Evod Magek.

Philip Cohran with harp and frankiphone, ca. 1966.
Collection of the AACM.

Advertising flyer for the first AACM events, in 1965. Courtesy of the Jamil B. Figi Collection, JIC Don DeMicheal Archives Collection, Chicago Jazz Archive, University of Chicago Library.

The Joseph Jarman Quintet, University of Chicago
Festival of the Arts, 1966: Charles Clark, bass;
Bill Brimfield, trumpet; Steve McCall, drums;
Joseph Jarman, alto saxophone; Fred Anderson,
tenor saxophone. Collection of Douglas Ewart.

OPPOSITE

The Joseph Jarman Quintet at the inaugural
AACM concert, Chicago, August 1965:
Charles Clark, Arthur Reed, Jarman, Bill
Brimfield, Fred Anderson. Photo by Muhal
Richard Abrams.

Outside Abraham Lincoln Center, Chicago, 1967.
Front row, left to right: unidentified young girl,
Richarda Abrams, Leroy Jenkins, John Shenoy
Jackson. *Back row, left to right:* Christopher Gaddy,
Leonard Jones, Anthony Braxton, Malachi Favors,
unidentified person, Martin "Sparx" Alexander,
Jodie Christian, Roscoe Mitchell. Photo by Peggy
Abrams.

CONCERT
THE EXPERIMENTAL BAND
Richard Abrams, Director

SUNDAY, APRIL 9, 1967   3:00 P.M. TIL 6:00 P.M.

AT LINCOLN CENTRE — 700 East Oakwood Boulevard

DONATION — $1.25 AT DOOR

Score excerpt, "Estivalf-" (1965) by Muhal Richard Abrams. Courtesy of Muhal Richard Abrams.

Nevin Wilson, Steve McCall, Gene
Dinwiddie, Reggie Willis, ca. 1967.
Photo by Muhal Richard Abrams.

Intermedia performance, Chicago, ca. 1968. Performers include Joseph
Jarman, clarinet (far left), and Douglas Ewart, saxophone (middle left).
Photo by Robert Abbott Sengstacke.

TOP

Performance with Amus Mor (David Moore), poet; Joseph Jarman, shakuhachi. Kathy Sinclair is seated fourth from left, and one of the saxophone-playing identical twins, Michael Cosmic or Phill Musra, is seated directly behind Jarman. Photo by Leonard Jones, 1968[?].

LEFT

Advertising flyer, John Cage, Joseph Jarman, and Roscoe Mitchell. Harper Theater, Chicago, 1965. Courtesy of the Jamil B. Figi Collection, JIC Don DeMicheal Archives Collection, Chicago Jazz Archive, University of Chicago Library.

Contrabass choir, ca. 1967.
Malachi Favors, Leonard
Jones, Charles Clark. Photo
by Robert Abbott Sengstacke.

A Cultural Event For All Ages

The AACM

PROUDLY PRESENT THE

TROY ROBINSON JR.
QUINTET

MONDAY, JANUARY 24, 1966 — 8:00 P.M.

ROSCOE MITCHELL
QUARTET

CLAUDINE MYERS, Vocalist

MONDAY, JANUARY 31, 1966 — 8:00 P.M.

AT

ST. JOHN GRAND LODGE — 7443 S. INGLESIDE AVE.

Advance Donation — $1.25   Donation at Door — $1.50

DONATION TICKETS MAY BE PURCHASED AT
Met Record Shops — 328 E. 58th St. — 8225 Cottage Grove
Gardner Record Distributors — 746 E. 75th Street
Ellis' Book Store — 831 East 61st Street

Advertising card for the AACM concert series
at St. John Grand Lodge, featuring the music
of Troy Robinson and Roscoe Mitchell, 1966.
Courtesy of the Jamil B. Figi Collection, JIC
Don DeMicheal Archives Collection, Chicago
Jazz Archive, University of Chicago Library.

Cover, AACM magazine, *The New Regime*, 1968. *Clockwise from lower left:* Roscoe Mitchell, Ajaramu, Lester Bowie, Muhal Richard Abrams, John Shenoy Jackson. Collection of Douglas Ewart.

New Orleans-style group photo in painter Wadsworth Jarrell's backyard, ca. 1968. The photo was used in the organization's first informational brochures. Wadsworth Jarrell's young son watches the proceedings. *Foreground, left to right:* Leo Smith (with bamboo flute), Sarnie Garrett, Muhal Richard Abrams, Wallace McMillan (with flute), Douglas Ewart (clarinet), John Stubblefield (little instruments), Steve McCall (with drumsticks), Henry Threadgill (clarinet). *Back row, on stairs:* Buford Kirkwood (alto saxophone), John Shenoy Jackson (trumpet), Lester Lashley, Martin "Sparx" Alexander (trombones). Collection of the AACM..

Teaching at the AACM School, ca. 1968. *Left to right:* Leroy Jenkins (reading from book); Ajaramu (with hat, partly obscured), M'Chaka Uba (with cello). Photo by Leonard Jones.

tem'67

OPPOSITE TOP

Performance at the University of Chicago, ca. 1968.
Left to right: Kalaparusha, tenor saxophone; Anthony
Braxton, alto saxophone; Alvin Fielder, drums.
Photo by Terry Martin.

OPPOSITE BOTTOM

The AACM Band in performance, Chicago, ca. 1968.
Left to right: Ajaramu, Anthony Braxton, Kalaparusha,
John Shenoy Jackson, Joseph Jarman, Leo Smith,
Henry Threadgill, Amina Claudine Myers (partly
obscured), Lester Lashley, Joel Brandon. Collection
of Oliver Lake.

FAREWELL CONCERT

Chicago &
Jazz new music jazz: AMER

AACM

Lester Bowie

Malachi Favors

OSCOE Mitchell

Joseph Jarman

The Art ensemble

a promise

THEY TOLD ME TO CONTINUE WHAT I WAS
DOING AND TO SPREAD JOY AND REVOLUTION.
I CHING

Saturday May 24, 8:00
The Blue Gargoyle
57th and University
$1.25

Flyer for a "farewell concert Chicago" of the Art Ensemble, May 1969. Courtesy of the Jamil B. Figi Collection, JIC Don DeMicheal Archives Collection, Chicago Jazz Archive, University of Chicago Library.

he Art Ensemble, September 1973.
itchell, Bowie, Jarman, Moye, Favors.
ioto © 2007 Michael Wilderman /
zzVisions.

he Art Ensemble of Chicago, 1973,
iris. *Left to right:* Roscoe Mitchell,
seph Jarman, Malachi Favors,
on Moye, and Lester Bowie. Photo
Leonard Jones.

Leonard Jones, Sarhanna Smith,
and Leo Smith, Germany, ca. 1971.
Collection of Wadada Leo Smith.

Lester Bowie, Paris, ca. 1970.
Photo by Leonard Jones.

Don Moye, Europe, ca. 1970.
Collection of Oliver Lake.

Rehearsal for the BYG/Actuel recording *Seasons* by Alan Silva's Celestial Communication Orchestra. *From left to right:* Ronnie Beer, Robin Kenyatta, Don Moye (mostly hidden), Roscoe Mitchell, Steve Lacy, Bernard Vitet, Joseph Jarman, Michel Portal (back to the camera), Alan Silva, Irene Aebi (mostly hidden), Malachi Favors. Maison de la Radio, Paris, December 24, 1970. Photo by Jacques Bisceglia/Vues sur scènes.

Joseph Jarman of the Art Ensemble in exultation. Festival d'Amougies, Belgium, October 25, 1969. Photo by Jacques Bisceglia/Vues sur scènes.

The AACM, ca. 1975. *Front row, left to right, partially standing or seated:* Joseph Jarman, Leroy Jenkins, Charles Wes Cochran, George Lewis, Douglas Ewart, Adegoke Steve Colson, Iqua Colson. *Back row, left to right:* Edward Wilkerson, Henry Threadgill, Leonard Jones, Kahil El'Zabar (face turned to the right), Muhal Richard Abrams, Famoudou Don Moye, Steve McCall, Roscoe Mitchell, Pete Cosey (partially obscured), Thurman Barker, John Stubblefield, James Johnson, Ajaramu, Amina Claudine Myers, Kalaparusha. Photo by Nancy Carter-Hill.

Chico Freeman, 11th Street Theatre, Chicago,
January 1978. Photo by Nancy Carter-Hill.

Wallace McMillan, ca. 1974. Photo by C. C. James.
Collection of the AACM.

OPPOSITE TOP LEFT

Rasul Siddik in performance, ca. 2000.
Photo by Lauren Deutsch.

OPPOSITE TOP RIGHT

Douglas Ewart with instruments, ca. 1975.
Photo by Nancy Carter-Hill.

OPPOSITE RIGHT

The cooperative trio Air in performance, 1975.
Steve McCall, drums; Fred Hopkins, bass;
Henry Threadgill, bass flute. Collection
of Evod Magek.

The Fred Anderson Sextet, Chicago, ca. 1975. *Left to right:* Douglas Ewart, George Lewis, Iqua Colson, Anderson, Soji Adebayo, Hank Drake, Felix Blackmon.

The Muhal Richard Abrams Big Band, Transitions East, Chicago, ca. 1975. *Left to right:* Rahmlee Michael Davis, George Lewis, Frank Gordon (partially obscured), Steve Galloway, Sabu Zawadi, Billy Howell, Walter Henderson (partially obscured), Eugene Easton, Henry Threadgill, Pete Cosey, Charles Wes Cochran (face obscured), Chico Freeman.

The new regime in New York, 1976.
Left to right: Vincent Chancey, Adegoke Steve Colson, Iqua Colson, Henry Threadgill, Steve McCall, Patricia Jones, Phillip Wilson, David Murray, Amra, Hamiet Bluiett. Collection of Iqua and Adegoke Steve Colson.

Advertising flyer for the concert series "The AACM at WKCR-FM" at Columbia University, New York, May 1977. Collection of George E. Lewis.

Mwata Bowden in rehearsal for the concert series "The AACM at WKCR-FM" at Columbia University, May 1977. Photo by Nancy Carter-Hill.

TOP

Rehearsal for the concert series "The AACM at WKCR-FM" at Columbia University, May 1977. *Left to right:* Vandy Harris, Douglas Ewart, Martin "Sparx" Alexander, James Johnson (bassoonist, obscured), and Mwata Bowden. Photo by Nancy Carter-Hill.

BOTTOM

George Lewis preparing for the premiere of his *Homage to Charles Parker*, AACM Summerfest, University of Chicago, 1978. Photo by Nancy Carter-Hill.

OPPOSITE

Recording session for Roscoe Mitchell composition, *The Maze* (1978). Collection of Roscoe Mitchell. Photo by Ann Nessa.

Score excerpt, *The Maze* (1978) for eight percussionists, by Roscoe Mitchell. Collection of Roscoe Mitchell.

The AACM National Conference, 1977. *Front row:* Adegoke Steve Colson, Douglas Ewart, Roscoe Mitchell. *Second row:* Iqua Colson, Thurman Barker, John Stubblefield, Steve McCall, Kahil El'Zabar. *Third row:* George Lewis, Ajaramu, Amina Claudine Myers, Leroy Jenkins, Kalaparusha, Charles Wes Cochran (partially obscured). *Standing:* Joseph Jarman, Pete Cosey, Henry Threadgill, Leonard Jones, Malachi Favors (partially obscured), Edward Wilkerson, James Johnson, Famoudou Don Moye, Muhal Richard Abrams.

The Ethnic Heritage Ensemble, Paris, ca. 1980. Edward Wilkerson, tenor saxophone; Kahil El'Zabar, hand drum; Light Henry Huff, soprano saxophone. Photo by Jacques Laurens.

Performance, music of Amina Claudine Myers, keyboards; Reggie Nicholson, drums; Jerome Harris, bass. Photo by Mauno Hamalainen, collection of Reggie Nicholson, 1980s.

TOP

Underground Fest, Chicago, 1983. *Left to right:* Rita Warford,
Rafael Garrett, and Mwata Bowden. Photo by Lauren Deutsch.

BOTTOM

George Lewis in his studio at the Institut de Recherche et
de Coordination Acoustique / Musique (IRCAM), Paris, 1984.
Collection of Cheryl Lewis.

RIGHT

The AACM Chicago Chapter, 1982. *Standing, left to right:*
Edward House, Iqua Colson, Dushun Mosley, Ajaramu,
Ameen Muhammad, Malachi Favors, Rita Warford,
Vandy Harris, Adegoke Steve Colson, John Shenoy Jackson.
Seated, left to right: Edward Wilkerson, Light Henry Huff,
M'Chaka Uba, Ernest Khabeer Dawkins, Reggie Willis,
Mwata Bowden, Reggie Nicholson, Douglas Ewart.
Photo by Floyd Webb.

Publicity photo for the New Horizons Ensemble, 1990s. *Left to right:* Ameen Muhammad, Avreeayl Ra, Yosef Ben Israel, Ernest Khabeer Dawkins, Steve Berry, Jeff Parker. Collection of the AACM. Photo by Donald Getsug.

The Ameen Muhammad Ensemble, with
Ameen Muhammad, trumpet solo. Collection of
the AACM, 1990s. Photo by James Hollis.

Ann Ward and Janis Lane-Ewart, ca. 1990s.
Collection of Janis Lane-Ewart.

Samana in rehearsal, ca. 1994. *Left to right:* Coco Elysses, Shanta Nurullah, Maia, Nicole Mitchell. Collection of Maia. Photo by Rose Blouin.

Nicole Mitchell, flute, AACM Thirty-fifth Anniversary Festival, 1990, accompanied by Ann Ward, Maggie Brown, and Coco Elysses, singers. Photo by Lauren Deutsch.

The Experimental Band, Chicago, 1995.
Left to right: Muhal Richard Abrams,
Eddie Allen, George Lewis, Joseph
Jarman, Wadada Leo Smith, Anthony
Braxton, Roscoe Mitchell, Reggie
Nicholson, Amina Claudine Myers,
Henry Threadgill, Leroy Jenkins,
Leonard Jones. Collection of Muhal
Richard Abrams.

AACM cofounder Jodie Christian in performance, ca. 1991.
Photo by Lauren Deutsch.

Transcription excerpt, tenor saxophone solo by Fred Ander-
son on his composition "December 4th," from the CD *Fred
Anderson Quartet Live at the Velvet Lounge,* vol. 2 (Asian Improv
AIR 0054). Transcription by Paul Steinbeck.

Ann Ward in performance, early 2000s. Photo by Lauren
Deutsch.

The Experimental Band, Society for Ethical Culture, New York City, 1995. *Left to right, back row:* Amina Claudine Myers, piano; Leonard Jones, bass; Reggie Nicholson, drums; Thurman Barker, marimba; Muhal Richard Abrams, piano. *Left to right, foreground:* Roscoe Mitchell, alto saxophone; Frank Gordon, trumpet; Wadada Leo Smith, trumpet; Joseph Jarman, tenor saxophone; Wallace McMillan, baritone saxophone; George Lewis, trombone; Henry Threadgill, flute; Leroy Jenkins, violin. Collection of Muhal Richard Abrams.

The AACM and friends in Chicago, ca. 2000. *Back row, standing, left to right:* Iqua Colson, Nicole Mitchell, Martin "Sparx" Alexander (mostly obscured), James Johnson, Wallace McMillan, Ben Ward, Ernest Khabeer Dawkins, G'Ra, Oliver Lake (partly obscured), Ann Ward, Art Turk Burton (partly obscured), Taalib-Din Ziyad, Dushun Mosley, Thurman Barker, Edward Wilkerson, Malachi Thompson, Hanah Jon Taylor. *Front, seated, left to right:* Ari Brown, Isaiah Jackson, Douglas Ewart, Mwata Bowden, Maia, Joseph Jarman, Leroy Jenkins, Ameen Muhammad. Photo by Lauren Deutsch.

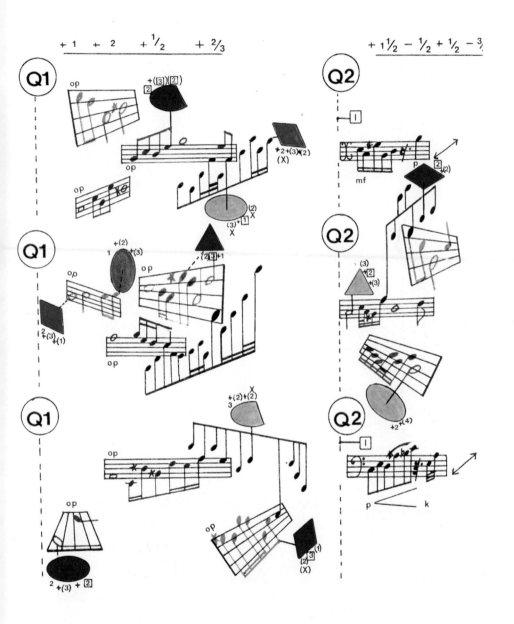

Score excerpt, *Composition no. 76*, by Anthony Braxton (1977). Courtesy of the composer.

Score excerpt, *Color Ankhrasmation-1: Universal Music of the Spheres, set 1–8* (1998), by Ishmael Wadada Leo Smith. Collection of George E. Lewis.

Douglas Ewart, *Duppy Conqueror*, mixed media. Collection of Douglas Ewart.
Photo by Warwick Green.

Samana, ca. 1990s. *Left to right:* Maia, Nicole Mitchell, Aquilla Sadalla, Coco Elysses, Shanta Nurullah.
Photo by Rose Blouin.

As the year 1969 emerged, the AACM was becoming a group of young and ambitious artists who were eager for their music to gain a hearing, and who had already gained some actual national and even international notoriety for their efforts, something that most musicians never achieve. As John Stubblefield put it, "Everybody felt that we had done a lot of things in Chicago. What more was left? Everybody was starting to branch out." Thus, as Bowie, always the practical one, realized, "The thing we were trying to figure out was how we were going to survive playing this music which was so different from anything else. To figure out a way to survive doing what we liked was the issue; and I've always been good at that sort of thing. Since I saw that we was a happening thing, then it was just a matter of logistics."[6]

Moreover, it was becoming clear to a number of AACM musicians that change was needed to nurture and sustain the atmosphere of openness and mobility that they had sought to foster. For those who left, this urge for change was undoubtedly deeply felt as a matter of sheer survival, both spiritually and physically. As Wadada Leo Smith recalled, the deaths of Clark and Gaddy made it imperative to "get the hell out of here, because we were dying." In 1967, some critics cited the lack of work in Chicago as evidence of the music's noncommercial bonafides, a prime criterion for framing the music as a species of art that was influenced by Frankfurt School critiques of mass culture.[7] Of course, the musicians felt differently. Bowie noted that "we couldn't make a living in Chicago. As long as we was in Chicago, Roscoe had to work his straight gig, I had to keep with Jackie Wilson or whoever. . . . We realized that we had to do our thing with a planetary approach. We had to hit the world market. We couldn't localize. It just could not be Chicago or New York. *The only way for us to survive was to develop a world audience.*"[8]

Some contention still exists among the older members of the collective concerning which AACM members had been the first to develop the idea of going to Europe. In fact, the answer is rather clear. Landing in a suburb of Amsterdam in 1967 with his wife Roberta and young daughter Chrissie, AACM cofounder Steve McCall was performing with the most illustrious of the previous generation of U.S. expatriates, Dexter Gordon and Don Byas. As McCall's mother told me, McCall quickly got to know Michiel de Ruyter, perhaps the most important postwar producer and radio personality in the Netherlands. "De Ruyter's mother lived on the outskirts of Amsterdam," Mrs. McCall told me. "Don Byas lived in the same area. She saw Steve, his wife, and baby, and said, 'You should not be living in a hotel with a wife and baby.' She turned her house over to him, left her house and everything in it."[9]

Except for Gene Dinwiddie and Sandra Lashley, there seemed to be little movement among AACM members toward New York, the traditional mecca for jazz-identified musicians. Perhaps the somewhat negative experiences that Jarman and Mitchell had at Slug's and other New York venues were less than encouraging. More crucial, however, was that unlike New York, the AACM had received an actual invitation to come to Europe. As Malachi Favors remembered it, sometime in the spring of 1969, the news that the Art Ensemble was headed for Europe electrified a midday AACM meeting.

Claude Delcloo, a Paris-based drummer, had been active as a producer for Actuel-BYG, a new French record label created in the wake of the events of May 1968 whose name bore the initials of its founders, producers Fernand Boruso, Jean-Luc Young, and Jean Georgakarakos. Delcloo had been listening to the AACM recordings and reading the reviews in European journals. A letter from Delcloo to the AACM is reprinted in the first issue of the AACM newsletter, *The New Regime,* published in 1968. The letter begins with the salutation "Dear Richard," indicating that in all probability, Delcloo and Muhal Richard Abrams were already in correspondence earlier that year. According to the letter, Delcloo had created his own magazine, *Actuel,* which had recently featured an article on the AACM. Delcloo projected future articles and reviews on Joseph Jarman and Leroy Jenkins, and indicated a willingness to publish articles by the members themselves. Wearing his producer hat, Delcloo requested that he be sent some AACM and Artistic Heritage Ensemble recordings, with a view toward selling them in France. What came next must have piqued great interest in that AACM meeting. "I think in a few time we'll have money enough to invite some American groups, and to give them some work," Delcloo wrote. "Sonny Murray is working with us and we're waiting for Alan Silva. I'm making a big band of 18 pieces and we're two drummers, Steve McCall and me. Ambrose Jackson is in the trumpet's section."[10]

Now Roscoe Mitchell, Lester Bowie, and Joseph Jarman were particularly excited about the prospect of taking their music to Europe, but Malachi Favors was somewhat less sanguine. For Favors and other qualified musicians who came of musical age in the 1950s, the South Side of Chicago had indeed been "the greatest entertainment section in the world."[11] "I wasn't for it at all," Favors told Chicago Beau in an interview. "The cats had to coax me into going. First of all I don't like planes. Second of all, I just felt that the music should stay where it is, and people should come and check out the music where it originates, which never really would have happened because of the poor interest in our community."[12] Indeed, anyone could see that the salad days of the South Side were now over. Moreover, for the adventurous and transgressive new music to which Favors and his AACM colleagues were now committed, those glory days had never really existed.

Anthony Braxton's recollection of the genesis of the European initiatives differs considerably from the most canonical account. "The idea of going to Europe wasn't the Art Ensemble's idea," he told me in our interview. "It was either my idea or Leo's idea or Leroy Jenkins's idea. We talked about it, planned the move, went and told the guys in the AACM, so that they would know what we were planning to do." The Braxton-Smith-Jenkins cooperative trio had already recorded *Three Compositions of New Jazz* under Braxton's name in 1968,[13] and Leroy Jenkins's recollection partly corroborates Braxton's account. "Braxton, Leo and myself were talking about going to Europe," Jenkins recalled. "What happened is that we were fatmouthing and told everybody that we were going to Europe. And the Art Ensemble was very competitive, always have been." From here, Braxton picks up the story:

> Bowie said, Aw man, you guys are thinking about going to Europe?
> We need you here. If you guys go, you're going to mess up the whole
> organization. We depended upon you guys. We need black power, we
> need solidarity. Right after that, the Art Ensemble sat down, created their
> strategy, got their buses, went into debt, got their instruments fixed. They
> informed us of their departure date about three or four days before they
> were about to leave. As they said goodbye to us, they said, "We're taking
> the AACM to Europe!" We said, What?

As Jenkins put it, "When they found out we were going—that's our concept of it—Bowie started selling his furniture in his house to get the money. Got them some money and went all on the move. The Art Ensemble beat us to the draw." Another, perhaps crucial, major change was that Mitchell, Favors, Bowie, and Jarman decided to transform their partnership into the kind of total collective that the AACM itself exemplified. To further this new conception, Mitchell apparently agreed that the name "Roscoe Mitchell Art Ensemble," signifying his personal leadership of the group, would be dropped. On May 28, 1969, four days after a Chicago farewell concert of the newly christened group, "The Art Ensemble"— Bowie, his wife Fontella Bass, Jarman, Mitchell, and Favors—boarded the S.S. *United States,* bound for France. According to *Down Beat,* the musicians planned to remain in Europe for "an indefinite period."[14]

Le Nouveau Paris Noir: Collectivity, Competition, and Excitement

Paris already enjoyed a long-standing reputation for welcoming black American culture, and was now perhaps the most accommodating of any city in the world to this newest American experimental music. However, despite the fact that black postbebop musicians of the 1960s had an enormous and lasting impact on Parisian cultural life, their activities are rarely mentioned in either historical or fictional accounts.[15] The omission seems particularly curious given the congruence of these musicians' histories with the city's traditional relationship with black expatriate artists and intellectuals, and perhaps should be considered in light of sociologist Bennetta Jules-Rosette's observation that the history of black American Paris is an ideologically constructed entity largely "based upon the cultural importance of the literary figures that it enshrines."[16] Here, according to Jules-Rosette, literary haunts once frequented by the likes of Chester Himes and James Baldwin became "sacralized" for tourist consumption,[17] and the sociologist's excellent survey of the literature leads one to conclude that for scholars working on histories of African Americans in Paris, the period between 1900 to the mid-1950s has been similarly sacralized in a way that post-1950s black histories have not been. In fact, the period from the 1960s onward appears to constitute a black hole as far as histories of African American Paris are concerned.

One possible reason for this takes into account the ways in which histories become mediated by generational, class, and social networks. Apparently, this newest group of late-1960s radical musicians developed a scene that rarely crossed with the earlier black expatriates. First of all, the post-1960s influx of black American musicians was younger, largely working-class, and less established than the writerly crowd. In addition, black American writers and black American musicians living in Paris pursued different métiers, placing them in dialogue with very different communities of practice, class, and social contact. For the most part, the earlier generation of black writers rarely met, socialized with, or wrote about the working-class black musicians arriving in Paris from all over the United States, as Famoudou Don Moye noticed.

There was a whole cadre of black writers, but that was a whole separate scene from "jazz" musicians. Subsequent readings of these cats, reading some of their novels and autobiographies, they talk about the music, but you can tell they didn't really know the musicians to be hanging out with them. We never really saw any of them that were like a fixture on the scene. They didn't go to any of the clubs we went to, but the clubs we went to weren't traditional jazz clubs anyway. We weren't the jazz establishment. We had our own little scene for the outcasts.

The major exceptions to this rule were poet Ted Joans, the creator of the world-famous slogan "Bird Lives," and James Baldwin. "Baldwin was on all scenes," remembered Moye. "Everybody knew him. He was a great cat. He was the leader of that black expatriate writers group. You would see him at openings and concerts, having dinner. He would show up all over the place, but not any of his boys." Joans lived in Paris and could be found at the famous Café Deux Magots, but was also a regular among the "outcasts" creating the new music. "Ted was *the* master traveler," said Moye. "I've run into him in the middle of Africa, the north of Norway. He had a house in Timbuktu. He might show up anywhere." For the most part, however, one is tempted to speculate that a major reason why these new musicians were considered outcasts in the black American expatriate community was the strong possibility that their music was very different from what that community (with the exceptions already cited) had grown up with or understood as black music.[18]

"From the 1920s onward," Jules-Rosette writes, "Paris was seen by the black American élite as the locus of artistic freedom and expansion."[19] Certainly, these newest, working-class artists shared that dream, and whether they knew it or not, the older generation of African American expatriate artists had now been joined by an astonishing array of the finest American musicians. Chicago blues harpist Lincoln "Chicago Beau" Beauchamp, in his book of interviews with the Art Ensemble of Chicago, provides one of the very few accounts of the black expatriate cultural scene in France that includes the experimental musicians as a significant component. Beauchamp arrived in Paris in August 1969, in the wake of the cataclysmic, Europe-wide student protests of May 1968. Paris, in Beauchamp's words, had become "a nurturing cauldron for artistic expression and ideas . . . Nearly every creative act contained an element of revolution, protest, discontent, or an appeal for peace."[20]

Once the word was out that a new and exciting group of musicians would soon arrive, more established French music magazines began to take notice. The Delmark and Nessa recordings by Jarman, Abrams, and Bowie were cited in the May 1969 edition of *Jazz Hot* as new events from "la nouvelle vague" and "l'école de Chicago."[21] Meanwhile, the Art Ensemble checked into a hotel in the Place St. Michel,[22] and immediately hit the streets to imbibe the exciting atmosphere. A Left Bank hotel such as the Buci was twenty francs a night for a room with a shared WC, and one quickly ran into the cream of the musicians who had spearheaded the free jazz revolution, such as pianists Bobby Few and Mal Waldron, saxophonists Frank Wright and Marion Brown, drummer Muhammad Ali, and bassist Alan Silva.[23] The AEC's first performance, at the Théâtre du Lucernaire in Montparnasse, took place on June 12, 1969, in a program opposite the "Free Action Music Orchestra" with pianist François Tusques, saxophonist Ken Terroade, trumpeter Bernard Vitet, bassist Beb Guérin, and drummer Claude Delcloo. The theater was already well known for presenting avant-garde musical and theatrical productions across a variety of genres, but had been presenting events under the banner of "experimental jazz" for only a couple of months at the time of the AEC events.[24]

The Art Ensemble concerts at the Lucernaire became an immediate sensation. The group's unusual hybrid of energy, multi-instrumentalism, humor, silence, found sounds and homemade instruments—and most crucially, extended collective improvisation instead of heroic individual solos—proved revelatory to European audiences. Writer Daniel Caux, reviewing a group whose name had suddenly become "The Art Ensemble of Chicago" at the Lucernaire, seemed overwhelmed at the complexity of the scene facing concertgoers:

> The stage of this curious, 140-seat theater is nearly entirely overrun by a multitude of instruments: xylophones, bassoon, sarrusophone, various saxophones, clarinets, banjo, cymbals, gongs, bells, bass drum, balafon, rattles etc. . . . The first night, listeners were surprised to see Joseph Jarman, his naked torso and his face painted, passing slowly through the aisles murmuring a poem while the bassist Malachi Favors, wearing a mask of terror, screamed curses at Lester Bowie, and Roscoe Mitchell operated various car horns.[25]

The writer of the program note for the Lucernaire performances could not resist framing the AEC in terms of an updated version of the "jungle" trope that had been active for black artists since the young Josephine Baker first wiggled her charming derriere in the faces of delighted 1920s Parisians. The invocation of La Baker underscored the writer's sense of fascination at the sheer experience of the spectacle:

> They are black. When you venture into their cave at the Lucernaire, rue Odessa, you believe that you are at a magical rite. Meditative and serious, four men explore a jungle of Baroque instruments: brass, strings, and all kinds of percussion. By turns austere, violent, reverent, and wild, such is the AACM of Chicago, which during July is presenting one of the most fantastic spectacles of free jazz that one could imagine.[26]

Attempting to describe the range of what a visitor to the Lucernaire might encounter, the writer wittily compares the Art Ensemble with European contemporary music, to the disadvantage of the latter's presumed aesthetic authority:

> It sounds like Xenakis. . . . Wait, there's Stockhausen, with a beat to boot—here a pop progression, there we're a bit bored—Klangfarben-melodie—etc., etc. The AACM does everything. Coming into the Lucernaire, watch out for how they're picking your pockets; you'll be beaten, robbed, then abused, and sent back totally naked and crying for your mother. But certainly not back home. . . . If you knew how to listen to the AACM of Chicago, you would become, all at once, a subversive terrorist. You'll see how intoxicating it is to kidnap Boulez, to kill Berio, or to beat up Xenakis.[27]

The description seems to support the notion that the work of the Art Ensemble of Chicago, where visual collage and historical montage combine, could exemplify Jacques Derrida's observation that collage/montage is the quintessential postmodern form of expression.[28] The depictive aspect of the work seems to lead inexorably to Lester Bowie's summary of their music as foreshortening the distance between art and the everyday world: "It's a music free and improvised, but difficult . . . like your life."[29]

Roscoe Mitchell saw Paris as "a total musical environment that existed twenty-four hours a day if you wanted to." Inevitably, however, after the first glow of Parisian nightlife, these sons of the Great Migration found it necessary to husband their resources. Searching for a cheaper place to live, the Art Ensemble met a music-loving doctor who, as Joseph Jarman recalled, presented them with a distinctive solution to their housing problem. "He said they had space at this insane asylum," Jarman told Chicago Beau. "It was probably illegal but we didn't care. I remember Alan Silva had stayed there. Becky Friend had stayed there. I recall we were out of funds, and staying there gave us an opportunity to gather some bucks. We stayed there and they would have lunch everyday."[30] The ironic gloss on Peter Weiss's *Marat/Sade* is hard to avoid here, and somehow seems fitting in the light of the unique relationship between art and life that the Art Ensemble's work asserted. "We could go in and out of that hospital, and you'd see the patients wandering around," said Jarman. "We were like patients too—it was weird. There were some restrictions there, but we were able to handle it. I remember this one woman used to walk past our room and glare in."[31]

Eventually the musicians found an old farmhouse in Saint-Leu-la-Forêt, about eighteen kilometers north of Paris, near Le Bourget, the old airport where Charles Lindbergh landed in 1927. The relative isolation in the area allowed greater individual privacy, as well as space to house and rehearse the increasingly extended instrumental setups the group was developing, where literally thousands of instruments of every description would be on-stage. The group was already well known for its extended daily rehearsals; as a program note affirmed, "They work at least five hours per day, five hours spent seeking new sonorities, to make the instruments say what they really aren't accustomed to saying."[32] In addition to offering space for rehearsals that would have been prohibitively expensive in the city, having a house in the country also removed the group from too-easy access to the Parisian nightlife scene, potentially fostering greater clarity in their business decisions.

The July-August edition of France's flagship magazine, *Jazz,* announced the early-June arrival in Paris of Roscoe Mitchell, Joseph Jarman, Malachi Favors, Lester Bowie, "and Mrs. Bowie (better known as a singer under the name of Fontella Bass)," as well as the imminent arrival, by the end of June, of Anthony Braxton, Leroy Jenkins, and Leo Smith.[33] Jenkins recalled that Braxton had been put a bit out of sorts by the Art Ensemble's move to Europe. "They got there, man. Braxton was so mad. . . . He was upset, terribly, because they had beat us there, because he was very competitive too, especially with Roscoe."[34] In any event, Braxton left for Paris soon after the Art Ensemble's departure, arriving just in time for one of their Lucernaire performances.

I said, you guys haven't seen the last of me. About a month later, in Montparnasse, I had one of those moments that I'll never forget. I'm walking down the street and there's Joseph coming to the Lucernaire. Joseph looked up and saw me, and his eyes got so big. I said, Hello Jarman. I told you, you hadn't seen the last of me. He could not believe it, because they thought they had done a number on us, and had left us.

Apparently, whatever dislocations existed were quickly patched up, and a three-day run at the American Center in Paris in late June 1969 featured Braxton performing with the Art Ensemble. A concert review described the overtly theatrical presentation as a "sensation": "They created an astounding, dream-like climate: confetti, streamers, and especially smoke (you couldn't see more than a meter away), musicians moving around the room, emerging abruptly from the smoke."[35] A month or so after Braxton's departure, Leroy Jenkins, Leo Smith, and Smith's future spouse Kathy Sinclair, the sister of John Sinclair, landed in Le Havre, and headed directly for Paris, where Steve McCall and his family had been based for at least a year, perhaps even living at the American Center.

"Braxton never really communicated back with us after he left," Smith recalled, "and we didn't have any phone numbers."

Nobody met us, so we got a hotel. The next day, early in the morning, we went trying to find anybody we could see. We walked past the American Center, and we saw some drums sitting out there. Leroy said, those are Steve McCall's drums. So we went in and found out that Steve had played there the night before, and they were in fact his drums, and that Steve was coming there sometime later, so we met Steve.[36]

McCall, always in touch with the situation, helped Smith and Jenkins find Braxton, who was staying with the Art Ensemble at the farmhouse in Saint-Leu-la-Forêt. The Art Ensemble farmhouse had plenty of space to welcome the three additional newcomers from home before they set out to locate their own, longer-term housing around Paris. Smith had saved enough money "to get by for maybe a month." Jenkins, who had worked steadily as a schoolteacher before coming to Paris, was in a somewhat less delicate financial position. Braxton and Jenkins elected to follow the Art Ensemble's example, first finding a place outside Paris and eventually moving into the city proper, but Smith decided to try to find an apartment in town right away. Smith noticed that finding suitable housing in Paris was complicated not only by his financial status, but by some of the same issues they had encountered in the United States, despite the rhetoric of the absence of such things in Europe.

> A lot of the places in the city had problems renting to black guys. Some of the places I went to, they were kind of like some of those places in America where you call up and talk about them, have somebody call and talk about them, then you go to deal it and it doesn't exist any more. One of the real estate people told me directly that certain areas, you could live in. You could live in an area where the Arabs lived in. Certain areas, you could get a place, but somebody would have to get it for you. I finally got a place at the end of town, Porte d'Orléans, good neighborhood. Steve [McCall] lived near there too. I rented from a British guy that was an absentee.

Like the Art Ensemble, the Paris debut of the Braxton-Smith-Jenkins-McCall quartet was a month-long stay at the Théâtre du Lucernaire,[37] which by now had become a showcase for the new music—"our Lincoln Center," as Leroy Jenkins put it. The bracing, even breathtaking attention that their music received lifted the spirits of the AACM musicians in Paris, as they realized that their music was succeeding in an international arena. It was evident to concertgoers that the music of "l'école de Chicago" had broken sharply with the sustained high-energy performances that characterized 1960s free jazz. Quick changes of mood were the rule, ranging from the reverent to the ludic. A quiet, sustained, "spiritual" texture offered by one musician might be rudely interrupted by an ah-ooh-gah horn or a field holler from another. A New Orleans–style brass fanfare would quickly be dunked in a roiling sea of tuned metal trash cans. An ironically demented fake-bebop theme could be cut up into a series of miniatures, punctuated by long silences and derisively terminated by a Marx Brothers raspberry.

This was deformation of mastery, indeed. No sound was excluded and no tradition was sacrosanct, and French audiences and the jazz press quickly fell in love with the ruptures and surprises. Leo Smith, speaking in 1999, said that "all of us for the first time could see that our music means something." The audiences for the events sometimes approached rock-concert levels. In the wake of Woodstock and May 1968, enormous festivals such as Actuel and Chateauvallon, combining musics of all kinds, drew hundreds of thousands from around Europe in this pre-Schengen era of closed borders between European countries. AACM musicians found themselves sharing the bill with Frank Zappa, with an equal claim to audience affection. Roscoe Mitchell recalls that "these were big events, where they had the police for crowds of this size. The stuff was starting to border on that kind of thing, like a rock concert. The music was exciting and everybody felt really excited about it, like this concert at the Maubert-Mutualité with Ornette's group and Braxton's group and the Art Ensemble. You had packed houses. You couldn't get in if you didn't get there in time."

Speaking in 1998, Lester Bowie recalled that "we were finally playing the music that we like to play. We were having a ball, I mean we were having a ball—the cats were going crazy. . . . Then there's just the idea that we were over there making it. We supported our families, we had a nice house."[38] As Leroy Jenkins summarized it, "Country boys from Chicago, we weren't used to that kind of thing."[39]

The Art Ensemble of Chicago was one of the AACM ensembles that most radically exemplified the collective conception of the AACM as a whole. Following the AACM model, decisions that impacted the group business were taken collectively in meetings. Roscoe Mitchell explained why:

> One of the reasons why the Art Ensemble was successful was because it was perceived as a unit and you had to deal with it as a unit. It's easier to do that kind of work when you're young. You have a certain goal as a collective. That put us in a better slot to take care of our business. By having a collective, we had our means to get around. We weren't just out there like—you know, somebody changes their mind and the only thing you got is a Metro ticket.

Braxton, Smith, Jenkins, and McCall had aspirations in the same direction, but in the Parisian pressure cooker, with the increased attention paid to particular members of the group, a collective orientation proved difficult to sustain. As Leroy Jenkins recalled of the group's 1968 Delmark recording, "Even though it was Braxton's recording date, *Three Compositions,* that started us off, we had decided that the group was going to be a co-op. But as it turned out, Braxton, being the more competitive, his name seemed to have gotten out there more easily than ours, so the group was quite often referred to as the Anthony Braxton Trio, or quartet, since we added Steve McCall when we got to Paris."

Moreover, according to Jenkins, "When we got there, Roscoe and the

Art Ensemble were entrenched. They had the connections right away, so we were always playing second fiddle to them, all the time we were there. That frustrated us a lot, Braxton more so than anybody." Published reviews comparing the Art Ensemble's work with that of Braxton-Jenkins-Smith-McCall were also a source of consternation, possibly destabilizing attempts at collectivity. Even so, as Leo Smith recalled, "We were quite popular. Every event had overflowing crowds. We had interviews, radio and papers."

Indeed, press reception for the AACM musicians in France was voluminous and overwhelmingly positive. Already in October 1969, a photo of Joseph Jarman on the cover of *Jazz Hot* announced a feature story on the AACM. Moreover, critical attention was by no means limited to the jazz press. One widely used quote from *Le Nouvel Observateur,* one of the leading French newsweeklies, likened the AEC's work to "a living sculpture."[40] On Christmas Eve 1969, a poem and essay by Joseph Jarman occupied an entire page in *Le monde,* the major French newspaper, on the occasion of the release of the Art Ensemble's Paris-recorded album, *People in Sorrow.*[41] A program note from a 1969 Lille concert quoted Philippe Adler in *L'express,* another important newsweekly, describing the Art Ensemble as creating "a music which seems to leave the earth, passionate and sumptuous." The author declared that the AEC "incorporate everything of value, classical, European, Hindu, African, seemingly without any prohibition against any kind of process of working with sound."[42] The Braxton-Smith-Jenkins-McCall performances garnered similar notice. The October 1969 issue of *Jazz* presented a rave review of a concert featuring the group (billed as the "Anthony Braxton Quartet"), along with the Art Ensemble of Chicago and the Ornette Coleman Quartet. In another article in the same issue, short photo profiles of Braxton, Jenkins, and Leo Smith were shown under the caption "The New Leaders of the New Music."[43]

The AACM musicians recorded prolifically during their Paris sojourn. A photo essay in the September 1969 issue of *Jazz* announced a massive recording project aimed at documenting the work of a number of "free jazz" musicians. The report stated that the impetus for the project had come from Jean Georgakarakos, the co-owner of BYG Records, and his producer, drummer Claude Delcloo. According to the article, BYG's aim was to record twenty albums within one month, and everything began when Delcloo "imported" (the article placed this term in quotes) the musicians from the AACM.[44] Large photos of Braxton, Mitchell, Bowie, and Favors were featured in the article; Bowie was shown behind his trumpet case with a Chicago-made AACM bumper sticker—"AACM: Music Power"—prominently showing.[45]

On July 7, barely a month after their arrival in Paris, Mitchell, Jarman, Favors, and Bowie recorded their first album. Four other Art Ensemble recording sessions quickly followed, including two for BYG, one for Polydor, and one for Le Chant du Monde, and the Braxton-Smith-Jenkins-McCall group recorded at least two BYG albums.[46] Others to be recorded included the Martinican trumpeter and composer Jacques Coursil, who recorded his *Black Suite* with Anthony Braxton, and most prominently, saxophonist Archie Shepp, who was working with pianist Dave Burrell, drummer Sunny Murray, trombonists Grachan Moncur and Clifford Thornton, and bassist Alan Silva. Moncur recorded an ensemble featuring Mitchell, Silva, Burrell, and drummer Andrew Cyrille.

As Leo Smith remembers, many of the BYG recording sessions had a kind of ad hoc, impromptu, even insouciant quality. "When we went to Paris," Smith recalled, "if you wanted a gig, you wanted to be on somebody's record, and you weren't invited, all you had to do was go to the BYG studio with your horn. The guy would say, Oh, you have your horn. Come and play on this piece. Sometimes you could go there without your horn and they'd give you a horn to play." That the now-prominent bright line between "inside" and "outside" musicians was viewed as something of a fabrication by the musicians working in Paris was evident from the personnel for another BYG Shepp recording, *Yasmina, A Black Woman*. The session featured, along with Bowie, Favors, and Mitchell, the finest of the 1950s generation of musicians, including saxophonist Hank Mobley, and drummers Philly Joe Jones and Arthur Taylor.[47]

The notion of a separate "Chicago school" with significant methodological and sonic differences from the older New York free jazz had taken hold by the time that writer Daniel Caux provided the first major European interview with AACM musicians in October 1969. The interviewer recognized that "whether in their music or in life, one will find among members of the AACM a marked distrust of any cult of personality, in favor of the collective spirit."[48] Thus, in that spirit, the interview itself would be a collective one, with input from most of the new arrivals. The interview participants included Lester Bowie, Malachi Favors, Joseph Jarman, Leroy Jenkins, Roscoe Mitchell, and Leo Smith, all of whom were pictured in the article. Although not present, Anthony Braxton and Steve McCall were also pictured, rounding out the AACM contingent in Paris. The interview took place in the Art

Ensemble compound in Saint-Leu-la-Forêt, and Lester Bowie was evidently designated by the musicians to handle informational questions, somewhat in the manner of a press secretary.

The discussion was frank, playful, and serious by turns, expressing the extreme optimism of the young musicians. They sought to throw off old stereotypes and comparisons with other musicians, and evinced a sophisticated media strategy that challenged the power of the press. The article begins with Bowie reciting eight of the nine purposes of the AACM, which the interviewer duly translated, more or less verbatim. Bowie follows the standard history in attributing the founding of the organization to Richard Abrams, Jodie Christian, Phil Cohran, and Steve McCall, and adds Malachi Favors (who in a later interview, denied having been a founder and names the other four).[49] Bowie further asserted that the trip to Europe had been "submitted to the board of directors" of the AACM, of which Bowie, as the article reminded the reader, was still the president.[50]

To the question of whether the AACM is "popular," Bowie responded that "if by 'popular' you mean money, well, no, the AACM doesn't make a lot of money . . . but the Association is well known in musical circles, all the musicians have heard of it."[51] Bowie also mentioned the St. Louis and Detroit movements, but in response to a question about contact with Archie Shepp, Albert Ayler, LeRoi Jones, or other New York figures, Joseph Jarman spoke up in a diplomatic tone. "We really tried to get together with people in New York, but apparently, there were problems. However, they are aware of the existence of the AACM; a move was made towards them. We don't want to attack people or tell them what to do. We're still waiting . . . maybe a day will appear and we'll able to establish a common program."[52]

The interviewer's query about connections between the AACM with the work of Sun Ra began by citing a frequent comparison, based on the notion of two groups coming from Chicago with superficially similar methods and provenance, such as multiple percussion, theatrical forms, and the fact of being black. While hastening to assure the musicians that "to us your approach seems radically different,"[53] the interviewer pops the question of Sun Ra's influence nonetheless. The musicians responded with more or less subtle assertions of distance that correspond well with their histories. Mitchell made the very obvious, timeline-based point that "when I was in the army, [Sun Ra] was still in Chicago, but when I came back, he was in New York."[54] Malachi Favors said, chuckling, that he attended only one rehearsal of the Arkestra. Leroy Jenkins spoke up for the first time on this question: "If we're influenced by Sun Ra, so we are, as much by all that we live, what we see, what we hear, what we feel. No force, no influence is predominant. In the course of my life, Johnny Griffin could have as much importance for me as Sun Ra."[55]

Jarman made the further point, evident to those who actually knew the music, that the Sun Ra who left Chicago in 1961 was not the New York Sun Ra of 1965: "It should be said that when he left Chicago, he was not yet the Sun Ra that we know from *Heliocentric Worlds,* the New York Sun Ra. His evolution and ours proceeded without intersecting."[56] The reference to a recording, rather than direct contact, strongly indicates that recordings were the major transmission route between the ideas of Sun Ra and this first generation of AACM musicians. At this point, Jarman decides to indulge in a bit of the antipatriarchal iconoclasm for which the AACM became noted. "In our eyes, heroes, gods, masters, do not exist," he intoned. "We love and respect every musician, whether from the past, the future or . . . someone who doesn't yet exist . . . just as much as birdsong interests us. To be here drinking a Coke can influence the process of musical creation as much as anything."[57]

At this point, the assembled musicians moved to reject the notion that their music "is associated nevertheless with what is called New Thing or Free Jazz. . . . What does tradition mean to you, the blues, for instance?"[58] Leo Smith declared his desire to integrate "all forms of music," without separating them in terms of fixed notions of "traditions," saying that "everything and anything is valuable." Jarman went further in an impassioned soliloquy: "We play the blues, we play jazz, rock, Spanish music, gypsy, African, classical music, contemporary European music, vodun . . . everything that you'll want . . . because finally, it's 'music' that we play: we create sounds, period."[59]

Inevitably, in the atmosphere of vicarious Black Power that had captured the French imagination, the interviewer asked about relationships to political organizations, "par example, les Black Panthers?" Jarman responded that direct affiliation with political associations would be "foreign to the intentions of the AACM."[60] Such associations, Jarman made clear, were strictly personal, rather than organizationally mandated. Rather, as Jarman put it, the nine purposes of the AACM comprised its social and political position: "The music is a response to these problems: that means that when people hear it, they can experience a reaction to these problems. Thanks to the music, they can in turn become more active and more responsible."[61]

Lester Bowie cautioned against the danger of connecting a given musician with a preconceived notion of the "correct" audience or the "proper" musical method: "It's dangerous to box a musician into a definition, to say that he plays in a particular way and that this way will be especially appreciated by a particular audience. We condemn this kind of attitude. The audience is everywhere. . . . We use everything that can serve our goals, our desires. There doesn't have to be a limit."[62] Soon after, Bowie turned the tables on the interviewer, subtly critiquing the relatively generic questions that had been asked, and calling for a new criticism to match this new music: "Basically, the jazz press needs to reevaluate what's happening now in the music. . . . We want people like you to go deeper into their way of writing about the music. You need to invent a new way of talking about things, to discover all this life in its originality. . . . For you also, that will be beneficial because it's life itself that this is about."[63]

With this, Bowie proclaimed that "we intend to establish the AACM everywhere, in every corner of the universe. That kind of ambition requires a serious approach to information."[64]

Black experimental musicians in Paris developed their own preferred environments that loomed far larger in their sight than places like the Café Deux Magots, the Brasserie Lipp, or Leroy Haynes's soul food restaurant, prominent among the locales that have now achieved canonical status for African American histories in the city. The nightclub most frequented by black American musicians was not the expensive Bricktop's, but the suitably funky Chat Qui Pêche. According to Malachi Favors, "Some of them cats down there were pugs, man, they'd fight quick. In fact it got to the place that they had an article in the paper which warned the French about the Chat Qui Pêche, because of the rough and tough musicians that were hanging out there. Man, there were rough cats hanging out down there: Philly Joe, Sunny Murray, Reverend Frank Wright; and you know he was rough."[65]

Clubs such as the Chat Qui Pêche and Storyville jostled for the attention of audiences and denizens of the scene with a new kind of venue, the American Center on Boulevard Raspail in the 14th arrondissement. "Everybody used to play there," Famoudou Don Moye recalled." The American Students and Artists Center was founded in 1931 by the dean of the American Episcopal Cathedral in Paris, Frederick Warren Beekman, who was said to "own" New York's *Social Register*. The center was modeled after the YMCA, and was intended to encourage Americans to experience French culture, while at the same time, in the declining days of American Prohibition, providing an alternative to the "corrupting" environment of the

Parisian cafe. Given its pedigree, the largely privately funded center quickly gained upper-class respectability. After World War II, however, the center became a haven for American experimental artists of the 1950s and 1960s, changing what one writer called its "Ivy-League, clubby atmosphere."[66]

In 1969, Henry Pillsbury, an heir to the Minneapolis flour fortune, took over as executive director of the center. Under his leadership, the center extended and broadened its focus as a prime meeting place for experimental musicians, choreographers, and visual, theater, and performance artists. The center presented concerts by experimental musicians from a variety of backgrounds, including the AACM musicians, the New York free jazz contingent, and musicians such as Musica Elettronica Viva, Terry Riley, and La Monte Young. Moreover, the center provided rehearsal space, and even temporary housing and storage space for artists. In the wake of May 1968, the center's bohemian image ("like a small Berkeley," as one person put it)[67] came in for considerable criticism. Pillsbury's own considerable personal reputation served to allay most concerns, as powerful people from all segments of the U.S. political spectrum found favor with his laid-back approach to running the center. Moreover, the center's highly favorable reputation as an important part of French cultural life was enhanced by both the concerts and the center's classes for art students, which along with concert ticket sales for events, grew to provide up to 80 percent of the center's operating budget.[68]

Creating relationships with more established artists proved far easier in Paris than in the early, brief visits to New York by Mitchell and Jarman. "In America," Jarman said in an interview with Chicago Beau, "the famous never spoke to us. They would put us down as a matter of fact: 'You guys ain't playing shit.'"[69] Now, Malachi Favors could say that in Paris, he "got to meet a bunch of cats that I had just heard of or read about."[70] In Europe, AACM members developed collaborative and personal relationships with many residents and frequent visitors to the continent who had already developed extensive contacts in Europe.[71] For Mitchell, "it was a time for the younger musicians to communicate with the older guys" such as Hank Mobley, Don Byas, Johnny Griffin, Dexter Gordon, Arthur Taylor, and Philly Joe Jones, and to meet a later generation of black experimentalists, such as Ornette Coleman, Archie Shepp, Cal Massey, Sunny Murray, Grachan Moncur, and Ed Blackwell. Steve McCall, already well known from having performed with so many of these musicians, helped the newcomers gain entrée into the expatriate and itinerant musicians' community in Paris.[72]

Braxton biographer Ronald Radano saw the AACM Paris trip as motivated by the musicians' desire to reap the rewards that a career in jazz offered. "Looking to the future for a career in jazz, they had met face to face with the reality of making a living in the music business, a world in which success required concessions to the market."[73] It is difficult to see, however, exactly what market the AACM Paris contingent might have been conceding to. On the contrary, on the basis of reception it would seem reasonable to conclude that rather than acceding to demands for sounds that articulated known forms, AACM musicians working in Paris simply presented their own music as they had been doing in Chicago. Moreover, rather than trying to fit in with an existing scene with defined borders of aesthetics, method, and practice, AACM musicians in Paris made no attempt to contextualize the work solely within the jazz art world. Rather, they took work wherever they could, and regularly moved outside the frame of jazz, collaborating with a wide range of artists.

"That scene that Joseph and I were on at that time was away from the music scene," remembered Smith in 1997. "We were making this kind of experimental French theater music. Joseph and I performed in their company, not music, but as actors." During the period, the Art Ensemble with Fontella Bass completed the soundtrack for the movie *Les Stances à Sophie*,[74] a recording whose power and lasting value outpaced the now nearly forgotten film that the music undergirded.[75] "We met some powerful directors," said Smith. "When I left, they gave a huge party in the French tradition." Jarman and Smith met the French experimental poet/chanson singer Brigitte Fontaine at a Lucernaire performance, and in November 1969, a collaborative recording session took place featuring the Art Ensemble, Fontaine, and her longtime musical partner, the percussionist and singer Areski.[76] The recording has since become an underground classic.[77] Fontaine remembers the origin of the collaboration in an Internet interview:

> It was the guy I was living with at that time, an American cameraman living in France. We were playing, Areski and me, in a theatre where the Art Ensemble of Chicago was scheduled at another hour. As it was a kind of improvised show, from time to time they happened to play a little something, as a duo or three at once. And so the guy had the idea to create a show and a record together with the Ensemble.[78]

The rather skeptical review of their first collaborative concert painted Fontaine in ironic terms as "the Kay Davis of today" (referring to one of Ellington's better-known collaborators) and claimed that the music of the Art Ensemble merely served as a foil and backdrop for Fontaine's exploitation. "She and Areski had no other ambition than to present a show where jazz is only invited, an element of the scene with the same status as the mimes, the poses, or the singer's black cape and bowler hat."[79] A later interviewer's attempt to stereotype the 1970 collaboration claimed common cause with Fontaine by noting that he himself was working with "musiciens de jazz." This viewpoint was immediately and sharply rebuffed by Fontaine, who contrasted the Art Ensemble's work with more conventional, generic musics. "Look, for me the Art Ensemble of Chicago aren't jazz musicians, just musicians. I don't like jazz, I detest jazz, I loathe jazz, jazz makes me puke. Except, of course, for the greats, those from when jazz was alive, that is, when I was very young: Thelonious Monk, Charlie Parker, Coltrane. . . . But for me, now, jazz means nothing any more."[80]

Some collaborations, particularly those that involved interfaces with the traditional infrastructure that supported European contemporary music, proved difficult or even impossible to pursue at the time. Anthony Braxton noted that "it became very clear to me that I could be successful if I would accept black exotica, but I could never have my notated music ever respected or performed. ORTF had set aside a sector, like [grotesque voice] 'Le Hot Jazz,' and it was going to be that or nothing."[81]

The Politics of Culture: Black Power and May 1968

For French intellectuals of the period, only one American critic-historian of black music really mattered: LeRoi Jones (later Amiri Baraka), whose book *Blues People* and subsequent essays were widely read and highly influential; a long entry devoted to his place in jazz history appears in a major French reference work on jazz.[82] Under the strong influence of Jones, many Parisian intellectuals, in and outside the jazz community, viewed "free jazz" in black cultural nationalist terms.[83] In 1971, *Jazz* magazine editor Philippe Carles and New Wave film director Jean-Louis Comolli, a founder of the film journal *Cahiers du Cinéma,* published the classic French treatise on the "new thing," *Free Jazz/Black Power.* The book is still practically unknown in the United States, since it was never translated into English.

More of a scholarly than a journalistic work, yet written in accessible language, *Free Jazz/Black Power* articulated a proto-postcolonial emphasis which stood in sharp contrast with nearly all Stateside accounts of the history of black music. Drawing on Jones and the work of historian Frank

Kofsky, in the Carles and Comolli account, the importance of black resistance, not only to racism, but also to a related economic and cultural imperialism from slavery forward, conditioned the emergence of black music in the United States. Black music, for Carles and Comolli, was "a music invented and played by Blacks but culturally and economically colonized by Whites."[84] Carles and Comolli were persuaded that "with free jazz, one is witness to a real political positioning of music, through the convergence of directly militant concerns, and their influence, also direct, on the very conception of the music and on its aesthetic explorations."[85]

Comparing this kind of francophone work with its U.S. counterpart, it is difficult to avoid the conclusion that analyses of the new music in French publications tended to be, if no less contentious, considerably more intellectually diverse. French jazz magazines gave wide latitude to authors to explore aesthetic issues at a theoretical depth that, except for the work of LeRoi Jones, rarely saw the light of day in the American press. Moreover, in contrast to much post-1990s American scholarship, French critiques of the 1970s positioned free jazz as a postmodernist, rather than a modernist phenomenon. Quoting Carles and Comolli concerning the "polymorphism" of the new music, the critic and musician Francis Marmande calls upon that critical language, seeing in the music a kind of rupture, "a certain lexical world that is constantly called upon ('collages,' 'mixtures,' 'borrowings' . . .), scrupulous inventories of 'quotations' or 'references' from which programs for free music records or concerts are woven."[86]

Carles and Comolli were critical of American jazz criticism for its apparent avoidance of discussions of American capitalism, as well as the field's emphasis on aesthetic autonomy to the exclusion of economic and political analysis. In part, this critique reflects the French belief that "European criticism has played—on the cultural plane if not directly on the commercial plane—a relatively more important role than American criticism."[87] At the same time, their view that mainstream U.S. critics were essentially complicit in systems of domination was rarely addressed in the United States, except by Jones and A. B. Spellman, another black critic who was highly influential in French circles. As Carles and Comolli maintained,

> Because the economic colonization of jazz by American capitalism is only one of the aspects of colonization, of the economic exploitation of Blacks by the same system: the awakening to the intolerable character of this exploitation leads the musicians, like the masses, to the need for revo-

lution. It is thus not by chance that the whole of jazz criticism, in its histories and commentaries (with the exception of black critics A. B. Spellman and LeRoi Jones), has—discreetly—said nothing about, or minimized in the name of aesthetic purism, the seriousness of the capitalist exploitation of jazz.[88]

Carles and Comolli extend Theodor Adorno's critique of the culture industry toward a direct engagement with race, by viewing the canonization and "mechanical" repetition of timeless, classical rules and aesthetic structures for jazz as an aspect of the political domination of African Americans. The two commentators were critical of both American and French commentators for their apparent insensitivity to this dynamic: "Jazz criticism, which emerged during the same era in both America and Europe, erects these dominant characteristics and, with a beautiful recklessness, elects them as transhistorical *values* of jazz; [and] blinding itself to these determinations and their historical, social, and ideological contingency, proposes them to musicians as references and models."[89]

Unlike Adorno, however, rather than condemning black musical culture for its "acceptance of castration,"[90] the French critics look directly at race as a critical component in that domination. Carles and Comolli note that the common origin myth of jazz as a harmonious "synthesis of Western and African influences" evades an examination of the economic violence and the asymmetries of power that marked that supposed synthesis. On this view, "Jazz is not an ecumenical music, but a music of divisions, of unresolved tensions and unhealed wounds."[91]

Moreover, unlike many U.S. jazz histories of the period, Carles and Comolli viewed hard bop's emphasis on "soul" not as a reaction to the "abstraction" of bebop or as nostalgic commercialism, but as an intensification of the celebration of the music's African roots that was already in place with bebop and its immediate descendants. For the French writers, Max Roach's "Garvey's Ghost" and Horace Silver's "Sister Sadie" were aspects of *le retour culturel,* a cultural homecoming, a "return to the source." Thus, in the soul music of the 1950s and 1960s, "Africanité, violence, négritude, beauté noire, nationalisme noir" [Africanity, violence, negritude, black beauty, and black nationalism] became "explicit affirmations of the new black consciousness, which extended the 'negrifying' action of *hard bop.*"[92]

This strain of jazz criticism was laudable in its inclusion of the social at a time when U.S. jazz writing followed traditional musicology in relying upon constructions of a radical autonomy of the artwork. Moreover, the two critics directly cite at length the nine AACM purposes to illustrate an important stage in the struggle against exploitation.[93] Nonetheless, some AACM musicians felt that this kind of theorizing sometimes devolved into reducing the music to an occasion for the presentation of social theory and exoticism, as well as constructing essentializing differences between various AACM approaches to music. As Leo Smith saw it, "A lot of the intellectuals on the academic scene hooked up with what was going on and there was a continuous argument about whether they liked us better than the Art Ensemble, whether one music was more 'African' than the other, or more 'contemporary'—all superficial kinds of things."

Meanwhile, a number of social theorists of the period, such as sociologist Alfred Willener, were turning to cultural production for clues to the meaning of the explosion that was May 1968. The relation between politics and emerging experimental movements often assumed center stage in such analyses. The Slovenian trombonist and composer Vinko Globokar, then resident in France, explicitly connected the activism of the period with developments in contemporary music, including an increased exploration of the possibilities of improvisation by performers and composers with a strong base in pan-European experimental music.[94] For many, however, European contemporary music, seemingly a creature of the upper classes, was hardly revolutionary. Instead, for Willener, it was the "new thing" that constituted "the most complete 'overthrow' imaginable, a revolution in earlier ways of thinking."[95] Moreover, the notion that "a kinship existed between May and various other movements, both earlier (Dada, Surrealism) and contemporary avant-garde movements in jazz, the theatre, and the cinema" led to Willener's audacious assertion that "May seemed, in turn, to explain Dada, Surrealism, Free Jazz, etc."[96]

Willener's analysis draws heavily upon Jones, as well as upon published interviews in French jazz magazines with the highly quotable Archie Shepp, himself closely aligned with Jones during this period. The idea of improvisation played a key role in Willener's analysis. "Whether collective or individual," Willener wrote, "improvisation presupposed the dialectical synthesis created by a group or an individual, redefining known elements, elements that have just been played and experienced, while inventing new elements in the course of the activity itself.[97] Asserting that the protesting students were practicing a form of collective improvisation, the practices of improvisation in jazz appeared to offer theorists such as Willener a window into the goals of the students. "There has appeared a variety of jazz, however—*free* jazz—

which claims to be revolutionary, both politically and artistically. This new departure should therefore provide a much closer parallel with a student movement that is also difficult to grasp as an entity, an *object* of projection on the part of the protagonists, and of its enemies and observers."[98]

For Willener, the abandonment of metric regularity in "free jazz" meant that "the principle of the dialectical interplay between integration and non-integration into an existing order is completely abandoned."[99] This phenomenon of "autonomization" seemed to parallel developments in May 1968 that abandoned accommodation with existing structures of authority, including those that had been traditionally constituted historically. Musicians, according to Willener, were

> improvising according to a personal itinerary, without referring, even implicitly, to an external order. This liberation through a very advanced autonomization is a movement towards individuality. Everyone has his own rhythm, his own harmony, his own *sound*. . . . The individual finds his *own* nature, and also that of many other individuals. The solution is not individualism, but the discovery through a process of creation—of the work and of oneself.[100]

For post-May society, on this view, the consequences of similar feelings of autonomization and the need for spontaneity were being experienced not by isolated individuals, but by an entire generation. Describing a kind of postmodernism, Willener maintains that the procedures of post-1960s African American improvisors announced the emergence of

> the image of a society in which great diversity and permanent change will be accepted. This new type of personality, opposed to rules, demands the non-fixation, even the diversity, of individuals, thus leading to constant redefinitions of what is ever only provisionally attained. The abandonment of a style that one has developed oneself (Coltrane), of an instrument that one knows very well (Coleman), and many other procedures reveal what, in May, was called "scuttling."[101]

Willener advances the notion that "free jazz" represented "an ever-changing, *immediate exteriorization* of life; it is therefore what, at a particular moment, those who are creating it (musicians and audience, in their reciprocal relations) *are*."[102] To this extent, Willener's ideas do not so much explain May 1968 as they take aspects of its behavior and graft them onto notions of jazz based in primitivism, exoticism, and immediate gratification. To be sure, Willener himself expressed the major caveat that "the politicization of a musical phenomenon, an abstract expression, does present problems."[103]

Although Willener was undoubtedly speaking of methodological and analytic issues, from the standpoint of the musicians, the nationalist straitjacket that the music of the AACM Paris contingent was being shoehorned into often served to limit the ways in which their music might be perceived and contextualized. For instance, a 1969 program note described the AACM itself as "an organization for struggle which brings young musicians together and adapts the principles of Black Power to the musical world: no more white intermediaries; jazz must be completely the business of Blacks."[104] Given that context, it was easy for Willener to psychologize that "the pointing of the instrument at the white audience may represent the brandishing of a machine-gun."[105] As quoted by Willener, Comolli's theory of free jazz involves a negative aesthetic: "Free jazz proceeds *by frustration*. By skilful gradations in the untenable, or the chaotic, it forces the listener to hope more and more desperately for an aesthetic solution, an ecstasy after anger, desires that it stimulates, but deliberately fails to satisfy, rejecting the satisfactions of balance as much as the graces of perfection."[106]

These and other reductivist accounts of their work were strongly resisted by AACM musicians working in Paris. For instance, despite the Art Ensemble slogan, "Great Black Music," the group's variegated visual and sonic iconography came from around the world, as Jarman explains:

> We were representing history, from the Ancient to the Future. . . . Malachi always represents the oldest entity . . . he would look like an African/ Egyptian shaman. . . . Moye was really in the midst of the African tradition, . . . not a single African tradition, but a total African tradition. . . . I was Eastern oriented. These three were the pantheistic element of Africa and Asia. Roscoe represented the main-stream sort of shaman, the Urban Delivery Man. . . . Lester was always the investigator, wearing cook clothes, which is healing, creating energy and food.[107]

Of course, this is not to say that AACM musicians in Paris avoided engagement with issues of blackness. In 1970, the Art Ensemble performed along with the Frank Wright Quartet and Daevid Allen's "Gong" in a benefit concert for the Black Panther Party.[108] Famoudou Don Moye's recollection went like this:

I'll tell you what happened. I was there. They had the Black Power thing, the Black Panthers, and we were at Mutualité, that hall around the bottom end of Boulevard St. Germain. It was a big hall and they had all kinds of political rallies, concerts. That was where they had all the rallies for the Black Panthers. Clifford Thornton got up and gave a speech, jack. The shit he was saying, even the Black Panther cats were like . . . [laughs]. The people went wild, but when he was leaving the stage, the special inspector cats met him and escorted him on out. The next thing I knew, he was living in Switzerland.[109]

By this time, news of the triumphs of the Art Ensemble in Paris had reached the U.S. magazine *Down Beat,* in the form of an article by British writer Valerie Wilmer. The day after the Black Panther benefit, a concert at the Théâtre du Vieux Colombier found the four Art Ensemble members augmented by singer Fontella Bass and Chicago-born drummer Jerome Cooper, who, according to the article, was living in Copenhagen at the time. In the article, Joseph Jarman is quoted as telling the audience, "The critics have called it avant garde, they've called it the New Thing," he said. "But we have only one name for it: Great Black Music."[110]

"And that, along with showing how the music still echoes the Black American struggle for survival, was what the concert was all about," Wilmer concluded. The writer waxed enthusiastic about how "Fontella came out there to tell it loud; to shout, scream and spew her mind out about blackness and pride. And she made the audience weep with her intensity," performing a piece titled "Black Is the Color of My True Love's Mind."[111]

For the most part, Braxton, Jenkins, Smith, and McCall eschewed the more overt visual, theatrical, and political presentations associated with the Art Ensemble. Daniel Caux's euphemistic observation that the Chicagoans "often keep their distance with regard to swing"[112] led inexorably to his impression, in which he was hardly alone, that the Braxton-Jenkins-Smith-McCall was "encore plus troublante"—even more troubling—than the Art Ensemble:

> Having completely deconstructed jazz, they rebuild it according to not very orthodox laws giving the best part to a concentration on sounds, and especially a discontinuity, a completely unusual splicing of time. . . . One would be wrong to reject this music, at once casual and dedicated, which, refusing all lyricism, demystifies at the same time Western serious music—a taboo area—and a "real jazz" with arbitrarily defined limits.[113]

Moreover, as Leo Smith noted, the group's lack of articulation of standard jazz practice, including its explicit avoidance of free-jazz performativity, puzzled musicians, critics, and producers, if not audiences. "Notions of silence, rhythmic design, directed motion, those kinds of things were very different from the notion of playing the greatest solo or cutting everybody to pieces that you're playing on the same stage with. We weren't interested in cutting anybody. We were like the outside guys anyway. We were known as 'the slide rule boys.'"

As they had in Chicago, Braxton-Jenkins-Smith-McCall frankly engaged tropes connected with pan-European high culture music. Bringing this conception to the metropole, the birthplace of that music, inevitably brought criticism. "They thought we were going after the Western tradition, for example," said Smith. "We challenged that tradition, but it wasn't our only investigation."

> From my recollection of interviews and interactions with people who were in the media system there, their questions were always limited to just the black issues, and what the music meant in those terms. Even though we would go into these areas of explorations, other ideas, they would always try to refocus it. Their idea was designed to present not just an artist, but a black artist in their society.

The emphasis on the new black music as an expression of black power was by no means limited to France. European commentators in other countries quickly signed on to this interpretation. Italian jazz journalist and historian Arrigo Polillo seemed to recapitulate the thrust of a 1966 *New York Times* magazine piece by Nat Hentoff[114] with his 1969 characterization of the "new thing" as "discordant, harsh, furious."[115] Like many French critics, Polillo naturalized the connection between what he heard as protest in the new black music to connect with "the young protesters of Central Europe."[116] Hardly a fan of the new music at the time, Polillo described its situation (at least in America) in terms that recalled the classic trope of the "tragic mulatto," a biracial waif caught between two social worlds without being truly accepted in either. "Paradoxically, in fact," Polillo wrote, "their music is not understood by most blacks, who prefer the easier and more amusing rhythm and blues . . . and it is not naturally loved by whites, who perceive its hostility."[117] Thus, the logical place for these liminal musicians to flourish was in Europe, "where their musical preaching, so often accompanied by speeches and declarations, has found ardent converts among young people, and in particular among those convinced that the world must be thrown to the winds as soon as possible."[118]

The inherent simplicity of the thesis itself was attractive enough, but the notion that black music was inevitably tied to a black nationalist politics also allowed Europeans in particular to defuse any larger challenges to methods and practices active in pan-European high-culture musics. At the same time, the thesis allowed Europe to be framed as a haven for black refugees from the corruption of U.S. society. Of course, those musicians who resisted this interpretation of their work were themselves often looked at askance. As Smith recalls, Parisian commentators tried mightily, but without much success, to frame the music of Braxton-Jenkins-Smith-McCall in terms of essentialist conceptions of the new black music as an articulation of protest and Black Power ideologies. "The music had a place in the environment, but it was a peculiarity," said Smith. "They took the music as an example of their protest against the society. That's the context that it was often forced into."

The controversies forced the musicians to sharpen their understandings of their work. Along the well-worn tradition of the "American in Paris," Smith recalled of the confrontation with the media that "you kind of grow up in a lot of different ways." On the other hand, their lack of accommodation to the political tropes swirling around their work meant that appearances by AACM-oriented musicians in Parisian venues were scarce. As Smith recalls it, most of the events took place outside Paris, and as in Chicago, most performances took place in theater spaces or alternative venues. The interface between the music and the clubs proved difficult and ultimately untenable, by mutual consent.

> We didn't really play any clubs. The New York guys would be playing the clubs. I don't think they really wanted the AACM music there. They didn't mind the kind of swing-type free music that was coming out of New York, with people still grooving and pretending that it was in another zone. But if you had Braxton, Jenkins, Smith, and McCall, and we would drop a silence bigger than a table, what do you do? Do you say, hey, gimme another drink, or what? The musical language didn't fit there, and we didn't try to seek it out either. I don't remember Braxton, Jenkins, Smith, and McCall playing in a club, ever.

In any case, for Smith, the grafting of '50s-era jam session and club thinking on their emerging new music was incongruous at the very least:

I've never been excited about sessions. I've been to quite a few, and was appalled that nothing took place other than a notion of authority and power. They play the same pieces all the time, and the same guys always trip people up. This whole notion of sessions has passed beyond its time, because it had this kind of competitive edge, kind of a bronco-busting competition. I think after people have gotten a little more used to deciding how they're going to present their stuff, they kind of drop that.

In fact, as Smith remembers it, even in Chicago the AACM rarely, if ever, organized jam sessions among its members. "The thing in the AACM was always to present something with a notion of concept," said Smith. "Not just the piece, but the whole performance, had to have some kind of conceptual design." Contrasting what he saw as a certain immaturity of the jamming-as-performance session culture with a more formally organized approach, Smith maintained that

we were looking at music in a much broader way than a lot of other people in the music community at that time. . . . That was why when you walk into that [BYG] studio, they would say, come on and play. An AACM guy would never do that. Basically, our thing was project-oriented. We did new music essentially every time we played; we had something we wanted to present, and we felt that nobody could really sit in with us unless they had rehearsed that music.

Ever since Phillip Wilson, the wizard of St. Louis, went off traveling with Gene Dinwiddie as part of the Paul Butterfield Blues Band, the Art Ensemble had encountered a number of musical problems that pointed up the need for a drummer. One day, on a trio event at American Center, Roscoe Mitchell, Joseph Jarman, and Malachi Favors were approached by a young man carrying a set of congas. Favors was somewhat skeptical at first:

All of a sudden this congo player came up and started setting his stuff up. I think Roscoe asked me if I knew him. I said I didn't know him. I asked Joseph if he knew him and he said no. . . . They asked me if I wanted him to play. I said OK, because I had played with a congo player when I was with Andrew Hill back in Chicago. . . . Afterwards I thought, yeah this cat sounds good.[119]

The young drummer, Donald Moye, was one of a number of artists who had been storing his equipment at the American Center. Moye was born in Rochester, New York, in 1946, and grew up in an ethnically mixed neighborhood very unlike the rigid segregation that most AACM musicians experienced. He never knew his father, who was stationed with the U.S. Army in Germany after World War II and died in the Ludwigsburg food riots in 1945.[120] Moye lived in a Rochester housing project, brought up by his mother. "She used to take us to the opera, Mahalia Jackson, Mormon Tabernacle Choir, the Modern Jazz Quartet. All kinds of concerts. My grandmother used to cook at the Elks Club. All the musicians used to come by and eat, the jazz cats—Jimmy McGriff, Kenny Burrell, Grant Green. So that was the beginning of the end [laughs]."[121]

The young Moye soon found another, less heralded site for musical learning. "I used to listen to gospel music," he recalled, "because I used to help out at the barbershop, and these cats were all Sanctified, Holy Rollers. They had all the Sanctified music, that's all they played. The singers would hang out there, so there was a whole scene." Moye went to Catholic grammar school and high school, where he became part of a drum and bugle corps, the Fabulous Crusaders, which won the 1965 American Legion National Championships. "That was a ticket out of the area. It gave us something to do, as opposed to hanging out on the stoop. I would get up in the morning at 6:30 and by 7 o'clock I'd be gone. Otherwise I probably would have been in one of them gangs. I'd be coming home with a big thing of books, Latin, French, calculus. These cats would come home from school, they'd be carrying a bottle of Wild Irish Rose."

Moye had also been playing congas, bongos, and drums with the Puerto Rican boys in the neighborhood, and at seventeen he got a scholarship to Central State University, a historically black school in Wilberforce, Ohio. He joined a group of African musicians and started a percussion ensemble, but his time at the school was relatively brief:

> If you were political, a musician, anybody who didn't want to join a fraternity, you were automatically ostracized. I got in trouble because I was hanging out with the blues cats in town. At school they took me on the rug about that—hanging out with blues dudes wasn't good for your English. The music school rehearsal facilities and auditorium were off-limits to people playing blues and "jungle music"—nigger music. The next year, the shit changed, because Ken McIntyre went down there. He was the band director, so they eased on up, but I was long gone by then.[122]

Moye transferred to Wayne State University in Detroit, where he studied at the school's experimental wing, Monteith College. Moye soon became a part of Detroit's multicultural experimental art and music scene, which in the late 1960s had become a hotbed of musical and poetic ferment. It was during these years that Moye met Joseph Jarman, who was a frequent visitor to the Detroit new music scene. As Moye remembers, "They had a poetry press and a couple of magazines, so I got involved in publishing and editing. Ginsberg was around, Diane DiPrima, Gregory Corso, Robert Creeley, Charles Olson, Timothy Leary. It was cats from England, Australia, Japan. I met all those cats, and I read all that stuff."

Moye became a member of the band Detroit Free Jazz, which took off for Europe in 1968. The band traveled around Europe and even played in Morocco, but dissolved in Copenhagen. Moye headed for Rome, where he met soprano saxophonist Steve Lacy. He became part of Lacy's ensemble, with vocalist Irene Aebi and bassist Marcello Melis, while serving as a house percussionist at the Italian Radio. Moye was with Lacy's group when the saxophonist decided to move to Paris in 1969. Staying at the Hotel Buci on the Left Bank, the young drummer quickly met the cream of black America's latest generation of expatriate musicians, the musicians who had spearheaded the free jazz revolution. Moye soon became a fixture at the American Center, where he and many other musicians rehearsed and stored their equipment.

> Everybody used to play there. Art Taylor, Johnny Griffin, Slide Hampton—the big boys. The real jazz cats, the official legends of the bebop. It wasn't that makeover shit. Dexter was around, Kenny Drew. I used to hang out with Papa Jo Jones whenever he came through. I used to go to Art Taylor's house every morning. He had a real slick apartment up in Montmartre. Him and Randy Weston, they were the slicksters. Randy had a villa in Morocco. Memphis Slim was there, he was clean all the time, had a Rolls-Royce and a big mansion out in the country. So those cats were like our heroes.

Paris was nothing if not cosmopolitan, and the young Moye was eager to explore.

> You know the Paris scene, it was people from all over the world. I was playing a lot with the drummers from Guinea, Senegal, and Ivory Coast. [Saxophonist] Manu Dibango had just come up from Cameroon. There

was a lot of stuff down where Les Halles is now. It was *the* market for
Paris, with artists, night people, stuff going on twenty-four hours a day.
It was jumping all the time. The women of the night, the hustlers, they
would come there late at night to eat at places like Le Pied de Cochon,
open twenty-four hours. I used to have a studio right there on Rue
St. Denis. There was this editor, Jerome Martineau. He had a bookstore,
and he owned the building. He was Melvin Van Peebles's first editor, and
also did André Gide. Oliver Johnson had a studio in the basement.

Moye began working with European and American musicians, but as he
recalled, "It wasn't clubs, it was more like concerts, or galleries, cultural centers. We weren't part of the club scene. We never worked, like, traditional
jazz clubs." Moye already knew about the Roscoe Mitchell Art Ensemble
from his time in Detroit, when Charles Moore introduced him to the members of the group. Moye "got hooked on the dream of playing with them
. . . the open ended creative aspect of what they were trying to do is what
hooked me."[123] Everyone had heard that the group was looking for a drummer, and since everybody in Paris had heard about the Art Ensemble, it
was clear that this new position had strong possibilities—or, as Moye put it,
"Cats was WERKIN!"[124] One day at the Center, early in 1970, Malachi Favors
walked in, and his ears pricked up as he heard something special: "I went
over to this club, and there Moye was playing with Mal Waldron. I asked
would he come out [to the AEC compound at Saint-Leu-la-Forêt,], we were
looking for a drummer, and he said yes. And that's what happened, he came
out, and that's the beginning of Moye."[125]

Die Emanzipation: The Rise of European Free Improvisation
There is a general agreement among scholars working on European improvised music that at the end of the 1950s, European jazz was in the throes
of an identity crisis. Music historian Ekkehard Jost describes the European
jazz of this era as "an exotic plant on barren soil . . . that must have seemed
as bizarre as British flamenco."[126] In thrall to what musicologist Wolfram
Knauer called an "epigonal Americanism,"[127] European jazz musicians were
said to inhabit a landscape in which aesthetic, methodological, and stylistic
direction flowed for the overwhelming part from the metropole of America
to the tributaries in their own lands.

The situation would eventually lead to a kind of declaration of independence from that hegemony. Beginning roughly in the mid-1960s, this
move toward aesthetic self-determination took musical form as musicians

combined extensions, ironic revisions, and outright rejections of American jazz styles with a self-conscious articulation of historical and cultural difference. Complicating the picture was the fact that starting in the 1950s, black American jazz, particularly bebop, was gaining acceptance as a form of art music. As such, this new music found itself in competition with the historically certified sonic products of Europe, and responses to this new competition, articulated from European soil, were sometimes just as extreme as they had been in the United States in the 1940s and 1950s.

Germany's annual Donaueschingen Festival of Contemporary Music was birthed in 1921 in the Black Forest residence of the Fürstenberg family, whose place in German nobility helped to launch the careers of composers such as Hanns Eisler and Ernst Krenek. After World War II, the Nazi-imposed ban on *entartete Kunst* ("degenerate art") gave way to Donaueschingen premieres of the new music of Karlheinz Stockhausen, Pierre Boulez, and Pierre Schaeffer, among many others. The influential German critic and producer, Joachim-Ernst Berendt, whose dialogues with Theodor Adorno about jazz are well known in contemporary German letters, directed the first jazz production at Donaueschingen in 1954.[128] A second production took place in 1957, and since 1967, the festival has included a small, but generally well-attended jazz component.

A 1977 article by Max Harrison in a British jazz journal described in no small detail the reception of the 1957 Donaueschingen appearance by the Modern Jazz Quartet, which thoroughly overshadowed the premiere of Igor Stravinsky's *Agon*. However, in an otherwise detailed review of a recording of this signal event, the writer gives no clue as to why, after such an enormously successful concert, jazz disappeared from the festival for ten years.[129] Joachim-Ernst Berendt himself provided the answer to this question, many years after the concert, in his own more detailed history of jazz at Donaueschingen. His account of the 1957 controversy over the Modern Jazz Quartet speaks volumes about the intensity of the European perception of competition between white European and black American art musics.

Where Harrison minimizes the effect of the 1957 concert except for its importance as an aesthetic object on recordings, Berendt cites German theater and classical music critic K. H. Ruppel's observation that the continent-wide importance of the Modern Jazz Quartet concert to the acceptance of jazz on the European concert stage recalled the impact of Benny Goodman's 1938 Carnegie Hall event.[130] The overshadowing of

Stravinsky, however, was an ominous sign. After the tabloid *Bild* summarized the comparison with the pithy headline, "King Jazz Dethrones King Twelve-Tone," jazz was simply frozen out of Donaueschingen for the next ten years.[131] Heinrich Strobel, the music director of the giant regional Südwestfunk radio network, who had originally planned to allow much more space for jazz, explained his change of heart shortly before he passed away, in something of a deathbed confession: "We must be careful that what actually matters to us is not pushed into the background by things that we certainly also love, but which are not in the center of what we want at Donaueschingen."[132] This attitude also seemed to explain in part why Ornette Coleman, who was well known for his notated works, never appeared in Donaueschingen.[133]

The 1967 appearances of German trumpeter Manfred Schoof with Swiss pianist Irene Schweizer, and the Globe Unity Orchestra of pianist Alexander von Schlippenbach (according to Berendt, "the first attempt to apply the experiences of Free Jazz to the composition of a modern orchestral work") finally broke the ice.[134] These musicians were part of the critically important first generation of musicians who confronted issues of European musical identity in jazz. They included Schlippenbach, Schoof, trombonist Albert Mangelsdorff, saxophonist Peter Brötzmann, pianist Karlhanns Berger, and vibraphonist Gunter Hampel in Germany; Schweizer and drummer Pierre Favre in Switzerland; pianist Fred van Hove in Belgium; saxophonist Willem Breuker, pianist Misha Mengelberg, and drummer Han Bennink in the Netherlands; and in Great Britain, drummers John Stevens and Tony Oxley, saxophonists Trevor Watts and Evan Parker, vocalist Maggie Nicols, trombonist Paul Rutherford, guitarist Derek Bailey, bassist Barry Guy, and trumpeter Kenny Wheeler. The French-based wing of the emerging European free jazz movement included drummers Aldo Romano and Claude Delcloo; trumpeter Bernard Vitet; French pianist François Tusques and German pianist Joachim Kühn, then resident in France; saxophonist/clarinetist Michel Portal; and bassists Beb Guérin, Barre Phillips, and Jean-François Jenny-Clark.

There is no question that the first generation of European free jazz improvisors was heavily influenced by now-canonical African American figures from the jazz tradition. Contemporaneous accounts represent this new breed of Europeans as having promulgated a new, specifically European style of "free jazz" that built upon the innovations in form, sound, method, and expression advanced by Ornette Coleman, Albert Ayler, Cecil Taylor,

John Coltrane, and other African American musicians of the early 1960s. Confounding simplistically linear and rigid notions of "roots" and "influence," as well as bombastic accusations of appropriation and perhaps even "theft," it is clear that at this early stage in the development of European free improvisation, the musicians made no attempt to deny the Afrological influence upon their work. Indeed, both critics and musicians have generally overlooked the crucial, ongoing investment by the current field of European free improvisation as a whole in fundamental notions of sonic personality based primarily in Afrological models. Later, the new European musicians were widely credited with the development of a more open conception of "free improvisation" that was generally acknowledged in Europe to have broken away from American stylistic directions and jazz signifiers. Borrowing from a critically important event in nineteenth-century American history, the end of chattel slavery, Joachim-Ernst Berendt, in a 1977 essay, called this declaration of difference and independence "the Emancipation" [*Die Emanzipation*], a term that has entered the general lexicon of German jazz historiography.[135]

Steve McCall's work with Gunter Hampel and Willem Breuker provided a link between the AACM and members of this first wave of European free jazz musicians. Hampel's important recording, *The 8th of July 1969*, with Breuker, McCall, Anthony Braxton, and singer Jeanne Lee, was recorded during this period.[136] Overall, however, there seemed to be relatively little interaction between AACM musicians in Paris and the European free jazz scene. As Leo Smith recalled, "It wasn't a deep participation. My participation with the French guys would be through somebody else's ensemble. I didn't do much of that, because I never hung out." In fact, most AACM musicians in Europe performed mainly with their AACM colleagues. As Lester Bowie saw it, this was a question of method, not race:

> No one really had our kind of approach. We were into all the music, whereas a lot of cats were into parts of it. The music of the AACM was all about everything. It could be African rhythm one thing, it could be show business the next thing. It could be R&B. It could be just about anything—experimental stuff, down-home stuff. We weren't musicians who said, we're blues cats or we're jazz cats. It was Great Black Music, Ancient to the Future. It was new for them.

In this context, it could be said that the unstable silences, sonic diversity, and performative imagery in the new Chicago music was posing new challenges to those European musicians who were just getting used to the older, frenetic style. One French drummer's sharp critique of Art Ensemble intermedia is worth quoting at length, as a marker of the distance between the AACM musicians and the European free jazz scene.

> I'm sorry, but that's all bullshit. The music is enough by itself. You don't need to see Coltrane or Ornette. These people are using the aesthetics with the music: it's uninteresting and that's why I don't like the A.A.C.M. If they didn't burn incense and paint their faces, their music would be dreary. . . . You don't have to be a clown to get your music accepted, unless you know that it isn't enough by itself. And then, it would be better just to be a whore and make real money![137]

The experiences of AACM musicians at the 1969 Baden-Baden Free Jazz Treffen in southern Germany seems to have constituted a signal event that set out the terms of many future encounters. Given his knowledge of the European music scene, Steve McCall could well have been in a position to suggest to festival organizer Joachim-Ernst Berendt that his fellow Chicagoans be invited to the 1969 edition of the meeting.[138] Besides McCall, three other members of the "Chicago avant-garde" who were living in Paris, Lester Bowie, Joseph Jarman, and Roscoe Mitchell, came to Baden-Baden for the event, along with the pianist Dave Burrell. Ensconced in the German Schwarzwald, they met sixteen European musicians, including trombonists Albert Mangelsdorff and Eje Thelin, saxophonists Alan Skidmore, Heinz Sauer, Gerd Dudek, John Surman, and Willem Breuker, guitarist Terje Rypdal, pianist Leo Cuypers, drummer Tony Oxley, and singer Karin Krog.

In hindsight, the Baden-Baden event could be viewed as an early example of an intercultural event between two emerging musical vanguards. A recording of several pieces that were created for the meeting survives, released under the name of Lester Bowie as *Gittin' to Know Y'all*. The album's pointedly ironic title seems to signify on the Chicagoans' quasi-immigrant status in Europe.[139] As Lester Bowie said in 1999, "We had been there awhile, and we were invited by Joachim Berendt to come over and do this piece, to work with these German musicians. I called it 'Gittin' to Know Y'all' because that's what it was—being acquainted with them, getting to know each other."

According to the review of the event in *Jazz Podium,* the most influential German-language jazz publication, Braxton, Smith, and Jenkins were both surprised and upset that they were not allowed to take part in the performance—although who barred their participation is not mentioned in the review.[140] In 1998, Braxton recalled that "I went to the rehearsals and I met Joachim Berendt. I thought he was an interesting guy, who later would become important to me again as I sought to understand what was happening in Europe." Leo Smith felt that

> Baden-Baden was an interesting zone. Braxton, Jenkins, Smith, and McCall weren't invited. McCall went away to play with Archie Shepp in Nigeria. We got this van from the record company and we drove to Baden-Baden from France. The Art Ensemble was there and there were a lot of other people from around the planet, most of them Europeans. They weren't people I had been listening to. It was a huge meeting. We went there essentially as observers, just to hang out. We did observe the rehearsals and the performance.

The *Jazz Podium* reviewer complained that during the course of the meeting, the six Chicagoans "separated themselves, formed a clique whose inapproachability stood in contrast to Bowie's certainly honorably intended work of contact, and somewhat disturbed the otherwise refreshingly familial character that distinguished the meeting." For this reviewer, the "one-big-happy-family" of musicians was destroyed by the *unzertrennliche Bruderschaft*—the inseparable brotherhood—exhibited by the Chicagoans. The review cited racism as the cause of the problems, and the clear implication was that the Chicago "clique" was to blame, as "the black-white problem spread over the event like a shadow."[141] This simplistic, race-based reproach, directed exclusively at the black musicians, effectively "e-raced" not only obvious creative differences, but the asymmetrical class differences, personally, historically. Even so, in Leo Smith's summary, the differences were largely methodological rather than racial, cultural, or economic:

> We were not knocked out by the areas of investigation that particular session was looking at. No one was doing anything with deep space. Most of those people were still suffering under the weight of Albert Ayler and those people at that time. I saw great musicians, but I was looking for something that was really very different from what was expected. The things that they looked at, other than some really nice blowing sessions, were very typical to the New York kind of presentation, where you mix a bunch of musicians together, and people do their solo thing. It wasn't very interactive, or looking at new ways of doing things. They had people

who were interesting in their own fields, but they didn't seem to think about ideas. People played together, and it felt to me like a session kind of a thing.

This, in turn, leads to an emerging notion of the AACM as simply *different*. "Our language is very different than the community language," Smith maintained. "What makes it very different is the kind of research that has been engaged in by Braxton, yourself, Roscoe, Muhal, myself, some other people. It has been a concerted thrust not just for new information, but how to make everything responsible to this whole urge to make art." Finally, Bowie's playful "confession" about Baden-Baden points to another kind of intercultural engagement with difference that could possibly have contributed to the reviewer's complaints: "I can't think of anything too much that happened, except that me and Karin Krog got caught. We had snuck off to one of the rooms, and Joachim Berendt peeped us kissing. I forgot about the rest of what happened there."

The first generation of European free jazz musicians was often heavily subsidized by the post–Marshall Plan social democratic states of Europe. A 1966 *Down Beat* column reported on the situation in the Netherlands, where, "thanks to a substantial subsidy from the Dutch government," Misha Mengelberg, Han Bennink, saxophonist Piet Noordijk, and bassist Rob Langereis and were brought to perform at the Newport Jazz Festival in July 1966.[142] In 1968, a German group including Albert Mangelsdorff, Gerd Dudek, Heinz Sauer, Peter Brötzmann, Manfred Schoof, clarinetist Rolf Kühn, and pianist Wolfgang Dauner toured South America under the aegis of the German internationalist cultural arm, the Goethe-Institute.[143] Of course, since the onset of the cold war, various branches of the U.S. government had long been actively subsidizing both American and European cultural production in Europe, both overtly, by the American Office of Military Government in Germany and the U.S. Department of State,[144] and covertly, via the Central Intelligence Agency and the dummy philanthropic foundations it created for the purpose.[145] However, nothing as audacious as U.S. free jazz, with its strong overtones of political and social rebellion, had ever been supported by U.S. government sources.

In a sense, the notion of "European jazz" itself began as a European internalization of American cultural hegemony that conflated all of the combined histories, languages, and styles of the continent into a single monolith. By the mid-1970s, however, the political stance of the new European musicians began to perform precisely that conflation, moving well beyond the notion of "European jazz" toward an emerging pan-European political and cultural nationalism that included a nativist politics that identified African American music and musicians as foreign competitors.[146] One of the central areas for the new pan-European movement for cultural nationalism in improvised music was Germany, and a central journalistic site for the movement was the Stuttgart-based magazine *Jazz Podium*. Prior to 1965, *Jazz Podium*'s editorial policy emphasized a clear pro-U.S. bias in its articles and reviews. With the rise of the first generation of European free jazz musicians, the magazine underwent radical revision under the leadership of editor-in-chief Dieter Zimmerle, who with his associate (and later editor-in-chief) Gudrun Endress, featured the new Europeans extensively in reviews, interviews, and cover articles.

By contrast with the French magazines, *Jazz Podium* ran relatively few feature articles, concert reviews, and record reviews of AACM musicians. One of the few such articles appeared under Endress's byline in 1970, in the wake of the controversial Baden-Baden event. For Endress, the AACM's emphasis on multi-instrumentalism presented the possibility that "the emphasis on sound is an escape from soloistic virtuosity, which they don't yet possess."[147] On the other hand, she offered the possibility that since the AACM represented, as it were, "the third generation of free jazz," their work had not really had time to mature. Much of the rest of the article was given over to essentially prosaic thumbnail sketches of the AACM Paris contingent, apparently compiled largely from secondary sources in the United States, Britain, and France.[148]

Homecoming

Despite their successes, by 1971 most of the AACM expatriates had left Europe. Leroy Jenkins, Leo Smith, and Anthony Braxton were the first to depart, returning to Chicago in early 1970. It is impossible to generalize about the reasons for the departures; Leroy Jenkins saw it rather prosaically. "I didn't want to be in Paris because I couldn't speak the language," he explained. "I was fairly illiterate, and I didn't like the idea of that, so I thought I'd make it on back to America." As Roscoe Mitchell saw it, "People weren't really from there. Either you did go back home, or you ended up staying in Paris like some people did. That was a hard choice for a lot of musicians. I had never intended on moving to Paris, having a permanent base. In the 1998 interview with Chicago Beau, Lester Bowie agreed with these assessments. "After a while it wears on you," Bowie reflected. "Different country, different land. You have to talk slow to be understood. I mean if you want to assimilate into their thing, like becoming French, that's another thing. To me it ain't no gas to be French. I like being an American Negro."[149] Following standard Art Ensemble procedure, the decision to leave was taken collectively. "I wasn't totally convinced that it was time to go back," said Mitchell, "but I was willing to go with the vote of the group. My take on it was that there was a lot more of the world to see. I was young and open to explore stuff."

Issues related to French taxes may have also played a role in the Art Ensemble's decision, as Don Moye made clear.

> We were ready to go back to the States in '71, but that's when the French authorities fabricated some tax shit, but all of our papers were in order. The French had confiscated all our instruments and put them in storage, but had to release our shit back because like I said, all of our shit was in order. In the process it occurred to us to let France go for awhile.[150]

In fact, according to Bowie, in the wake of the tax issue, the group was actually "kicked out of France" in the summer of 1970. It was becoming apparent that the establishment's romance with black revolution was waning:

> There was a radio program about us on Radio Luxembourg; it was just about us. The show portrayed us as revolutionaries, damn-near Black Panthers, and by the way, they happen to live in St. Leu la Forêt. So the big boys in St. Leu were like "What, they live here?" The next day after the broadcast the police showed up at our door. They told us if we didn't leave town they would escort us to the border.[151]

British journalist Val Wilmer's memoir of the period, which included accounts of her encounters with AACM musicians and their music, observed that

> By 1970 the racial climate had changed considerably from the tolerant one that had seemed so attractive to expatriate Blacks of an earlier generation. Following the war in Algeria, open hostility was directed against North Africans and anyone with a dark skin not dressed conservative. And the Black man/pimp:white woman/whore stereotype persisted wherever interracial couples were found. Taxis in Pigalle [Paris evening entertainment district] were a problem. My aid was enlisted to hail a cab by a musician en route to a concert; he skulked in a doorway while I stopped it. "He'll think I'm one of them Algerians," was his jocular comment.

"As time went on and the revolutionary fervor died down," Wilmer concluded, "many found themselves as unwelcome as the Algerians had become."[152]

"We were ready to go back," Moye recalled. "We had to stay in Europe some more months to build our stash back up to get back. The fine ate up the money we had budgeted for the trans-Atlantic transportation, the boat and everything. I mean we had three trucks, personal stuff, equipment, and children. So we finally went back on the SS Rafaello out of Geneva."[153]

AACM members living in Europe vigorously promoted the AACM name and philosophy as they presented performances throughout the continent. Interviews with European-based AACM members in French journals brought other, still relatively unknown Chicago-based members to the attention of European promoters and journalists, preparing the ground for future generations of AACM members to receive a hearing. These interviews also invariably mentioned the AACM itself as an important source of strength and nurturance. On the other hand, it was not uncommon for writers to conflate the AACM with the Art Ensemble of Chicago, as one 1970 program note did: "The Art Ensemble of Chicago is often referred to—as is usual as far as jazz or pop music are concerned—by the initials A.A.C.M., Association for the Advancement of Creative Musicians." The program note went on to describe the goals and purposes of the AACM more or less accurately as "this independent organization bringing together, in a kind of community or cooperative, a certain number of American musicians working regularly together, linked by the love of the music, by research, and by the intention to control without market middlemen (producers and publishers) their own productions."[154]

Articles such as this led some AACM members, both in Paris and at home in Chicago, to feel that the Art Ensemble itself had been responsible for the confusion, to the detriment of other AACM members based in Paris. Even in 1998, Anthony Braxton's understanding was that the Art Ensemble "started selling themselves immediately as the AACM." A more charitable interpretation, which seems supported by the foregoing reception review, indicates that some reviewers made little distinction between one AACM group and another, describing any new music from Chicago as emanating from "l'A.A.C.M."

In any event, Roscoe Mitchell's understanding was that the Art Ensemble had indeed played an important role in bringing the AACM as a whole to the attention of an international public. By most indications, the same could be said of all the AACM musicians who went to Paris. Moreover, at least the public transcript of the Paris period indicates that cooperation among AACM members in Paris seemed to play a more public role than intragroup factionalism. As Mitchell put it,

The Art Ensemble went out there and carried the banner of the AACM and established a strong foundation for musicians to go over there and do different things. So the younger guys who came after us—George Lewis and all those people—didn't really have to do it in the same way. Whereas we had to go out there and live on people's floors and do this and do that and pave the way for people who came along after us and were able to take advantage of that. I wonder how many people working now even realize that's what happened?[155]

8

THE AACM'S NEXT WAVE

More from the Midwest: The Black Artists Group

Back to the United States. We didn't work for a couple of years, but
we were rehearsing nearly every day.
—Joseph Jarman, radio interview

The warmth of the AACM's European reception provided a sharp
contrast with the paucity of Stateside work; even so, there was no
wholesale rush to Europe among AACM musicians. Relatively few
AACM musicians could have sustained the costs of a short-term European residency, and the idea of actually relocating there was even
less appealing to most. One exception was Leonard Jones, who left
Chicago for Germany in 1969, not long after the departure of the first
wave of Europe-bound AACM members.[1]

For those who were returning from Europe, the thought of remaining in Chicago was, quite understandably, far from uppermost
in their minds. As Anthony Braxton commented, "'The music was
taken out of the community'—that's a great phrase, but in fact that's
not what happened. The musicians go where the gigs are." Thus,
Braxton, Leo Smith, and Leroy Jenkins returned to Chicago for only a
brief period. As Jenkins related, "I just went back to collect my retirement money from the teaching job that I had, a couple of thousand.
I figured I'd go to New York, because when I came back to Chicago I

knew I wouldn't be able to go there any more. So I decided I'd go to New York, in February 1970. Braxton and I came together. We drove up."

Leo Smith remembers his departure from Paris as the result of a collective decision that had been conceived by the trio in Paris.

> We decided that we wanted to live on the East Coast. All of us went back to Chicago first, and one by one, all of us left out. Braxton and Kathy and I came back to Chicago together, and I functioned [as an AACM member]. I left in August. Braxton and Leroy had already gone back to New York when I left. I went to Connecticut and Braxton and Leroy ended up in Manhattan.

Along the way, the trio's collaboration became a casualty of experience and maturity. "When we got back," Smith mused, "I don't think we had an idea that Braxton, Jenkins, Smith was going to move any further. I think the moment we got back we realized that we weren't going to play together any more."

Roscoe Mitchell noted that "I didn't stay in Chicago too long, about a month or so. I was starting to get back on my track of, you know, maybe I ought to get on out into the country so I can see what's going on with *me*, have a look in the mirror at myself." Lester Bowie and his family returned to St. Louis, and were soon joined by Mitchell and Don Moye, who worked with members of the Black Artists Group (BAG). Don Moye began exchanging studies with the St. Louis–based Senegalese percussionist, Mor Thiam. Moye saw BAG as "a totally creative environment of musicians, dancers, actors, poets, and painters. . . . We used to have concerts called the Sunrise Series. We'd start one day at noon and play all the way through till the sun came up the next day with continuous music featuring all the different groups and combinations."[2]

In 1968, three years after the AACM was founded, the young painter Emilio Cruz had just come back from Europe. Born in 1938 in New York, Cruz took the artist's path early on. "I was in my teens when I went into the art world," Cruz said in our interview. "I entered it when I was about eighteen, nineteen, being around [theater artists] Julian Beck and Judith Malina. I had been doing these things at the Judson Church. Really, it was because I didn't have any money, so I ended up in the center of the avant-garde."[3] Cruz was going to art school in New York, but a friend advised him to go to Provincetown, Massachusetts, a resort town in the Cape Cod area that was a traditional haven for artists. "That was the center of the avant-garde at that moment," Cruz said.

> From the Black Mountain people, you had Charles Olson, and Franz Kline. Happenings were taking place at that time, and Red Grooms. So I ended up being one of the artists, with Bob Thompson, who had just had a show at the Whitney. I met Bob in Provincetown. Baraka became a very good friend of mine. So I was very much steeped in the avant-garde in ways that most people were not. Jack Kerouac, I knew all those people.

"From practically being homeless," he marveled, "I had made myself an established painter in New York City. . . . I had broken through to the galleries and the museums. I had just come back from Europe." By the mid-1960s, Cruz had established a relationship with the curator Richard Bellamy, the founder of the important Green Gallery in New York, who had shown works by Richard Serra, Robert Morris, Dan Flavin, Claes Oldenburg, James Rosenquist, Donald Judd, and Lucas Samaras, among others. "Dick Bellamy was really the most important person in terms of art dealers in the avant-garde at that point," Cruz pointed out. At the same time, pursuing his lifelong love of music, Cruz also got to know musicians such as Archie Shepp, Cecil Taylor, Ornette Coleman, and Don Cherry.

In the meantime, the saxophonist Julius Hemphill had come to St. Louis from his hometown of Fort Worth, Texas. During the "Long, Hot Summer," the U.S. urban rebellions of 1968, he was living in an apartment in St. Louis right across from Fairground Park, the site of public events in the nineteenth century.[4] This was the era of Lyndon Johnson's "Great Society," a post–New Deal vision of America that ultimately drowned in the shallow rice paddies of Vietnam. In 1964, a new housing development, Laclede Town, had been conceived as a racially integrated urban redevelopment project that would revitalize what was becoming known as St. Louis's "inner city," or to many, "the black ghetto."[5] Hemphill had just earned a music education degree from all-black Lincoln University in Jefferson City, Missouri. He was working for the local Model Cities agency in Laclede Town, and editing a newspaper called the *Model City Voice,* out of an office right across the street from Maurice's Gold Coast, a well-visited cocktail lounge. The Model Cities Program was a classic Great Society urban renewal program, an artifact of Johnson's alternately celebrated and maligned "War on Poverty."

"St. Louis was having a crisis," Cruz recalled. "You had urban flight. They were losing their population, and people were going to the suburbs. They had to show that the inner city was not only a nice place to go, but that artists were living there." As it happened, Richard Bellamy found out about a Model Cities job for an artist in St. Louis, and suggested to Cruz that he might be ideal for the position.

> They kept asking me and asking me and asking me, and I kept saying, no, no, no. One day I'm sitting in my studio, and somebody knocks on my door. It's this big tall guy wearing combat boots. He looks like somebody who just came out of the wilderness. And he's with this very short guy, dwarf-like. I said, who are you? He said, my name is Julius Hemphill . . . and my name is Malinke. We're from St. Louis.

"As you know," Cruz told me in 1999, "Julius Hemphill was kind of a magnetic person. Julius was without a doubt extraordinarily gifted, brilliantly talented. I needed money, and could use a year of working, and getting some support, and being free of economic problems." Cruz's friend, the painter Bob Thompson, had died of a heroin overdose in 1966, which precipitated an emotional crisis in Cruz's life. On the other hand, Cruz had just met his future spouse and soul mate, the theater artist who became Patricia Cruz. Like Patricia, Malinke Robert Elliott was a theater artist. The trio hit it off immediately. "When Julius came in, we became more than fast friends," Cruz said. "I had just met Pat, and Julius and I spent the day laughing and talking, and imagining all the things that we, as black artists, could create together."

Even though Cruz considered himself part of the New York avant-garde, it had become clear to him that his connections in that regard were going to be limited by the fact of his being of African descent. "When I was a part of the other avant-garde, I was an interloper," he observed. "The idea of not being an interloper, but of putting my foot down and saying, this was my territory, was extremely appealing to me." Pat and Emilio Cruz headed for St. Louis.

Oliver Gene Lake, born in Arkansas in 1942, grew up in St. Louis in an area known as "The Ville," near Homer G. Phillips Hospital, the African American health facility where so many black St. Louisans had drawn their first breaths. Tina Turner lived a few doors away, and like Lake, attended Sumner High, which ended up producing so many of St. Louis's best musicians, including mezzo-soprano Grace Bumbry, drummer Phillip Wilson, trumpeter Floyd LeFlore, and pianist John Hicks.[6]

Lake grew up with the St. Louis version of urban segregation, and his first-person description is only too well known. "Black people weren't permitted to go to certain businesses that were owned by whites. You couldn't go to a white lawyer if you needed a lawyer. You couldn't go to a white restaurant if you wanted to eat. You had to go only in the segregated area, only where the black people were. I thought segregation was written into the law."[7] On the other hand, said Lake, "it was before the integration stuff, so there were all these black businesses. It was lively, wonderful, in my memory of going out and seeing all the stores—black beauty shops, black restaurants. That whole block was alive, with tons of people walking back and forth." Lake's mother owned a restaurant that served delicacies such as barbecue and pig's feet, and his stepfather owned several businesses himself, including a car wash, a shoe shine parlor, and a poolroom. Lake also worked on weekends in various establishments owned by his parents. "There was a liquor store on the corner," Lake observed, "so everybody would be drinking, and then they'd have to get them some ribs and pig ears, and then get their shoes shined, get their car washed, and then go shoot some pool. We had that corner going."

As a child, Lake's family listened to Hank Ballard and the Midnighters, as well as "Muddy Waters, Lightnin' Hopkins, all those gutbucket guys" at home, and in the poolroom. At fourteen, Lake joined an all-black drum and bugle corps sponsored by the Denver-based American Woodmen insurance company. That allowed him to travel outside St. Louis, and the responsibilities of corps membership kept Lake, like Don Moye, safe from the attractions of street life. The drum and bugle corps activity also introduced him to older teenagers who were developing as musicians, and he would attend jam sessions, armed with a present from his mother, one of the portable Japanese transistorized tape recorders that were then sweeping the United States. One of the jammers, a saxophonist, suggested,

> Hey man, why don't you get a saxophone? He was in the Columbia Jazz Record Club, and they sent him Paul Desmond records for free. He said, man, I don't like this stuff, you take this. He gave me all of Paul Desmond's records. He picked up his tenor and played *Oleo*. It blew me away. Then he played Charlie Parker for me. This was all revolutionary stuff for me, I hadn't heard any of it. I really dug the alto, so I said, I think I want

to get a horn. My youngest aunt's husband had an alto sitting up in his closet that he wasn't playing, and I begged him for that. I started taking lessons, and joined the high-school band.

"But I never practiced," Lake admitted. "I learned the C scale and that was it." Lake graduated from high school in 1961, and started working in the post office. "I got married, had a couple of kids, and decided to go back to school." He entered Stowe Teachers College, but flunked out of a biology program. He decided to start practicing again, and after an intense summer, he enrolled in a music education program in Lincoln University. "Julius Hemphill had been there," Lake laughed. "When I went there he was in the service, but his stories persisted, no doubt about it. He was an incredible saxophonist, but most of the stories were about him getting drunk, and the wild shit he would do, staying up for three days, and the things he would say to instructors. But mainly the fact that he was a genius."

"It was very difficult," Lake recalled of his own experience in the program. "They didn't consider jazz as music, and if they heard you playing jazz, you would be admonished. We would have to wait until all the instructors were gone, and then we'd start jamming."

> This guy used to double around and come back and see that we were doing it, and come in and bust us. He kept doing it and kept doing it, and eventually I stepped out of my student teacher thing and went man to man with him. I called him over to the side and said, look man, I'm going to play this music, no matter what you say. You cannot stop me. So every time you come here and do this, it's not like you "caught" me. This is what I'm going to do.

Lake and his new family moved to the newly opened Laclede Town complex. Jerry Berger, the highly respected and well-remembered manager of Laclede Town, was busy creating a space for artists to live there. "He said that he was going to make an ideal community, so he needed X amount of artists, X amount of blue-collar people. So he said, all musicians who want to live here, you get the first two months free if you move in. So we all moved in, brand-new houses, three-story town houses." Now back in St. Louis, Lake met the cream of the local musicians at places like the Fat States Lounge—bassist John Mixon, the young Lester Bowie, who had been on the road with Oliver Sain and Albert King, and the saxophonist Freddie Washington, Jr., with whom Lake began studying. In the summers, the younger musicians, such as Hemphill, trumpeter Floyd LeFlore, drummers Leonard Smith and Charles Bobo Shaw, and Lester Bowie's younger, trombone-prodigy brother, Joseph, would stage jam sessions in the expansive spaces of the city's well-maintained Forest Park. Lake remembers the musicians "experimenting, playing more open. Somebody might start a tune, and it would end up being more open than how it started out. Or sometimes we wouldn't say anything. We'd just start playing, and have a long improvised piece, and everybody would play."

At Laclede Town's Circle Coffee House, Lake began playing with LeFlore and Smith, and accompanying poets with music, a postbeat practice with simultaneous roots in the black church that was fairly common as an artifact of the Black Power movement. As historian George Lipsitz notes, community activists such as Percy Green and Ivory Perry also lived in Laclede Town, and the Circle Coffee House quickly became a site for "politically charged artistic expression as well as a locus for political consciousness-raising." As Lipsitz points out, the venue "enabled people to put on their own readings and concerts in a place outside the control of commercial entrepreneurs and cultural institutions alike."[8]

The great choreographer Katherine Dunham was based in the area, and according to Lipsitz,

> Members of the Circle Coffee House group developed ties with dancers trained at Katherine Dunham's art institute and community center in East St. Louis, with visual artists trained at the WPA-originated People's Art Center in north St. Louis, with musicians from local jazz and rhythm-and-blues ensembles, and with artists engaged in preschool education and academic enrichment through the city school system and the St. Louis programs supervised by the federal government's Office of Economic Opportunity's "war on poverty."[9]

Perhaps the critical catalyzing event that brought the future members of BAG together, as many of its founders report, was a Webster College production of Jean Genet's play, *The Blacks*. "I think Oliver Lake had the band, provided the music," recalled Hemphill.[10] "Julius was writing the music," remembered Lake. Whoever was responsible for the music, the event brought together musicians, artists, composers, theater artists, choreographers, and dancers from all around St. Louis.

After the play's run ended, Lake decided to head north for a while. "I think Lester had moved to Chicago and started playing in Roscoe's group,"

Lake recalled. "I went there to visit Lester, and that's when I got introduced to the AACM. The revelation was that we were doing similar things, but we didn't have it organized. We didn't have the music organized, nor did we have ourselves organized. Yet, we had a core group of people. It was very exciting to hear original compositions in a more open format, and that musicians were presenting themselves and doing their own thing."

"When I got back to St. Louis, I was turned on," Lake remembered. "I called up Julius, I called up Floyd. I said, look, why don't we become a branch of the AACM?" Hemphill had also recently visited the AACM along with Phillip Wilson, and while he was similarly impressed and had inquired about joining, he remembered that "they had a lot of rules and stipulations, and I had just gotten out of the army, and I wasn't excited about having a whole lot of rules applied to me."[11]

"Julius said, we don't need to do that," Lake recounted. "Why should we be a branch of them? They only have musicians. We hang out with actors, poets. Why don't we start our own group, and involve everybody? We just finished doing this project and we've got all this expertise of the best actors and dancers in St. Louis. I said, great."

> It had to do specifically with the fact of all those genres being brought together—theater, music, dance, poetry. So we just sat around in a meeting saying, what can we name the group? Well, we got a group of artists here. Somebody said, it's a black artist group. What would be the initials? BAG? That sounds great, as an acronym. I don't know who started it. It was a group of us that just kept brainstorming. I think BAG stuck more. So we thought up our own name, Black Artists Group."[12]

The founding members, according to Lake, were Floyd LeFlore, Julius Hemphill, Malinke Robert Elliott, poet and drummer Ajule Rutlin, and Lake himself. "I think, we were trying to—again like the AACM model we used—we were trying to become self-sufficient," explained Hemphill in a 1994 interview with George Lipsitz. "Instead of satisfying the desires of somebody in a club, whether it was the owner, the patrons, or whoever, we decided we could hire a hall, and give a concert, hopefully draw an audience. And we got up pretty well." Oliver Lake also made the connection between self-production and necessity. In St. Louis, Lake observed, "The only kinds of club settings were more traditional jazz, bebop, and we weren't invited in those spaces. It wasn't our audience, and that's why it made so much sense that we presented ourselves. Otherwise we weren't getting any work."

The former Elbert Jimmy Carroll, born in Homer G. Phillips Hospital in 1947, was also present at the creation of BAG. Like Lester Bowie, Carroll had played with Oliver Sain and Albert King, and around this time he had changed his name to the self-created Baikida, with an Arabic-sounding last name of Yaseen that he later dropped in favor of the family name Carroll. Like most U.S. cities (with the striking exception of New York) St. Louis had separate black and white musicians' unions at the time, and it was at the black union's rehearsal hall, rehearsing with the All-City jazz band, that Carroll met the slightly older Bowie for the first time.

> We would rehearse on Saturdays. Oliver Nelson donated the charts, and he would come by. We'd read through all those great charts. The older guys would come by, [trumpeter and bandleader] George Hudson, and listen and talk to us and give us little pointers. Lester and I were third and fourth chair trumpet. I was about sixteen, sitting in that place, listening to Lester telling jokes. Later, he came to me and said, I got a gig that you might want to play on. I think Fonnie's *Rescue Me* had just come out. They may have been married then, but they were together. He asked me to play on that gig, and that was my first professional gig.[13]

In 1968, Carroll moved into Laclede Town after a stint in the army, where he had been stationed in Germany with an army band. Before his German posting, Carroll was lucky enough to get into the Armed Forces School of Music program in Norfolk, Virginia. "Basically, in 1965," he explained, "anyone from eighteen to thirty-five, draft age, was trying to get in that school to keep from going to Saigon. So you had the best, people who were graduates of Juilliard trying to get in, from all over the country." In Germany, Carroll started "a big band, an avant-garde band. We would write charts, and I was conducting at that point. So when I got back to St. Louis, I said, I don't want to go back to blues bands and chitlin circuit bands." As a means of relief during the hot and humid St. Louis summers, Carroll would practice outdoors in Forest Park. "So I'm sitting upside a tree, practicing, and there were these rolling hills. I see this tiny figure, and he's walking toward me. Seemed like it took like an hour for him to get there. Next thing I know this huge guy is standing in front of me. He says, you sound really good. We're starting this organization, you should come by and check it out, and see if you like it." "I went over with him, and that was Julius Hemphill, with that Texas drawl," Carroll laughed. "So I ended up staying in St. Louis for those three years, for the advent of the Black Artists Group. After being in the army, I wanted to go to New York and get involved in Eric Dolphy and all that type of stuff. I had no intention of staying, but after meeting Julius and Oliver, I said, well, there was another type of music out there."

At the height of the War on Poverty, substantial funding from various sources for the arts was being directed to inner-city areas, and St. Louis's Arts and Education Council received grants from the Rockefeller Foundation and the Danforth Foundation for "an experimental program of community cultural enrichment," providing classes in dance, theater, and music for two thousand children and young adults in St. Louis and East St. Louis. "Malinke was instrumental in writing that grant," recalled Lake. "There were no other black cultural groups organized in St. Louis who had applied for grants at that time, which was totally strange. So we were the only organized group who had applied for this particular grant. So we ended up splitting a portion of the grant with Katherine Dunham on the east side, and us in St. Louis." Hemphill was appointed director of the St. Louis program, and set up instructional programs in all of the arts represented in the new organization—dance, music, drama, poetry, and visual art. The collective moved quickly, using the funding to rehabilitate an old auditorium building near Laclede Town, where the collective set up studios and performance spaces. Hemphill estimated the building's usable floor space at around five thousand square feet on each of two floors.

According to Hemphill, dislocations soon arose between BAG and Dunham's organization, which was planning to set up shop at the Gateway Theatre. "Initially the idea was that we were supposed to work under Miss Dunham's supervision," Hemphill recalled, "but that wasn't really satisfactory."

> Our whole thrust was in conflict, you might say, as aesthetics go, with what she was proposing. The cross-disciplinary aspect was not in keeping with her program. Her program was primarily about dance—her dance. That involved a little costume and stuff, but she was trying to rekindle interest in subject matter that, me personally, I didn't find interesting. We were talking about approaching the unknown, and she was talking about strictly dealing with the known. So we got permission, we agreed that we would work with her, but we wouldn't work for her.

"I think in our goals we had some way of knowing that we were playing our part in the revolution through our culture," Lake observed. "We were teaching kids music, theater, dance, and poetry. Everybody had classes and students. And, we were all being compensated for that through our grants." Part of the money was used to bring in outside artists. "When we received that big grant the second year," said Lake, "we brought in Emilio Cruz from New York as an artist in residence. Emilio turned out masses of work. He was incredible." There was even enough money available to allow visiting artists Emilio and Pat Cruz, who also participated in BAG, to live in Laclede Town rent-free. Other critically important early BAG artists were Carroll, Joseph Bowie, drummers Bensid Thigpen and Charles Bobo Shaw, painter Oliver Jackson, theater artist Vincent Terrell, clarinetist J. D. Parran, dance artist Georgia Collins, baritone saxophonist Hamiet Bluiett, and composer and saxophonist James Jabbo Ware. In 1970, Hemphill served as BAG's chair; Malinke Robert Elliott (then Malinke Kenyatta) was executive director, Lake was treasurer, and Jackson served as artistic advisor.[14]

By 1970, BAG was running a multidepartmental, community-based alternative arts education facility with salaried instructors and an operational budget of around $65,000 (in 1970s dollars) that was organized into practice-based departments.[15] Elliott, who also taught vocal production, headed the "Theatre Course." As Oliver Lake remembers it, "Most of the theater was so-called revolutionary, or things that were going to expose different white myths about our society, things like that." Elliott and Muthal Naidoo taught "interpretation," Georgia Collins and Cathy Allen taught movement and dance, Portia Hunt and Liz Carpentier taught improvisation, and Emilio Cruz taught visual design.

The music faculty was headed by Lake, with Thigpen, Carroll, Hemphill, J. D. Parran, Floyd LeFlore, and trombonist Robert "Happy Tooth" Edwards. Carroll taught theory, and Hemphill taught composition. Their students, according to Carroll, included trumpeters George Sams, Miles Davis's son Gregory Davis, future AACM member Rasul Siddik, and Bruce Purse—"He was a kid in high school. Bruce was really hard core, very conscientious." According to Baikida Carroll, he, Hemphill, and Bluiett led BAG big bands. "[Bluiett] would do graph charts, very little written music, if any at all. We had a certain way we would practice. But right after that, he got the gig with Mingus, so he left St. Louis."[16]

The goals of the music program were summarized in a BAG internal grant proposal document:

> The music course of the school emphasizes involvement, with applied music at its foundation. Students work individually with their teachers and the understanding gained from this type of teaching has enabled the students and teachers to get together in the best possible combinations

and ensembles. Throughout music history, musicians have continually experimented with different instrumentations to achieve new sounds and textures. BAG continues with this experiment and the exciting sounds and forms complement the innovative teaching concept used throughout the school. The musicians create music among and for themselves but also contribute to the drama, dance, and poetry productions, so it is especially important that the communication within the school's faculty is an open and vital force.[17]

"We used ingenuity, not necessarily money," Hemphill told George Lipsitz. "We all worked together, no matter what the project happened to be, whether it was a concert, a play, a dance program. Whatever was needed, we all went out into the community and dug it up. For sets, hanging lights, selling tickets, whatever needed to be done, somebody in the group did it. We were reinforcing each others' efforts that way. Consequently, we all learned a lot, just from hands-on participating."

For Oliver Jackson, BAG's interdisciplinary environment was an important source of learning:

> Working with musicians taught me about the whole matter of *time* in a painting, the need to eliminate the dead spots, the parts that don't move. From musicians, I learned how to get into a painting, to find an opening. And the most important thing you learn from the best musicians is: just play the tune. There are some tunes, certain thematic ideas, that call for lots of notes and speed and intricacy. Others simply have to be done with very few, and very simply. The same is true of a painting.[18]

The connection with the AACM was quickly established with a series of jointly organized concerts in Chicago and St. Louis, one of which, in 1971 or 1972, I participated in. The first of these exchange events took place in the spring of 1969 at the Parkway Community House. Two of the three evenings of an AACM "Mid-Winter Festival" were given over to the work of BAG members Lake, Hemphill, Rutlin, bassist Carl Richardson, and drummer Jerome Harris. Lake's performances, according to the experienced listener John Litweiler, were "stunning, a revelation of agility, melodic power, and a definite sense of careful exploration," while Hemphill's duo with Harris exhibited "fluency, melodic resourcefulness, and care for sound."[19]

"We cut across all these compartments," observed Hemphill. "I tried some experiments in working out plays with music and language in a kind of duet," Hemphill remembered. "They didn't attract so much attention, but we did do it."

> Obviously the musicians were musicians, and the actors [were actors], but we sometimes were able to put ourselves in their shoes, so to speak, and to watch them rehearse, and to make suggestions about—well, if the set included this and that, it might make it more interesting. It was a healthy exchange of ideas, and we learned which of our ideas were hogwash, too. The test is, will it stand up before an audience?

By 1971, the Black Artists Group was flourishing in St. Louis, but unbeknownst to its membership, the seeds of its ultimate demise had already been planted. Emilio Cruz's recollection expressed the optimism with which the organization was suffused:

> What we decided to do was to take all the money and do something serious, in the hope that we would establish not just a thing that would last for one year, which was how long the grant was, but something that would last for many years, and would serve as a teaching institution, and a performing arts institution. The people who started it would go on their way, and it would continue without us.

"That never came about," Cruz explained. The reasons for BAG's demise were complex, and until recently, partly opaque to the artists themselves. One major, perhaps overdetermining, reason involved the sudden withdrawal of the foundation funding that had nurtured BAG's ambitious plans. Of course, the spectre of race, as always, critically informed the proceedings. As George Lipsitz found in his archival research, officials from the Danforth and Rockefeller foundations were "deeply disappointed in the practices that emerged from BAG." The original announcement of the grant to the collective proclaimed, "We believe that the arts, thought of in the broadest sense, do offer a direct remedy for some of the underlying ills—voicelessness, isolation, depersonalization—that affect the economically underprivileged members of our urban society." Funding for the African American arts from white-run foundations was already a major anomaly, and while telling themselves that their purpose in funding the collective was to enhance interracial understanding, foundation officials complained that the BAG programs were "mainly for blacks, not whites. Therefore the effect on black-white understanding has been very limited."[20] Thus, from the foundations' perspective, the critical issue was apparently the fact that BAG programs did not place white concerns at center stage.

Presaging 1990s debates over the politicization of cultural production, foundation officials decried the possibility that "certain artists have been more interested in social reform than in art."[21] BAG's support for a rent strike against the squalid, publicly funded Pruitt-Igoe housing project, one of the worst in the nation, was certainly one of the actions the officials had in mind. As Emilio Cruz maintained, however, "To communicate with the black neighborhoods, you have to address them not in terms of what you would like, but what their needs are."

"I come from the poor," Cruz explained, "and prior to this we lived in Spanish Harlem and that was one of the most devastating experiences I've ever had, seeing absolute, collective despair."

> But when I went to St. Louis, I saw collective despair in ways that I was not prepared for. That had to be addressed. You could just cry when you saw what was happening with all these people. In Pruitt-Igoe, the windows were all knocked out in the dead of the winter, and so the pipes broke, and there was an iceberg that went from the top floor, which was about twenty stories up, all the way down to the bottom. People were living there like animals.

"We decided that we would go in support of the rent strikers," Cruz recalled. "I decided to put together this thing that would meet down at BAG once a week."

> It was called the Citizens' Forum. Pat [Cruz] had a background in civil rights work, and she was extraordinarily articulate. She was only about twenty at the time. So she became the head of this organization. We decided to rent a flatbed truck, and those things are expensive. We turned it into a stage, and once a week we'd go down to political rallies in these various housing projects.

"Now this was exactly what they didn't want us to do," Cruz intoned matter-of-factly. While for Cruz, "they" were the funders, the painter also noted that "some people in BAG, they thought of themselves as artists and felt like, well, this is an imposition. But Hamiet Bluiett and Bobo [Shaw], they were all willing, so we got everybody. Pat, Julius and I went around to all the churches and tried to get them to contribute."[22] Ultimately, as

Lipsitz found, BAG's work was judged as "not conforming to the definitions of urban problems and their desired solutions as envisioned by officials at the Danforth and Rockefeller Foundations,"[23] a judgment that resulted in the termination of the organization's funding. As Lipsitz notes, this came in the midst of "a general attack on the institutions that generated and sustained the civil rights and black power movements in St. Louis"[24] and, I would add, other major U.S. cities.

As Lipsitz and BAG chronicler Benjamin Looker discovered, the internal foundation debates were apparently hidden from the artists. Looker writes, "The charge that BAG exacerbated racial tensions, claims [Malinke] Elliott, never was expressed to the group's leadership, instead being voiced only in a series of private memos and telephone conversations between Danforth and Rockefeller personnel and their consultants."[25] In the absence of this knowledge, in keeping with the general ethos of personal responsibility and self-determination that motivated collectives such as BAG and the AACM, Carroll, Lake, Hemphill, and other BAG artists placed major responsibility for the demise of BAG at their own door. "When that whole period ran out, we couldn't maintain the building any more, not based on concerts," Baikida Carroll observed in our interview, "because it wasn't popular music. We did have a good audience, but it was not enough to sustain that lifestyle for a thirty-nine-thousand-square-foot building."

Oliver Lake pointed to the difficulty of maintaining unity across the panoply of artistic practices that BAG tried to bring together, especially in the absence of the kind of relatively stable social democratic funding base that had nurtured European free improvisation practically from its origins.

> It ended up being the musicians against the actors. That's how the group broke up. I can't remember the real argument, but we ended up being separated for a while. The musicians had always been the administrators, running the group, and the actors were upset about something. There was a truce, and they came back to the musicians and said, OK, we want to rejoin the group, and the musicians refused it. When we refused it, that was the end of the group. That really broke the group down as we knew it.

By this time, the artists of BAG were already looking outward. The South African Muthal Naidoo, of East Indian descent, was part of the theater wing, and an opportunity to develop a more expansive notion of blackness, perhaps along the lines of 1980s British society, was lost when Naidoo left the collective in 1972, feeling that "not being racially African American became a problem as some members . . . were moving the group towards a more exclusive understanding of what it meant to be black." In what was probably a substantial blow to the organization's stability, Malinke Robert Elliott had already left St. Louis in mid-1970, studying theater in Denmark and Sweden, where he was joined by Portia Hunt, Darryl Harris, and for a brief time, Julius Hemphill.[26] Hamiet Bluiett was receiving important work and critical notice since moving to New York, and in 1972, at Bluiett's urging, James Jabbo Ware moved to New York as well. Hemphill arrived in New York in 1973. "I had a notion that I could do better," Hemphill told George Lipsitz in 1994. "I could make money in New York. It was a little more difficult than I thought, but not impossible. I kind of carried the notion that formed in my mind in St. Louis and the Black Artists Group, and kind of brought that here."

Oliver Lake, Floyd LeFlore, Baikida Carroll, Charles Bobo Shaw, and Joseph Bowie (the latter fresh out of high school), drew upon the AACM's example, as well as the contacts that the Art Ensemble had developed. "They gave me the name of their agent, Michel Salou, and a friend of Jarman's," recalled Lake. "We had two vans. We landed at Le Havre. I had four kids and my wife with me, and the band. My youngest kid was six months old. We hauled those two vans off the boat, and drove from Le Havre to Paris, checked into a little tiny hotel. Next day I called Michel, and we kind of eked our way from that."

Bowie, LeFlore, and Shaw soon returned to the United States, but Carroll and Lake stayed for nearly two years.[27] In France, the group was generally billed as "The Black Artists Group of St. Louis." For the most part, the St. Louis musicians, like their Chicago counterparts, did not perform or record very much with French or other European musicians; one exception was Carroll's unusually pensive recording, *Orange Fish Tears*.[28] The group received some excellent notices in the French press, but inevitably, as Lake tells it, "They looked at us like, they're kind of another version of like the Art Ensemble. We had all these instruments, all these percussion instruments. I had every saxophone, alto, soprano, tenor and flute, and vibes. But we were still exciting to the French audience. They were on us with interviews, and filling up our concerts. It was like, wow, look at all these people."

"Then you'd have another gig six weeks later," Lake noted dryly. The lack of steady work, combined with the problems associated with expatriate life, particularly as persons of color, were daunting at times. "I had money, but I couldn't find a place to live," Lake observed. "Paris was crowded, I had four kids and a wife, and I was a black musician. Who was going to give me an apartment?"

> The first place we found was about a hundred miles outside of Paris, on a farm. We lived there for about three or four months, and it was so far away from Paris that the guys, they ended up with girlfriends or somebody to stay with in Paris, and when we got a gig I would drive in, get them, and go do it. Then we found another place in a suburb of Paris, at the end of the subway line. That's where we spent the majority of the time.

"We did end up playing on these huge festivals with our idols. It was like, 'Herbie Hancock, and the Black Artists Group,' We hadn't even been to New York, and we were playing on these major festivals." At times, the experience seemed to justify Lester Bowie's encouraging words about the European situation: "Just get there—you'll work."[29] For the most part, however, as Lake tells it, "It was a very difficult time. We were scratching. We worked, but there was a lot of space in between. If I hadn't had the amount of money I had with me to buy food, to pay rent in advance . . ." Anthony Braxton, who was living at the Cité des Arts, was an artist in residence at the American Center, and when he left the position he successfully recommended Lake. The position included "a stipend of about 400 francs a month. You wouldn't believe how that 400 francs was saving me. Between that and the private students I had, and the few gigs that we got, I was able to eke my way out."

Ultimately, however, the compounding of professional and family instabilities forced Lake to leave Europe. "It was too much for me," Lake admitted, "having those kids there, being a father to my family and a father to the band. I sent my van back on the boat and took the plane back. We left the van there because it cost $500 to get it out and we didn't have it. By then my wife had a nervous breakdown. I had to get out of Paris because she was gone. I moved my wife in with my mother, and my mother took care of her."

Lake moved to New York in 1974. By that time, only the memory of BAG remained in St. Louis. "We didn't leave any younger Black Artists Group to continue," said Lake. "Our audiences had died. We lost the building, we lost

the funding, we lost the group, we lost everything." For Hemphill, "one of
the glaring missed opportunities was to develop a group of people to come
along behind the originals."

"Nineteen sixty-eight. I was thirty years old," observed Hemphill. "I
made some mistakes, but they were honest mistakes."

New Elbows on the Table: The AACM's Second Wave

Ronald Radano's understanding in his 1993 Braxton biography that the
AACM's organizational unity "collapsed" in the wake of the Paris trip seems
at variance with the documentary evidence, including regular concert announcements in *Down Beat*'s "Strictly Ad Lib" column.[30] In fact, the AACM,
including Claudine Myers (now Amina Claudine Myers), Henry Threadgill,
Wallace McMillan, Muhal Richard Abrams, Kalaparusha Maurice McIntyre,
and Thurman Barker, continued to hold meetings, present concerts, and
conduct classes at the school. As Barker told me in 1998, "when the move
happened, those people were not around, and other people began to be active. Leroy, M'Chaka Uba, John Jackson, Stubblefield . . ."[31]

Nonetheless, there was little question that the loss of some of the
AACM's leading members was a major cause for concern that could have
developed into a full-blown crisis. "When you lose your leadership all at
once," observed Leo Smith in retrospect, "the plane drops until the next
guy takes the wheel. I don't think there was any moment of the organization failing, but it put it in a crisis to steer it again." In fact, the Paris trip was
only one of the sources of this organizational instability. For Leonard Jones,
devastated at the loss of Christopher Gaddy and Charles Clark, leaving the
United States

> had nothing to do with a musical exodus. It was an exodus from America
> for me. I didn't go to Paris, I went to Hamburg to be with my wife-to-be.
> I went to Paris in 1970 to visit the Art Ensemble, but I didn't do any play-
> ing because I had stopped playing. I've been knowing Peter Kowald since
> 1969, when he was playing with Peter Brötzmann, Fred van Hove, and
> Han Bennink. I never mentioned anything about being a musician. I had
> no desire to play.

The example of the European sojourn seemed to spur other attempts
to spread out beyond Chicago, amounting to a developing AACM diaspora
that threatened to leave Chicago bereft of some of its most promising experimental musicians. John Stubblefield's 1971 attempt to establish him-

self in New York was relatively successful. M'Chaka Uba left for the West, and Ajaramu, Amina Claudine Myers, and Kalaparusha Maurice McIntyre settled briefly in Newark.[32] Henry Threadgill tried New York briefly, sending back glowing reports about the possibilities there. As he tells it, his Chicago-based colleagues were inexplicably underwhelmed by his enthusiasm, and Threadgill himself soon returned to Chicago.

During this unstable period, Leo Smith felt, "Muhal had to rescue it." This apparent reassertion by Abrams of crucial leadership was accompanied by the arrival of new members, such as saxophonist Vandy Harris, and trumpeters Frank Gordon (who had also tried New York briefly), and Bata Rutlin, the brother of Ajule Rutlin. These musicians sustained the organization's activities, continuing to present concerts as always, and conducting the AACM School's Saturday morning music classes. Another new member was guitarist Pete Cosey, who was associated with the "Afro-Jazz" ensemble, the Pharaohs. The group, which included saxophonist Don Myrick, Derf Reklaw-Raheem on flute, saxophone, and percussion, Aaron Dodd on tuba, Black Herman Waterford on saxophone, and Big Willie Woods on trombone, had just released its first, self-produced album, *Awakening,* in early 1972.[33]

The renewal of the AACM intensified after 1970, as what came to be regarded as a "second wave" of younger musicians appeared. The more experienced members enculturated these newcomers into the set of values developed in the AACM's self-realized atmospheric hothouse: economic and musical collectivity, a composer-centered ideology, methodological diversity, and freedom of cultural reference. Douglas Ewart is undoubtedly a critically important pivotal figure in this second wave.

Ewart was born in 1946 in Kingston, Jamaica. His father, Tom Ewart, was one of cricket's most internationally celebrated professional umpires, eventually earning induction into the Cricket Hall of Fame. His aunt, Iris King, was a leading member of the People's National Party, then headed by Norman Manley, the national hero who negotiated the island nation's independence. She became a member of the House of Representatives, and later, the first woman mayor in Jamaica. Mrs. King's son, Herman, or "Woody," as he is known, influenced the young Ewart in a number of ways. Woody was a ship's pilot, an important and well-compensated occupation on the island. "He was a very progressive thinker," said Ewart. "He was involved in organizing labor and was very political. He was a member of the Rastafarian movement. He associated with people from all walks of life. This fascinated me as a child."[34]

In Jamaica, hard times were endemic, and there was tremendous economic pressure to emigrate to the United States, which Ewart's mother Sybil did, with the family's support, when Ewart was nine years old. Ewart's father "was around, but he wasn't a caregiver in that kind of way," so Ewart grew up in his grandmother's house, on an acre of land that opened out onto the Caribbean Sea. Ewart's grandmother, a Seventh-Day Adventist, ran a tight ship. The wakeup call came at 5:00 a.m., and after morning prayers and chores, the children would walk to school. When the Sabbath began on Friday evening, "from six o'clock, no radio, no playing of any kind—card games, any kind of games. We sat in a circle, and she had these 'quarterlies,' which were supplements for the Bible study."

Ewart grew up under British colonial rule, and when he was nearing his teens, the Rastafarian movement began to pique his interest. "One of the things that drew me to the movement," he recalled, "was the Afrocentricity of it and the anti-British feeling, which I had at a very early age. In movie houses during those days, the movie was prefaced by playing the national anthem of England, and you'd have to stand. Well, I decided I wasn't going to stand for the queen, and they would throw you out if you refused to stand."

Another element in the attractiveness of the Rasta camps was the music. Early on, the young Ewart was a frequent visitor at drummer Count Ossie's celebrated "grounations," gatherings with music where people came together in large numbers to discuss politics, culture, everything. "Count knew our family, and so we were always welcomed." It could be said that Ewart's musical career started right there. "My entry into music was trying to drum, and of course, nobody gave lessons or anything like that. I started beating on large cans." Eventually, Ewart received the occasional opportunity to play drums at Count Ossie's camp, where he met some of the musicians who would create the music later known around the world as ska, including trombonists Don Drummond and Rico Rodriguez, saxophonist Roland Alphonso, and trumpeter Dizzy Johnny (Johnny Moore).[35]

Ultimately, both home and school became less interesting for Ewart, so one day he ran away from home to a Rasta camp. The Rastas took him in, but any illusions regarding a carefree life were quickly dispelled.

> There was no running water, no plumbing of any kind. I had to carry a five-gallon bucket of water, and you had to learn the skill of persuading somebody to give a Rasta water. Some people were very happy to give you water, and some people would curse you. I slept on a bed that was

basically cardboard, and we didn't have any blankets or anything like that. It was pretty much open, and in a good rain you would get wet. Of course you had to eat, so you had to find some way to help contribute. Periodically I'd go home and raid our pantry, and bring back what would be my contributions to the rations.

Ewart was saved from being sent to reform school by his cousin Woody, who took him in, placated his exasperated grandmother, and exposed him to a wide range of musics. Another cousin, Errol Lazarus, was a seaman who brought back recordings for Cousin Woody that were difficult to find in Jamaica—Charles Mingus, Clifford Brown, Charlie Parker, John Coltrane, Sarah Vaughan, Ella Fitzgerald, Billy Eckstine, and Sonny Boy Williamson, as well as classical European music. Eventually, the family enrolled Ewart at Cobbla Camp, a military-style school where he became interested in farming. Meanwhile, Ewart's mother, who originally went to New York on a vacation visa, found a job doing housework. She overstayed her time, however, and was turned in to U.S. immigration, possibly by her neighbors. She skipped her appointment with the immigration authorities in favor of joining a relative in Chicago, where in 1963, she found another job, and sent for Ewart and his sister.

Ewart took up tailoring at Dunbar Vocational High School on Chicago's South Side, graduating in 1967. He was still excited about music, however, and it was a classmate, flutist Joel Brandon, who introduced him to the first concerts of the AACM at Abraham Lincoln Center. It was around this time that he met Joseph Jarman and Fred Anderson. "I was drawn to the music because it was very different from what I had been listening to," Ewart said. "Even though I wasn't a musician yet, I'd go and watch them at rehearsals at Gordon Emanuel's house, and I'd see people like Braxton and Wadada Leo Smith." Dizzy Gillespie's example had already kindled in Ewart a desire to play the trumpet, and Ewart soon went to the local pawnshop to purchase a horn. To his surprise, however, the trumpet seemed intractable to him. Jarman came to the rescue by introducing Ewart to John Shenoy Jackson, the trumpeter and behind-the-scenes administrative wizard of the AACM, who sold him a Buescher alto saxophone for $90. Ewart began taking private lessons with Jarman. "Joseph was my mentor, more so than any member of the association I can think of," Ewart affirmed. "I liked what Joseph did as an artist, multidimensionally, and philosophically, we found common ground. I was very much involved in Baha'i at that time. He was into Buddhism, and there were similarities there with the Baha'i faith. We did breathing exercises, stretching exercises, silent meditation."

Ewart began attending classes at the newly opened AACM School, and in our interview, described at some length its composer-centered pedagogical methods. The first class of the day, music theory, started at 9:00 a.m. "One of the interesting things about going to the AACM School is that we began composing immediately. We'd be given a melody or a cantus firmus, and then we'd write the chords, or you'd be given a scale and you'd learn how to compose from that. The AACM had concerts for the students, so we performed our compositions that we had written in the class."

Ewart marveled that even in Chicago's bitterly cold winters, "Everybody was there every week, thirty, forty below. We didn't even pay for chalk, and it was an endless semester. The musicians were serious, and if you weren't serious, you got kicked out." Ewart added flute and clarinet to his instrumental palette, and began to learn about the business of self-promotion, using the same persuasive skills that he had learned in obtaining water for his Rasta camp.

As he remembers it, Ewart was never formally inducted into the AACM, and he was not listed among the members in the 1968 issue of the *New Regime.* "I just started going to meetings, being involved, helping to put the magazine together, distributing posters, working at the door." In terms of rehearsing and performing with the AACM, Ewart remembers a process of critical engagement.

> People in the group would say, hey, I'd like you to use more of the material that we've utilized within the composition, rather than falling back on older ideas of how one might improvise on a piece. Or, if it was open improvisation, they would not tell the person what to do, but mainly point out that there were a lot more avenues to take, and that it was important that you really exercise your creativity, to be more discerning, to create greater variety.

It was clear to Ewart that "the idea of making a true departure from what had gone before was something that was definitely considered." At the same time, however, "In trying to forge new ground, cats were not in any way trying to undermine what had gone before. People were listening to Louis Armstrong, James P. Johnson, Fatha Hines, Duke Ellington, Basie, the Lunceford work. Cats were looking at Erik Satie, Balinese music, Burmese music, the I Ching. They said, the cats set a pace for us, and we got to keep up with this pace."

In the summer of 1971, I was a native South Sider, a member of Cook County Hospital's class of 1952. My father and mother, part of the great exodus from the South, had met in Chicago around 1950. My father had gotten a job in the post office around that time, and was still working there in 1970 when he and my mother purchased their first home on 88th Street near Stony Island Avenue. We had come a long way from our first abode, a two-room Woodlawn apartment with a Murphy bed in the living room, on a dead-end street in the shadow of the Illinois Central tracks.

My mother liked John Lee Hooker and B. B. King, Charles Brown at Christmastime, and Sam Cooke at any time, as well as Little Johnny Taylor and R&B in general. My father had two passions: electronics, which he had studied under the GI Bill, and the kind of jazz that was popular among his generation of African Americans—Buddy Johnson, Tab Smith, Cleanhead Vinson, Brother Jack McDuff. On the radio, we would listen to Marty Faye, and later to Dick Buckley, and my dad's endless lectures about hearing Erskine Hawkins, Lionel Hampton, and Illinois Jacquet live as a young navy seaman were made all the more vivid by the fact that he never played any records by any of them. Like a radio play, you could use your imagination.

At the neighborhood school I was one of those children who attended in half-day shifts to relieve "overcrowding," or rather, to facilitate de facto segregation.[36] An African American teacher, whom I remember as Miss Vining, took an interest in my education and told my parents about scholarships at the University of Chicago Laboratory School. When they heard about the cost, even with the scholarship, they were pretty daunted. Miss Vining was not to be denied, however, and when I got to the Lab School in 1961, I was one of a very small complement of black pupils, mostly children of professional people. Two amazing teachers were crucial to my life there: Louise Pliss, who for two years did everything she could to facilitate my transition from ghetto school to Lab School, and the Lab School band instructor, Frank Tirro, the well-known jazz historian, who was then working on his PhD. That was also where the whole formal business of music started for me.

I didn't know anything about instruments, but my parents thought that music would be a way to make friends. I think I picked the trombone mainly because it looked big, shiny, and weird. It cost around $150, and my mother paid for it on time, five dollars or so every month. I played in the school orchestra and the concert band, and later took private lessons from University of Chicago graduate students, where we read Arban, Rochut, and Bach cello suites, standard fare for trombonists. Carrying this unwieldy instrument, I would walk twice daily across the Midway, the arboreal southern border between the nice, pleasant campus and what was then being called "the ghetto."

Around high school, Mr. Tirro and a new teacher, Dean Hey, started a jazz band at the Lab School, and we started going to stage band contests. Mr. Hey, whose training was in both contemporary classical music and jazz, wanted everyone to improvise instead of playing the written-out solos that were typical of school-band arrangements, so he started an improvisation class. His jazz-band pupils also presented Allan Kaprow–style happenings, which I guess some people today would complain about, since this was not part of "the tradition." I began studying trombone privately with Mr. Hey, and at the same time, I discovered some records at home that my father never played—Max Roach with J. J. Johnson, Miles Davis with John Coltrane, and Lester Young with Oscar Peterson. The Lab School librarian, Win Poole, one of the few African Americans on staff there, introduced me to Charlie Parker and Thelonious Monk, as well as tape music from the University of Illinois electronic music studios. A fellow student, Carolyn Wilkins,[37] introduced me to late Coltrane, via his *Live at the Village Vanguard Again*, which elicited a very strong and lasting emotional reaction. After hearing that record, I started to get interested in trying to play that sort of thing. As it happens, I started playing music at the same time as trombonist Ray Anderson, and around 1968, Ray took me to hear Fred Anderson at an AACM concert at the Parkway Community House. I was totally baffled— what was it?

About a year later I saw flyers posted around the school advertising a group called the "Art Ensemble." The concert took place at the University's Ida Noyes Hall, right there on campus. I was stunned by Joseph Jarman's body-painted arms, attacking a vibraphone with mallets swishing dangerously close to my nose. I remember being so frightened that I literally seemed to faint. When I came to, Lester Bowie's trumpet squeals and raspberries were leading to long drone sections where Malachi Favors's bass unwound long strings of melody, while Roscoe Mitchell contentedly puttered about in a secret garden of percussion.

Accepted to Yale in 1969, I was going to major in "prelaw," but I also took music theory. That first year, people like Sam Rivers, Keith Jarrett, and Archie Shepp, with Sunny Murray, Alan Silva, and saxophonist Byard Lancaster, all came to the school. After the Shepp concert, Murray, Lancaster, and Silva hosted a sort of jam session, where I met a piano player, Anthony Davis, who was a music major. He was composing music and leading his own groups, and we started playing together a lot after that—oh, for the next thirty-five years or so. During my second year I took more music theory and history, but then I became disinterested in school, and I took a year off. This was probably a foolhardy move, since you could be reclassified 1-A and sent to Vietnam. For some reason, though, that didn't happen.

So one typically humid Chicago summer afternoon in 1971, free from school and the draft, I was riding home from a summer job on the North Side of Chicago. Usually I rode the Stony Island bus to 87th Street, but that day I took the Jeffery Express bus, and began walking west toward my parents' house, where I had been living. Along the way, I heard an unusual sound. Searching for its source, I peeked through the window of a two-story red brick building that looked like a school, and saw a group of musicians, including a tall, bespectacled fellow, wearing a brightly colored dashiki and holding, of all things, a trombone. I decided to go inside to listen. The music was fascinating, and when they took a break I went up to the bandleader, who wore a darker-colored dashiki, and asked him how one might join the group. "You have to be known as a musician," he said gravely. A dashiki-clad guitarist with an enormous Afro looked a bit skeptical as well, but a more welcoming, expansive person, wearing thick-rimmed glasses and an oxford shirt and carrying a trumpet, came up and said something like "Hey, Richard, what do you want to do with these parts?"

"Are you Richard Abrams?" I said. The bandleader nodded, but I think he was a bit startled by my query, as if he hadn't expected that someone outside the circle of musicians might know of him. I told him that I lived right around the corner, and I had heard *Levels and Degrees of Light*. In this way, I was introduced to Muhal, the oxford-shirt fellow, John Shenoy Jackson, and the guitarist, Pete Cosey. They had a short private conference, and agreed that I should come to a rehearsal they were holding in the same building that coming Saturday. I went home and told my parents and my sister excitedly that I had met some real musicians, and that I was going to rehearse with them.

On Friday, I got a call from Jackson, who apologized for having to cancel the Saturday rehearsal. He suggested that on the following Monday I should come to the venue where they were performing, a nightspot called the Pumpkin Room, on 71st and Jeffery, on the South Side, not far from my neighborhood.[38] My parents were a bit concerned, since the Pumpkin

Room was a tavern, and at nineteen, I was not of legal age. They demanded to go along. Just before the big event I got a call from Anthony Davis, who was driving west to Iowa, where his parents were living. Could he, his girl-friend Debbie, and his brother Kip crash at our house for a couple of days? There were no objections, and I added that, as it happened, I had this "gig" at the Pumpkin Room and we could all go on Monday night.

So at the appointed hour, Tony, Debbie, Kip, my father and mother, and I clambered into the family car and headed for 71st Street. I went backstage with my horn and met Abrams and Jackson. Seeming surprised, Jackson told me, "We thought you should just come to listen." Abrams, in a rather authoritative voice, said, "But are you ready to play?" Up to that point, I thought I was ready to play, but the word "yes" wouldn't come out of my mouth.

"Well, are you ready to play?" Muhal demanded again.

"Yes," I said softly.

"OK, get ready. Jackson, give him the charts."

I was warming up and looking over the music when I saw somebody I thought I recognized from that scary Ida Noyes event in 1969. Pulling out his saxophone, he looked me over briefly, but said nothing. Other musicians began to file in. "Is that Joseph Jarman?" I asked Jackson hesitantly. Jackson nodded.

It was time to go onstage. We took our seats, and Abrams told the band to get out "Mood 2." I looked through the charts and didn't find it. Steve Galloway, the tall trombonist who I had seen that first day, found it and pulled it out. The name on the title page didn't look anything like "Mood 2." Instead, the letters were scrambled—"ᴏᴍᴅᴏ II"—with long dashes over the two *O*s.

That's about all I remember; I don't remember, for example, the tall, muscular, and very congenial cross-dresser everybody talked about who served as the club's bouncer. I do remember that an arrangement of Thelo-nious Monk's "Round Midnight" was called, and somebody named Kala-parusha stood up and played an incredible tenor saxophone solo. The other thing I remember was playing "Blues Forever." Noticing the key signature, D-flat, I recalled all of my struggles with that particular key. As soon as we finished the head, Abrams pointed at me to play. Evidently, these struggles were to become quite public.

After the ordeal was over, I thought that I had definitely blown it, but the band's drummer, a very kindly and engaging man, introduced himself as Steve McCall. "Hey, man, are you working next week?" I thought about

my summer job; I didn't understand musician-speak. Since the job was ending, I answered truthfully. Steve said that he was organizing a concert at
McCormick Place, Chicago's convention center, and asked me to be part
of it. We exchanged numbers, and at the rehearsal, I was introduced to Jarman, Roscoe Mitchell, Malachi Favors, a second drummer, Sabu Toyozumi,
a tuba player, Aaron Dodd, and yet another dashiki-wearing person, who
introduced himself as Douglas Ewart. Douglas invited me to his house after the rehearsal, and that was the start of a lifelong friendship. Everybody
had heard of McCormick Place, and so my parents came to see me a second
time. The event made the Chicago *Defender,* complete with pictures of all
of us.[39]

I don't remember how I was introduced to the AACM per se, but I
started going to the Saturday morning theory classes, and shortly thereafter, Jackson suggested that I apply for AACM membership. The one-page
application asked for a mix of personal information and aesthetic and career aspirations. I was accepted, and perhaps even that same day, was voted
recording secretary. I began taking minutes of the weekly meetings—a
kind of apprenticeship that went beyond the purely musical, as the gruff,
erudite, and broadly humorous Jackson began to teach me the realities of
how an organization is run.

The visibility of AACM musicians was rising sharply, both in the United
States and in Europe, and AACM members began to appear more frequently in the *Down Beat* Critics and Readers Polls. In 1970, the "Talent Deserving of Wider Recognition" (TDWR) section of the Critics Poll named
Lester Lashley as the winner in the trombone category, well ahead of Basie
stalwart Al Grey. The Art Ensemble of Chicago finished just below the top
of the combo category; Roscoe Mitchell also placed in the alto saxophone
section; the soprano saxophone section named both Mitchell and Joseph
Jarman; and Lester Bowie received notice in the trumpet section. AACM
musicians who had not gone to Europe were also recognized, including
Richard Abrams, Joel Brandon, and Maurice McIntyre. In the category of
tenor saxophone, McIntyre placed in the company of Sam Rivers, Pharoah
Sanders, Chicago expatriate Johnny Griffin, and the winner, Albert Ayler,
who was found dead in New York's East River the following year. The
AACM Big Band, an ensemble with varying instrumentation composed
simply of the membership itself, was recognized along with Sun Ra in the
band category, even in the absence of a released recording.[40]

Nineteen seventy was also the era of the emergence of jazz-rock fusion, and *Down Beat* readers ignored criticisms of Miles Davis as a "commercial sellout," selecting him in the magazine's Readers Poll that year as (in the gendered language of the period) "Jazzman of the Year." The readers also weighed in with limited recognition of still-emerging AACM artists such as Mitchell, who was recommended by thirty readers for the same honor. The AACM Big Band made a showing in the category of "Big Band of the Year"; the Art Ensemble of Chicago was also recognized, along with Chicago-based Lester Lashley and Maurice McIntyre, and the European so-journers Lester Bowie, Joseph Jarman, and Malachi Favors.[41]

In addition to wider recognition within the jazz world, by 1970, various AACM musicians were pursuing a Chicago-based insurgency beyond that world that was bearing fruit in various interdisciplinary arenas. Henry Threadgill and Joseph Jarman were working in collaboration with surrealist performance artist Franklin Rosemont, theater artist Kim An Wang, and the emerging local theater group, Kingston Mines. The group Integral, with Threadgill, Lester Lashley, and Leo Smith, worked with Threadgill's first wife, theater artist Catherine Slade, at venues such as the Museum of Contemporary Art. Threadgill also worked with Smith and John Stubblefield in the Free Theater's performance of William Burroughs's *Naked Lunch*.[42]

Despite the enhanced public profile of the AACM and a number of its members, performance opportunities for black experimental music, particularly in Chicago, remained scarce. The University of Chicago and other midwestern campuses occasionally presented AACM music, but these infrequent performances were hardly sufficient to guarantee a living. Musicians made up the financial slack in a variety of ways. Older, more connected members, particularly those who had come up under the earlier bebop-dominated period, such as Steve McCall and Muhal Richard Abrams, were able to eke out a living with combinations of club dates and standards, including performances with their longtime associate and fellow experimenter, saxophonist Eddie Harris.[43] Amina Claudine Myers and Ajaramu toured from time to time with Gene Ammons, including a month in New York in 1971, and a trip to Los Angeles.

The Art Ensemble of Chicago, with its orientation toward collective business practices, worked more frequently than many. Thurman Barker enjoyed something of a sinecure in Chicago's musical theater scene, and trombonist Martin Alexander pursued his métier as a trained electrical engineer. For many younger musicians, less connected with insider networks and/or unwilling to take regular employment, the situation was far more precarious. Some attempted a variety of small-business enterprises. Trombonist Lester Lashley, who held an MFA from the School of the Art Institute, sold his visual art and crafts privately, as did painter and clarinetist Jose Williams, an AACM member during the late 1960s who gave frequent concerts with his Gallery Ensemble at his own AFAM Gallery on the South Side.[44]

Joseph Jarman credits trumpeter John Shenoy Jackson as a critical element in the survival strategies of many AACM musicians. Jackson had risen to a position of influence in the Chicago-area public assistance administration, and was able to place a number of AACM musicians on the public aid rolls.[45] Some members, such as Jodie Christian and Fred Anderson, became amicably separated from day-to-day AACM activities. Christian had achieved stature as one of the area's best known and most highly respected musicians, performing in the style he and others of his generation had perfected at the Cotton Club sessions in the 1950s. Anderson, never one to attend regular AACM meetings, lived in Evanston, far from the AACM's South Side staging ground, with his wife, Bernice, and their three rapidly growing sons. After completing his daily tasks at a rug company, Anderson would rehearse and occasionally perform publicly with Lester Lashley, Steve McCall, and his old friend Bill Brimfield, among others.

Anderson's freely offered tutelage was a key factor in the development of several AACM members, and in 1971, he was playing a particularly vital role in the development of two young university students, Steve Colson, and Earl Lavon Freeman, known since childhood as "Chico." Both Freeman and Colson were born in 1949. Colson's father, who had some college background, was employed at Newark Airport as a cargo loader for United Airlines. Colson's mother, a high-school graduate, eventually became executive secretary to the director of the Port Authority of New York and New Jersey. A partial list of the music he and his parents listened to would include Beethoven symphonies, Ella Fitzgerald, Illinois Jacquet, Count Basie, Ezio Pinza, King Pleasure, the Temptations, Smokey Robinson, Stevie Wonder, and Mary Martin. Colson started piano lessons in junior high school, practicing Chopin waltzes and Bach preludes, and trying to learn to improvise. He was also becoming an avid connoisseur of recordings by Art Blakey, Horace Silver, Ornette Coleman, Andrew Hill, and Eric Dolphy.

In 1967, Colson was admitted to the Northwestern School of Music in the Chicago suburb of Evanston. There, he met Chico Freeman, whose father, Earl Sr., generally known in the world of music as Von Freeman, is widely recognized as one of the most important Chicago saxophonists. "I've seen the musician's life from both sides," said Chico Freeman in our interview, "from the side of being at home waiting, and now, being a musician and going out."[46] The Freeman family has lived in the same South Side house for a generation, and when Freeman was growing up, crossing certain borders was asking for trouble. "At the time, I wasn't aware of it," Freeman remembered. "When I saw white people, I didn't think, they're white and I'm black. Not until a few incidents happened to me. I was with some friends and we rode our bikes into a white neighborhood and they tried to kill us."

One could not gainsay the home-grown variety of trouble either. Freeman's neighborhood high school, like many on the South Side, was disputed gang turf, with the Blackstone Rangers and the East Side Disciples as the two primary contenders. "You had to be a part of it, or you couldn't survive," Freeman said. "I never got involved in their criminal activities, but I found myself having more altercations than I would have liked." Nonetheless, by all accounts, Freeman was a good student, with German and advanced mathematics as particular interests. Freeman started on piano at the age of five, played trumpet in his elementary school band, and sang in numerous singing groups, including the choir at his grandmother's Sanctified church. "I wasn't interested in jazz," said Freeman. "I was interested in Jerry Butler, the Impressions, the Temptations, and things like that. I went to school with the Emotions. Those were my peers. I was singing on the street corners, in the school hallways."

Most music in the Freeman family residence itself was heard live, made either by his grandmother, who played guitar and sang gospel songs, or by his father and his many musical colleagues, including Andrew Hill, Malachi Favors, Pat Patrick, John Gilmore, bassist David Shipp, and Freeman's uncles, guitarist George Freeman and drummer Bruz Freeman. According to Freeman, his father "hardly owned any" records, but one of them, Miles Davis's *Kind of Blue,* was "the record that made me want to become a musician."

> One day nobody was home except me, or I got up in the middle of the night. We lived in a pretty crowded house, and that was the only time I could have that space. I put on this record. I didn't even know what it was. I just grabbed it and put it on, and it touched me. That's why I started playing trumpet, six, seven, eight years old.

In high school, the pressure of carrying several advanced mathematics courses, along with a desire to play basketball, induced Freeman to give up the trumpet. Moreover, Freeman's singing was going well. "I almost had a recording contract with Brunswick Records, the same people who had Jackie Wilson, Curtis Mayfield," he recalled. "Vietnam stopped that. I didn't go, but everybody in my singing group did. They all got drafted." One of the few ways of avoiding being sucked into the jungle was a college deferment, and Freeman accepted a mathematics scholarship to Northwestern University. Rather quickly, however, "the music bug took over again, and I ended up leaving the math school for the music school," where he met Steve Colson, who was taking composition and theory. Freeman resumed his trumpet studies and got into the concert band. His trumpet instructors, however, did not share his love of Miles Davis: "I brought this to my teacher, who was teaching me all the classical stuff. He was a good guy. But when I brought Miles Davis to him, he said, he played out of tune. He didn't like his tone. I sat there and I thought, wow, maybe this is not going to work out for me. But I continued."

In the late 1960s, Northwestern University, like many predominantly white academic institutions, was struggling with integration. In practice, this meant that African American students bore the brunt of the cultural and social contention that engaged the community as a whole.[47] Certainly, the university exposed Freeman to another America that simply didn't exist on the South Side. "The music that was played on campus was mostly music that white communities liked, which we had never heard before," said Freeman. "I had never heard white rock—Cream; Crosby, Stills, and Nash; Janis Joplin. And, of course, there were the classical concerts. Motown hadn't crossed over yet." In this way, one of the biggest fears of doctrinaire cultural nationalists of any race—miscegenation—was slowly being realized in sound. "I had white roommates," said Freeman, "and one day I found myself starting to like some of this music. I became a Crosby, Stills, and Nash fan."

New musical influences not withstanding, one receives the impression that for African American students during this period, Northwestern was very stressful indeed. "I had more fights, physical fights, in college than I did in high school," Freeman recalled. "Being attacked by groups of whites, attempts to run us over with cars on the campus. Fights in the gym, namecalling we got walking down the street. The university hadn't been doing anything. So finally a threat was made that if they didn't do something there were going to be problems." Inevitably, one day there was a major incident: "It appeared that a white guy from a pretty racist fraternity there fired a gun at one of the black basketball players at Northwestern. Phone calls went out to everybody. Each person said, make a phone call to who you know in Chicago, and get them up here."

"Who you know" meant the gangs, which in this case performed their traditional function of neighborhood protection.

> On the South Side there were the Blackstone Rangers. They wore red berets. The Disciples wore blue berets. On the West Side there were the Egyptian Cobras and the Vice Lords. The Vice Lords wore yellow, and the Cobras wore green. Within one hour, there were red, blue, green, yellow, and black berets, a sea of them on the campus. That was the first time the university began to change their policies. It didn't change fast enough, ultimately.

By this time, both Freeman and Steve Colson, as well as Anthony Porter (later Soji Adebayo), who had become a pianist, were actively composing and studying in the music school, one of many sites where the tiny minority of African American students at Northwestern (some students recalled a total population of under one hundred out of ten thousand) saw their culture being ignored and even actively disparaged. As Steve Colson recalled,

> You didn't want to be heard playing any jazz. You're supposed to be here to learn, you know, whatever the classical piece was. . . . In the history class they said, OK, you can write a paper on a twentieth-century composer. Somebody tried to write something on Bird, and they said, what are you doing? We're talking about Bartok, not Dizzy Gillespie.

Unlike the situation in Walter Dyett's era, however, students in this period were not content to limit their encounters with black music to extracurricular activities. "The current of the time had changed by then," Colson recalled, "because we were in negotiations, saying, look, we want some black studies courses." In 1968, Colson was part of the student organization that was pursuing these negotiations. He also recalled the presence of James Turner, who later coined the term "Africana Studies," and initiated Cornell University's Africana Studies and Research Center. "At some point," Colson related,

> They decided, let's do something a little bit more dramatic than talk. It was decided to take over the Bursar's Office [chuckles]. Nobody'd be get-

ting their checks, you know, and the professors would be ticked off. Early one morning, everybody just started to walk towards this certain area. At a certain point, two guys went over and kind of hoodwinked the guards.

"It was national," Colson recalled. "The state troopers and everything, the National Guard was getting ready to come in. We had chained ourselves in." According to one *New York Times* article, the students demanded "more and better scholarships for Negroes, with a gradual increase in the number of Negro students . . . separate living units for black students by the fall quarter . . . [and] courses in 'black literature' and 'black art' taught by professors approved by Negro students." The accompanying picture featured a sign demanding "Black Autonomy" and "Black Self-Determination."[48] Thirty-six hours later, according to a UPI wire report from May 5, 1968, "The university met almost every demand of the 100 Negro students in some form." The demands, according to the article, included "racially segregated living quarters" and a demand for half of future black admits to come from inner-city school systems.[49] "We wound up getting the university to give us a location which we called the Black House," said Colson. "We got a dean that was specific to us as blacks on campus. So we got a black dean."[50]

In the wake of this and other student protests, particularly at Rutgers and Cornell universities, demands for black studies courses grew, led by both students and African American scholars, including Nathan Hare, who organized the first such program in the United States in 1969. This movement fostered entirely new academic disciplines, including ethnic studies and gender studies, and reformed the research canons of older, more established fields, paving the way for wide-ranging changes in U.S. education at all levels.[51] Nonetheless, the old structures were still in place, as Steve Colson remembers, at once ruefully and whimsically. "My English teacher," he recalled, "used to brag about how his great-grandpappy started the Ku Klux Klan."

During what was supposed to be Colson's final year on campus, he met a young music school freshman named Kristine Browne. "My little joke about Northwestern," said Browne, "is that the only thing I got out of Northwestern was that I met my husband there. I'm walking down the steps from the music school. He comes around from the basement. He looks up and says, *You* are in the music school?" Those were the first words he said to me. He kind of looked at me because I wasn't the usual—I wasn't *straight*. I had the big Afro and the earrings and the attitude."[52] The young singer, now known as Iqua Colson, was born in Provident Hospital, the black-run hospital on Chicago's South Side, and grew up in arguably upper-middle-class circumstances in the University of Chicago's constructed bedroom community of Hyde Park. Her mother, a talented pianist with a master's degree in administration, headed the guidance department at Orr High School on the Far South Side. Her father was a chemical engineer who worked on projects (some of which were possibly classified) at Argonne National Laboratory.

The young Kristine spent summers with her parents and relatives at their summer home in Idlewild, a middle-class resort town in Michigan, where she knew Robert Stepto, who published a memoir of his Idlewild experience, *Blue as the Lake.*[53] Her uncles were economist Robert Browne, who was part of president Bill Clinton's economic liaison to postapartheid South Africa, and Warren Bacon, a well-known Chicago businessman and community leader who was an important element in the 1983 election of Chicago's first African American mayor, Harold Washington, who is still regarded with reverence and awe in Chicago's black community for breaking the white stranglehold on political power in the city.

Young middle-class African Americans definitely felt the sting of the major *Verbot* on black middle-class values put forward during the cultural nationalist era, supported ethnographically by black sociologist E. Franklin Frazier's scathing 1957 portrayal in *Black Bourgeoisie.*[54] Of course, nobody wanted to be a *boojie.* "My Aunt Mary Lou said, isn't Kris going to come out for the Links?[55] Don't you want to be in Jack and Jill? I was like, absolutely not." For many people throughout the United States at this time, black consciousness was visually symbolized by clothing and hairstyles. "I had the huge Afro, and the multiple ear-piercings, and we went on and pierced our noses," Colson recalled. "We knew how to wrap our heads, even in high school." As a high schooler, she would skip choir practice to serve breakfast to young children at the Black Panther school, and tried to engineer a one-day school holiday at Kenwood High School in memory of Malcolm X's birthday.

Colson's father was fond of Gene Ammons and Count Basie, and Colson herself had been taking classical piano since age six. At Kenwood High School, she studied music with the legendary Lena McLin, an accomplished composer who taught generations of young people in the Chicago Public Schools over a thirty-six-year tenure. After a period of disaffection from music—"It became this chore that my mother insisted that I do"—Colson suddenly developed a desire to sing, inspired by "Motown stuff, Isaac Hayes, Aretha, [Oscar Brown, Jr.'s] Signifying Monkey, [Nancy Wilson's] 'Guess

Who I Saw Today.'" She began performing with alacrity in the numerous choral arrangements crafted by McLin for her students, while also studying piano privately to prepare for her entrance auditions at Northwestern.

Arriving on the Evanston campus, Colson was subject to the same kinds of dislocations that other black students were experiencing. For black women in particular, the situation was compounded by the general curiosity factor of whites—again, often symbolized by hair. "I was going through campus like, grrr, what am I doing here," recalled Iqua. "I had professors touching my hair—you know, just ignorant crap." Moreover, even though in the wake of the black student protests, jazz was now being included in the curriculum, the standards for admission seemed variable, to put it charitably. Steve Colson remembered that "Neither Chico nor I could get into the jazz band that they had started while we were there. The guy says, 'I want you to play a jazz piece—but no blues.' So I said OK. I'm thinking, I'll play 'Dat Dere,' which is not a blues. That was the first piece I had learned, in high school. He says, 'I told you, not a blues.' So I didn't get in." Thus, Steve Colson and Chico Freeman learned jazz in exactly the same way that their forebears had learned it. "Some things were trial and error," Colson observed, "but I was like, I'm at least playing jazz as well as the people that you have playing it—although I was actually doing fairly well in some courses until [laughs] after we took over the Bursar's Office."

During Colson's sophomore year, he and Freeman were drawn to the AACM's Evanston "chapter," headed by Fred Anderson and Bill Brimfield. The two Evanstonians took the young musicians under their tutelage, and it should come as no surprise to those who know Anderson that they were listening closely to Charlie Parker. "We stayed over there and listened to records until we actually fell asleep on the floor," Colson recalled. "His wife must have got tired of us because we spent the night often," said Freeman. "We were like his kids. He'd show us how to practice. We would just be playing with Fred all night."

Adopting the music education track, like many black students across the United States, Freeman was exposed to a variety of brass, string, and reed instruments. At a woodwind class, he tried a saxophone for the first time. "I asked my teacher, would it be all right if I took this tenor home during spring break. He said yeah, and I took it home and practiced eight, twelve hours a day, every day. I just couldn't put the horn down." Freeman came back to school and told the band director that he wanted to play saxophone in the band. "He said, how long have you been playing saxophone. I said, two weeks. He said, are you crazy? This is Northwestern University. This is not your high school band." In the end, however, Freeman passed the audition, and he became a saxophonist in the Northwestern University concert band. He began studying with the well-known classical saxophonist, Fred Hemke, and a renewed interest in jazz made it natural for Freeman to visit the South Side frequently to sit in with his dad Von at his jam sessions. "He would often charge only a dollar at the door," the younger Freeman remembered. "I'd collect the money, or I'd bartend for him, and sometimes jammed."[56]

By this time, Steve Colson and Kristine Browne were joining Freeman on his South Side visits to his father's 75th Street jam sessions. "Von was like, I'm putting you on the stand," remembered Iqua. "I was not really into scat, and I said, no, don't do that. Von said, I'm doing it. He called 'Night in Tunisia,' and when they hit the break, guess who was out there. That's how Von did you." On another of those visits, the young singer stopped by an African shop on 53rd Street, near her home.

> I wasn't looking for a change of name. . . . This guy says to me, you're a singer. You're Iqua. And I said, what does that mean? He wrote it down, and he said, Iqua is a name we give women in our village who sing. He was from Nigeria. He said, it has two meanings—either you are a singer, and/or one whose mother has sung for her or prayed for her. It fit because of the singing, and "Kristine" always seemed just a little stern and proper for where my head was. Slowly, my brother started calling me that, my husband started calling me that, and I started using it. Now, everyone calls me Iqua—except my mother [laughs].

Eventually, her mother relented when she and Steve Colson, who had taken the name "Adegoke," were married. "Trying to take on a new name," he said in our interview, "is partly to try and gain a new perspective on yourself, and also to portray yourself to others more in line with what you think your values are." In his words, his adopted name, Adegoke [ah-DAY-go-KAY], incorporates a Yoruba translation of "Steven," which is derived from the Greek word for "crown," to signify "the crown that has been exalted." At the same time, like many black Americans who adopted African names, he kept the Colson name as a mark of respect for his family history.

It was Fred Anderson who suggested that the three musicians get in touch with Muhal Richard Abrams and find out about the AACM. "Adegoke and I went together," Freeman recalled. "We said, Fred Anderson sent us, and we might want to join. He said, come to the class. We went to the class, and he was teaching the Schillinger stuff, you know. I was totally—it was too cool." As Colson recalled, "We would get off into some philosophical stuff, as well as the whole mathematics of music. We'd sit around talking about the Schillinger system, Hindemith, tone rows. I was looking at it like this was a continuation of what I was doing in school, except that this was more open for people to contribute what they thought."

I met Chico at Muhal's classes. We went to AACM classes together, performed concerts together, and outside of class, shared both an ardent love of Coltrane and expansive visions of the future. Chico was zealous about mouthpieces, which was where I learned to parse quite subtle (if not entirely chimerical) timbral differences between the Otto Link, Brilhart, and other tenor saxophone mouthpieces. Like all of us, Freeman admired Abrams. "I found him to be, if not the wisest person I know of, one of them for sure, somebody very special. I was at his house all the time. My father loved him too, and when my father found out that I was hanging out with him, he liked that." Von Sr. corroborated his son's account in a 1987 interview with radio host Ted Panken, an authority on postwar Chicago jazz. "Richard is a very dedicated man," the elder Freeman said. "And hey, man, what can I say about him? He's a great musician, and I love him—plus, he taught my son. I got to love him! Taught him well, too."[57]

In 1972, the Colsons decided to move to Hyde Park, and by the end of that year, the Colsons and Freeman became AACM members. The admittance of the two men was relatively unproblematic, but in Iqua's case, "I made my application, and it never occurred to me that it would be controversial." As she put it,

> I think one of the things that was being argued was that sometimes women could come into an organization and offer a certain kind of organizational sense that maybe men aren't going to focus on in that way, and therefore, it's a complement to have them. The way they were behaving was as though women hadn't been in, or shouldn't be in. But I always knew Peggy [Abrams] and Amina were involved. Of course, I wasn't at the meeting, and I don't know what all was said, but it was close, and I ended up being voted in.

"It was kind of a general back and forth," recalled Steve Colson in my interview with him and Iqua Colson, "with different people just throwing ideas out there, like, do we want a woman in. I don't remember some of the specifics, except that I got the feeling that some people just felt that it might interfere with, I guess, the camaraderie, the 'male bonding.' But once the vote was taken and she got in, then I was thinking, well, those people who had reservations, they'll accept it."

"Was it close," asked Iqua, "or was that just in my . . ."

"No, I think it was close," Steve responded. "Probably the individuals did relinquish some of those feelings."

Throughout this period, the AACM was receiving important press support from the North Side–based weekly free paper, the *Chicago Reader*. The paper was difficult or impossible to find on the black-dominated South Side, except in Hyde Park, home to the University of Chicago, and considered one of the few integrated neighborhoods in Chicago. In September 1972, the *Reader* named the Art Ensemble of Chicago as one of Chicago's "Heavy Sixty" of influential local cultural figures.[58] In October 1972, Fred Anderson and his quartet, with Steve McCall, Lester Lashley, and Bill Brimfield, received front-page coverage in the *Reader*, as a preview of an upcoming event. J. B. Figi, a long time supporter of the AACM's music, borrowed a phrase attributed to Jack Kerouac in describing trumpeter Bill Brimfield's bravura virtuosity as "metallic cocaine bebop."[59] Many reviewers described Anderson's sound as analogous to his body type—"brawny," "burly," "working like a heavyweight at a bodybag," trying to express in words something of the visceral intensity of his tenor saxophone sound.

Near the end of 1972, the AEC received a standing ovation at the Ann Arbor Blues and Jazz Festival, organized by John Sinclair and a group called the Rainbow People's Party.[60] This extremely diverse event exemplified Sinclair's aim of using music as a means of bringing people together to act (literally) in concert. The festival recalled similar events taking place in Europe, and as with the European festivals, Sinclair and his associates sought to encourage diversity in audience taste. "We want to get blues fans into jazz, jazz fans into blues, and rock fans into both musics," Sinclair announced, and to that end, Muddy Waters, Hound Dog Taylor, Mighty Joe Young, Sippi Wallace, Lucille Spann, Luther Allison, Junior Walker, Bobby Blue Bland, Otis Rush, Freddie King, Dr. John, and Bonnie Raitt (described in the review as "a Radcliffe student who tried to do some blues") shared the environment with the Art Ensemble of Chicago, Leo Smith, Detroit's Contemporary Jazz Quintet, Pharoah Sanders, Archie Shepp, the Sun Ra Arkestra, and Miles Davis, at this time in fully controversial electric effect with wah-wah-articulated trumpet.[61] Kalaparusha Maurice McIntyre, who had recently gained highly favorable critical attention with his first Delmark recording, *Humility in the Light of the Creator,* also performed at the festival.[62] This description of a Kalaparusha event seems particularly apt: "Difda's sense of black humor and irony vies with a pure, though gnarled, lyricism. . . . The internal logic of his constructions is usually as solid as a pit in a peach, the motive usually a dramatic kind of cubist vision."[63]

In the United States, however, the diversity strategy seemed doomed, and Ann Arbor was one of the last festivals of its kind. Attitudes, values, and lifestyles were hardening, and the incipient balkanization of musics into ever narrower idiomatic and commercial slots, a fact of life at the onset of the twenty-first century, simply steamrollered this alternative vision, first in concerts, and later on U.S. radio and television. As a review of the Revolutionary Ensemble's 1973 Ann Arbor performance had it, "The festival is quietly forgotten by many blues purists who feel uncomfortable rubbing elbows with common pop concert-goers . . . jazz aficionados find the affair a bit too grubby for their liking . . . the biggest turn-off feature for many staunch jazz fans . . . is the obvious favoring of the avant-garde."[64]

At least in Chicago, the demise of South Side jazz clubs had already forced changes in the strategies by which black musicians found work. Radio, which in the 1950s and 1960s had provided exposure for up-and-coming black artists at the local and national levels, was becoming increasingly corporatized, with Big Rock as an overdetermining force. This led to something of a paradox for many observers at a time before the notion of jazz's "lack of commercial appeal" had become canonical. "Ask the program director of any major Chicago radio station about the jazz radio audience in the city," said one critic in the *Reader.* "Seems like all those hundreds of thousands of Chicagoans who used to dig jazz aren't around anymore. Of course, someone is buying jazz records in unprecedented amounts. Miles Davis sells millions, and Pharoah Sanders, John McLaughlin, Freddie Hubbard, and others aren't too far behind."[65]

For Charles Suber, who was quoted in the article, racism was a factor, even trumping economics. "To a lot of radio stations, jazz means black, and there's quite a few stations in Chicago that refuse to cater to black people. The fact is that jazz has no meaning at all to the people that own most of the stations in town. They don't know about it, and they don't care. So it's been left to the black stations to carry it on."[66] WBEE-AM had become the major jazz station in town, broadcasting from predominantly black south suburban Harvey. The station was limited to daylight hours, however, and broadcast on a frequency at the top end of the AM dial that was difficult to receive beyond the South Side of Chicago. WNUR-FM, a student-run station at Northwestern, exhibited the reverse problem, being received mainly on the North Side due to its very low power. The student-run University of Chicago station, WHPK-FM, even had an AACM show, but was similarly restricted in range.

The year 1972 saw the emergence of the Muhal Richard Abrams Sextet, an all-AACM group with early AACM member Reggie Willis on bass, Steve McCall on drums, and a forest of woodwind and saxophones, played by Henry Threadgill, Kalaparusha Difda, and Wallace McMillan. I heard this amazing, diverse ensemble on numerous occasions, and performed with them at least once, on their regular Sunday afternoon performances at the auditorium of Child City, a South Side daycare center headed by the mother of AACM guitarist Pete Cosey, where AACM functions were headquartered. *Coda* magazine's detailed three-page review of the sextet's December 1972 performance at Chicago's Jazz Showcase is perhaps the best published description of the group's music. What the reviewer described as a "rare northside AACM concert" lasted for four nights, and featured Abrams on electric guitar as well as acoustic and electric piano. The group played along with an electronic tape collage that "sounded like Nixon or a Nixon put-on, but the audibility was too muffled to tell for certain"; of course, "everyone went wild on bells, thousands of little bells!"[67]

The sextet played to excited audiences at the 1973 Berlin Jazz Festival, the first international performance for everyone except McCall. Although AACM musicians performed frequently in West Germany, in contrast to the alacrity with which their work was received in France, AACM music was still not often reviewed in the canonical German jazz magazine, *Jazz Podium*. Steve McCall's report of the warmth of the Abrams Sextet's reception in this cold war–divided city[68] was countered by the *Jazz Podium* review, which complained that "between the chaotic collective [improvisations], pastoral sections, and African percussion sounds, there were certainly too many solos from the saxophonists, whose now already conventional noodling became almost formless through the lack of dynamics and adherence to the same processes."[69]

Nonetheless, the reputation of the AACM in Europe was still growing, and some commentators were becoming interested in what other undiscovered gems might be found in Chicago. In March 1973, *Jazz* magazine published a feature article introducing Abrams, whose work, according to the author, was practically unknown in France. The article, which apparently drew from the published work of Terry Martin, as well as J. B. Figi's liner notes, argued that it was the forays into Europe by the younger AACM musicians that had created curiosity regarding Abrams's work—certainly as much or more than Abrams's Delmark recordings, *Levels and Degrees of Light* and *Young at Heart, Wise in Time,* which were difficult to obtain in Europe. Comparing "The Bird Song" from *Levels and Degrees of Light* to the Velvet Underground's dense "Sister Ray,"[70] the article described Abrams as "to a great extent at the origin of the work of Roscoe Mitchell, Lester Bowie, Anthony Braxton, gifted individuals whose European success could make one forget that they are not all that is the AACM."[71]

This article apparently whetted the appetite of the magazine's editors for more. In the spring of 1973, *Jazz* magazine editor Philippe Carles, along with the British magazine *Melody Maker*'s Richard Williams, interrupted the jazz world's traditional fascination with New York by making the trek to Chicago, a city that was rising to prominence in the world of music in the wake of the AACM's innovations. The two writers had the misfortune to visit during one of Chicago's legendary subzero spells, a regular feature of the landscape that always makes a strong impression upon the uninitiated. Carles commented upon the cold at considerable length, *à la façon anthropologique,* noting that at these times, "activities and entertainment for Chicagoans are limited to well heated buildings. . . . The cold would even be a decisive factor: the importance of 'thermodynamic' phenomena in Chicago blues would correspond . . . to the need for working-class blacks to make up for the absence of central heating."[72]

Besides the weather, Carles also commented frankly on another frigid local phenomenon—namely, the city's extreme segregation, a social factor that, even following a decade of civil rights activism, seemed to have hardly budged since Gene Lees's description in *Down Beat* nearly fifteen years earlier. "Despite some attempts at integration," Carles observed, "the social/racial barriers that divide the city seem not to have lost any of their effectiveness."[73] By way of example, the writer described his visit to a 75th Street night spot where Von Freeman was performing "for a dozen patrons, and we were the only whites."[74]

The Chicago experience of urban segregation as musical determinant posed obvious challenges to those who had been weaned on social histories of jazz that celebrated the Greenwich Village integrationist subcultures surrounding the Beats. Carles's South Side expedition included visits to well-known blues clubs, such as Teresa's, with an all-black clientele which had not yet experienced the influx of white patrons that accompanied the later "blues revival." Searching for "the only place where blacks and whites seemed to have some chance of meeting,"[75] Carles found the Joe-Segal run

Jazz Showcase, and Bob Koester's Jazz Record Mart. The French writer observed that while it was easy to find the AACM musicians themselves, it was in fact difficult to find a place to hear the new music in its hometown. During their Chicago visit, Carles and his cohort attended a Child City AACM concert of a group led by Muhal Richard Abrams, and noticed that "in the house: family and friends of the musicians. Entrance fee: an optional donation for expenses."[76] This was one of the first descriptions of a Chicago-based AACM event published in any European journal. The reportage began by noting how the musicians "faced the East" before performing:

> Before playing, the musicians, backs turned to the audience, remain motionless for a few minutes. Then they turn to approach their instruments: all are wearing rubber masks worthy of a horror film. Gong (Abrams), electronic sounds, a dancer starts to outline very slow movements. Little by little, via small percussion, whistles, and toy instruments, the space becomes a kind of immense birdcage. Once the "birds" have disappeared, a mass of percussion develops, starting from the gong. Duration of the first piece: half an hour.[77]

Throughout the piece, the writer noted, "silence is valorized, and the tiniest changes of sound become decisive."[78]

During his Chicago visit, Carles theorized that not only economic conditions, but also "the ideological uniformity of the media" (*l'uniformité idéologique des 'media'*) were prime factors that tended to marginalize this new music. This point, among many others, was touched upon in a wide-ranging interview with Abrams that followed the setting of the scene in Chicago. The interview itself provided an occasion for Abrams to describe the administrative structure of the AACM and its school for young musicians. One additional benefit of the interview is that French readers discovered the meaning of the name Muhal: "number one."

Asked whether the school taught Mozart, "par example," the pianist and composer pointed out that the classical tradition was already taught in every school and disseminated across a wide range of media. In contrast, making young black musicians more aware of the products of their own culture was a key to their empowerment as artists and as human beings: "The investigation and transcription of all musics are also part of our program . . . but if you want to give yourself the means to succeed, in any field, it is essential to start from where you are." After all, Abrams remarked, referring to the Middle Passage experience, "we all got on the same boat."[79] Nonetheless, asked about going to Africa, Abrams, who had never visited the continent, replied that it was not a question of "returning to the source," but of recognizing the importance of the African imaginary. For Abrams at that time, "Africa . . . is a mixture of a lot of things, especially after having come through the colonial period. . . . What's important is not a physical but a mental return."[80]

The 1973 edition of the Newport Jazz Festival was the first to feature representatives of the AACM—namely, the Art Ensemble of Chicago, who had recently acquired a major-label recording contract with Atlantic Records. Carles's subsequent interview with Joseph Jarman in the September 1973 issue of *Jazz* highlighted that fact that, from a French perspective, the appearance of the AEC was seen as a belated recognition by U.S. musical culture of the importance of the AACM itself. The Newport event had been the first AEC concert in nearly a year, and for Jarman, the power simply to wait out the long periods of inactivity rested with the group's principle of collective organization and responsibility.

> The Art Ensemble always tried to alter the relationships with organizers, agents, etc. We refuse certain things, we require certain working conditions. . . . If people refuse our principles, we refuse theirs. Our lives are more important. In Paris, we should play in places like the Opera, where concerts of classical music take place. The clubs, the Latin Quarter, that's OK, but that's not where things should happen any more.

Jarman's optimism led him to affirm to Carles that "I think that the Art Ensemble of Chicago will exist as long as we live."[81] The recording contract itself, however, did not exhibit a similar longevity. In 1974, it was reported that the Art Ensemble "severed relations with Atlantic Records and plan to form their own company in the near future."[82] Nonetheless, 1974 was the prelude to a major year for AACM musicians. The New Year was rung in with a *Down Beat* cover profile of Lester Bowie, who described his incipient postmodernism by observing, "One thing wrong with a lot of people is that they limit themselves to a certain style of playing or they limit themselves to wanting only a certain type of sound. I like all the styles and all the sounds, so I'm completely free. I can do whatever I want to."[83]

With the demise of Chicago's South Side scenes, and then its Near North Side Wells Street club scenes, the area around North Lincoln Avenue was becoming a more prominent location for music, with events by people such as Fred Anderson and Muhal Richard Abrams. The year 1974 also saw the first *Down Beat* mentions of George Lewis, who was performing with Chico Freeman (still called "Von Jr.") at a South Side lounge.[84] In March 1974, the Abrams Sextet and the Art Ensemble had been named by the *Chicago Reader*'s Pop Poll as among Chicago's best jazz groups. Abrams himself was named Most Valuable Player on the Chicago Music Scene, and the sextet was named Chicago Jazz Artist of the Year, followed by the Art Ensemble, with Henry Threadgill not far behind. The Expatriate of the Year award went to Anthony Braxton in a three-way tie, with Roscoe Mitchell and Sun Ra in another three-way tie for fifth place. In September 1973 and the following year, the AACM's tenth anniversary, the AACM as a collective was named as one of the "Heavy 75," a "Who's Who in the Chicago Alternative Culture."[85]

A major feature on Muhal Richard Abrams, his first since 1967, appeared in *Down Beat* in August 1974. For this reviewer, the sextet's 1973 Berlin performance marked the group as "the most exciting, cohesive and musically significant ensemble to emerge from the AACM since the initial appearance of the Art Ensemble."[86] Abrams's solo concert at the 1974 edition of the Montreux Jazz Festival was a great success, and he accompanied the Art Ensemble on a European tour that same year.[87] Arista Records, founded by former Columbia Records producer Clive Davis, was recording jazz-identified music, and the AEC soon established a relationship with Arista's "second-line" company, Arista-Freedom, after their relationship with Atlantic Records ended.

I spent the year away from Yale playing in the Muhal Richard Abrams Big Band, which performed on Monday nights at the new, expanded Transitions East Juice Bar. Transitions East, which had moved from its original location on 1823 E. 79th to 8236 S. Cottage Grove, was a popular South Side cultural center and performance space. The space was run in part by future AACM member and drummer Afifi Willel, and frequently featured the Pharaohs, as well as a number of AACM groups, such as Amina Claudine Myers, and saxophonist and pianist Ari Brown's "Ultimate Frontier." Founded by the Hebrew Israelite community in the city, the atmosphere at Transitions East eschewed alcohol in favor of health foods, juices, and Afrodiasporic décor, which served to heighten the irony of having Leon's Bar-B-Q across the street, where the acrid smell of pork ribs clashed with the healthy juices and cakes from the redoubtable Brother Tim's bakery.

The Abrams band came off the stand around 2:00 a.m., and I would help

Muhal fold up the stands and pack away the sound system and the tape recorder; Muhal recorded each week's concert, probably on the same Sony reel-to-reel recorder that he used to tape the AACM meetings in 1965. Then I would race home to take a nap before rising at 5:30 to make my 7:00 a.m. laborer's job at Illinois Slag and Ballast Company, for which I had to become a member of the United Steelworkers union. I returned to Yale in the fall of 1972, just as Professor Willie Ruff (Yale '57) was founding the Duke Ellington Fellowship Program, a "conservatory without walls" whose goals were "to encourage the study of Afro-American music and recognize and perpetuate the jazz, blues and gospel traditions."[88] Some of the greatest musicians in the United States were made Duke Ellington Fellows, where they interacted with Yale students. Professor Ruff and his associate, pianist Dwike Mitchell, based the program at Branford, one of Yale's residential colleges, where I happened to be in residence. We had dinner in the dining hall with Dizzy Gillespie and William Warfield, and went to cocktail parties with Duke Ellington, Charles Mingus, and Max Roach—*all in the same room.* We listened to and talked personally with Papa Jo Jones, Willie "The Lion" Smith, Marion Williams, and of course, the Duke himself. Perhaps the greatest impact was when Anthony Davis and I were privileged to play "Ornithology" with Tony Williams and Slam Stewart.

And then there was Davis's father, Charles, the innovator of African American studies, the teacher of Henry Louis Gates, and a great pianist to boot. Robert Farris Thompson and Houston Baker were there, and I took classes with them. The students, undergraduate and graduate, were people like Anthony, flutist Robert Dick, saxophonist and divinity student Dwight Andrews, composer Alvin Singleton, violinist Miles Hoffman (my roommate), bassist Mark Helias, and saxophonist Jane Ira Bloom. Even Jon Pareles, now a *New York Times* music critic, was playing flute. Other musicians in the area included bassist Wes Brown and vibraphonist Jay Hoggard, who were students at Wesleyan; vibraphonist Bobby Naughton, and drummers Pheeroan AkLaff (or Paul Maddox, as he was known then), and Gerry Hemingway, a native of the New Haven area.

Leo Smith had married Kathy Sinclair, and the couple and their two daughters had settled in a suburb of New Haven, Connecticut. Of course, Leo was kind of a legend for me, someone I had heard about that entire year in Chicago, and I think he was surprised and not a little pleased to discover someone of a younger generation, who was not there when he was in Chicago, who claimed to be an AACM member. Of course, as Smith himself recalled our first meeting,

I was standing up on the street, and George was going, and he said, "Hey, are you Leo Smith?" And I said, "Yeah. How are you doing?" We talked for a few minutes, and he said, "Well, I know the AACM," and blah-blah-blah, and then he gave me his room number, and I think in the next couple of days I came by. . . . Because basically, I couldn't visit nobody in town. There was nobody to talk to except Marion Brown. And when George came to town, I went by George's and hung out there, and turned him over and he turned me over. Then I'd go by and hang out with Anthony Davis. And after that, that was it.[89]

Usually Leo came over quite early, around 7:00 a.m. One morning he came by with an interesting-looking composition written on a single sheet of paper, using a new notational concept called "rhythm-units," written in a system he was developing called "Akreanvention" that he documented in a self-published book of difficult exercises/solo compositions that recalled Olivier Messiaen's "Technique de mon langage musicale."[90] Somewhat later, Smith self-published his first book, *Notes (8 pieces) source a new world music: creative music.* This text, insightful and laconic in the fashion of Leo's own playing, was one of the first I had seen that sought to theorize African American experimental music in the context of global creativity.[91] Smith's 1974 article, "(M1) American Music," published in a respected academic journal, intervened in the process of canon formation in an early call for a composite, multiculturalist notion of American music, as well as a non-nativist awareness of the cultural change that marked the advent of globalization.[92] As Smith declared in a 1975 interview with Bill Smith, "A world music will happen. A world art will happen. A world dance will happen. A world philosophy will develop." Smith cautions, however, that "by this I do not mean a leveling out of all the cultures into one. That is where you kill the human being. Then you don't have the beautiful reality of the African, you don't have the beautiful reality of the Asian, all you have is a motivating force that would control the world culture. . . . That's the point of the universality of European standards as a measure for what happens on earth."[93]

Smith's identification in his texts of a functional role for "the improvisor" in the composite music of the West was an important discursive step that antedated Derek Bailey's far more widely disseminated 1980 work by a number of years.[94] Of course, Smith's frank discussion of the artifacts of race as a determinant of musical canons, discourses, and infrastructure is not to be found in the Bailey text; certainly, as art historian Robert Farris Thompson wrote in an extended review of Smith's book in *Coda* from 1975, Smith was posing sharp historiographical challenges. "But what he is really saying," Thompson noted, "is let everyone move to a higher plane of expositions: *a new art of writing about music.* . . . Create with equal intensity and respect in the art by which you verbally remember what you hear our music saying and we shall welcome you as comrade."[95]

When I returned to the AACM in the summer of 1973, I met two new faces, Edward Wilkerson and Rasul Siddik. Wilkerson was born in 1953, to college-educated, upper-middle-class parents who came up through what he called "the old black aristocracy." His mother held a master's degree in child psychology from the University of Minnesota, which Wilkerson described as "one of the few liberal schools where black people could go to graduate school."[96] His father, an orphan, lived with relatives, and after college at the University of Iowa, attended Meharry Medical College in Nashville, Tennessee, an historically black institution that trained many of America's African American physicians. The family settled in the Kinsman area of Cleveland, where his father hung out his shingle as a general practitioner. The neighborhood was rapidly deteriorating, however, and as its population dropped, changed complexion from white to black, and became steadily poorer, the area gradually became known as the "Forgotten Triangle." In the mid-1960s the family moved to the affluent, largely white Cleveland suburb of Shaker Heights, where Wilkerson and his three sisters spent their formative years.

The family listened to both Western classical music and jazz at home. Wilkerson's mother had a strong interest in music and the theater, and all the children took music lessons. The family had a piano, and even before taking formal lessons, Wilkerson was familiarizing himself with it. Shaker Heights had arguably one of the best public school systems in the United States, and an arrangement with the Cleveland Institute of Music allowed Wilkerson to begin basic solfège, as well as formal lessons on clarinet, at nine years of age. At thirteen, he began taking private lessons on saxophone, listening to Charlie Parker and Stanley Turrentine, and writing arrangements for small groups in which he was performing.

Wilkerson was determined to major in music in college, and was accepted at Cornell University and the University of Chicago, where he landed in the fall of 1971.

> I knew the U of C was not a performance-oriented kind of thing. I was really interested in theory and analysis, and I wanted to write. For me, a

lot of it was being in Chicago, and I wanted to be in a school that had a certain academic standing. The whole thing of the "life of the mind," that kind of monk-like existence, no social activities, the whole thing with the gargoyles, I kind of liked that.

By this time, Wilkerson was aware of his primary orientation toward jazz. Nonetheless, he saw the pan-European orientation of music study at the university as "a good grounding for me. I knew I wasn't going to learn anything about improvisation or performance, but I really wanted to have what I thought was a fundamental basis." Despite not having had the same background in classical European music as some of the other students, he adapted quickly to the standard studies in Grout's *History of Western Music*, the Walter Piston harmony text, and Schenkerian analysis. Wilkerson also regularly attended the concerts by the university's Contemporary Chamber Players, which had so excited the young Henry Threadgill years before.

Wilkerson knew Chicago's reputation as "a blues mecca," but had never heard of the AACM. At some point in 1972, he became part of a "free-form" improvisation group with Danny Riperton, the pianist and brother of the singer Minnie Riperton, and his fellow student Sonja Williams, a clarinetist.[97] As Wilkerson recalled in our interview,

> One day Sonja said she was going to this class on Saturday mornings. It was over at this place called Child City, and Muhal Richard Abrams was teaching. So we just took the bus out to Stony Island. We go there, and it was weird, the strangest scene. Sonja was there, Rah-Bird, Shanta, Chico, Douglas. You might have been there. They had these tiny kids' desks, and you paid a dollar, and Muhal—it was really just an eye-opener, the way he approached music. The classes were about writing, composing.

Wilkerson and Williams became regulars at AACM concerts, including the legendary 1972 Mandel Hall concert of the Art Ensemble of Chicago,[98] and the Monday night marathons with the Muhal Richard Abrams Big Band at Transitions East that began in that same year. Eventually, Wilkerson was called to substitute for Transitions East band members who had conflicting engagements on Monday nights.

Rasul Siddik came to Chicago in 1970 as Jan Corlus Mahr, the fifth of eight children who grew up in the black inner city of St. Louis. Siddik's parents were staunch Catholics, but their son and his friends regularly opted for a different kind of religious experience. "We'd start out for church, then get out of sight and detour," Siddik said in our interview. "We'd go around the corner to the gospel place. They had the whole band in there, drums and bass, and they'd be getting down, getting the Holy Ghost. We would hang out until it was time to come back home from church."[99] Siddik's uncle, John Sanders, a jazz saxophonist, visited the household frequently with new LPs. The Mahr family would visit local theaters such as the Comet to hear the music revues, with groups such as the Temptations, Gladys Knight, Sam and Dave, and the Impressions. There was a piano in the home, and Siddik's sister was an active pianist. His father "was into all different kinds of music, everything from Nelson Riddle to Lawrence Welk, but he had a record collection of all the jazz greats, too."

Siddik's history with his chosen instrument, the trumpet, is largely autodidactic. His older brother bequeathed his trumpet to young Jan, who started taking lessons at the community music school, but he was unhappy with his teacher. Shortly after, his trumpet was stolen, and the family wasn't able to acquire a replacement for a couple of years, when his junior high school started a band. "By this time I'm already listening to real music— Trane, Dolphy, Cannonball, as well as the Top 40 stuff. We're playing all this old concert music. You got all these little kids trying to play violins and— *squeak!* It was torture. I stayed in there and learned reading and stuff, then I couldn't take it no more and I quit. I just started practicing on my own."

Siddik entered a Catholic high school, but soon transferred to a vocational school, O'Fallon Tech, where his study of pre-engineering ended when the teacher informed him, "I don't think you're engineering material. I understand that you're on academic probation. If you don't get enough F's, *I'm* going to fail you." Siddik eventually received his General Equivalency Diploma, but like other young men of his generation, he faced the draft and the Vietnam War. "As you know, they were drafting all the black people, and sending them straight to Vietnam," Siddik recalled. "I couldn't see going to another country fighting people when we weren't free at home. They were sending the draft order, so I split. That's how I wound up in Chicago."[100] Another reason for coming to Chicago was the AACM. In St. Louis, Siddik was part of the extended artistic family that had converged around the Black Artists Group. "I knew Quincy Troupe, he knew my family," Siddik affirmed. Even before the formal emergence of BAG, Siddik attended self-produced events by Leonard Smith, Bobo Shaw, Floyd LeFlore, and Joseph Bowie, among others.

For Siddik, in the early 1970s, "The South Side was jumping." Philip Cohran's Affro-Arts Theater was in full effect, and although the 63rd Street nightlife scene was a fading memory, the 75th Street scene, with black clubs such as the Apartment and the El Matador, where Von Freeman had steady work, was showing promise. Siddik also began coming to Abrams's Saturday classes at the AACM School, which was probably where we met each other. Siddik lived with his aunt and his saxophone-playing uncle, who had actually built a nightclub in the basement of one of the fine old mansions on South Park Way (now Martin Luther King Drive), where Siddik would practice and watch the musicians rehearse. Just around the corner, on 47th Street and Drexel Avenue, a musicians' building had developed, where Troy Robinson, bassist Milton Suggs, and the young trumpeter Malachi Thompson were all living. Saxophonists Edwin Daugherty, Henry Threadgill, and John Stubblefield, and trumpeter Frank Gordon would come by, as well as up-and-coming young musicians such as pianist Koco Calvin Brunson and guitarist Dale Williams. Bassist Fred Hopkins lived next door, as well as the beloved Chicago trumpeter, pianist, and composer Hobie James, with whom Siddik studied "for about a year, to get techniques in approaching changes. Great teacher. He loved Booker Little, so he would always play Booker Little for me after the lessons." Siddik's close friend, the saxophonist and bass clarinetist Harlan Robinson, came to Chicago from St. Louis soon after Siddik. Robinson had studied with Julius Hemphill, and became widely admired in the South Side musical community. In the end, however, Robinson became so engrossed in the spiritual life that he apparently decided to leave music altogether. "He got heavily involved in Islam, and he just went the other way with it. He kind of alienated himself from his friends."

It was in Chicago that Jan Corlus Mahr, looking for alternatives as were so many other African Americans, became Rasul Olufemi Siddik. Like another St. Louis trumpeter, Philip Cohran, Siddik began a period of intense study and introspection, part of a personal transformation. "I had a friend who was into Islam, heavily, and we would talk about it a lot. I was starting to check it out more and more, reading the Koran. "I was still 'Jan' when my younger brother came and visited me. He said, I've got a name for you. He gave me a list of names, and told me, I already picked it out, but I want to see if you know who you are. He knew me better than anybody in the world, and we both picked out the same name."

When Siddik's oldest brother suffered life-threatening injuries in an automobile accident, Siddik went back to St. Louis, only to discover that he appeared to be on the list of the Army's Most Wanted. "My friend came and told me, they're looking for you at the house. You can't go home, because they're waiting for you. I had to literally sneak out of town." Siddik returned to Chicago to find that his aunt had rented his room. "I was actually living on the street for a few weeks, homeless, crashing here and there at somebody's house." After finding a steady home, Siddik entered Malcolm X College in 1971, armed with his GED and a new determination. At this time, however, the old draft issue surfaced again. "First I was a conscientious objector, and they just said, 1-A. I was studying Islam, I didn't believe in war. They didn't care. Plus, I had flat feet, heart murmur. I was ineligible, but they were just sending all black people over there. It was like a genocidal process." The final resolution of the draft matter unfolded in St. Louis, and in the end, Siddik's last-stand resistance strategy recalled the one that Emanuel Cranshaw described from the 1950s:

> I went down there looking like one of Sun Ra's boys—space suit, an Indian robe, and a poncho. I had my hair all braided up, a little space hat. I went back to my revolutionary thing—I can't wait to get to boot camp so I can shoot me some honkies and rednecks, I can't stand white people, I can't take orders from no white man, blah blah blah. I was acting my ass off. It was an Academy Award performance.[101]

The exasperated army official told Siddik, "You went through a lot to stay out of the army. I guess you'll be happy to know you succeeded. He stamped the thing 4-F. I looked at him: 'Fuck you!' and walked out. The funniest part was when I left the induction center, walking down the street in downtown St. Louis with all this crazy shit on."[102]

Bandleader Charles Walton was recruiting the best of Chicago's South Side musicians for his program at Malcolm X College, including saxophonists Sabu Zawadi (later a member of the AACM), Ahmad Salaheldeen, Sonny Seals, and Ari Richard Brown, bassist and trombonist Louis Satterfield, trumpeter Rahmlee Michael Davis, trombonist Billy Howell, and the enigmatic young saxophonist Khusenaton, who played with Sun Ra before his untimely death. Walton's pedagogical strategy of preparing students for careers in music education was a time-tested one for African American musicians. Another Chicago-area school, Governors State University, was founded in 1969 near the South Chicago suburb of Park Forest. Under the direction of Warrick Carter, the school created a jazz program that pursued an agenda similar to Walton's. By 1973, the program had attracted a large group of excellent Chicago musicians who were pursuing music education credentials, while playing in one of the country's most powerful collegiate big bands. Muhal and I were studying electronic music at Governors State with Richard McCreary, a graduate of the experimental music program at the University of Iowa, who had outfitted a large studio with an ARP 2500 modular synthesizer.[103]

Art Burton, a percussionist, was one of the students in the music education program, which included AACM members such as Vandy Harris, Chico Freeman, Billy Howell, and Frank Gordon. At the time, Gordon was recording with Eddie Harris, and a Gordon trumpet solo from *Hear, Sense, and Feel*, a 1972 recording by the Awakening, was transcribed and published in *Down Beat*.[104] Gordon, a mainstay of Abrams's Transitions East ensemble, was presented in the article as a well-studied musician with a degree in composition from Chicago's Roosevelt University, and the two-page transcription was presented as evidence that Gordon had "a lot of things covered that some better-known players do not . . . potentially one of the future giants on his instrument."[105]

Burton himself had just joined the AACM around this time. Born Arthur Theodore Burton in Chicago's Provident Hospital in 1949, he eventually became one of the world's leading authorities on the black West. His two best-known books, *Black, Red, and Deadly* and *Black, Buckskin, and Blue*, chronicled black and Indian gunfighters, outlaws, and lawmen in the Old West, such as Bass Reeves, a deputy U.S. marshal for thirty-two years who was, for Burton, "as great as any lawman in the history of the Wild West." This historical work emerged from his personal research into his family's background in Oklahoma, as well as an early and abiding interest in history more generally.[106]

Burton is known to his friends and musical colleagues as "Turk," a name that he somehow picked up in grade school. His mother's side of the family went to Oklahoma around 1890, the prestatehood moment when the territory was opened for settlement; his mother was born there in 1917. Burton's father, a Pullman porter, was born in 1903 and grew up in the Mississippi Delta—evidently a very unpleasant experience, as it was for the many blacks who left en masse during the first phases of the Great Migration. Burton described it as "a horror show. He never wanted to go back to Mississippi." Burton's parents settled first in Chicago, then in the predominantly black South Chicago suburb of Phoenix, Illinois, where Burton grew up. Contributing to his parents' decision to leave Chicago was the omnipresent threat of the Bomb that permeated the U.S. national consciousness in the 1950s. "People always said, well, if we have a war, they would drop the bomb on downtown Chicago, and it would radiate so much into the city," Burton noted. "So he felt that moving to the suburbs, it would be a buffer against atomic warfare. That was his mindset."[107]

In the fifties, as Burton recalls, Phoenix was a rural community. Many residents owned livestock, and Burton's family had chickens, ducks, pigeons, and a large garden, all of which provided food for the family table. City life was represented by the White Rose nightclub, a regular stopover for artists such as Muddy Waters, Howlin' Wolf, and B. B. King. That was of relatively little import to Burton's parents, however. "My father wasn't too much into music," Burton recalled. "My mother was real staunch into the church, so they didn't nightclub at all. They went to church and went to work, and that was about it." Burton's mother did play the piano, however, and on visits to his aunt in Chicago, she would play "The St. Louis Blues" for the family. An Oklahoma-based uncle played guitar and piano, and was originally from Mississippi, where he came up in the now little-known African American fife-and-drum tradition, which predated the blues and which Burton described as "a cross between military music and African music."[108] By the time the young Burton got to grade school, he was eager to play drums, having seen Lionel Hampton on television.

In fifth grade he started with the snare drum, but in short order his musical trajectory hit a bit of a snag. "They told us that if we wanted to stay in the band, we had to buy a drum set. It was $300, and my father pretty much told me I was crazy. Then he talked about the nefarious life of musicians, which was on the side of hell." As an alternative, his father offered to buy him a set of bongos, which he had located in a Portland, Oregon, pawnshop for a much more reasonable price of eight dollars. At first, Burton was reluctant, but soon changed his mind.

> There was a small group of boys at school one day who gave a concert in class. That was the first time I'd heard the bongo drums being played live. I had heard music from Latin America and it sounded good, but when I heard these boys playing it live, I felt like this was something I could do, so I told my dad to go ahead and get the bongos.

Burton began playing for talent shows and dancers, and added the conga drum to his arsenal. Burton became excited about jazz, particularly the soulful, organ-trio variety played by Jack McDuff, Charles Earland, and Jimmy Smith that was popular in black communities across the United States, and which retains its hold on black midwestern audiences to this day. Burton began to notice the great musicians who, in the 1950s, could still be seen on television—Candido, Mongo Santamaria, Art Blakey with Lee Morgan and Wayne Shorter, Ray Barretto with Wes Montgomery, and Cannonball Adderley—artists who were to completely disappear from the screen when, as media historian J. Fred MacDonald noted, white-run media companies had resolved "to keep blacks off national television as much as possible."[109]

Burton briefly moved to Oklahoma City, where he completed his secondary school education. There, a cousin introduced him to "Trane, Horace Silver, Dexter Gordon, jazz that was a little bit beyond what I had listened to when I was in Chicago. . . . I knew Trane's music was heavy; I just couldn't understand what he was playing." Returning to Chicago after high school, Burton started an R&B band with a group of young musicians in his neighborhood. Their first gig was at the White Rose, which was owned by the father of one of the band members. A larger band that Burton joined, the Soul Naturals, won the Illinois State Battle of the Bands in 1969, which earned Burton and the other musicians a trip to the national competition in Raleigh, North Carolina. The band broke up when most of its members were drafted and sent to Vietnam.

Burton, who was not drafted, met and studied with Philip Cohran for a year, and worked with a future AACM member, Avreeayl Ra. Ra, who later became a drummer, was playing saxophone at the time, in the footsteps of his celebrated father, Swing Lee O'Neil, a decorated veteran of the Cotton Club sessions. "Phil was very interesting because he talked a lot of music history, a lot of metaphysics," said Burton. "I thought he wrote very interesting compositions. The majority of his music, I guess, has never been heard." Meeting a founding member of the AACM was perhaps the best preparation for becoming involved with the AACM itself, for which he received encouragement from none other than Rahsaan Roland Kirk, who Burton met at a South Side event that also included AACM music by Henry Threadgill, Ajaramu, and Amina Claudine Myers. "Rahsaan made a lot of good comments about the association and about Muhal," recalled Burton, "so I said, the AACM must really be important for Rahsaan to be saying this. He was saying, these people you need to stay close to, because they're doing some important stuff."

Burton met the drummer and professional boxer known around Chicago as Amen-Ra, who was a member of the AACM for a period of time around the mid-1970s. Amen-Ra invited him to perform on an AACM concert, and around 1973, he became an AACM member himself. Burton began substituting for Don Moye with Abrams's big band at Transitions East, and since

Moye was becoming increasingly busy, Abrams passed the percussion chair to Burton. "That has to be one of the pinnacles of my musical life," said Burton. "To this day I probably have never heard any music as intense as what we played with Muhal's band, as a collective, big band type of experience. In Muhal's orchestra we played everything, and then went beyond that."

Ten Years After: The Association Comes of Age

In 1975, the AACM was ten years old, and AACM members were frequently represented in *Down Beat* Readers and Critics Polls, including more established members, such as Leroy Jenkins, Kalaparusha, Muhal Richard Abrams, and the members of the Art Ensemble, and a new figure, George Lewis, the first of the younger AACM generation to receive this kind of recognition. Even so, the collective was struggling with the loss of its Child City venue. The new home of the organization was the All Souls First Universalist Church on 910 East 83rd Street in the Chatham area. As a Unitarian denomination with an integrated congregation, the All Souls Church was highly anomalous in Chicago's black community. The weekly Sunday afternoon concerts were going well in the church's spacious auditorium, and other AACM events were taking place at the new NAME Gallery, an artist-run gallery and performance space at 203 West Lake in the Loop area.[110]

The AACM's tenth year of existence culminated in the first of its many subsequent anniversary festivals. The four-night AACM Tenth Anniversary Festival, held at Transitions East on the South Side, was perhaps the largest-scale event ever attempted by the organization. Steve McCall, speaking with an Italian journalist in 1974, had already remarked that "the fact that the A.A.C.M. is well and stronger after living ten years, almost ignored, is a very important sign."[111] As Douglas Ewart saw it in retrospect, "With everybody recognizing the importance of the association, that the organization had made a contribution, it was time we started celebrating ourselves, recognizing what we were about. It was also a good way, by combining all those groups, to draw a good crowd."[112]

The program book for the four-day festival featured Don Moye, holding a long horn that held a banner titled "AACM Tenth Anniversary." The front cover proclaimed a commitment to "Past, Present, and Future Liberation." Performing on the first night of this four-day festival were a panoply of AACM artists, including Kahil El'Zabar, an increasingly influential voice in the organization, and Rita Frances Warford, named on Kalaparusha's second album as "Rita Omolokun." Warford was a 1945 Cook County Hospital baby, and like Douglas Ewart, is a contemporary of first-wave AACM people such as Anthony Braxton and Henry Threadgill. She grew up on 40th and Vincennes in Bronzeville, and remembers her neighborhood as a far cry from the image of the detritus-filled inner city that predominates now. "We had nice lawns, and flowers in the yard, and everything was well maintained," she told me. "A child could feel safe, because if your parents weren't there to look after you, the other people in the neighborhood were."[113]

Although in simplistic media pieces regarding the demise of U.S. black urban communities, the exodus of the black middle-class serves as the major villain, Warford, a mother and grandmother, provides an explanation for the exodus that is notable for its direct practicality. "The more affluent segment of the population," she observed, "found that it was time to do something else too, because if you're in a neighborhood and you have something and somebody else doesn't have anything, you could become prey."

Warford's mother came to Chicago as a child, as part of the earliest wave of the migration. She was raised in a house surrounded by extended family, except for her father, who was not in the home. The elder Warford was a pool shark with the professional moniker "Sharp Eye," who was noted, according to his daughter, for having played the legendary Minnesota Fats. The young Warford would go along with him to the poolrooms: "He set me on top of the bar, and all these people were coming at me, saying, 'Oh Sharp Eye, she's so cute.' Their faces looked like those mirrors you see in amusement parks, where everything looks all grotesque and distorted. They had these different smells, alcohol, and perfume. They were hugging me and kissing me, and I was terrified."

The upright piano in the Warford home was a great attraction. On a given evening, her uncle might be found playing stride, and her mother might present renditions of Billie Holiday songs. "I don't remember her singing nursery rhymes to me. When I would go to bed, my mother would tell me stories about Billie Holiday, and sing Billie Holiday tunes to me until I went to sleep. I think there's some type of emotional content in Billie's music, the genuineness, the sincerity in her sound, that draws little children. They'll sit and listen to Billie, girls and boys."

Warford was already playing rhythm instruments in the Baptist church, but when she entered a Catholic school near her home, she received more formal training in piano and violin, which she continued through high school. When Warford was in her teens, her family moved to the West Side, where she attended a newly integrated school. Experiencing all the tensions that integration entailed at the time. "Instead of going to school, my girl-friends and I started hanging out with these grown men, drinking wine in this one guy's basement that he had fixed up like a night club. One of them was what they call an albino, and he played saxophone. Instead of going to school we would just hang down there and listen to Charlie Parker."

"Times were so different then," Warford marveled. "We were high-school girls, and none of those men ever touched us, or approached us like that. We were just hanging." Warford's frequent truancy, however, led to her being expelled from school, and briefly sent to a school for "bad girls." Her mother intervened, however, and sent Warford to live with an aunt in New York. It was during her years in Harlem that Warford's interest in the arts blossomed. The panoply of expressive cultures she experienced there included "West Indian dancing at the Audubon, Tito Puente at the Pavilion, the Metropolitan Opera, or Olatunji's dance company—a rich cultural ex-perience I had never been exposed to in Chicago." In one sense, Warford's aunt could fairly be characterized as strict, and she forbade Warford from wearing the then-popular Afro hairstyle. In another sense,

> although she was conservative, she was also a gambler, and on the week-ends she would go and stay in the gambling houses over in New Jersey. So on the weekends I would wash my hair and wear it natural, go get me a pack of cigarettes and a six-pack of beer, and as often as I could, spend time in the Village. I was looking old for my age, and I hung out a little bit in Small's, local people, even though I was only fifteen or sixteen years old.

Her aunt had also counseled her against involvement with the civil rights movement, but when she returned to Chicago, she began singing with the well-known Thompson Community Singers. At one event she met some-one who introduced her to the Congress of Racial Equality. She sang at fund-raisers and on the picket lines, while raising a four-year-old son. Some of Warford's Chicago friends had been listening to the work of John Col-trane, Eric Dolphy, Archie Shepp, so it seemed somehow inevitable that one of them would introduce her to Leroy Jenkins, who had just returned to Chicago and joined the complement of first-wave AACM musicians.

> By the time I got to the AACM, I felt that I was really ready for what they were doing. Leroy took me to a Roscoe Mitchell concert, and Roscoe and

a number of other reedmen were playing in a semicircle. I can't say I totally understood it, but it was something I totally enjoyed. Because I had been listening to all this other stuff, I was ready for it.

She began performing with Jenkins, Mitchell, Muhal Richard Abrams, and Joseph Jarman, as well as vocalists Sherri Scott, Penelope Taylor, and the late dancer Rosetta Ewing, who took part in many first-wave AACM events. She studied with Abrams as well, "mostly vocal exercises, keyboard skills, listening, a little theory. It was never a formal thing. I could call him up and go over different stuff here and there."

Kahil El'Zabar, closer in age than Warford to second-wave AACM members, was born Clifton Henry Blackburn, Jr., in 1953, to parents who were part of the second wave of migrants from the South. Blackburn Senior was a sergeant in the United States Army, and as a toddler, El'Zabar lived in Europe with his parents, who were on army business. When El'Zabar was five years old, the family came to Chicago, where his father got a job with the Chicago Police Department. The family lived first in Englewood, and then in the somewhat more middle-class Chatham neighborhood, where some of the black community's cognoscenti, such as the Boutté and Johnson families (of Ultra Sheen fame) were living.

The theorist bell hooks's remembrance of her early years resonates well with El'Zabar's experience of a performative childhood. "As young black children raised in the post slavery southern culture of apartheid," hooks writes, "we were taught to appreciate and participate in 'live arts,' Organised stage shows were one of the primary places where we were encouraged to display talent. . . . We performed for ourselves as subjects, not as objects seeking approval from the dominant culture."[114] El'Zabar's parents manifested that same kind of energy, and El'Zabar himself remembered a kind of ring shout atmosphere at family gatherings. "We used to do things where they'd throw the kids out in a circle and let them dance or sing or just get into these energies," he remembered. "There was always an appreciation for self-expression."[115]

"In our all-black schools and churches," hooks continues, "performance was a place of celebration, a ritual play wherein one announced liberatory subjectivity."[116] El'Zabar's father exemplified that celebration in every way, introducing him both to the music and to the social atmosphere that nurtured it. "My father was hip," El'Zabar declared with pride. "He had all the right hats, the right pleated pants. He could scat, that's how I learned to scat. He would take me to Chan's restaurant, Chinese restaurant, where there was this guy called the Sandman, and Jug, Von, George [Freeman]. All these cats would go down there after their gig."

In contrast, El'Zabar was at best ambivalent about the cultural atmosphere in Chatham, which he associated with the worst aspects of what E. Franklin Frazier identified as the "black bourgeoisie," such as an emphasis on acquired wealth and professional position as markers of status. The ostensible restrictions on self-expression, performed in apparent imitation of how white middle-class families were thought to be behaving, were perhaps even more chafing, and seemed to El'Zabar to be at variance with fundamental aspects of African American history and culture. "I always danced wild," observed El'Zabar. "I always played basketball loud, a lot of things that were about a certain emotional physicality that didn't seem to get appreciated in the same way as a more delicate, controlled sense of expression."

"The kids called me a gangbanger, with my little Quo Vadis hairdo, with a relaxer. Yech! Look at that gangbanger." So for El'Zabar himself, in retrospect, the task in facing the middle-class sons and daughters of black privilege was twofold—first, "to learn how to articulate. I'm going to learn how to be an Ivy Leaguer, and I'm not going to let these kids limit me from being successful in their environment. At the same time, I ain't going to let go of this gutbucket energy." El'Zabar's father had a set of drums in his basement, which his uncle, the drummer Candy Finch, would come by and play. El'Zabar himself started playing those drums at age four, "just going in the basement, acting crazy." Meanwhile, El'Zabar was being enculturated by his father into the world of jazz.

> Most of my friends were basically trying to deal the Sly and the Family Stone, Earth, Wind, and Fire type energies, the Bar-Kays, but my father had already indoctrinated me. I could only listen to WVON when my father wasn't home. When he got home, I could only listen to WCFL ("The Voice of Labor"), which had Jesse Owens, Sid McCoy, Yvonne Daniels. All they did was play jazz.

El'Zabar switched to hand percussion at fourteen, playing (and dancing) as part of the celebrated dance troupe of his cousin, Darlene Blackburn. Through his cousin, he met a group of Chicago musicians who eventually became known as the Sun Drummer, "Sun Drummer was an organization of percussionists that started in the '60s," El'Zabar explained. "Harold Murray, who was called Black Harold, played with Phil Cohran, Sun Ra. That was my percussion teacher."[117] El'Zabar's father bought him a fiberglass conga drum, "but the guys said, that ain't a real drum. By sixteen, I had to make a drum, and start really getting into it. They were teaching me these principles. By sixteen I didn't touch traps." Soon, El'Zabar was playing talent shows at the Regal Theater, and sitting in with the Pharaohs, substituting for one temporarily absent member or another. By the early 1970s, he was doing recording sessions, going on the road with Donny Hathaway and working with the Pharaohs, the Sun Drummers, Gene Chandler, Pete Cosey, and the Hebrew Israelite bands. El'Zabar got to know the musicians in Philip Cohran's circle, including Master Henry Gibson, who worked with Cohran and then with Curtis Mayfield, and Derf Reklaw-Raheem, a member of the Pharaohs who played with Ramsey Lewis and Eddie Harris. "Gigs Derf didn't do, I got." At around that same time, Kahil became part of the AACM milieu, both as a performer and as one of the members who worked at self-production in the concerts. "It meant a lot for me the first time I was able to put up some chairs at Child City," he recalled. "That was like, damn, these are like great motherfuckers and I'm in some shit here that's really special."

The Tenth Anniversary Festival was celebratory in the fashion that bell hooks suggests. On the first night, there was an ensemble led by Chico Freeman, with Henry Threadgill, Frank Gordon, Adegoke, Leonard Jones, Don Moye, drummer Ben Montgomery, and performing poet G'Ra. After that, the Muhal Richard Abrams Big Band performed, with Freeman, Ari Brown, Charles Wes Cochran, Gene Easton, and Sabu Zawadi, saxophones; Steve Galloway, Billy Howell, Lester Lashley, and George Lewis, trombones; Gordon, Bill Brimfield, Rahmlee Michael Davis, Walter Henderson, and John Shenoy Jackson, trumpet; Amina Claudine Myers, piano; Fred Hopkins, bass; Moye and Ajaramu, percussion; and Tamu, dance. The second night featured Joseph Jarman's "Return from Exile," with Freeman, James Johnson on saxophone and bassoon; Vela Sengstacke, harp; Vandy Harris, reeds; Evod Magek, piano; Malachi Favors, bass; Aye Aton, percussion; and Iqua Colson, voice; and "Amina and Company," with Threadgill, Davis, Ajaramu, El'Zabar, and three voices: Iqua, Rita Warford, and Rrata Christine Jones (later Christina Jones-Stewart). The third night featured Fred Anderson's ensemble, with Lewis, Iqua Colson, Douglas Ewart, Salim (later Soji Adebayo) on piano; Hank (later Hamid) Drake, drums; Felix Blackmon, electric bass; and Marilyn Lashley as dancer; and the Muhal Richard Abrams ensemble, with Lewis, Harris, Brimfield, Threadgill, Ajaramu, Favors, Moye, and Wallace McMillan.

The final performance day included the Black Artists Group of Chicago, with Zawadi, Montgomery, Turk Burton, Rasul Siddik, Harlan Robinson, pianist Calvin Brunson (later Koco), piano, bassist Rudolph Penson, and vocalist Bernard Mixon, who was briefly an AACM member in the mid-1970s. Tamu was once again the featured dancer. The AACM Big Band, directed by Abrams, concluded the festival, with the reeds of Cochran, Ewart, Freeman, Harris, Johnson, Zawadi, Michael Danzy, Edward Wilkerson, and artist-musician Seitu Nurullah; Lewis and long-time AACM trombonist Martin Alexander; two pianists, Amina and Adegoke; Favors on bass; two percussionists, Ajaramu and Moye; and Mixon.

As with future AACM festival booklets, this one did not forget the members who had passed away. Obituaries of Charles Clark and Christopher Gaddy were reprinted on the first two pages, right after the list of nine AACM purposes, printed on the inside front cover. As the organization's chair, I had the last word on the last page. Expressing "unshakable faith in the power of Great Black Music," I wrote that the "common purpose" of the AACM was "the creation of new cultural values, and the acceptance of responsibility for the creation of these values. As members and supporters of the Association for the Advancement of Creative Musicians, none of us should settle for less than this."[118]

The *Chicago Reader* published three articles on the eve of the anniversary festival. AACM chronicler John Litweiler wrote a pensive piece recalling the early excitement of the AACM, who "made discoveries that created shock waves through all the rest of jazz. . . . Some of these AACM players acquired what passes for fame in the jazz business." The Art Ensemble of Chicago was said to command "rock-group prices for concerts," while Abrams, Braxton, McCall, and Kalaparusha were now "important figures on the European grand tour of American jazz musicians."[119] One of the new generation of Chicago critics of the period, Neil Tesser, called the AACM "a symbol of committed excellence," where "the effect of finding the letters 'A.A.C.M' after a musician's name is not unlike that of finding 'PhD' or some other designation of achievement after the name of a statesman or novelist." Tesser observed that the work of the AACM "literally put Chicago on the worldwide jazz map of the last decade." Key to this reputation, according to Tesser, was that the AACM "remains an important source of experimentation. . . . The A.A.C.M. has encouraged the progression implicit in experimentation, and is thus now an organization focused largely on the new innovators," including the organization's "second generation" of newer and/or younger members.[120]

In hindsight, it was Litweiler's interview with Abrams in the same issue that could be seen as announcing the collective's future.

> The AACM is on the move. Anything that lasts 10 years in this society, especially any black independent group, has to have the sanction of some force that's much more relevant than this society. It has touched what's produced us. I can say "God," "Allah," "Jehovah," but all people don't relate to that. Everybody relates to change, and I think change is synonymous with any conception of the deity. It's something basic to mankind, it's in the physical make-up, the deterioration and rebuilding of the cells, and there's no thing man-made that gets beyond change. So the AACM has been used by change as a channel, a willing channel.[121]

An article under Tesser's byline had appeared in the *Reader* well before the anniversary festival, offering a thoughtful and probing analysis of this emerging evolution. Writing in 1975, Tesser anticipated saxophonist and cultural theorist Salim Washington's similar meditation on the meaning of the term "avant-garde"[122] in observing that in jazz, the term had been "robbed of its infinity, its relativity, its value as a word descriptive of the leading trend at a given moment. It is now rooted to a certain musical genre, which was most prevalent in the last decade."[123] In refuting the impression that this reification had, in fact, killed the new music, Tesser pointed to two recent events. The first was a Roscoe Mitchell solo saxophone concert at the Museum of Contemporary Art, in which the entire evening consisted of "written compositions, with sections of improvisation or improvisational techniques." Mitchell also performed Albert Ayler's "Ghosts," along with pieces by Anthony Braxton, Muhal Richard Abrams, and Henry Threadgill. Tesser described a new Mitchell piece, "Cards," as "an aleatory piece written on several pieces of music paper, which are then shuffled, overlapped, even turned upside down, during the performance. The resulting music owes as much to chance as to the performer or composer." The sound of the piece, however, owed little to previous aleatory efforts. Tesser vividly describes Mitchell's sound as "ferocious notes bitten sharply out of the alto saxophone's mouthpiece, angrily alive with guttural squawks and sounds of pain, intermixed with dreamy sections of spaced softness. These throaty eruptions of noise and catatonically wandering atonal melodies fill much of Mitchell's work."[124]

The second event referred to by Tesser, a three-hour concert by the Fred Anderson Sextet, took place at J's Place, a juice bar set up by an entity called the "Foundation Church" in the fading Wells Street entertainment district at 1529 N. Wells. Now, between the unholy hours of midnight and 5:00 a.m., Anderson was surrounded by what Tesser describes as "children half his age," youngsters barely out of their teens—me, singer Iqua Colson, electric bassist Felix Blackmon, drummer Hank (later Hamid) Drake, and the elder statesman of the group at thirty, Douglas Ewart. Instead of to the friendly church members, all wearing rather severe blue suits, Tesser's attention was turned to a duo between Douglas and me: "They interact, first in question-and-answer form, then in dialogue, heads bobbing up and down in unison, the music similarly rising and falling in emotion and intensity." As Tesser affirmed, Anderson "gives more of the solo space to Lewis and Ewart, and enjoys watching them grow."[125] In fact, I had probably played with Fred more than anybody else during my years in Chicago—after (naturally) taking his introductory course on the music of Charlie Parker. Fred let you play as long as you wanted, and you could try out anything. There is no question that it was the many rehearsals and concerts with Fred, along with the concerts with Muhal's Transitions East Big Band, that played a major role in solidifying both my musicianship and my conception of form.

In a *Reader* article written in late 1975, in the wake of the Tenth Anniversary Festival, Tesser hinted at a the possibility of a renewed exodus of musicians from Chicago, noting that "many of names associated with the A.A.C.M have migrated to other cities (not one member of the original Art Ensemble still plays regularly in Chicago). . . . Younger members, such as trombonist George Lewis, saxophonist Chico Freeman, and pianist Steve Colson, . . . need a regular showcase as soon as possible." Tesser recounted the by now familiar tale of the decline of jazz: the relatively few (but "healthy") radio outlets, including Tesser's own weekend offering at the time on WNIB-FM (no one even mentioned television, which was presumed to be forever closed to jazz-identified musics), and the paucity of performances, particularly on the South Side. ("When it does appear, it's most often the music of the A.A.C.M.") The writer concluded by pointing out the fragile and tenuous nature of the Chicago jazz scene: "Chicago jazz drifts along, in and out of good times and bad, picking up steam and then losing momentum in a twinkling. . . . You'll never know, abracadabra— when it'll drop out of sight again."[126]

In fact, the music of the AACM was changing and expanding rapidly. A thoughtful Litweiler review of a 1975 Roscoe Mitchell event at Michigan State University described the changes that were in motion, noting that these new Mitchell works featured "highly controlled situations . . . a far cry from 'old' Mitchell." Here, Litweiler noted, "much of the improvisation occurs within strictly delineated outlines."[127] The program featured seven Mitchell compositions for the most diverse formations: a large ensemble with members of the Creative Arts Collective, the AACM-like collective that Mitchell had formed in the Detroit area with A. Spencer Barefield, Anthony Holland, and others; a saxophone quartet with Jarman, Threadgill, and McMillan; a trio with Abrams and Barefield; a quartet for two bass saxophones and two trombones, including me and CAC member William Townley on trombones; and an even larger intermedia ensemble including a choir and dancers.[128] Mitchell made explicit use of the kiva-like in-the-round setting of the MSU performance space as part of an antiphonal approach to the saxophone and trombone–bass saxophone formations, as well as the large ensembles. Foreshadowing by at least twenty-five years the advent of "lower-case" or "reductionist" quiet improvisations, Mitchell's saxophone playing at this time was described by Litweiler as "playing *very* sparsely . . . his hard sound grew breathy, quieter, the sense of melodic fragmentation enhanced by the evolution of silence in his line."[129] Similarly, *Tahquemenon*, on which I performed, was said to explore "a quiet place."[130]

Most important in the evolution of the work of AACM composers was Litweiler's observation that "Mitchell's division of score/improvisation, invention/interpretation is to a large extent no division at all. The act of creation—or more accurately, revelation—encompasses all these now, and it's rather a blow to absolutist theorists."[131] A review of the same event by Bill Smith in the Canadian magazine *Coda* was even more detailed, and more sensitive to the intermedia nature of the event. Photographs of the working processes of Jarman, Mitchell, Lewis, McMillan, Threadgill, Abrams, and Favors were included, and the work of the choir and the dancers, particularly the "astounding" Rrata Christine Jones, was also described. The article highlighted a growing affinity for the AACM and its music by Smith and the magazine generally; this affinity was reflected in the offerings of his recording company, Sackville, which featured releases by Braxton, Mitchell, and myself in particular.[132]

In September 1975, a lengthy interview with Roscoe Mitchell appeared in *Coda,* complete with a detailed discography that included *Coda* editor Bill Smith's 1974 Sackville-produced recording of Mitchell's solo saxophone compositions.[133] The interview functioned as a kind of biographical sketch, a forum for discussions of aesthetics, and a site for airing the problems with category and genre classifications that were endemic to AACM musicians. Late in the article, Mitchell describes the first fruits of his ongoing research collaboration in computer interactivity with the psychoacoustician and computer musician David Wessel, who was then teaching at Michigan State, and who set up the CAC/AACM event.

The AACM Tenth Anniversary Festival had been a watershed event in many respects, but in retrospect, it could be said to have foreshadowed certain changes in the consciousness of many members, including myself as the organization's chair. In a telephone conversation I had with Douglas Ewart in 2004, we tried to reconstruct the events of 1975:

> EWART: It was the first time to my knowledge that the association had ever made that kind of money, and from their own endeavors, not from a gig. . . . It was around fifteen hundred dollars or more. That was a fair amount of money at the time, but what started to happen was, people started to create these "expenses."[134] People got traffic tickets on "AACM business" and suddenly the organization should pay for that. . . . I remember Jackson saying that as president, the money should go with you, that you should take responsibility. I remember [various members] calling your house. Your parents became concerned. I think it was your mom that called me. She said, I don't know what's going on, but it was becoming a problem, and could I think about something that should be done. I called you and I said, you know, you should just give them the money because it's not worth all this. To me, it was stupid. You had just become president, we had this new kind of fervor about moving forward, and it seemed as though it was kind of like the old attitudes. These have been the similar kinds of riffs that have occurred over the years in one form or another.
>
> LEWIS: There was a certain naiveté about my activity, and others might have understood things better than I did. I was living at home, I had a job. It was a whole different thing for me. . . . You would think that being out of the system meant that you could be more impartial, but in fact it meant that you just weren't aware of certain things that were important. I said, I understand this, but I can't go along with it. I think we should use this money to try and invest it in some way. So when I got the call from the membership about the money, I just said, probably the best thing for me to do is resign. . . . I guess the money kind of got dissipated, but resigning was the best thing to do. . . . I could see where my lack of experience was really hurting the situation, in retrospect. Rather than cause a big split in the organization, just accept the limits of the confidence people have in your leadership. But it didn't

make me think, well, I'm leaving the AACM or anything. Maybe someone else could do what they felt needed to be done with majority support. I hadn't heard the part about people scaring my parents, though.

EWART: It [anniversary festivals] became an annual thing after that. . . .
This was the first one, and it was crucial.

LEWIS: When I looked at it, it wasn't a failure, because a lot of things came
out of it. Things changed rapidly from this point. But, you know, it
was an important learning experience. I wasn't quite as trusting of
some people after that.

9

THE AACM IN NEW YORK

Migration and Invasion

John Stubblefield and drummer Phillip Wilson were already on hand when Anthony Braxton and Leroy Jenkins returned from Europe in early 1970 to pursue an encounter with New York City. In a 1978 interview, Jenkins described his earliest days in New York:

> We stayed downstairs at Ornette's Artist House, which at the time wasn't decorated. It was cold down there, where we slept. Ornette gave us a mattress but he didn't realize how cold it was. One night something happened and he came downstairs to wake us up. He said, "Wow, you cats better come upstairs." We stayed there and that's when I went to the University of Ornette. He put the finishing touches on me. I spent three months up there, staying at his house, doing everything. Answering the door, helping him copy music, arguing about his harmolodic theory.[1]

"When I came to New York, I didn't have a gig," recalled John Stubblefield. "Mary Lou Williams gave me my first job. I came when there was a telephone strike, and I went eight months without a telephone." Although performance opportunities and press coverage were relatively sparse, these AACM musicians performed with many of the more established experimentalists of the period, such as Marion Brown, Rahsaan Roland Kirk, Sam Rivers, Chick Corea, Ornette Coleman, and Archie Shepp. In many cases, these encounters simply extended the relationships AACM members had initiated in Paris.

The first wave of New York–based AACM musicians presented their own work in concert programs of both contemporary notated music and improvised music. In May 1970, promoter Kunle M'wanga organized perhaps the first AACM concert in New York, at the Washington Square Methodist Church (Peace Church) in the West Village. Featured was the "Creative Construction Company," consisting of Leroy Jenkins, Anthony Braxton, Muhal Richard Abrams, Steve McCall, Leo Smith, and Chicago-born bassist Richard Davis.[2] By 1973 Anthony Braxton had managed to garner notice in the *New York Times* for an Alice Tully Hall performance of his chamber work, "L-J-637/C."[3] The year before, he had followed in the footsteps of Ornette Coleman by renting Town Hall for a performance of his work.

Jenkins worked with Archie Shepp, whom he had met in Paris, and was also a participant in the Carla Bley/Paul Haines collaboration, *Escalator over the Hill,* a kind of postbeat jazz opera that incorporated a highly diverse group of artists.[4] The Jazz Composer's Orchestra workshop, formed by composer-pianist Carla Bley and trumpeter Mike Mantler in the wake of the demise of the Jazz Composers Guild, presented Jenkins and Smith in successive events at CAMI Hall.[5] In 1973, Smith was part of the Jazz Composer's Orchestra's five-evening performance of Don Cherry's *Relativity Suite* at New York University. The reviewer commented that "anyone with some knowledge of the new music will see from the personnel that just about every important name in the new music field who happened to be available was in attendance, and those not playing showed up in the audience during one of the five nights, including Ornette Coleman and Anthony Braxton."[6]

The Revolutionary Ensemble, one of the signal groups of the period, was formed around this time, when M'wanga introduced Jenkins to bassist Sirone. The first concerts included drummer Frank Clayton, and when Chicagoan Jerome Cooper joined the group, the reformulated trio took off. The ensemble presented a concert at Ornette Coleman's Artist's House, located on Prince Street in New York City's Soho district. The review served as something of an introduction to the group, noting that it had been formed nearly two years prior. According to the review, the ambiance of Artist's House included African décor and original paintings. The reviewer concluded that seeing the Revolutionary Ensemble "might teach you something horribly true about yourself."[7] Earlier that year, the group performed at the Public Theater,[8] founded in 1967 by producer and entrepreneur Joseph Papp. Seeking to build upon his successful New York Shakespeare Festival, which had been running since 1954, Papp dedicated the Public Theater to experimental drama, often with a musical component.

The work of Anthony Braxton was beginning to emerge in U.S. reviews, including a mention in the 1971 *Down Beat* Reader's Poll. Braxton's self-engineered two-LP set of unaccompanied alto saxophone solos, *For Alto,*[9] had been released in 1968 as part of the Delmark AACM series, but received a five-star *Down Beat* review only four years later. The audacity of the attempt alone struck that reviewer favorably, in contrast to a musician's review in Leonard Feather's "Blindfold Test," which once again served as the vehicle of generational conflict over aesthetics. Saxophonist Phil Woods, a self-described acolyte of Charlie Parker, was seemingly nonplussed by the Braxton track he was introduced to, and indeed, the entire concept of unaccompanied saxophone improvisations. Woods denounced the Braxton recording in colorful language, while recognizing implicitly that somehow, this threat to musical order seemed "beyond category":

> It's not jazzy, it's not classical . . . it's dull . . . it's not well done, he doesn't breathe properly. I'm sure his fingers wave off the keyboard. I'm sure he hasn't studied the saxophone. This doesn't bother me, there's a lot of primitives that play and get a lot of exciting music; but this is such an ego trip, that you can think that you're so much of a bitch that you can do a solo album.

Woods concluded by saying that "I don't even want to guess who it is, because I might hate him."[10]

Braxton received far more sympathetic press in France, where he was in residence at the Cité Internationale des Arts in Paris, writing the texts and developing the philosophical concepts that would eventually emerge in the mid-1980s as the massive, 1,800-page, three-volume *Tri-Axium Writings.*[11] Over the course of the early 1970s, the composer and saxophonist received considerably more coverage than any other AACM musician in the pages of the French magazine *Jazz Hot,* as well as receiving sustained and substantial notices in the Paris-published magazine *Jazz.* As was typical of French jazz journals of the period, many of the articles included detailed analyses of Braxton's music. The 1971 formation of Circle, the famous but short-lived quartet with Braxton, drummer Barry Altschul, bassist Dave Holland, and pianist Chick Corea, augmented Braxton's visibility still further, culminating in a watershed Paris concert, a recording of which was eventually released on ECM.[12]

Following this increased visibility was a long interview with Braxton in the April 1971 issue of *Jazz Hot,* with interviewer François Postif's questions apparently edited out. Here, Braxton described the AACM as an organization devoted to "la musique contemporaine noire" [black contemporary music]. Apparently the reviewer noticed this, and in answer to the textually absent, yet all too present query, Braxton had this to say: "You will notice that I do not use the word 'jazz' to speak about my music. However, I like the word 'jazz,' It sounds good, it's a great invention as a term, but I don't consider myself to be a jazz musician—and I'm in the process of asking myself if I'm even a musician at all."[13]

While U.S. president Richard Nixon was pursuing a covert war in Cambodia, the postwar economic boom that had been kept alive by the Vietnam War was fading, replaced by rising unemployment and "stagflation," a stagnant economy with rampant inflation that the administration's wage and price controls had done little to ameliorate. Thus, collectivity was in the air, as New York–based musicians sought new answers to the perennial problem of work, which was becoming ever scarcer. A "New York Musicians' Association" had already organized an independent "off"-festival of "younger and more avant garde oriented players," held concurrently with, and in apparent reaction to, the Newport Jazz Festival. Concerts were held at the jazz club Slug's, the Studio Museum in Harlem, Studio WIS (founded by Chicago-born percussionist Warren Smith), and playwright and director Woodie King, Jr.'s New Federal Theater. The concerts included drummer Milford Graves; saxophonists Anthony Braxton, Clifford Jordan, Frank Foster, Archie Shepp, and Byard Lancaster; trumpeters Bill Hardman, Tommy Turrentine, Cal Massey, and Ted Daniel; bassists Wilbur Ware and David Izenzon; and organist Larry Young. The festival was run by the musicians themselves, "with proceeds divided on an equitable basis."[14]

In New York, collective strategies were being most prominently pursued by the Collective Black Artists, which had strong roots in New York's black community, particularly in Brooklyn and Manhattan.[15] The CBA, which included bassist Reggie Workman, trumpeters Donald Byrd and Jimmy Owens, pianist Stanley Cowell, and saxophonist Bill Barron, presented a "Symposium of Creative Musicians" in Brooklyn's Bedford-Stuyvesant section in April 1972, with discussions of the music business by Owens, and seminars in improvisation and black music history by Barron and Byrd.[16] Dizzy Gillespie, who spoke on a panel at the meeting, was paraphrased in a review of the event as observing that "by establishing a pecking order of stardom, by singling out individual musicians for particular elevation, musicians themselves have often played into the hands of a destructive competitive attitude instead of realizing that there is a bond between all creative musicians."[17]

The explicit presence of the word "Black" in the organization's name was of no small import at a time when melting-pot and integrationist ideologies were being challenged by political and cultural stances influenced by Black Power. The review characterized Workman as observing that the emphasis on blackness was "a manifestation not of cultural separatism, but of a certain socio-cultural realism."[18]

> We are focusing on black artists because whites and blacks have different problems unique to their different cultures and life styles. We started out as an interracial group, but nothing was happening because of those differences. . . . Eventually, blacks and whites will come together, but for now it's more important to establish a firm base, do our homework, and work out our own problems individually.[19]

In July 1973, the first New York concert of the Art Ensemble of Chicago took place at Columbia University's Wollman Auditorium, as part of promoter George Wein's Newport Jazz Festival. An advance article about the festival was written by *New York Times* critic Robert Palmer, a member of an emerging advance guard that was promulgating new ways of writing about improvised music in the New York press. Palmer describes some of the Art Ensemble's musical methods as reminiscent of various elements of black jazz and R&B traditions, but avoids traditional jazz journalism's tendency to deploy historical jazz icons as a means of quickly, yet all too neatly, contextualizing a particular performer's work within a constructed jazz tradition. Rather, evoking a postmodernist contextualization, the article descriptively expands the frame of reference, comparing the Art Ensemble's work to "developments in the visual arts; themes, variations, solos and ensemble passages alternate in a continuous flow that is comparable to a collage of apparently disparate objects and images."[20]

Even the fabled sophistication of the New York cultural community, however, was challenged by the AEC's "unpredictability and steadfast refusal to be stereotyped" during their first extended club engagement in late 1975. At the Five Spot Café, where John Coltrane and Thelonious Monk once held audiences spellbound, according to one press account, "most New Yorkers didn't know quite what to make of their audio-visual performances."[21]

> Bowie came out first, sporting a casino dealer's visor on his head and drinking from a pint of whiskey. Jarman and Moye staggered across the club like two winos, holding each other for balance, shooting off streamers and mumbling nonsensically. Bowie spotted them and yelled, "Over here! None of this music shit, we're gonna play cards!" Somehow they found their way to a table set up in front of the stage, where a deck of cards was produced. Bowie proceeded to deal furiously, cards flying everywhere, the three drinking and cursing each other in a hilarious parody of a seedy card game perhaps, or a parody of a jazz club.[22]

Between 1973 and 1977, it was clear that a sudden and dramatic shift was occurring in experimental music in New York, in which the AACM was to play a crucial role. Samuel Gilmore's sociological analysis of the New York "concert music world" of the early 1980s (i.e., ostensibly excluding jazz, pop, or other "vernacular" genres) draws upon the methods of symbolic interactionism in identifying three major art world divisions—uptown, midtown, and downtown, that even by the early 1970s, were fairly well defined, if "imagined," communities. While at this writing the terms "uptown," "midtown," and "downtown" are still used in New York, it must be emphasized that in the 1970s, as now, the art worlds to which they refer interpenetrated one another to a considerable extent to form an overall "art music" scene in New York. Gilmore viewed the term "midtown" as denoting major symphony orchestras, touring soloists, and chamber groups active in large, well-funded, commercially oriented performing spaces, such as Lincoln Center and Carnegie Hall. "Uptown" referred to academically situated composers "of whom the public has rarely heard . . . but who win the Pulitzer Prize every year."[23] For Gilmore, these representative "uptown" composers included Milton Babbitt and Elliott Carter; representative performance ensembles included the Group for Contemporary Music, then directed by composers Harvey Sollberger and Charles Wuorinen; and Speculum Musicae, which then featured the very diverse and insightful pianist, Ursula Oppens.

Gilmore identified the term "downtown" as referring to "the composer / performer, living in small performance lofts in Soho, Tribeca, and near alternative performance spaces in Greenwich Village." Representative venues included the Kitchen, the multidisciplinary performance space founded in 1971 by the video artists Steina and Woody Vasulka, which by 1975 had become a central part of New York's new music scene; intermedia artist Phill Niblock's Experimental Intermedia Foundation; and later, Roulette, founded by trombonist Jim Staley and sound artist David Weinstein. Representative composers active in this downtown art world included John Cage, Philip Glass, Philip Corner, Robert Ashley, and La Monte Young. These artists, and others in their circle, might be brought under the heading of "Downtown I," to distinguish their putative post-Cage commonality from the post-1980 construction of "downtown," or "Downtown II," most prominently represented by saxophonist John Zorn, vocalist Shelley Hirsch, sound artist David Moss, and guitarists Fred Frith, Eugene Chadbourne, and Elliott Sharp, among many others.[24] Both Downtown I and Downtown II are generally racially coded in press accounts as white, and by the late 1980s, such accounts routinely portrayed Downtown II as the logical successor to Downtown I's connection with pan-European high culture.

Both chronicling and contributing to the shifting currents in musical experimentalism were new ideas emerging in the critical domain. The younger *Times* music writers, including Robert Palmer, John Rockwell, and Jon Pareles, were acquainted with a wide range of musical aesthetics and practices, and thus less invested in maintaining traditional taxonomies. In a review of Lincoln Center's 1974 "New and Newer Music" Festival, Rockwell announced (some might say "warned of") changes in the relationship of jazz with "serious contemporary music." Rockwell contrasted the standard bebop-era image of "somber-looking black men wearing berets," playing in "dim, smoky clubs," with that of "short-haired white people peering industriously through their spectacles at densely notated pages of . . . genteelly complex music in genteelly academic environments." The writer went on to note that the border between "experimental jazz" and contemporary music was routinely being crossed in the "downtown" environment. "For several years in downtown lofts," the article observed, "the same faces have been turning up among the performers at avant-garde jazz concerts and avant-garde 'serious' new-music concerts."[25]

Rockwell went on to present an optimistically color-blind analysis of the situation: "The National Endowment for the Arts, the New York State Council on the Arts [and] the Guggenheim Foundation are just as likely to give their grants to Ornette Coleman as to Charles Wuorinen."[26] Of course, the real situation was far less sanguine. In 1971, the Jazz and People's Movement, organized by Rahsaan Roland Kirk, Roswell Rudd, and Archie Shepp, had staged a "play-in" at the offices of the John Simon Guggenheim Foundation in New York, "demanding an end to the obvious and blatant racist policies . . . in the allocation of awards."[27] Indeed, NEA funding for music was hypersegregated according to racialized categories of "jazz/folk/ethnic" and "music," with the latter category apparently intended to denote, to recall Rockwell's phrase, "short-haired white people" creating "genteelly complex music in genteelly academic environments."

In 1973, the NEA disbursed over $225,000 to 165 individuals and organizations applying to its "jazz-folk-ethnic" category. Composition grants for commissioning new works were provided, but no grant exceeded $2,000, including those given to such important artists as pianist Cedar Walton, saxophonist Clifford Jordan, and composer Duke Jordan. Several AACM members received grants, including Lester Bowie ($750), Malachi Favors ($1,000), Joseph Jarman ($1,000), Leroy Jenkins ($2,000), Roscoe Mitchell ($1,000), Don Moye ($1,000), Leo Smith ($1,000) and trumpeter Frank Gordon ($1,500).[28] The next year, the new "composer-librettist" category—as it happens, one of the less well funded among the several categories under which pan-European music could be supported—was allocated nearly twice the amount allotted to the jazz-folk-ethnic category, with grants of $10,000 to George Rochberg and John Harbison. Other grants were received by Vladimir Ussachevsky ($7,500), Charles Wuorinen ($3,500), Morton Subotnick ($7,000), Charles Dodge ($4,500), Steve Reich ($2,000), Otto Luening ($6,000), and Barbara Kolb ($2,000).[29]

Despite the obvious presence of the border in terms of financial support, in other respects, many of the changes Rockwell had announced were in the air. The "New and Newer Music" taking place at Ornette Coleman's Prince Street performance loft, Artist's House, featured works by Coleman, Carla Bley, and Frederic Rzewski—"successive evenings of jazz and classical avant-garde, and works that fuse the two."[30] By 1975, black experimental music was starting to be featured at such midtown venues as Carnegie Recital Hall. Writers Gary Giddins and Peter Occhiogrosso, and later Stanley Crouch, publishing in both the *Village Voice* and the now-defunct *Soho Weekly News,* were becoming instrumental in covering this newest black experimental music, which they discursively folded into the previous decade's conception of "avant-garde jazz." Their articles came sporadically, perhaps every other month or so; certainly there was no concentrated, dedicated press coverage of these black experimentalists that could be considered analogous to composer Tom Johnson's weekly *Voice* columns on Downtown I, which were instrumental in furthering the careers of Robert Ashley,

Steve Reich, Meredith Monk, Philip Glass, Pauline Oliveros, Glenn Branca, and others.[31]

Even a small amount of publicity for a musician, however is like an infusion of life-giving oxygen in outer space—or as Art Blakey is said to have observed, "If you don't appear, you disappear." Partially as a result of this press coverage, word was getting back to AACM members in Chicago through the musician's grapevine that New York was beckoning, with potential opportunities far beyond what was available in Chicago at the time. Between 1975 and 1977, it seemed to a Chicago-based musician like me that one was hearing something exciting about New York every week. Glowing, if often apocryphal, reports came back from New York about playing with famous musicians, enthusiastic audiences, opportunities for foreign travel, and so on. At the same time, it was becoming clear to many who tried that it was not very realistic to try to organize events in New York from afar using the same techniques one used for finding work in other American cities. As one person asked me over the phone: "Are you in New York? No? Well, we'll talk when you get here."

Kalaparusha Maurice McIntyre left Chicago in 1974. "Jack DeJohnette had got the vibe that I was coming East," Kalaparusha recalled, "so he told me not to go to New York, but to come up there [to Woodstock]. I met Karl Berger and the other people in the Creative Music Studio," the experimental-music institute that Berger, his spouse Ingrid, and Ornette Coleman had founded in 1972.[32] After trying upstate New York for a fair period of time, it became apparent to Kalaparusha that change was needed. "People in Woodstock were rich," he said in our interview. "I didn't have no money to stay up there. I moved to Brooklyn in '76, basically to be in New York City. It was basically the loft scene at that time. I did a lot of working out of Sam Rivers' Studio Rivbea. Seventy-seven was the year that I went to Nancy with Sam Rivers' big band."[33]

In a sense, the pressure was becoming unbearable, and perhaps these hopeful signs served to "set people flowin'," to borrow Farah Jasmine Griffin's phrase about African American migration narratives.[34] After the fashion of a river overflowing its banks, members of the AACM's second wave, along with the Chicago-based remnants of the first wave—including, most importantly, founder Muhal Richard Abrams—moved to New York, seemingly en masse. Joining those already on the East Coast, this grand wave, including Kalaparusha, Lester Bowie, Amina Claudine Myers, Henry Threadgill, Steve McCall, Fred Hopkins, Chico Freeman, Malachi Thompson, Iqua Colson, Adegoke Colson, and me, all moved to Manhattan or the New York area during this time. Members of BAG, including Charles Bobo Shaw, Baikida E. J. Carroll, Oliver Lake, Julius Hemphill, Hamiet Bluiett, J. D. Parran, Joseph Bowie, Patricia Cruz, Emilio Cruz, and James Jabbo Ware, had all arrived in New York before this mass migration, forming a powerful group of midwestern colleagues.

Leonard Jones came back to Chicago from Germany in July 1974, and was soon swept up in the New York fever. "I left for New York in August of '77," Jones recalled in our 1998 interview in his home in Ratingen, Germany, near Düsseldorf. "You remember that terrible car ride," I laughed, referring to our cross-country trip to the East Coast in my super-flaky Ford Pinto, "in Pennsylvania, where the electrical system crapped out."

"Yes, part of it we experienced together," Jones chuckled.

"I remember the period, because New York was poppin' and jumpin'," said Chico Freeman, who moved to New York in 1976.

> It was exciting, this big pioneer thing. We were a cooperative kind of an organization that was coming with this concept, the whole AACM way of thinking, and all these different groups and musicians, that for some reason, migrated at the same time. We all went to everybody's concerts. Then we found other supporters that had already been here, like [bassist] Cecil McBee, that were already established, but who became involved.

For newcomers to New York, the expense and complexity of finding a suitable place to live can be daunting. Luckily, a number of AACM and BAG musicians found apartments in the newly erected, federally subsidized Manhattan Plaza apartment complex near Times Square, which opened its doors in 1977.[35] These included Chico Freeman, Amina Claudine Myers, Frank Gordon, J. D. Parran, Luther Thomas, Joseph Bowie, myself, and Muhal Richard Abrams, whose departure from Chicago in 1976, according to Martin "Sparx" Alexander, was particularly surprising.

> Muhal was well established around Chicago, so I was very surprised when he moved to New York. I figured he might be like Von or something, become an institution in Chicago. This situation he was in here was just sapping his energy, and he wasn't really able to provide for his family. He was doing what he wanted to do here, and it wasn't really supporting him. New York was much more viable for him to put some bread on the table.

Abrams had been coming to New York off and on since a 1959 appearance with Eddie Harris at Harlem's Club Baron. Now, with the increased visibility of the new music he had been instrumental in promulgating, Abrams was a frequent visitor, at the behest of Anthony Braxton in particular, with whom he performed at Carnegie Hall. "I was living with Barry Altschul, and partly in that loft that Jerome Cooper used to have, and that Steve McCall ended up getting," Abrams recalled. "Then in the fall of '77 I moved the family here."

> Basically I felt I needed to—as others had done before me, but not so much because of that—to make a presence, to follow the reputation that we had garnered through our activities. And, to expand my business base, because Chicago was no longer challenging me as a musician. The most cutting edge stuff in every place is around here, or if it's not, it's headed here from someplace else. If I need a saxophone player who plays all the reeds, he's a phone call and subway ride away.

"I was confident that I had made the right move," Abrams affirmed. "There were no gigs or nothing. We were just hanging around in those lofts. We were getting fairly good press, Gary Giddins, mostly, and I was doing a recording each year with Black Saint." At the same time, as Abrams saw it, "We came to grips with the fact that we had removed ourselves from the black community in terms of presence, because we didn't come here and go to Harlem. We came to Manhattan. The reason we came to Manhattan is because the center of the business was in Manhattan, and it still is. The dictates of necessity had to be the basis of it."

The audience makeup was different," Abrams said.

> The black content of the audience diminished, because of the location where we performed. . . . The mixture was much more varied. A lot of times it wasn't a mixture of black people and white people, but white people and different other kinds of people. Here in Manhattan you don't have a big concentration of black people that attend those kinds of things. You can walk down the street into Birdland any night of the week. Not a lot of black people in it.

As Lester Bowie recalled, AACM-style collectivity played an important role in finding opportunities in New York.

All the [Midwest] cats peeped that there was availability at the building over on 43rd Street [Manhattan Plaza]. They knew about it before the New York cats did, and that's what pissed New York off. The motherfucking word got out and all the cats, J. D. [Parran], Muhal—I didn't think Muhal would ever leave Chicago. Everybody got them apartments, like, quick! Nice apartment, nice view, cool. Cats put their applications in, and they were here, paying cheap rent. They just came and got them a place to stay first, which was hip. That's the first thing to do, then start doing our own thing again, playing with some people, playing around, but also creating your own shit too.[36]

In addition to this contingent, there was a group of new and exciting Californians, in large part the products of pianist Horace Tapscott's Los Angeles-based UGMAA, such as saxophonists Arthur Blythe and David Murray, flutist James Newton, and trumpeter Lawrence "Butch" Morris. Also associated with UGMAA was the writer Stanley Crouch, who presented many of the new experimentalists in his role as music director at the loft/club on the Bowery, the Tin Palace.[37] "The Tin Palace was a place where the gamut of the music was played, mainstream all up to open," remembered Muhal Richard Abrams. "The audience came in for all of it. Some cats came in playing changes, but I think the majority of it was cats playing open." Crouch also ran a performance series, Studio Infinity, out of his own upstairs loft at the same Bowery location. "They used to have jams up there, and he was trying to play drums," Abrams recalled. "We used to always say that it sounded like he was moving furniture. But one thing he could do and still do. Stanley Crouch can go to the piano and write very unique melodies. He's very good at it. He had a natural talent for it."

Chico Freeman was part of Warrick Carter's Governors State University Jazz Band, which was winning collegiate competitions around the country. Engaged to go to Brazil with the band in 1976, Freeman decided to stop off briefly in New York. Freeman's very positive experiences in New York, fortuitous as they were, were far from atypical for the period.

Fred [Hopkins] was sharing a loft with David Murray and Stanley Crouch over the Tin Palace. For three days I stayed in the loft with them, to see what New York was like. Henry [Threadgill] was playing at the Tin Palace with Jeanne Lee. For some reason he had to go back to Chicago, so he asked me to take his place that weekend. So my three days turned into a week. At the end of the week I said, I'll go back, but at the Tin Palace, they had such a good turnout for Jeanne Lee that they asked her back for the next weekend. She liked me, and so she asked me to do the gig again. So now that week's turning into another week.

"While that's happening, I ran into Olu Dara," Freeman continued. "Olu said, I'm working at this place with [bassist] Mickey Bass and [drummer] Michael Carvin and [trombonist] Kiane Zawadi. Come on up and hang out."

So I went up there, and they invite me to sit in. I sit in, and Mickey Bass hires me for this gig he's got every weekend for a month. Now my two weeks are turning into a month, and I told Fred three days. I told them, look, I need a little more time to start looking for something. They said OK, and I became friends with David and Stanley. During this month, I'm playing avant-garde music with Jeanne Lee and bebop with Mickey Bass.

"Then I met Cecil McBee," Freeman went on. "John Stubblefield was the saxophone player, and he had just gotten the call to go out with [trumpeter] Nat Adderley. So John called me to take his place with Cecil. I sat in and Cecil hired me and I became part of Cecil's group. He had a thing where he would be working for the next three months, so I knew I had to get a place.

"I never went back," Freeman concluded. "I ended up joining Sun Ra, and eventually I found a place." In fact, even more was in store for Freeman, when he visited the venerable Village Vanguard to sit in with the great drummer Elvin Jones.

As soon as I went in, Keiko [Jones, Elvin's spouse] was like, Argh! You're late! I was totally shocked. She said, take your horn out! Take your horn out! It was like I was already hired, but I didn't know this. I took my horn out, put it together, and stepped onto the bandstand—in the middle of the song. She was like, get out there. Then Elvin looked at me, like "Solo!" So I just started playing, and played the rest of the set. I didn't hold back at all. I went all the way out there, and started to pack my horn, because I just knew, you know. Got off the bandstand, and Keiko came up and said, OK, OK. So, you want a job? I said, yeah. She said, OK, play the next set. So I played the week. I got hired at the Vanguard on the spot, and I was with Elvin.

Europe and the Lofts

The new music of the AACM, BAG, and the Californians was in the process of becoming widely influential. Robert Palmer wrote of the AACM and BAG that "their originality becomes more and more evident. Their improvisation ranges from solo saxophone recitals to little-tried combinations of horns, rhythm instruments and electronics. They have rendered the clamorous playing characteristic of much of New York's jazz avant-garde all but obsolete with their more thoughtful approaches to improvisational structure and content."[38]

"Chicago developed a school that was totally different from the New York school," Roscoe Mitchell observed. In response to my query as to what was really different about the music, Lester Bowie's mock-prosaic characterization was illuminating: "The main difference was that we would stop. We had rests. We had whole notes. We were dealing with some melodies. People would say to the Art Ensemble, how do you do it? We said, we do it like everybody else—we practice. We play it over and over again and get it right. Using the palette, the colors. They still can't really see it."

The arrival in New York of AACM cofounder Muhal Richard Abrams provided an occasion for perhaps the most extensive *Village Voice* article on the AACM's growing influence on black experimentalism. In a May 1977 article, Giddins declared that "[Abrams's] presence here is a crest on the wave of immigrant musicians recently arrived from St. Louis, Los Angeles, and especially Chicago." The article's focus on the history of the AACM sought "to get to the bottom of why an inner-city organization from the Midwest founded in 1965 should revitalize New York's music scene a decade later." Giddins observed that "a distinguishing characteristic of the new movement is that it isn't a movement at all, at least not one with closed stylistic parameters."[39] The writer's quote from Leo Smith summarized well the intentions of this nonmovement: "[The AACM] represents the control of destiny for the music and the artist."[40]

In 1977, Smith and John Stubblefield received profiles in *Down Beat,* and Air, which later garnered an Arista contract in the same year, was the subject of a concert review and an extended *Down Beat* article, courtesy of the Chicago-based AACM supporters' circle at the magazine. The Fred Anderson Sextet, with Douglas Ewart, Hank (later Hamid) Drake, Bill Brimfield, Felix Blackmon, and Ajaramu, also received a performance review.[41] Numerous recordings featuring Leroy Jenkins were also reviewed, including the Creative Construction Company's 1970 Washington Square Church concert, recordings of the Revolutionary Ensemble, and Jenkins's own composition for the Jazz Composer's Orchestra, *For Players Only.*[42] The increased attention to new things Chicago could have even played a role in *Down Beat*'s publication of an article on saxophonist Von Freeman, whose son, Chico, was part of the AACM exodus to New York. By 1980, a *Down Beat* article featured the two of them together.[43]

Anthony Braxton had already been having a banner period, with a major label recording contract with Arista that came with a number of perks, including full-page advertisements in trade publications, five-star reviews, a multipage interview in *Down Beat,* and two sympathetic and hard-working producers, Steve Backer and Michael Cuscuna.[44] Braxton was putting his contract to good use in ways that recalled the Yoruba image of the trickster. "The challenge of the Arista association," Braxton recalled to interviewer Graham Lock, "was to feed them the quartet music and slip them some of my other projects 'under the rug.'"[45] Displaying the diversity of cultural reference that was fairly typical of first-generation AACM musicians, Braxton used his vastly increased visibility and heightened infrastructure to reveal a seeming torrent of ideas—pieces for a hundred tubas, parade music, electronic music, his tripartite systems of repetition forms, and his interest in the work of John Cage, Earle Brown, Karlheinz Stockhausen, Morton Feldman, and Buckminster Fuller. Other projects included a concerto grosso with himself and me as soloists.[46]

My own personal and collegial association with Braxton began in 1975, at the sessions for his watershed Arista recording, *Creative Orchestra Music 1976.* For the session, Braxton had assembled a diverse group of musicians. There was Seldon Powell, an ace of the studio scene, who played either lead or second alto saxophone along with Anthony, as well as two generations of trombonist-arrangers in Earl McIntyre and the gracious, avuncular Jack Jeffers. Also present were a number of Chicago-identified musicians: the AACM contingent, including me, Leo Smith, Muhal Richard Abrams, Roscoe Mitchell, and drummer Phillip Wilson, whom I had never met; two members of the amazing Bridgewater musical family, trumpeter Cecil and saxophonist Ron; and the versatile and insightful percussionist Warren Smith, who had performed and recorded the music of Harry Partch at the University of Illinois.

There was Braxton's Woodstock neighbor, Karl Berger; and Braxton's extensive connections with exponents of post-Cage white American experimentalism were reflected here in the work of trombonist Garrett List, pianist Frederic Rzewski, and synthesizer pioneer Richard Teitelbaum, all of whom had been part of the improvisation group Musica Elettronica Viva.

I stayed at Richard's apartment and discussed synthesizers with him, having never seen a modular Moog up close, and eventually, he and electronic composer David Behrman became important mentors, collaborators, and friends for me as I explored the complexity of New York art worlds. Also on hand were the members of the Braxton Quartet, whose records I had been practically devouring, including bassist Dave Holland, who had come to prominence working with Miles Davis during his electric period; drummer Barry Altschul; and trumpeter Kenny Wheeler, who, along with vibraphonist Gunter Hampel, was one of the first-generation of European free jazz/free improvisation musicians. Finally, the atmosphere at the session was greatly leavened by the ironic, dark humor of Jon Faddis, who contributed the amazing quasi-Corelli piccolo trumpet solo at the end of the march piece.

The tension in the session was heightened by the extraordinary difficulty of the written music. Particularly for some of the jazz-trained studio musicians, who were used to one-take sessions of the sort that had dominated jazz recording for decades, Braxton's ironic treatment of standard jazz big-band tropes, which drew upon post-1950s practices in new music, proved difficult to negotiate. The frequent presence of the homophonic passages that still dominated big-band writing in the early twenty-first century was scarcely reassuring amid the wide-intervals leaps, long lines of stuttering rhythms that seemed not to repeat for many pages, and the frequent irruptions of complex, tuplet-strewn counterpoint. In the midst of one particularly difficult session, one of the musicians declared a certain passage unplayable and left the studio. Braxton came to me in a panic, handed me the part and asked me to try to learn it in time for the next take. The musician returned to find a trombonist playing his part, and decided to try again, realizing that if one could negotiate the section with a trombone, an instrument noted for its relative intractability in fast-moving passages, maybe it wasn't that hard after all. The incident was part of the overall dynamic of the session in prompting substantial revision of the notion, active at the time in those New York circles that had adopted critic Stanley Dance's view of themselves as "mainstream," that "free jazz" musicians lacked musicianship.

The hybridity evident in the Braxton session called for a new kind of musician, one whose mobility of reference encompassed many histories and perspectives. Recent antecedents for this approach did not, for example, include Third Stream ideas, whose approach to performance was culturally collagist rather than interpenetrative. In contrast, William Grant Still's optimistic 1930s belief in the viability of a "Negro Symphony Orchestra," based on his own experience as both composer and performer in classical, jazz, and popular idioms, presaged by more than thirty years ethnomusicologist Mantle Hood's coining of the term "bimusicality" to describe musicians trained in two performance traditions. Still predicted that for the players in such an orchestra, "their training in the jazz world will even have enhanced their virtuosity, and they will be able to play perfectly passages that would be difficult for a man trained only in the usual academic way."[47] In fact, many musicians trained in jazz were already well known as early practitioners of the bimusical, and by the time of the 1975 session, the AACM musicians had been exploring a similar strain of multiple musicality for years, one that incorporated compositional as well as improvisative practices. Braxton's approach to composition, while perhaps anomalous to standard jazz practice of the period, was certainly no surprise to the AACM musicians, from whose milieu these approaches originally sprang. Their musical interests and backgrounds dovetailed neatly with those of the post-Cageians.

On a personal note, the period around 1975 was a breakout moment for me, as for the AACM more generally. In the spring of 1976, after I left the Count Basie band at the end of a two-month tour of the United States, Canada, and Japan, Braxton called again, and asked me to come to New York for rehearsals prior to his engagement at the Jazz Workshop in Boston. When I got to New York, I was warmly received in the loft of drummer Barry Altschul, who provided me with my first sustained understanding of what New York was about, including a trip to a famous deli on the corner of Canal and Broadway for a chocolate egg cream. Braxton had left about thirty or forty trumpet parts with Barry, numbered starting with "1"; despite Braxton's reputation for complex diagrammatics, there were no "mathematical" markings on any of the music I saw. I spent the next two days transposing the music for trombone. Since I knew all of the Braxton Arista recordings, when I got to number 8, I recognized it as the fearsomely fast theme that had been recorded as "Cut 1, Side 1" on *New York, Fall 1974*.[48] We negotiated that one successfully the second night, and I think that it was at that point that Braxton started to think that having trombone instead of trumpet in the quartet might be a viable option.

In 1976, Braxton asked me to join him in a Moers duo performance, my first trip to Europe. After we left the stage in Moers that afternoon in May 1976, nothing in this world was the same for me, as reviewers made comments (all hyperbole admitted) such as the following, by Braxton's long-time friend, *Jazz Hot* editor Laurent Goddet: "After George Lewis, one will not be able to play the trombone as before."[49] In any event, for me, my work together with Braxton achieved a rare commonality of intent, based on an empathy that the scholar in me is reluctantly obliged to call "transcendent." Goddet referred to "a diabolical understanding between the two men," a description that I find apt.[50]

Braxton's work was respected across a broad spectrum of experimental fields, but he remained something of a polarizing figure as far as the jazz world was concerned. For some, adjectives such as "mathematical" and "Varese-like" served to problematize his jazz bonafides, as critics suspended the more typically macho language related to swinging, punching, and driving in favor of musicologically influenced depictions of the music's structure and organization. For others, Braxton was simply "overrated and overpublicized."[51] His June 27 Newport Jazz Festival appearance, in which I participated along with Dave Holland and Barry Altschul, featured a fifty-page, nearly fully notated composition that the reviewer characterized as having a "dry, ascetic quality . . . punctuated by primordial bleeps and blats."[52]

Braxton's "under the rug" strategy reflected a reality with which he would soon become all too familiar. One of the last Arista projects, from 1978, was a massive, three-LP piece for 160 musicians grouped into four orchestras, with a 300-page score.[53] "We had to rush the recording because the record company, of course, thought it was going to be a 'jazz' record, and we kind of *snuck* it in."[54] His producers understood the strategy, Braxton observed, but he felt that upper management, including president Clive Davis, was skeptical. "For an African American, you know, a young man . . . I was thirty, thirty-one, with visions of a piece for four orchestras, a three-record set: how many projects like that do you see released? The record companies aren't going to do it." Braxton joked that "as the records came out, my name would go up in the polls, but when it became apparent what I was *really* about, I dropped from maybe third or fourth in *Downbeat* to 500th!"[55] In the end, only two-thirds of the four-orchestra work, performed by students at the Oberlin Conservatory of Music, actually made it onto vinyl. Braxton invested $25,000 of his own funds in the project, but despite a five-star review in *Down Beat* from Chicago-based critic and poet Art Lange,[56] the record was released for six months before being deleted from the Arista catalog.[57] "I wanted to use the platform while it was there," Braxton concluded. "I knew it wouldn't last."[58]

The experience seemed emblematic of the ambivalence some AACM members felt about their new situation, as well as about being based in

New York. Those New York–based members who did comment on their experiences in the city valued above all their access to colleagues of the highest quality, and proximity to business opportunities. In a French-language interview in 1977, Abrams said that "it's good for work. In the United States, New York is an important market; if you want to be known beyond your local area, sooner or later you have to have business in New York."[59] Kalaparusha was of the same opinion: "New York is a business center, the capital of the music business, that's all. That's why most musicians who want to live from their work are in New York."[60]

On the other hand, in an interview with Valerie Wilmer, Amina Claudine Myers noted that many of the promotional strategies and collegialities that had worked in the Chicago days of the AACM were far less effective in the very different and unfamiliar environment of New York: "In Chicago when I wanted to do a concert, I'd just set it up. I'd go out and put up my flyers. Now you can do this in New York but it's definitely not that easy. Chicago has a large black population but New York is altogether a different thing. The pressures are much different."[61] Some of these pressures, of course, were gender-related: "I was always encouraged, except for one time. That was in New York about two years ago when I ran across a male ego. . . . I ran across some real games that some of the men musicians played in New York."[62]

Furthermore, even as they acknowledged the central role that New York has traditionally played in musicians' aspirations, AACM members tended to challenge that role when it conflicted with their ideals of methodological mobility. As in Chicago, some AACM artists in New York saw the jazz community as it was then constructed as only a part of their overall reference base. Pursuing membership to varying degrees in a panoply of sociomusical and career networks, including those traditionally centering on high-culture "art music," AACM musicians in New York articulated a definitional shift away from rigidly defined and racialized notions of lineage and tradition, toward a more fluid, dialogic relationship with a variety of musical practices that problematized the putative "jazz" label as it was applied to them. For these musicians, pan-European contemporary music was not a distant, disembodied influence, nor was it something to be feared, avoided, or worshiped. Rather, musicians articulated participation across genres, as well as exchanges of musical methods. To advance notions of hybridity and mobility across and through media, traditions, and materials meant not only the freedom to draw from a potentially infinite number of musical sources, but also the freedom to explore a diverse array of infrastructures, social and professional lecturers, and modes of presentation.

In May 1977, the AACM, seeking to do in New York what some of its members had done in Paris—that is, bring to the fore AACM musicians who were not as well known—collaborated with Taylor Storer, then a student worker at Columbia University's radio station, WKCR, to produce an ambitious four-day concert series at Wollman Auditorium. WKCR was already one of New York's most adventurous radio stations, programming a wide variety of musics that rarely received a hearing on commercial outlets. As a preview of the festival, billed as "Chicago Comes to New York," the station broadcast ninety consecutive hours of music, interviews, and unpublished recordings of AACM members.[63] Thus, one sunny Chicago afternoon, a contingent of AACM members, associates, and family (including one-month-old Issa Colson, son of Adegoke and Iqua) loaded their instruments and suitcases onto a rented Greyhound-style bus bound for New York. On board were a large number of musicians who had seldom performed in New York up to that time, or who were just then trying to become established there.[64]

On the final evening of the "Chicago Comes to New York" event, the AACM Orchestra, conducted by Muhal Richard Abrams, gave a performance of a single untitled work lasting one and one-half hours. The piece, which featured all of the members who had been present, included an instrumental complement of eight reeds, two trumpets, two trombones, four percussionists, three pianists, and three singers.[65] This performance, as well as the festival as a whole, was the subject of a long, searching article in the *New Yorker*, written by veteran jazz writer Whitney Balliett, that presented a context and history of the AACM as he saw it. The article, which reports on each of the concerts in great detail, provides what is perhaps one of the most meticulous and richly contextualized accounts of AACM musical performances to appear in any American publication. Describing some of the music heard in the ninety-hour radio broadcast as "beautiful, infuriating, savage, surrealistic, boring, and often highly original," the writer described his conception of the AACM's composite vision: "The broadcast revealed a ferocious determination to bring into being a new and durable music—a hard-nosed utopian music, without racial stigmata, without clichés, and without commercialism."[66]

By the late 1970s, both the promotional and musical efforts of the first and second waves of AACM musicians had born fruit in Europe. In September 1979, *Down Beat's* first issue in its new monthly format featured an announcement affirming that AACM musicians had become a major part of the European festival circuit. "All of us are over here," observed Kalaparusha Maurice McIntyre with no small degree of exultation. Other AACM musicians traipsing around Austria, Belgium, France, West Germany, the Netherlands, Italy, Norway, and Switzerland, according to the article, were Muhal Richard Abrams, Thurman Barker, Chico Freeman, Lester Bowie, Wallace McMillan, Steve McCall, and me, as well as the creative orchestras of Roscoe Mitchell and Leo Smith.[67]

One of the most important festivals for new music was the Moers "New Jazz" Festival, founded in 1972 by Burkhard Hennen, a former sympathizer with radical post-May 1968 activist Rudi Dutschke. Moers, a friendly town of around a hundred thousand inhabitants at the time, nestled in the West German Ruhrgebiet, surprised itself in becoming the site of perhaps the leading festival for European free jazz. Born in Moers, Hennen began by starting a *Kneipe* called Die Röhre ("The Tube"), which served as the base for his first forays into music production. With West German government support, as well as the support of the town of Moers itself, Hennen built the festival into one of the largest in Europe, and Die Röhre functioned as an after-hours meeting place for an event that, for several days a year, transformed the plucky working-class German town into a kind of mini-Woodstock or Chateauvallon. The four-day outdoor event, which attracted up to five thousand listeners per day, rain or shine (and it rained often) became a focal point for breaking out new artists in the European theater of operations, and in 1974, Anthony Braxton's growing business relationship with Hennen encompassed not only festival appearances, but also releases of multidisc recordings of Braxton's music. Hennen organized extended tours of Europe for Braxton's quartet (which by 1976 included me), often driving the van himself over long distances across Germany's furious autobahn traffic, and as far north as Sweden.

The 1977 edition of the Moers festival was the first to feature heavy participation by AACM musicians, and its connections with other festivals, particularly the Groningen Jazzmarathon in the Netherlands, helped to attract press from across Europe and even in Japan; *Swing Journal*'s Teruto Soejima was a fixture at Moers for years. Arguably, the 1977 Moers festival raised the profile of the AACM, not least in Germany, where it had been more difficult for the AACM to find performances, but also across northern and southern Europe. At this time, a group of young intellectuals and music enthusiasts, including Nicola Tessitore, Roberto Terlizzi, Ugo Fadini, Massimo de Carlo, and Michele Mannucci, as well as promoters such as Isio Saba, were active in bringing AACM music to Italy. An important, if neglected, work from this period is Franco Bolelli's book *Musica creativa,* which drew heavily upon French poststructuralist and psychoanalytic thought, including the work of Jacques Lacan, Gilles Deleuze, and Félix Guattari, to illuminate improvised music in a way that did not recur until the mid-1990s turn to theory in jazz studies. Despite his lack of published work at the time, Anthony Braxton's ideas, transmitted via lengthy interviews in various European magazines during the early 1970s, were a major inspiration for Bolelli's theorizing. Bolelli himself centers the AACM in his analysis, and in a sense, the book served as a kind of dialogic response to Braxton's ideas in particular.[68]

Moreover, it was at these early European festivals that I became acquainted with the work of the first-generation European free improvisors. I still remember Evan Parker introducing himself and asking, seemingly almost apologetically, if I might like to play with him and Derek Bailey sometime. In 1980, the two of them brought me to London, where we formed a quartet with Dave Holland at a performance space in Charing Cross Hospital, in the Fulham area of west London, as part of that year's edition of Derek's influential "Company Week" series of free improvisation meetings. This was the start of a long-standing collaboration and friendship between us;[69] like many others, I was greatly inspired by Evan and Derek's organic intellectualism, which reminded me of what I had encountered with Leo Smith and Anthony Braxton.[70]

Becoming the cover boy for jazz publications across Europe was as heady an experience for me as it must have been for my older AACM colleagues, who were certainly feeling that, at least for the moment, the destiny of music seemed to be in their hands as much as anyone's. Alex Dutilh's comment on the 1977 edition of the Moers Festival was typical:

> They have arrived! If last year the Moers Festival showed European improvised musics, this year it was incontestably the theatre of a thoroughgoing onslaught from the new generation of Americans. Emerging for the most part from the A.A.C.M., all these musicians reside in New York. They proved superbly the point that the music that is being done there is, all at once, alive, accomplished and multifaceted.[71]

A 1978 *Jazz Hot* article featured a picture of me with a Moog synthesizer. The picture of me with technology is quite unusual, particularly in the world of jazz photography, despite my definitive subsequent engagement with the analog and digital worlds, and my projection of desire to work with computers is one that predates my having actually owned one. At the time, the enthusiasm and optimism that I and other AACM people felt about electronics seemed to overflow all talk of genres.

> Now there are [computers] of reasonable size that seem very fast. I am convinced that it is possible to create a program so that the computer can dialogue with one or more improvisors. . . . I don't think that it should be that difficult to think of controlling this new instrument. . . . In reality, we know that behind the computer is a person. . . . Why not be that person and make use of this instrument for musical ends?[72]

For my part, the integration of electronics into my work was already in progress, and I saw an opportunity to use whatever notoriety I had achieved as a springboard to support for further experimentation. Within the cadre of jazz, however, the use of electronics seemed quite often (Goddet excepted) to exceed the limits of what the otherwise relatively sonically open critical fraternity was willing to accept, at least from young African Americans who were supposed to be representing acoustic purity and the natural. Thus, an Italian critique of my Moers performance of 1977 with Douglas Ewart, in which my work *Homage to Charles Parker* used live electronic synthesis and timbral modification of percussion and trombone, seemed to reprise the early reception of Muhal Richard Abrams's 1967 *Levels and Degrees of Light:* "At Moers, however, his duo performance left me perplexed: in the concert Lewis used rather complex electronic instrumentation, consisting in particular of a foundation prerecorded on tape and some equipment that modified the natural timbre of the trombone."[73]

Nonetheless, our enthusiasm remained undimmed (perhaps because few among us, Famoudou Moye excepted, could read Italian), reaching a point that was unimaginable even to those AACM musicians who had been so well received in France in 1969, and culminating in a critical event that remains unprecedented. "The idea was in gestation for a long time," wrote Alex Dutilh, a member of *Jazz Hot*'s editorial board, in 1978. "It was on our return to this year's Moers Festival that it appeared to us to be needed. It was absolutely necessary to devote a special issue to the A.A.C.M." For Dutilh, this extraordinary double issue of *Jazz Hot,* which included long interviews with Leo Smith, Chico Freeman, the members of the Art Ensemble of Chicago, and Muhal Richard Abrams (featured on the cover) was entirely justified, on an international level:

The most advanced forms of improvised music are all, in one or more aspects, indebted to the A.A.C.M., just as with the maintenance of the Negro-American cultural tradition, to which the Chicago Association actively contributes. Moreover, if New York has once again, in the past two or three years, become the site of musical activity overflowing with creativity, a field of experiment undoubtedly as concentrated as during the bebop era, this is equally due in large measure to the invasion by A.A.C.M. musicians.[74]

The writer's account of the collective's origins, history, orientation, and goals involved not only the music itself, but also the AACM School, as having the important potential to "bring to young blacks a music which is theirs and which is not offered by the media or the official cultural institutions. This course of action is rich with potential, because it is addressed to young people deprived of references, for whom the concepts of "avant-garde" or "experimental" or "creative" music lose their meaning."[75]

Dutilh's cover article mentioned not only first-wavers such as the Art Ensemble of Chicago, Air, Leroy Jenkins, Leo Smith, Amina Claudine Myers, Anthony Braxton, Kalaparusha, and Thurman Barker, but also second-wave musicians and groups, including the Ethnic Heritage Ensemble, Douglas Ewart, Chico Freeman, and me. For Dutilh, the ideal of the AACM's "collective ardor" had managed to avoid many of the issues that plagued other large formulations of musicians, such as the earlier Jazz Composers Guild, which had been "corroded by people problems." Dutilh contrasted the collective quasi-leaderless spirit of the AACM with the Sun Ra Arkestra, an ensemble that operated "in an introverted and centralized way." As the writer saw it, "The AACM knew how to protect itself from these pitfalls. Systematically practicing cross-fertilization among all its members . . . posing, as a rule, mutual respect among musicians. In this way, all its members have, at one moment or another, selectively or regularly, played music(s) by the others."[76]

"In the final analysis," wrote Dutilh, "the only constant of the A.A.C.M. is its categorical refusal of constancy. . . . The influences, the instruments, the orchestral conceptions, the harmonic, rhythmic, or compositional approaches, the connections with other arts, with other musics, with other musicians, with those who belong to the association . . . all those (and other elements) try to be resolutely plural."[77]

Abrams's November 1977 solo performance in Bologna was lionized in a 1978 interview with the writer Valerio Tura, who wrote in the Italian monthly *Musica Jazz* that "the concert that was given (if I do say so) on that occasion was surely one of the most extraordinary musical events we have attended in Italy over the last few years."[78] In the interview, Abrams declined to take credit for the by now worldwide reputation of the collective.

> I didn't invent anything. The AACM couldn't have been born without everybody's collaboration and also sacrifices, and certainly not without great will and determination. But look, if the things that we have created are moving forward, then you want to say that they were right, good; there are lots of young musicians of great value whose names you don't know here in Europe, who have grown up with us since they were children—you can tell it yourself—and now they are among the best musicians from every point of view.[79]

Back in New York, the most radical experimental work was taking place in small performance lofts and other alternative spaces. The loft network developed as part of the general move among experimental musicians to develop performance environments that eschewed the codes and genre-policing of conventional jazz and classical performance. Thus, Ornette Coleman's Artist's House was started for many of the same reasons as the Kitchen—namely (recalling the AACM press release of 1965), "to provide an atmosphere that is conducive to serious music." These newer art worlds needed alternative spaces in order to get their experimental work before the public, expanding the set of positions available for the music.

The venues and social networks to which these new spaces constituted "alternatives," however, were vastly different according to genre, and most frequently, race as well. Until the mid-1960s, "serious," that is, pan-European new music, including the early work of John Cage and the New York School, was conceived largely for traditional concert halls, a legacy bequeathed by previous generations within this overall art world. Countering the dominant upper-class ideology which maintained that such halls were the venue of choice for "serious" music—and, incidentally, only for that music and no other—younger artists of the 1960s began experimenting with gallery spaces, specially designed site-specific spaces, outdoor spaces, and the like.[80]

For jazz-identified black musicians, on the other hand, the club, rather than the concert hall, had been heavily ideologized as the ideal, even the genetically best suited space for their music. Naturalizing propaganda in favor of clubs continues to be strenuously asserted, both in journalistic commentary and in latter-day academic scholarship. Historian Scott DeVeaux's remarks seem to reinscribe the standard trope: "That bebop would quickly find its way into the concert hall seems, in retrospect, inevitable. . . . Still, for all its complexity, bebop never entirely became a music of the concert hall. The natural milieu for the bop combo was—and to a large extent remains—the more informal surroundings of the nightclub, where spontaneity could be given free rein and its subtlety observed at close range."[81]

It was considered axiomatic that later generations of musicians would fold themselves neatly into that model. Early on, however, a newer generation of black experimentalists realized that serious engagement with theater and performance, painting, poetry, electronics, and other interdisciplinary expressions that require extensive infrastructure, would be generally rendered ineffective or even impossible by the jazz club model. In this light, the supposed advantages of performing in clubs began to appear as a kind of unwanted surveillance of the black creative body.

The newcomers from the Midwest and the West were now being represented in the New York, European, and Asian press as part of an emerging movement which came to be called "loft jazz," a term that appeared to be recycled from a 1960s instantiation.[82] By 1976 the loft was being touted in the New York alternative press as the new jazz club, inheriting from its predecessor the minimal infrastructure and the related discourse of "intimacy." Indeed, some of the early lofts sought to emulate traditional jazz club environments, with tables, drink minimums, and smoking, but many others provided versions of a concert environment, with concert seating and, at times, light refreshments.[83] Musician-organized or directed lofts included the La Mama Children's Workshop Theatre, where La Mama Theatre Workshop founder Ellen Stewart worked with BAG drummer Charles Bobo Shaw; the Brook, run by saxophonist Charles Tyler; pianist John Fischer's "Environ"; drummer Rashied Ali's Studio 77 ("Ali's Alley"); and perhaps the most adventurous and long-lived of the improvisors' lofts, Sam and Bea Rivers's Studio Rivbea, which had been founded in the early 1970s. Loft proprietors would often band together to present "alternative" festivals that featured musical approaches that were either poorly represented or completely excluded by the ordinarily "mainstream" jazz policy of the Newport Jazz Festival.[84]

The collection *Wildflowers: The New York Loft Jazz Sessions*, recorded at Studio Rivbea's 1976 Spring Music Festival and originally released in 1977, constitutes a handy summary of some of the ideas and practices about im-

provisation that were being explored during this period by the loosely associated group of musicians dubbed "the loft generation"—a term whose
ephemerality the musicians are no doubt quite grateful for today. On these
recordings, the newcomers from the Midwest and the West were heavily
represented. Among the AACM musicians presented were Roscoe Mitchell,
Anthony Braxton, Kalaparusha Maurice McIntyre, Don Moye, Leo Smith,
and myself as trombonist, as well as the collective Air, with Henry Threadgill, Fred Hopkins, and Steve McCall. From the BAG diaspora came Charles
Bobo Shaw, Oliver Lake, Julius Hemphill, Hamiet Bluiett, and cellist Abdul
Wadud.[85] In his regular monthly column in the now-defunct men's magazine *Players* (a kind of African American *Playboy*), Stanley Crouch, who performed on drums in several of the performances on *Wildflowers,* reviewed
the live performances that the recordings later documented. Crouch hailed
the new music on these recordings as "significant for its variety, its crafts-
manship, and finally, its often breathtaking beauty and clarity of its artistry."
For Crouch, Hemphill was "masterful," while Mitchell's performance was
"almost as exciting and great as anything I've heard from Coltrane, Rollins
and Ornette Coleman."[86]

Even the major U.S. media of the period picked up on the phenomenon.
Riffing on one of U.S. public culture's periodic tropes heralding one or another "revival" of jazz, a *Newsweek* cover story in August 1977 declared that
"All of a sudden, le jazz is hot."[87] According to the article, most of the heat
was being generated by the music's encounter with rock, as represented
by Herbie Hancock and the originary jazz-fusion band Weather Report.
Also featured in the article as key players in the "avant-garde" section of the
revival were Sam Rivers and the AACM, including Muhal Richard Abrams
and Anthony Braxton, both of whom were being recorded on major-label
Arista Records at the time.

It can fairly be said that the loft period provided entry-level support for
an emerging multiracial network of musicians. Key players in this network
included not only the Californians, BAG, and the AACM, but also many
others, both black and white.[88] Many of these musicians deeply resented
the reduction of the diversity of their approaches to the term "loft jazz."
Chico Freeman's reaction was typical: "Then, and I don't know where it
came from, somebody came up with this term, 'loft jazz.' Not just me, but
every musician who was involved in it vehemently opposed that."[89] Not
only was there little or no agreement as to what methods or sounds were
being described by the term, but as bassist Fred Hopkins related in a 1984
interview, "The funniest thing was, the musicians never considered it a

movement."[90] Musicians pointed out that this label, by framing their music as requiring minimal infrastructural investment, was used to disconnect them from more lucrative economic possibilities. A 1977 *Voice* article reported the concerns of musicians that "constant press association with lofts has undermined their commercial viability with European promoters, since lofts have come to be synonymous with percentage-of-the door payments."[91]

"When they started calling it loft jazz, I stopped going into places," observed Abrams. *"Swing Journal* [Japanese-language periodical] had pictures of a lot of us and the caption 'Loft Jazz.' We got enough names, and if they accept that, I'm not playing in these lofts any more. If I call you Jack S., I got you. When I want to eliminate Jack S., well, I created it, didn't I? I can eliminate it, and you along with it." Nonetheless, critics defended the label, and felt confident in assigning musicians to this amorphous category, while at the same time admitting its descriptive inadequacies. For instance, in countering what he viewed as "misconceptions," Giddins asserted the tautology that "there is neither a loft nor an AACM style of jazz. Loft jazz is any jazz played in a loft."[92] With this, the taxonomic policing mechanism that at once connected the signifiers "AACM," "loft," and "jazz" created a tightly bound, multiply mediated corset that the AACM's mobility and border-crossing strategies were already shredding.

At any rate, by the early 1980s the loft jazz phenomenon was all but dead in New York, the victim of competition for the attention of the new musicians from better-funded, higher-infrastructure New York spaces, such as Broadway producer Joseph Papp's Public Theater; midtown spaces such as Carnegie Recital Hall; and downtown lofts such as the Kitchen, all of which had engagement policies that mirrored to some extent those of the lofts.[93] Even rock spaces such as CBGB briefly featured loft-jazz veterans alongside the "art-rock" of groups like the Theoretical Girls. Also important were issues of individual support; it is not difficult to imagine that it could have proved daunting for individual musicians such as Sam Rivers to compose and perform new work while directing an ongoing concert series. Moreover, the more established artists could obtain work at traditional club spaces, such as Sweet Basil and the Village Gate, to say nothing of the expanded opportunities then becoming available in Europe. "We started to hook up overseas," Abrams recalled. "First I went over there with Braxton. Braxton took me to Verona with him. That was my first time in Italy."

Finally, issues of aesthetic and methodological burnout began to arise. In Chico Freeman's view, "After a while, the music got—I don't want to say stale, but it stopped changing. It was out, but the experimentation had gotten old in the methods. Those things were new, they hadn't been done in those ways, but after a while we had done them in so many ways that the music stopped growing. . . . The enthusiasm seemed to wane, as we were getting more individual-minded."

"We got older, and our priorities changed," Freeman concluded.

Beyond a Binary: The AACM and the Crisis in Criticism

As early as 1975, it was becoming increasingly unclear as to exactly whose purview it would be to chronicle and critique the new hybrid music. *Voice* writer Gary Giddins mused openly on how the blurring of boundaries that was taking place across ethnic and genre divides was affecting critical commentary. He began with an admission: "I know something of John Cage's theories, but virtually nothing of his music as a living thing. This is pretty strange when you consider how many of the people I write about acknowledge Cage as an influence." Giddins went on to acknowledge the asymmetrical power dynamic symbolized by the separation of genres in his own newspaper, with its twin headings of "Music," that is, reviews of work from the high culture West, and "Riffs," the low-culture, diminutively imaged Rest.

Noticing that "much avant-garde music, whether jazz or classicist, is moving in similar directions," the article suggested that Tom Johnson, then the *Voice*'s "downtown" critic, might move outside his normative "Music" purview to investigate Anthony Braxton, while he, as a "Riffs" columnist, would discover Philip Glass. Giddins even invoked a version of the one-drop rule (that holdover from America's high eugenics era that decreed that a single blood drop of "Negro ancestry" was enough to render anyone a Negro) to speculate (perhaps with a naïve humor) about what would happen if Glass and Braxton made a recording together: "Since black blood is more powerful than white, as any mulatto will attest, Braxton would presumably render Glass non-Music and both would be filed as a Riff."[94]

Eventually, Giddins and Johnson, among many others, would be obliged to journalistically encounter music that incorporated references outside their usually defined spheres of study. In particular, it was becoming obvious that AACM events were presented in a great diversity of spaces— jazz and new music lofts, clubs, concert halls, and parks. Inevitably, just as the black community of Chicago broke out of the South Side Bantustan to which restrictive covenants and discriminatory law had confined its members, the AACM was destined to run roughshod over many conventional assumptions about infrastructure, reference, and place.

At first, these determined efforts to produce new music that blurred boundaries and exhibited multiplicity of reference were lauded, particularly in the jazz press, as the number of AACM and BAG musicians listed in the *Down Beat* polls continued to rise. Often listed in multiple categories, new names such as those of the trio Air, Fred Hopkins, Henry Threadgill, Julius Hemphill, Leo Smith, Oliver Lake, Hamiet Bluiett, Don Moye, Joseph Bowie, and my own, all appeared. In 1978, Air's recording, *Air Time,* was produced by Chuck Nessa, and in 1980, the group's *Air Lore,* devoted to reimaginings of Scott Joplin and Jelly Roll Morton, was selected as the *Down Beat* critics' Record of the Year.[95] In 1977, Braxton's *Creative Orchestra Music 1976* was the Critics' Poll Record of the Year, and over the next few years, Amina Claudine Myers, Steve McCall, Abdul Wadud, Douglas Ewart, and Chico Freeman found places in the poll listings. Chico Freeman's first recording of his own compositions appeared in 1978, and Fred Anderson, still based in Chicago, nonetheless received a good deal of notice, with a 1978 recording of his own quintet, with Bill Brimfield on trumpet and Hamid Drake on drums, live at a major German festival, as well as a major *Down Beat* article.[96]

Thus, it would appear that at least at first, the business gamble of so many midwestern musicians had paid off. In time, however, some aspects of the evolution of their music met with considerable resistance from a variety of entrenched sectors of New York's jazz and new music communities. Bogged down in binary systems—black/white, jazz/classical, high culture/low culture—critical reception in particular eventually became quite often frankly dismissive of the extensive engagement with extended notated form, electronics and computers, graphic scores and traditionally notated works (with or without improvisation) realized by AACM musicians and others. Moreover, some musicians may have been chagrined by what they felt was excessive attention paid to the new midwesterners at the expense of more established musicians based in New York. As early as 1971, Lester Bowie noticed that "some of them dig us but some of 'em don't. . . . But most that we've met, the personal relationship has been good. Some of them view us as a threat, but really they shouldn't because we're not a threat to their existence. Our music is an expansion; it's meant to really lift everyone."[97]

In an interview published in the jazz magazine *Cadence* in 1990, bassist William Parker, born in 1952 in the Bronx, remembered the situation this way:

In the early '70s what had happened to a lot of New York musicians was, Sam Rivers did this series with Douglas Records called "Wildflowers." That sort of began to mark the turning point where you had all the musicians who were in New York working, who were sort of put for some reason in the background and the musicians from Chicago and St. Louis were pushed up and took advantage of whatever advantages there were.[98]

Parker connected this changed dynamic with the breakdown of the traditional systems of inheritance—largely patrilineal to be sure—that had heretofore been in force on the New York jazz scene. Asked whether the strategies were economic or musical, Parker replied,

> Well, it could have been they came at the right time when people started to write about the music or people began to want to record the music. And they had more energy to put into business because they came to New York and they looked at it differently than the musicians perhaps who were here, living here all the time and were thinking, if you played with Miles Davis in the '50s, the piano player could get a record date, the bass player could get a record date, the drummer could get a record date, and the tenor could get a record date, and eventually you could step out from Miles and begin to . . . it was sort of a step system. And that sort of happened, you could play at Studio Rivbea and then move to the Tin Palace and then move to the Public Theatre and get a gig and get a record date, but after a few years that stopped. There was no Public Theatre and after the Public Theatre there was no record date, and if you played with well known artists there was no guarantee, unless it was Miles Davis or that crowd, that you were going to step up. It's like being with a company, you've done 10 years or 15 years service then you would be promoted, like 'now we're going to expose him to the public.' And that stopped happening.[99]

The quote appears to support a contention that a breakdown in the traditional structure of generational authority was in process even before the advent of the midwesterners. The writer Jimmy Stewart, speaking of the 1960s in 1971, identified a similar breakdown in an article "Black Aesthetics in Music": "The music of the sixties represents a cleavage with the past in this essential and fundamental sense, in that Ornette and those who are considered as forerunners of the new Black music did not 'earn' their leadership status in any of the ways by which leadership was 'earned' in our music previously, from New Orleans to the present."[100] To be sure, the roots of this authority complex run very deep. The late Betty Carter complained about the "loft generation" in a 1979 *Down Beat* article: "You're gonna sit in a loft and say, 'I'm a genius?' You don't say that. *We* tell you that—after you have done your groundwork and your on the job training on stage. In front of us you make mistakes; you do your thing and you grow."[101] Amina Claudine Myers's early experiences in New York provide additional corroboration of this dynamic:

> Milt Jackson was there one time. I said, "Hello, Mr. Jackson. My name is Amina Claudine Myers and I used to play with Gene Ammons and Sonny Stitt." I went on for about five minutes. "I would love to play with you." He said, "Excuse me?" I knew he was playing that old-school game— "How dare you come up and approach me." Betty Carter used to do that stuff too. They weren't friendly and outgoing, but I was always the type to walk up and introduce myself and talk to musicians. Here's a young woman on the scene, somebody new, but I think they want you to pay dues and go through changes. Somebody's been out there a long time, they're established and known, and here you are, naïve, "Hi." They want to make you struggle and scuffle and not be feeling so secure. You just can't walk up and be "in." I saw Milt Jackson sometime after that and he was a wonderful, friendly man.

On the other hand, as Stewart notes, "what can be stated as 'revolutionary' involves more than technical innovation. It involves the temerity of these men to suggest that all the assumptions, or at least some of the basic and most fundamental ones, which I've recounted above, had to be discarded."[102] In this sense, the new music scene that was creating so much controversy in the New York of Parker's teenage years, the one in which he was destined to become a major figure in the 1980s and 1990s, actually fostered the very same breakdown of traditional generational change that prompted his criticism.

Finally, the question of economic competition was undoubtedly a factor. Ethnomusicologist David Such, writing on the work of Parker and others in the early 1990s, provided a glimpse of the extremely precarious economic situation that musicians faced during the loft jazz era and after.[103] The *Cadence* colloquy between Parker and his interviewer explored this issue at some length:

CAD.: It seems from my vantage point, the music, particularly in New
York, seems to be sometimes somewhat dependent or carried by
cliques. You suggested that there [were] times you wished you were
from Chicago and had AACM affiliations, you would have found it
easier to get work.

W.P.: Well, I don't know. I was always loyal to who I was associated with.
It was just an observation that it was a time where being a member of
the AACM could be profitable, it was very profitable.

CAD.: . . . Is there a period even in so-called Creative Improvised Music
where non-aesthetic things may have an effect on what one hears[?]

W.P.: Yeah. I don't think it had so much to do with the music, it probably
had very little to do with the actual sounds, because it's hard to put actual values on what one person makes and another person makes. It's
sort of what promoters and people who . . . this is referring to Europe
now, because in America I don't think there are that many promoters
and it doesn't make that much of a difference because I still think the
AACM and *all* musicians living in America, they still probably make
75% of their money in Europe, whether recording for a European
company or touring. [104]

Certainly, the high profile at *Down Beat* of two generations of Chicago-
based critics who had close associations with the AACM, including John
Litweiler, Neil Tesser, Howard Mandel, and Larry Kart, among others,
contributed to this perception. At the same time, Anthony Braxton could
observe in 1976 that "it wasn't like God just smiled on me or something. I
went over to Europe with $50 in my pocket. Some nice things happened,
but a lot of hard times happened, too."[105]

"When I first came to New York," Chico Freeman noted, "I noticed that
Air had come with the same AACM attitude of independence. By that, I
mean, Henry was trying to do his own concerts. He wasn't waiting for anybody to call him and hire him for a gig." Muhal Richard Abrams observed
that "the gigging around here was mostly the things we [the AACM] were
doing, not any particularly mainstream stuff like in the early days in Chicago." In our interview from 1999, Wadada Leo Smith presented a related
viewpoint. "We weren't sanctioned by New York when we first got there,"
he recalled. "They have their own cliques and beliefs too. Almost anyplace
that we've gone, there is some tension from the fact that we didn't all live
in New York City and come through Ornette Coleman and Sun Ra and

those people." In our interview from 1998, Lester Bowie agreed. "There was probably some resentment, because cats were playing different shit, and getting a lot of play," Bowie recalled. "They had raised a bunch of cats in New York, had them thinking that they should be jealous, when they should be praising the music, rather than trying to shun it, pretend that it didn't exist. They should have said, yeah, let me try that shit. But they didn't do that."

The cultural and methodological issues that informed the work of AACM composers were often obscured by discussions of whether or not their music was truly "jazz." A *Voice* review of a 1978 Leroy Jenkins concert at Carnegie Recital Hall became the occasion for critic Giddins to confront some of the same questions that had dogged Ellington forty years earlier: "How does this music relate to the jazz tradition? At what point can jazz be wrenched from its idiomatic integrity?"[106] A related trope informing critical reception on the jazz side articulated concerns about the "authenticity" of hybrid musics—particularly those that incorporate sources from jazz's great competitor, pan-European classical music. In this regard, the opinions that saw the light of day in the New York press of the period exhibited remarkable, even uncanny unanimity. Reviewing a Muhal Richard Abrams recording, Giddins expresses "some sympathy for the complaint that extra-jazz influences water down the idiom." In 1979, Rafi Zabor wrote that "one of the hazards this music may be facing now is the ingestion of a fatal dose of root-devouring Western intellectual hunger."[107]

As Leroy Jenkins put it in a 1997 interview, however, these "labels" (in musician parlance) were flexible and not necessarily related to actual musical directions or content, but rather to the potential for obtaining work and commissions. "Since I didn't seem to be welcome with so-called Jazz," Jenkins reasoned, "I thought I would deal with 'new music.' . . . I don't mind the labels; they can put the labels one right after the other; if it will get me work. But then, on the other hand, if it's going to keep me from getting work, I don't want to be put in that position."[108] In fact, the discomfort among this generation of jazz critics with the notion that any kind of breakdown between high and low culture might be asserted by these musicians seemed almost palpable. Among Muhal Richard Abrams's recordings for Arista, the 1978 *Lifea Blinec* (pronounced "Lifeline A-B-C") elicited particular opprobrium from *Down Beat* reviewer Chip Stern. The controversy continued into 1979 when a reader's letter pointedly called the reviewer to account for the negative review. The critic held and even intensified his ground, referring to "listeners who would rationalize guano droppings into high art if it came from an avant garde hero."[109] Peter Occhiogrosso, reviewing a Roscoe Mitchell concert in 1978, declared that Mitchell's work was "uninspired, boring music, music that belongs in the conservatory, music that will hopefully soon go the way of third stream, electronic music and conceptual art . . . [it] should be left to academics and people like Philip Glass."[110]

Jacques Attali has maintained that the emergence of "free jazz" represented "a profound attempt to win creative autonomy."[111] Certainly, Ornette Coleman was acknowledged by a number of early AACM members as one of the critical forerunners in asserting this autonomy, for challenging the policing of the creative black body, and for asserting freedom of reference. In Abrams's view, "Ornette is the only one that really had been an inspiration for the whole field. . . . Ornette was the first to take the risk."[112] Coleman, then as now, sought to involve himself not so much in "extending the boundaries of jazz," but in erasing the barriers placed around African American creativity generally, and around his work in particular. Coleman saw himself very early on as in international dialogue with musicians from every field; his string trios and quartets, as well as his 1972 orchestral work, *Skies of America,* served to challenge notions of black nonentitlement to the infrastructural means of experimental music production, and to the impulse of experimentalism itself.

At first, Coleman's compositions became associated with the Third Stream practices of composer and conductor Gunther Schuller; some AACM practices would later be described as congruent with this tradition. Schuller's 1961 explication of the concept implicitly recognized that the decades-long contention between pan-European classical music and African American jazz was coming to a head. For much of the twentieth century, the boundary between high and low culture in the United States had been symbolized musically by the great competition between the jazz and classical traditions, a discursive stand-in for a more fundamental cultural struggle. Proposing a performative amalgamation of these traditions in the late 1950s, Schuller wrote that

> by designating this music as a separate, third stream, the two other main-streams could go their way unaffected by attempts at fusion. I had hoped that in this way the old prejudices, old worries about the purity of the two main streams that have greeted attempts to bring jazz and "classical" music together could, for once, be avoided. This, however, has not been the case.[113]

In retrospect, perhaps Schuller's pluralist hope was bound to founder on the shoals of existing discourses of the era that foregrounded competing cultural nationalisms. Moreover, while Third Stream infrastructure may well have been attractive in the undercapitalized field of jazz, its ideology was seen by some as reifying racialized notions of classical and jazz methodology in a way that, as John Coltrane observed, was "an attempt to create something, I think, more with labels, you see, than true evolution."[114] In this kind of pluralism, as art critic Hal Foster has pointed out, "minor deviation is allowed to resist radical change."[115]

Thus, by 1974, John Rockwell could quote conductor Dennis Russell Davies to the effect that the new jazz-classical mixes were not like "the old so-called 'Third Stream.'" For Carla Bley, quoted in the same article, Third Stream practice meant that "the old forms of jazz were put together with the old forms of the other."[116] As Bley clearly implies, by this time Third Stream concepts of musical form had already been overtaken by more radical experiments in indeterminacy, improvisation, and other forms of real-time music making, as in the work of Coleman, Coltrane, Ayler, and Taylor, as well as Christian Wolff, Earle Brown, Morton Feldman, John Cage, and Pauline Oliveros. For many black artists, as "a metaphor for jazz reaching outside itself and incorporating other elements, to broaden and diversify" (as a *New York Times* critic put it in a 2001 retrospective article),[117] Third Stream could be viewed as a form of liberal racial uplift. To white artists and audiences, Third Stream could propose a sublimated image of "miscegenation" with jazz as a source of renewal of the European tradition, proposing a way out of the dilemma of the alienated listener, for which European high modernist composition was being blamed.[118]

Post-1960s African American artists like Coltrane, however, were understandably reluctant to commit to a musical movement in which their culture was considered a junior partner. Most crucially, the Third Stream movement failed to realize or support the complexity of black musical culture's independent development of a black experimentalism that, while in dialogue with white high culture, was, like the New Negroes of the Harlem Renaissance, strongly insistent upon the inclusion of the black vernacular, including the imperative of improvisation. Moreover, unlike the Third Stream movement, this independent black experimentalism challenged the centrality of pan-Europeanism to the notion of the experimental itself, instead advancing the notion that experimentalism was becoming "creolized."

In this light, the unitary focus in standard histories on the role of improvisor, a trope that has become standard in the historiography and criticism of black American music, cannot account for the diversity of black musical subjectivity exemplified by the AACM. As we can see from the following meeting excerpt, the dominant focus of the AACM as strongly *composer*-centered was fostered right from the start. To emphasize this, it is worth reprising my chapter 4 discussion of the May 15, 1965, AACM organizational meeting, at which Abrams exhorted the assembled musicians to take up composition. "You may not be Duke Ellington, but you got some kind of ideas, and now is the time to put 'em in," he insisted. "Wake yourself up. This is an awakening we're trying to bring about."[119] One can certainly identify a connection between this (and later dialogues) and the extensive engagement with notation in the later works of a number of AACM composers. Moreover, in the context of the 1960s, Abrams's reference to bringing about "an awakening" through composition recognizes that this simple assertion by Afro-Americans—defining oneself as a composer—constitutes a challenge to the social and historical order of things.

The reference to Ellington is understandable on a number of levels, given the fact that throughout his career, Ellington's image of himself as a composer working with and through African American forms was constantly challenged, stigmatized, and stereotyped.[120] Moreover, even African American composers who had grown up with "classical" training were similarly burdened with ethnic stereotyping and channeling.[121] Thus, Ellington could be viewed as a symbol not only of excellence and innovation, but also optimistic perseverance. Moreover, as some AACM composers explored the more restricted, Dahlhausian notion of composition as a dialectic with notation,[122] modernist black classical composers, such as Ulysses Kay, Olly Wilson, Talib Rasul Hakim, and Hale Smith, provided models for emulation and vindication.

Like the modernist black composers, AACM composers often sought to place their work in dialogue with diasporic traditions and histories from both Africa and Europe. At the same time, the ongoing binary opposition between composition and improvisation, present as an important trope in both modernist and postmodernist pan-European practice, lacked any real force among AACM composers, who were often drawn to collage and interpenetration strategies that blended, opposed, or ironically juxtaposed the two disciplines. Thus, as with Ellington, as well as later white American experimentalism, the definition of "composition" could be a fluid one, appropriating and simultaneously challenging and revising various pan-European models, dialoguing with African, Asian, and Pacific music traditions, and employing compositional methods that did not necessarily privilege either conventionally notated scores, or the single, heroic creator figure so beloved by jazz historiography.

During this period, the work of a number of AACM composers, both in their compositions and in improvisative performances, placed great emphasis on multiplicities of timbre, exemplifying what AACM members have termed "multi-instrumentalism." The extension into multi-instrumentalism saw a number of AACM improvisors, including Leo Smith, Henry Threadgill, Douglas Ewart, Anthony Braxton, Roscoe Mitchell, and Joseph Jarman, develop multiple voices on a wide variety of instruments. This multiplicity of voices, embedded within an already highly collective ensemble orientation, permitted the timbral diversity of the whole group to exceed the sum of its instrumental parts. Art Ensemble percussionist Famoudou Don Moye would bring literally hundreds of drums and percussion instruments to the stage; Jarman and Mitchell would be responsible not only for the entire saxophone, flute, and clarinet families, but for percussion as well.

Multi-instrumentalism as a practice strongly asserts that as each musician moves toward proficiency on a variety of instruments, the group as a whole is afforded a wider palette of potential orchestrations to explore. Such multi-instrumental improvisors as Eric Dolphy (flute, alto saxophone, and bass clarinet) and Ornette Coleman (alto saxophone, trumpet, and violin) undoubtedly provided crucial impetus for the AACM's radical extension of the practice; less often cited, but hardly less influential in terms of the concept, are Ellington's early ensembles, as well as the early New Orleans musicians, who were often fluent on a variety of unusual instruments, as with Sidney Bechet's 1924 sarrusophone solo on "Mandy, Make Up Your Mind" with Clarence Williams's Blue Five.[123]

As a practice, multi-instrumentalism can easily be read as confounding the commodificatory constructions of instrumental taxonomies that persist in jazz journalism as remnants of the "star system" so often decried by AACM artists. These heroic categories, recast as "lineages," are at variance with the fact that improvisors do not limit themselves to the study of the heritage of their own instrument. Rather, the central mantra/maxim, usually handed down as a word to the wise from experienced musicians to newcomers, is that one should "listen to everyone." Gradually, this imperative migrates toward a practice of "listening to everything," as expressed through both the "little instruments" that have been so strongly identified with AACM practice, and the use of electronics, an important feature of the recordings of Muhal Richard Abrams, as well as my own work. In the end, the goal and outcome is the attainment of mobility as a spiritual resource. As Joseph Jarman wonders aloud in a poem:

> I seek new sounds
> because new sounds
> seek me
> Why, please tell me
> must I limit myself
> to a saxophone or clarinet!
> All the rhythm of All
> the universe is flowing
> through me—through all
> things, why must I become
> "a master"—of anything
> when all sound all movement
> springs from the same
> breath.[124]

In this way, the focus of expressive articulation shifts from the commodificatory construction of the heroic individual instrumentalist to primordial forms of sound, rhythm and movement, which are given life through "breath." At the same time, although Jarman's phrases assert resistance to the language of mastery, control, and commodification, in my own experience, the use of little instruments was not necessarily intended as an escape from the challenge of virtuosity. As the great Javanese court musician Hardja Susilo has maintained: "Indeed, to learn to strike a gong only takes about one minute! To learn to play a gong, however, is quite another matter."[125] This view appears in sharp contradistinction to notions of improvisation emanating from those Cage-influenced quarters that seek spontaneity and novelty through the abnegation of the will, as exemplified by the composer's own view from the 1980s:

> It is at the point of spontaneity that the performer is most apt to have
> recourse to his memory. He is not apt to make a discovery spontaneously.
> I want to find ways of discovering something you don't know at the time
> that you improvise—that is to say, the same time you're doing something
> that's not written down, or decided upon ahead of time. The first way
> is to play an instrument over which you have no control, or less control
> than usual.[126]

In contrast, AACM improvisors viewed even an instrument as "little" as a triangle, or as large and seemingly unlikely as the set of tuned "garbage cans" that Anthony Braxton shipped to Europe in the 1970s,[127] as embodying potential for sonic invention that could be fully realized through the familiarization process known as "practicing." On this view, which sees pure spontaneity as a chimerical ideal of autonomy that has little to do with the historical, social, and cultural situatedness of actual improvisation, sustained and rigorous study is generally seen as the most likely way to "discover something you don't know." To use the everyday phrase, "chance favors the prepared mind."

The more elaborate fruits of these preparations began to appear in the late 1970s. Roscoe Mitchell's 1978 recording of *The Maze* featured a meditative composition for eight percussionists—or rather, eight musicians who had developed unique, personal setups of found objects and homemade instruments. Mitchell created the work expressly for these musicians, and the work itself introduced the AACM-based practice of working with "little instruments" to contemporary percussion practice. Muhal Richard Abrams's 1978 *1-QOA+19* juxtaposed complex written passages with propulsive rhythms, while his *Lifea Blinec,* recorded in the same year, presented multi-instrumentalism, text-sound, and electronic textures. Anthony Braxton's *Composition 76* for multi-instrumentalists was released on Arista in 1978 as the album *For Trio.* The album presented two performances of the work, one with Roscoe Mitchell and Joseph Jarman, and the other with Douglas Ewart and Henry Threadgill.[128] In 1979, Leo Smith recorded a long-form notated work for trumpet and three harps, *The Burning of Stones;* Chico Freeman was working with contemporary jazz quartet forms, and in 1979's *Air Lore,* the trio Air was recasting older, pre–New Orleans African American forms; and my own work from the period, including the 1977 *Chicago Slow Dance* and the 1979 *Homage to Charles Parker,* combined minimalism, open improvisation, and both tape and live electronics.[129]

Muhal Richard Abrams noted that the exploration of extended forms was a long-standing direction among AACM composers. "In Chicago," he observed, "we were already looking at these things, and equipped to deal with them when we came here [to New York]."

> In this city you come in contact with classical musicians. You might be invited to write a string quartet. [The previous generation of musicians] were not dealing in those kinds of forms. They've never displayed the extent of orchestrational and compositional abilities such as the AACM.

When we came along, there was a whole sea change, a glitch, something that wasn't there before. The compositions themselves showed that they were outside of the mainstream of jazz, and notice was taken by classical people. You can get access to these ensembles, and it started to happen.

"We wrote those pieces without having any talk of a performance," Wadada Leo Smith told me in our 1999 interview. "Of our people, Braxton was the first to have success in that area. That came when you started playing with Braxton. One of the first ones was the duo solos with the chamber orchestra."[130] Despite the favorable assessments of his peers, however, Braxton continued to have trouble having his notated music taken seriously. At the 1976 Berlin Jazz Days, the work Smith referred to, a double concerto with Braxton and me as soloists, was termed "as problem-ridden as all fusion attempts between jazz and modern classical music have been in the past." However, given the reviewer's understanding that "Lewis created the impression that not one, but about a dozen different trombonists were at work," it was difficult to see just what the issue was with the work.[131] As Henry Threadgill saw it,

> At first we had these people who were writing and playing music that was still under the umbrella of jazz. They were called outbound jazz, free jazz or whatever. As the years passed, these guys branched out and started getting commissions, writing for dance companies and theater companies, chamber groups, orchestras. These people kept going beyond where they were initially, but they're still under that umbrella of the playing part and a certain music that's got this historical base of collective improvisation and jazz. But they completely branched all the way out into something that's got nothing to do with that. They've completely crossed over into the other category, into the classical music world category. Anthony Davis, Braxton, everybody has been doing things that take us completely out of the so-called straight jazz category, and all of these people have been writers too.

Following Kobena Mercer, this kind of critical dialogism asserts a kind of creolization of the field of music composition, while at the same moment affirming the heterogeneity and polyphony of black identity. Indeed, what Mercer calls the overturning of "hegemonic boundary maintenance" was a critical element of the Ellington and AACM projects. The frequent disclaimers by black musicians of the classification "jazz" can be seen as an expression of this desire for genre and methodological mobility, and in this context, as Threadgill noted, the practice of composition itself takes on a strongly instrumental dimension in terms of aesthetic, methodological, professional, and social mobility. Thus, as Ellington remarked in 1962, after a lifetime of evading labels, "Let's not worry about whether the result is jazz or this or that type of performance. Let's just say that what we're all trying to create, in one way or another, is music."[132]

That having been said, experimental musicians who were familiar with the important earlier work of the influential critic and activist Amiri Baraka might have been particularly surprised at the vehemence with which he denounced the hybrid new music of the AACM in a collection of his 1980s critical essays on music. Baraka disparages an unnamed violinist (probably Leroy Jenkins) as a member of what he calls the "Tail Europe" school, whose members were presumably unduly influenced by European modernism. According to Baraka, the project of "Tail Europe" was to "take music on a tired old trip, deliberately trying to *declass* the music, transforming it into a secondary appendage of European concert music, rather than the heroic expression of the folk and classical music of the African American majority as well as the spirit of a progressive and populist high art." Baraka holds up the work of saxophonist David Murray as an example of "redefining the spiritual aesthetic of a whole people," while another, unnamed saxophonist—almost certainly Anthony Braxton—"wants to show us that he's heard Berg and Webern and Stockhausen . . . showing white folks how intelligent he (they) is."[133]

Even at the time that it was written, this updated Dionysian/Apollonian binary, along with its evocation of the "heroic" and "the majority," is difficult to understand as anything other than a certain nostalgia for a bygone moment. Jazz had by this time long since ceased to be a music of the black majority, but here, the music is reenlisted in the quest for that elusive being, a democratic and populist high art. Moreover, this discussion points to the fact that, despite the best efforts of black scholars such as Eileen Southern and long-time *New York Amsterdam News* music critic Raoul Abdul, the black classical composer has been almost entirely ignored by black cultural critics. The reasons for this disavowal are complex, even as Southern warned in 1973, "If we black folk are serious about our commitment to the rediscovery and the redefining of our heritage in the fine arts, our scholars must take upon themselves the responsibility for developing an appropriate and exemplary literature."[134] To the extent that these composers problematized constructions of a pure, uncontaminated black aesthetic self that had been promulgated by both black and white scholars and journalists, theorizing the reasons for the apparent disregard of their work can provide an expanded context for exploring the impact of black musical experimentalism more generally.

This responsibility has not, for the most part, been taken up by the field of academic popular culture studies, which, by downplaying or even actively disparaging the utility, purpose, and influence of those indigenously black musics that are not obviously or predominantly based in or represented as mass culture, has effectively ignored the diversity of black musical engagement, and in particular, has been largely unprepared to theorize the seeming anomaly of a nonvernacular music produced from working-class roots. Put more accurately, what emerges is a distinct reluctance to interrogate the constructions of the notion of the vernacular, or to investigate the discursive processes through which particular notions of the vernacular become naturalized. On this view, what is needed is a local and contingent articulation of the vernacular, one that responds to particular persons, histories, and social conditions, rather than a universalizing and essentializing conception of the vernacular that is permanently identified with whatever the black popular music of the moment might be, as gleaned from sales figures. Such a conception of the vernacular need not be defined in reaction to a similarly fixed notion of high culture, and would, moreover, be immune to the high/low class and race binaries that currently animate the cultivated/vernacular distinction.

Thus, to the extent that certain oppositional black musical forms have been generally ignored or dismissed by academic theorists, the idea is thereby perpetuated that there is no necessarily noncommercial space for black musical production. In contextualizing the development of African American music, this intellectual climate supports Andrew Ross's commercial/social Darwinist framing of soul music as having forged "a more successful cultural union." In fact, Ross's brief critique of "avant-garde jazz" as having "gone beyond the realm of popular taste" moves well past Baraka's in advancing the notion that marginalized, oppositional, subaltern, corporate-ignored or otherwise nonmainstream forms of black cultural production should be ignored, if not altogether erased.[135]

In this context, the entry into classical music by black composers, rather than being a form of bourgeois assimilationism as it is often portrayed, becomes an oppositional stance. In fact, the very existence of the black classical composer not only problematizes dominant conceptions of black music, but challenges fixed notions of high and low, black and white. For the most part, black classical composers active since 1930, coming out of the tradition of William Grant Still, have never been as dismissive of popular music as their white colleagues. Black classical music-making, from Still's 1930 *Afro-American Symphony* to Hale Smith's 1975 *Ritual and Incantations,* continued to reference elements of vernacular black life, both in recognition of the continuing dialogue between black culture and European traditions, and as an articulation of the composers' connection to an African diasporic sonic culture whose worldwide influence throughout the twentieth century and into the twenty-first can hardly be overstated.

Baraka's 1980s definition of the directions in African American music as overdetermined by "wherever the masses of the African American people have gone"[136] recapitulates the thrust of his famous 1966 essay, "The Changing Same (R&B and New Black Music)."[137] In such an atmosphere, the African American composer trained in the Western European "art" tradition is troped as a tragic mulatto figure—shunned by white-dominated systems of cultural support, and supposedly a nonfactor in black culture as well. It seemed plain enough to Muhal Richard Abrams, however, that "there are different types of black life, and therefore we know that there are different kinds of black music. Because black music comes forth from black life."[138] What the Baraka of the mid-1980s did not notice was a certain reversed dynamic relative to the 1960s, when resistance to dominant narratives included a strategy of refusal of the "bourgeois" values of classical music in favor of the advocacy of vernacular musics such as jazz, blues, and R&B. Attali's notion of the economy of repetition, however, identifies the deployment of an amorphous construction of "the masses" as useful precisely for the same dominant economic interests who have, according to need, alternately exploited and erased black musical expression. Far from articulating resistance or class struggle, those who import the bourgeois-versus-vernacular binary dialectic unblinkingly into the complex world of black musical expression run the risk of inadvertently serving as the ventriloquist's dummy for corporate megamedia.

A conception of black cultural history that is forced to deny engagement with or influence from pan-European traditions would look absurd if it were applied to black writers or visual artists. Such a perspective cannot account for the complexity of experience that characterizes multiple, contemporary black lives. Thus, this particular formulation of resistance, in advancing (strategically) essentialist notions of black music practice and reference, enforced an aesthetic rigidity that minimized the complexity and catholicity of a composite black musical tradition that includes Nathaniel

Dett, James Reese Europe, Will Marion Cook, H. T. Burleigh, Florence Price, Ulysses Kay, Olly Wilson, Dorothy Rudd Moore, Hale Smith, Primous Fountain III, Wendell Logan, and Jeffrey Mumford. A trope that uses overly broad strokes to posit a classical-jazz binary cannot account for those who, like Sun Ra, John Coltrane, Miles Davis, Bud Powell, and many others, were extremely respectful of and eager to learn from the achievements in pan-European music—and all other musics—while rejecting Western aesthetic hegemony. On this view, the AACM's engagement with Europe was simply the next step in a long history of exchange that, as with such AACM composers as Roscoe Mitchell, Joseph Jarman, Henry Threadgill, Malachi Favors, Anthony Braxton, and others, included formal academic study.

AACM musicians pursued not only practices of exchange and creolization, but also strategies of deauthorization, as expressed in Lester Bowie's signifying:

> I mean most Europeans' background is one of wars and colonization of Africa. I mean really, they've dogged a lot of people. And they have this kind of presumed intelligence, they presume that they're really cultured. And they are in a certain sense, but in other ways they're really barbaric, crude. Most western nations are like that. They didn't get to be big western nations walking on roses or no shit like that. I mean they became France by cutting off motherfuckers' heads.[139]

Thus, I would advance the notion that what is particularly striking about some AACM music is not how much it sounded like white European and American experimentalism, but how little. Reading many of the "Tail Europe"–style critiques, it became clear to musicians that many jazz critics were simply not prepared for the full impact of the postmodern multi-instrumentalism of the AACM, with its tremendous range of references from around the world. Moreover, if we can take Giddins's and even Baraka's remarks as symptomatic, the high modernist and postmodernist music being performed in New York in the 1970s and 1980s, from Sollberger to Ashley to Reich to Oliveros to Rzewski, was unfamiliar to many jazz writers, even those who were living in New York. In the final analysis, those who thought that Anthony Braxton sounded like Karlheinz Stockhausen or Anton Webern could not be said to have truly heard much of either.

AACM musicians had been inculcated into a set of values that saw constructed distinctions between musicians, such as those advanced by Baraka between Murray and Braxton, as a form of divide-and-conquer, regardless of the race of the person articulating them. Thus, Steve McCall, one of Baraka's frequent 1980s collaborators, nonetheless said this about New York jazz writers: "Something that irritates me about many people who write about jazz here is the fact that they think that when they praise one music, then they have to downgrade another. I don't like that at all! Because that is completely unnecessary."[140] Accordingly, those who were looking for divisions between AACM members based on the "Tail Europe" issue were undoubtedly disappointed in Lester Bowie's response to an interviewer's claim that Anthony Braxton, Douglas Ewart, and I "ignore a whole lot of the cultural background of jazz": "There's a whole branch of that, I call it neo-classical. They're in touch with this kind of thing and I feel it's very valid and very cool. . . . they are developing other areas that are just as valid and just as culturally expressive of our time and age. The music is spreading to encompass all of these areas."[141]

Where Baraka sees overt class struggle in the composition, performance, appreciation, analysis, and critical writing about the music,[142] I would maintain that on this very view, the AACM represents an indigenous working-class attempt to open up the space of popular culture to new forms of expression, blurring the boundaries between popular and high culture. As African American musicians sought the same mobility across the breadth of their field that (for example) African American writers and visual artists were striving for, engagement with contemporary pan-European music became a form of boundary-blurring resistance to efforts to restrict the mobility of black musicians, rather than a capitulation to bourgeois values. AACM musicians felt that experimentalism in music need not be bound to particular ideologies, methods, or slogans. Rather, it could take many forms, draw from many histories (including the blues), confront different methodological challenges, and manifest a self-awareness as being in dialogue with the music of the whole earth. Thus, Lester Bowie could affirm the excellence of his "neo-classical" colleagues while locating himself solidly in a different area within this vast field of musical riches: "I am from a different kind of thing. I deal purely with ass-kicking. Period. Just good old country ass-kicking."[143]

Diversity and Its Discontents: New American Music after the Jazz Age

In the context of American musicology, communication between white, high-culture composition and black music is most frequently discussed in terms of a relatively narrow period between 1920 and the putative end of the Swing Era in the early 1940s. During this period and after, however, radical experiments were going on in classical music, including the hotly contested "end of tonality" and the advent of indeterminacy. Jazz-identified musicians were by no means isolated from these far-reaching developments, and classical-identified musicians were hardly unaware of the innovative paths that the newly christened "jazz" music was taking.

If the 1940s were indeed a period in which, as Amiri Baraka observed, "Negro music had to reflect the growing openness of communication with white America,"[144] then the early AACM composers, steeped in the practices of bebop and its 1950s extensions, were heirs to that openness, as well as to the breakdown of genre definitions and the mobility of practice that appeared on the horizon at that historical moment. Understanding the directions taken by black experimental music of the late twentieth century necessitates a closer examination of both the historical events and historiographical tropes that informed the landscape in which these musicians founded their organization.

It is well known, though not widely discussed in histories of American music, that European composers of the 1920s and 1930s felt strongly that jazz could form the basis for a uniquely American music that could emancipate itself from European models. According to musicologist Carol Oja, whose treatment of the issue is one of the most detailed, European composers visiting the United States, including Maurice Ravel, Igor Stravinsky, Darius Milhaud, and Béla Bartók, were "eager to hear jazz, which for them represented the core of American music."[145] In contrast to their strong interest in jazz, "visiting European luminaries such as Ravel seemed to pay little attention to American composers of concert music—at least there is scant record of it."[146] Both at home and abroad, indigenous American classical music was widely seen as the embodiment of epigonality vis-à-vis the products of Europe. Visiting the United States in 1928, Ravel critiqued what he saw as the derivative nature of American composers, saying that "I think you have too little realization of yourselves and that you still look too far away over the water." Ravel exhorted his American counterparts to open their ears to the new sounds in their midst, declaring, "I am waiting to see more Americans appear with the honesty and vision to realize the significance of their popular product, and the technic and imagination to base an original and creative art upon it."[147]

Most historical accounts of this crucial period in the formation of an American classical music give little or no notice to the ferment in black intellectual circles on this issue. In this light, the words of Alain Locke, the great philosopher of the Harlem Renaissance, could be seen as even more challenging than Ravel's. "Certainly for the last fifty years," Locke remarked, "the Negro has been the main source of America's popular music, and promises, as we shall see, to become one of the main sources of America's serious or classical music, at least that part which strives to be natively American and not derivative of European types of music.[148] Ernst Krenek was among the European composers who engaged most directly with the new black sounds. In 1927, Krenek premiered a shocking "jazz opera," *Jonny Spielt Auf,* which combined the new extended tonality with transformations of blues harmonies and forms. The work's portrayal of interracial sex symbolized the confrontation between Old Europe and the new American cultural vitality. Locke quotes the London-born conductor of the Philadelphia Orchestra, Leopold Stokowski, as saying that Negro and American influences would "have the same revivifying effect as the injection of new, and in the larger sense, vulgar blood into dying aristocracy."[149] Drawing on a similar, and at the time very common eugenics-based discourse of "hybrid vigor," American composer George Antheil, according to Locke, declared that European music had grown "weak, miserable and anaemic," needing "the stalwart shoulders of a younger race to hold the cart awhile till we had gotten the wheel back on."[150]

The notion that jazz could become an avatar for American music itself was deeply troubling to Paul Rosenfeld, perhaps the most influential American critic of the period, who railed continually against this upstart competitor as "the greatest threat" to the nascent American concert idiom. "American music is not jazz," went a typical Rosenfeld pronouncement. "Jazz is not music. Jazz remains a striking indigenous product, a small, sounding folk-chaos, counterpart of other national developments."[151] Some American composers, including Charles Ives and Henry Cowell, were also troubled by the rise of jazz. Cowell, a leader of a self-consciously "ultramodern" school of American composition, advocated the construction of "a usable past" for American music that would elicit respect from the mavens of European high culture. Fashioning Charles Ives as "the father of indigenous American art-music" served this need.[152] At the same time, Cowell shared the elder composer's fear that their efforts to define an "American" music would be overwhelmed by the strong worldwide interest in jazz as constitutive of the best of American musical creativity.

Thus, as a matter of self-preservation, Cowell and Ives, both publicly and privately, self-consciously asserted a kind of competition for the minds of Europeans between American classical music and American jazz. A biography of Cowell, part of a program for a 1931 Town Hall concert, lauded the composer for "helping to offset the notion abroad that there is nothing new or of value in American music but jazz."[153] A sample solicitation letter from Cowell to Ives expressed concern that Europeans were gleaning an incorrect picture of American music. "It is unfortunately the case that the few American compositions which have been performed in Europe have rarely been our most serious or most original works." Ives himself edited Cowell's next passage to read, "We have gained the reputation in Europe of being able to produce only jazz—or conventional imitations of European music and music of a rather trivial order."[154]

Ironically, one could read Alain Locke as making a kind of common cause with Ives and Cowell, albeit from a distinctly different subject position, as well as a different set of premises and goals. Although, as musicologist Samuel Floyd notes, "the idea that black music was America's only distinctive contribution to American and world musical culture was accepted and emphasized by Harlem Renaissance leaders,"[155] Locke declared that "neither America nor the Negro can rest content as long as it can be said: 'Jazz is America's outstanding contribution, so far, to world music.'"[156] Thus, in the 1930s, Locke became interested in the development of something he called "symphonic jazz." For Locke, the work of George Gershwin, William Grant Still, and William Dawson could elevate jazz to the status of classical European music.[157] The philosopher also held out some hope for Duke Ellington as "one of the persons most likely to create the classical jazz toward which so many are striving. He plans a symphonic suite and an African opera, both of which will prove a test of his ability to carry native jazz through to this higher level."[158]

Musicologist Oja sees critic Rosenfeld as caught in a paradox: namely, that "American modernism must conform to long-established European standards at the same time as it found its own distinctive manifestations."[159] This Eurocentricity was in collision with potent social forces that were already transforming the American political, cultural, and social landscapes, such as the Great Migration, the massive influx of immigrants from eastern and southern Europe, and the advent of powerful new media technologies such as radio. These factors, according to Oja, were gradually taking the United States toward a pluralist conception of its own culture;[160] American composer Roger Sessions was even able to assert in 1927 that "America is no longer an Anglo-Saxon country."[161] The modernism envisioned by Cowell, however, drew in part upon a notion of whiteness as fundamental to an indigenous American modernism. In a 1930 essay called "Three Native Composers," Cowell argued that jazz had led American composers astray, and posed the question, "What have Anglo-Saxon Americans done in the way of original composition?" As musicologist Beth Levy points out, Cowell felt that "listeners did not usually perceive Anglo-Saxons as a well-defined American group." The listening public, Cowell believed, was unaware of "what to look for in them."[162]

Well after the Jazz Age and the Swing Era ended, there was still a great deal more exchange between black and white modernisms than is reflected in the most commonly referenced historical accounts of black music. For instance, Amiri Baraka's claim in *Blues People* that "the influence of European and Euro-American classical music during the forties was indirect, and not consciously utilized in the music of the boppers"[163] was fatally compromised at the time of its writing, not only by the sounds in the music itself, but by the direct statements of the musicians. As historian Ted Gioia and many others have noted, improvisations by Parker and many others frequently quoted passages from classical compositions, and bebop musicians routinely transcribed classical recordings for practice purposes.[164] A 1953 radio interview with Parker revealed a witty, urbane man, knowledgeable about contemporary classical music. Bird declared that Bartók was "beyond a doubt one of the most finished and accomplished musicians that ever lived," and expresses his disappointment at not having been able to meet the composer before his death.

At the same time, the interview should have allayed any fears that Parker might be in denial regarding the provenance of his music. The interviewer had been persistent in repeating the same question regarding developments in the new music, each time with a slightly different spin. "How much of this change that you were responsible for," the host ventured, "do you feel was spontaneous experimentation with your own ideas, and how much was the adaptation of the ideas of your classical predecessors, for example as in Bartok?" In response, Bird adopted a pointed tone that exhibited only partially mock exasperation. "The things which are happening now known as progressive music, or by the trade name Bebop, not a bit of it was inspired, or adapted, from the music of our predecessors Bach, Brahms, Beethoven, Chopin, Ravel, Debussy, Shostakovich, Stravinsky, etc." From this pithy history lesson, the saxophonist went on to name the musicians—all African Americans—whom he regarded as central to the new developments: "Dizzy Gillespie, Thelonious Monk, Kenny Clarke, there was Charlie Christian—'37, I guess—there was Bud Powell, Don Byas, Ben Webster, yours truly . . ."[165]

On one view, Parker's cultivation of an extensive knowledge of classical music could be interpreted as an implicit bid for the authority that derived from high art status. At the same time, however, as historian Scott De-Veaux's analysis of the historiography of jazz maintains, for the dominant culture to accept jazz as a kind of classical music, a very high discursive "entrance fee" would be demanded. The music would have to be reimagined as having "outgrown its origins in a particular ethnic subculture and could now be thought of as the abstract manipulation of style and technique. Jazz was now to be measured against the 'absolute' standards of greatness of the European tradition." On this view, "Jazz was a music of promise, but it still had a long way to go, and the only way to get there was to acknowledge the priority of European music."[166]

While seeking to connect his work with other intellectual currents of the time, however, Parker's insistence on an African American source for his music advances the more radical notion of a modernist high art based in black culture. In effect, Parker and many other musicians simply refused to pay the "entrance fee." The Parker example exposes music historiography's general lack of a framework for examining post–Jazz Age interpenetrations between jazz-identified musics and contemporary European American musical experimentalism. This lacuna, for example, precludes references to composers such as Edgard Varese, one of the most influential ultramodernists of the twentieth century. William Grant Still had worked closely as Varese's student before his definitive turn away from ultramodernism toward his own musical path.[167] Parker had arranged to study with Varese shortly before the saxophonist's passing,[168] and as Parker related it, "He wants to write for me"—a tantalizing prospect indeed.[169]

At the same time, the saxophonist was certainly well aware of his own role as one of the progenitors of a new experimental practice, a role analogous to Varese's own. Thus, rather than an expression of epigonality vis-à-vis his own musical traditions, Bird's move to work with Varese constituted an assumption of collegiality, as well as an assertion of mobility of reference and practice. Indeed, Parker could have seen in Still a kindred spirit who crossed boundaries with alacrity; after all, as musicologist Oja observed,

> In the early 1920s he [Still] was doing it all—playing in the orchestra of the historic Eubie Blake and Noble Sissle musical *Shuffle Along;* working for the Pace and Handy Music Company, subsequently for the Black Swan

phonograph company; producing arrangements for black revues; and beginning to compose concert music, first studying in Boston with George Wakefield Chadwick and then in New York with Edgard Varese.[170]

There is little question that Parker, Gillespie, and other beboppers were moving to assert the same mobility expressed by Scott Joplin's opera *Treemonisha,* James P. Johnson's magnificently orchestrated yet rarely heard orchestral suites, and the oeuvre of Duke Ellington. Eric Porter points out that Mary Lou Williams, who composed her twelve-part extended composition *Zodiac Suite* in 1946, "demonstrated discomfort with the constraints that generic categories placed on music and musicians. Jazz could be celebrated as black musical culture, but it signified the primitivist expectations of its audience as well [and] also symbolized the limitations on where black musicians could perform."[171]

In the end, bebop's project of mobility contained the seeds of its own fragmentation, and was soon to undergo centrifugal forces of frightening magnitude. For one thing, bebop, though based in the blues, was anything but a popular, vernacular form, and by the early 1950s, its proponents were being blamed for the loss of jazz's position as a music of mass attention, particularly with black audiences, a fact commonly framed as evidence of the music's "decline." Writing in 1963, Baraka declared that "the most expressive Negro music of any given period will be an exact reflection of what the Negro himself is."[172] On this view, this fundamental black self was an outgrowth of "the poor Negro," based in folk culture. Quoting Ralph Ellison, Jones named this construct "the blues people," meaning "those who accepted and lived close to their folk experience."[173]

This framing of the presumed target demographic for any music made by black people is critiqued by historian Scott DeVeaux as operating "as the center of an essentialist conception of black identity."[174] Nonetheless, a cryptically asserted, class-and-market-based essentializing of black musical authenticity is widespread in academic popular culture studies. The ongoing effort to chain the ideas of black musicians to the demands of vox populi has assumed many forms, but one of the most widely used tropes draws upon confidently asserted readings of the will of "the black masses." Baraka's later definition of the directions in African American music as overdetermined by "wherever the masses of the African American people have gone" is but one such example.[175] Whether based on essentialist identity projections or record sales figures and other commercial data, presumptions of a necessary, authenticating relation of identity between black music and mass culture abound in recent histories of jazz.

Perhaps inevitably, the entertainer/artist divide that bebop brought to the fore became a metaphor encompassing constructions of low and high culture, blackness and whiteness, working class and middle class. No less a personage than Ralph Ellison became a pungent critic, not only of the musical values of the beboppers, but of their rejection of the entertainer role. As Ellison saw it, the critique of Louis Armstrong's seemingly minstrelized onstage persona constituted a denial of the music's working-class roots. "By rejecting Armstrong," Ellison wrote in 1962, "[beboppers] thought to rid themselves of the entertainer's role. And by getting rid of the role they demanded, in the name of their racial identity, a purity of status which by definition is impossible for the performing artist."[176]

Even DeVeaux easily asserts that "if bop was a revolution, it was hardly a revolution aimed directly at the black masses, who insisted on a music that satisfied their taste for bluesy dance and entertainment."[177] In support of this thesis, DeVeaux turns to historian Gerald Early's similar construction of an Armstrong-bebop binary.

> To Armstrong and to the black masses, the concept of the artist and of art as it is generally fixed by Euro-American standards is, quite frankly, incomprehensible. Armstrong saw himself as an entertainer who must, by any means, please his audience. And to the black masses generally there would scarcely be a reason for the public performer to exist if he did not feel that pleasing his audience was the prime directive.[178]

Early's suggestion that musicians who fail to obey this "prime directive" really should not exist at all is undermined by the fact that bop emerged from the same working-class masses who are being romanticized as bearers of authenticity in his thesis. Further pressure is placed on this unreflective ventriloquizing of the "black masses" by subsequent events that made it clear that neither Armstrong nor Parker could realistically be said to represent that demographic. In the end, the complex network of black sonic positionalities emerging during this period could not be accounted for by spurious binaries as "Euro/Afro"—or for that matter, "artist/entertainer."

By the mid-1950s, black music was being rapidly transformed from a passive source of raw materials for the experiments of pan-European composers to a feared competitor offering a trenchant alternative to the latest products of the pan-European high art tradition. Moreover, this radical, improvised upstart appeared to many to be fast gaining the upper hand in an era when both American ultramodernism and European experimentalism were highly controversial. Some critics, such as Henry Pleasants, declared the European tradition all but dead, and proposed jazz as the music most likely to replace it.[179] Thus, at the conclusion of the fifties, Rosenfeld's project of decisively separating "high" from "low," heretofore seen as central to the project of creating an American art music, appeared to be in grave danger.

This threat to the centered position of pan-European musical culture was coming to the fore at precisely the same moment that a number of Euro-American composers became perhaps the first to break through the European perception of American epigonality. Elliott Carter, Milton Babbitt, and the New York School of John Cage, Morton Feldman, Christian Wolff, David Tudor, and others, part of a group of composers whose work had only recently achieved a tenuous claim to art music status, had every reason to deploy Rosenfeldian tropes to ward off future competition. These composers did so by articulating a model of American music that eschewed any contact with African American forms. However inadvertently, Catherine Cameron's work provides a glimpse into how white experimentalist composers across a wide aesthetic spectrum tended to situate themselves as American exponents of a unitary European art music tradition.[180] In this regard, Cage's "History of Experimental Music in the United States," part of his early, widely influential 1961 manifesto, *Silence*, continues to serve as a "readymade" touchstone for later histories, reference works, reviews, and retrospectives that tend to define "experimental music" in terms of a set of acceptable methodologies, people, sites, and venues available to pan-European high-culture music.[181] In the essay, the composer explicitly asserted a strong relationship to the European Dada movement, European experimentalists such as Pierre Boulez, Karlheinz Stockhausen, Luigi Nono and Luciano Berio, and Cowell's generation of ultramodernists.[182]

Already preempting the New York School's later attempts at expropriating the trope of experimentalism, however, was Alain Locke, who in the 1930s located musicians like Louis Armstrong, Fletcher Henderson, Earl Hines, "Fats" Waller, Cab Calloway, Don Redman, Jimmy Lunceford, and Duke Ellington at the nexus of "feverish experimenting."[183] In later years, the denial of race as an aspect of the historiography of experimental music (viewed not only in the U.S. context, but internationally), tended to separate work on new music from contemporary scholarship and criticism in visual art, literature, and dance. More centrally, it could be said that part of white-coded experimentalism's ongoing identity formation project depended upon an Othering of its great and arguably equally influential competitor, the jazz tradition, which is also widely viewed (and views itself) as explicitly experimental. The transcribed orature of musicians endorsing the importance of exploration, discovery, and experiment is quite vast and easy to access; it spans virtually every era of jazz music, and includes nearly every improvisor of canonical stature before the rise of Wynton Marsalis in the mid-1980s.[184]

As Oja notes, the older American ultramoderns whom Cage took as his spiritual fathers had already asserted the absence of an indigenous high-art tradition in American music.[185] This "lack of tradition" is inscribed as the trope of the tabula rasa that animated the American frontier project, which, as historian William Appleman Williams maintains, often serves as a representation of an American exceptionalism based in innovation and limitless growth.[186] A similar trope was used by Alain Locke to describe jazz, supported by a quote from the conductor Leopold Stokowski: "The Negro musicians of America are playing a great part in this change. They have an open mind and unbiased outlook. They are not hampered by conventions or traditions, and with their new ideas, their constant experiment, they are causing new blood to flow in the veins of music."[187]

Cage and his cohorts articulated a musical version of this "frontier thesis." As one Cage story had it, "Once, in Amsterdam, a Dutch musician said to me, 'It must be very difficult for you in America to write music, for you are so far away from the centers of tradition.' I had to say, 'It must be very difficult for you in Europe to write music, for you are so close to the centers of tradition.'"[188] For Cage and many of his colleagues, however, the vitality of the frontier trope in musical experimentalism depended crucially on a strategy of ignoring or denigrating the contributions of their major competitor, the African American tradition.[189] African Americans became, in historian David Noble's words, "people without history,"[190] and those seeking to construct a "usable past" for American music claimed to have little to learn from these domestic subalterns. As Cage declared in 1961, "Jazz per se derives from serious music. And when serious music derives from it, the situation becomes rather silly."[191]

In the final analysis, as Ralph Ellison noted in a 1976 interview, white American composers were "mixed in their attitudes" toward black music: "They accepted its resources, but when it came to identifying it as a viable part of American music they were hindered by racial considerations."[192]

Nonetheless, by 1950, improvisative methods and processes, problematized by European music for the previous one hundred years, were now challenging the methods and practices of that music at its core. Compounding the issue was the fact that this challenge was once again coming in large measure from a culture whose inferiority—in terms of class and race—had up to this point been assumed.

Following on the pursuit of cultural pluralism that was a marker of American music in the 1920s and 1930s, white American composers traveled the world in search for alternatives that would preserve the Rosenfeldian high/low divide. Cowell, the pre-1950s Cage, and later, Lou Harrison, engaged with the court musics of Asia in search of a high-culture, non-European source for their music. At the same time, their pluralist adventures were tempered by a staunch refusal to countenance either Ravel's or Locke's vision of African diasporic sounds and practices as a foundation for an indigenous American high-culture music.[193] Indeed, any imputation of influence from African American sources was generally simply denied, ignored, or actively denigrated.

Despite this massive resistance, however, it was becoming clear that traditional Eurological methods needed to be revised to confront the new realities that bebop had placed on the table. In this context, "indeterminacy" became a compositional method that could embrace the new spontaneity, while preserving both the primacy of core Eurological aesthetic and formal values, and the associated high/low divide. In furtherance of the theory of indeterminacy, Cage proclaimed that "composing's one thing, performing's another, listening's a third. What can they have to do with one another?"[194] While Daniel Belgrad sees irony in this famous declaration, at the most fundamental level this triumvirate of practice appears to describe improvisation rather well. The fact that most critics and commentators seemed not to notice this serves as the real irony, an index of how distant their work had become from those indigenous American musical forms based in black culture.

Among the indeterminists, there was considerable debate as to the nature, psychology, form, and social function of spontaneous music-making. For instance, the important pianist David Tudor realized several indeterminate works by producing secondary performance scores, using older dodecaphonic methods for generating harmony and voice-leading. In performance, the artists realized these scores more or less to the letter. Some, such as Earle Brown and Christian Wolff, were critical of the secondary score approach for its avoidance of the spontaneous, but Tudor resisted such on-the-spot decision-making. The pianist made it clear that he "would not accept a performance that happened by chance, just simply because I happened to read something on the spur of the moment."[195] Nonetheless, Frank O'Hara's 1959 description of Morton Feldman's "Intersection 3" constitutes an early example of the long list of accounts crediting the musical New York School with the articulation of spontaneous music-making. O'Hara's representation of the work as featuring "improvisatory collaboration, with its call on musical creativity as well as interpretive understanding" is undercut not only by the existence of Tudor's secondary score, but also by the fact that Feldman was well known for his dislike of improvisation. In fact, O'Hara's description seems far more congruent with the musical practices of the bebop that he knew and loved.[196]

As George Lipsitz has said, "Struggles over meaning are inevitably struggles over resources."[197] The sociologist Howard Becker illuminated the issue in terms of art world competition for resources and redefinition of discourses, showing that in fact, meaning itself constitutes a resource:

> If I can argue cogently that jazz merits as serious consideration on aesthetic grounds as other forms of art music, then I can compete, as a jazz player, for grants and fellowships from the National Endowment for the Arts and faculty positions in music schools, perform in the same halls as symphony orchestras, and require the same attention to the nuances of my work as the most serious classical composer.[198]

As Ekkehard Jost notes, however, the music of this generation of black experimentalists, in addition to being both financially and ideologically unattractive to the emerging U.S. media corporations, lay

> outside of the officially recognized culture promoted by subsidies and scholarships. It took many more years and substantial efforts on the part of this new generation of jazz musicians to break apart the established educational system's constricted notion of culture in such a way that not only John Cage, but also Cecil Taylor could benefit from it—to a lesser degree, of course.[199]

In contrast, for white American composers, academia had become a useful refuge from the market. In 1961, John Cage asked, "Why is experimental music so lacking in strength politically (I mean unsupported by those with money—individuals and foundations, unpublished, undiscussed, ignored)."[200]

These cavils notwithstanding, Cage himself benefited from numerous temporary university appointments and residencies.[201] In the postwar boom economy, major private foundations and the U.S. government, moving to project high culture as an expression of American freedom and democracy, created new teaching posts and residencies. New sources of support for commissions came forth, and composers and performers received tenured professorships and endowed chairs at major public and private universities. Universities subsidized new music journals, performance ensembles, and record companies, and expensive electronic music studios were installed at institutions across the country.[202]

In contrast, the musician and scholar Leslie B. Rout objected in 1969 that "Disgracefully, jazz, perhaps American's only art form, had to wait until 1968 before an individual jazzman, Ornette Coleman, received a Guggenheim Foundation fellowship. Bear in mind that classical musicians and composers had been happily drawing similar kinds of stipends for years."[203] Similarly, Andrew Hill asked in 1966, "If a place like Lincoln Center can be built for classical music, why can't another place be built for people who are a product of this society?"[204] By the late 1960s, Hill's argument was being advanced with increasing urgency, often drawing upon the same Americanist/nativist trope that moved John Cage and his associates to situate themselves in distinction to European culture. In Cage's case, however, the distinction is undercut by his simultaneous sense of familial reverence for Europe. Hill's quote, in contrast, advances a notion of the indigenousness of African American music as a criterion for receiving support.

Some jazz critics accepted the jazz-as-art claim to a limited extent, while justifying differences in infrastructure in various ways. By 1967, Leonard Feather had discovered German avant-garde composer Karlheinz Stockhausen, whom he promptly proclaimed as being, along with John Cage, "many years ahead of jazz musicians, who only in the 1960s have begun to discover and toy with the potentialities of sound beyond the long-accepted boundaries of music. . . . Around 1950 most jazz musicians had barely reached Stravinsky in their training and thinking."[205] Of course, the tendency to make pan-European music the measure of all things, as Feather does here with his infantilization of the musicians, was precisely what the new black musicians were challenging. At the same time, the comment underscores the extent to which competition between the trans-European and the trans-African, already in evidence since the 1920s, was now reaching a dramatic new stage. The new musicians' awareness that their already influential work had become a species of art music made the extreme contrast between the conditions they experienced and those enjoyed by composers and performers of white experimentalist "new music" even more glaring and obvious.

Even as both uptown and downtown musics of the 1980s sought to challenge prevailing wisdom in so many areas, the dominant response of white American experimentalism to the new opportunities for hybridity that were being presented displayed an ongoing fealty to the erasure of African American cultural production from the very definition of "experimental."[206] This stance, however, was radically challenged by the diversity movement in experimental music. For Attali, free jazz "eliminated the distinctions between popular music and learned music, broke down the repetitive hierarchy,"[207] and as we have noted already, the AACM's revision of the relationship between composition and improvisation lies on an unstable fault line between the new black music and the new white music.

This border was again brought to light in the late 1970s, as the work of AACM, BAG, and other black experimentalist composers began to receive limited exposure in some of the same venues, and support from some of the same sources, as white experimental composers. Thus, for a short period between 1976 and 1978, trombonist Garrett List, as music director of the Kitchen in the mid-1970s, was particularly active in moving toward a nonracialized, barrier-breaking conception of new music. Members of the new generation of black experimentalists, such as Anthony Braxton, Leo Smith, Oliver Lake, and the Art Ensemble of Chicago, were presented in Kitchen concerts during List's tenure, though few of these events were ever reviewed. At this time, *New York Times* critic Rockwell could even write of a largely black vanguard, an idea that scarcely survived the advent of Wynton Marsalis.

> These jazz musicians make their improvised music in the jazz tradition in performance spaces that also cater to conventional "new music"; they compete for the same grant monies, and they interact with improvising or non-improvising composers who don't stem from the jazz tradition at all. Indeed, except that they may hope to supplement their incomes with the occasional jazz gig, or invest their music with intimations of the black experience, these musicians are inseparable from any other sort of new-music composer. Good examples of this sort of overt art-jazz would be Ornette Coleman, the Art Ensemble of Chicago, the World Saxophone Quartet, Leroy Jenkins, Anthony Braxton, Garrett List and, perhaps most

notable of all in his steady move into the territory of the non-jazz avant-garde, George Lewis.[208]

By 1980, my own two-year tenure as music curator of the Kitchen could be viewed as helping to shift the debate around border crossing to a stage where whiteness-based constructions of American experimentalism were being fundamentally problematized. Both the *Village Voice* and the *New York Times* announced the new Kitchen regime in bold letters. The *Times* presented a large picture of the new curator, accompanied by the Kitchen's Wales-born director, Mary MacArthur, in its Sunday Arts and Leisure section.[209] *Voice* writer Tom Johnson's review of my first curated event described a double bill of a collaboration between synthesist Tom Hamilton and Black Artists Group woodwind improvisor J. D. Parran, followed by a John Zorn "opera" for improvisors, *Jai Alai*. For Johnson, the salient feature of this event was expressed in the headline "The Kitchen Improvises." Johnson admitted that while the previous Kitchen concert policy had been a valuable forum for "many fine minimalist works requiring long spans of time and complete composer control," it had nonetheless "tended to shut out new music involving improvising groups." The writer predicted that the direction of the Kitchen's programming, "assuming that these opening concerts are symptomatic, is to open the door to new forms of improvising."[210] Even so, the jazz side of the *Voice* took little, if any, notice of events at the Kitchen; a full five years after the earlier musings of Gary Giddins about border crossing, the venue was still not considered part of the jazz "turf."

My presence at the Kitchen was one small artifact of an era in which African American musical histories and practices came into dialogue with white-coded American experimentalism's methods, practices, and not incidentally, its sources of support, right in the center of New York City's downtown art world, one of the most publicly charged arenas to be found anywhere. The Kitchen, with its relatively extensive infrastructure, its large presentation and commissioning budgets, and its commitment to experimental work, had a long history of supporting complex projects that other spaces would not or could not bring to fruition. The new curatorial direction promised to make that infrastructure welcoming to African American artists who sought to present that kind of demanding hybrid work. Perhaps realizing this, Johnson goes on to warn his readers, many of whom were presumably regular Kitchen concertgoers, that the apparent broadening of scope and altering of focus was going to require some adjustments, particularly in dialogue with a cultural institution whose overall budget at the time was over half a million dollars. "When it is decided that previously ne-glected formats will open the season at a place like the Kitchen, that means a lot," Johnson observed. "It's not just someone's opinions but an actual fact, and everyone concerned must adjust to it."[211]

The new hybridity reflected in the Kitchen's programming was part of an emerging challenge to journalistic, critical, social, and historical dis-courses that presented as entirely natural the musical separation of black and white, low and high, uptown and downtown, popular and serious, "Music" and "Riffs." Lacking a language adequate to the task of describing and contextualizing the new diversity, critical reception eventually settled on the notion that the Kitchen was now "concentrating" on jazz, which seemed putatively defined as new music by black people, and/or which fea-tured improvisation—a framing that updated, but ultimately preserved the old racializations. While the number of Kitchen events featuring African Americans or improvised music had indeed increased sharply from prior years, "concentration" was far too strong a term; the complement of artists presented could not be subsumed under any generalizations about ethnic-ity, race, gender, or musical method.[212]

Eventually, the *Voice,* which had faithfully covered Kitchen events for years, virtually ceased covering them. The *Soho Weekly News* followed suit until its demise in 1981, preferring (mostly negative) articles about its "up-town" relatives to boundary-crossing engagement with black forms that had started to come under attack on the jazz side of the paper. *Voice* jazz critics practically never ventured to the Kitchen, and Gregory Sandow, the eventual replacement for Tom Johnson, bravely stepped into the breach to review a 1981 Julius Hemphill/Anthony Davis double bill, where he found that "the new music crowd found at the Kitchen on other nights stayed away."[213]

There are several reasons for the asymmetrical dynamic regarding criti-cal support for experimental forms in New York. First, critical commentary on the work of the Downtown I avant-garde was most often written by composers, such as Johnson and Sandow, who were regarded as members of that community. As a result most *Voice* articles were not simply nonad-versarial, but were, in a sense, insider reports, where the voices of the art-ists themselves were always centered.[214] With the support of a sympathetic publisher, the clear purpose was to build a community, even as the articles tended to implicitly define Downtown I's methodological, ethnic, and class boundaries. In contrast, writing on black experimental music came not from among the musicians themselves, but from a cadre of more or less professional writers. Few black musicians had the kind of relatively unmediated access to publication that the white experimentalists enjoyed; for a brief period, guitarist Vernon Reid, later a founding member of the Black Rock Coalition and the important heavy metal band, Living Colour, wrote *Voice* reviews.

However, resistance to diversity, while dominant, was hardly monolithic. The central role of leadership exercised by musicians themselves was vital in envisioning the end of "hegemonic boundary maintenance." The Creative Music Studio (CMS), located in Woodstock, New York, was a grassroots initiative of vocalist Ingrid Berger and her partner, Karl Berger, a vibraphonist and academically trained philosopher who had performed with Eric Dolphy.[215] Inspired by both Black Mountain College and trumpeter Don Cherry's cross-cultural vision of new music, the Bergers' creolizing conception brought together members of various experimentalisms. This hybrid conception from the 1970s constituted one obvious model for John Zorn's 1986 declaration that "we should take advantage of all the great music and musicians in the world without fear of musical barriers."[216]

A typical visitor to CMS might encounter a conversation or performance among a diverse array of musicians, including members of the AACM, such as Roscoe Mitchell and Woodstock neighbor Anthony Braxton, Indian flutist G. S. Sachdev, Japanese Zen shakuhachi artist Watazumi-doso, Senegalese drummer Aiyb Dieng, Brazilian multi-instrumentalist Nana Vasconcelos, and composer and improvisor Pauline Oliveros, a CMS neighbor and frequent participant, who collaborated there with the African American choreographer Ione in creating an opera about Angolan Queen Nzinga's resistance to Portuguese colonial domination. Other area residents, such as bassist Dave Holland and drummer Jack DeJohnette, were regular visitors and instructors, as were the members of the best known of the live electronic music ensembles, Musica Elettronica Viva. These politically engaged composer-performers—pianists Alvin Curran and Frederic Rzewski, synthesizer player Richard Teitelbaum, and trombonist Garrett List—had for many years actively sought alliances with improvisors from different traditions, recognizing early on that musicians of all backgrounds and ethnicities were exchanging sounds, styles, materials, and methodologies.[217]

The high point of this early diversity movement produced the New Music America Festival, perhaps one of the first attempts to codify, in a performance network, an avant-garde that drew from a wide variety of sources. The festival's immediate predecessor was 1979's "New Music, New York," a week-long series of concerts and symposia sponsored by the Kitchen during composer Rhys Chatham's tenure as music curator. Beginning in 1980, the New Music America Festival sought to expand on the success of "New Music, New York," aiming at the creation of nothing less than an annual national showcase for experimental music. Over the fourteen-year lifespan of the festival, large-scale festivals were held in such major cities as Chicago, San Francisco, Miami, and Montreal.

While a 1992 monograph summarizing New Music America's history is suitably multicultural in tone and presentation,[218] it could well be said that the reality of inclusion never quite caught up to the rhetoric. The fifty-four composers listed in advertisements for the original "New Music, New York" constituted a veritable catalog of Downtown I artists; just three, however, were African American: Don Cherry, Leo Smith, and myself.[219] Thus, at several of the panel discussions accompanying the New York festival, criticisms were made concerning the overwhelming whiteness of the version of experimental music being presented as "diverse." The few nonwhite composers featured, however, exercised influence far out of proportion to their numbers, not least because for perhaps the very first time, their presence obliged the "downtown" art world to touch upon, however gingerly, the complex relationship between race, culture, music, method, and art world rewards. Describing the furor, *Voice* reviewer Johnson, while admitting that "the festival was clearly weighted toward white musicians," felt nonetheless that this had "more to do with recent history than with overt racism."[220]

Johnson's acknowledgment that "the black-dominated loft jazz scene has evolved right alongside the white-dominated experimental scene throughout this decade" was perhaps one of the few such admissions to appear in any New York paper. For Johnson, however, an attempt by the Kitchen to engage with this black experimental music "would be far more patronizing than constructive . . . a truly ecumenical festival of new music in New York would have to include some of the klezmer musicians . . . along with shakuhachi players, kamancheh players, Irish groups, Balkan groups, and so on."[221] This strategy of unfurling the banners of pluralism and color-blindness to mask this astonishing conflation of diverse musics under the heading of "Other" begs questions of affinity, collaboration, and competition between black and white experimentalism that were already being articulated all over New York, right under the noses of media commentators supposedly "representing" both camps.

In any event, AACM and BAG artists constituted a clear majority of the very few African American composers featured in New Music America events over the succeeding years. For NMA 1980 in Minneapolis, the only

African Americans invited were Douglas Ewart, the Art Ensemble of Chicago, a duo of Oliver Lake and Leroy Jenkins, and former SUNY Buffalo Creative Associate Julius Eastman, out of forty-seven events listed. Despite the presence of two AACM members (Douglas Ewart and me) on the advisory board of the Chicago-based 1982 NMA festival, just four performances by African Americans were featured, of the approximately sixty-five presented. These included an orchestral work by Muhal Richard Abrams, and chamber works by Douglas Ewart and Roscoe Mitchell. Particularly telling, in the founding city of the AACM itself, with an African American population of over 40 percent, was a panel discussion, titled "New Music and Our Changing Culture," in which all of the participants—David Behrman, John Cage, Dan Graham, Ben Johnston, Marjorie Perloff, and Christian Wolff—were white.

10

THE NEW REGIME IN CHICAGO

Generational Shifts in the Collective

In the wake of the artistically successful AACM Tenth Anniversary Festival, a number of new Chicago-based members came to the fore. One of the most influential on subsequent AACM generations has been the clarinetist and saxophonist Mwata Bowden, who joined the AACM in 1975, just after the festival. Born in Memphis in 1947, Bowden was just slightly younger than some of the youngest first-wave AACM members, such as Henry Threadgill and Anthony Braxton. Bowden's family came to Chicago when he was ten, part of the last major wave of the Great Migration. The family settled with relatives at 46th and Vincennes, in a basement apartment right in the middle of Bronzeville, now increasingly referred to as "the ghetto." The family lived a block away from the Regal Theater, where Bowden would go to see stage shows unaccompanied by his parents, and the 63rd Street club scene was still in force when Bowden was a teenager.[1]

At the age of twelve, Bowden began taking clarinet lessons at Ebenezer Baptist Church, right in the neighborhood on 45th and Vincennes, where the young Dinah Washington, then known as Ruth Jones, had accompanied the even younger Leroy Jenkins twenty years before. At Forrestville, the same elementary school that Ajaramu had attended in the 1930s, Bowden joined the instrumental music program, where the legendary Chicago drummer and bandleader George Hunter, a student of Captain Walter Dyett, was now the band director. Music kept Bowden away from the blandishments that ghetto life offered, and eventually Hunter sent Bowden on to his master's bailiwick at DuSable High, where Cap was as irascible as ever. Dyett's jazz band, previously an extracurricular activity, was now a part of the standard school curriculum, and featured a number of future musical leaders, including bassist Fred Hopkins, saxophonist Edwin Daugherty, drummer Jerome Cooper, and the Galloway brothers, trumpeter Tim and trombonist Steve. Even so, Bowden was not as excited about jazz band as some people might have expected. "I liked concert band, because it challenged me as a clarinetist," he recalled. "I wasn't into saxophone then." Alongside his clarinet studies, at Cap's behest Bowden took theory lessons at Sherwood Conservatory.

Besides music, Bowden was interested in oceanography. "I would have gone to college in San Diego or somewhere," he remembered—except that there was no money for college. Meanwhile, nearly five hundred thousand troops were in Southeast Asia in 1969. In that same year, a draft lottery was established for the first time since World War II, and Bowden's lucky number was 237, which meant that instead of serving and possibly dying, he went to the American Conservatory with the goal of becoming a symphony clarinetist. Along the way, however, Bowden began to understand that his public-high-school path to music, though earnest and nurturing, had not prepared him for orchestral performance. Thus, by 1972 Bowden was following the practical path trod by generations of black classically trained musicians—earning a degree in music education. Even so, his continued pursuit of a career as a clarinetist seemed utterly quixotic to Charles Walton, an important Chicago musician and educator with whom Bowden had been working. "When are you going to come to your senses?" Walton told the young musician. "He finally sat me down and said, Here, take this horn. He gave me a baritone saxophone. He said, rehearsal is this coming Monday. That was the start of it. I picked up a saxophone, and started playing in his band."

In Walton's band, based at Malcolm X College on the South Side, Bowden met some of Chicago's more experienced younger musicians, including saxophonist Sonny Seals and trumpeter and trombonist Billy Howell. As for the baritone saxophone, however, "I didn't like it at all. Clarinet was an instrument I knew. Baritone—the finger span was too wide, it took too much air, the mouthpiece was *this big,* it was heavy as hell, and I sounded like a damn beginner. It crushed my ego." Nonetheless, Bowden began working steadily as a part of Chicago's still-hot R&B circuit. One day, he met an unusually charismatic individual who said,

> Hey man, would you like to come over and practice? That was the first time anybody on the R&B circuit had said, let's practice. The R&B cats were like, go to the gig. So I said, real cool. We're practicing, and we started talking some stuff, and he said, let's take a break and listen to some music. He put on some John Coltrane, and it started to blow me away. This was Rasul Siddik.

As Bowden explained it, "It was this one cat who began to turn me on to the hip stuff, the out stuff. I got excited again about music." Bowden began meeting other musicians of the AACM's second wave, including me, Edward Wilkerson, and Douglas Ewart, for whom the AACM School, rather than the jam sessions of yore, had become a prime meeting place for the exploration of new ideas, unfamiliar methods, and new technical challenges. Especially exciting was the fact that given the expanded instrumental palette being explored by AACM musicians, Bowden was finally able to give his clarinet dreams full rein.

Although the music was artistically satisfying, "We were really building a family, and I needed a consistent income." Calling upon his degree in music education, Bowden got a job at King Junior High School in Harvey, a largely black suburb just south of Chicago. He continued his work on the R&B circuit, notably in a backup band for the Chi-Lites, but by 1976, he had reached an impasse with the R&B circuit, so he signed on as a student in the burgeoning music program at Governors State. The program was already populated by other AACM musicians, including Vandy Harris, Frank Gordon, Chico Freeman, and Billy Howell, and with scholarship funds and the support of his spouse, Judy, Bowden was able to concentrate full time on music. It was around that time that Bowden became a founder of the collective wind quartet Quadrisect, along with James Johnson, Douglas Ewart, and me. The quartet featured compositions by each of its members, and exemplified an egalitarian spirit that animated the hybrid combination of free improvisation and composed forms that comprised much of the ensemble's concert performances. The group made a successful European debut in 1977, performing at the Moers New Jazz Festival in West Germany and the Groningen Jazzmarathon in the Netherlands.

Edward Wilkerson finally joined the AACM in 1975, upon the completion of his undergraduate studies. Up to that time, he was active in the AACM both as occasional performer and as volunteer.[2] By this time, few first-wave AACM members still lived in Chicago, and several second-wave members, notably Chico Freeman and I, had moved away as well. The geographic distance between me and my Chicago-based Quadrisect colleagues proved insuperable, and the ensemble disbanded soon after its European trip. The breakup was characteristic of the strains of collectivity that the AACM endured in the late 1970s, but the new challenges were far more acute than anything experienced during the period of first contact with Europe in 1969. This was in no small measure because so many of the founding members of the organization were no longer available. Despite the departures, the organization as a whole was still perceived by its members (as well as the musical world in general) as having Chicago as its home base. Thus, influenced in part by ideologies of "giving back to the community," AACM members living and working on the East Coast (and as far away as Europe) frequently returned to Chicago, taking part in anniversary festivals produced by Chicago-based AACM members.

One such festival, in August 1977, was held in tandem with a three-day AACM "national conference" that explored the implications of the expanded possibilities for black experimental music—including increasing opportunities for performances in Europe—that were perceived to be emerging in the wake of the New York exodus. The meeting evinced the diversity of experience and interest that was emerging within the AACM. The participants, some of whom were meeting each other for the first time, can be roughly separated into four loosely defined, overlapping sets or positions. One group was comprised of the earlier generation of Europe-based expatriates, along with those who had moved to the East Coast before the AACM migration of 1975–77; this group included Anthony Braxton, Leroy Jenkins, Leonard Jones, John Stubblefield, Steve McCall, Leo Smith, Malachi Favors, Roscoe Mitchell, Famoudou Don Moye, and Joseph Jarman. Another contingent included those who had recently moved to the eastern seaboard, including myself, Kalaparusha, Henry Threadgill, Steve McCall, Amina Claudine Myers, and Muhal Richard Abrams, who chaired the meeting.[3]

A third, smaller group of musicians, most of whom had been part of the AACM since the late 1960s, included Douglas Ewart, Evod Magek, Thurman Barker, Ajaramu, John Shenoy Jackson, Wallace McMillan, and Pete Cosey. This group, which had declined for various reasons to join the New

York exodus, served as a source of continuity for a fourth group of younger Chicago-based members who had joined the AACM between 1972 and 1977, including saxophonist Charles "Wes" Cochran, Mwata Bowden, Rasul Siddik, Iqua Colson, Adegoke Steve Colson, Edward Wilkerson, and Kahil El'Zabar, who had become the organization's chair in 1976.[4] Most of these musicians had never met the members of the first contingent of East Coast and Europe-based musicians. On the other hand, these were among the last of the AACM's second-wave members to have experienced working at first hand with some of the founding and original members.

This first national meeting, as might be expected at a major homecoming and reunion, was warm, lively, and often jocular, even as serious business was being planned. The participants organized themselves into several smaller caucuses that explored a variety of issues over the three days, after which each caucus presented its findings for general discussion. The need for AACM unity and solidarity across geographic lines was generally acknowledged, and the role of the Chicago-based membership in maintaining the AACM's organizational and community service aspects was recognized by those who had left the region. At the same time, in the course of the meeting, it became clear that with the departure of these founding and original members, significant shifts across the generations had already emerged regarding musical concepts, practices of collective governance, conceptions of and experiences with the music business, and overall goals for the organization as a whole.

Douglas Ewart's succinct and well-organized presentation on the expansion and reorganization of the AACM School drew applause from the assembled body. My subsequent presentation from the finance committee explored grants and the possibility of forming a kind of clearinghouse for publishing AACM music in various forms. Later in the meeting, as a member of the media caucus, I brought up the issue of emerging technologies for music dissemination, which at this predigital moment included the emerging videocassette medium. Don Moye reported on the AACM Building Fund, a self-help savings initiative toward the purchase of a building that would house AACM concerts and pedagogical activities, archives, and more. With the loss of the BAG space due to fickle funders,[5] a number of AACM members felt that the only viable route was total self-sufficiency, and the Building Fund was one initiative informed by that notion of uplift.

A philosophy caucus, comprising Moye, Kalaparusha, and Kahil El'Zabar, was chaired by Leroy Jenkins. One of the issues discussed in this committee concerned what Jenkins called "musical intent." As Moye put it,

> We were saying that one of the primary factors in the awareness of the self is to be able to identify what you're doing, for the person himself to be able to say what he's doing, not what everybody else has said. So that's why we felt the need for a label to be created, and that label that we had discussed in the caucus was that of Great Black Music, as a descriptive term of what the AACM music was about.

Despite the reputation of the AACM as a black-nationalist organization, there was considerable and very vocal resistance in the meeting to the idea of "Great Black Music" as an overarching description of the AACM's music—not least because the promulgation of a single label (whatever its provenance) seemed to many to be at variance with the ideals of artistic and discursive mobility. In fact, Abrams, who had to gavel the meeting back to order because of the ensuing tumult, was less than enthusiastic himself about the label. An interview with Ekkehard Jost published in 1982 seems to reflect his point of view. "The only reason we call it black music," he explained, "is to distinguish it from all the musical horrors you have around here. Otherwise we wouldn't call it black music at all. We'd just call it music. Because in the end, that's what it is. It's music that proceeds from the universe. That's exactly what it is! So we can just take all the other names that people put on this music, we can call all these names and throw them in the garbage and let them stay there.[6]

The second aspect of the philosophy caucus report—what Jenkins reported as "the social, which is, the black and white issue"—was arguably even more explosive. As Kahil El'Zabar put it, "We brought this up yesterday, and we had come to the point where I had stated about our ethnic purity." "Ethnic purity" was a phrase made notorious by Jimmy Carter in a *Playboy* magazine interview in November 1976, in which he apparently defended the maintenance of "neighborhood ethnic purity,"[7] a remark that was widely interpreted by blacks as cryptically sanctioning and naturalizing what was then called "de facto" segregation. The reversal of this remark to apply to black "ethnic purity," in the form of collective self-determination rather than externally imposed segregation, was clearly contemplated, in this caucus at least. In contrast to the situation in the late twentieth century, in which ethnically exclusive organizations were regarded as part of an overall notion of multiculturalism (even given the attendant dangers associated with the possible revocation of cultural mobility), at this time, the spectre of an all-black organization was still troubling to many. On the outside, as El'Zabar strongly implied, resistance to all-black organizations was asserted; El'Zabar advocated a kind of cryptic strategy in response. "We know this area can become touchy," El'Zabar observed, "and we can develop a policy also in how we deal with this situation. We don't have to go out to the world telling them that this is an all-black organization, because that just wouldn't work."

The idea that members might forge a common front regarding artists' fees was also explored by this caucus, but as Leroy Jenkins pointed out,

> Since the members in this group are so diverse in many ways, we couldn't really put out any basic figures for them to go by, but to try to get the most out of whatever they were doing. . . . It so happens that some of the members in our own caucus had situations whereby you wouldn't expect them to go along with a minimum wage, let's say, because it was necessary for them to take whatever they could get.

The observation recalls the failed attempt by Bill Dixon to convince his fellow Jazz Composers Guild member, Archie Shepp, to refuse a major-label recording contract. The range of fees that AACM artists were commanding at this time could be wide indeed—from the major-label recording contracts to which both the Art Ensemble and Braxton were signed, to the loft events in New York City, as well as the AACM events being self-produced in Chicago by the younger, emerging members with almost no industry or grant support. In that context, redefining and maintaining collectivity was made much more complex. In general, however, the meeting resonated with the members' ongoing belief in the efficacy and desirability of combining individual and collective strategies. The issue of publishing seemed directly related to this belief, as Henry Threadgill's caucus report made clear. "First thing is that we form a cooperation of all the publishing companies that we have in the AACM," Threadgill declared. "We can form a large enough account where it becomes attractive to large rights-collecting organizations."

The increasing availability of grants for jazz music during this period can be seen as representative of a breakdown of borders between high and low culture that was in progress in the West more generally. As a result, AACM experimentalists, who generally were classified by the dominant musical culture as "jazz" musicians, began to receive fellowships from the National Endowment for the Arts. This increased support was undoubtedly spurred by Muhal Richard Abrams, who was now serving on NEA peer-review panels. Moreover, there was little question that living in the New York area constituted a significant advantage for attracting the attention of NEA peer panels. For example, in 1980, artists living in New York and its environs received more than half of the seventy-eight NEA individual-artist grants to jazz musicians given that year.[8] Most AACM musicians were emerging artists, and while finding support was difficult for emerging artists of all kinds, those who were "naturally" perceived as representing "high culture," whether by dint of genre, ethnicity, or musical practice, had greater access to networks that distributed grant support. In this regard, Threadgill raised the very pertinent issue of the gate-keeping functions of genre classifications and labels.

> They shove your music in certain categories, so therefore, certain grants aren't available to you. Number one, a lot of people had trouble with the National Endowment for the Arts, simply because the music was evaluated by people who said that this music wasn't, quote, "jazz." And even if it ain't, quote, "jazz," it ain't going to be evaluated in terms of no classical music. That's out of the question.

"I was just thinking that what you said was a very good point about us being classified as, our music not being classified as jazz," Roscoe Mitchell responded. "Maybe the caucus could work on that. We could draft some kind of letter to let these people know what we're thinking about, and let them know that I actually feel that they *are* trying to categorize us." In an echo of the 1960s Jazz Artists Guild's call for direct action, Threadgill suggested going further: "We need to apply in every one of those categories, and send all our work in, and let them know that we are AACM people," he declared. "And then, when we get rejections, we got a platform to make a revolt against how our music is being assessed."

The Two Cultures and a New Chapter

> Everybody was migrating from Chicago . . . David [Murray], the loft thing.
> Muhal had finally moved here. We were talking about starting an AACM
> in New York, because we were feeling like, what's going to happen to the
> chapter in Chicago?
> —Chico Freeman

The 1977 meeting's government caucus, chaired by Anthony Braxton, suggested a kind of "national expansion" of the AACM, with chapters in various locations where members were living. As Braxton put it in his verbal report, the task was "to finalize this East Coast charter, and to begin to work for further expansion in terms of, we have members of the AACM on the West Coast, and on various parts of the planet."[9] The written version of the caucus recommendation suggested that the collective should "begin completion of east coast charter and begin work for further expansion."[10] Various versions of a "national headquarters" for the AACM were being proposed, as well as an AACM National Council, which was envisioned as an umbrella board of representatives who would be drawn from all chapters.[11] This board would govern the creation of any future AACM chapters in different cities, and would coordinate joint fund-raising strategies. The first two chapters would be the Chicago and New York chapters; the National Council would be charged with raising funds that could be routed to any chapter.[12]

The original chapter relationship appeared as a "hub-and-spokes" organizational scheme, and perhaps the most contentious issue concerned whether the national hub would be based in Chicago, the organization's birthplace, or in New York, where many of the AACM musicians who had come to prominence had recently resettled. "I feel," said Kahil El'Zabar, a leading younger-generation, Chicago-based member who was serving as the organization's chair, "that Chicago should always be the headquarters for the entering of new members."

"Meaning they'd have to come to Chicago?" asked Roscoe Mitchell.

"Right."

Kalaparusha, now living in New York, responded with alarm, "That's not possible," amid the general tumult that El'Zabar's remark elicited. "Point of order," Abrams declared above the uproar. The debate over governance brought a major and growing tension within the organization out into the open. With the departure from Chicago of so many older members, "we were left without certain kinds of group experience," recalled Douglas Ewart. "The AACM had to regroup, to come of age. Anybody that had been there for any length of time, they had to then come forward with whatever knowledge they had acquired over the years. We did come together, and we were able to maintain the school of music. We maintained the concert series."

Indeed, by 1977, those who were based in Chicago, particularly the younger musicians, had become used to working independently, and had begun to rethink the institutional aspects of the AACM. In effect, from their point of view, the collective was now being led by a new generation. Edward Wilkerson, who became chair in late 1977, observed later that "our thing was like, someone is passing the torch on to us and we have to maintain the torch." More pointedly, Iqua Colson observed that "there was a New York contingent of folks who had been in and out, but there had been enough of us in Chicago doing things so that we kind of had an idea of how things should go."

Among the first of this new generation to arrive was drummer Dushun Mosley, who was born in 1948 in Chicago Heights, Illinois, in the St. James Infirmary. "Yes, the one in the song," Mosley laughed in our interview. "That was the only place you could have black children in that area of the South Side in that day."[13] His mother studied "comptometry," a special skill suited to the Victor Company's keypunch machines, whose trade name was "Comptometers." For the most part, however, she raised her children at home rather than entering the workforce. Mosley's father was a construction contractor who built his own house, as well as a motel in Chicago Heights.

Mosley himself was brought up in Phoenix, Illinois, the same area that gave birth to his second-wave AACM contemporary, Art Turk Burton. Like Burton, Mosley also remembered the White Rose Tavern, which was only a few blocks away. Mosley's grandfather played piano, his grandmother played banjo, and his father was a blues and jazz drummer who even played with Muddy Waters on occasion. "We used to listen to a lot of Stan Kenton, a lot of Miles Davis, Erroll Garner," remembered Mosley, who originally wanted to play trumpet in the school band. His mother demurred at the expense, reminding young Dushun that a full set of drums was already in the house. "So I said, OK, I'll play drums."

By his own estimation, Mosley "grew up fairly comfortably." When he was sixteen, the family sold the Chicago Heights hotel, generating enough capital to acquire 170 acres of land near Fenwick, Michigan, where his father established one of the first resort hotels after Idlewild for African Americans in the area. Mosley started his own band in high school, playing "stuff by Ramsey Lewis, Dionne Warwick, and Herb Alpert" at school dances and even the odd bar. Even so, "it was tough on us trying to assimilate. You couldn't get a job in the town at the local stores. I remember not being able to date—no dating. I knew not to date, because . . . [laughs]. Finally in my last year we did find a black family within about sixty, seventy miles, so I finally had a date."

Mosley considered music as a career, but his first experiences, like Lester Bowie's before him, were sobering.

I was in the "B" band at Motown, which played for the Whispers and some other groups. We would do Motown revues at these small towns, like Kokomo, Indiana. I was nineteen, twenty years old. We toured with these guys, which was an experience that let me know that I didn't want to do that. You rehearse with these guys the day of the concert. People would be coming in and we would be behind closed doors trying to rehearse these steps. You look the way the Motown people looked. You put on costumes, outfits.

"They put the whole band in one hotel suite, along with all of our instruments," Mosley marveled. "Luckily, the manager had smarts enough to say, look, we want to have our money up front before we go on tour. That was the last money we saw." Mosley also played with guitarist Grant Green, as well as rock bands and jazz-rock fusion groups. "I had a big 'Fro, played Cream, Jumpin' Jack Flash. They had the big Marshall amps, and I remember that I had to put cotton in my ears, because it was so loud, I couldn't hold my drumsticks." In the end, Mosley decided to study technology, eventually earning a degree in computer science from Michigan State University in 1975. While there, musical change came in the person of Roscoe Mitchell, who had moved to Michigan in the early 1970s. Mitchell was in residence at Michigan State, at the behest of faculty member and computer musician David Wessel. "Roscoe began to organize this new music I had never heard before," Mosley recalled. "The first time I remember looking at Roscoe's music, I just didn't know what it was [laughs]. "3 X 4 Eye," I said, what is this?[14] It was a whole new experience that I took to like a duck in water." Mitchell's initiative and that of the young musicians around him led to the formation of a new organization, the Creative Arts Collective.

> Roscoe actually started it. The first meeting was Roscoe, [pianist] Henry Butler, myself, Kenneth Green, Spencer Barefield, Tony Holland. Also, Les Rout was there. Of course, Roscoe already knew how to do this by being in the AACM, so he laid down some guidelines. He helped us lay out things like by-laws, so we had some guidance in doing this, because we knew nothing.

Like the AACM, the CAC held regular meetings, followed a collective-governance model, and was chartered as a nonprofit, tax-exempt corporation. "We wanted to be as extraordinary as the AACM," said Mosley. "We knew that the AACM had a huge great caliber of musicians, and we felt that we had a good caliber of musicians too, and we were trying to hold to that." The early days of the CAC culminated in a joint AACM/CAC concert at Michigan State University, organized by Mitchell and Wessel, with seven Mitchell compositions for the most diverse formations. "We were in awe of you guys," said Mosley. The vagaries of the musician's life, however, can place strains on any geographically situated group. "A lot of people moved away, several people graduated," noted Mosley. "Henry Butler went back to New Orleans." Nonetheless, through various changes in personnel and structure, the CAC, under Barefield's leadership, continues to present events as of this writing in 2005 . Mosley himself moved to Chicago in 1976, with the goal of becoming a studio musician, "but in '76, that whole thing started breaking up. By '77, '78, it was all gone." In 1977 he became an AACM member. His earlier connections with the AACM had already led to his becoming part of the Colson Unity Troupe, which made its first recording with Mosley in 1978.[15]

Form and Funding: Philanthropy and Black Music in the 1970s

By this time, Abrams was already well known at the National Endowment for the Arts, where he was serving on the jazz peer-review panels. As a Chicagoan who was identified with experimental music, yet who was respected by the ancien regime, Abrams was uniquely positioned to take a leading role in guiding the broad changes in both the demographics and the aesthetic directions of the panels that gradually took place.

Black musicians in particular took note of the extent of the racialized basis upon which both public and private arts funding was distributed in the United States. It can fairly be said that in the 1970s, private philanthropy lagged well behind Southern lunch counters in responding to the desegregation efforts of the previous decade. Meanwhile, both the university composer system of the 1960s and the private foundation subsidy system were regarded, both by their supporters and many of the almost exclusively white beneficiaries, as forestalling wholesale assaults on Western civilization by barbarians at the gates. In the 1960s and 1970s, jazz-identified musicians were undoubtedly the least well supported of those musical artists for whom the term "art," with its concomitant membership admission to well-endowed funding circles, was said to apply. Unlike other forms of American music, private foundation support for jazz (and black music more generally) was practically nonexistent.[16] The most prestigious award, the Pulitzer Prize, was completely closed to jazz-classified improvisors and composers; no black composer had ever won the award.

One small exception was the Guggenheim, which by 1971 had given just eight of its important awards to jazz-identified artists. A demonstration in front of the foundation's New York offices in 1971 was headed by the Jazz and People's Movement and Black Artists for Community Action, a group headed by Archie Shepp. The demonstrators called for an end to "the obvious and blatant racist policies" of the foundation, which was accused of excluding "artists representative of the black culture and the black experience." The fact that of the many awards given by the foundation each year, just three had gone to black musicians, including Ornette Coleman, George Russell, and Charles Mingus, was seen as evidence of a "policy of tokenism designed to assuage and silence the black community."[17]

Thus, during the 1970s, the National Endowment for the Arts developed into a critically important source of support for jazz and its offshoots. As Muhal Richard Abrams remembered, "In terms of jazz, we knew that the NEA was about the only funding source. We found out that other entities had in their guidelines that they did not fund jazz. . . . The notion was that jazz was public entertainment, and it was commercially able to support itself." Abrams's experience finds support in the contemporary scholarly literature. For instance, Paul DiMaggio, one of the major research sociologists of art, found that up to 1986, "only a small share of the foundation dollar goes to experimental arts organizations, minority arts organizations, artists, or community-oriented organizations."[18] Of course, this provided another reason for yet another generation of musicians to attempt to remove themselves from the already economically disadvantaged "jazz" label. As Abrams put it, "It's still used for racial purposes, to say, this doesn't deserve what concert music deserves. They make that distinction when they get ready to give out monetary awards. We know that from being on panels . . . they're going to use that word anyway to separate you from the white people."

The first stirrings of the NEA's multiculturalism and regionalism were evident in the expansion of NEA music funding to include a "jazz/folk/ ethnic" section, moving beyond the Arnoldian Eurocentricity that was dominant during the agency's earliest years. Nonetheless, in these early years, the NEA's jazz peer-review panels were practically all male, and dominated by East Coast–based musicians and critics. Moreover, the aesthetic direction of the panels, according to Abrams, was "staunch, hardcore, mainstream bebop." Inevitably, the guidelines for jazz grants, which were written to favor particular aesthetic and methodological directions, were challenged. The guidelines were written in the explicit belief that they fostered the preservation of African American tradition. However, the construction of that tradition, as it was embedded in the guidelines, led to some curious contradictions. For instance, applicants in jazz composition were required to submit work samples comprising at least sixty-four bars of music, realized using common-practice European notation. In contrast, the NEA's "classical" composition panel did not specify notation styles at all, and was therefore presumably open to practices also being explored by jazz-identified experimentalists, such as intermedia, graphic notation, text-based scores, electronic music, sonograms, conceptual art, and other forms of performance and composition—as well as improvisation, a practice widely seen as central to the identity of jazz. Thus, as Abrams saw it, "they had to expand what the guidelines said."

> The guidelines used to describe what they fund—music that's done in the African-American tradition, and that shows proper knowledge about chord changes, etc. . . . We took that out. I said, to some people these guidelines tell them, don't apply. This is the NEA, a government wing. We have to invite all these people in here. The so-called jazz world is producing all kinds of innovations. We have to recognize that. We cannot sit here and resist based on some empirical notions concerning swing and tempo and chord changes. The music has developed out of that into other things.

"It was a heck of a war," Abrams observed in retrospect. "Even though the cats respected me, because they knew I knew all about the mainstream, they still resisted. After a year or so, they started to have more respect for the AACM stuff. They didn't like it, but they respected me. When the AACM stuff came across the table, they wouldn't say, 'Who?'" The fact that jazz-identified composers and improvisors, as with other experimental musicians, were challenging fixed genre hierarchies, and asserting freedom of aesthetic, historical, cultural, and methodological reference, was also challenging the NEA's music panel, which was practically exclusively comprised of white male academic composers.[19] "Anything that came through classical that they thought didn't meet their [requirements]," Abrams recalled, "they sent it over to jazz. With the introduction of the AACM in the process, they started getting requests for music that they weren't prepared to deal with, even the jazz panel. The fact that I was there changed that, because I could be there to talk."

Even as granting practices and infrastructure access based upon racialized genre categories increasingly came to be seen as illogical and untenable, some critics were skeptical about the purposes behind the new dynamics of genre instability. According to Stanley Crouch's 1980 review of a series of public workshops sponsored by the Detroit Council of the Arts,

> The most controversy took place during the discussion on "The National Endowment for the Arts and Jazz," when the question was raised whether there should be a non-idiomatic panel at the Endowment for those musicians who say they don't play jazz and don't know what it is, but are always sending applications to the jazz panel and jump at any jazz job offered if it pays enough, from festival to club.[20]

Nonetheless, as Abrams saw it, "This whole thing opened up for people sending in new music, which necessitated that they get people from all areas on the panel. . . . Being there, I had access to the process, so that I could facilitate getting the AACM its first funding. . . . No question about it, I represented the AACM." As a result, by the late 1970s, not only were AACM musicians regular recipients of NEA grants, but the organization itself, with the support of writer A. B. Spellman, the director of the NEA's Expansion Arts program, was being viewed as a prime candidate for institutional funding. Expansion Arts was founded in 1970 as a multigenre program rather than one earmarked for jazz.[21] Spellman, author of an important book on black music, *Four Lives in the Bebop Business,* had known Abrams since the late 1960s; in 1969, the writer had managed to place an extensive article about the new black music, including Abrams and other Chicagoans, in the otherwise conservative African American–owned national magazine, *Ebony.*[22]

Expansion Arts was one of a number of NEA programs designed with the intention of redressing race-based distributional inequities in arts funding. According to sociologist Samuel Gilmore, the programs sought to "find, evaluate, and encourage high-quality applicants in a pre-selection process that has the added benefit of helping peer panels find appropriate criteria for evaluation." This strategy, which Gilmore called "awareness" in an article on race-based distribution asymmetries at the NEA, was deemed "particularly effective among artists and arts organizations who are outside mainstream arts networks." Further, Gilmore predicted that in the United States, the initial stage in a coming shift from "a single, dominant, Eurocentric programming focus to a focus on multiple artistic traditions," would feature a "transition to a multicultural art world . . . through the emergence of well-sponsored 'culturally specific' arts organizations, through which traditionally underserved minority communities will gradually become more integrated and visible in the art world through identification processes."[23]

The Expansion Arts program's target funding profile exemplified this trend, given its what Gilmore called its concentration on "smaller arts organizations that focus on a minority population, support aspiring professionals, are community-based in a rural or urban area, or are education-oriented."[24] According to Gilmore, Expansion Arts staff "relied heavily on community contact people to find appropriate applicants."[25] Certainly, Abrams was such a contact, and on this view, the AACM appeared to fit at least some of the Expansion Arts program's target criteria. To fully qualify, however, as Abrams remembered, it was deemed necessary that the collective's manner of operation, its business and accounting practices, and its interfaces with other institutions, would need extensive revision.

In some arts funding circles, this kind of expansion, which in the case of the NEA was termed "technical assistance," was seen as the performance of social work, albeit in a higher register than before. Ethnomusicologist Ellen Weller, in an unpublished dissertation on 1990s-era arts funding in San Diego, enumerated the problems of mid-level arts organizations in qualifying for this kind of funding. Weller noted that many granting institutions in the area demanded that smaller arts organizations adopt rigid, hierarchical, corporatized organizational models as a condition of funding. This placed these smaller, grass-roots organizations at a severe disadvantage by forcing them into direct and expensive competition with the largest and best-funded high-culture institutions, many of which had extensive private donor support and could call upon networks of expertise that were unavailable to organizations comprised of people of color. In some cases, according to Weller, the organizations themselves were fatally affected.[26]

In 1979, the AACM moved to a South Side location at 7058 S. Chappel, in a deteriorating section of South Shore, now part of an expanded Bronzeville. The relatively spacious converted apartment allowed rehearsals, concerts, administrative duties, and the operation of the AACM School, even through periodic burglaries and thefts of equipment and instruments. Central to the fortunes of the organization at this time was a still newer generation of AACM musicians who were just becoming active. This generation had a very different experience in the organization from perhaps any previous membership wave, not least because most of the members who had defined the collective's early directions were no longer present on a regular basis. Saxophonist Ernest Dawkins and trumpeter Ameen Muhammad were among the most influential of this newer group.

Muhammad was born Curtis Allen in 1954, in Clarksdale, Mississippi. When his mother, who was "a laborer most of her life," remarried, he became Curtis Chapman, part of a family of nine children. Like another AACM trumpeter, Wadada Leo Smith, Muhammad grew up around the blues. Young Curtis's barber happened to be Wade Walton, the well-known blues performer who was famous for playing a harmonica tied to a brace around his neck and beating out rhythms on the razor strap, all while he was cutting your hair. "When he got finished with your haircut, he would start playing the guitar, or the squeeze-box," Muhammad marveled. "I would just be in awe."[27]

One day young Curtis spied an older fellow in the neighborhood, washing his car. During breaks from the work, the man would play his trumpet.

> He turned and spoke to me, and asked me if I wanted to play this thing. I told him, yeah. I had been standing there watching him, and I heard what was going on inside the sound. I was actually hearing how that sound was being produced. So when he gave me the trumpet, I could blow it, with no instruction. I just knew what to do. He said, you should be playing trumpet. But there wasn't no money, so there wasn't no trumpet.

When Muhammad was in the second grade, his family came to Chicago. "I really grew up under my mom," he recalled. Like Henry Threadgill, Muhammad's stepfather was "basically a gambler. The night scene was his scene, so I guess that's why he was into jazz [laughs]."

> I began to get into jazz because that's what was at the house. In Mississippi I had listened to all the hip gospel cats, Golden Gate, Five Blind Boys, the Gospel Hummingbirds. When I came to Chicago, my mom was into Lou Donaldson and Gene Ammons, Louis Jordan, folks like that, so I started hearing all that stuff. I started hearing Coltrane and different folks, and it just snowballed.

Around that time, the young Curtis met Ernest Dawkins, who was born in Cook County Hospital in 1953. "We smoked our first joint together," Muhammad laughed. Dawkins's father was also Mississippi-born, and despite a sixth-grade education, forged a career as a real estate broker. His mother, who attended Wendell Phillips High School, became an administrator. The family lived a relatively comfortable middle-class life in Chatham, the same community where Kahil El'Zabar grew up—that is, until Dawkins's parents divorced, and his mother took him, his grandmother, and a large array of relatives to an apartment that Dawkins described as "close to what we would refer to as the ghetto," a relatively spacious apartment at 60th and Michigan. This was the neighborhood where Anthony Braxton grew up, and Muhammad joined the drum and bugle corps at Braxton's old grammar school, Betsy Ross. The funds to purchase a real trumpet were still lacking, but his mother bought him a Sears Silvertone guitar. Meanwhile, Dawkins was playing the electric bass.

Curtis and Ernest would spend hours practicing on tunes like "Green Onions." The transistor radio was a fact of life now, and Dawkins and Muhammad were regular listeners, not only to WVON-AM, the local African American "soul" station, but also to Jimi Hendrix, Led Zeppelin, and Iron Butterfly—guitar-hero music. Dawkins was also becoming a regular client of Met Music on 58th Street, the record store that Braxton and so many others credited as a major aspect of their early musical educations. Another important means to musical knowledge involved attendance at—what else?—the stage shows at the Regal Theater. On "official" trips to the Regal, his father would take Dawkins to hear Count Basie and Duke Ellington, but on Sundays the young man would sneak out of church to see Gene Chandler, Jackie Wilson, Mary Wells, the Temptations, the Miracles, the Four Tops, and many others.

Like Chico Freeman, who was just a few years older, the two teenagers, as Muhammad remembered, "lived in a community where it was the Disciples, so we were Disciples, and if anybody bothered us, this is how we came out."

> We had guns that we could go and put our hands on if we needed them. We were more sports-minded than violence-minded, but we didn't let nobody bother us, either. You couldn't get away from it, because folks would come down into your community to do things to you. We played sports and music, and did our drinking and drugging, smoking herb.

In high school, Muhammad was playing defensive tackle on the Dunbar Vocational High School football team, which left no time to join the school band. Dawkins played on the offensive line for Chicago Vocational High School, or CVS, which Braxton had attended years earlier. Dawkins and Muhammad also became involved with the Black Panther Party. As Muhammad noted, "The Panther thing really became heavy-moving after [Martin Luther] King's death. It was not identified with being a gangbanger."

> A peace thing came on the scene after the so-called Prince of Peace had gotten killed, and a lot of the gangs went into a truce bag. That little narrow thread of peace was enough for the people who didn't want to stay in that unstable situation—where you either had to be a gangbanger or a pimp or a hustler or a dope fiend—to escape and be a recognized person in the community who was striving for your own people.

"We read a lot too," said Dawkins. "When they came out with the *Red Book* [Mao Zedong] we read that. We read *Manchild in the Promised Land*, *Soul on Ice*, James Baldwin, Richard Wright. *Jet* used to have *Black World*, *Negro Digest*. They had *Africa World*." The heightened awareness of the importance of community service also fostered critical thinking in other important areas. "We started getting interested in other religions," Dawkins remembered. "We got into reading the *Bhagavad Gita*, a lot of stuff."

Eventually, Dawkins and Muhammad began to explore the tenets of Islam. "A guy introduced the imam to us. We'd talk and read, that kind of thing," said Dawkins. "I read Malcolm's *Autobiography* as a sophomore in high school, and it answered a lot of the things I had been seeking," said Muhammad. "At that point I knew the direction I wanted to go in. Within a year's time after I made that decision, that I considered myself to be Muslim, I started doing a lot of studying." Dawkins and Muhammad began attending a mosque on the West Side of Chicago. "The name 'Ameen Muhammad' was given to me by my peers. It means 'one who strives for honesty and sincerity.'" The imam gave Dawkins the name "Khabeer." In Egypt, according to Dawkins, "they interpret 'Khabeer' as 'big man'—big in essence, stature, but not physical stature." Around 1971, the two young men also met Rasul Siddik, who had come to Chicago the year before. It was Siddik who provided Muhammad and Dawkins with their first exposure to the AACM, which was by that time not only internationally prominent in music circles, but also a well-respected South Side community institution.

The two friends separated for a while when Dawkins, suspended from CVS for various indiscretions, was summarily packed off to St. Emma's Military Academy, an African American school in Virginia. "That's probably the best thing that ever happened to me," Dawkins commented. "It gave me another perspective, and kind of got me away from the neighborhood, away from those influences." The Vietnam War appeared to be waning somewhat, and for some reason, Dawkins's draft status was 1-H, meaning "not subject to processing for induction." Meanwhile, Muhammad secured a football scholarship to Alcorn A&M University, and the student deferment allowed him to avoid military service. Echoing the well-known example of Muhammad Ali, Muhammad felt that "I had gone through stuff like the Panther Party and I just couldn't see going to sign up to wage battle against somebody when a battle was being waged against me."

A different kind of battle was ahead, however. Once more, Muhammad was back in the heart of the Mississippi Delta, but with a signal difference. "I'm used to like, black folks helping black folks and working with black folks," he recalled.

> All of a sudden, I'm around nothing but black folks, but I'm different. You're from the North. They're calling each other "homeboy," and I'm "Al Capone." In 1972 in Mississippi, they were in a time warp as far as I was concerned. Coming from Chicago and having been active in the kinds of things I had been active in, I got down there and it was like it was still the Civil War.

The social atmosphere was further complicated by the seeming indifference on the part of the coaches to the scholarship aspect of the term "football scholarship," particularly given Muhammad's desired choice of major.

> If you were on the football team, you couldn't take any music classes. Those cats like to fell out when I told them I wanted to major in music. They asked me was I gay, and all that kind of shit. So I started asking them about different cats. Are you hip to John Coltrane, Dexter Gordon, Ben Webster? Of course, they weren't, and I said, I don't think you really know nothing about musicians.

"They laughed that under the covers," said Muhammad. "They said, we'll give you the classes that 'you need.'"

> We'd go down to practice three times a day—in the morning before school started, you go at three o'clock when you got out of school, and you went back at seven. You didn't finish until ten, and lights out at ten-thirty. Just like the army. So I told them, I don't have time to study. The coach said, well, what does your scholarship say you're here for?

Muhammad soon left Alcorn for Wright Junior College in Chicago, where he studied music composition and theory, while earning an associate's degree in electrical engineering. Dawkins had returned from military school, and the two began to intensify their musical concerns. Dawkins was becoming fascinated by the sound of the saxophone, and in particular, the music of Chicago altoist Guido Sinclair.

> He played a lot like Bird. I thought, man, I'd like to do that. So one of my friends said, my old man has one of those saxophones at home. You wanna buy it? I said yeah, how much you wanna sell it for? He said, fifteen dollars. Right after that, my girlfriend, her father had a clarinet. I bought that, and then somebody else had a flute, so within a couple of weeks I had a saxophone, a clarinet, and a flute—for about twenty-five dollars.

Dawkins enrolled in the VanderCook School of Music. "I'd only been playing three months," he noted. "They were whupping my butt down there, but I caught up after about a year or two." Financial issues obliged him to transfer to the public Olive-Harvey College, and from there to Governors State, the school that was becoming a major jazz powerhouse under the direction of Warrick Carter. By 1983, Dawkins, prudently, had earned a master's degree in music education. Meanwhile, Muhammad had a clarinet that he bought for five dollars, carrying it around in a trumpet gig bag. He met Rahmlee (Michael Davis), the young virtuoso Chicago trumpeter who had performed with Earth, Wind, and Fire, among many others. Rahmlee invited Muhammad to a concert he was giving at Dunbar, and told him, "I'm gonna blow a vibe on you."

> And sure enough, he did. The next day, there was a group of us, Dawkins and a couple more of the cats, that as a result of hanging around Rasul and them, had begun to learn our scales and theory. My brother—we grew up to be brothers, but I was an only child—was playing trumpet, and I was playing clarinet. I asked him, can I see your trumpet for a minute. So I blew it for about two hours straight. That let me know that this was my instrument. Then all this other stuff from earlier popped back into my head. Dawkins and all of them were saying, man, trumpet is what you're supposed to play. I had about two bucks in my pocket, but I said, if it's meant for me, a way will come where I'll get one.

"The next day," marveled Muhammad, "I got $317 in the mail, an income tax refund check. I went that day to the pawnshop and bought me a trumpet. I've been playing trumpet ever since." By this time, Muhammad and Dawkins were regulars at the AACM School and the concerts, as well as at the Muhal Richard Abrams Big Band events at Transitions East, "Those were the cats that inspired me to want to be in that music," Muhammad told me in our interview. "Rahmlee, Billy Brimfield, Rasul, John Jackson, and Frank Gordon, those were the basic trumpet cats, and Walter Henderson. You and Billy Howell and Steve Galloway, those were the trombones, and Threadgill, Wes Cochran, Muhal, Chico, Gene Easton, Ari [Brown]." Muhammad was studying with both AACM saxophonist-composer Vandy Harris (at the AACM School), and Harris's teacher, trumpeter and composer Hobie James.

Dawkins was studying with AACM saxophonist and composer Charles Wes Cochran, for whom Harris was both mentor and close friend. At the time, Harris, Cochran, and Edward Wilkerson were the primary teachers at the AACM School, and Cochran and Dawkins practiced together at Cochran's studio at the intersection of 71st Street and Cottage Grove. The membership was shocked and saddened when Cochran, a quiet and unassuming man born in Chicago in 1947, suddenly passed away in Chicago in September 1978. "Wes was a Vietnam vet," remembered Dawkins. "That's where they say that he may have contracted meningitis," which eventually felled him. According to his obituary, Cochran spent four years in the U.S. Air Force, then studied music at Loop Junior College and Governors State University. Rita Warford and Adegoke Colson performed at the funeral service, John Shenoy Jackson contributed remarks, and Vandy Harris served as a pallbearer.[28]

Dawkins began studying with Douglas Ewart shortly thereafter, and joined the AACM in 1978. Muhammad, who was working at Argonne National Laboratories, joined the collective a year later. For Muhammad, the AACM was in line with "my greatest ambition, which was to make an impact within my own community. That's what I saw them doing." For Dawkins, "it was kind of like a training ground, because I didn't come in as an experienced musician. I came in more like learning, kind of beginner, intermediate kind of level."

What Muhammad called the "New York exodus" had occurred three or four years before, and for this generation of AACM musicians, Siddik, Douglas Ewart, and Mwata Bowden were influential elder statesmen. Edward Wilkerson, a second-wave member, was serving as chair, following

Kahil El'Zabar. Other active members, part of a second wave, were Adegoke and Iqua Colson, Wallace McMillan, Art Turk Burton, Rita Warford, and Vandy Harris. Also present were early members M'Chaka Uba and Martin Sparx Alexander, as well as Malachi Favors, who lived in Chicago but traveled extensively. Henry Threadgill, though transitioning to New York, was active in Chicago. In these circumstances, a major remaining link to AACM histories, traditions, aspirations, and governance practices was John Shenoy Jackson. "Jackson became our godfather," Dawkins remembered fondly. "Jackson was a big influence on me, because he made me study," said Muhammad. "John Jackson," noted Douglas Ewart, "was our most important elder, and someone that everybody paid attention to."

In the wake of the transition of so many AACM musicians to the East Coast, a rising tide of international interest in the collective soon washed up on the shores of Lake Michigan. Now, journals in Europe and Japan, wishing to see for themselves the birthplace of these new forms, and also to determine how deep the wellsprings ran, were trying to cover new music events in Chicago. This was something new for the international critical community in the jazz field, which to this point had tended toward the understanding that all one had to do to understand the musical culture of the United States was to visit its largest city, New York. The tide even lifted the boats of the Chicago independent record companies Delmark and Nessa, who received feature articles in French magazines pursuant to having recorded AACM musicians.[29]

Articles on the 1978 AACM Summer Festival in Chicago were published in French and Italian. Renzo Pognant Gros's article in the Italian magazine *Musica Jazz* praised the work of Rrata Christine Jones, who danced in the second section of the premiere of my piece, *Homage to Charles Parker*.[30] The writer Brent Staples, then a graduate student at the University of Chicago, had gotten to know fellow U of C student Edward Wilkerson, as well as some of the other second generation AACM members. Staples was writing commentary on the AACM for local media, and developed an insider's understanding of the AACM's second generation. Staples's article on the festival, published in the French magazine *Jazz*, noted that "most of the music for this celebration of the AACM's thirteenth birthday was produced by the second generation of AACM members."[31] Both Staples and Gros highlighted AACM musicians who had spent most of their musical careers in Chicago—the original members such as Reggie Willis, Ajaramu, and Lester Lashley; second-wave members such as myself, Adegoke and Iqua Colson, Wallace McMillan, Evod Magek, Vandy Harris, James Johnson, and

Rita Warford; and a still newer generation represented by Dushun Mosley. Some, like Fred Anderson and Bill Brimfield, were invited to the Moers Festival for the first time that year.[32]

Among the youngest of the third-wave AACM members was Reginald "Reggie" Nicholson, who was born in Chicago in 1957. The young Nicholson lived with his father at 43rd and Ellis, an area that in the early 1960s was only beginning to experience the kind of urban decay that later claimed much of historic Bronzeville. Through his father's job at a local 47th Street grocery store, Nicholson made important cultural connections with the neighborhood. "My father was like a clerk there, and also a delivery boy in the area," Nicholson remembered. The famous Sutherland Hotel was still attracting major musical artists to the area, and his father got to meet many of them.

> One day my father noticed that I was really into the drums, and my first album he bought for me had a lot of African drums. It also had Candido. My father knew him. Candido actually made a hand drum for me, a conga drum. It was real skin, and wood, and you could see the nails around the edge to keep the head on. That was the beginning of me playing hand drums, and drums in general. I used to play along with his records.[33]

Unfortunately, the young boy misplaced the drum. "I couldn't have been more than seven or eight. I was too young to understand the value of it." Soon, however, Nicholson joined his grade school band—but not as a drummer. "Everybody wanted to play drums. I said, aw man, I'm not gonna get a chance to play. So I applied for saxophone."

> I tried it for a little while, then I told the band director, I really play drums. He said, OK, let me hear you. So I played, and he heard me play something on the conga drums, and he said, yeah, you can play. Do you know how to play with drumsticks? I said, no, I had never really tried it. So he gave me a pair of drumsticks, and that was it.

In Nicholson's teenage years, his father sent him to live with his aunt on 77th and Dobson, in the shadow of Hirsch High School, which he attended. "That was the beginning of the white flight out there," he recalled. My father thought it would be safer to go to school out there than to stay around 43rd Street, which was becoming increasingly intense with crime and problems." On the other hand, their new home was hardly problem-free.

I remember we all drove out from 43rd to see the new house. I stepped out on the porch and saw this massive park, you know. So I went across the street, and I noticed this yellow writing on the ground near the entrance. I was curious, so I walked toward the yellow writing and looked down, and it read, "No Niggers." It blew me away. I had never seen anything like that. It was like, painted in bright yellow letters. As we walked around the park, I saw that every entrance had this yellow warning: "No Niggers."

On 43rd Street, the blues and black music had been all around the young Nicholson, but now, recorded music at home and on the radio served as lifelines. "I grew up on WVON—Herb Kent, Butterball, Lucky Cordell," he recalled, "listening to all the famous soul singers—Sam Cooke and Jackie Wilson, Walter Jackson, and all the Motown greats." Nicholson joined the concert band at Hirsch, where George Hunter, who had taught Mwata Bowden at Forrestville Elementary a decade before, was now the band director, performing arrangements by Neal Hefti and Quincy Jones—"my first encounter with playing drum set in a jazz form, a groove." On occasion, he also attended an African Methodist Episcopal church with his mother, but "I wasn't really into it."

My father wasn't into it. He got into the Black Hebrew Israelites, the Black Hebrew sect. Actually, we grew up as Jews—as Hebrews—as kids. He had these mezuzahs. Each one had a little scripture on it. We never ate pork. He was always into the Jewish beliefs, but he never followed the whole traditional way of honoring Jewish holidays. He would always say that the black Jews were the true chosen people.

Nicholson was already excited about playing drums, but a chance encounter in his new and rapidly changing neighborhood, when he was around eleven or twelve years old, seemed to consummate his engagement. "Three houses down, I used to always hear this guy playing on the drum set. One day I struck up the nerve and went to the back of the house, and there was Brother Su-Ra." Formerly known as Paul Ramsey, then Paul Ramses, this highly respected musician and artist was a member of the AACM for a brief period during the 1970s, and again in the early twenty-first century. "In terms of learning jazz and how to play on the trap drum set, Su-Ra was the main influence on me," Nicholson affirmed. "I used to take my conga drum down and play along with him. I was very shy, and it took a lot for me to ask him questions. I'd sit and listen to him and watch him. He had incense blowing all the time, and he had these grains and health food all around the house."

Later, Su-Ra switched to conga drums, which he pursued extensively during his period of association with the AACM. By this time, Nicholson had begun playing traps, and Su-Ra encouraged him by letting him play his trap set. Nicholson eventually became part of a neighborhood band, playing tunes by the Ohio Players; Earth, Wind, and Fire; B.T. Express; Mandrill; Chicago; Blood, Sweat, and Tears; and "James Brown, naturally. 'Cold Sweat' was my first drum solo I had to learn. I was into Parliament/Funkadelic. Jimi Hendrix was the ultimate, Buddy Miles. I was into rock, Led Zeppelin, Iron Butterfly, Yes, Black Sabbath, Frank Zappa, all those crazy periods of music. Pink Floyd, Grand Funk Railroad. 'In-a-Gadda-da-Vida' was the other drum solo I had to learn. [Sings] Ba-DUM! Bu-Be-DUM!"

Nicholson's progression as a musician reflects the autodidact tradition that lies at the root of so much American improvisation. "I never had a private teacher," he observed. "I guess Su-Ra was the closest, but he never really showed me anything. He'd just let me get on the drums and play. He never showed me what to play or how to play it. I'm indebted to him." Nicholson learned enough from Su-Ra to obtain a music scholarship to Chicago State University. After a brief detour as a business major at the behest of his father—"Parents always do that, I guess [laughs]"—hanging around the recital hall sparked a longing for music study. With the support of his dad, Nicholson started a program in music education. Cutbacks in the program, however, obliged him to switch his major to performing arts, graduating in 1981 with percussion as his area of concentration.

The percussion teacher was Hal Russell, the founder of the NRG Ensemble,[34] and one of Chicago's most intrepid experimentalists. "I didn't know until later that he was the guy responsible for NRG," said Nicholson. "He was really strict with the lessons. He had this really eccentric way of teaching, but it was really fun. He did a concert at the school one time with his band, and that's when I realized that he was *out*." Saxophonist Bunky Green was the jazz teacher, and for Nicholson, his presence raised the bar in terms of his study of the idiom. Green led Chicago State's popular jazz ensemble, and after a period of apprenticeship, Nicholson became the number one drummer in the ensemble. He also performed in the concert band under Marcellus Brown, a classical trumpeter—"very technical, very precise, and he took the time to rehearse the parts. He made sure that we played our parts correctly. He was a very serious cat, and I admired that."

Nicholson began performing around the city, and around 1978, a friend recommended him to Rita Warford and Mwata Bowden, leading to his first performance encounter with AACM musicians. The concert, which also featured M'Chaka Uba on bass, took place at the University of Chicago's Blue Gargoyle, which was now hosting second-wave AACM musicians. "This was my first encounter with really playing, like, free," Nicholson remembered.

> I came in and asked Mwata and Rita, what do you want from me? They said, just play. Doing that first gig with Mwata and Rita made me realize that music does not have barriers. It kind of made me open up more to the idea that you could express yourself without being structured in a traditional sense. It turned my whole life around.

Bowden and Warford sponsored Nicholson for AACM membership, and in 1979, he became a member: "I'll never forget the day I got my letter from John Jackson." Nicholson was one of the first of the new generation of AACM musicians who had never met founder Muhal Richard Abrams or any of the first-wave members. "I had no idea what the AACM was about. I was only familiar with the people who were around."

Nonetheless, Nicholson became one of the few third-wave AACM musicians who worked extensively with the first wave.

> That's how I got in touch with the members who weren't there any more, by playing in their bands when they came through Chicago. I got to play with Muhal, Threadgill, and Amina, Joseph Jarman. I learned their music and their concepts. Then I got more into listening to the music after I had experienced playing the music. It was like a crash course with each member that I worked with. When I first worked with Braxton, with all these symbols and directions, I said, man, what is this?

During the late 1970s, Douglas Ewart, one of the first students in the AACM School, gradually emerged as a highly influential leadership figure in the Chicago Chapter. In 1980, Ewart became AACM chair, and Muhammad was voted in as vice president. Now an experienced composer and performer with an international reputation, Ewart began to be selected for NEA peer panels. Reflecting the broadening of the NEA peer-review processes, Ewart first served not on jazz panels, but on "new music" and interdisciplinary panels. "I was being schooled in how one operates in the world of funding," said Ewart. "You get to meet people, and the association's name was growing."

One of the first and most essential tasks Ewart and Muhammad faced was the reconstruction of the AACM financial records, which were in extreme disarray. "When cats left Chicago, this New York exodus, as it has been termed in history," Muhammad noted, "it's not like they said, A, B, C, and D have to be done, and we're leaving this in your hands."

> On an organizational level, we were attempting to make our structure more viable for the sake of funding. We had put a lot of time into getting things acceptable and accredited—not just for the sake of making our community a certain thing, because in our own hearts we knew what our community was and is. It was being able to stretch the boundaries of what we do, so that we could be able to do more in our community.

At the same time, Muhammad's sharp critical eye connected the struggle for arts funding with a species of minstrelsy. "You had to put on, like Bert Williams did, blackface," Muhammad opined. "Bert Williams got paid for putting on blackface, where he wouldn't have gotten paid for coming out there in his own black face. I said that to a group of folks on a panel, man, and they were like, get that shit out of here."

Following the recommendations of the 1977 caucuses, between 1978 and 1985 an AACM New York Chapter began to take shape, including New York and East Coast–based musicians such as Abrams, Henry Threadgill, Fred Hopkins, Lester Bowie, Leroy Jenkins, Joseph Jarman, Anthony Braxton, Kalaparusha, Chico Freeman, Frank Gordon, Steve McCall, Amina Claudine Myers, Leo Smith, John Stubblefield, and me.[35] On January 24, 1978, according to an internal memo written by AACM chair Edward Wilkerson, various East Coast–based AACM members met (probably in New York) to finalize the results of 1977's government caucus. Wilkerson's six-point memo, in apparent response to a New York Chapter communication, reflected the sense of an AACM meeting held in Chicago on February 14 in setting out points of disagreement between what was now called "the Chicago Chapter" and the emerging "New York Chapter."[36]

In particular, the Chicago membership, pointing to the government caucus's written report, objected to the New York meeting's contention that approval of its new members need not be secured from Chicago, a point of contention that had already emerged in the 1977 national meeting. From the Chicago Chapter's point of view, a New York Chapter would be a subsidiary to a national AACM headquarters based in Chicago: "This concept of having a national chapter in Chgo. with various subsidiary chapters is very important to establish early in the development of the first regional chapter."[37] The New York Chapter, however, explicitly challenged both the hub-and-spokes model of organization, and Chicago's attempted assignation of New York's board, eliciting strong disagreement from the Chicago-based membership:

> On _____ a letter was sent to Muhal Richard Abrams specifying board members for the New York Chapter. This procedure is well within the guidelines outlined in POINT I H of the CAUCUS RESULTS. In a meeting between the Chicago Board and MUHAL RICHARD ABRAMS acting as representative for the New York Chptr. he stated that the Chicago Chapter should not do this. We disagree with the manner in which our suggestions were totally disregarded.[38]

Moreover, Wilkerson's letter appeared to intimate that the New York Chapter's action was taken without the full consent of all its members: "Various members from New York have informed us that they had no knowledge of the first New York Meeting." In any event, it is not clear from the documentation just how New York's board was selected, but the Wilkerson memo referred to a New York Chapter leadership comprised of Abrams (chair), Steve McCall (vice chair), Leo Smith (treasurer), and Leroy Jenkins (recording secretary).

Probably the most contentious of the points in the Wilkerson memo, particularly in the highly competitive environment of New York, was the Chicago Chapter's fifth point:

> The Chicago Chapter therefore advises the members in New York to hold off temporarily on the solicitation of any national funds. Further study of the relationship of the two chapters and applications for grants must be undertaken in order to avoid any blunders, which might affect our ability in the future to receive grants. Contact will be made soon with the New York Chapter to begin study of this complex and important problem.[39]

Reading the documentary record shows that whatever dislocations that existed between the two chapters regarding governance were resolved by

1980, when NEA Expansion Arts, which at Abrams's suggestion had identified the AACM as a candidate for reorganization, provided funds to engage endowment-approved consultants. These consultants, working together with AACM musicians based in both Chicago and New York, helped the AACM set up its first National Council, as well as the New York Chapter's state charter and its federally tax-exempt, 501c3 status with the Internal Revenue Service, a necessity for arts organizations by the early 1980s.[40] Thus, in final realization of the initiatives first discussed at the 1977 national meeting, the National Council of the Association for the Advancement of Creative Musicians was chartered as a nonprofit, tax-exempt corporation by the State of New York in November 1982. Signatories to the charter included East Coast–based members Chico Freeman, Amina Claudine Myers, Frank Gordon, Joseph Jarman, Leo Smith, Fred Hopkins, Henry Threadgill, and Muhal Richard Abrams, and Chicago-based members Famoudou Don Moye, Iqua Colson, and Adegoke Colson. In addition to the original nine AACM purposes from 1965, the National Council's objectives were:

- To function as the policy making, chartering, regulating, and general coordinating body for the various chapters of The Association for the Advancement of Creative Musicians (AACM)
- To aid in fund development for AACM chapters
- To develop and secure funding for AACM programs with National and International Focus
- To carry out the program and organizational mandates established by the membership.[41]

Three years later, the National Council was similarly certified at the federal level.[42]

In the NEA's funding model, subsidies were in fact going both to the organization being assisted in its expansion, and to high-priced and presumably well-trained consultants who were to lead the process. Thus, by May 1980, while no musicians in the organization were receiving salaries, and no portion of the NEA assistance was earmarked for artistic production, the AACM suddenly had an NEA-funded administrator-fundraiser. The formal agreement for the position specified a thirty-hour workweek, ten paid vacation days per year, sick leave, and salary continuance in the event of hospitalization. The duties for the position included audience development, concert promotion, budgeting, and staff management, the preparation of quarterly reports, and fund-raising, for which, in addition to the salary, the administrator would receive 10 percent of the funds raised. The powers of the office also included hiring and firing of administrative staff as needed, with the approval of the AACM's board of directors.

The musicians were nothing if not relieved at having these new resources placed at their disposal. "When we got the administrator, it was like, whew, we don't have to do that, too," remembered Ameen Muhammad. In fact, the corporatization of the musicians was proceeding apace. The organization experimented with sending member artists "performance evaluations," with categories such as "attendance," "revenue generation," "administrative functioning," "project development" and "task completion ratio."[43] In July 1980, the NEA-funded consultant convened a five-day meeting in Chicago, with Muhal Richard Abrams, Douglas Ewart, Edward Wilkerson, saxophonist Light Henry Huff, Kahil El'Zabar, and the AACM's administrator in attendance. A twenty-five-page outline of the meeting's agenda, complete with complex, tree-structured charts, covered such items as the nature of nonprofit corporations, tax exemptions, fund-raising, budgeting, accounting, contracts, personnel management, audience development, market analysis, public relations, board development, community organizing, governance, facilities and real estate, and much more. Curiously, a two-year budget projection amounting to nearly $150,000 included funds for various administrative personnel, as well as for rental of concert spaces, but nothing at all for artists' fees and expenses, or the purchase of instruments for the AACM School.[44]

Nonetheless, this corporatization could be seen as an attempt to realize two of the long-standing stated purposes of the AACM. Certainly, this kind of work could serve to "increase mutual respect between creative musicians and musical trades persons." If creative musicians were shown to be not only capable of performing at a high level, but also equally facile with complex business matters, the organization's members would be less susceptible to music industry rip-offs. More important, a kind of moral transformation was also at work. The notion that musicians were "taking care of business" was considered to be not only a pragmatic strategy, but also a good in itself—an adoption of the classically American/Puritan work ethic that would, in the words of one of the AACM purposes, "set an example of high moral standards for musicians and . . . uplift the image of creative musicians." Not all musicians, however, were equally capable in the ways of corporate administration. As a result, the idea was developing within the organization that those who were more capable would take care of the organization's operation—in DuBoisian terms, a kind of AACM "Talented Tenth." Eventually, it was envisioned, this leading group would be able to implement an organizational structure that would permit the artists to totally recuse themselves from business matters. Musicians would create, and administrators would administrate—an entirely natural division of labor on this view.

Strains, Swirls, and Splits

The Chicago Jazz Festival, founded in 1979, quickly grew into one of the largest such events in the United States. Upward of fifty thousand people would lounge in beautiful Grant Park to hear local and national artists, even braving the park's typical evening onslaught of aggressive lakefront mosquitoes—perhaps a legacy from the city's past as what the Algonquin Indians termed "the onion swamp." The festival featured completely free admission, and the local NPR outlet, WBEZ-FM, broadcast the festival from start to finish. That year, a series of entrepreneurial conversations developed among AACM members Kahil El'Zabar, Adegoke Steve Colson, and Iqua Colson, joined by El'Zabar's then spouse, Kai, and three friends, businessmen Henry Rock, Bruce Montgomery, and Robert Johnson. "The idea was simple, you know," remembered Iqua Colson. "There's fifty thousand people on the lake in Grant Park at this jazz festival. It's eleven o'clock at night and they're all hepped up and want something else to do."

"And they didn't pay any money to listen," added Adegoke Colson, "so whatever money they've got, they've still got it."

"So let's give them something to do," concluded Iqua. The group felt that the Chicago festival at that time was very nearly closed to the kinds of music represented by the AACM. "They might put one or two of 'us' avant-gardist-types," said Iqua, "but basically they were going for a more traditional thing." The parties to the conversation decided to found a new organization to sponsor performance events. Called Forum for the Evolution of Progressive Arts, or FEPA (pronounced *Fay*-pah), the new organization's first brainchild took place in conjunction with 1979's Chicago Jazz Festival. FEPA's "Underground Festival" took place at a local performance space immediately following the close of each night's Grant Park festivities. Antecedents for the Underground Festival included a similar event created by New York musicians in 1972 in response to the Newport Jazz Festival, as well as an event created by the German organization, FMP (Free Music Production/Freie Musik Produktion) as a response to the Berlin Jazz Festival's lockout of European experimental musicians.

The advent of FEPA, however, exposed strains in the collectivity of the AACM, ironically because most of the artists FEPA proposed to present were AACM members. FEPA was heavily criticized within the association, where it was felt that the new group, even though it maintained separate administration and financial remuneration networks, was utilizing—for its own benefit—contacts and resources that the AACM had developed. Further complicating matters was the fact that some of the Chicago-based AACM musicians, particularly those with somewhat more prominent public profiles, were receiving more performance opportunities pursuant to these collectively developed resources than others. Thus, as Rasul Siddik saw it, the new organization's Underground Festival constituted a new and needed performance opportunity for "people that nobody in the AACM was hiring. They weren't getting none of the concerts. The big-name people were getting all the stuff. So, it was musicians trying to work, as hard as it is in the world to work." Moreover, as Adegoke Colson saw it, a kind of hypocrisy was at work behind the complaints. "They got mad because I brought up the fact that we had basically hired all of them," Colson observed. "At one point we had hired just about everybody in the room that was complaining about FEPA. You accepted the gig, and now you're coming back later, mad because we started this stuff."

Kahil El'Zabar, who had worked closely with AACM founder Philip Cohran, had assumed a leadership role in FEPA, both in programming artists and in planning the overall direction of the organization. In fact, El'Zabar had floated the idea of including non-AACM musicians in AACM festivals, receiving a generally lukewarm response.

> No one wanted to do that, but I wanted to do that, so I went and put together a festival, and that was the Underground Fest—the AACM plus other people that I respected, to try and find a different showcase that the city seemed to not do for artists from our community. My whole thing was, somebody didn't want to do something, that's cool, I'll just do it myself.[45]

Moreover, as Iqua Colson indicated, frustrations with the slow process of collective decision-making were compounded by the oft-noted gap between the formulation of decisions in meetings and their effective implementation on the ground.

There was some disgust in the AACM that we didn't make that happen through the AACM, but there was some frustration on our part at having to quibble and argue every little thing that just seemed like common sense, and to go forward, put the egos aside, and just get something done, make events happen that would actually be beneficial to everybody's careers. There were just six of us, and we could do exactly what we wanted to do, and not just feature AACM artists either. We had Von [Freeman], we had David [Murray]. We did Pharoah.

"I could understand [Kahil's] frustration," Douglas Ewart remarked.

Often it took votes to implement certain conduct, only to have those same people who voted not be there to do any work. However, if you were going to rule with the idea that it was an inclusive organization, you couldn't just run away and leave the pack. You had to run away and then come back, sort of like a wolf going hunting and then bringing back some of the food.

By all accounts, the Underground Festival was a smashing success each year that it was presented, and its echoes remained for many years in various "afterfests" around the city. The Chicago-based musicians who were presented included AACM musicians such as Chico Freeman, Edward Wilkerson, M'Chaka Uba, Don Moye, Bill Brimfield, Light Henry Huff, Ari Brown, and Hanah Jon Taylor, as well as noted local artists such as singers Bernard Mixon and Luba Raashiek, and pianist Soji Adebayo, among many others.[46] FEPA endured until 1988, reaching a high-water budget of $140,000 per year, according to El'Zabar, and sponsoring not only music, but various kinds of cultural and academic forums, film festivals, and a magazine.

The resentments surrounding FEPA and other matters finally broke out into the open at another "national meeting," which took place in December 1981. By the time this meeting took place, the already-present gulf in perceptions between Chicago-based members and their counterparts living on the East Coast had come to be metonymized by a new version of the binary opposition of "Chicago vs. New York" that had long informed Chicago musical discourse. Here, "Chicago" meant younger members, or anyone based in Chicago, while "New York," referred to older, more established members based elsewhere, whether they were actually living in New York or not.

The meeting was held in conjunction with the production of the collective's Sixteenth Anniversary Festival. Both the meeting and the concerts were held at Northeastern Illinois University's Center for Inner-City Studies on Chicago's South Side. In attendance and in performance were both Chicago members and New York members Kalaparusha, Muhal Richard Abrams, Amina Claudine Myers, Fred Hopkins, Chico Freeman, Steve McCall, Leo Smith, and Henry Threadgill, among others.[47] Up to this point, the AACM had been able to assimilate radical difference as a part of its strength. Now, however, the pressures of the music industry were seeping into cracks in the discursive wall of solidarity that the AACM had so painstakingly constructed. Nonetheless, the members in attendance had high hopes that this deepening deterioration would be arrested.

"It was the big meeting where we were supposed to get together and unite and move forward," recalled Rasul Siddik, "but it divided us, I think, more than anything. The thing was, the New York members came back with this gangster attitude, like, they were going to control the meeting. That meeting was like the meeting from hell." In Douglas Ewart's recollection,

> When the cats came from New York, they came to point out our inadequacies when they came. The idea was that cats here were still evolving musically, and that the cats there were more advanced musically, and they were more advanced as business people. They were more qualified to lead than we were. It was like, don't worry, we're here to save the day. We gon show y'all how to take care of business [laughs].

"All this time," Douglas Ewart pointed out, "we've been bringing cats back and running the organization. The school was running at full force. We had over forty or fifty pupils, a full Saturday class, from nine o'clock in the morning to sometime in the afternoon. We acquired five pianos."

"They had this argument going on that New York is the business capital of the world," Rasul Siddik remarked. "But Chicago had been the backbone in terms of keeping the [AACM] stuff alive." Thus, as Dushun Mosley pointed out, this perception of disregard for the work of the Chicago-based members led to "really bad feeling among the Chicago group. . . . Even though Muhal and some others had the musicians' status, they shouldn't come back and tell us what we can do." This perception led many East Coast members to a conclusion that unsettled many in Chicago, as Ewart recalled. "The idea was that Chicago would no longer be the headquarters of the AACM. The AACM would be officially moved to New York, because the people who were recognized as being the major part of the association were living in New York. They were the spearheads of this music. That way, it could almost become like a brokerage house for the AACM."

Among the very few Chicago-based members who consistently managed to surface in the United States and international press were the members of the Ethnic Heritage Ensemble, led by Kahil El'Zabar and featuring multi-reedists Light Henry Huff and Edward Wilkerson, and the Colson Unity Troupe, an intergenerational AACM ensemble with Adegoke and Iqua Colson, Dushun Mosley, Wallace McMillan, and original AACM member Reggie Willis. In 1979, the Ensemble and the Unity Troupe became the first of the Chicago-based, post–New York migration AACM ensembles to tour Europe; the next year, the Unity Troupe toured Europe, performing at the North Sea Jazz Festival in The Hague.[48] During a return visit the following year, the group recorded for the Italian Black Saint label.[49]

In 1980, Burkhard Hennen, director of the Moers New Jazz Festival, engaged the Ethnic Heritage Ensemble as part of their first European tour. The Moers concert was well reviewed by Joachim-Ernst Berendt, who commented that "Muhal Richard Abrams's Chicago school seems to have an endless capacity for finding new talent."[50] Perhaps in the wake of this and other positive notices, in 1981 Hennen's Moers Music label released the EHE's first recording, *Three Gentlemen from Chicago*.[51]

The musicians of the ensemble were presented in a French magazine as "the third generation of the AACM" ["la troisième generation de l'A.A.C.M."], and for the writer of the review, who hadn't heard of the group before their appearance in a local club, the newcomers' bonafides seemed assured by the very fact of their membership in the collective: "The AACM of Chicago, of which they are part (Kahil El'Zabar and Edward Wilkerson were presidents) has already proved itself, and this 'label' is now a guarantee of quality."[52] This theme of the name "AACM" as a mark of quality music, also noted by Ekkehard Jost, was continued in another rave French review of the ensemble. Calling their work "a limpid music, as if born from the depths of eternity but trembling with emotion and deeply original," the writer explained that there was "nothing surprising about that: the three musicians come from Chicago, two coming from the third generation of the AACM."[53]

Still, it was beyond question that the public (and particularly the music industry) image of the AACM at this time was bound up in large measure with the names of those who had made the treks to New York and the European continent. For the most part, local and national press reviews of Chicago-based members between 1977 and 1983 were few and far between, a fact that contributed to Amina Claudine Myers's perception in our interview that "most people, when they think about the AACM, they think about the older members, like Braxton or Muhal. They're known more." In Muhal Richard Abrams's reflection, the interface with larger networks in the music industry and among the performance-going public contributed to the dislocations within the collective. "They were just young cats," Abrams said of the younger members. "There was always this jealousy and fear of the cats that went before, that if we come to town, it would overshadow them because people knew more about us than them, or people would react to us in a different way. Some of it subsided and settled, fortunately."

Certainly, younger members did not feel that they had a share in the apparent largesse of press attention and performance opportunities that were coming the way of other AACM members in the wake of the increased visibility that the collective was enjoying. At least on paper, New York members were thought to be doing better than their Chicago-based fellow collectivists, even as Amina Claudine Myers cautioned, "The younger people—I don't know, they feel like they're left out. They think that we're up here getting all the work and doing so much, but we're all struggling up here." Indeed, all was not sweetness and light, even in Europe. The important Italian jazz critic Arrigo Polillo, who was probably unaware of the collective's internal generational struggles, roundly condemned central representatives of both generations on their 1981 appearances in Milan. For Polillo, the festival in question had

> begun most poorly, with the Ethnic Heritage Ensemble, who due to the fact of having emerged from the AACM, and due to the gullibility of certain cultural operators that we all know, have a most undeserved international reputation. In reality the three of the E.H.E are the poor and inexperienced who are deluding themselves as presenting a refined cultural operation by dressing up as Africans (the leader calls himself Kahil El Zabar) and playing a bit of exotic music mixed together with very bad free jazz. Musicians in the subway could call them colleagues; I concur. The fact that certain people could be writing [about them] here and in Europe (also at the "new jazz" festival of Moers) is indeed an ugly sign.[54]

Of Abrams, Polillo had this to say: "Atrocious disappointment the next evening, with Muhal Richard Abrams, guru of the AACM, confirmed that this association has manufactured—in the field of Afro-American music— more myths about anything that can come to mind. In fact, Muhal played for a hour straight, demonstrating technical poverty and an inconceivable destitution of ideas."[55]

Lacking access to these kinds of reviews, which were equally uncomplimentary of both Chicago and New York, Chicago members at the 1981 meeting faulted their New York colleagues for a lack of reciprocity regarding the sharing of performance opportunities, a dynamic that amounted to a kind of destructive autoimmune response to conditions that neither group fully understood at the time. Here, Reggie Nicholson's view is illuminating:

> You know, like in Chicago, we used to bring everybody from New York in to do concerts. We'd get a budget and bring everybody in to do the festivals. You know, spreading the work around, trying to involve the whole organization in all the activities of the AACM, in New York and Chicago. There was a lot of resentment among the cats there [in Chicago] who never performed in New York.

Most of the Chicago AACM members present at that meeting, including Ernest Dawkins, Ameen Muhammad, Reggie Nicholson, and Dushun Mosley, were not yet part of the organization when members from New York and Chicago took part in the AACM's 1977 "AACM in New York" event at Columbia University. Thus, the divide between Chicago and New York was compounded by the fact that many older members, some of whom had left Chicago as far back as 1969, had little opportunity to get to know younger members musically—either in performance, or in formal and informal settings in which musical, aesthetic, and other kinds of ideas could be exchanged. "I know Douglas, I know you, Light Henry Huff, Edward Wilkerson," Anthony Braxton told me in an interview. "I don't know the next generation. We never had real experiences." For Thurman Barker, it was "Reggie Nicholson, Douglas Ewart, Mwata Bowden. Those are the ones I really know. I know there are a lot of others. I've heard about [bassist] Yosef Ben Israel, and I've even hired him. There's this other guy, Ameen Muhammad, who acts as a roadie for the Art Ensemble."[56]

An important corollary to this dynamic of mutual estrangement was the view of many Chicago members—developed in relative isolation from their older cohorts—that the collectivist direction of the AACM necessarily included a form of intragroup networking that should have extended to "sending for" AACM members in Chicago, in the manner that family members who came to Chicago during the Great Migration sent for their kin who remained in the South. This understanding was further supported by a particular ideology regarding black citizen mobility that had developed during the 1960s: that those who left the "community"—in particular, members of the often vilified black middle class—should recognize their responsibility to "give back" to those who remained at home.

On the other hand, many New York–based AACM musicians felt, in effect, that "those who remained" were in fact free to leave. Nobody brought us to New York, we took ourselves—or so the thinking went. If you want to come to New York, just come, and when you get here, you can become a part of the scene. In fact, Reggie Nicholson did move to New York in the late 1980s. For whatever reasons, however (and of course these reasons are infinitely varied), very few Chicago-based AACM musicians, particularly of the younger generation, followed him in making the trek. As Kahil El'Zabar observed, "I chose not to do it that way because I was living better in Chicago. I didn't feel like going through what I saw guys going through in New York."

Keeping in touch across borders of time, age, personal history, and geography proved difficult in many cases. As Iqua Colson recalled, "I was in the AACM with a nucleus of people for a very long time before I met the whole Art Ensemble clan, because they weren't around. I don't know Dawkins and Ameen like I know Dushun and Kahil." Even in 1998, New York member Leonard Jones (who actually lives in Germany) said, "Out of the people that are in Chicago now, the only ones that I can say I basically know a little bit about are Ed Wilkerson, Kahil, Mwata, and Douglas." To the names of Ernest Dawkins, Ameen Muhammad, and Dushun Mosley, he replied, "Who?"

Some New York members also felt that perhaps the estrangement was mutual. "I think that the younger people who joined don't know too much about us, and we don't know about them," said Amina Claudine Myers. "I know Dawkins a little bit, Ed. Maybe we seem foreign to them." On the other hand, Chico Freeman felt that the onus for any estrangement could have been mutual as well, at least in part.

> When I go back to Chicago, I don't see any of the [Chicago AACM].
> I went back to Chicago and played Orchestra Hall, my band, and Chick
> Corea's band. Sold out. None of them showed up, except Turk [Burton].
> Maybe they don't know who I am. I think they know who I am maybe

on a national level, if they're keeping up with what we're doing in New York, but they don't relate to us as AACM, I don't think. I've never kept in touch with them. I don't call them. I don't know who's president.

"There was never any kind of real communication or real sharing or real exchange, per se, between the Chicago Chapter and the New York Chapter," Ernest Dawkins felt. "When I say real exchange, I'm talking about musician exchange, where we do, say, three workshops with the New York Chapter here and they do three workshops for us there. That was supposed to happen." Here, there is little question that economic factors played an important role. Many Chicago-based members, particularly those who had never left the Chicago area for concerts, or toured with non-AACM ensembles, seemed unaware of just how little infrastructural support was actually available for some of the highly publicized engagements in New York spaces. Moreover, few seemed aware of the costs involved in producing an event in New York, a factor that tended to discourage the kinds of independent concert promotion that had been a relatively simple matter in Chicago.

When all the AACM musicians were active in Chicago, it was a relatively simple and inexpensive matter to engage new, untried musicians, but the costs of transport and accommodations over great geographical distances (for European concerts in particular) often rendered such ventures difficult to realize, particularly when experienced musicians were available just a subway ride away. Here, the aspect of competition between musicians in different geographic locales constituted one factor that tended, in an environment of scarcity, to trump the desires of New York–based AACM musicians to collectivize their efforts with their Chicago-based colleagues. Many musicians (perhaps most) were reluctant to take a chance on hiring people simply because of AACM membership, without actually hearing their music. Moreover, the New York Chapter, which was never well funded, actually produced very few concerts during its early years of existence. Its first concerts took place at Symphony Space on Manhattan's Upper West Side in 1982, barely a year after the acrimony in Chicago took place.[57]

Nonetheless, it was clear that by 1981, the traditional grapevine that in 1975 allowed me to be hired by Anthony Braxton simply on the advice of his AACM peers had broken down. Perhaps inevitably, many younger AACM musicians interpreted the lack of musical interchange as a lack of respect for them as qualified musicians. Nicholson plainly recalled "a kind of resent-

ment for that, toward Muhal and everybody else who didn't really acknowledge the cats in Chicago as the next wave, or generation, of the music." As
Ernest Dawkins mused, "They probably felt that the musicians that came
after them were of a lesser caliber, conceptual-wise. They probably felt that
we hadn't been exposed to whatever they had been exposed to."

At the national meeting, the flap over FEPA reemerged as a source of
conflict between the two chapters—not least because FEPA was now competing for national grants with the AACM, while proposing a lineup that
included nearly exclusively AACM members. Thus, as Adegoke Colson recalled, non-FEPA AACM people "were saying that we would be fighting
the AACM for whatever grant monies were available." Moreover, it was
rumored that questions were raised in NEA panel meetings as to whether
FEPA was a separate organization, or a subterfuge designed to garner additional funds for the AACM itself. According to Ameen Muhammad, "Muhal
and them came and jumped down on us, like it was something that we had
contrived. They came here and lumped everybody in that bag. Then the
shit just exploded and went into some heavy finger-pointing, and airing out
of feelings. Personal attacks began to ensue."

"The actual outcome of the meeting," said Muhal Richard Abrams, "was
a split."

In 1979, the young Janis Carolyne Lane, already deeply affected by the music of the AACM, saw an opportunity to fold volunteer work for the organization into her studies as part of the University of Chicago's MA-PhD
program in sociology. Lane was born in Chicago in 1953. She was raised
by foster parents; her mother was a housewife, her father a police officer.
Lane grew up in Woodlawn, where she attended McCosh Elementary, an
all-black school on 65th and Champlain. Like most of her young neighborhood peers, "I was completely enveloped in R&B and soul music," Lane
recalled.[58] She and her three older siblings loved to dance, and "doo-wop"
was the order of the day, both on records, and via the radiophonic ministrations of Herb Kent, the smooth-talking "Cool Gent" on WVON-AM.
When Lane entered Chicago's Lindblom Technical High School, the school
sat on the dividing line between the white community to the West and a
Bronzeville that was exploding beyond its custom-imposed territories. That
line was slowly being pushed westward from Ashland Avenue to Damen
Avenue—a mere four city blocks—and the dynamics of resistance to what
Lane called the "fight for Damen" often played themselves out on the side-
walks outside the school.

> There used to be fights at 63rd and Damen between the surrounding
> white community boys and the black boys who went to Lindblom. You
> could take the bus without a fight if you walked to Ashland but if you
> took the bus at Damen you were going to have to duke it out. The black
> boys were particularly protective of the black girls who went to Lind-
> blom, so we were never in a fight, but we were often shielded from the
> fights. We were very aware that they were taking place, and that they
> were racially motivated.

As a high schooler, Lane was sensitive to the need to affirm her identity
as an African American. "Particularly being in a physical community where
blacks and whites were fighting over the neighborhood, I always felt, we
have a right to be here," she commented. Lane remembers disturbances
around the school in the wake of Martin Luther King's assassination in
1968, albeit of a rather different character than that which had generally
come down through mainstream media reports. "People were throwing
bricks at us," she recalled. "We couldn't get on the bus to get home."

A self-confessed "nerd," Lane graduated in 1971, and was accepted at
Northwestern University, where several of her friends had also been admitted. She went with the intention of studying political science, with the career goal of becoming an attorney. There were very few African American
students on campus; she knew of future AACM members Chico Freeman,
Steve Colson, and Kris Browne, but they were "far enough ahead of me
that my presence as a lowly freshman was not on their radar." Lane remembers her own sympathy with the goals of the black student protesters at
Northwestern. Nonetheless, "I was very concerned with being here on a
scholarship and afraid that if I didn't go to class and try to keep my grades,
I'd get kicked out."

Lane pledged the local chapter of Alpha Kappa Alpha sorority, the oldest
African American Greek sorority in the United States, which was founded
in 1908. For Lane, sorority membership offered several advantages:

> I needed to have some commonality with, a physical closeness with other
> women. Having grown up in a foster family, having grown up as the first
> person in my foster family or my regular family to go to college, being a
> bit isolated, being working-class poor—I had a scholarship but I had to
> work, and I had to really budget and I had to pay attention to what I could
> have and what I couldn't have. So joining a sorority had a lot of add-ons
> for me—the add-on of friendship, commonality, a sense of being wanted

and needed, and being useful in a community because at that time there was a real emphasis on community service.

"It was a focal point for social activity, particularly in Evanston, where there was still a predominantly white influence." Indeed, having grown up in an essentially all-black environment, Lane's first semester at Northwestern "was very unusual for me, because it was my first long-term contact with a white person, up close and personal. For a whole year, we shared a room together. Prior to that point I had never spent more than maybe a classroom setting, forty-five minutes, with a white person." Her African American student colleagues were listening mainly to R&B and gospel music, but in Lane's sophomore year, Lane discovered the listening library, where Pharoah Sanders's "The Creator Has a Master Plan," became " the most significant recording for me at that time. . . . I would listen to that religiously for three or four hours. I enjoyed the meditative quality, I enjoyed the message from the lyrics. It was different from anything else I had been accustomed to, and I found it very intriguing."

Lane dropped out of Northwestern for personal reasons, and finished her bachelor's degree at the University of Illinois Chicago Circle campus in 1978. By this time, she had discovered another completely new kind of music. At the Whole Earth Bookstore in Evanston, she heard an all-AACM ensemble that included Douglas Ewart, Edward Wilkerson, James Johnson, Hamid Drake, pianist Evod Magek, and bassist Mike Logan.

> The music was fascinating. It was my first experience at knowing that
> I heard all original compositions. It was so different that I continued to
> tell myself that I couldn't leave because I needed to know what else they
> could do that could be any more different from what they did fifteen min-
> utes ago. There was an array of instruments, and I did not know many of
> them. I was mesmerized.

Ewart became an important connection between her and this strange new scene. "I was twenty-three at the time. I can honestly say that I was into *GQ*, tall, dark, black, and handsome," Lane remembered. "So when this person came up to me—much shorter than I was, not *GQ*, quite Bohemian, playing a thousand instruments—I was quite taken aback." Nonetheless, Lane began going to more AACM events. "The challenge of trying to understand even one-eighth of it," Lane remembers, "might have been finally what took me back to hear some more." She heard Air, the trio of Fred

Hopkins, Steve McCall, and Henry Threadgill, as well as Fred Anderson;
the experiences reminded her of "the kind of musical experience I'd had
as a child in church, where I would feel myself get shivers, goose bumps
on my arms. I could close my eyes and sort of rock and feel immersed in
the total sound envelope of the music." As she became closer with Ewart,
whom she married in 1983, Lane could still observe that

> The originality of the music was the major factor in continuing to have
> me listen to it. Certainly somebody else might discuss the budding love
> interest, but I have to say, at the time I felt completely sure of myself and
> what I wanted to do. I didn't stop listening to other kinds of music, and I
> don't think that at the time I would have totally given myself just because
> of love to something that was so "out."

Around 1978, Lane began volunteering at AACM concerts and "mailing
parties," where food, stories, and conversation would be shared among the
AACM's second wave—Ewart, Kai and Kahil El'Zabar, Adegoke and Iqua
Colson, Vandy Harris, and John Shenoy Jackson, whom everyone valued as
a redoubtable raconteur who would regale the youngsters with what Lane
whimsically recalled as "some historical event from a concert or a general
BS story." Lane began to learn about the mission and philosophy of the collective, and took classes with Harris, Rita Warford, and Light Henry Huff
at the AACM School. "I became totally immersed in the sense of the collective," Lane recalled, "and the more they raised money for more programming and other events, the more I volunteered." Soon, Lane became a part-
time assistant to the AACM's Washington, D.C.–based consultant:

> He would make certain proclamations about what had to happen, and
> then I would physically be the person to pull all this together—the pa-
> perwork, whatever written materials needed to be done. After that went
> on for about twelve to eighteen months, there was some disillusionment
> with his performance as a director, and what he was physically able to put
> out, particularly because he was not in Chicago and didn't have day-to-
> day contact with the organization.

Indeed, a sense of unease with the work of the AACM's highly paid consultant was growing. Douglas Ewart felt that "in the end he actually became a burden to the organization in terms of the amount of money we

had to pay him and what we were getting back." In Ameen Muhammad's acerbic recollection,

> We got a lot of positive paperwork—for about twenty thousand dollars. It was very positive, but we didn't have the people to actually make this paperwork do what it had the potential to do. It was just a twenty thousand dollar pile of paper. It was guidelines, the components that you need for a successful organization. He had given us all this hip spiel about how he could put our stuff back together and get us in favor with the funders.

The Chicago AACM leadership was also unhappy with the work of its administrator. "We went on into teaching in the school and playing and running around the world," said Muhammad, "but all of a sudden a year had passed and we didn't have nothing to show for it." A major problem, according to Lane, was that despite the stated duties of his position, "he was not actively working to fund-raise. He was shuffling papers and not being effective in pushing forward to the concert series or the school. He was also not working to get a building, which at that time was a major thrust." Ameen Muhammad was scathing. "The cat didn't do nothing," he maintained. "He was getting paid thirty grand a year, but he didn't have good administrative skills."

"This is one of the first beginnings of where Chicago and New York did not concur," Ewart recalled, "because my feeling at that point was to fire him immediately." Ewart continued, "Because we were getting funded from the NEA, and people felt that the organization had just come into these circumstances, they felt that we shouldn't rock the boat by firing anybody." Nonetheless, Ewart and Muhammad began developing the necessary documentation to justify the actions that they felt were becoming necessary. "We started watching him closely," remembered Muhammad, "letting him know what we wanted done, and seeing how that would materialize. It wasn't materializing, so then we had to really kind of come down on this cat." In late 1982, AACM chair Ewart dismissed both the consultant and the administrator, whereupon the organization discovered, to its chagrin, that "by the time [the administrator] left, the money for administration was gone, and there was no money to hire anybody."[59]

"It was suggested that what I was doing could just as well serve at what he was doing," Lane said. "I had the organizational skills. I had the writing skills. I could write a good letter. I knew how to type. I was people-oriented and I knew how to move among a group of men musicians and get things done." Lane became the AACM's administrative director in 1983. Her duties, according to a letter to the organization from Ewart, included being an "administrator, janitor, errand runner, school administrator, bookkeeper, receptionist, corresponding secretary, etc., etc., etc."[60] Nonetheless, as some had predicted, an ill wind from the NEA did indeed materialize. "We became a case on their docket to be penalized, but we hadn't done anything wrong," said Muhammad. Nonetheless, the NEA decided to cut the purse strings, despite the organization's protests.

> We went through many hours of gathering documentation to prove that, but when we sent it to them, they went through another change of administration, and all that stuff got put on hold. The new administration wasn't interested in going through all these bags of information we had sent them, so they basically left us on a list of not being able to be funded. We fell through the cracks.

The New York Chapter managed to avoid becoming entangled in these issues. According to Abrams, the endowment asked the New York Chapter "if there was any connection between the financial setups of the two chapters. We told them, absolutely not." This declaration, more than anything else, symbolized the split. "Effectively, there are now two separately chartered AACM chapters, with no formal coordination, though there are certainly informal links," Abrams explained to me in 1999. "The AACM is one unit with two different setups. The stability of each unit is a question of individualism. An individual chapter's welfare is dependent on what they actually do themselves in their own community."

The AACM is nothing if not self-critical, and it is this tradition of sometimes painful introspection (even if the standards to which the collective's members often hold themselves are nearly impossible to attain) that Anthony Braxton drew upon when he said to me that even if he knew few, if any, of the younger Chicago musicians, for him, these sometimes turbulent AACM histories invited contrasts with the Wynton Marsalis phenomenon that was emerging during this same period.

> Say what you want about Mr. Marsalis, but I'll give him this: He came to New York, the political scene was set up for him, he went into the position, fulfilled it, did his best at it. But, he also brought in his people, and

endorsed his people, even now. In many ways, the New Orleans guys have shown the Chicago guys what it's all about: solidarity. We did not have that. We came from a more desperate environment, but in the end, we had enough information about what was happening in the East and in Paris. For the dissension that took place in the AACM we have no one to blame but ourselves.

Joseph Jarman, who as an older member was frequently counted as part of the New York contingent, felt in retrospect that the AACM membership at this time was succumbing to the collectivity-killing blandishments of commercialism:

Those issues of class only manifest later on, as the individuals begin to identify themselves with social elements and social forms—their goals of identity, as far as their individuality, their race, and class. This might have happened as much as fifteen years after the input of the organizational consciousness of the AACM, beginning to think in terms of social goals—I should have this, and I should do that. But there's nothing wrong with that, because everyone has the right to pursue their own vision. If one's vision is to be a very wealthy materialist, then one should devote one's effort to that. In music this takes not genius, but manipulable skill, how to make the necessary connections to achieve what it is that we want, who to actually meet and engage a business relationship with. It's things like this that began the expansion and bickering over class and struggle. Prior to this the whole AACM was still a committed, hardcore, philosophically oriented group. But about fifteen years after its founding, we can begin to speculate on why these variants begin to occur.

However, Chico Freeman, another New York member, felt that "it wasn't as simple as a power struggle. There were differences in direction, just finding out who wanted to make certain levels of investment and who didn't, and what people were looking for as a result of their input and investment." For Freeman, a major issue was that "there was no longer the single vision that was there before. The organization was a means to get the same things that it was started for to accomplish. Later, other people didn't have that same vision. They wanted other things." Indeed, perhaps the push for a viable business structure, in a world in which the social democratic arts largesse of Europe was nonexistent, could have distracted the membership from the business of creating music. "That's what I remember during that period," Edward Wilkerson concluded, "a lot of meetings about business, and less and less playing and performing together." Even so, in the 1982–83 season, the Chicago-based AACM sponsored twenty-two concerts that drew an average of ninety persons per event, with a diverse array of Chicago artists, including Vandy Harris, Rita Warford, Light Henry Huff, drummer Avreeayl Ra, bassist Yosef Ben Israel, trombonist Isaiah Jackson, trumpeter Malachi Thompson, and many others. A concert of Muhal Richard Abrams and Anthony Braxton drew an audience of nearly seven hundred, and a two-day AACM Festival drew over twelve hundred.[61] The AACM School held three ten-week semesters during this same period, with an average enrollment of forty-five students.[62]

As Muhal Richard Abrams saw it, younger members were the recipients of a legacy that the older musicians had passed down to them. "Most of those guys got their notoriety from being AACM, from what we had done. People always look to Chicago for the AACM. They saw those guys down there. They started getting trips overseas because they were AACM. They had no records, no way for people to know what they sounded like, except for people who may have passed through Chicago."

On the other hand, many younger members expressed sentiments similar to this one from Dawkins, pointing out the difference between a largely conceptual legacy and one articulated through face-to-face interaction:

> I felt that what happened in my career, if I didn't do it, it wouldn't have happened, 'cause I didn't get much help. I got help from Chicago members, but I didn't get a lot of help from the New York members. The only time I may have played with the New York members is when they came here for a festival or something. I've never been asked to perform in New York at the AACM series, or played with somebody up there.

In 1998 Abrams still felt that the generational shift that took place during these years was inevitable.

> How could you expect the people who didn't interact with us at close quarters to understand what we were about? They could understand what we were about in terms of that which has resulted and has accrued to them as the AACM. They might say, I can imagine what these cats might have been doing to hold this thing together, to bring it to what it is— producing concerts, just the idea of doing that.

At the same time, however, Abrams admitted that "I don't blame them in terms of more communication. We have to take some blame for that too."

"Man, the AACM creates such idealism out of us," Ameen Muhammad observed. "We want shit to be so ideal, but life ain't that way, so what makes us think that the AACM is going to be that way?"

"I don't have any hard feelings or resentments," Ernest Dawkins concluded. "I said, let's move on."

11

INTO THE THIRD DECADE

The 1980s: Canons and Heterophony

> Here I looked around one day, and said, Damn! The AACM's been in
> existence over twenty years!
> —M'Chaka Uba

Indeed, by the mid-1980s the AACM had survived five U.S. presidents.
At the same time, to many observers, the AACM of 1985 barely resembled its 1965 version. Its Chicago and New York chapters were
widely divergent in age, aesthetic orientations, economic bases, connections to the music industry, and connections to local communities. John Shenoy Jackson, the gruff yet jocularly avuncular trumpeter who taught generations of AACM musicians the practicalities
of administration, was still active in the AACM, and also serving as
executive secretary for the Art Ensemble of Chicago, when he suddenly passed away in September 1985. To younger members of the
collective, Jackson, as he was universally known, embodied historical
continuity with its original and founding members. As Ernest Dawkins put it, "Jackson became our godfather," and his passing affected
the membership deeply. As the Art Ensemble put it in their 1969 Paris
recording, *A Jackson in Your House:* "Jackson, that cat is something."

In many ways, Jackson's passing symbolized a renewed coming-
of-age of the collective itself. Particularly in Chicago, younger mem-

bers, many of whom were unknown to the New York cohort, were developing approaches to music and its role in the local community that diverged markedly from their older colleagues. Even more crucially, these younger, Chicago-based musicians were becoming known to the public in their hometown as "the AACM." Local newspaper accounts of the organization were as likely to address the work of Ernest Dawkins, Ameen Muhammad, Edward Wilkerson, Douglas Ewart, and Mwata Bowden as that of the New York–based members.[1]

Ewart had already released a number of recordings of his own music by this time, beginning with the George Lewis/Douglas Ewart duo album in 1979. In 1983 Ewart founded his own label, Aarawak, on which he released albums such as *Red Hills* and *Bamboo Meditations at Banff,* a series of pieces that electronically transformed Ewart's bamboo wind and percussion instruments.[2] In 1985 Wilkerson formed the important bands Shadow Vignettes and 8 Bold Souls, whose first recordings, *Birth of a Notion* and *8 Bold Souls,* emerged in 1988.[3]

In the meantime, in 1982 the New York Chapter had already begun presenting concerts, beginning with a two-day event at the Upper West Side theater, Symphony Space, that included the trio Air, duos by Anthony Braxton and Leroy Jenkins, and Muhal Richard Abrams and Amina Claudine Myers; an ensemble led by Frank Gordon; and two AACM large ensembles, performing pieces by Jenkins, Abrams, Gordon, and Braxton, that included Abrams, Myers, Braxton, Jenkins, Douglas Ewart, Warren Smith, Fred Hopkins, Lester Bowie, Brian Smith, Steve McCall, Craig Harris, Kalaparusha, Thurman Barker, and me. After federal certification of its nonprofit tax status in 1985, the New York Chapter began presenting several concerts yearly, as budgets permitted, in the far more expensive environment of Manhattan. These included an AACM Twentieth Anniversary Celebration in December 1985 that included cellist Abdul Wadud and trombonists Steve Turre and Dick Griffin as guest artists; a twenty-fifth anniversary event at Merkin Concert Hall, one of the leading venues in the city for new music; and finally, its ongoing four-concert season, first at the New York Society for Ethical Culture, and subsequently at the Community Church of New York. The New York Chapter also presented Chicago-based AACM musicians, including Wallace McMillan, Edward Wilkerson, Douglas Ewart, Rita Warford, and Fred Anderson, and its concert series eventually moved to include the work of non-AACM composers, including Warren Smith, saxophonist Marty Ehrlich, percussionist Andrew Cyrille, cellist Nioka Workman, and others.[4] The series also presented large-form notated works by Abrams, Jenkins, Jarman, and me, performed by conductor and composer Petr Kotik's S.E.M. Ensemble.

From 1982 to 1987, I was living in Europe, deeply involved with musical environments in which jazz-identified discourses were absent as a matter of course, or in which the pressure to conform to jazz-historical reproduction standards had not arrived. For those black experimental musicians who were based on the East Coast, however, the situation was becoming more and more difficult, particularly with the rise of the so-called neoclassical movement in jazz, which placed musicians, critics, and audiences on the horns of at least two dilemmas: between tradition and innovation, and between classical music and jazz. Trumpeter Wynton Marsalis, who possessed expertise in both jazz and classical traditions, soon emerged as the leading spokesperson for this movement. Marsalis, who had already won Grammy awards in both classical and jazz categories—in the same year—began working with New York's Lincoln Center, home to the Metropolitan Opera and the New York Philharmonic, to produce a series called "Classical Jazz," a title that seemed tailored to Marsalis's rapidly growing public image. In fact, Alina Bloomgarden, a Lincoln Center employee, had been promoting the idea as far back as 1983; for the post of "artistic advisor" she recruited Marsalis, who in turn recruited writer Stanley Crouch.[5]

Up to this point, a unique aspect of the debate over borders between classical music and jazz in the United States was that its most publicly prominent conceptual leadership came disproportionately from the black experimental music community. A 1987 *New York Times* article by Jon Pareles, viewing Marsalis's double releases of classical concertos and jazz recordings as "superficial" and "a gimmick," framed AACM composers Roscoe Mitchell and Anthony Braxton, along with Ornette Coleman, James Newton, Anthony Davis, and Butch Morris, as "experimental hybrids [who] have to battle on both the jazz and classical fronts," but who were nonetheless key to the emergence of a new synthesis of classical music and jazz.[6]

The alacrity with which this interpretation of classical-jazz fusion was simply swept from the discursive chessboard is fascinating to review. The promulgation of a revisionist canon that emphasized a unitary, "classic" tradition of jazz eventually took on an institutionalized cast with the 1991 creation of Jazz at Lincoln Center (JALC), arguably the most heavily funded jazz institution in history. The JALC approach to the classicization of jazz had its antecedents in many earlier classicizing projects, but this new version sought not to problematize or transgress barriers between jazz and classical music, as the AACM and others had tried to do, but to uphold and nurture them. In a critical discursive shift, the term "classical" became less a description of a musical tradition than of an attitude—one of reverence and preservation. Stanley Crouch, formerly one of the most vocal supporters of the 1970s black experimentalists, had shifted ground by the early 1980s. Influenced by the heroic modernism of writer Albert Murray, Crouch became heavily critical of the new music,[7] and declared in the liner notes to a Marsalis recording of "jazz standards" that the new challenge for black musicians would be "to learn how to redefine the fundamentals while maintaining the essences that give the art its scope and grandeur."[8]

Ironically, JALC's construction of the jazz canon (at least up to 1960) would be fully congruent with that of the first-wave AACM members, who had all grown up revering the same artists—Louis Armstrong, Jelly Roll Morton, Art Tatum, Duke Ellington, Charlie Parker, Thelonious Monk, and others—that the neoclassicists held dear. For years, prior to coming to New York, Henry Threadgill had been combing the Joplin repertoire, Muhal Richard Abrams was mining and recasting stride, and Roscoe Mitchell was making ironic references to R&B. Interestingly, no less a personage than the critic Dan Morgenstern cited Air's reimaginings of Scott Joplin, declaring that "though it was little understood at the time, respect for (and understanding of) the roots of jazz was a key characteristic of the AACM's musics (the plural is intentional) from the start."[9]

In fact, the issue of "standard music" versus "original music" had already been a central aspect of the discussions in the initial meeting of the AACM on May 8, 1965. As Steve McCall noted on that day, "The standard music, we've all played it."[10] Thus, one can imagine the puzzlement of AACM experimentalists when a new breed of New York–based journalists, critics, and musicians advanced the claim that those who had been creating the new music had "no respect for tradition." Curiously, this discourse is hardly to be found in other musical genres. Jimi Hendrix was not critiqued on his ability to sound like Little Richard, nor was Reba McEntire challenged on her ability to sing like Patsy Cline. On the other hand, these musics did not, until recently, witness the kind of radical challenge to traditional modes of musical aesthetics that jazz did. When transgressive musics eventually came along in other fields—punk, techno, grunge, thrash—those critical communities did not, for the most part, critique these musics on the grounds that they did not sound like the Beatles, or insist that they cover a Hall and Oates tune as part of their legitimation strategy. This is to say nothing of contemporary pan-European art music, where present-day composers are not judged on their ability to incorporate the sounds of Vivaldi into their work, though they are free to do so if they wish.

In contrast, the fact that the new musicians of the AACM chose definition over redefinition, by presenting their own music as they had done since their Chicago days, now became an issue for much critical reception, at least in the jazz world. In fact, the presentation of "original music" was now used as prima facie confirmation of a "lack of respect." For some, this "evidence" made the "no respect" claim easier to substantiate than the simultaneous recycling of the older canard that the "free" musicians "couldn't play," since many AACM musicians had worked with some of the most traditionally respected musicians—Mercer Ellington performing Muhal Richard Abrams's Duke Ellington arrangements; Lester Bowie with Albert King; Leo Smith with Little Milton; Pete Cosey with Miles Davis, Steve McCall with Dexter Gordon; Amina Claudine Myers with Gene Ammons and Sonny Stitt; my work with Count Basie and Gil Evans; and so on.

A signal difference between the pre- and post-Marsalis framings of African American musical tradition, however, was that the AACM musicians were taking what was up to that time an unchallenged view—that the jazz music now regarded as "classical" was originally the product of innovation, that is, "finding one's own sound." On this view, the musician's attitude of experiment and self-realization was one of the crucial reasons for the importance of the work itself. A 1995 article on Marsalis in the *New York Times Magazine* challenges this view, accusing those who valorized innovation as appealing to outdated notions of "progress" in the arts:

> Have we had progress in poetry, in the novel, in painting or in dance? I don't think so. . . . The way to strengthen one's ability to tell the difference between progress and evolution is to study the canon—that music which has had the longest and deepest influence—because the canon contains the evolutionary signposts and implies how jazz can spiral outward without losing its identity. . . . One of the most important missions of Jazz at Lincoln Center is to lay down a foundation for the future of jazz by presenting important works from the canon with all the passion and intelligence that can be brought to bear.[11]

While the new canon seemed lacking in a number of important respects, such as the apparent exclusion of the work of people like Ornette Coleman, Cecil Taylor, post-*Ascension* Coltrane and other black experimental musicians, Farah Jasmine Griffin points out that "had Marsalis not struck such a conservative stance, whereby some of the most innovative practitioners are left out of the jazz canon, it is highly unlikely he would have been able to acquire the resources necessary to do the kind of work on behalf of the music that he has done."[12] Certainly, in the severely undercapitalized field of jazz, the advent of JALC, with the massive resources to which Griffin refers, had much the same effect as the introduction of a Wal-Mart Super-center into a community of mom-and-pop businesses.[13] Taking advantage of a regular media presence, as well as backing from major corporations for his music and his JALC events, Marsalis eventually took on a role as authoritative spokesperson for the future of music itself, taking as his primary mission the creation of an atmosphere in which jazz was finally to be treated with "the same respect" as classical music.

Prominent black intellectuals who had generally been associated with progressive political stances signed on. Some, like philosopher Cornel West, did so enthusiastically, even calling Marsalis an "intellectual freedom fighter," determined to "keep alive potent traditions of critique and resistance."[14] Others, like Amiri Baraka, acknowledged a certain ambivalence. In a 1995 German-language interview, Baraka avows that "I want to be completely honest there—I would rather hear Wynton Marsalis in an Ellington concert than what [Lester] Bowie or [Henry] Threadgill do. Even when I value them for certain things that they have brought into being." In the very next breath, Baraka emphasizes the issue of self-determination, which the AACM had also sought to bring forth—an idea with which Baraka himself, with his long history of political activism, had inspired many: "Yes, they [Bowie and Threadgill] should have regular stages too, and I wish that Sonny Rollins had one. But the problem will present itself as long as we do not have our own independent institutions. Until then I can only say: it is to be welcomed that the Afro-American tradition is being preserved by Wynton Marsalis. I would even describe his work in these times as progressive."[15]

Despite Baraka's assertion in the interview that "there is no point on which we agree," on the issue of black experimental music aesthetics, he and Stanley Crouch found common ground at this moment in their disapprobation of black music that exhibited too much "European influence"—a criticism that, given their own (and Marsalis's) use of European tropes, appears particularly curious, even contradictory. Thus, it became evident that this "progressive" motif of preservation and protection did not extend to the products of the black experimentalists. As early as 1982, discussions of black new music were beginning to disappear from the New York "alternative" press. AACM-oriented ideas of diversity, mobility, and innovation came under withering attack, not only from an emerging politically and culturally conservative aesthetic movement, but from the black political left wing as well. As Anthony Braxton noted,

> After the sixties, research and development was X-ed out as being a component of the black creative music experience. It was redefined as, you have to be a legitimate black person, and to be legitimately into the music, you had to have this position and this position, and you had to play idiomatically, as opposed to finding yourselves. Some of these problems were not coming from racism in the white community, as much as from a complex understanding of blackness in the black community. We were rejected by the black intellectuals, not just the young boy and girl on the street listening to Sam Cooke or hip-hop.

A supremely supportive press generally dismissed criticisms of Marsalis's approach to the canon, and naysayers were admonished to (as the title of a 1995 *New York Times Magazine* piece had it) "Stop Nitpicking a Genius."[16] Nonetheless, many musicians were resistant to the new regime. Even as he was being widely touted as an up-and-coming "Young Lion in the Tradition," composer Anthony Davis, who collaborated extensively with a number of AACM artists, expressed the views of many when he was quoted as saying that the notion of "tradition" was being used "essentially as a vehicle for conservatism," and "as a means of maintaining the status quo, of limiting your own personal connection."[17] A number of AACM musicians, moreover, detected the hand of corporate megamedia stirring the new traditionalism's soup kettle. Roscoe Mitchell warned that

> What we've seen happen between the 60s and now is the commercial machine expanding and dominating the scene. . . . We've seen the institutionalizing of so-called "jazz." We've seen a general turning away of new ideas and sounds. . . . [Young musicians] are getting these messages from the media that they should do such-and-such to re-create the tradition. But the tradition will never be re-created as strongly as it was by the people who invented it.[18]

In this respect, Leroy Jenkins's comment is worth considering at length:

In the 1980s, so-called avant-garde music took a fall in terms of concert opportunities and recordings. This has a lot to do with record labels pursuing younger musicians playing music more familiar to the people. Younger musicians who were trained in the colleges. The result was players sounding like young Coltrane and Miles Davis. It was a repeat of people doing things that need to be done; the things I had listened to in my youth. But it was commercially viable to the commercial recording industries. These same executives were raised on this kind of music, so they thought, "this is what should sell."[19]

Indeed, the marketing strategy around the heavily advertised and corporate-supported Ken Burns film *Jazz* exhibited a remarkable marketing synergy, with DVDs and CDs bearing the "Ken Burns Jazz" logo available immediately following the airing of the first episode.[20] Thus, Mitchell was certainly expressing a common view, neatly encapsulated in a 1994 *New York Times* headline announcing a "Classical Jazz" event: "Jazz, Classical, Art, Business: A Series Wraps All into One."[21]

It is worth noting that up to this point in time, Lincoln Center had never been a significant long-term supporter of musical experimentalism; why so many people in the jazz community thought that a Lincoln Center jazz program would be any different might be explained with reference to a certain lack of experience with the histories and practices of this and other high-culture institutions. Moreover, despite Marsalis's reputation as an interpreter in both jazz and classical idioms, his public pronouncements regarding method and canon were somehow essentially limited to the jazz side of his work. Finally, in contrast to the ideologically charged atmosphere on Lincoln Center's jazz side, its classical side tended to avoid extensive public critiques of experimental music in its chosen, European-based tradition. In fact, composers seen as "fringe" elements were quietly supported, even as it was acknowledged that the public was not necessarily excited about their music. Nonetheless, the belief that actually hearing the work might alienate donors was sufficiently widespread that to keep donations flowing, patrons were discouraged from attending new-music events.[22]

In the wake of this changed atmosphere, by the mid-1980s, when one of the new black experimentalists presented an event deemed as falling outside the social or methodological frame of jazz, neither the jazz writers nor the new music writers would cover it. In the jazz press, those among the black experimentalists who "refused to swing" or were "too European" were routinely savaged, with little hope of succor from the "new music" press, which simply ignored them as it had done earlier. Black composers framed as "jazz" who dared to present transgressive new work at spaces like the Kitchen would be covered only when they chose to return to their "natural" home in a local club. As Attali says of free jazz, the work of these musicians was "contained, repressed, limited, censored, expelled."[23]

However, the increasingly interdisciplinary and multicultural landscape in which present-day artists find themselves wreaks havoc with the logic of those who would confine African American musicians to nativist (re) presentations of a narrowly constructed "blues idiom" while arrogating to themselves the right to consider Picasso, Rothko, de Kooning, Proust, Joyce, Eliot, Melville, Kerouac, Burroughs, Wagner, Schoenberg, and Stravinsky salient to their deliberations. Throughout the past century, African American musical artists have pursued an ongoing engagement not only with Eurological forms, but also with the world of art and music as a whole, in full awareness of their position in a world of art-making traditions. As with the work of earlier generations of African American artists, the current generation is free to assimilate sounds from all over the world, even as they situate their work in a complexly articulated African American intellectual, social, and sonic matrix. In this regard, Julius Hemphill's challenge was particularly apt: "Well, you often hear people nowadays talking about the tradition, tradition, tradition. But they have tunnel vision in this tradition. Because tradition in African American music is as wide as all outdoors. . . . Music is much bigger than bebop changes. I don't feel like being trapped in those halls of harmony."[24]

Outside New York, the neoclassical jazz movement never succeeded in marginalizing its experimental predecessors. Rather, a kind of aesthetic pluralism and mobility that included new musical practices was on display around the United States and beyond. Muhal Richard Abrams saw this pluralism as particularly characteristic of Chicago. "People experimenting was not strange around there," Abrams told me in 1998. "Nobody bothered you about that. Everybody respected each other. That's how we were able to develop." Even so, the adoption of an arguably "avant-garde" or "experimental" musical practice as a populist marker of Chicago's innovative soul, equal in historical importance, if not in popular appeal, to such more established Chicago-identified musical genres as the blues, could hardly have been expected by the AACM's founding and original members. Indeed, not only were the Chicago-based AACM musicians spared the vitriolic denunciations to which their East Coast colleagues were subjected, but in the Chicago mediascape, a new generation of local critics, led by Chicago *Tribune* writer Howard Reich, saw the music of the AACM largely as most of the rest of the music world beyond Jazz at Lincoln Center saw it—as one of the most important contributions of the latter half of the twentieth century to jazz, and even to world music history writ large.

In Chicago, media accounts ignored the AACM's internal politics of place, making no distinction at all between New York and Chicago, while portraying Chicago-based AACM musicians—even those who, like Vandy Harris, were as old as some of the departed New Yorkers—as part of a newer generation or "third wave" of the AACM that was continuing its tradition of innovation. In this context, Fred Anderson was becoming a hero to the younger generation, a symbol of the combination of personal tenacity, historical continuity, and radical musical integrity that many younger Chicago musicians, both within and outside the AACM, were inspired by. One reason for this respect was the Chicago community's perception that Anderson had continually sought to put into practice AACM tenets of self-reliance and independence.

A 1979 *Down Beat* article by Sharon Friedman and Larry Birnbaum detailed Anderson's first attempt to create a performance space. The Birdhouse was founded by Anderson and Friedman in May 1977 in a German American neighborhood in the 4500 block of North Lincoln Avenue. For Anderson, the storefront space's reasonable rent, location, and good acoustics were ideal for an independent music space named after Charlie Parker, but his neighbors saw things very differently. Plagued with problems arising from Chicago's arcane and highly racialized neighborhood folkways, the Birdhouse operated but intermittently from its inception. Police doubted the authenticity of Anderson's stated purpose; his neighborhood alderman perceived the jazz music workshop as a place out of sync with the German American stores and Asian restaurants already on the street; city building inspectors "studied" the Birdhouse's zoning and architectural plans and called for expensive renovations. Anderson's legal counsel advised the Birdhouse to maintain a low profile, a seeming impossibility, and faced with rising costs, numerous unscheduled closings, scarce audiences, and governmental harassment, the Birdhouse closed at the end of June 1978.[25]

Beginning in the mid-1980s, "Great Black Music," along with its corollary, "Ancient to the Future," was deployed in Chicago by both musicians and critics in constructing a kind of Afrodiasporic canon, redoubling the AACM's historicity. Moreover, the fact that this movement, unlike the previous historical construction of "Chicago jazz," had emerged from the African American working-class community in Chicago, and by all accounts continued to attract support and respect from that community, powerfully contradicted the received wisdom that the music had no black audience. In turn, this meant that charges by outsiders that the music lacked historical importance could be construed as an attack on Chicago's black community more broadly, even for those who did not personally subscribe to the experimentalist aesthetic. As a result of this unusual conflation of populism and racialism, no amount of pressure from anywhere was going to shake the locally held conviction that the AACM had staked post-1950s Chicago's claim to making jazz history; those who persisted in denying the collective's importance risked losing credibility as authorities on the music.

The phenomenon was part of an overall decentralization of U.S. expressive culture, in which artists increasingly avoided the rent and housing bubbles of Manhattan and Brooklyn in favor of establishing local communities as bases in which they could thrive, and from which they could launch national and international initiatives. Further contributing to the shift in the power dynamic was the fact that AACM musicians, particularly in the first and second waves, had created so many networks outside the purview of the jazz world that the power of jazz world discourses to channel their energies had become circumscribed. In the end, many people felt able to ignore the "Young Lions" and subsequent trends in favor of continuing to work on their music in their own ways, finding support from alternative sectors as musicians have done throughout history.

Great Black Music: The Local and the Global

With the emerging multiculturalism of the 1980s, even the embrace of the term "Great Black Music" by younger, Chicago-based AACM artists did not seem nearly as threatening or radical as it had a generation ago, when the term itself was often construed first as merely a synonym for jazz, and more ominously, as a form of racism. In Lester Bowie's view, however, Great Black Music constituted a broadly internationalist, Afrodiasporic reading of the black music tradition that was, in the words of a 1996 essay of mine, historically emergent rather than ethnically essential.[26] As a result, the term could easily encompass nonblack musicians and nonjazz music within its purview, as Bowie noticed: "This Great Black Music doesn't belong only to the Art Ensemble. . . . Mahalia, Aretha, Woody Herman, Stan Kenton, Duke Ellington, Louis Armstrong, Bessie Smith, all of them are playing Great Black Music, they all have their roots in Great Black Music."[27] Following on Bowie's observation, and anticipating by at least ten years the Black Rock Coalition's (BRC) reclaiming of rock as a black space, Malachi

Favors included rock as a part of Great Black Music: "What they call 'rock and roll,' for instance, comes from the black churches. . . . After that they named their music 'rock music.' It was Great Black Music, but nobody recognized that."[28] In fact, as Black Rock Coalition chronicler Maureen Mahon observed, "Many BRC members described the AACM as an example that inspired the formation of the BRC."[29]

In any case, the racial politics seemingly evoked by the term "Great Black Music" are very difficult to unpack. Most deconstructions of the term begin with a stress upon the "Black" part of the slogan. For example, writer Jason Berry felt that "Great Black Music's emphasis on black [is] a uniformity of aspirations and belief systems rooted in ethnicity."[30] In contrast, we have Roscoe Mitchell's typically laconic reply to my interview query concerning why the Art Ensemble created the term: "Well, nobody was calling the music great."[31] Here, the term revises deeply embedded discourses that portray the juxtaposition of "black" and great" as naturally oxymoronic.

Like Berry, Paul Gilroy was rightly remonstrative where racial essentialisms are promulgated from within the black community. Particularly skeptical of the notion of appropriation, or "cultural theft," Gilroy reminds us that "the important lesson music still has to teach us is that its inner secrets and its ethnic rules can be taught and learned. The spectral figures of half-known or half-remembered musicians like Bobby Eli, Steve Cropper, Tim Drummond, Andy Newmark, John Robinson and Rod Temperton appear at my shoulder to nod their mute assent to this verdict."[32]

In fact, this "lesson" would not seem particularly unusual or trenchant to many among the generations of black musicians who have seen that, given time, nurturance, and opportunity—the same possibilities that the AACM sought to make available to members of the black community—anyone can play any music. As Muhal Richard Abrams told Ekkehard Jost in 1984, "Music is here for everyone. And when you let it be heard once, then it's public property. So you can't say: So and so should not play such and such music."[33] At the same time, Phil Cohran's 1965 observation, made in an early AACM meeting, brings the real issue to the table. "We can all create music and somebody else can take it and use it," Cohran noted. "The musicians are the ones who need the help."[34] Cohran's remark reminds us that the process of critiquing racialized notions of authenticity and cultural theft should not obscure the possibility that theft is nonetheless taking place—more precisely, a theft of the positional diversity of the black musical subject, especially with regard to reward structures and documentation, but even more crucially, with respect to aesthetics, style, and methodology.

Here, the real culprit is not Elvis Presley or Mick Jagger, but the institutional and societal investment in white positional diversity, with its complementary disinvestment in black subjectivity. In such a socially articulated institutional framework, an individual Beatles member is merely enabled to take advantage of this asymmetrical investment structure—and why not?

While the assertion of simplistic homologies between the producers of music, the sounds that they make, and their ethnicities is fanciful, to say the least, these homologies often emerge with particular urgency once it is noticed that a statement like Bowie's includes white Californian Stan Kenton as part of the Great Black Music tradition. Indeed, as both studies and the economics of the music business have repeatedly shown, black musicians and audiences, as well as any others, are more than willing to accept "black" sounds from "nonblack" people, from the New Kids on the Block to the phenomenally successful white rapper and film star Eminem, who was "discovered" by the already successful African American rap artist and producer, Dr. Dre. In the face of this audience willingness to accept supposedly "nonauthentic" sources of black music, perhaps the most effective recourse that a conventional U.S. black cultural nationalism might have would be to create, as with African American sexual politics, the social conditions whereby musical miscegenation would result in social and economic death for its black purveyors.

In both cases, however, these matters have proven very difficult to police. Given the model of Jacques Attali's "economy of repetition," in which sounds are stockpiled, endlessly recycled, and continuously commodified,[35] the impact of Gilroy's observation is that the network of sonic discourses is too vast, too rhizomatic, to even allow discourses of authenticity to gain a foothold. Moreover, the simple face-to-face, human exchange of sonic narratives in countless performances, public and personal, naturally plays a critical role in the breakdown of narrow imputations of the authentic. In this regard, the reaction of Famoudou Don Moye to a 1974 interview question was typical. The interviewers, noting that "many young European musicians were influenced by your work," asked Moye, "Do you think that these musicians should seek their own 'roots'?"[36] Here, Moye was very clear and direct: "No, 'their own roots,' there's no such thing. We don't have particular roots. What's decisive is the environment, the feelings, the way of life, of seeing. . . . You can find ideas anywhere in life."[37]

The notion of musicoracial authenticity of which Gilroy is so critical nonetheless proceeds from black cultural nationalism's noblest motive— the drive for self-determination for African Americans. In musical terms, however, as Attali finds, this goal amounts to a takeover of power, a prospect that the economist finds dim:

> Literally speaking, "taking power" is no longer possible in a repetitive society, in which the carefully preserved theater of politics is only sustained to mask the dissolution of institutional places of power. . . . The only possible challenge to repetitive power takes the route of a breach in social repetition and the control of noisemaking . . . the permanent affirmation of the right to be different.[38]

On this view, supporting a vision of aesthetic mobility would be potentially much more powerful than appeals to an impossibly monolithic, and therefore easily subverted, Maginot Line vision of "black unity." Even after "having failed as a takeover of power in repetitive society," as Attali has it, the new music nonetheless functioned as "the herald of another kind of music, a mode of production outside repetition."[39]

In 1977, before the Ethnic Heritage Ensemble made its first European tour, Muhal Richard Abrams presented to a French interviewer an image of the AACM as multiple, expressing the hope that information about the Chicago-based artists would eventually filter out across the Atlantic and the Pacific:

> There's only one AACM, but it has two different sides. An international side, with the musicians you know—myself, the Art Ensemble, and so on—and then, there's the local side. Some of these musicians are completely eminent. But they were not launched on the national or international scene. One can say, in a way, that there are these two parts which can only form a unity together. One of the original goals of the AACM was to encourage information about music . . . and to spread this music throughout the whole world.[40]

The other side of the coin was equally complex, in that a decade later, far more was written about Chicago-based AACM members in Chicago than elsewhere. Perhaps returning the favor, after 1985 the Chicago Chapter tended to turn its attention away from both the international music industry and the New York/Chicago binary, in favor of reasserting the AACM's original heritage as an organization with strong local community roots. Moreover, the Chicago Chapter's local fund-raising strategies were bearing fruit, with matching grants from the MacArthur Foundation and the NEA. Other local donations came from Soft Sheen, the African American hair care firm, and the Chicago Council on Fine Arts. The African American leadership of the Chicago Chapter's board of directors, as exercised by board members such as Janis Lane-Ewart, playwright Paul Carter Harrison, local politician Richard Newhouse, lawyers Doris Whalum, Cheryl I. Harris, and Yvonne King, dancer Gloria Lewis (an early AACM associate), graphic artist Floyd Webb, journalist Earl Calloway, and founder Philip Cohran, functioned smoothly with white members, such as the widely admired Larayne Black and Howard Greisler.[41]

It is arguable that these local initiatives were reflected in the music of the younger generation, as the "split" between Chicago and New York came to embody not only organizational differences, but methodological and aesthetic ones as well. "When the New York people left, a certain aspect of the AACM's concept left," Ernest Dawkins observed. "The people that were here kind of developed their own concept of what the music was. I think that's generational," Dawkins concluded. "The people who were in Chicago, I guess we were more conservative with our approach, I don't know."

The flux of musical identity being faced by the Chicago AACM came to renewed international attention in 1986, when a large group of AACM musicians from Chicago came to Moers. By this time, the AACM was considered a major force in music; as Ekkehard Jost observed in 1991, the name AACM had become "something like a guarantee of quality for a creative music of the first rank."[42] Most of this generation of musicians, however, were new to European critics, and the less-than-enthusiastic reviews of the Moers event may have reflected in part a certain discomfort with the substantial differences from earlier AACM practice articulated by the younger Chicago-based musicians. For the important French critic and photographer Gérard Rouy, for example, with the exception of work by Edward Wilkerson, and the work of musicians already known in Europe, such as Muhal Richard Abrams and Douglas Ewart, the AACM events at Moers "did not fail to bore. A weariness caused by too great a similarity of inspiration. This direction of 'one foot in the tradition, one foot in the avant-garde' [was] a little aggravating, [and] the compositions [were] often not very attractive, with soloists who have certainly broken with all the disciplines but were often lacking groove and assertive personality."[43]

The Rouy review credited trombonist Craig Harris with presenting "a music appreciably different from that of his Chicago confreres, freed from all the phony Africanisms (in dress and instruments)."[44] Similarly, a review of their events by British critic Steve Lake characterized most of the AACM performances at Moers as "paradoxically conservative," citing a "dreary insistence on little instruments" in advancing the view that "much of the music of the Chicago bands is now a celebration of their own history, merely retrospective. . . . Chicago music has come to be about craft as these cats settle into professionalism."[45] As it happened, in our interview, which took place over a decade later, Edward Wilkerson was critical of similar tendencies he saw developing at that time, particularly in the Chicago context:

> At some point we have to question certain things that we have accepted as part of what the AACM is about, certain things that have become our AACM trademarks, like the little instruments and stuff. Just the way they're used musically, it's become a standard kind of trademark. I remember somebody did a concert, and he said, I don't wanna hear none of them little bells! I was like, yeah! Because it was accepted that there's going to be certain textures, a certain approach. It was adventurous maybe twenty years ago, but I think we haven't really been trying to challenge that with something to replace it or make it more current—I don't know, more something. I think that's the danger of having an old organization like this. At some point you have to sit down and reevaluate, and I don't think we do that often enough.

Nonetheless, in this context, it might be useful to explore the extent to which critic Lake's characterization of "conservative" could be read as referring to the assertion of explicit references to jazz and/or African American tradition, and concomitantly, a relatively distanced relationship to European cultural references, including the Euro-style free jazz and noise music that by this time was constitutive of a kind of tradition as well. For example, it was soon after these European events that Ernest Dawkins began his international collaborations with important South African improvisors, including saxophonist Zim Ngqawana and drummer Louis Moholo-Moholo. These collaborations, as well as such Dawkins recordings as the 2000 *Jo'Burg Jump,* were presaged by the Art Ensemble's work with the Amabutho Male Chorus on the 1990 recording, *Art Ensemble of Soweto,* whose title seemed to extend the Afrocentric wordplay of their 1970 *Chi-Congo.*[46]

My interview with Dawkins seemed to reinforce the view that aesthetic experimentation need not preclude a strong relationship to jazz, particularly for those who assert that tradition as central to their cultural identity.

In our conversation, I asked, "What was original music? That was the debate, and what originality was had a lot of different definitions. Let's say, using Stockhausen as a symbol, people came at a certain point who were not terribly interested in that. Are we saying that by extension, that entire European composed tradition, that influence is not very prevalent in the AACM after a certain point?"

"I think it's still there, but it's not dominant," Dawkins replied. "It's not the dominant factor in the conceptualizing of what original music is. I think people use it less now than they did then."

> The people that were in the AACM before my generation came in, around the late '70s or early '80s, concentrated more on the Schillinger techniques, more so than the people that were left behind here. . . . Maybe some people that left before didn't necessarily deal with traditional harmony and melody and rhythm concepts as related to what we call jazz. Some did, some didn't. The people who were left behind here were interested in more quote "traditional" harmony and melody—nontraditional, but dealing with the concepts of harmony and melody.

Indeed, in 1996, critic Bill Shoemaker heard a recording by Dawkins's New Horizons Ensemble as exemplifying a "populist trend" among the younger generation of AACM musicians.[47] Like Muhal Richard Abrams before him, however, Dawkins appealed to a notion of pluralism in defining the notions of "experimental" and "creative" that seems to recapitulate the discussions in the very first organizational meetings of the AACM, about the many kinds of music that could be subsumed under an umbrella of an organization dedicated to creative music:

> Sometimes we get blinded as far as what we think this creative person should be. It's an association of creative musicians, period. It don't say nothing about you can't do this or you can't do that, or you should do this or you should do that. It don't say nothing about what kind of musician you have to be, or you can be, or you should be. It's supposed to be about experimental tradition, yeah. That's underlying what the name says. But if you look at the name, it didn't say, "Association of Experimental Creative Musicians."

The aesthetic dislocations between many of the musicians in the Chicago AACM and other recent currents in experimental music-making became more evident with the 1995 attempt to promote a concert bringing the collective together with two generations of European improvisors, including guitarists Stephan Wittwer and Hans Reichel, saxophonist Rüdiger Carl, drummer Paul Lovens, bassist Peter Kowald, violinist Philipp Wachsmann, pianist Irene Schweizer, and the American bassist Barre Phillips, long based in Europe. The concert was billed as representing the Freie Musik Produktion (FMP), the erstwhile collective of European musicians that by this time had gradually been transformed into a recording company devoted to European free improvisation. FMP was then operated by its founder Jost Gebers and his spouse, Dagmar Gebers, who exhibited her photographs in Chicago as part of the festival.[48]

Presaging this visit by almost a decade was the 1987 performance of the Globe Unity Orchestra at the Chicago Jazz Festival, part of their first-ever American tour. The event, in which I participated, was quizzically received by a fair portion of my hometown's festival audience, many of whom were undoubtedly experiencing European free improvisation for the first time. According to a reviewer, the music headed "immediately into free form sonic territory, much to most of the audience's dismay. In perhaps the weekend's only open display of audience rudeness, many literally waved white flags of surrender and booed."[49] The comments of *Chicago Sun-Times* critic Lloyd Sachs allow us to understand that this performance in particular was one of the most controversial ever to hit the festival, perhaps since its inception. Sachs's commentary offers a rare perspective on the backroom talk of the jazz art world:

> WBEZ's Dick Buckley, hopelessly deaf to new music, huffily argued on the air that GUO should have explained their music to the crowd before their performance. . . . Other serious jazz observers favored a softening of the music for the mass audience. Even esteemed jazz authority Dan Morgenstern, Sunday's co-emcee, was heard to complain that GUO had violated a rule of jazz by not building to a strong finish.[50]

Sachs reported that even the festival presenters "regretted the booking of Globe Unity"; in turn, the writer himself regretted hearing that "the mass annoyance caused by Globe Unity Orchestra threatens future bookings of experimental bands."[51] Over the ensuing years, moreover, Sachs returned from time to time to the motif of the dropping jaws induced by Globe Unity. At the same time, however, less prominent Chicago venues had been enthusiastically hosting European improvisors, and the 1995 return to Chicago by a large assemblage of European musicians was one of the signal events that opened the door to regular touring of the United States by European improvisors after years of nonreciprocity in which Europe served as a crucial source of employment for U.S. musicians while Europeans were locked out of the U.S. market. The FMP event also represented the growing interest in European free music among younger Chicago musicians, particularly in the white community, where an improvisors' scene was nascent. A number of musicians from this newest branch of Chicago's experimental music community, such as saxophonist Ken Vandermark, pianist Jim Baker, bassist Kent Kessler, violinist Terri Kapsalis, clarinetist Gene Coleman, oboist Robbie Hunsinger, and guitarists Kevin Drumm and Jim O'Rourke, were also advertised as performing, along with New York–based singer Shelley Hirsch.[52]

As it happened, the fit between the FMP and the AACM was less than optimal—in fact, something far less extensive than the advertised meeting actually took place. The situation as it developed seemed to represent an eerie reprise of an earlier meeting between AACM musicians and European improvisors—Lester Bowie's *Gittin' to Know Y'All* sessions in Baden-Baden in 1969. Indeed, the dislocations that developed seemed to turn on many of the same kinds of creative and cultural differences and variant perspectives that marked the earlier meeting.[53] Some of the European musicians who came to Chicago, such as Peter Brötzmann and Evan Parker, were of that same first generation of European free jazz musicians who were part of the Baden-Baden event. A panel discussion, called "Impressions on Post 1960's Free Improvised Music: The AACM Meets the FMP," featuring music critics John Corbett and Bill Smith, and musicians Douglas Ewart, Evan Parker, and Brötzmann, seemed in retrospect to evoke the memory of the 1969 event, however unwittingly.[54] At the same time, it is doubtful that many Chicago-based AACM members (or the audiences that they had nurtured in Chicago) had significant contact with European improvisors. Fred Anderson, who performed at the event, observed that

> if I name some of the European cats to some of these black musicians around here, they don't even know who they are. But the Northwestern radio station plays a lot of European music, so they're hip to the Europeans. They come over here to play, and they get an audience. Peter Kowald played on a Monday night, and there were so many people you couldn't get in here [Anderson's performance space, the Velvet Lounge].

From the perspective of some Chicago AACM members, part of the issue turned on the distribution of artist's fees. Certainly, it was reasonable to assume that the Europeans were being compensated in some monetary way for their performances. Often, these funds came from European governmental sources, an aspect of cultural support that is far less developed in the United States. In this case, the poster listed support from the German/American Arts Foundation, the Goethe Institut Chicago, and Lufthansa.[55] In Ernest Dawkins's account, that support base was not being shared with the Chicago collective:

> They wanted us to play at the University of Chicago for free. We came to a consensus in the meeting that we weren't going to deal with it if they weren't offering any money. There were no contracts ever signed, there was no written communication, nothing like that. It was like word-of-mouth—do y'all want to do this? The next thing we know, flyers are out with your name on it.

In the course of events it became evident that the work of the Chicago AACM musicians exhibited major differences from both the Europeans and earlier AACM generations. Both in 1969 and in the 1990s, the AACM's composer-centered aesthetic included free improvisation among its practices, but unlike that of the Europeans, did not foreground it as a predominant practice. In that context, one possible explanation of the dislocations that ensued is that the 1995 event's apparent assumption that European-derived discourses and practices of "improvised music" would be the lingua franca connecting the two groups was a faulty, perhaps a fatal, miscalculation that could have been avoided with a more nuanced view of the relationship between composed and improvised elements in AACM music-making. The failure to take that history into account may have been seen as limiting the expressive possibilities of the AACM musicians, thereby limiting the possibilities for collaboration between the two groups of artists.

Nonetheless, the "FMP meets AACM" event, held in November 1995 at the University of Chicago's Goodspeed Hall, undoubtedly drew upon the historical synergy developed through the AACM's long association with the university. The small AACM contingent on hand included Fred Anderson (in duo with Hamid Drake), and Douglas Ewart, who played with Irene Schweizer and Kent Kessler. The African American bassist Harrison Bankhead played what must have been a very interesting duo with singer Shelley

Hirsch. Most of the other events were held at the HotHouse, a jazz performance space operated by the energetic presenter, Marguerite Horberg.[56]
As in 1969, the "diplomatic meeting" model of improvisation's role became
unwittingly problematic. For instance, despite the presence of black Chicagoans such as Fred Anderson, Hamid Drake, and Harrison Bankhead, only
white improvisors from Europe were listed on the poster advertising the
event, an unfortunate recapitulation of the "Schwarz-Weiss Problem" that
overshadowed the 1969 Baden-Baden meeting.

"They had a reception," remembered Dawkins. "I went, but I didn't play."

Leading the Third Wave: The New Women of the AACM

The extreme flux of identity experienced by the collective, both in the Midwest and on the East Coast, now included the dynamics and ideologies of
gender to an extent never before faced by the organization. Up to this point,
the major route taken by AACM musicians toward working with women
artists involved woman-led dance companies and woman soloists, rather
than instrumentalists. Among the most fondly remembered of these collaborations were those with the dance troupes of Darlene Blackburn in the
mid-1960s, and in the 1970s, with the dancer and choreographer Tamu. The
connections AACM members established with dancers and choreographers
had strong (and heavily gendered) roots in the South Side club culture of
the 1950s, where male musicians such as Sun Ra accompanied shows featuring female dancers.

My 1999 interview with Ernest Dawkins, who was serving as AACM
chair at the time, explored gender issues at some length. "Most of these
art-based organizations," Dawkins ventured, "particularly in the African
American community, that are doing these wonderful and great things, are
female-run organizations. We're the only male-driven organization—male-
driven, conceptually, and predominantly, through the years—the only African American male-driven organization." I couldn't resist asking Dawkins
a follow-up question. "In a male-driven organization," I ventured, "what's
the role of women?"

"Well, we're making a conscious effort to get more women in the organization," he replied. "Now we have four. I think we're bringing in another one, or two, so it will be about five or six. I don't think that it was
anything that was conscious. I think that's just what happened." Even so,
as Joseph Jarman noted in our October 1998 interview, at one time, "all of
the women who became members were somehow connected with already
active male members," including Amina Claudine Myers, who was married

to Ajaramu, and Iqua Colson, who was married to Adegoke Steve Colson. "Subconsciously that aspect of blackness was being manifested in the organization," Jarman remarked. "It wasn't perceived that the women had the strength and energy to be full-time up front. This is something that feeds into black culture, and is condoned by the general American society. I don't think any of us ever thought of that, but it was a part of the collective consciousness that we didn't really view."

"Amina already had a reputation as a powerful musician, and she was probably accepted right off the top," Jarman continued. "The others were, from the organization's point of view, unknown and starting. Of course, the vast majority of the organization was unknown and starting, but because of the male egotistical bullshit in identity, the females were just not permitted the same opportunities as the males who made application to join."

When Iqua and Adegoke Colson left the AACM in 1982, in the wake of the acrimonious FEPA issue, the singer Rita Warford, who was not in an intimate relationship with any AACM member, became the sole woman member of the AACM's Chicago Chapter. The New York Chapter had Amina Claudine Myers and Peggy Abrams, and, as Warford observed, "There were always women on the AACM scene." She named in particular two dancers—Gloria Lewis, and Marilyn Lashley, the former spouse of Lester Lashley, who performed at the Tenth Anniversary Festival and later became a professor of communications at Howard University. "I was just totally fascinated by Amina," said Warford. "Here was this woman who could swing so hard, play the organ with her shoes off." Despite the obvious fact that the complement of women associated with the AACM was rather small, Warford echoed Dawkins in her understanding that "I don't think that the AACM thought about [gender issues] that much. I don't think that there were gender issues. Maybe I'm just romanticizing about the period, but everybody was so into encouraging each other to have this original expression that I don't think that they thought about it that much in terms of gender."[57]

Regarding gender bias per se, Warford's recollections and experiences were somewhat at variance with those of Dawkins. "I can't say that it does not exist with certain individuals, but it was certainly not an institutional thing," she concluded. At the same time, she admitted that "I was around the AACM for a very long time before I became a formal member." After a very long, seemingly emotional pause, she continued. "I was always around, but I just never tried to formally join until years later. It might have been ten years later." Warford did not become a formal member until 1977, after many of the first-wave musicians with whom she had worked had left Chicago.

For Dawkins, the fact was that "women are being attracted to the organization. There's Rita, and after Rita, there was Ann Ward. Ann's been around for about fifteen years." As Janis Lane-Ewart saw it, however, resistance to the presence of women was endemic to the AACM throughout the 1970s and 1980s.

> I have to say that I still find it perplexing and reminiscent of an overly
> macho organization that having been in contact with the organization
> since 1977, there were at least three woman musicians that were actively
> involved—Rita Warford, Iqua Colson, and Amina Claudine Myers, and
> then to move to a point by 1986 where the only musician involved was
> Ann Ward. All the other women have been—I don't want to say pushed
> out. It's quite perplexing how women have moved in and out of the orga-
> nization—and most often, out of the organization.

Ann Ward was born in Chicago in 1949, part of a highly musical family that encouraged her to start piano lessons at the age of four. "I had an eclectic music experience," she recalled. "We listened to everybody—jazz, classical, choral, Whiffenpoofs songs. [Sings] "We're pooor little laaaambs who've looost their waaaay, Baaaa, Baaaaa, Baaaaa . . ."[58] Ward's devout Christian family members were also regulars for the weekly radio programs broadcast throughout Chicago by the Moody Bible Institute. Her father, an avid jazz aficionado, taught himself to play the piano, and her maternal grandfather was a member of the Chicago Umbrian Glee Club, a tradition-ally all-male black choral group founded in 1895 to foster performances of classical music and spirituals (or black classical music).[59] Ward's grandfather, a violinist as well as a singer, trained her mother as a classical violinist who went on to perform in the Chicago Civic Orchestra, but when she entered Chicago's Morgan Park High School, the dislocations of racism converged to block her aspirations.

> My mother was first chair at Morgan Park, although they tried to keep
> her from being first chair. They held her back, you know, the white
> people. When a visiting musician from Europe came through, a violinist,
> he wanted to see all the top people in the orchestra. They didn't introduce
> him to my mother. They snubbed her. She was very distraught about it,

so she went to her father, and he was irate. He was a social activist, so he went up to the school, wrote newspaper articles in the *Defender*, and made a big stink. What the school wound up doing was that the musician presented my mother with an apology, and a very special music box that is still in the family.

By all accounts, Ward was a diligent student, graduating from Englewood High School in 1967. At the same time, she was also attending Chicago Musical College, the same institution where Muhal Richard Abrams received his only formal musical training. Her rocky relationship with her teacher, however, soured her daily twenty-five-cent jitney rides downtown. "I knew she didn't care about me," Ward recalled. "I would play hooky, or go late, hang out at the Art Institute." Then one day, the teacher gave her scores of Stravinsky and Chopin, and played Debussy for her. Ward was fascinated. At the time, Ward was also active as an organist, playing a "rickety pipe organ" at services at her grandmother's church. She received a four-year music scholarship in piano at Kentucky State College (now Kentucky State University), a historically black institution founded in 1886 in Frankfort as the "State Normal School for Colored Persons." "The music department was very limited. I didn't find that out until I got there. They had a marching band program and a choral department, but they really didn't have the music department for a music major. I got there on a piano-organ scholarship, but they didn't have an organ. They had a Hammond B-3. I didn't know what it was."

"When I got to college, they put me on the track to a fine arts degree," Ward observed. "I wanted to be a composer, not a teacher," an aspiration that was at variance with the career counseling that the vast majority of African American musicians with postsecondary training received. Her goal was furthered by study with the composer Frederick Tillis. "He was my mentor," recalled Ward. "I got to take his composition class, and he taught theory. He saw the potential in me. He introduced me to Ulysses Kay. This is where they started throwing Stockhausen at me."

In one respect, Ward's college experience recalled that of Amina Claudine Myers in the 1950s. "When I got to school in Kentucky, girls did not wear pants on Sunday," Ward laughed. "You had to wear a dress on Sunday, and you had to go to chapel. The school was angry at me because I was wearing pants, desert mules, and a poncho." Students of the sixties inevitably found ways around the strictures. "We had a dormitory matron who looked like Cruella DeVil, but folks was gettin' down all over the campus. You couldn't walk in a dark spot." The assassination of Martin Luther King became the occasion for student unrest and activism. "We were from Detroit, Cincinnati, Chicago, Philadelphia, New York—big city kids, all dumped down here in Frankfort, so we were pretty volatile. We had formed a black student union. Now we were into Black Power, and we knew the King Alfred Plan."[60]

"Gospel music was frowned on," Ward remembered. "It was not 'cultured.'" In that context, forming a gospel choir at Kentucky State became another form of activist resistance—but the study of Euro-American contemporary composers, the bearers of another set of dangerous new ideas, could become equally transgressive. "Frederick Tillis brought us John Cage," Ward noted, "but other folks who were looking at notes and Gregorian chant were saying, uh-uh." After two years, Tillis left, and Ward soon followed suit, returning to Chicago to study composition and electronic music at Roosevelt, and in 1973 she decided to audition as a singer for the pianist and composer Ken Chaney, an original member of the AACM who was seeking to expand the strong local following he had developed with his remarkable compositions.

For three years, Ward, her aunt, and her uncle sang as part of the expanded Ken Chaney Experience, but by 1976 it was all over, the result of a European tour that was unfortunately truncated. Ward began modeling and working part-time as a cocktail waitress to make ends meet, and in the meantime, decided that she was going address a practice that even as a young person, she felt that she needed to engage. Here, her dilemma recalled Amina Claudine Myers's early struggles with jazz. "I wanted to play in these supper clubs, but I didn't know how to do standards," Ward noted, so she placed herself under the tutelage of the vocalist and keyboardist Gloria Morgan. "I decided that no one was going to teach me about jazz but me, so I started listening. I got all those David Baker and Jerry Coker improvisation books and transcriptions of Bill Evans."

It was through one of the many jobs that Ward was holding down that she met Mwata Bowden, who had become a central member of the Chicago Chapter.

> [Trombonist] Steve Berry had tried to push me into joining the AACM, but I said, I'm not what they want. I play theater music. I'm not "outside," as they say. It was fun to play creatively. I never thought I could just do that. I did it all the time by myself at home, but I never really went outside. I was still trying to just find my way in voicing.

Nonetheless, the sponsorship of Rita Warford—"Rita started pulling me"—and the support of AACM administrator Janis Lane-Ewart convinced Ward to join the organization in 1981. She quickly utilized what she saw as her "extremely strong culture in terms of classical and church music from the black perspective" to transform the AACM School as a teacher, eventually becoming the dean of the school at the behest of Mwata Bowden, who had become the organization's chair in 1990, shortly before the arrival of the young flutist and composer Nicole Margaret Mitchell.

Born in 1967, Mitchell's arrival signaled the advent of a new generation of AACM musician. Her father, an electronics engineer, and her mother, a writer and painter, hailed from the northeastern and midwestern United States, and were college-educated members of the same generation as the AACM's founding members. When Mitchell was eight years old, the family moved from Syracuse, New York, where Mitchell was born, to Anaheim, California, where her father took up a job with a major aviation technology firm. Mitchell went to segregated schools in her formative years—hardly unknown in the United States—but the racial makeup of these institutions was of a very different cast from what we have seen with most AACM musicians, in that the schools, like the surrounding high suburbia, were virtually all-white. The young girl's daily reality in the shadow of Disneyland was hardly the stuff of Disney image. "It was a very hostile environment," Mitchell recalled. "People would spit in my face. I would get in fights in school every day. It was a constant, daily battle, every time I left my house. The neighbors, if I stopped in front of their house, they would tell me to move away from their house because I was downgrading the value of their property."[61]

Mitchell's parents, raised as Christians, exposed the young Nicole and her two older brothers to art, music, and theater, as well as some of the same alternative spiritual explorations that the early AACM members engaged with. With her mother, Mitchell often attended the Self-Realization Fellowship, founded by Paramahansa Yogananda, whose classic *Autobiography of a Yogi* had been so influential on Muhal Richard Abrams many years before. Mitchell began taking music lessons—first on the piano, and then the viola. "Then I heard the flute, and that was it," Mitchell recalled, "but my parents didn't want me to play it because I was already taking piano lessons and I already had a viola, and I was taking dance. It took about four years to convince them. I gave up the piano lessons and the dance thing to do the flute. I listened for a long time before I got the flute, dreaming of when I could play it." Finally, at age fifteen, Mitchell, by now an honor student in high school, realized her desire, playing flute in the school's various performing ensembles.

After high school, Mitchell was admitted to the University of California, San Diego, one of the top public universities in the United States. UCSD was a heavily science-oriented school, and Mitchell matriculated as a computer science major, but "it wasn't in my heart." Within a year, she switched to music, where, "I looked up, and I was in a white world again." Nonetheless, she felt that the quality of instruction was excellent, particularly with flutists John Fonville and Sebastian Winston, even if "it was definitely more focused on the grad students. For the undergrads there wasn't a lot of direction. I think I might have been one of the only students who practiced. I would be in the practice rooms all by myself." In Mitchell's recollection, the departmental curriculum was largely oriented toward experimental Euro-American music, and Mitchell often attended events by UCSD's contemporary music ensemble, SONOR.

At UCSD, there was also "just a little bit going on with the jazz," a small opening that proved decisive for her. The trombonist and arranger Jimmy Cheatham, who came to UCSD in the mid-1970s, was only the second African American hired by the music department in a full-time capacity; the first, pianist Cecil Lytle, who later became provost of one of UCSD's colleges, had won first prize at the Franz Liszt International Piano Competition in 1970.[62] Cheatham had already started a jazz program that, by the time of his retirement in 2005, had trained literally hundreds of students. His zealous attention to student needs, often expressed as a kind of tough love, inspired devotion among his students. Mitchell remembers Cheatham's improvisation classes this way:

> I remember one day he wrote the word "permutation" on the board. Everybody said, what is that? He was real mystical about it. That was one of his ways to say that there were unlimited possibilities for what you could do with improvisation. He would just have us play, and make us listen. He would say that if you can't sing it, you can't play it. You gotta be able to sing what you hear.[63]

"It was just an introduction, and it was so strange when I started improvising," Mitchell recalled. "It was like learning how to crawl and walk all over again. It definitely fit more with who I am as a person." Mitchell began looking for other outlets for her creative and intellectual pursuits. Her nascent engagement with black consciousness began at UCSD with the symbolically important refusal to straighten her hair, and continued with her performances in a band that included members of the All African Peoples Revolutionary Party, founded by Kwame Ture (née Stokely Carmichael).

After two years at UCSD, Mitchell transferred to Ohio's Oberlin College as a physics major, quickly taking up residence in the school's African Heritage House. "Bell hooks had just gotten hired, Gloria Watkins. She was one of my mentors. She was just real cool. She would let us hang out at her house. The jazz department, Wendell Logan, was great, and Kenny Davis, a trumpet player from Cleveland." She studied with trumpeter Donald Byrd, who "was great as a teacher and mentor" as a sabbatical replacement for Logan. "It was still another protected environment," Mitchell commented, "but at the same time there was a lot of support and a lot of nurturing— like a black family at last, where I felt some acceptance." At Oberlin, Mitchell started writing music and poetry, but after a year, the financial strain became too great, and she moved back to UCSD briefly before rematriculating at Oberlin—this time as a jazz major.

Nominally closer to a form that would allow greater expressive latitude, Mitchell nonetheless grew relatively distant from the music department; for her, these issues were gendered as well as raced. "I had a confidence problem," she admitted, "and I've learned that in order to be a black woman doing music—especially jazz—you just have to be really aggressive, and I wasn't ready to be aggressive, and I didn't believe in myself enough. I really didn't have any support." In the end, however, it was again the financial strain that caused Mitchell to leave the program.[64] She went to Chicago in 1990, where she met up with "my 'family,' this group of artists that I'm still close to now." Rather than go to jam sessions, Mitchell frequently played on the street during her first summer, and one day she met an intense young woman named Maia.

> I had seen her before on the train and I just really knew that she was going to be someone significant in my life. She was going to the Art Institute, studying art, not music. She called me and I did a show with her at the Art Institute, this multimedia performance, with people drawing, taking pictures, singing, dancing, playing, all at the same time. That had a big impact on me.

Maia (without surname) was born in Atlanta in 1953. Eloise Kathleen Hubert was her birth name, but "when I turned a year old, my father renamed me Sonjia Denise, after Sonja Henie. He says that she was the most beautiful woman to him. She was a skater, she was famous, and that's what he wanted for me."[65] The Hubert family, Maia recalls, "is a very historic family. Growing up, I had teachers tell me about my family." Zack Hubert, a former slave, was one of the first African American landowners in central Georgia, having bought land near what is now Springfield, Georgia, in the early 1870s. Succeeding generations of the Hubert family continued to prosper, and the original Hubert homestead is now listed in the United States National Register of Historic Places.[66] Maia's father, holder of a master's degree in mathematics, taught high-school math and coached football and track in the Atlanta public schools. Young Sonjia grew up in the all-black Joyland area of southeast Atlanta with, as she puts it, "middle-class attitudes, but not always middle-class pockets."

Maia's only formal music training took place in high school. Her family evinced considerable musical talent. Her father was a singer who loved Nat King Cole; her mother, a classical pianist. Her grandmother, a Seventh-Day Adventist, would begin her radio listening day each morning with the six o'clock gospel program on WSB-AM. In high school, her older sisters were in choir and band, so it seemed natural for young Sonjia to follow suit, when (not for the first time) the long arm of gender intervened:

> I told the band director I wanted to be in the band, and that I wanted to play the drums. He said, no, he will not have any girls playing drums in his band. You have to pick the French horn or the flute. I said, OK, I'll take the flute. About two weeks after I started, I brought it back to him in tears. I said, I can't play this. He said, OK, well, you'll be the first one in your family to have ever quit. My ego couldn't take that. I went back and I took those books and sat in a room and learned that flute.

Maia attended all-black schools throughout her early years, including the period when Lester "Ax Handle" Maddox's unique combination of fried chicken promotion and unrepentant racism won him a stint in the governor's office between 1967 and 1971. Thus, as Maia remembered of those days before the emergence of the "New South," "we really couldn't go downtown and go to all those restaurants and stuff." Maia was fifteen when Martin Luther King was assassinated, and for her, that was "very significant." Malcolm X had been murdered three years before, but in Maia's family, "we were taught against Malcolm. He was the demon. He was a Muslim." In this complex social environment, the black awareness that Maia was gradually coming to grips with was not just a matter of collective social concern, but even more crucially, a question of personal identity. "I stopped using my last name when I was sixteen," she remarked.

> I was raised to believe that I was better than other people because I was a Hubert, because I was from an educated family, and I was light-skinned. I was fighting that. I could see myself getting arrested with my big Afro so that I could be on TV like Angela Davis, fighting for the cause of black people. I was into my revolutionary thing, and when I say revolutionary, it wasn't just black revolution. It was a revolution in me, of trying to find who I am and what I'm here for.

"I never had real contact with white people until I left home at eighteen," Maia recalled. A school-sponsored trip to New York became an occasion for reflections on how hairstyle could become a site for reconceptualizing identity. "We saw excerpts of 'Hair,'" Maia remembered. "I saw those Afros, and I said, that's how I'm going to wear my hair. I cut my hair off—oh, my daddy had a fit. You know, long hair, light skin, and I'm talking about, I'm black. I started seeing Nina Simone on TV, and little by little, the Afrocentricity started becoming more evident." Entering college, Sonjia Hubert intended to be an architect, but the excitement of being away from home, with all those new possibilities, tended to supersede her interest in studying. As Maia put it simply, "I had a full scholarship to the University of Pennsylvania. I partied it away." Moreover, she had internalized and personalized the understandable resentment of white power in ways that she later felt the need to move away from. On the other hand, it cannot be said that her sojourn on the East Coast bore no fruit.

> When I look at it on a higher level, what I was taken to Philly for was to find who I really am. I got into African culture there. I was in West Philly, and they had this dance class. I didn't know anything about Africa, and that's where I learned about Africa, after I stopped partying and getting high. I got into culture there. Some of my friends started reading *Muhammad Speaks,* and the Panthers had a lot of literature.[67]

It was around this time that Maia first encountered jazz, in the form of Miles Davis's *Bitches Brew.* She began listening to Ornette Coleman, Archie Shepp, and Max Roach, as well as Jean Carn, whose work had inspired Iqua Colson as well. In 1975, Maia went to Chicago to help her sister take care of her first child, and rapidly became enveloped in the Chicago version of the Afrocentric environment she had first encountered in Philadelphia. It was there that she first came across the music of the AACM, including the Transitions East concerts with the Muhal Richard Abrams Big Band. It was at the East, around 1976, that she met a person who would change her life forever.

> We went to Transitions East for a smorgasbord. And there, written on the wall, was that Phil Cohran was going to be there. My friend knew I played the flute and he introduced me to Phil, and I'm listening to myself say, Do you have a workshop or anything like that? He said, yeah, I have a workshop on Sundays. I said, well, is there a fee? He said it was three dollars. I was like, where am I going to get three dollars? But I got my little three dollars together.

At Cohran's workshop, the charisma that had been a crucial factor twenty years before in the formation of the AACM was in full effect.

> Of course Phil lectured, and he went way out in space somewhere. But I was out in space, so I was like, Yes! Here's somebody who knows what I'm thinking! He was talking about stars and how sound is hooked up with stars. Then he had us do a long tone, then the pentatonic, and he was explaining how it was connected to African people. I just felt that here I had found what I had prayed for.

What Sonjia had found, in effect, was a new identity. After numerous name changes, finally, in 1977, Sonjia Hubert became Maia at Cohran's behest.

> Maia stuck because it had the meaning that I needed to take me to where I felt I needed to go. Maia is "great mother." That's the biggest part of my personality. I am a very nurturing, motherly type of person, and I aspire to be that. I don't think that there's any greater thing a woman can be than a mother. I always say, Maia is my title. It's almost like "President."

Maia's relationship with Cohran progressed from mentorship to a collegial, musical, and personal intimacy that lasted fifteen years, produced two children, and was key to her development as a musician.[68] For Maia, coming up in "Phil's school" meant developing a balanced conception of sonic form:

I'm out, but I'm very rooted, because that's my training. I believe in
what Phil said about that earth connection, that music has always got to
be grounded with that earth beat, because African people have always
thrived on that constant beat. But I also balance it. According to what I
learned with Phil, chromatics are supposed to bring up demons and all of
these things. Well, what if a demon is necessary? It's not negative or positive, but what is appropriate.

Maia became a multi-instrumentalist and composer, performing on
vibraphone, flute, and as a vocalist. She performed as a dancer with Darlene
Blackburn's important dance troupe, but "musically, I had a verbal contract
to only perform with Phil." No published recordings emerged from the relationship, but as Maia explained, the archive of their work together should
be impressive, since Cohran recorded every concert. Notably, Maia performed with Cohran at the 1985 Chicago Jazz Festival and the Twenty-fifth
Anniversary AACM Festival in 1990.

In the late 1980s, Maia decided to work toward a BFA at the School of the
Art Institute of Chicago, where I met her while serving as a visiting artist
instructor in SAIC's Time Arts and Art and Technology areas. In addition
to her studies, Maia was taking the time to contemplate her past, present,
and future.

I was twenty-two when I met Phil. I was a child—a very bright child, but
a child. My whole world was built from his perspective. Even though I
had my opinions, little by little if you buy into something, and you do
something long enough, that becomes what you know. What I knew had
nothing to do with everything else that was going on out here. I didn't
know that.

The gradual discovery of how isolated she had been over the past fifteen
years informed her decision to leave Cohran in 1991 and strike out on her
own. There can be no question that gender issues crucially informed the
reasoning behind her departure. "I asked Phil, some years back, when we
as black people reach Utopia, reach this point that we're reaching for, is that
when you're going to deal with this issue that we have between men and
women? Because the black revolution is more about the revolution of black
men. The problems that exist between men and women existed before racism came about."

That same year, 1991, Nicole Mitchell, Maia, and the bassist, sitarist, and storyteller Shanta Nurullah formed the all-women multi-instrumentalists' ensemble, Samana. Regarding the origin of the name, Nurullah explained that the group's name was taken from the initials of its founding members: S(a) for her, M(a) for Maia, and N(a) for Nicole. Nurullah recalls an alternative explanation for the name with no small degree of amusement. "Maia was thinking about manna from heaven, in her own perky way—"Some manna" [laughs]."[69]

"After coming up with the name," Shanta added, "someone told us that in Hermann Hesse's *Siddhartha,* the Samana were the wandering holy people." In 1996, the group self-published its only recording, *Samana.*[70]

"Before Samana," Rita Warford reminded me, "there was a group called Sojourner," named for abolitionist Sojourner Truth.

> I was a member of Sojourner, and that's when I began to realize that I was getting something so totally different out of this all-female experience than I was getting out of a male experience. I know that playing with a women's ensemble is so different from playing with a men's ensemble, and I think that the more women come into it, the more women need to honor and support that female voice. I'm not talking about singing. I'm just saying that I think that what women bring to it is different.

Sojourner was active between 1982 and 1986. From Chicago, there was Shanta Nurullah, bass and sitar; Sherri Weathersby, electric bass; the singer Chavunduka; and Warford. From Detroit, there was Elrita Dodd, tenor, alto, and baritone saxophones and flute; Gayla McKinney, drums; Kafi Patrice Masuma, flute and harp; and Barbara Huey.

"We were like these little stars, these headliners, especially for most of the women's festivals," Warford recalled. "They're all over the country. They're just not considered mainstream because they're women."

> The one that stands out strongest in my mind is the one in Michigan, the Michigan Womyn's Music Festival, spelled w-o-m-y-n. They didn't want to have nothing to do with men, so they even spelled it differently. It's on this vast site, for miles and miles and miles. You just see thousands and thousands of women who come from all over the place, with their crafts, and their political agendas and materials. Many of them are camping out. All the tech, all the food, everything is run by women. We had nice cot-

tages by the lake, and even a separate cottage for rehearsing. They fed us four vegetarian meals every day, sumptuous meals. Everything was just so together. I was really impressed.

"It's quite incredible, but it's something that you would never see," Warford told me—gently but pointedly—"because they don't have men at the festival at all."

At a lot of those festivals, the women would approach you and say, look, these are the places that are available for you to work in my city. I will agree to set up X number of jobs for you if you will agree to do the same thing in your city. The kind of networking I found them to be doing, I thought was very interesting. I had never seen men talk to each other like that.

"There were women of all races and nationalities, Hispanic, Asian," Warford noted, "but it was definitely a predominantly white women's scene," Warford noted. In that context, Sojourner's performance iconography made perfect sense:

You know that we wore our colorful African clothes. When we would play with Sojourner, the cameras would just rush to the stage. We were always the headliners. I thought this was interesting because, OK, this is nice, but the mainstream they still considered to be that predominantly male environment. Although we're smoking on this women's scene, what would we do if we were on this male scene, this supposedly mainstream scene. That was not our intention, but they [the women's scene] started calling us more than anybody else.

"Shanta always says that it was my idea to put the group together," Warford observed, "but she really did all the work in terms of keeping everybody together. . . . Samana grew out of Sojourner, and the backbone of it all was Shanta." Shanta Nurullah was born Velma Patrice Neal in Chicago's Provident Hospital in 1950. Shanta's mother was born in Chicago in 1926, eventually becoming a secretary for the Chicago Housing Authority. Her father, who owned a tailor shop on 63rd Street until, according to Shanta, "readymade suits came on the market," was born in 1920 in Tulsa. His family migrated to the Midwest, and from there to Chicago, in the aftermath of Tulsa's devastating antiblack pogrom of 1921.[71] In Chicago, Shanta's family eventually became sufficiently stable to allow a move to the black middle-class Chatham area on Chicago's South Side, the same area where Clifton Blackburn, Jr., was becoming Kahil El'Zabar. As Shanta recalls, "I definitely remember white flight. We moved into this neighborhood, and one by one all the white neighbors left. We saw them run from us.[72]

Shanta's maternal grandfather was a choir director, and her great-aunt was "a classical pianist who never ever quite made it," but who "made sure we went to Orchestra Hall and heard concerts. There was a lot of emphasis on being well rounded and well bred." She took piano lessons from the age of five throughout her high-school years, and took tap dance at the South Side's Mayfair Academy from its founder, dance master Tommy Sutton, who was a friend of her father. Shanta was justly proud of the opportunity to work with Sutton, who had worked on Broadway with Mike Todd, as well as with Duke Ellington, Count Basie, Cab Calloway, Fats Waller, and Bill "Bojangles" Robinson.[73] Shanta remembered "a steady stream of Ramsey Lewis, Nancy Wilson," perhaps as part of the family's Saturday "special music days," where her mother would "put on a stack of records in the morning—Jackie Gleason, Frank Sinatra, Ramsey Lewis—and then we would clean house and dance and sing along with records. . . . Every Friday we would buy the new 45s, new things from Motown, Smokey Robinson, Mary Wells."

The young Velma graduated from Hirsch High School at sixteen, as class valedictorian, in January 1967, just around the time of the legendary Great Chicago Snowstorm. She was recruited by Carleton College in Northfield, Minnesota, but when she arrived, she quickly realized her lack of preparation for this very different world. "Academically, I felt overwhelmed. Here I was, valedictorian of my high-school class, and went up to this place and felt totally unprepared for what awaited me. I was totally miserable up there, but afterwards came to really value that education. Initially I just wanted to come home, but managed to persevere and make it through."

Academic life was hardly the only challenge facing her, as part of the advance guard of African Americans who were laying their bodies and personalities on the line for integration: "My freshman class brought the total number of black students to twenty-four. By the time I left black enrollment was up to about a hundred. So socially it was the pits. There were always more girls than guys within the black population, and at least some of the guys went for the white girls, you know. The dating situation was all out of whack." Even piano lessons were problematic. "The teacher had me like, everything I did was wrong. I was sitting wrong, I was holding my hands wrong, I was attacking the keys wrong. I was like, later for this. I'm not going to start all over again. That was a very demoralizing experience—basically the end of my formal music education." Instead, Shanta got involved in musical theater, doing "consciousness-raising" plays on racism in churches and community centers, while at the same time encountering the frequent insensitivity of her white fellow students to issues of race. "After a summer of coming in contact with [raises voice pitch in parody] 'What can we do?' I went back sophomore year angry and with my Afro [laughs]. I had read a lot of the stuff that was coming out that year, 1968—*Black Power* by Stokely Carmichael. That was the summer of my radicalization."

The situation was ripe for change, and by happenstance, the young Velma learned of a junior-year abroad program in India. She "didn't even know where India was," but she applied and was accepted, and spent six months in Pune. "That's where I heard the sitar and just fell in love. I was in political science, studying the 'untouchables.' When I heard the sitar, I fought with the chairman of the program to change my project to music." She began studying sitar, learning the intricacies of Indian classical music with Bhaskar Chandavarkar, a well-known film composer who had been a student of both Ravi Shankar and Dutch contemporary composer Ton De Leeuw.

If the young college student had been expecting that her sense of isolation would be somehow assuaged in a country of close to a billion people, the reality of her signal difference soon came home to her.

> My experience in India was different from everybody else's. For one thing, I had my Afro. The people there just couldn't get with it. Complexion-wise, I looked like them, but I had this *hair*. When I would get on the bus, the entire bus would turn around and laugh and look and stare. When people would ask me where I was from and I would say "America," they would say, oh, no, you're not. Maybe you're from Africa, but people from America are white.

"I was nineteen years old, half way around the world, and feeling really isolated," Shanta remembered, somewhat ruefully. "The other people in the group with me"—that is, white students—"were entertained by my experience, but they were not empathetic."

Emotionally it was a very hard experience. Indian people really didn't treat me very well, for the most part, with the exception of my teacher and a few others. The people who were warmest to me were the untouchables. When I came back, I didn't want to talk about my experience. I just wanted to put it behind me, except for the sitar. I would sit around playing the blues on the sitar.

She returned to Chicago in 1971 with a degree in English and a desire to "get involved in the black cultural movement," which was in full swing at the time. She joined theater artist Val Gray Ward's Kuumba Workshop, performing plays and "rituals" at the South Side Community Art Center on 38th Street and Michigan Avenue, and meeting writers such as Gwendolyn Brooks, Mari Evans, and Haki Madhubuti. The former Crane Junior College was now Malcolm X College, and teaching freshman English there brought Velma in contact with the vibrant, questing scene surrounding black cultural nationalism in Chicago. "We were celebrating ourselves, and discovering that we were beautiful and powerful and had something to say. It was a loving time, celebrating our discovery of our African connection, the revelation that there were all these advanced civilizations going on in Africa, and the fascination with the way our history had been hidden and distorted."

One day, in a health food store in downtown Chicago, she met a somewhat older man with a piercing eye and charismatic mien, a textile artist who had renamed himself from Robert Lewis to "Rah-Bird." Born in Indianapolis in 1941, Rah-Bird came to Chicago at the onset of his teenage years, attending Dunbar Vocational High School and the School of the Art Institute of Chicago, where he got to know AACM trombonist and fellow visual artist Lester Lashley. Later, he earned a master of arts in teaching at the University of Chicago. "I'd never met anybody talking so crazy," Shanta marveled. "I was fascinated with the way his mind worked." After joining her over a glass of carrot juice, Rah-Bird offered to accompany her to her appointment with Dr. Roland Sidney, the well-known Chicago naprapath visited by many health-conscious members of the African American cultural community. Later, Rah-Bird came to her performances at Kuumba. "We hooked up shortly thereafter, and almost immediately got on the babymaking trail," eventually producing three children. It was during her pregnancy with her first child, who was born in 1972, that Velma Patrice Neal became Shanta Sabriya Fehmiye Nurullah, and Robert Lewis became Seitu

Nurullah. "We had said we were going to change our names before the baby was born," she recalled.

> At the moment Mansur emerged, his name flashed across my mind like it was a neon sign—all spelled out. We found it later in the book. It was an Arabic name that meant "victorious" and "supported by God." I kept getting this "Mansur-Allah . . ." And so we then found "Nurullah"— "Light of God." And then found our names to go along with that. I was looking for an African name, and couldn't find anything. I kept on being pulled back to Shanta, which in the Indian classical system is the ninth or the highest emotion that can be expressed in music, which is peace. It was also the name of one person in India who was really good to me. So basically my name means, "to attain peace through the Light of God."

It was during this time that I met Shanta, when Rah-Bird and I were attending the Saturday classes at the AACM School. Then, in addition to the sitar, she was learning the electric bass, a present from saxophonist Roberta Ingram. She took lessons with AACM guitarist Pete Cosey, who introduced her to AACM founder Phil Cohran, who was holding his "Black Music Workshop" in the city. "When I first went up in Phil's workshop." Shanta recalled, "I told him I had a sitar. You have a sitar? You gotta bring it!" She said to Cohran that "they told me that I couldn't really play it unless I had studied for five years, and I've only had six months on it. Phil said, Sister, that sitar's from Africa and so are you. Just express yourself. That was all I needed, permission to play the instrument. I brought it out, and Phil wrote music for it. We did some wonderful sitar-harp duets." In India, Shanta had been fascinated with the odd meters, such as the seven-beat Rupaktal. "So when I hooked up with Phil Cohran," she found, "sevens and fives were his specialty. It was like, oh, I'm at home." For nearly four years, from 1972 to 1976, Shanta was a part of Cohran's workshop.

As it was practiced in those years, African American cultural nationalism often featured a complex convolution of gender, race, class, and economics, a dynamic that Shanta experienced both personally and professionally. The spectre of class—or rather, class-baiting—loomed particularly large. "Once I got out on my own and got into the cultural and nationalist movement, then I started trying to deny my upbringing," Shanta related. "I was called 'bourgeois' so much that I tried to run from that. I was told that the problem with me was how I grew up and how I was raised. I didn't have enough soul, I guess [laughs]. I hadn't had enough hard times to qualify as really black, you know."

We have already seen that first-generation AACM musicians had severe doubts concerning the ethical propriety and political effectiveness of pursuing careers in music in the midst of high American capitalism. In particular, my interview with Lester Lashley confirmed a discussion reported by Leslie Rout in 1967, in which many AACM musicians were said to be opposed to "taking Whitey's dirty money" in the form of foundation grants.[74] One seemingly more ethical and culturally viable alternative would be for cultural organizations to rely upon African American philanthropy exclusively. As Shanta Nurullah observed, the issue was still in play a decade later; there was a definitely an air of

> not wanting to be a part of the system, to go the white man's way. We would go our own way, and a lot of us fell on our faces economically. Phil used to preach that the black community should support the black musicians, and you shouldn't have to do anything else but your music. We had these great, talented people, and the world owed us recognition and money. I bought into that, and it was definitely downhill from there. You can't demand that the community support you. Nobody owes you anything.

For some, a search for black identity that naturally included spiritual matters seemed to devolve into a kind of ad hoc religiosity that identified blackness with a basis in gender inequity. "Man is king and master, and woman must submit," Shanta recalled ruefully of the period. "[Her husband] had me in turtlenecks and long dresses, so that no part of my body would be exposed except my face and my hands. No pants." Also touted at times as part of the new blackness was polygamy. In Shanta's recollection, she was often informed that "it is the black man's nature to have more than one woman. . . . Oftentimes the polygamous marriages were funded by public aid [laughs], and that's the part that they didn't seem to get out of Islam, where it says that you can have as many wives as you can *afford*." The strains led to the dissolution of Shanta's marriage. "The women were definitely in a second-class position," Shanta recalled.[75] Even so, Seitu Nurullah "was remarkably supportive of my efforts to play." Perhaps this was due to her husband's deep love of music and of the AACM, which he joined in the mid-1970s as a clarinetist.

In the late 1980s, Shanta met Maia, along with the vocalist and multi-instrumentalist Aquilla Sadalla, in the context of the Cohran workshop. By 1992, both Maia and Shanta had left Cohran's ensemble, and were in the process of forming Samana with Nicole Mitchell. The advent of Samana was happening just as the issue of the complement of women in the AACM was becoming more acute. "I would bring it out [in the meetings]," recalled Ann Ward. "We don't have any women." Maia was the first of the Samana group to apply for AACM membership. As Dushun Mosley remembered, "We had some real battles there. There was the whole thing left over about this being an all-male group, and some of the members didn't want any women." The matter recalled Iqua Colson's difficulties with being accepted into the AACM twenty years before. "Maia had written her letter," recalled Ward, "so we said we're going to bring Maia in. She brought in Niki, and finally Shanta." Maia's reasons for joining were pragmatic:

> AACM was an organization of artists. I saw this as a base from which to create. AACM was visible and historic, a base to create and then be seen. I saw AACM as these *bodies*. I'd like to be a composer for the big band. It thrills me to be able to have my music played by a large ensemble. I saw it more or less as a springboard to get more visibility, from a selfish point, and credibility, because in working with more people you're going to grow and be more credible. I had heard so much about the AACM that it seemed that the AACM was the stuff. It's an honor to be associated with such fine and historic figures. I was looking to run with the big dogs.

By all accounts, Maia also saw the pragmatic value of a collective entry of Samana as a group of women into the AACM. "At first I didn't really see the point," Shanta Nurullah recalled, perhaps understanding more than the others the history of the organization. "I didn't really like parts of it. But she thought it was a good move, and it turned out to be. We claim to be the first all-women's ensemble to have emerged from the AACM." In addition to the women who were members of the AACM, Samana embraced other women performers who were not members, including Chavunduka, Aquilla Sadalla, and percussionist and actor Coco Elysses.[76] At the same time, as the number of women in the AACM rose, new issues emerged that the overwhelmingly male membership had arguably been insensitive to. When the three newcomers entered the meeting room, they quickly learned from their female counterparts about the folkways of their male colleagues. "Ann and Rita used to say, we didn't have any support," said Maia. "We never had enough women to support us. A lot of times, Ann was the only woman there, so when she'd state an opinion, sometimes they just may not hear it."

"My experiences with women, it seems like the women listen to each other better," Warford extrapolated from her years with Sojourner. "The women get into those little subtleties and textures and little fine points a little bit better than the cats." As Maia saw it, "by having other women to even say things in a different way, somehow we're being able to be heard a little bit more, and then, after the habit is there, the men are listening more." Shanta Nurullah voiced a similar impression, but with greater caution. "I think that us being in the AACM caused them to tone down some of their stuff and reconsider," she noted. At the same time, this generation of AACM women was critical of their male colleagues for not including them in performance opportunities. "It's an old boy's club, you know," Nurullah observed. "You know how they call on each other to do things. I'm not on that list."

For Janis Lane-Ewart, "There is still some sense of men not really wanting to accept the creative power of and musical abilities of their female counterparts."

> I was at a concert where Samana was the reason why there were so many people in the audience, and the men were standing in the back talking during the performance, not even being respectful. It was disgusting. Many of the musicians in that band played three or four instruments well, write original compositions, and take their art form very seriously, but they are not embraced or even put forward as even—they don't even exploit the group in a way that would bring greater notoriety to the organization.

"I'm not willing to say that it's because I'm female," Nurullah mused. "I can say that it's either because they don't consider my musicianship up to snuff, or they haven't even bothered to hear me play, or they just want to keep doing what they're doing. If I wasn't in Samana, I wouldn't be working. So we created our own opportunities."

"Another aspect of the AACM to me," Ameen Muhammad observed in 1999, "was that it was primarily a lot of strong men. That was another great attraction for me." Maia echoed Muhammad from a very different standpoint, deploying a matter-of-fact recontextualization. "The AACM came up in a time when the focus was revolution," she noted, "but the revolution was about black men. Nobody meant women any harm. But if you don't have on a fire suit, you ain't gonna go into no fire. It may have been open to women, but if it is not inviting to women, women are not going to come." Douglas Ewart's analysis seemed to agree. "People's thought about the AACM, that it's a man's club, might have caused [women] to not pursue getting into the organization," he ventured. At the same time, Ewart pointed to the ways in which women had already manifested a nascent AACM presence. "A lot of the spouses of these men helped to maintain the organization in indirect fashion. Women have been there, helping at the concerts, helping with the infrastructure of the organization. I know Peggy Abrams is an indelible part of the AACM. You can't say 'Muhal' without 'Peggy,' at least I can't. I couldn't say 'AACM' without saying 'Janis Lane-Ewart.'"

For Maia, however, "Our women's presence in the AACM—our leadership presence—has been more visible with the presence of Samana," concluded Maia.

> We do have a lot of say-so. We've shaped the thinking to consider us a lot more, because we have definitely talked about that. Like, they're still calling everybody "the cats." I say, OK, well, I guess that includes us, right? I know the brothers don't mean any harm, but in the whole world scheme of things, men have had to come up to the times. Women have to be considered in everything, and considered differently than we used to be. So AACM just reflects the times.

"So we make an effort," concluded Dawkins in 1999. "Change comes slowly, and not without a fight sometimes." Even so, the nature of that battle is different for women. The close intertwining of art-making with personal relationships and family among women artists was a theme that came up repeatedly in my conversations with women AACM members.

"Women have a hard time holding onto their art," observed Maia. "We fall in love, we miss concerts because this man got on my nerves, then we have a baby and the children are getting on our nerves. We allow other things to distract us, so I feel really great just to have survived with my art through all the obstacles plus my family issues, my children."

12

TRANSITION AND REFLECTIONS

New York in Transition

John Stubblefield passed away on July 4, 2005, and a memorial for him was held in late September at St. Peter's Church on Lexington Avenue and 54th Street in his adopted home base of New York City. The previous pastor of St. Peter's, the Reverend John Gensel, had made the church well known for its extensive engagement with jazz events; musicians knew the church and its pastor, and services for musicians were frequently held there, including the memorial for Lester Bowie in 1999. At these times, one line of conversation is inevitable:

"What's happening with so-and-so?"

"Aw man, he passed."

"What?"

Indeed, a number of AACM musicians have passed away since I began my work on this book—Stub, Lester, Eugene Easton, Joel Brandon, Malachi Thompson, Emanuel Cranshaw, and even the young Ameen Muhammad. I was just hoping that no more would join them before the work was done and in print, so that those who remain and those who have yet to arrive could have the possibility of experiencing this tangible historical evidence of their achievements. The first of the AACM founders to pass away was Steve McCall; his funeral on the South Side of Chicago in May 1989 was attended by hundreds of people, myself among them. In 1992, the drummer Phillip Wilson, who was associated with the Art Ensemble in its formative years, died in New York City from injuries sustained in a home invasion. In 1993, saxophonist Light Henry Huff, born in 1950, passed away due to a mysterious ailment.[1] Fred Hopkins, who passed away in 1999, cofounded the trio Air. A student of Walter Dyett, Fred was the first recipient of the Chicago Civic Orchestra's Charles Clark Memorial Scholarship.[2] The flutist and virtuoso whistler Joel Brandon, an early AACM musician who introduced Douglas Ewart to the organization, passed away in 2003.[3]

I was unable to get to New York for Lester's service, but I was asked to send along a short text to be read there. That text, along with others, was published in a March 2000 *Down Beat* tribute to Lester.

> Right after he heard me play for the first time, in one of my first AACM concerts, he was nice enough (or concerned enough) to take me aside. He said something like, "You know, George, you don't have to do this. You could give up music now while you still have time. After a while, it'll be too late." (Now I hear that he told all the young musicians that.)[4]

Somewhat late, I climbed out of a taxi on 54th and Lex to find the singer Sathima Bea Benjamin at the church door, one of literally hundreds of musicians who were crowding around the door and congregating in the anteroom next to the spacious main chapel. Important chapters of my life came flooding back; I hadn't seen some of these colleagues and friends since the late 1980s, when the composer Peter Gena raptured me out of New York for my first academic job at the Art Institute of Chicago.

After a suitable interval greeting old friends and colleagues, including Kunle M'wanga, who organized the first AACM concert in New York in 1970, I made my way to the chapel, where the Reverend Dale Lind, who took over the pastorship after the passing of Father Gensel, was concluding his opening remarks. Father Lind had continued the church's engagement with jazz, and the chapel was packed with a multiethnic throng of friends, listeners, still more musicians, and others wishing to pay their respects. Stubblefield loved all kinds of music. He was respected by all for his grace and musicianship, and he managed to avoid becoming part of the cliques and cabals that seem a necessary evil of professional life in "The City." Accordingly, his wife Katherine, seemingly talking to everyone present with a similar grace, addressed the assembly with a plea for potential bone marrow donors. I found a seat next to Muhal Richard Abrams (whose daughter Richarda, an actress and singer, was serving as master of ceremonies) just as Sathima was starting an absolutely riveting and totally non-standard rendition of Ellington's "Come Sunday" that perfectly exemplified her Cape Town–rooted aesthetic, which she called simply the "Southern Touch."[5] "Duke would have loved what she did with that melody," Muhal exclaimed.

For nearly three hours, a flood of tributes ensued. The pianist Sonelius Smith commented simply, "In the last few months I've lost quite a few people. . . . Death brings people together." Certainly a generational shift was being expressed, as when Randy Brecker, whose brother Michael was undergoing a calamitous health crisis, observed jocularly of the assembled gathering of artists, "When I met a lot of these people, they were in their prime," speaking of the many heads and beards of gray among the audience members. Rufus Reid joked about a picture of himself with Don Byas that Stub had given him, depicting a time "when I had black hair."[6]

Jazz, like any music—all posturing by pan-European high culture aside—is founded on soul-infused bodies. But bodies change, learn, grow, and decline, and all the musicians can do to keep "tradition" alive is to create the conditions under which new bodies consecrate themselves to the musical act. Inexorably, even those bodies move toward states in which the soul can be said to depart, and it is at these times the jazz world draws upon its African American soul, articulated across a network of breath, metal, bone, and gut, rather than ostensibly disembodied electronic sounds. Stubblefield's was the generation born ten years before my own, a generation that dreamed of playing with Miles, Blakey, Mingus, or Trane. Some, like Stub himself, actually did. Most, however, had to make their own way in the wake of the *Götterdämmerung* of the seventies, when so many of the old verities and heroic postures of jazz were succumbing to the imperatives of postmodernity.

Amina Claudine Myers, who met Stub when she was a college student in Arkansas, was reassuring in her tribute, drawing upon the rich depth of her gospel soul with her own composition, "It's All Right Now." "Can't nobody do that like her," Muhal marveled, as Amina launched into "Dino," a piece that Stub had written for her. Another great pianist, Donal Fox, presented a piece by Stub's beloved William Grant Still. The drummer Billy Hart played with just about everyone present. People would get on the stage and announce, "Where's Billy Hart?" They wanted to take this opportunity to perform with one of the truly great musicians of our time.

Stub was a product of the experimentalist AACM, and that legacy was brought to the pulpit by Henry Threadgill, who reminisced about the earlier times in Chicago when he and Stub would compete to see who could write the most music in a week—an anecdote that illuminated the two artists' long relationship with the AACM's composer-centered aesthetic, which for Henry, was "founded on searching and learning and advancing." This kind of experimental practice, as Dick Griffin observed in his remarks that evening, required the tenacity emblematic of a person whom Dick jokingly referred to as "John Stubbornfield." Henry then pointed out another aspect that was perfectly congruent with a core AACM value—not aesthetic spiritualism, but aesthetic range and diversity. Stub "crossed a lot of lines—different genres, as they say," Henry remarked. This seemed like an ideal introduction to the music of Andrew Cyrille and Oliver Lake, whose intricate and pensive free improvisation—the evening's first—led to a blues-imbued performance of Stub's "Baby Man," a piece that had once been performed by an old friend of his family, the great pianist and composer Mary Lou Williams.

Thurman Barker mentioned Stub's presence with him on Joseph Jarman's classic AACM recording, *As If It Were the Seasons,* before proceeding with a solo drum performance "in memory of John, who gave me my first gig in New York." It was a ritual work with the formal clarity and timbral subtlety of a Max Roach. Thurman's playing moved me to reflect that so much of what one can accomplish as an artist depends on the kindnesses of friends, colleagues, and even strangers who love sound—a place to stay, a word of advice, a telephone number, an introduction. Then, by way of conclusion, after calling John Stubblefield "a great historian," Muhal Richard Abrams announced that he would play "two chords for John," perhaps in response to the often lengthy musical tributes that had been offered, some far exceeding the nominal five minute allotment to which everyone had agreed. Actually, Muhal's minimalist performance comprised three of his signature chordal flourishes, the third of which reprised the first. James Jabbo Ware and I turned to each other and simultaneously said, "A-B-A form."

In mid-November of that year, the AACM's New York Chapter presented Muhal's solo and ensemble music as a part of its fortieth anniversary celebration. The chapter had been doing a four-concert season for the last several years, presenting not only AACM members' works, but also those of compatible colleagues, such as bassist Mark Dresser and saxophonist Oliver Lake. Beginning with the fall 2003 season, the concerts moved from the Society for Ethical Culture on West 64th Street in Manhattan to the Community Church of New York on East 35th Street. Both spaces were spacious, sonically generous, and congenial places to listen to music. Now, as in 1965, the goal of the AACM concert series was the same: "to provide an atmosphere that is conducive to serious music and performing new unrecorded compositions; we hope to create a spontaneous atmosphere that is unique to our heritage and to the performing artist. Our aim is universal in its appeal and is necessary for the advancement, development and understanding of new music."[7]

That evening, Muhal's solo piano piece was unusually pensive, lasting about thirty-five minutes and drawing upon a manner of performance atmosphere that he had been developing over the past several years that for lack of a better adjective, I'm going to call his "transcendental" manner. After an interval, an ensemble of New York–based supermusicians appeared: Bob de Bellis, Marty Ehrlich, Enrique Fernandez, Aaron Stewart, and Howard Johnson, saxophones and woodwinds; Al Patterson, Art Baron, Jack Jeffers, trombones; Bob Milligan, Cecil Bridgewater, Jack Walrath, Eddie E. J. Allen, trumpets; Bryan Carrott, vibes; Saadi Zain, bass; Andrew Cyrille, drums. The ensemble performed a series of Muhal's beautifully orchestrated tone poems, some recent, some decades old. The pieces did *not* draw upon "the full range of the jazz tradition," a chimerical entity that is not only impossible to delimit, but far too frequently referenced to be anything but a cliché. Instead, what was on view was the full range of Abrams's extraordinary imagination, seeking out the hidden corners of consciousness. Ruminative and ebullient by turns, the ensemble elicited two standing ovations in the often unforgiving climate of New York City on this, the fortieth year of the AACM.

Chicago in Reflection

On Saturday, May 7, and Sunday, May 8, 2005, the actual anniversary of the first organizational meeting that led to the formation of the AACM, another AACM Fortieth Anniversary Festival took place at Chicago's Museum of Contemporary Art. Before a standing-room-only audience, Chicago-based AACM musicians, including Edward Wilkerson, Douglas Ewart, Nicole Mitchell, Isaiah Jackson, Ann Ward, and singer Dee Alexander, presented the face of the AACM in 2005. The newly formed "Great Black Music Ensemble," led by Mwata Bowden and comprising fifty-plus musicians, showed how the possibilities of new improvised music on a truly orchestral scale depend critically upon the construction of new communities. That these imagined communities have important musical consequences is at the heart of what the AACM meant to both musicians and audience.

How the AACM draws so much of its spiritual sustenance from this central destination for the Great Migration may be usefully explored with reference to the black church. Indeed, it remains a source of curiosity that despite the strong roots of many AACM members in African American religious traditions, few historical or critical accounts connect the AACM or other black experimental musics with this critically important black community institution. For instance, the famous article by Amiri Baraka, "The Changing Same (R&B and New Black Music)" theorizes that "it was the more emotional Blacker churches that the blues people were members of, rather than the usually whiter, more middle-class churches the jazz people went to."[8]

Earlier in the essay, Baraka asserted that "the new jazz people are usually much more self-consciously concerned about 'God' than the R&B folks. But most of the R&B people were *really* in the church at one time, and sang there first, only to drift or rush away later."[9] This asserted binary, however, seems a bit out of place given the inconvenient fact that many radical black musicians of the period, including most first-generation AACM musicians, came overwhelmingly from working-class, churchgoing, God-fearing stock, and grew up with a deep understanding of black popular musical culture. Certainly in 1940s Bronzeville, where the roots of so many of the earliest generation of AACM members lay, spiritual matters were traditionally taken with the utmost seriousness.

Malachi Favors came up with his father and uncle in the relatively strict Pentecostal denomination known formally as the Church of God in Christ (COGIC), founded in 1897 by the African American religious visionary Charles Harrison Mason. Mason was a former Baptist minister, originally based in Arkansas, who was expelled from both his church and the state Baptist Association for his belief in the Wesleyan-Methodist doctrine of sanctification. Mason's sect eventually grew to become not only one of the largest Pentecostal denominations in the United States, but an international church with more than 8.7 million members in more than fifty-two countries as of 1995. Over 5 million of these are in the United States alone, making COGIC the largest Pentecostal denomination in the country.

Mason pursued his original vision of a multiracial congregation in part through his ordaining of white ministers, many of whom split from COGIC in 1914 to organize an all-white denomination, the Assemblies of God, now the largest white Pentecostal denomination. This is in keeping with Favors's own understanding of church history: "They said that at one time white people did belong, but the white people split off. . . . But in recent years, they wanted fellowship again."[10]

The church forbade the use of nicotine and alcohol, and there were strict limits, particularly for women, on dress, deportment, and makeup. There were relatively few restrictions on overt expressions of the spirit, however, and the church is widely credited with popularizing "witnessing," the introduction of spontaneous exclamations of emotional and spiritual fervor during worship services. Mason himself referred to the exclamation "Yes, Lord!" as "the Church of God in Christ national anthem."[11]

The young Favors grew up with the history that his family had been present at the beginning of the church. His parents had emigrated to Chicago from Lexington, Mississippi, in the 1930s. His great-uncle had been established in Chicago for some time, and Favors's father eventually became the pastor of a church that started on 37th Street, and then moved a few blocks north to 35th. Favors remembers music as an integral and critically important aspect of worship in his father's church:

> The Church of God in Christ brought with it in its praise the use of all musical instruments. Tambourine, guitar, you name it. Also in the praise there was testifying, singing, dancing, shouting, clapping of hands, speaking in tongues, and great congregational praise. You could play any instrument you wanted. Most other churches didn't have nothing but the organ or the piano. During the testimony service, anybody can get up and express their spiritual communications with God, or they can get up and sing. Any person that sings a tune, after they finish they might testify too. And some of the greatest dancers I've seen in my life were in the church.

Favors remembers that Sister Rosetta Tharpe, the great gospel singer, was a member of the church pastored by Favors's uncle. In the church, "she played her steel guitar, and her mother played the ukulele." As Tharpe became famous, however—"singing out in the world, as they called it," according to Favors—one of Favors's relatives went backstage after a performance at the Regal Theater and told the singer, "You should be ashamed of yourself—out here like this, doing this kind of work for the devil."

With religious practice thus centered in the life of his family, Favors would spend several evenings per week at worship services that involved trance and glossolalia, a central tenet of Charles Harrison Mason's vision, and one that split the church in its early years. Favors remembers that other children would make fun of his mother and father as "Holy Rollers," but for Favors and his family it was a question of how people "moved in the spirit." Favors saw the church's communal spirit as "more or less an African tradition—not exactly like being in Africa, but the spirit. If you listen to a black preacher, it's like the griot—he sings his message." According to Favors, Bishop Louis Henry Ford, the presiding bishop of the Churches of God in Christ from 1990 to his passing in 1995, stated at the time of his death that "he was inspired by God through the Bible to continue some more of our African traditions of praise to the creator."

In early February 2004, I was preparing to fly from San Diego to Chicago for the memorial service for Malachi Favors Maghostut. I had spoken with Malachi only the week before, when I'd heard that he had entered the hospital with a "stomach virus" that turned out to be inoperable pancreatic cancer of a particularly aggressive type. He seemed fine on the telephone from the hospital, and at one point he talked about his military service—a fact that had escaped our interview for the book. The dates he gave for his service would have placed him in the Korean War, which was unlikely for someone who, as he always claimed, was born in 1937. Favors's tendency to dissemble about his age was a well-known source of mirth to fellow musicians of his generation, who frequently told whomever would listen that Favors was "older than dirt." When I mentioned the discrepancy, Favors joked, "Aah, you're not going to get that out of me."

The service was held on February 4, 2004, at the Love Community Church of God in Christ in south suburban Chicago.[12] The poet and community activist Haki Madhubuti was just one of the eminent Chicago community figures who spoke before the more than five hundred people in attendance. Favors was universally known in Chicago as a race man—a far cry from his early days as a gangbanger (1940s style), but fully in keeping with the history of so many of those adolescent miscreants—such as Malcolm X, or, closer to home, Ernest Dawkins, Ameen Muhammad, and Muhal Richard Abrams. Favors's longtime Art Ensemble friend and colleague Famoudou Don Moye had trouble keeping his composure during his particularly moving speech, and to see the genuine grief on the faces of Chuck Nessa, John Litweiler, and Terry Martin made me realize how the dislocations of race, class, gender, and profession can be redressed, if only for a brief moment, in the presence of loss or the possibility of rebirth.

The eulogy was delivered by Favors's nephew, the Reverend E. M. Walker, who took as his inspirational text a curious encounter with his uncle. "You may know," Pastor Walker revealed, "that Brother Favors performed a type of music that is not sanctioned by the Church of God in Christ. At those times," the pastor continued, "Brother Favors and I agreed that we just wouldn't talk about it." Somehow, the minister wove this theme of forbearance into a fascinating moral text, which was prefaced by Roscoe Mitchell's obsessively repeated and achingly moving blues line on alto saxophone—as we've learned from Henry Threadgill, the *only* saxophone for church people. A company of African-inspired drummers, organized by Moye, was apparently not permitted to play inside the church itself, although at the end of the service, a recessional of drums seemed to occur anyway, despite the church's proscription.

At the end of the service, I decided to follow Douglas Ewart and Lester Lashley, along with Pastor Walker and his cohort, to the site of interment, where Favors was buried with military honors. As Pastor Walker completed his oration, a bitterly cold wind whipped around those present. Suddenly, without warning, Lashley pulled out a set of "little instruments," whose concept Favors had been instrumental in initiating. He passed the instruments to Douglas and some others, and those of us without instruments clapped, shouted, and chanted as Favors's casket lay in the ground, to the apparent discomfiture of the religious contingent, who hurried away, leaving us, his colleagues and friends, to celebrate yet another side of Malachi Favors.

At 10 a.m. on August 5, 2005, I answered the "Call to Worship" at Trinity United Church of Christ, where a "Homegoing Service" was being conducted for the saxophonist and composer Vandy Harris, who was part of the AACM when I joined in 1971. I had performed with Vandy on numerous occasions during those early years, and his signature work of those years was "Valley of the Dry Bones," a kind of oratorio situated firmly within the African American tradition of using biblical texts as an allegorical means of raising black consciousness. When the AACM's Great Black Music Ensemble, led for the occasion by Ernest Dawkins, intoned the opening strains of the piece, I turned to saxophonist David Boykin, a musician still in his thirties, and remarked that my generation, like his, learned how to play by playing Vandy's music. He smiled. The seemingly inevitable graying of the AACM at forty was being forestalled right before my eyes by the Great Black Music Ensemble, where musicians in their sixties and beyond, such as Pete Cosey, performed alongside musicians in their twenties and even younger, all in the service of a continually renewable notion of Great Black Music in which the ensemble demographic seemed to add yet another meaning to the Art Ensemble's corollary slogan, "Ancient to the Future."

Art "Turk" Burton spoke gravely and at length about Vandy's contribution to the community, after which the obituary was read silently:

> Vandy Harris, Jr.—educator, multi-instrumentalist, composer, arranger, vocalist, jazz choral director, and band leader whose active music career spanned four decades—was born July 25, 1941 in Wisner, Louisiana to Vandy Harris, Sr. and Elmaree Daniels Harris (both deceased). In 1946 the family moved to Chicago. Vandy was baptized at Mt. Eagle Baptist Church in 1969. Since 1998, he and his wife Izabel have been members of Trinity United Church of Christ.[13]

The Reverend Quiller Harris, an older gentleman of serious mien, like Vandy himself, gave an oration about Vandy during the service. I realized that I had met only one other person named Quiller—my maternal grandfather. Later, my uncle Lonnie, whose father was my grandfather, was astonished to hear of another person named Quiller—evidently a name with deep Southern black roots of which both of us were only vaguely aware.

> When he was 12, the family got a piano and Vandy started lessons. When he heard a tenor saxophone, he set his dream on playing that instrument. He went on to play several instruments, specializing on the saxophone. Vandy earned a B.A. from Chicago Teachers College (1966) (now Chicago State University). Soon thereafter, although a conscientious objector, he was drafted and sent to Vietnam, where he served two years, and returned home a decorated soldier with an honorable discharge in 1969.[14]

When I read that passage, I thought of Rasul Siddik's experience with attempting conscientious objection. Probably it was around that time that Vandy joined the AACM, just before I came in 1971. The pastor of Trinity, the Reverend Jeremiah Wright, was known as a highly articulate firebrand, perhaps in the tradition of Albert Cleage and the black radical ministers who developed their own version of black liberation theology.[15] Pastor Wright's concluding "Words of Comfort" did not disappoint. He chose a biblical text that I am at pains to remember now; all I can recall is that the pastor made it clear to all that he, like Vandy, was deploying a biblical text in the service of a disquieting allegory. Wright framed the United States' contemporaneous difficulties in Iraq as a symbol of an overweening arrogance at the highest levels of power for which one could find obvious precedent in Scripture—leading one inevitably to the question of why a political culture that claimed to be led by the Bible could not divine the implications of such a text.

In pursuing his music, Vandy played with many well-known jazz musicians and was active in the Association for the Advancement of Creative Musicians (AACM) and the Jazz Institute. With his own group, The Front Burners, he produced two CDs: 'Pure Fire' (1996) and 'The Lighthouse Keeper' (1999). He also created The Obade Ensemble (Vocal Group). [16]

Vandy's demeanor was always pleasant and open, his saxophone playing virtuosic, with lots of altissimo, as if he were Dr. J playing above the rim. His compositions were technically demanding, and he was personally intense and serious, once demanding in an AACM meeting (that I attended) that musicians who did not meet their obligations regarding work for the organization be subject to corporal punishment. Needless to say, that motion did not pass, but I'm sure that many people who remember that meeting wonder (at least jocularly) what might have been in that regard.

> From 1979 to 2001, he taught in the Chicago Public Schools, kindergarten through high school. While getting an M.A. in Music Composition at Governors State University (1979), Vandy went with that school's jazz band on a 1976 tour to Brazil, where in Sao Paulo he met his future wife, Maria Izabel Leme; they married in 1994. When his health deteriorated in 2001, Vandy chose to move to Brazil, a country he loved. He made his transition on July 24, 2005, the day before his 64th birthday.[17]

A host of small signs during these services caused me to consider the possibility that even though the multiracial congregation in attendance at the Chicago services might have resembled that of St. Peter's in some respects, the cosmopolitan, Manhattan-based, New York professional musical community was nonetheless deterritorialized—relative to my perspective—in a way that Chicago's black musical community will never be. I remember Vandy's joy at meeting the beautifully gentle Izabel, and when pianist Koco Calvin Brunson and bassist Cecile Savage, a Frenchwoman who put down permanent musical roots in the South Side's black community many years ago, played Antonio Carlos Jobim's classic "Insensatez," Izabel wept quietly, as I listened in the company of Larayne Black and Doris Whalum, two of the AACM's staunchest supporters. "Larayne was like a mother to the AACM," said Muhal Richard Abrams, and for those who came later, Doris, with her legal brilliance and love of photography, was equally influential. In deterritorialized space, I ventured to myself, home is where the funeral is. Genre-busting goes so far, and then the homegoing takes over, where it becomes evident as to who your real community is, the one that will take care of you no matter what.

That sense was certainly on view at the services for the forty-nine-year-old Ameen Muhammad in February 2003. The large number of people who came to a South Side chapel to mark one of the most tragic passings in the recent history of the AACM heard musical offerings by the collective, as well as tributes by those closest to him: Ernest Dawkins, and Bonita McCall, actress, pianist, and sister of AACM founder Steve McCall. Ameen's pall-bearers were nearly all Chicago AACM members: Ernest Khabeer Dawkins, Dushun Mosley, Edward Wilkerson, Mwata Bowden, Douglas Ewart, trombonist Steve Berry, and singer Taalib'Din Ziyad. Traditionally, African American funerals are concluded with an offering of food, usually known as the "repast." This repast was held at Northeastern College on Chicago's South Side, a center for the study of black political and cultural issues. According to one report I found on the Web, the event included music by Ziyad, Ann Ward, Isaiah Jackson, Douglas Ewart, trumpeter Bob Griffin, and violinist Savoir Faire.[18]

Also contributing to the service for Ameen was the One Family Band, an ensemble founded by the AACM pianist and composer Evod Magek, whose single self-published recording, *Through Love to Freedom,* featured the late Oscar Brown III as well as myself, Duke Payne, Koco Calvin Brunson, and Curtis Prince.[19] Born David Maggard in Indianapolis in 1926, Magek (whom his bandmates called "The Chief") said that the Creator assigned him his name: "Evod (Dove for peace) and Magek (because to us the spirit is like magic)."[20] Magek lived most of his life in Chicago, where in the 1970s he attended the AACM School, eventually becoming chair of the AACM during that period. A World War II veteran, during a period of incarceration he taught himself music with the help of exchanges of letters with Eddie Harris, a journey that was chronicled in a set of prison journals he compiled and kept with him throughout his life. Magek was a unique and highly respected figure in Chicago's African American community, known for his intense and unwavering love for black people. When he himself passed away in October 2005, the performance tributes at his "homegoing" came from AACM cofounder Kelan Phil Cohran, pianist Robert Irving III and members of the Muntu Dance Theater. Both his own One Family Band and a large ensemble from the AACM led by Mwata Bowden performed a suite of his compositions.

For Rita Warford, the AACM is "a highly respected organization in the black community," even if "the black community never totally cared for the music that much." At the same time, she felt that "in any environment there's going to be, if not a whole lot of people, at least some people that like what you're doing." Ultimately, Warford felt that the "wholesome' effect that the AACM had on the black community was best symbolized by a story that Joseph Jarman brought to her.

> The Art Ensemble, they were just in the heart of the community, before they started traveling to Europe and everything. It might have been down on 43rd and Indiana or something. There was this one guy who used to come in and sit at the bar and eat a sweet potato pie. He eventually told them one night, he said, yeah, I used to be out shooting drugs and drinking all night long, but since you all have been playing down here, I just sit at the bar and eat this sweet potato pie.

Evod's life and work exemplified an important strain within the AACM—musicians who, rather than trying to become known in the international arena that is presumed to be a universal goal, instead sought to sustain and support their local community. In fact, this overall goal, supported by the collective's Chicago-based members, has played a crucial role in keeping the AACM alive as a black community institution since the departure of most of its original members in the late 1970s, nearly thirty years ago. In the end, some of the musicians whom some of the oldest AACM members call "the younger members" are in fact grandparents themselves.

J'ai deux amours . . .

When I returned to New York in 2004, after living in California throughout the 1990s, I was fortunate to be very graciously greeted by many people. It made me feel good to have my old friend and musical associate John Zorn say to me, more or less, "Get out of San Diego and come on back home," or to have Joan Logue, David Behrman, and Terri Hanlon ask how it felt to be home; or to ponder J. D. Parran's words about bringing up his son as a New Yorker, as I am doing now with my son.

At Stub's service, I saw so many musicians I knew, many of whom I had played with: Leroy Jenkins, Brian Smith, Reggie Workman, Steve Slagle, Mark Helias, Joe Lovano, Victor Lewis, Eli Fountain, Bill Lowe, Maxine Gordon, Ted Daniel, Kunle M'wanga, Salim Washington, E. J. Allen, Rufus Reid, Warren Smith, Patience Higgins, Hilton Ruiz, Clifton Anderson, Michelle Rosewoman, Cecil Bridgewater, and Bill Saxton, among others. I'm aware that for some in the jazz community, I have the image of the prodigal son, but somehow, the post-1980s genre policing seems terribly unimportant at these times, as the musicians' community simply welcomes you home. Indeed, for me the New York artist's community is home, and yet AACM concerts in Chicago are also homecomings of a very different sort.

Ultimately, the reasons why the AACM has become integral to the cultural identity of Chicago are relatively prosaic and can be enumerated at greater or lesser length. The deeper and more challenging question of why, despite the AACM's international, cross-generational multigenre purview, the crucible of Chicago continues to be integral to AACM identity, can only be hinted at in a narrative such as this one.

While waiting for the start of composer Alvin Singleton's seminar at the Juilliard School of Music, Henry Threadgill and I started talking about Ajaramu, who had passed away in Detroit in December 2006.

"Let me show you something," I said, opening up my laptop to a PDF file I had made from Ajaramu's obituary. Seeing the picture, Henry remarked, "That looks like Ajaramu—but who is Joseph A. Shelton, Jr.?"

"That's Ajaramu—his real name."

"What happened to 'Jerol Donavon'?" Henry asked, incredulous.

"That's just one of the many surprises I've gotten in writing this book," I said. "He never told you, and he never told me."

"Maybe he was in some kind of trouble. We've seen that before," Henry ventured.

"Whatever it was, he definitely kept it to himself," I observed. "Now, Henry, you don't have any surprises for me, do you?" We laughed heartily.[21]

On the morning of February 24, 2007, Henry phoned to say that Joseph Shelton became Jerol Donavon at the behest of Gene Ammons, who suggested that he needed a more exciting stage name. Henry then informed me that Leroy Jenkins had passed away that morning.

I was stunned. I had phoned Leroy in the hospital less than a week before, and he sounded optimistic about his prognosis. Yes, he had cancer in one lung, he said, but he was receiving daily visits and phone calls, and was going home that day. Another friend of his told me that he had even been shoveling snow a few days before.

A private service was held in Leroy's adopted New York City, at the Judson Church on West 4th and Thompson. Leroy's two sisters and nephew came from California, and I was asked to serve as compere. Various forms of appreciation, spoken, danced, and played, came from Muhal Richard Abrams, Alvin Singleton, Henry Threadgill, Kunle M'wanga, Jerome Cooper, Anthony Braxton, Felicia Norton, Mary Griffin, Brandon Ross, John Blake, Larry Fink and Rev. Shaku Joseph Jarman. The attendees at the service, from Ornette Coleman to Thomas Buckner to "Blue" Gene Tyranny, reflected a complex, multiethnic crosscut of the New York experimental music scene, and Leroy's lifelong embodiment of those ideals.

Someone who was at Leroy's bedside the night before his passing told me that at one point, he suddenly awakened and announced to everyone what he wanted at his memorial: "Improvisation . . . and white horses." He paused for effect. Then, seeing a group of quizzical faces, he added, laughing, "Just kidding."

Later, he awoke again and exclaimed, "Well, I'm ready to go—where are the horses?"

afterword

The Way of the Arranger

A few years back, the saxophonist and electronic musician Steve Coleman was in constant communication with my UCSD graduate students. One of his e-mails to them contained the reminder that in evaluating the impact of a musical movement (or perhaps any movement), one was obliged to consider not only what the movement did, but also what it tried (and perhaps failed) to do. As we have seen, one major thing that AACM musicians "tried" to do was to survive and even thrive while (a) pursuing their art and (b) controlling the means of its production. These goals are, in fact, intertwined with another important goal—that of affecting the discourses surrounding and mediating the activity of the African American artist.

In fact, none of these goals are likely to be realized without pursuing the others, and I'd like to invoke James Clifford's influential essay "On Ethnographic Authority" as a touchstone for establishing my working method for an interim evaluation of the collective's legacy. "One increasingly common way to manifest the collaborative production of ethnographic knowledge," Clifford writes, "is to quote regularly and at length from informants."

> But such quotations are always staged by the quoter, and tend to serve merely as examples, or confirming testimonies. Looking

beyond quotation, one might imagine a more radical polyphony . . . but this, too, would only displace ethnographic authority, still confirming the final, virtuoso orchestration by a single author of all the discourses in his or her text.[1]

Indeed, I cannot but admit my presence throughout this book an as orchestrator, an arranger of confirmatory (and sometimes conflicting) stories. However, what is on offer in the final few pages of this history of the Association for the Advancement of Creative Musicians is an unstable polyphony of quoted voices, a kind of virtual AACM meeting sampled from the many self-critical musings that I heard in my interviews with my colleagues and friends in the collective. The AACM often turned its critical eye on itself, sometimes without understanding that realizations of radical projects so often fall short of what was dreamed. All of the parties to this virtual discussion, I imagine, would recognize the mode of critique as typically AACM, even if some of the parties to the discussion have never met, and others only contributed their ancestral traces to the enterprise.

Again following Clifford, I openly admit my *prise de pouvoir* at this stage of the production of the narrative. Here, I wanted to use the narrative medium to imagine what an AACM meeting might be like with everyone present, living and ancestral. I do so, however, in the hope that this power that I have taken might be returned and shared at a different moment in the life of the text. The goal of the slave's narrative was not always vindication, but quite often, a moral plea for responsible chronicling. Underlying it all is the conviction that if you get written out of a history in which you were very evidently present, you can just write yourself back in.

The Individual

"You can't say, 'Where did the AACM music come from?'" Muhal's tone was forceful. "The AACM is a collection of individuals!"

"You have the original, and then you have this constant desire to recreate the original," Roscoe observed. "Now, somewhere that gets really watered down. The AACM was more aimed at creating an individual than an assembly line."

"But we have something in common!" Muhal was excited now. "For example, we are in agreement that we should further develop our music."[2]

"The purpose of [the AACM] was for musicians to come together and develop music, and have freedom to perform new music, in a creative environment," Thurman declared. "Those are the purposes that are on the charter of the organization, but those purposes, to me, are very real out here."

"We formed the AACM to have a power base from which we could play our music," said Muhal, "but we also took on other vibrations, some of which we hadn't anticipated when we got started. . . . Let me give you an example. The seventh item [in the AACM purposes] is 'to increase mutual respect between creative artists and musical tradesmen, booking agents, managers, promoters and instrument manufacturers.' In that department, we found that the only way to create mutual respect between artists and musical tradesmen was for us to become both the artists and the tradesmen."[3]

"I don't think anybody could have anticipated it going for thirty-five years," marveled Jodie. "Maybe a few months, or a year or so. Maybe somebody envisioned that, but I wasn't one of them. I'm not a visionary."

The Book

"If they want the real story," Lester Bowie told George, "your book will give more insight. The Art Ensemble book gives insight on how cats really think. That's why we wanted to do it that way."

"That was one reason why Muhal said that somebody in the organization should write the book," Jodie pointed out. "Because then you could really talk about it to them. When people called me to talk, I referred them to somebody else, because I didn't really want to talk about it to them. I don't think they would have understood what I was trying to say, or I was afraid that they'd take it somewhere else."

"I would never have some writer doing my autobiography," Lester continued. "They wouldn't know what to do with it. They wouldn't have it down right. I couldn't even tell them the shit that I could tell you. I wouldn't want to tell them the shit that I would tell you."

"[The book] is a part of the kinds of situations that you and I and a lot of the cats have talked about a lot of years," said Wallace, "a situation about a collective that should have been saving this kind of business years and years ago. . . . When we look around, there are people that have more documents on us than we have on ourselves."

Expansion and Sacrifice

Joseph pointed with pride to "all of our people who came out of there who are engaged in world-class academia. Even though they are working for these institutions and they have limits, and they have the policies of the institutions to adhere to, subconsciously they are still pushing that AACM ideal of freedom of expression and imagination, of search. Find out what's going on, don't be afraid to experiment. They're telling all their students this, and that's what the AACM was all about. These students, even if you have only one out of a thousand, subconsciously that one out of a thousand is going to be carrying the purposes, or the essence of the cause of this organization, on and on and on. So it's going to never die."

"We used to go by Muhal's house, and I can remember Roscoe saying, well, if he couldn't make it playing music, then he wasn't going to make it," recalled Sparx. "All them cats had to tighten their belts. I worked for the Edison Company for a number of years, and I used to look at them cats and wonder how they made it, because they had a lot of lean years, you know?"

"When the AACM started getting a name, certain kinds of jealousy erupted from the white community, that we didn't have no whites in there," Henry observed. "The reason was that they could hear that the music was crossing over into their shit. They knew that we were going to be up into their shit, any minute. And they were right. As soon as we would start to do something that didn't fall under the heading of so-called jazz, it would come up: 'What are y'all doing? You don't have any whites in there.'"

"Well, a lot of white people couldn't get into the AACM," Fred pointed out. "Ken Vandermark, all them cats that come out of Hal Russell's movement. I guess a lot of guys felt that they didn't want these [white] people to control it. They didn't want the Man to control the stuff."

"For a while," Ann reminded everyone, "the AACM School had white faculty and students, which was considered problematic by some members."

"But you have to keep expanding, and there are other musicians," Rasul replied. "The thing about guarding it is that so many things have been taken away from us."

"I personally didn't want to deal with white people in jazz," said Kelan. "It's my thinking that music is the language of a people, and I was interested in what the language could do for black people. I wasn't interested in what it could do for whites."

"From the very outset, there have been supporters of the organization who are Caucasian," Douglas pointed out. "As patrons or as audience, there have always been white folks there, even as board members, and the sky did not fall, and we did not disintegrate as a black group. They lent not only their moral support and intellectual support, they lent their financial support."

"I didn't have nothing against whites," Kelan replied. "I didn't like the idea that here we are over here, working to get our thing together and the scene had dried up. It didn't dry up for white musicians. They didn't have to go to New York. It had dried up for blacks, because they had decided to take our music and they purposely cut our thing down."

"Our idea of bringing the AACM together was to control our destiny as a people," Sparx said, "rather than be depending on the venues that were open to them at that time. It's obvious what has happened to us historically, so it was kind of a move in that direction, primarily for black music as such. That was predicated on what has happened in the past to a lot of artists, in terms of their creations, and what they got from that materially."

"The sacrifices that the founders had to go through and still go through, that's still valid." Maia was pensive. "Racism has not gone away. We have more opportunities in some ways and we have less in other ways."

"The organization has existed as a means of sustaining oneself, one's culture," Douglas replied. "It's been an important institution for black people. We've been a source for music, for employment, for education. We've been a support system, emotional, intellectual, and spiritual. That's not to say that it couldn't make a transformation, but it would certainly change the nature of what the AACM is."

"I think it's important to have organizations that are all male, and organizations that are all female, because of the nature of what the purpose of those organizations are," Maia replied. "I don't have a problem with those things. I do have a problem with not being able to relate. Be flexible. There are ways to incorporate other nationalities into the organization."

"But in the larger society," said Douglas, "the reason why the organization was founded, to me, still exists. That is, black people still don't have a lot of structures that enable them to work as artists on a certain level, and to be able to determine their own destiny."

"The reason why it was founded like that from the beginning, I don't know enough about, except for what I can see from the outside," Maia said. "What I see from the outside is that black people didn't have enough opportunities to have control over what we do, what we put out, what is considered valid music. I don't see that as being one hundred percent changed, so it may still be important."

"For me, as someone who really sees himself as a universalist and open, I think that I have my own consternation about having the thing opened up," Douglas felt. "Why? Because what the organization was founded for, we've not been able to achieve that. Maybe we won't ever be able to achieve it."

"But it didn't say, the Association for the Advancement of Creative Black Musicians," Fred responded. "If we were responsible for coming up with the idea as black people, anybody could contribute to the cause. They had white people marching with Martin Luther King." Janis agreed. "When I go back to the purposes, not one of them said, we are here to create original music for the total and exclusive enjoyment of African Americans."

"Music's for everybody," Rasul said simply. "You live and you learn that you can't discriminate on people from wherever they're from. They're human beings. We have to be more human. I learn to be more human and more tolerant as I get older, and some of your philosophy of the way we were brought up changes, as you get older. As you mature, you see that we all need to be more tolerant of each other as people, as humanity."

After a long silence, Joseph spoke. "I think that the AACM was always sort of afraid of integration, subconsciously, because of what it did to the society at large," he observed softly. "I went to an integrated high school and an integrated grammar school too, but when the society at large was integrated, it put the black people in second place again, although they had the illusion of being in equal place. It caused much more pain than the separation had caused, because the black community began to lose its identity."

"At this point in time," began Anthony, "we can talk of a global community of global musics. Part of the significance of the open improvisational music has been its ability to provide a forum for interactive experiences for people from different parts of the planet, which lends itself to transglobal, transvibrational experiences."

"I work with musicians from everywhere, from all different parts of the world, and the color issue is not an issue," said Rasul, expressing the reality of his long experience as a resident of Paris. "But the AACM . . . that's a tough one, because the color issue still exists here, in the United States, differently than it does in other places. We're still pretty much kind of segregated, more than other places in the world."

"We've had such global experiences," Anthony ventured, "that we can't then suddenly separate ourselves from our experience and try to be back on the South Side of Chicago and look at things from that perspective. I wish I could, but I can't."

"That's right," said Rasul. "A lot of people haven't been able to go to other countries, and they don't see the humanity in the people from all places in the world. After you travel, a lot of this stuff, you have to throw it out the window, man."

"This issue is going to be ongoing until the first generation passes," said Joseph. "The fourth generation will revise the laws and there will be a rainbow organization. The third generation cannot do it, but the fourth generation can. These are very young people who are maturing, but in twenty years they will be responsible and they're going to have to decide, because the first and second generation, ninety-eight percent of it will be gone. In order for the organization to survive, that third generation will have to make the necessary decisions as to how to move it on."

"But everybody in the group is forty or over," Dushun broke in. "We have nowhere to pass this down to, and we don't know our history."

"Wait a minute," said George. "What about Matana Roberts, Corey Wilkes, Dee Alexander, Jeff Parker? Chad Taylor, Savoir Faire, Darius Savage? Plus you have people who have been around a while, like Robert Griffin, Ike Jackson, Steve Berry, Yosef Ben Israel, Avreeayl Ra, Taalib'Din Ziyad, and people like Ari Brown who have reconnected, providing their experience. Then, you've got Mwata's son Khari B with his 'discopoetics,' and Maia's children, and Phil's, who formed that band and went to New York. All you have to do is pop over to the Velvet Lounge and talk to Fred. He seems to be the central mentor now. Everybody looks up to him."[4]

"Coming in new, though, you feel like they want you to do a lot of stuff, but it's kind of like a generation gap," said Nicole. "People here in Chicago, from the generation before me, have all their old garbage issues with each other, like an old family. They've been working together for a really long time, and it's hard for the new people to really find a place in the organization."

"Still, what we have to do in the AACM right now is bring in a whole new crop," Dushun replied. "We're getting to be the Gray Panthers in a minute," joked Ernest. "I think it's going to be a real problem. That's why we're attempting to recruit new members. We have to."

"I think it should spread worldwide," said Rasul with alacrity, echoing a phrase Lester Bowie often used about the AACM.

Emilio Cruz, who was visiting the meeting as a representative of BAG, stood up and lent his perspective as an elder. "To be sophisticated, to function in the world," he began gravely, "in every avenue that you step into, there exists paradox. What makes a person naïve is that they don't have an understanding of paradox. The idea of having an all-black organization has a great deal of vitality to it, and when you are struggling to create an identity and opportunity that won't exist anywhere, what you have to do is to cast down your bucket where you are. You have to take in the resources that are necessary. That idea in itself is not a bad idea. In that, you build up your strength.

"But in terms of recognizing how one deals in the world realistically, the road that you take in order to better yourself, to realize your dreams, cannot be one that is a direct reaction to the brutality that has been placed upon you. You're doing this because it is a matter of self-defense. Self-defense is always reasonable. But then I have to know clearly what it is I'm defending myself against. I'm defending myself against injustice. That doesn't mean that to defend myself against injustice, I become a perpetrator of injustice.

"I don't want to be like my enemy. I want to be better than my enemy. Every time I get to be like my enemy, I end up joining my enemy, and I join my enemy against myself.

"All of these things," Emilio sat down wearily, "involve a recognition that life is very complicated."

Boxing with Tradition

"Is it important that new members stem from the jazz tradition?" George asked. "What about people doing other kinds of black music?"

"That's not necessarily important, that they stem from the jazz tradition, but it always helps," said Ernest. "Now, if they want to come in and be a part of the AACM and play this music, that's a different story. As long as they express a desire to come in and play this music, I think we can work with them. But probably it's best suited for somebody that, quote-unquote has come from the so-called jazz tradition."

"But the problem is like what Duke said once," George pointed out. "'It is becoming increasingly difficult to decide where jazz starts or where it stops.'"[5]

"Jazz, for me, was a form that addressed many different things." Anthony waxed analytic. "But the most important thing for me is that jazz expressed the intellectual, esoteric, vibrational, spiritual, and emotional aspirations that have always existed from a tricentric perspective in an African or Afrocentric thought unit.

"On the other hand," he continued, "playing with Evan Parker in that context, is it still jazz? I would say that it is jazz and it's not jazz. Once people start playing whatever they want to play, it gets kind of complex. I'm playing my music, and I'm approaching it from my so-called aesthetic and psychology, but I'm playing with a person who has different experiences, who in an open improvisation, can express that just like I can. I don't think that I can call that 'jazz' without violating that person on some level, because everybody has music."

"That's why Great Black Music is such a great term," Lester said, "because if they can acknowledge that, they're giving us respect, and they're actually atoning for calling it jazz. They're actually freeing themselves. They acknowledge it as being great, they acknowledge it as being black, and everybody knows its musicality. If they can relate to jazz, they can relate to Great Black Music. If they can relate to blues, they can relate to Great Black Music. As long as they say 'jazz,' they're not really apologizing. When they say 'Great Black Music,' that means 'I apologize,' and everything can move forward from that."

"Really, Great Black Music is an aspect of the Holy Ghost, for us as a people," Ameen observed. "It's the music that brought us into existence. Great Black Music is one of the blessings that came with us standing up to a white world and saying, we're going to do what we want to do, despite what you try to do to us. Great Black Music is a result of us having the courage to use our Great Blackness, and realizing that this is our only power."

Regrets

"It's quite perplexing to me," Janis began, "to see the organization reaching its thirty-fifth anniversary and it still had not gotten its physical building. It still has not owned its own property."

"Well, very few musicians' collectives have their own building, not to mention bands," George ventured. "I don't think Duke had a building for his orchestra. Sometimes we can be pretty hard on ourselves."

"The AACM had a building fund, so the AACM should have had a building," Fred reasoned directly. Jodie agreed, "Any organization that's thirty-five years old, that's the least they should expect. The reason why they don't have a space is because the musicians haven't come together."

"You can't say that we didn't have the ideas and plans, but our focus on the music as individuals took up our time," Muhal observed. "We talked about getting our own building, and even set up a building fund. We talked about doing our own recording. But we were consumed by our individual achievement as musicians, and we didn't give enough time to the other."

"That question has been posed to us a couple of times," responded Ernest. "Do you want to operate as an organization and develop this stuff into an institution, or do you want to be this loosely based band of musicians who band together to produce their own concerts, etc., etc.? We've been operating as a member-driven organization, which is cool, and the members individually have made great strides, but the organization hasn't been put in a place to make it work for the members. We need to get the organization to a place where it helps the members—all the members. We want to move to the final stages of where it should be, which is the true institutional stage."

"We should have," Anthony reflected, "but we couldn't have done it because there was still one stratum of trust that we were not able to cross."

"One of the reasons why we haven't achieved more than we have is because of a lack of unity," Douglas felt. "The way our society has developed, this is a very difficult thing to obtain." Ernest's observation turned on this point. "Everybody comes in with their own concept of what the AACM is, which is cool," said Ernest, "but then, maybe the organization doesn't move in the direction it needs to move in because everybody has their own concept of what it is."

"Certainly there are a lot of valid concepts," Roscoe responded. "The problem comes when you get too fixated on one concept as being the only concept. You don't have to throw away one concept in order to try out another." Anthony agreed. "The AACM was transidiomatic. It was not about a style that everyone could hum and be a part of. It was a thought process. It was a recognition of transformal dynamics, of an emerging global platform, and all that would imply in terms of a challenge to definitions of identity."

"I guess that makes a lot of sense," George said, "but I remember reading somewhere about how you called the Great Black Music idea 'racist.'"[6]

"I quit the AACM several times," said Anthony, "but in fact, in the end, I see all of that as irrelevant." Ameen agreed strongly. "The music has got to prevail over all things else—environmental discrepancies, personal discrepancies, all of those little tribal differences."

"What has kept the organization alive was what I wanted to keep alive," said Jodie. "My youngest son's wife called me. She said, do you know any place where they give piano lessons? I thought, the AACM, that's what they do. If that ever dies, then the AACM dies. That's what's holding it together. That, to me, is the backbone of the AACM.

"All these groups that come historically before the AACM, their agenda was often the motivation of their own art," Wadada pointed out. "Our agenda was not only to motivate our own art, but you notice that a clause in our by-laws clearly connected us to service to a community. To get into the collectivism that was expressed in the design of the organization hasn't been totally achieved, but the kind of achievement has let us know that this is the right future."

Survival

"Somehow . . ." Edward paused for emphasis. "Somehow, we decided that the organization had to live forever. Is that really necessary? We've accepted that the organization should always be around. Nobody has ever considered that maybe there's going to be a last AACM meeting one day." Fred's response was kindly, but firm. "The name of the game out here is survival, and any way that you can, you keep your music and keep everything going," he said pointedly. "You have to be able to maneuver through this system, because we all know what's happening."

"Those that survived probably have no idea how long it would take to finally come into yourself," Henry said. "They succeeded because it was a rare combination of unique people that got tossed together, a bunch of hard-nosed, hard-ass, determined-ass individuals that had something in them creatively and musically."

"Let us go back to the blues and before the blues, before that word existed, back to the cotton fields. Survival was laid out right there," Muhal said gravely. "The way to survive is to stop trying to be like other people and just follow the thought of who you are."[7]

"That required a certain type of character," said Henry. "These people are still here, and they kept stretching their own boundaries, in spite of adversity, and with great bulldog tenacity, have forged ahead when there was no payday, through all these years, and have not fallen by the wayside into obscurity, or into a permanent position in the underground."

"The AACM will survive because we're still surviving," Rasul declared. "I think that anybody who really cared about it and was directly involved in it will keep it alive, keep the spirit of it alive. That's what I try to do in my travels. I talk about the AACM, my experiences with it, and the need for it, and in the music that we do, too. It's a direct part of my affiliation with it."

Contemplating the Postjazz Continuum

In 1977, Muhal Richard Abrams predicted that the AACM's influence would empower other musicians and groups. "A lot of people will pick up on the example and do very well with it," Abrams said. "A lot of people that are not AACM people. Now who those people will be a couple of years from now, who knows?"[8] This prediction proved prescient as New York experimental music movements emerging in the late 1980s, such as the movements of Downtown II and "totalism," adopted the language of diversity.[9] Improvisor and composer John Zorn, arguably the most well-known artist to emerge from Downtown II, connected this articulation of diversity directly with the AACM, an important influence on his work. In discovering Braxton and the Art Ensemble, Zorn noticed that "the guy's [Braxton] got a great head, he's listening to all this different music. It all connected up."[10] Echoing long-standing AACM premises, Zorn declared that "I want to break all these hierarchies: the idea that classical music is better than jazz, that jazz is better than rock. I don't think that way."[11]

Downtown II artists, who were never subjected to the discourses of canonization and "roots" that were being used to police the work of black experimental musicians, were able to take full advantage of their relative freedom from cultural arbitration. Thus, contemporaneous commentary on Zorn and other Downtown II artists celebrated this diversity of sonic and cultural reference in their work, even as comparable efforts by black experimentalists were being routinely condemned. In 1988 John Rockwell found no particular difficulty in declaring that Zorn not only "transcends categories; better, he's made a notable career crashing them together and grinding them to dust."[12] In contrast, a 1982 Rockwell piece could insist of Anthony Braxton that "however much he may resist categories, Mr. Braxton's background is in jazz, which means an improvisatory tradition," an evocation in a single sentence of the eugenicist power of the one-drop rule which revoked, rather than celebrated, Braxton's mobility.[13]

Finally, unlike the black artists who preceded and influenced them, Downtown II artists were routinely framed as transcending race as well as genre. By 1989, a *New York Times* reviewer could declare that the repertory of Zorn's "Naked City" project

> mirrors a typically modern sensibility, in which the culture of our grandparents—whether it's defined by race, religion or nationality—is abandoned, or at least tempered, in favor of the possibilities of endless information. Eclecticism isn't simply a position for some composers: it's the only position. It's the only culture that makes sense to them, that they can depend on—a culture of musical literacy.[14]

Downtown II's press coding as white, however, was not only at variance with this image of transcendence, but seemed to have little basis in either New York City's geography or musical affinities. African American saxophonist Greg Osby's acerbic observation neatly encapsulated the issue:

"I played with all the downtown cats but nobody called *me* a downtown cat"—a statement that some AACM members could have made twenty years before.[15]

Jazz critic Bill Shoemaker has shown the outlines of an already emerging postjazz, post–new music network for improvised music that moves beyond gatekeeping authorities, aiming toward the creation of an environment where canonizing pronouncements are both powerless and meaningless. For Shoemaker, the old idea of the "avant-garde" as a "style" of jazz has fallen by the wayside in the course of social, collegial, technological, and economic developments. In fact, Shoemaker's claim is that jazz and the avant-garde are, in effect, becoming separate entities: "It is a mistake to conclude that avant-garde music has been assimilated into a jazz melting pot. On the contrary, the avant-garde has moved on—and jazz is the poorer for it, as now little more than business considerations and the inertia of a blemished shared history prevent jazz and what it claims as its avant-garde from rupturing irrevocably."[16]

There is much to commend this view; in fact, there is no reason to view the jazz tradition as somehow exempt from the fragmentation and instability that has been endemic to the condition of postmodernity, particularly when, as Shoemaker notes, "Successive waves of musicians—proponents of the AACM-articulated idea of creative music, the Downtown NYC experimental scene, the largely European improvised-music network and others—were increasingly emphatic in disassociating themselves from jazz."[17] Moreover, in the wake of the AACM's 1969 gamble on Paris and the European free improvisation *Emanzipation,* it was evident that, in Shoemaker's words, "the movements spawned in Amsterdam, Berlin, Chicago and London have redrawn the map, removing New York from the center of the avant-garde world. Unsurprisingly, artist collectives figure prominently in most of these movements—the AACM, Amsterdam's BIM, the London Musicians Collection [*sic*] . . ."[18] For Shoemaker, the technoscape, represented by the World Wide Web, electronic mail, and listservs, has been a critically important factor in the globalization of the avant-garde, as well as the panoply of new artist-run labels that accompanied the demise of relatively expensive vinyl fabrication in favor of cheap CD reproduction. In Europe, for instance, many of these labels come together via the Internet on the *European Free Improvisation Pages.*[19]

This emerging, globalized community of new music would need to draw upon the widest range of traditions, while not being tied to any one. Perhaps, as Attali would have it, such music would exist "in a multifaceted time in which rhythms, styles, and codes diverge, interdependencies become more burdensome, and rules dissolve"—a "new noise."[20] What will not produce a new noise, however, is the ongoing tendency to frame as canonical what I have called elsewhere "a composite construction of a whiteness-based, transnational, pan-European experimental aesthetic that would frame as axiomatic the permanent marginalization of African American agency."[21] This is the danger Morgan Craft pointed out when he wrote to the British magazine *Wire*, "I'm constantly fed this steady stream of future thinking folks from Germany, Japan, UK, Norway, etc, but when it comes to America all I hear about is the genius that is free folk or if it's black it must be hiphop, jazz, or long dead. How many more articles on Albert Ayler do we really need?"[22]

Indeed, if jazz, the "avant-garde," and other musical movements have become part of a larger network in which no one scene is dominant, resistance to the essentializing impulses that discursively block freely forming conceptual, financial, social, and cultural flows is critically important. At the same time, Craft does not see the problem as based solely on racialized dislocations of discourse and power. In addition, he points to the assumption of responsibility and agency by African American experimental artists as crucial to the emergence of new noise:

> What does the black American musician do now with the space s/he has been given? Hiphop, jazz and blues existed. Improvisation and resourcefulness are present. The awareness of European and Asian traditions informs our approaches. Technology is within reach. The hype of the interconnectedness of individuals is here. What does the black American do with all of this? What do we do now that sample culture is so prominent and success comes before an actual gestation period with our materials? What is the black American working on in terms of taking sound forward? Where is the next generation willing to dig deep and come back with the new blueprints we desperately need?[23]

My 1999 interview with Edward Wilkerson affirmed some of the dangers to which creative musicians could be exposed when we fail to engage this kind of radically open dialogue and self-critique:

> I don't think the organization is as exposed musically as it used to be. I don't think cats are as aware as they were of as much music as cats used to be when I first started coming around the AACM, aware of what's going

on musically around the world. People are more concerned with paying the bills, their jobs. The AACM has become more insular, more like a church group now. I'm talking mainly from here [Chicago].

Whether or not one agrees with this assessment, its frankness resonates with the willingness of AACM members to confront both the successes and the failures of the movement. In fact, new noises are being realized on an ongoing basis, and at Shoemaker's writing, these included "John Zorn's hardcore entente and his Radical Jewish Culture faction, David S. Ware and Matthew Shipp's respective tenures with indie-rock labels, and champions like Sonic Youth's Thurston Moore."[24] Of course, many more new noises have emerged since that time, and it would seem self-evident that many of these, as Shoemaker notes, have "a growing audience that has little or no connection with the jazz mainstream."[25]

The network Shoemaker describes can be viewed in the same terms as those used by theorists Michael Hardt and Antonio Negri to discuss the antiglobalization movement, which for them constitutes a new form of challenge to centralized authority. For Hardt and Negri, the movement "is not defined by any single identity, but can discover commonality in its multiplicity."[26] Similarly, Muhal Richard Abrams declared more than twenty years ago, "First we make for ourselves an atmosphere, in which we can survive, in spite of this environment—simply through that which we have in common. We have something in common! For example, we are in agreement that we should further develop our music. Whatever else we do outside of our central development, we will not let this central development be destroyed."[27]

Ultimately, the AACM's gamble can be viewed as pointing the way toward a mobile, boundary-crossing experimentalism that exemplifies these notions of commonality in multiplicity and individuality within the aggregate. The example of the AACM has been central to the coming canonization, not of a new musical aesthetic with defined borders, but of a new kind of musician who works across genres with fluidity, grace, discernment, and trenchancy. After nearly forty years of a living AACM presence, the significance of what these new musicians have done up to now, as well as what they might create in the future, is only now beginning to be understood.

Atmospheres

"The AACM helped me to feel that I came out of something, a generation or an area, that people know about," Thurman said softly. "It probably played more of a role in me feeling confident in this business. It has played a strong part in helping me to feel that I was a part of something that was bigger than I realized. I would meet people here, in Europe or wherever, and they would remind me of how great the music was."

"We take for granted the power of what music really is," agreed Nicole. "It's not about trying to make a few dollars at some concert. It's not about, do we have a crowd, or do I have an image, or have I, quote-unquote, made it."

"The AACM taught me love of my fellow musicians," Alvin continued. "I feel as though I can make music with anyone—with a child, or with the most accomplished musicians."

"It opened me up to be more open-minded about music and all of its different approaches," Stub said. "It's not regimented, but as disciplined as the organization was, it mirrored the discipline in my personal life. It surpassed the individual self into the realm of sincerity, from then to now. I'm very emotional about it."

"As I was talking to Peggy [Abrams] the other day," Joseph began, "she remarked that even though we don't see each other as often as we'd like to, or even though we don't communicate as often as we'd like to, that link is still there. There is a psychic energy that binds all of these people together. The energy is circular. It keeps going around and around and it's also expanding."

Ann Ward followed with a little story. "One day AJ [Ajaramu] came into the meeting, and I said, why would anybody want to be a part of the AACM? He gave me a speech that would bring tears to your eyes. He said, what do you mean? Do you know what kind of history we're talking here? He laid it out, to the gist that it's bigger than all of us, or any one of us will ever be, no matter how successful we get. He said that this music, this collective, was born of a faith and a strength and a belief in creativity that is millenniums old—this is our culture, from Africa. He said that it was greater than any of us because it was a collective, it was all of us. If we couldn't all be there, it wasn't AACM."

"It's about independence, too," Nicole added. "It's about each person knowing that they have the power to create their own reality through the world of music, and that they should do that, instead of following whatever's been done before, and at the same time, being grounded in the tradition, but really trying to reach inside themselves to create—it's like creating another universe, really."

"The AACM brought out the creativity in me," Amina reflected. "It was there all along, but I was so naïve. It was a way for me to open up to the fact that I had something to offer. The AACM showed me who I was as a person, and it opened me up to all kinds of possibilities. It was a great thing to happen; I don't know if it will ever happen again."

"The AACM has been the ultimate musical experience in my life," Alvin declared to the membership. "I've lived my life according to AACM standards. It's prepared me to play with Kidd [Jordan], to be close to Billy Higgins, to Vernel Fournier. It has allowed me to play what I want to play with no compromise. You don't compromise the music. I'd quit first."

Futures

In 1982, Fred Anderson, undaunted after his convoluted 1977 experience with his Birdhouse performance space, took over the Velvet Lounge, an ancient bar on Indiana Avenue near Cermak Road, and transformed it into an internationally known center for improvised music. When the building housing the Velvet was finally condemned amid the wild real estate speculation in the area, Fred simply moved the Velvet around the corner to 67 E. Cermak Road, where it opened in 2006. "Innovation cannot be stopped," Muhal commented. "It can be sidetracked, tampered with in a million different ways, but it cannot be stopped from getting to its rightful position according to what it has generated. It may be me, you, your kids, or even their kids. It doesn't have to happen to me."

"As I see it," said George, "the organization will probably outlive the people who started it. I think that's scary for some people." Nicole Mitchell, always community-minded, was one of the earliest supporters and fundraisers for the new Velvet, which she accomplished in the midst of a burgeoning international career and her new position as copresident of the AACM along with Douglas Ewart, the first time that a woman had held the top position of leadership and service in the collective. "I see the AACM as a movement, part of the whole Black Arts Movement, part of a movement to uplift a people, to help us to heal ourselves as a people," said Nicole. "That was the purpose of the music."

"Secrets pervade the African continent on many different levels," Braxton intoned, "and I feel that AACM consists of a group of people who, in a strange kind of way, are the existential inheritors of a possibility to build new spiritual and processual systems. The AACM is a reappearance of the esoteric musics and informations, and each of the primary people would all evolve themselves to the point where they each got a key. Somewhere in the third millennium, I believe that the AACM will be a point of definition for those individuals who would like to find out what each key activated. The summation effect of all twelve keys will fulfill some esoteric component related to some cosmic something. That will make it apparent that our group did exist in this time period, and that the work we were doing was serious work."

"The people who called some of us charlatans, a lot of those people are dead," Threadgill remarked. "A lot of them don't want you to remember that they even said these things."

"I believe in something that is bigger than I am as a musician," Muhal agreed. "I am optimistic and fully confident that my participation in the process will bring humans to an understanding of how great their individual contribution can be."

"I think of one of the slogans in the beginning—Power Stronger Than Itself,'" Jones mused softly. "That might absolutely be a truth." Jarman agreed. "Regardless of what we've gone through, we're still a part of the power that's stronger than itself. Even though all of the primary elements may shift, and even maybe one day the name changes, it's still there forever, it's in, plugged into history."

"We were never concerned with how it was going to come off," Muhal said with a definitive air. "We were just concerned with the fact that we were going to do it, and that it was going to happen. Whatever takes place up there, that's it. There's nothing that can go wrong, because there're nothing to compare it with."

appendix a

INTERVIEWS CONDUCTED BY THE AUTHOR

Abrams, Muhal Richard. Chicago, Illinois, December 26, 1997; New York City,
    June 23, 1998; June 24, 1998; June 25, 1998; October 29, 1998; July 19, 1999;
    July 29, 1999.

Ajaramu. Chicago, Illinois, July 12, 1998.

Alexander, Martin "Sparx." Chicago, Illinois, December 31, 1997.

Anderson, Fred. Chicago, Illinois, July 8, 1998; February 9, 1999.

Barefield, A. Spencer. Detroit, Michigan, October 14, 2000.

Barker, Thurman. Jeffersonville, New York, October 24, 1998.

Berry, Fred. San Mateo, California, February 6, 1999.

Black, Larayne. Chicago, Illinois, February 15, 1999.

Bluiett, Hamiet. San Diego, California, March 5, 2000.

Bowden, Mwata. Chicago, Illinois, June 18, 1999.

Bowie, Lester. New York City, July 22, 1999.

Braxton, Anthony. Middletown, Connecticut, June 27, 1998; October 23, 1998.

Burton, Art Turk. Chicago, Illinois, June 28, 1999.

Carroll, Baikida. La Jolla, California, April 8, 2000; Woodstock, New York, July 1,
    2000.

Christian, Jodie. Chicago, Illinois, June 10, 1998.

Cohran, Kelan Phil. Chicago, Illinois, February 14, 1999.

Colson, Iqua, and Adegoke Steve Colson. Montclair, N.J., October 21, 1998.

Cranshaw, Emanuel. Chicago, Illinois, February 11, 1999.

Cruz, Emilio. New York City, July 24, 1999.

Dawkins, Ernest Khabeer. Chicago, Illinois, June 24, 1999.

Difda, Kalaparusha Ahrah. Bronx, New York, July 22, 1999.

Dinwiddie, Flo and Gene. La Puente, California, July 8, 1999.

Ehrlich, Marty. New York City, July 20, 1999.

El'Zabar, Kahil. Chicago, Illinois, February 4, 1999.

Ewart, Douglas. Chicago, Illinois, December 26, 1997; Oakland, California, February 7, 1999.

Ewart, Douglas. Telephone interview. March 3, 2004.

Favors Maghostut, Malachi. Chicago, Illinois, July 12, 1998.

Fielder, Alvin. New Orleans, Louisiana, August 16, 2003.

Freeman, Chico. New York City, July 24, 1999.

Gordon, Frank. Maplewood, N.J., October 19, 1998.

Jarman, Shaku Joseph. Brooklyn, New York, June 26, 1998; October 22, 1998.

Jenkins, Leroy. Brooklyn, New York, June 25, 1998; October 27, 1998.

Jones, Leonard. Ratingen, Germany, September 18, 1998.

Lake, Oliver. Montclair, N.J., October 18, 1998; July 25, 1999.

Lane-Ewart, Janis. Chicago, Illinois. June 21, 1999.

Lashley, Lester. Chicago, Illinois, August 7, 2005.

Lashley, Marilyn. San Diego, California, August 16, 2003.

Litweiler, John. Chicago, Illinois, February 13, 1999.

Magek, Evod. Chicago, Illinois, February 11, 1999.

Maia. Chicago, Illinois, June 25, 1999.

McMillan, Wallace LaRoy. Chicago, Illinois, June 18, 1999.

Mitchell, Nicole. Chicago, Illinois, September 9, 1999.

Mitchell, Roscoe. Madison, Wisconsin, December 27 and 28, 1997.

Mock, King. Amsterdam, The Netherlands, September 22, 1998.

Mosley, Dushun. AACM School, Chicago, Illinois, February 13, 1999.

Moye, Famoudou Don. Chicago, Illinois, February 10, 1999; June 21, 1999.

Muhammad, Ameen. Chicago, Illinois, February 10, 1999.

Myers, Amina Claudine. New York City, June 26, 1998; October 27, 1998.

Nicholson, Reggie. New York City, October 19, 1998.

Nurullah, Shanta. Chicago, Illinois, February 14, 1999.

Parker, Jeff. Chicago, Illinois, September 3, 1999.

Parran, J. D. New York City, April 19, 1999.

Robinson, Troy. North Hills, California, July 7, 1999.

Siddik, Rasul. Los Angeles, California, October 7, 1998.

Smith, Wadada Leo. Fillmore, California, December 20 and 21, 1997; Sespe, California. December 21, 1997; La Jolla, California, March 7, 1999.

Stubblefield, John. New York City, October 22, 1998.

Thompson, Malachi. Telephone interview, August 15, 2005.

Threadgill, Henry. New York City, June 24, 1998; October 18, 1998.

Toyozumi, Rochelle, and Mrs. Willa McCall, Chicago, Illinois. June 22, 1999.

Uba, M'Chaka. San Diego, California, March 16, 1999.

Ward, Ann. Chicago, Illinois, February 15, 1999.

Ware, James Jabbo. New York City, July 20, 1999.

Warford, Rita. New York City, November 1, 1999.

Wilkerson, Edward. Chicago, Illinois, February 11, 1999.

Willis, Reginald. Chicago, Illinois, June 20, 1999.

appendix b

SELECTED AACM RECORDINGS

8 Bold Souls. *8 Bold Souls*. Sessoms, 1987.

———. *Ant Farm*. Arabesque Recordings, 1994. Compact disc.

———. *Last Option*. Thrill Jockey Records 071, 1999. Compact disc.

Abrams, Muhal Richard. *1–OQA+19*. Black Saint 120017-2, 1978. Compact disc.

———. *Levels and Degrees of Light*. Delmark DS-413, 1967. Vinyl disc. Delmark DD-413, 1967. Compact disc.

———. *Lifea Blinec*. Arista Novus AN3000, 1978. Vinyl disc.

———. *One Line, Two Views*. New World Records 80469-2, 1995. Compact disc.

———. *Spihumonesty*. Black Saint 120032, 1980. Compact disc.

———. *Things to Come from Those Now Gone*. Delmark DE-430, 1972. Compact disc.

———. *The UMO Jazz Orchestra Plays the Music of Muhal Richard Abrams*. Slam CD 506, 1999. Compact disc.

———. *The Visibility of Thought*. Mutable Music MM17502-2, 2001. Compact disc.

Abrams, Muhal Richard, and Amina Claudine Myers. *Duet*. Black Saint 120051, 1993. Compact disc.

Abrams, Muhal Richard, George Lewis, and Roscoe Mitchell. *Streaming*. PI Recordings PI 22, 2006. Compact disc.

Air. *Air Lore*. Arista Novus AN3014, 1980. Vinyl disc.

———. *Air Raid*. Trio Records PA-7156, 1979. Compact disc.

———. *Air Song*. Trio PA-7120, 1975. Compact disc.

———. *Air Time*. Nessa N-12, 1978. Vinyl disc.

———. *Air Time*. Nessa NCD-12, 1996. Compact disc.

Anderson, Fred. *Another Place*. Moers Music 01058, 1978. Vinyl disc.

————. *Fred Anderson Quartet Live at the Velvet Lounge*. Vol. 2. Asian Improv AIR 0054, 2000. Compact disc.

————. *Live at the Velvet Lounge*. OkkaDisk OD12023, 1998. Compact disc.

————. *Timeless: Live at the Velvet Lounge*. Delmark DVD 1568, 2006. DVD-Video disc.

Anderson, Fred, Marilyn Crispell, and Hamid Drake. *Destiny*. OkkaDisk OD12003, 1994. Compact disc.

Art Ensemble of Chicago. *A.A.C.M. Great Black Music/Message to Our Folks*. Spot 549, [1969] 2004. Compact disc.

————. *A.A.C.M. Great Black Music: Reese and the Smooth Ones* (BYG-Actuel GET 329, 1969). Vinyl disc.

————. *The Art Ensemble of Chicago in Concert*. EFOR Films 2869005, [1981] 2004. DVD-Video disc.

————. *The Art Ensemble of Chicago with Fontella Bass*. Verve 067865, 1971. Compact disc.

————. *Art Ensemble of Soweto*. DIW 52954, 1992. Compact disc.

————. *The Art Ensemble: 1967/68*. Nessa NCD-2500 A/B/C, 1993. Three compact discs.

————. *Chi-Congo*. Varese Sarabande (USA) VSD 3020615282, [1970] 2005. Compact disc.

————. *Coming Home Jamaica*. Atlantic/WEA, 1998. Compact disc.

————. *A Jackson in Your House*. Affinity AFF 752, [1969] 1989. Compact disc.

————. *Les stances à Sophie*. Emi Pathe CO62 11365, 1970. Compact disc.

————. *Live at Mandel Hall*. Delmark DE-432, 1972. Compact disc.

————. *Live in Paris*. Fuel 2000 302 061 383 2, [1969] 2004. Compact disc.

————. *People in Sorrow*. Nessa N-3, 1969. Vinyl disc.

————. *Swim: A Musical Adventure*. Kultur Video D4009, 2005. DVD-Video disc.

Barker, Thurman. *Strike Force: The Thurman Barker Percussion Quintet*. Uptee Productions, 2004. Compact disc.

Bowie, Lester. *Avant Pop*. ECM 13326, 1986. Compact disc.

————. *Gittin' to Know Y'all*. MPS 15269,15038, 1970. Vinyl disc.

————. *Numbers 1&2*. Nessa N-1, 1967. Compact disc.

Braxton, Anthony. *B-Xo/ N-O-1-47A*. Get Back GET 315, 1969. Compact disc.

————. *Composition no. 247*. Leo Records LR 306, 2001. Compact disc.

————. *Creative Orchestra Music 1976*. Arista AL4080, 1976. Vinyl disc.

————. *For Alto*. Delmark DE-420, 1969. Compact disc.

————. *For Four Orchestras*. Arista A3L 8900, 1978. Three vinyl discs.

————. *For Trio*. Arista AB 4181, 1978. Vinyl disc.

————. *The Montreux/Berlin Concerts*. Arista AL 5002, 1976. Two vinyl discs.

————. *New York, Fall 1974*. Arista AL 4032, 1975. Vinyl disc.

————. *This Time*. Get Back GET 347, 1970. Compact disc.

————. *Three Compositions of New Jazz*. Delmark DD-415, 1968. Compact disc.

————. *Town Hall (Trio & Quintet) 1972*. hatART 6119, 1972. Compact disc.

————. *Trillium R, Composition no. 162 (Opera in Four Acts): Shala Fears for the Poor*. Braxton House BH-008, 1999. Four compact discs.

————. *Trio and Duet*. Sackville 3007, 1974. Vinyl disc.

Braxton, Anthony, and George Lewis. *Elements of Surprise.* Moers Music 01036, 1977. Vinyl disc.

Brown, Ari. *Venus.* Delmark DE-504, 1998. Compact disc.

Christian, Jodie. *Soul Fountain.* Delmark DE-498, 1997. Compact disc.

Circle. *Paris-Concert.* ECM 1018, 1971. Compact disc.

Cohran, Philip, and the Artistic Heritage Ensemble. *On The Beach.* Chicago: Zulu Records, 1967. Vinyl disc.

Colson, Steve and Iqua. *Hope for Love.* Silver Sphinx, 2003. Compact disc.

Colson Unity Troupe. *No Reservation.* Black Saint 120043, 1980. Vinyl disc.

————. *Triumph!* Silver Sphinx, 1978. Vinyl disc.

Creative Construction Company. *Creative Construction Company.* Vol. 1. Muse Records MR 5071, 1975. Vinyl disc.

————. *Creative Construction Company.* Vol. 2. Muse Records MR 5097, 1976. Vinyl disc.

Dawkins, Ernest, and the New Horizons Ensemble. *30 Years of Great Black Music: Chicago Now.* Vol. 1. Silkheart SHCD140, 1995. Compact disc.

————. *30 Years of Great Black Music: Chicago Now.* Vol. 2. Silkheart SHCD141, 1997. Compact disc.

————. *After the Dawn Has Risen: Live at Leverkusener Jazztage.* Open Minds/Sound Aspects, 1992. Compact disc.

————. *Cape Town Shuffle: Live at Hothouse.* Delmark DG-545, 2003. Compact disc.

————. *Jo'Burg Jump.* Delmark DE-524, 2000. Compact disc.

Drake, Hamid, and Peter Brötzmann. *The Dried Rat-Dog.* Okka Disk OD 120004, 1994. Compact disc.

Equal Interest. *Equal Interest.* OmniTone 12001, 1999. Compact disc.

Ethnic Heritage Ensemble. *Ka-Real.* Silkheart SHCD150, 2000. Compact disc.

————. *Three Gentlemen from Chicago.* Moers Music 1076, 1981.

Ewart, Douglas. *Bamboo Meditations at Banff.* Aarawak 003, 1994. Compact disc.

————. *Red Hills.* Aarawak 001, 1983. Audiocassette.

————. *Songs of Sunlife: Inside the Didjeridu.* Innova 594, 2003. Compact disc.

Ewart, Douglas, and Inventions (Clarinet Choir). *Angles of Entrance.* Aarawak 004, 1996. Compact disc.

Fontaine, Brigitte. *Comme à la Radio.* Saravah SHL1018, 1970. Compact disc.

Freeman, Chico. *Chico.* India Navigation IN 1031, 1977. Vinyl disc.

————. *Live at Ronnie Scott's.* DRG Records S1425, 1986. Compact disc.

————. *You'll Know When You Get There.* Black Saint 120128, 1988. Compact disc.

Freeman, Chico, featuring Arthur Blythe. *Focus.* Contemporary, 1995. Compact disc.

Freeman, Chico, and Von Freeman. *Freeman and Freeman.* India Navigation IN 1070, [1981] 1989. Compact disc.

Gordon, Frank. *Clarion Echoes.* Soul Note 121096, [1985] 1993. Compact disc.

Harris, Vandy. *Pure Fire.* Self-published, 1996. Compact disc.

Isotope 217. *Utonian_Automatic.* Thrill Jockey 063, 1999. Compact disc.

Jarman, Joseph. *As If It Were the Seasons.* Delmark DD-417, 1968. Compact disc.

————. *Pachinko Dream Track 10.* Music & Arts 1040, 1999. Compact disc.

————. *Song For.* Delmark DD-410, 1967. Compact disc.

Jarman, Joseph, and Famoudou Don Moye. *Egwu-Anwu (Sun Song).* India Navigation, 1978. Vinyl disc.

Jenkins, Leroy. *For Players Only.* JCOA LP 1010, 1975.

————. *Leroy Jenkins' Driftwood: The Art of Improvisation.* Mutable Music 17523-2, 2005. Compact disc.

————. *Leroy Jenkins' Sting: Urban Blues.* Black Saint 120083, 1984. Compact disc.

————. *Mixed Quintet.* Black Saint 120060, 1979. Compact disc.

————. *Space Minds, New Worlds, Survival of America.* Tomato TOM-2032, [1978] 2003. Compact disc.

————. *Themes and Improvisations on the Blues.* CRI CR663, 1994. Compact disc.

Lewis, George. *Changing with the Times.* New World Records 80434-2, 1993. Compact disc.

————. *Chicago Slow Dance.* Lovely Music LP 1101, 1977. Vinyl disc.

————. *Endless Shout.* Tzadik 7054, 2000. Compact disc.

————. *The George Lewis Solo Trombone Record.* Sackville 3012, 1976. Compact disc.

————. *Homage to Charles Parker.* Black Saint 120029, 1980. Compact disc.

————. *Sequel (For Lester Bowie): A Composition for Cybernetic Improvisors.* Intakt CD 111, 2006. Compact disc.

————. *The Shadowgraph Series: Compositions for Creative Orchestra.* Spool Line 13, 2001. Compact disc.

Lewis, George, and Douglas Ewart. *George Lewis/Douglas Ewart.* Black Saint 120026, 1979. Compact disc.

Magek, Evod. *Through Love to Freedom.* Vol. 1. Black Pot Records, 1998. Compact disc.

Maia. *Introducing . . . Maia.* M'Ladiah Productions MBM 105, 2000. Compact disc.

McIntyre, Kalaparusha Maurice. *Humility in the Light of the Creator.* Delmark DD-419, 1969. Compact disc.

————. *Morning Song.* Delmark DG-553, 2004. Compact disc.

————. *Peace and Blessings.* Black Saint 120037, 1979. Compact disc.

————. *Ram's Run.* Cadence CJR1009, 1982. Vinyl disc.

McIntyre, Kalaparusha Maurice, and the Light. *South Eastern.* CIMP 247, 2002. Compact disc.

Mitchell, Nicole. *Nicole Mitchell/Black Earth Ensemble: Afrika Rising.* Dreamtime 004, 2002. Compact disc.

————. *Nicole Mitchell/Black Earth Ensemble: Vision Quest.* Dreamtime Records, 2001. Compact disc.

Mitchell, Roscoe. *Congliptious.* Nessa N-2, 1968. Compact disc.

————. *L-R-G; The Maze; SII Examples.* Nessa NCD-14, 1978. Compact disc.

————. *Nonaah.* Nessa 9/10, 1977. Vinyl disc.

————. *Quartet Featuring Muhal Richard Abrams.* Sackville 2009, 1975. Compact disc.

————. *The Roscoe Mitchell Solo Saxophone Concerts.* Sackville 2006, 1974. Vinyl disc.

————. *Solo [3].* Mutable Music 17515, 2004. Three compact discs.

————. *Sound.* Delmark DD-408, 1966. Compact disc.

Mitchell, Roscoe, and Muhal Richard Abrams. *Duets and Solos.* Black Saint 120133, 1993. Compact disc.

Mitchell, Roscoe, and the Sound Ensemble. *3 X 4 Eye.* Black Saint 120050, 1994. Compact disc.

MJT+3. *Daddy-O Presents MJT+3.* Cadet LP 621, 1957. Vinyl disc.

Moye, Famoudou Don, and Enoch Williamson. *Afrikan Song.* AECO/Southport 3009, 1998. Compact disc.

Murray, Diedre, and Fred Hopkins. *Stringology.* Black Saint 120143, 1993. Compact disc.

Myers, Amina Claudine. *Amina Claudine Myers Salutes Bessie Smith.* Leo Records, 1980. Compact disc.

———. *Jumping in the Sugar Bowl.* Minor Music, 1984. Compact disc.

———. *Women in (E)motion.* Tradition und Moderne T&M 102, 1993. Compact disc.

Nicholson, Reggie. *Solo Concept.* Abstract Recordings 02, 2005. Compact disc.

Revolutionary Ensemble. *The Psyche.* Mutable Music 17514-2, [1975] 2002. Compact disc.

Russell, Hal. *Hal Russell NRG Ensemble.* Nessa ncd-21 (1981). Compact disc.

Samana. *Samana.* Storywiz, 1996. Compact disc.

Smith, Leo. *Spirit Catcher.* Nessa N-19, 1979. Vinyl disc.

Smith, Wadada Leo. *Golden Quartet: The Year of the Elephant.* PI Recordings PI 04, 2002. Compact disc.

———. *Kabell Years 1971–1979.* Tzadik TZ 7610-4, 2004. Four compact discs.

———. *Tao-Njia.* Tzadik 7017, 1996. Compact disc.

Sticks and Stones. *Sticks and Stones.* 482 Music, 482-1012, 2002. Compact disc.

Stubblefield, John. *Morning Song.* Enja ENJ-8036-2, 1993. Compact disc.

Thompson, Malachi. *Buddy Bolden's Rag.* Delmark DE-481, 1995. Compact disc.

Threadgill, Henry. *Henry Threadgill's Zooid: Up Popped the Two Lips.* PI Recordings PI 02, 2001. Compact disc.

Threadgill, Henry, and Make a Move. *Everybody's Mouth's a Book.* PI Recordings PI 01, 2001. Compact disc.

———. *Where's Your Cup?* Columbia 67617, 1996. Compact disc.

Wildflowers: The New York Loft Jazz Sessions. Vols. 1–5. Casablanca/Douglas NBLP 7045, 7046, 7047, 7048, 7049, 1977. Vinyl discs.

Wildflowers: The New York Loft Jazz Sessions. Vols. 1–5. KnitClassics 3037, 2000. Compact discs.

Wilkerson, Edward, and Shadow Vignettes. *Birth of a Notion.* Sessoms, 1985.

notes

PREFACE

1. Muhal Richard Abrams and John Shenoy Jackson, "Association for the Advancement of Creative Musicians," *Black World*, November 1973, 72.

2. Ken Burns, "Jazz: A History of America's Music, Episode 10" (2000).

3. "Die Bedeutung und der internationale Ruf der AACM resultierten nicht nur aus ihrer Effektivität im Organisatorischen, sondern vor allem auch aus ihrem musikalischen Ertrag, der aus der Bezeichnung AACM so etwas wie ein Gütezeichen für eine kreative Musik ersten Ranges machte." Ekkehard Jost, *Sozialgeschichte des Jazz in den USA* (Frankfurt am Main: Wolke-Verlag, 1991), 215. A first-person account of the AACM is found in Anthony Braxton, *Tri-Axium Writings*, vol. 1 (Dartmouth: Synthesis/Frog Peak, 1985). Other accounts of the AACM's early activity, philosophies, and musical approaches are to be found in Ekkehard Jost, *Free Jazz* (New York: Da Capo Press, [1975] 1994); John Litweiler, *The Freedom Principle: Jazz after 1958* (New York: Da Capo, 1984); Benjamin Looker, *BAG: "Point from Which Creation Begins": The Black Artists Group of St. Louis.* (St. Louis: Missouri Historical Society Press, 2004); Ronald M. Radano, *New Musical Figurations: Anthony Braxton's Cultural Critique* (Chicago: University of Chicago Press, 1993); Valerie Wilmer, *As Serious As Your Life: The Story of the New Jazz* (London and New York: Serpent's Tail, [1977] 1992).

4. Sidney W. Mintz and Richard Price, *The Birth of African-American Culture: An Anthropological Perspective* (Boston: Beacon Press, 1992), 40.

5. Lydia Goehr, *The Imaginary Museum of Musical Works: An Essay in the Philosophy of Music* (Oxford: Oxford University Press, 1992), 243.

6. Mintz and Price, *The Birth of African-American Culture,* 43. Emphasis in the original.

7. Lincoln T. Beauchamp, Jr., ed., *Art Ensemble of Chicago: Great Black Music; Ancient to the Future* (Chicago: Art Ensemble of Chicago, 1998), 56. Italics in the original.

8. John Szwed, "Josef Skvorecky and the Tradition of Jazz Literature," *World Literature Today* 54, no. 4 (1980): 588.

9. Samuel A. Floyd, Jr., *The Power of Black Music: Interpreting Its History from Africa to the United States* (New York: Oxford University Press, 1995), 228.

10. Eileen Southern, "Music Research and the Black Aesthetic," *Black World*, November 1973, 5.

11. Ibid., 5–6.

12. Ibid., 6.

13. George E. Lewis, "Afterword to 'Improvised Music after 1950': The Changing Same," and "Improvised Music after 1950: Afrological and Eurological Perspectives," both in *The Other Side of Nowhere: Jazz, Improvisation, and Communities in Dialogue*, ed. Daniel Fischlin and Ajay Heble (Middletown, Conn.: Wesleyan University Press, 2004).

14. See, for example, the issue featuring improvisation in the November 2000 issue of *MusikTexte* (Heft 86/87), which, rather than being exceptional, merely constitutes one of the more egregious recent examples.

15. Newer histories of the period often uncritically recapitulate the corporate-supported tale told by the heavily funded Ken Burns *Jazz* series, a story which goes something like this: John Coltrane went mad in 1965, and a mysterious virus that he and others were carrying killed hundreds of musicians until Wynton Marsalis arrived in 1983, carrying a powerful mojo from the birthplace of jazz that put the deadly germ and its carriers to flight.

ACKNOWLEDGMENTS

1. See Ajay Heble, *Landing on the Wrong Note: Jazz, Dissonance, and Critical Practice* (New York: Routledge, 2000); Mike Heffley, *Northern Sun, Southern Moon: Europe's Reinvention of Jazz* (New Haven: Yale University Press, 2005); Eric Porter, *What Is This Thing Called Jazz? African American Musicians as Artists, Critics, and Activists* (Berkeley: University of California Press, 2002).

2. See Herman S. Gray, *Cultural Moves: African Americans and the Politics of Representation* (Berkeley: University of California Press, 2005); Deborah Anne Wong, *Speak It Louder: Asian Americans Making Music* (New York: Routledge, 2004).

3. See Daniel Fischlin and Ajay Heble, eds., *The Other Side of Nowhere: Jazz, Improvisation, and Communities in Dialogue* (Middletown: Wesleyan University Press, 2004); Robert G. O'Meally, Brent Hayes Edwards, and Farah Jasmine Griffin, eds., *Uptown Conversation: The New Jazz Studies* (New York: Columbia University Press, 2004).

4. Charlie Parker and John McLellan, interview with Charlie Parker, June 13, 1953 (accessed November 17, 2005); available from http://www.plosin.com/milesAhead/BirdInterviews.html#530600.

5. For a theory of the "American maverick" that seems to locate little substantive place for African American music, see Michael Broyles, *Mavericks and Other Traditions in American Music* (New Haven: Yale University Press, 2004). A common thread in scholarship on American music draws upon western or frontier tropes that assume whiteness as

a constitutive element. See, for example, Beth E. Levy, "'The White Hope of American Music'; or, How Roy Harris Became Western," *American Music* 19, no. 2 (2001).

6. Muhal Richard Abrams, interview with the author, New York City, July 19, 1999.

INTRODUCTION

1. F. Richard Moore, *Elements of Computer Music* (Englewood Cliffs, N.J.: Prentice-Hall, 1990).

2. Joseph Jarman, "AACM History: Interview with Leo Smith," tape recording, January 2, 1981, New York City, Collection of Shaku Joseph Jarman.

3. Except as noted, quotes and narratives from Jodie Christian hereafter come from Jodie Christian, interview with the author, Chicago, Illinois, July 10, 1998.

4. Muhal Richard Abrams, interview with the author, New York City, October 29, 1998.

5. Whitney Balliett, "Jazz: New York Notes," *New Yorker,* June 20, 1977, 92.

6. Charles T. Davis and Henry Louis Gates, Jr., *The Slave's Narrative* (Oxford and New York: Oxford University Press, 1985); Sarah Louise Delany and A. Elizabeth Delany, with Amy Hill Hearth, *Having Our Say: The Delany Sisters' First 100 Years* (New York: Kodansha International, 1993); Alex Haley, *Roots* (Garden City, N.Y.: Doubleday, 1976); James Weldon Johnson, edited with an introduction by William L. Andrews, *The Autobiography of an Ex-Colored Man* (New York: Penguin Books, [1912] 1990); Malcolm X, with the assistance of Alex Haley, *The Autobiography of Malcolm X* (New York: Ballantine Books, 1973).

7. Jon Michael Spencer, *The New Negroes and Their Music: The Success of the Harlem Renaissance* (Knoxville: University of Tennessee Press, 1997).

8. Burton W. Peretti, "Oral Histories of Jazz Musicians: The NEA Transcripts as Texts in Context," in *Jazz among the Discourses,* ed. Krin Gabbard (Durham: Duke University Press, 1995), 122.

9. See James Clifford, "On Ethnographic Authority," *Representations* 2 (1983).

10. See Amiri Baraka, "Jazz and the White Critic," in *The Jazz Cadence of American Culture,* ed. Robert G. O'Meally (New York: Columbia University Press, 1998).

11. Arthur Taylor, *Notes and Tones* (New York: Da Capo Press, [1977] 1993).

12. Leo Smith, *Notes (8 pieces) source a new world music: creative music* (Self-published, 1973). Leo Smith, "(M1) American Music," *Black Perspective in Music* 2, no. 2, (Autumn 1974).

13. See Amiri Baraka, *Blues People: The Negro Experience in White America and The Music That Developed from It* (New York: Morrow Quill Paperbacks, 1963); Anthony Braxton, *Tri-Axium Writings,* vols. 1–3 (Dartmouth: Synthesis/Frog Peak, 1985); John Cage, *Silence* (Middletown: Wesleyan University Press, 1961); Karlheinz Stockhausen, *Texte zur Musik* (Köln: M.D. Schauberg, 1963); Derek Bailey, *Improvisation: Its Nature and Practice in Music* (Ashbourne: Moorland Publishing, 1980).

14. Stanley Dance, Review of *Representing Jazz* and *Jazz among the Discourses,* by Krin Gabbard, *Jazz Times,* November 1995, 75.

15. To judge for yourself, see Krin Gabbard, *Jazz among the Discourses* (Durham: Duke University Press, 1995); Krin Gabbard, *Representing Jazz* (Durham: Duke University Press, 1995).

16. Radano, *New Musical Figurations.*

17. Morgan Craft, "Towards a New Consciousness," *Wire* 260, October 2005.

18. Fred Moten, *In the Break: The Aesthetics of the Black Radical Tradition* (Minneapolis: University of Minnesota, 2003), 32.

19. Jacques Attali, translated by Brian Massumi, *Noise: The Political Economy of Music* (Minneapolis: University of Minnesota Press, 1989), 140.

20. Ibid., 133.

CHAPTER SUMMARIES

1. Joseph Jarman, interview with the author, Brooklyn, New York, June 28, 1998.

2. Farah Jasmine Griffin, *"Who Set You Flowin'?": The African-American Migration Narrative* (New York: Oxford University Press, 1995).

3. I am using the term "avant-garde" in the sense that Peter Bürger and Renato Poggioli made use of it in their separate books on the subject, rather than in the jazz-historical sense of the word as denoting either a particular network of musicians, or the presence or absence of specific musical practices. For a critical account of canonical jazz usage of the term, see Salim Washington, "'All the Things You Could Be by Now': Charles Mingus Presents Charles Mingus and the Limits of Avant-Garde Jazz," in *Uptown Conversation: The New Jazz Studies,* ed. Robert G. O'Meally, Brent Hayes Edwards, and Farah Jasmine Griffin (New York: Columbia University Press, 2004). For the nonjazz uses of the term, see Renato Poggioli, *The Theory of the Avant-Garde,* translated from the Italian by Gerald Fitzgerald (Cambridge: Belknap Press of Harvard University Press, 1968).

4. Babatunde Olatunji, with Robert Atkinson, assisted by Akinsola Akiwowo, *The Beat of My Drum: An Autobiography* (Philadelphia: Temple University Press, 2005).

5. The collective's own lore generally acknowledges Abrams, Christian, Cohran, and McCall as cofounders. From my research, I trace this acknowledgment to the role played by these musicians in organizing the first meetings and recruiting musicians to the collective's ranks. Outside the organization, Fred Anderson is frequently represented in non-AACM publicity as a founder of the AACM. In our 1998 interview, however, Anderson's reply to my direct question on this issue pointed to two of the four acknowledged founders, rather than to himself. "Muhal was the first one who mentioned it to me," he responded. "Jodie was talking about it." Fred Anderson, interview with the author, July 8, 1998, and February 9, 1999.

6. Smith, *Notes (8 pieces) source a new world music.*

7. E. Franklin Frazier, *Black Bourgeoisie: The Rise of a New Middle Class in the United States* (New York: Collier Books, [1957] 1969).

8. See George E. Lewis, "'Gittin' to Know Y'All': Von improvisierter Musik, vom Treffen der Kulturen und von der 'racial imagination,'" in *Jazz und Gesellschaft: Sozialgeschichtliche Aspekte des Jazz,* ed. Wolfram Knauer (Hofheim: Wolke-Verlag, 2002).

9. For an account of this reception in France, see Stephen H. Lehman, *I Love You with an Asterisk: African-American Experimental Composers and the French Jazz Press, 1970–1980* (2004 [accessed November 22, 2005]); available from http://repository.lib.uoguelph.ca/ojs/index.php, 2005, 38–53.

10. Looker, *BAG: "Point from Which Creation Begins."*

11. See Leroi Jones, "New York Loft and Coffee Shop Jazz," *Down Beat,* May 9, 1963.

CHAPTER 1

1. For an extensive account of these and other issues facing prospective migrants, see Leon F. Litwack, *Trouble in Mind: Black Southerners in the Age of Jim Crow* (New York: Alfred A. Knopf, 1998).

2. James R. Grossman, *Land of Hope: Chicago, Black Southerners, and the Great Migration* (Chicago: University of Chicago Press, 1989), 17. This kind of land grab was hardly limited to the South. A three-part *Los Angeles Times* series from 2001, "'Torn from the Land,'" documented how black Americans all across the United States lost family land that is now worth millions of dollars. One site taken from a black family was sold to the Los Angeles Dodgers baseball team. See Dolores Barclay, Todd Lewan, and Allan G. Breed, "Prosperity Made Blacks a Target for Land Grabs; History: Specter of lynching boosted impact of lesser threats," *Los Angeles Times*, December 9, 2001; Todd Lewan and Dolores Barclay, "'When They Steal Your Land, They Steal Your Future'; History: Study details black landowners' losses, now worth millions," *Los Angeles Times*, December 2, 2001.

3. Except as noted, quotes and narratives from Kelan Phil Cohran hereafter come from Kelan Phil Cohran, interview with the author, Chicago, Illinois, February 14, 1999.

4. Except as noted, quotes and narratives from Jerol Donavon (Ajaramu) hereafter come from Ajaramu Jerol Donavon, interview with the author, Chicago, Illinois, July 12, 1998.

5. Carl E. Baugher, *Turning Corners: The Life and Music of Leroy Jenkins* (Redwood, N.Y.: Cadence Jazz Books, 2000), 1–2; Except as noted, quotes and narratives from Leroy Jenkins hereafter come from Leroy Jenkins, interview with the author, Brooklyn, New York, June 25, 1998.

6. Arnold R. Hirsch, *Making the Second Ghetto: Race and Housing in Chicago, 1940–1960* (Chicago: University of Chicago Press, [1983] 1998), 4.

7. St. Clair Drake and Horace R. Cayton, *Black Metropolis: A Study of Negro Life in a Northern City* (Chicago: University of Chicago Press, [1945] 1970), 12.

8. Ibid, Grossman, *Land of Hope*, 185.

9. Drake, *Black Metropolis*, 383.

10. Ibid., 379–80.

11. Novelist Richard Wright described the economics of the kitchenette in a 1941 narrative accompanied by a series of poignant pictures of the inhabitants. Wright described the kitchenette as "our prison, our death sentence without trial, the new form of mob violence that assaults not only the lone individual, but all of us." Richard Wright, *12 Million Black Voices* (New York: Thunder's Mouth Press, [1941] 1988), 106.

12. Baugher, *Turning Corners*, 2; Jenkins interview.

13. Hirsch, *Making the Second Ghetto*, 18.

14. Arna Bontemps and Jack Conroy, *Anyplace but Here* (New York: Hill and Wang, 1966), 329.

15. Except as noted, hereafter quotes and narratives from Rochelle Toyozumi and Willa McCall, come from Rochelle Toyozumi and Willa McCall, interview with the author, Chicago, Illinois, June 22, 1999.

16. Except as noted, hereafter quotes and narratives from Muhal Richard Abrams come from Muhal Richard Abrams, interview with the author, Chicago, Illinois, December 26, 1997.

17. Favors was in the habit of postdating himself, and most biographies and dictionary entries follow suit in placing his birth year as 1937. As Famoudou Don Moye cautioned me in our 1999 interview, "Did Favors give you his right date? Because he used to add ten years [laughs]. It's '27, not '37. For the record, it's 1927." Except as noted, hereafter, quotes and narratives from Famoudou Don Moye come from Famoudou Don Moye, interview with the author, Chicago, Illinois, June 21, 1999.

18. Except as noted, hereafter quotes and narratives from Malachi Favors Maghostut come from Malachi Favors Maghostut, interview with the author, Chicago, Illinois, July 12, 1998.

19. Hirsch, *Making the Second Ghetto,* 26–27.

20. Ibid., 25.

21. Drake, *Black Metropolis,* 112; Dempsey J. Travis, *An Autobiography of Black Chicago* (Chicago: Urban Research Press, 1981), 47.

22. Leroy Jenkins, interview with the author, Brooklyn, New York, October 27, 1998.

23. Works Progress Administration, a Depression-era New Deal employment program.

24. Rufus Schatzberg and Robert J. Kelly, *African-American Organized Crime: A Social History* (New Brunswick: Rutgers University Press, 1996), 10.

25. Wilmot Alfred Fraser, "Jazzology: A Study of the Tradition in Which Jazz Musicians Learn to Improvise" (PhD dissertation, University of Pennsylvania, 1983).

26. Darlene Clark Hine, "Black Migration to the Urban Midwest," in *The Great Migration in Historical Perspective,* ed. Joe William Trotter (Bloomington: Indiana University Press, 1991), 134.

27. Jenkins interview.

28. See Carol Oja, *Making Music Modern: New York in the 1920s* (New York: Oxford University Press, 2000).

29. Kathryn Talalay, *Composition in Black and White: The Life of Philippa Schuyler* (New York: Oxford University Press, 1995), 111.

30. Baugher, *Turning Corners,* 2–4, Jenkins. One of Frederick's slightly older violin students was Ellas McDaniel, later known as Bo Diddley. See Nadine Cohodas, *Spinning Blues into Gold: The Chess Brothers and the Legendary Chess Records* (New York: St Martin's Press), 101.

31. bell hooks, "Performance Practice as a Site of Opposition," in *Let's Get It On: The Politics of Black Performance,* ed. Catherine Ugwu (Seattle: Bay Press, 1995).

32. For discussions of the two band directors, see Dempsey J. Travis, *An Autobiography of Black Jazz* (Chicago: Urban Research Press, 1983).

33. Ted Panken, radio interview with Eddie Harris (WKCR-FM, New York City, June 24, 1994 [accessed December 1, 2005]), transcript, available from http://www.jazzhouse.org/library/.

34. Ted Panken, radio interview with Richard Davis (WKCR-FM, New York City, [accessed August 18, 1993]), transcript, available from http://www.jazzhouse.org/library/.

35. John Szwed's contention that "many of the key players" in the AACM were Dyett students appears considerably overstated, although at least three of the nearly thirty first-wave AACM musicians came up under Dyett's tutelage. See John F. Szwed, *Space*

Is the Place: The Lives and Times of Sun Ra (New York: Pantheon Books, 1997), 87. Joseph Jarman was active as a percussionist at DuSable, and while Dyett was impressed with the young Leroy Jenkins, the band program could not support string performance, so Jenkins played saxophone, clarinet, and bassoon. Later, Henry Threadgill and second-wave AACM members Mwata Bowden and James Johnson studied under Dyett, as well as non-AACM drummer Jerome Cooper, a Chicago native who later cofounded the Revolutionary Ensemble with Leroy Jenkins and bassist Sirone.

36. Frances Stonor Saunders, *The Cultural Cold War: The CIA and the World of Arts and Letters* (New York: New Press, 1999).

37. Clovis E. Semmes, "The Dialectics of Cultural Survival and the Community Artist: Phil Cohran and the Affro-Arts Theater," *Journal of Black Studies* 24, no. 4 (1994): 451.

38. Semmes, "The Dialectics of Cultural Survival," 451.

39. Paul Berliner, *Thinking in Jazz: The Infinite Art of Improvisation* (Chicago: University of Chicago Press, 1994); Fraser, "Jazzology."

40. Beauchamp, *Art Ensemble of Chicago*, 28.

41. Ted Panken, radio interview with Von Freeman (WKCR-FM, New York City, June 7, 1987 [accessed November 30, 2005]), transcript, available from http://www .jazzhouse.org/library/index.php3?sel=Interviews.

42. Ralph Ellison, "On Bird, Bird-Watching, and Jazz," in *Living with Music: Ralph Ellison's Jazz Writings*, ed. Robert G. O'Meally (New York: Modern Library, [1962] 2001), xxviii.

43. Except as noted, hereafter quotes and narratives from Martin "Sparx" Alexander come from Martin "Sparx" Alexander, interview with the author, Chicago, Illinois, December 31, 1997.

44. Donavon interview. Among the many musicians active on the scene were Von, George, and Bruz Freeman, Victor Sproles, Chris Anderson, John Young, Willie Pickens, Billy Wallace, John Gilmore, Nicky Hill, Rafael Garrett, Ira Sullivan, Wilbur Campbell, King Fleming, William Jackson, Gene Ammons, Johnny Griffin, Sonny Stitt, Ike Day, Tom Archia, Henry "Hen-Pie" Prior, Red Saunders, Pat Patrick, Julian Priester, Sun Ra, Walter Perkins, Eddie Buster, Andrew Hill, Ahmad Jamal, George Coleman, Paul Serrano, Booker Little, Harold Mabern, Frank Strozier, Richard Davis, Charles Davis, Clifford Jordan, Wilbur Ware, Leo Blevins, Leroy Jackson, Eddie Harris, Claude McLin, Larry Jackson, Phil Thomas, Vernel Fournier. Of course, even this relatively long list of musicians active on the South Side in the 1950s is far from exhaustive.

45. Ted Panken, radio interview with Alvin Fielder, transcript, July 1, 2002, WKCR-FM, New York City, Collection of Ted Panken.

46. Ibid.

47. Wilbur Ware, *The Chicago Sound* (Riverside OJCCD-1737-2, 1957), compact disc.

48. Jost, *Sozialgeschichte des Jazz in den USA*, 86.

49. Scott DeVeaux, *The Birth of Bebop: A Social and Musical History* (Berkeley: University of California Press, 1997), 203.

50. Critic Leonard Feather's *Inside Jazz*, which first appeared in 1949 as *Inside Be-bop*, provides a musically literate summary of bebop forms that provides some index of how much standardization had already developed by the early 1950s. Leonard Feather, *Inside Jazz* (New York: Da Capo Press, [1949] 1976).

51. DeVeaux, *The Birth of Bebop*, 207.

52. Ralph Ellison, "The Golden Age, Time Past," in *The Jazz Cadence of American Culture*, ed. Robert G. O'Meally (New York: Columbia University Press, 1998), 454.

53. Porter, *What Is This Thing Called Jazz?*, 81.

54. Ibid., 82.

55. Arthur C. Cromwell, "Jazz Mecca: An Ethnographic Study of Chicago's South Side Jazz Community" (PhD dissertation, Ohio University, 1998), 101.

56. Ellison, "The Golden Age, Time Past," 454.

57. Quotes and narratives from Emanuel Cranshaw throughout this book come from Emanuel Cranshaw, interview with the author, Chicago, Illinois, February 11, 1999.

58. Donald Spivey, *Union and the Black Musician: The Narrative of William Everett Samuels and Chicago Local 208* (Lanham: University Press of America, 1984), 9–10.

59. Ibid., 46.

60. Ibid., 53.

61. Ibid., 93.

62. Jost, *Sozialgeschichte des Jazz in den USA*, 109.

63. "Strictly Ad Lib: Chicago [announcement of the passing of Nicky Hill]," *Down Beat*, August 1, 1963.

64. Cohran, Semmes, "The Dialectics of Cultural Survival," 451.

65. Ted Panken, radio interview with Johnny Griffin, transcript, April 18, 1990, WKCR-FM, New York City, Collection of Ted Panken.

66. Hine, "Black Migration to the Urban Midwest," 129–30. According to Hine, "the ceiling on black women's job opportunities was secured tight by the opposition of white women. . . . Employers seeking to avert threatened walkouts, slowdowns, and violence caved in to white women's objections to working beside or, most particularly, sharing restroom and toilet facilities with black women."

67. Ibid., 140.

68. Except as noted, quotes and narratives from Fred Anderson come from Fred Anderson, interview with the author, Chicago, Illinois, July 8, 1998.

69. "Biography of William Brimfield," dated April 15, 1975, Collection of Muhal Richard Abrams.

70. Ibid.

71. DeVeaux, *The Birth of Bebop*, 298.

CHAPTER 2

1. Daniel Belgrad, *The Culture of Spontaneity: Improvisation and the Arts in Postwar America* (Chicago: University of Chicago Press, 1998), 5.

2. Ronald Sukenick, *Down and In: Life in the Underground* (New York: William Morrow, 1987), 58.

3. Belgrad, *The Culture of Spontaneity*, 194–95.

4. Ibid., 195.

5. Sukenick, *Down and In*, 84.

6. Eric Lott, "Double V, Double-Time: Bebop's Politics of Style," in *The Jazz Cadence*

of American Culture, ed. Robert G. O'Meally (New York: Columbia University Press, 1998), 464.

7. Moten, *In the Break,* 32.

8. Baraka, *Blues People,* 231.

9. Sally Banes, *Greenwich Village 1963: Avant-Garde Performance and the Effervescent Body* (Durham: Duke University Press, 1993), 146.

10. Ibid., 111.

11. Jon Panish, *The Color of Jazz: Race and Representation in Postwar American Culture* (Jackson: University of Mississippi Press, 1997), 19.

12. Banes, *Greenwich Village 1963,* 146.

13. Panish, *The Color of Jazz,* 18.

14. Sukenick, *Down and In,* 86.

15. Leroi Jones, "Tokenism: 300 Years for Five Cents," in *Home: Social Essays* (New York: William Morrow, 1966). For other autobiographical and historical perspectives on progressive African American artists working in New York at this time, see Rashidah Ismaeli Abu Bakr, "Slightly Autobiographical: The 1960s on the Lower East Side," *African American Review* 27, no. 4 (1993); Calvin Hernton, "Umbra: A Personal Recounting," *African American Review* 27, no. 4 (1993); Mike Sells, *Avant-Garde Performance and the Limits of Criticism: Approaching the Living Theatre, Happenings/Fluxus, and the Black Arts Movement* (Ann Arbor: University of Michigan Press, 2005); Lorenzo Thomas, "Alea's Children: The Avant-Garde on the Lower East Side, 1960–1970," *African American Review* 27, no. 4 (1993).

16. "Jazzy Beat Poet Known for 'Bird Lives' Graffiti, Dies," *New York Times,* May 18, 2003.

17. Hettie Jones, *How I Became Hettie Jones* (New York: E. P. Dutton, 1990), 47.

18. Belgrad, *The Culture of Spontaneity,* 210.

19. Sukenick, *Down and In,* 20.

20. Amiri Baraka, *The Autobiography of Leroi Jones* (Chicago: Lawrence Hill Books, 1984), 186–87.

21. Ibid., 187.

22. Ibid., 255–56.

23. Banes, *Greenwich Village 1963,* 147.

24. Ibid., 146.

25. Ibid., 110–11.

26. Ibid., 158.

27. Ibid., 111.

28. Ibid., 110.

29. Ibid., 111.

30. Baraka, *The Autobiography of Leroi Jones,* 262.

31. This is not to say that the early '60s New York avant-garde completely eschewed contact with black perspectives or issues. The Banes account lists a number of engagements by white artists with the civil rights movement, such as the "Two Sunday Evenings for Mississippi," as well as work by painter James Rosenquist, Fluxus musician Dick Higgins, and the political work of Jackson MacLow and Philip Corner. Banes, *Greenwich Village 1963,* 154–55. Although these kinds of activities cannot be said to play a large or

generally discussed role in the history of the period, Banes is to be congratulated for at least raising issues that most other historians and critics working on the avant-garde could not see at all.

32. "Events/Comments: Is New Music Being Used for Political or Social Ends?" Source: *Music of the Avant Garde* 3, no. 2(6) (1969): 7.

33. Ibid., 90.

34. Ibid., 91.

35. Ibid.

36. Ibid., 9.

37. Ibid.

38. Banes, *Greenwich Village 1963*, 156.

39. Ibid., 157.

40. Ibid., 156.

41. Ibid., 158.

42. Michael Kimmelman, "The Dia Generation," *New York Times*, April 6, 2003.

43. Forays by artists from other sectors into the murky world of the jazz club, such as longtime Greenwich Village resident Edgard Varese's 1958 "smash hit" Village Gate performance of his "Poème Eléctronique," were exceptions that proved the prevailing rule. Few white avant-garde classicists took up the concert reviewer's enthusiastic suggestion that composers should "turn the tables on the jazzmen and invade the night clubs, as jazz invaded the concert hall." H. B. Lutz, "Varese at the Gate: Brief but Potent," *Village Voice*, November 19, 1958.

44. Sukenick, *Down and In*, 221.

45. Baraka, *The Autobiography of Leroi Jones*, 187.

46. For a forthright account of the struggles of black artists against erasure from rock histories, see Maureen Mahon, *Right to Rock: The Black Rock Coalition and the Cultural Politics of Race* (Durham: Duke University Press, 2004).

47. Bill Coss, "Cecil Taylor's Struggle for Existence," *Down Beat*, October 26, 1961, 20.

48. For more detailed treatment of the musical techniques being explored during this time, see Michael J. Budds, *Jazz in the Sixties: The Expansion of Musical Resources and Techniques: An Expanded Edition* (Iowa City: University of Iowa Press, 1990); Roger Dean, *New Structures in Jazz and Improvised Music since 1960* (Milton Keynes and Philadelphia: Open University Press, 1992).

49. For an account of how pan-Africanist intercultural music-making, dating from the 1940s, had profound consequences for American experimentalism more generally, see Jason Stanyek, "Transmissions of an Interculture: Pan-African Jazz and Intercultural Improvisation," in *The Other Side of Nowhere: Jazz, Improvisation, and Communities in Dialogue*, ed. Daniel Fischlin and Ajay Heble (Middletown: Wesleyan University Press, 2004).

50. For Gunther Schuller's analysis of motivic form in Rollins, see Gunther Schuller, "Sonny Rollins and the Challenge of Thematic Improvisation," in *Musings: The Musical Worlds of Gunther Schuller* (Oxford: Oxford University Press, [1958] 1986). For a recent reconsideration of structure in Coleman, see Eric Charry, "Freedom and Form in Ornette Coleman's Early Atlantic Recordings," *Annual Review of Jazz Studies* 9 (1997–1998).

51. Jost, *Free Jazz*, 21–23.

52. New York Art Quartet, *New York Art Quartet* (ESP Records, 1964).

53. Frank Kofsky, *Black Nationalism and the Revolution in Music* (New York: Pathfinder, 1970), 228.

54. "Quatre musiciens qui sont parmi les plus importantes du monde contemporaine *dans la domaine du jazz*" (transcription and emphasis by the author). The introduction and the performance can be heard on John Coltrane, *A Love Supreme: Deluxe Edition* (Impulse 314 589 945-2, [1964] 2002), two compact discs.

55. "John Coltrane interpretera un theme . . . en fait, une *composition* en plusieurs mouvements" (transcription, translation, and emphasis by the author). Ibid.

56. Ibid.

57. Even sympathetic analysts tended to assume an absence of harmonic frameworks in the work of artists such as Ornette Coleman. In this sense, the critics may have been seduced by the statements of the new musicians themselves. In a 1960 *New York Times* article, Coleman said, "Before we start out to play . . . we do not have any idea of what the end result will be. Each player is free to contribute what he feels in the music at any given moment. We do not begin with a preconceived notion as to what kind of effect we will achieve." John S. Wilson, "Jazz Played on a Plastic Sax," *New York Times*, July 31, 1960. As ethnomusicologist Eric Charry has shown, however, prestructured elements, including old-style AABA and blues forms, abound in recorded performances of the early Ornette Coleman groups—with the notable exception of the double-quartet recording *Free Jazz*. Nonetheless, artist's statements such as Coleman's, while sometimes apocryphal (as with statements concerning the "improvisational spontaneity" of Cageian indeterminacy), inspired countless aspiring experimentalists to assume that the ideas behind them were actually being done *now*, and could therefore be extended and revised in the future. See Charry, "Freedom and Form in Ornette Coleman's Early Atlantic Recordings."

58. See Charles Ives, *Ives Plays Ives* (CRI CD 837 DDD, 1999), compact disc; Lennie Tristano, *Intuition* (Capitol Jazz CDP 7243 8 52771 2 2, 1949), compact disc.

59. See Joe Harriott, *Abstract* (Polygram/Redial 538183, 1962), compact disc; Joe Harriott, *Free Form* (Polygram/Redial 538184, 1961), compact disc. For a discussion of Harriott's work as a "forgotten message" presaging the rise of European free jazz, see Ekkehard Jost, *Europas Jazz, 1960–80* (Frankfurt am Main: Fischer Taschenbuch Verlag, 1987).

60. Jost, *Free Jazz*, 11–12.

61. Scott DeVeaux, "Constructing the Jazz Tradition," in *The Jazz Cadence of American Culture*, ed. Robert G. O'Meally (New York: Columbia University Press, 1998), 502.

62. Jost, *Sozialgeschichte des Jazz in den USA*, 180–81.

63. Nat Hentoff, "The New Jazz: Black, Angry and Hard to Understand," *New York Times Magazine*, December 23, 1966, 34.

64. Ibid.

65. Ibid., 34–35.

66. Ingrid Monson, *Saying Something: Jazz Improvisation and Interaction* (Chicago: University of Chicago Press, 1996).

67. Baraka, *The Autobiography of Leroi Jones*, 257.

68. Jones, *How I Became Hettie Jones*, 172. For journalistic accounts of the 1960s affinities between the abstract artists of Greenwich Village and musicians such as Cecil Tay-

lor, Charles Mingus, Randy Weston, Thelonious Monk, as well as a description of local Village nightclubs such as the Five Spot Café and the Half Note, see John S. Wilson, "'Village' Becomes Focal Point for Modern Jazz: Five Spot Café and the Half Note Spur the Move Downtown," *New York Times*, October 27, 1960.

69. Baraka, *The Autobiography of Leroi Jones*, 262.

70. Ibid., 265.

71. Hentoff, "The New Jazz:," 36.

72. Wilmer, *As Serious as Your Life*, 258.

73. "Der Bebop war in gewissem Sinne sehr romantisch. Er sprach über heroische Aktionen, über Dinge, die politisch *und* musikalisch zu tun seien; aber er *tat* sie nicht. Im Grunde ging es im Bebop eher um die *Idee* dessen, was zu tun sei, als darum, tatsächlich etwas zu tun. Wir tun es jetzt." Quoted in Jost, *Sozialgeschichte des Jazz in den USA*, 92. The original English version is in Robert Levin, "The Emergence of Jimmy Lyons," in *Music and Politics*, ed. John Sinclair and Robert Levin (New York and Cleveland: World Publishing, 1971), 90, which I have not been able to find.

74. DeVeaux, "Constructing the Jazz Tradition," 502.

75. Hentoff, "The New Jazz," 34.

76. Baraka, *The Autobiography of Leroi Jones*, 261.

77. Ibid., 266–67.

78. DeVeaux, "Constructing the Jazz Tradition," 503.

79. Hentoff, "The New Jazz," 34.

80. Ibid.

81. Leroi Jones, *Dutchman*, in *Political Stages: Plays That Shaped a Century*, ed. Emily Mann and David Roessel (New York: Applause Theater and Cinema Books, [1964] 2002), 157.

82. Jon Cruz, *Culture on the Margins: The Black Diaspora and the Rise of American Cultural Interpretation* (Princeton: Princeton University Press, 1999), 43.

83. Ibid., 47.

84. Don DeMicheal, "John Coltrane and Eric Dolphy Answer the Jazz Critics," *Down Beat*, April 12 1962, 22.

85. Dan Morgenstern, "Caught in the Act: Titans of the Tenor Sax," *Down Beat*, April 7, 1966, 36.

86. "Was der großen konservativen Fraktion der Jazzkritik der 60er Jahre außerordentlich gelegen kam, war, daß mit dem Anbruch des Free Jazz die Solidarität des Schweigens unter den Jazzmusikern ein Ende fand. Hätten es früher die Musiker meist sorgfältig vermieden, vor einem Mann von der Presse oder sonst einem Außenseiter etwas Negatives über einen Kollegen zu außern, so öffnete der Free Jazz alle Schleusen der Zurückhaltung. Ältere Musiker bezeichneten jüngere als Scharlatane, die ihr Handwerk nicht verstünden, die mutwillig den Jazz zerstörten, nicht swingen würden." Jost, *Sozialgeschichte des Jazz in den USA*, 182. Translations throughout the book are by the author unless otherwise noted.

87. Leonard Feather, "The Blindfold Test: Ruby Braff," *Down Beat*, January 21, 1960.

88. Leonard Feather, "The Blindfold Test: Miles Davis," *Down Beat*, June 18, 1964.

89. Ibid.

90. Leonard Feather, "The Blindfold Test: Benny Carter," *Down Beat,* November 23, 1961.

91. Sonny Rollins, *Our Man in Jazz* (BMG 7 4321 19256-2, 1962).

92. "Strictly Ad Lib [Sonny Rollins performance announcement]," *Down Beat,* June 6, 1963.

93. Leonard Feather, "Sonny Rollins: Blindfold Test, Part Two," *Down Beat,* August 16, 1962.

94. Charles Mingus, "Another View of Coleman," *Down Beat,* May 26, 1960. "Symphony Sid" Torin (1909–84) was an important jazz disk jockey in Boston and later New York, during the forties, fifties, and sixties.

95. Ronald M. Radano, "The Jazz Avant-Garde and the Jazz Community: Action and Reaction," in *Annual Review of Jazz Studies 3,* ed. Dan Morgenstern, Charles Nanry, and David A. Cayer (New Brunswick: Transaction Books, 1985), 71.

96. Ibid., 74.

97. Ibid., 75.

98. Kofsky, *Black Nationalism and the Revolution in Music.*

99. Radano, "The Jazz Avant-Garde and the Jazz Community," 76.

100. Ibid., 74.

101. See Don DeMicheal, review of Ornette Coleman recording, *This Is Our Music, Down Beat,* May 11, 1961.

102. Martin Williams, "The Bystander," *Down Beat,* May 10, 1962.

103. John Tynan, "Take 5," *Down Beat,* November 23, 1961.

104. Leonard Feather, "Feather's Nest," *Down Beat,* February 15, 1962.

105. DeMicheal, "John Coltrane and Eric Dolphy Answer the Jazz Critics," 21.

106. Ibid., 23.

107. Ibid.

108. Radano, "The Jazz Avant-Garde and the Jazz Community," 74.

109. DeMicheal, review of Ornette Coleman recording, *This Is Our Music.*

110. John Tynan, review of Ornette Coleman recording, *Free Jazz, Down Beat,* January 18, 1962.

111. Morgenstern, "Caught in the Act," 35.

112. "Sie würde nichts anderes zu Tage fördern als die Ignoranz und—möglicherweise unbewusste—Infamie grosser Teile der amerikanischen Jazzkritik und ihren Leichtsinn im Umgang mit den elementärsten Regeln ihres Handwerks. Natürlich gab es auch eine Reihe von Kritikern, die dem Neuen Jazz mit Sympathie gegenüberstanden, sei es aus immanent musikalischen Gründen, sei es auch nur aus ideologischen. Jedoch waren sie in der Minderheit und publizierten selten in den massgeblichen Journalen." Jost, *Sozialgeschichte des Jazz in den USA,* 182.

113. Radano, "The Jazz Avant-Garde and the Jazz Community," 77.

114. Ibid., 76.

115. LeRoi Jones, "Jazz and the White Critic: A Provocative Essay on the Situation of Jazz Criticism," *Down Beat,* August 15, 1963. Reprinted as Baraka, "Jazz and the White Critic."

116. Jones, "Jazz and the White Critic," 16.

117. Ibid., 17.

118. Ibid., 16.

119. In fact, Jones's argument that in music, "each note *means something* quite in addition to musical notation" was highly suspect in the field of musicology at the time his piece appeared. Jones's view is closer to the notion of "music-in-culture" that had been developing in what was variously called "the anthropology of music," "comparative musicology," or "ethnomusicology." See ibid., 17.

120. Ibid., 34.

121. Ibid.

122. Bontemps and Conroy, *Anyplace but Here*, 323.

123. According to Grossman, the university even created its own "independent" commission to "create an economically upgraded and predominantly white neighborhood. If the racial homogeneity of the area could no longer be maintained, class could still be used to assure the 'quality' of those nonwhites permitted to remain." This strategy, of course, encountered considerable breakage. For instance, black sociologist and academic St. Clair Drake, the most prominent chronicler of the Black Belt's rise, was denied the opportunity to purchase a home in a "restricted" area of Hyde Park; see Grossman, *Land of Hope*, 136–37, 184.

124. Hirsch, *Making the Second Ghetto*, 41.

125. Mary Lui, interview with Jamil B. Figi, transcript (Chicago Historical Society, Chicago, Illinois, October 29 and November 6, 1998), 18–19.

126. Ibid., 16–17.

127. Ibid., 17–18.

128. "Strictly Ad Lib: Chicago [Report on Ira Sullivan–Roland Kirk Quintet]," *Down Beat*, September 29, 1960.

129. Don DeMicheal, "Ira Sullivan: Legend in the Making," *Down Beat*, September 15, 1960, 18.

130. See Gene Lees, *You Can't Steal a Gift* (Lincoln and London: University of Nebraska Press, 2001), 31.

131. Gene Lees, *Cats of Any Color: Jazz Black and White* (New York: Oxford University Press, 1994).

132. Gene Lees, "Report on Chicago," *Down Beat*, February 18, 1960, 19. By the turn of the new century, Lees was more comfortable with the terminology of blackness and whiteness, admitting gingerly in a 2001 book that "the city tended to be divided in two, the North Side, whose population was white, and the South Side, whose population was black" (Lees, *You Can't Steal a Gift*, 31). On the other hand, his recollection in the same paragraph that segregated locals in the Chicago musicians' union had been abolished by the time he came to the city is incorrect; the black Local 208, and the white Local 10 merged in 1965.

133. Lees, "Report on Chicago," 19.

134. Ibid., 10.

135. Ibid., 20.

136. "Ad Lib: Chicago [Report on the Richard Abrams Trio]," *Down Beat*, July 21, 1960.

137. Lees, "Report on Chicago," 21.

138. Eddie Harris, *Exodus to Jazz* (Collectables 7145, 1960), compact disc.

139. Lees, "Report on Chicago."

CHAPTER 3

1. Szwed, *Space Is the Place*, 83.

2. Szwed, *Space Is the Place*, 111.

3. Ibid., 94.

4. Ibid., 111.

5. Panken, radio interview with Alvin Fielder.

6. Szwed, *Space Is the Place*, 183.

7. John S. Wilson, "Space Age Jazz Lacks Boosters: Cosmic Group Fails to Orbit with Rhythmic Propulsion," *New York Times*, February 19, 1962. "The Sun Also Rises," *Down Beat*, March 29, 1962.

8. Szwed, *Space Is the Place*, 176.

9. Peter Shapiro, "Blues and the Abstract Truth: Phil Cohran," *Wire*, May 2001, 29.

10. Paramahansa Yogananda, an Indian spiritual teacher of worldwide influence, founded the "Self-Realization Fellowship" in 1920. See Paramahansa Yogananda, *Autobiography of a Yogi* (Los Angeles: Self-Realization Fellowship, [1946] 1981).

11. Abrams interview. Also see Robert L. Campbell, Robert Pruter, and Armin Büttner, *The King Fleming Discography* (accessed November 25, 2005); available from http://hubcap.clemson.edu/~campber/fleming.html.

12. MJT+3, *Daddy-O Presents MJT+3* (Cadet LP 621, 1957), vinyl disc.

13. The piece was later renamed "Great Life" on a 1995 recording by the King Fleming Trio. Hear King Fleming, *King! The King Fleming Songbook* (Southport Records S-SSD 0041, 1995), compact disc.

14. Henry Cowell, *New Musical Resources* (Cambridge and New York: Cambridge University Press, [1930] 1996).

15. Edwin Black, "For the Record: Charles Stepney," *Down Beat*, November 26, 1970.

16. Abrams interview.

17. See *Facts about Berklee* (accessed July 3, 2006); available from http://www.berklee.edu/about/facts.html. For a short essay on the connection between Schillinger and Berklee, see Ted Pease, *The Schillinger/Berklee Connection* (accessed July 3 2006); available from http://www.berklee.edu/bt/122/connection.html. Thanks to John Litweiler for calling this to my attention.

18. Olivier Messiaen, *Technique de mon langage musical* (Paris: A. Leduc, 1944); Olivier Messiaen, *The Technique of My Musical Language*, trans. John Satterfield (Paris: A. Leduc, 1956).

19. Xenakis composed *Achoripsis* in 1956–57 and documented his methods in a 1963 French-language volume on "formalized musics" (*musiques formelles*). See Iannis Xenakis, "Musiques formelles," *La Revue Musicale* 253–54 (1963). The articles later appeared in book form. See Iannis Xenakis, *Formalized Music: Thought and Mathematics in Composition* (Bloomington: Indiana University Press, 1972).

20. Joseph Schillinger, *The Schillinger System of Musical Composition* (New York: Da Capo Press, [1941] 1978), x.

21. Ibid.

22. Joseph Schillinger, *The Mathematical Basis of the Arts* (New York: Philosophical Library, [1948] 1966).

23. Toyozumi interview.

24. John Litweiler, "Air: Uncommon Ensemble Excitement from the Streets of Chicago," *Chicago Reader,* December 17, 1976; Toyozumi interview.

25. Philippe Carles, Andre Clergeat, and Jean-Louis Comolli, eds., *Dictionnaire du jazz, nouvelle édition augmentée* (Paris: Robert Laffont, 1994). Toyozumi interview.

26. John B. Litweiler, "Air: Impossible to Pigeonhole," *Down Beat,* December 16, 1976. Toyozumi interview.

27. DeVeaux, *The Birth of Bebop,* 212.

28. Panken, radio interview with Eddie Harris.

29. Ibid.

30. At the same time, by Charles Walton's own account, there was more to this arts patronage than met the ear: "Chuck could easily not care whether there were patrons in the club because he was dealing in all kinds of illegal things on the club premises. This subsidized the music. I heard that a person could buy anything in the C&C basement. Some years later, Chuck was indicted as a drug dealer and murderer. He died before he went to court." Charles Walton, *Dr. William "Bill" Fielder: Trumpeter and Jazz Improvisor* (2004 [accessed November 25, 2005]); available from http://www.jazzinchicago.org/Internal/Articles/tabid/43/ctl/ArticleView/mid/522/articleId/115/DrWilliamBill Fieldertrumpeterandjazzimprovisor.aspx.

31. Panken, radio interview with Eddie Harris.

32. Except as noted, quotes and narratives from Roscoe Mitchell throughout this book come from Roscoe Mitchell, interview with the author, Madison, Wisconsin, December 27, 1997.

33. Drake, *Black Metropolis,* 380; Mitchell interview.

34. Except as noted, quotes and narratives from Shaku Joseph Jarman throughout this book come from the author's interviews with Jarman in Brooklyn, New York, June 26, 1998, and October 22, 1998.

35. Information on black performers on U.S. national television in this chapter is found in J. Fred MacDonald, *Blacks and White TV: African Americans in Television since 1948,* 2nd ed. (Chicago: Nelson-Hall Publishers, 1992).

36. Ibid., 70.

37. Lipsitz, quoted in Belgrad, *The Culture of Spontaneity,* 300.

38. Robin D. G. Kelley, "Dig They Freedom: Meditations on History and the Black Avant-Garde," *Lenox Avenue: A Journal of Interartistic Inquiry* 3 (1997): 18.

39. Jarman, "AACM History: Interview with Leo Smith."

40. Jarman interview.

41. Richard Wang, "Lecture by Dr. Richard Wang" (paper presented at the Trading Fours: Jazz and Its Milieu, University of Chicago, May 11, 2001).

42. Terry Martin, "Blowing Out in Chicago: Roscoe Mitchell," *Down Beat,* April 6, 1967, 21.

43. Panken, radio interview with Alvin Fielder.

44. Alvin Fielder, interview with the author, New Orleans, Louisiana, August 16, 2003.

45. Panken, radio interview with Alvin Fielder.

46. Ibid. An unpublished tape of Mitchell's music, which Roscoe Mitchell dates from 1962, seems to corroborate Fielder's account. Roscoe Mitchell, "Quartet Recording," unreleased tape recording, 1962, Collection of Roscoe Mitchell.

47. Panken, radio interview with Alvin Fielder.

48. John Litweiler, "The Chicago Scene," *Coda,* May 1967, 38.

49. Roscoe Mitchell, *Nonaah* (Nessa 9/10, 1977), vinyl disc.

50. Quotes and narratives throughout this book from Gene Dinwiddie come from Gene and Flo Dinwiddie, interview with the author, La Puente, California, July 8, 1999.

51. Quotes and narratives throughout this book from Flo Dinwiddie come from Gene and Flo Dinwiddie, interview with the author, La Puente, California, July 8, 1999.

52. Except as noted, quotes and narratives throughout this book from Troy Robinson come from Troy Robinson, interview with the author, North Hills, California, July 7, 1999.

53. Except as noted, quotes and narratives throughout this book from Thurman Barker come from Thurman Barker, interview with the author, Jeffersonville, New York, October 24, 1998; Robinson interview.

54. Except as noted, quotes and narratives throughout this book from Henry Threadgill come from Henry Threadgill, interview with the author, New York City, June 24, 1998, and October 18, 1998.

55. For an account of Still's early studies with Edgard Varese, see Gayle Murchison, "'Dean of Afro-American Composers' or 'Harlem Renaissance Man': The New Negro and the Musical Poetics of William Grant Still," in *William Grant Still: A Study in Contradictions,* ed. Catherine Parsons Smith (Berkeley: University of California Press, 2000).

56. Except as noted, quotes and narratives throughout this book from Leonard Jones come from Leonard Jones, interview with the author, Ratingen, Germany, September 18, 1998.

57. "Chicago Exodus: AACM Members Off to Paris," *Down Beat,* June 26, 1969.

58. Saxophonist Abshalom Ben Shlomo, né Virgil Pumphrey, was one of the early AACM musicians.

59. See James W. Loewen, *The Mississippi Chinese: Between Black and White* (Prospect Heights: Waveland Press, 1988).

60. Except as noted, quotes and narratives throughout this book from M'Chaka Uba come from M'Chaka Uba, interview with the author, San Diego, California, March 16, 1999.

61. Ted Panken, radio interview with Thurman Barker (WKCR-FM, New York City, February 15, 1995 (accessed December 1, 2005), transcript, available from http://www.jazzhouse.org/library/.

62. "Ad Lib: Chicago [Experimental Band announcement]." *Down Beat,* May 9, 1963; J. B. Figi, "Chicago/Wild Onions," *Change* 2 (Spring/Summer 1966): 21.

CHAPTER 4

1. Drake, *Black Metropolis,* 794.

2. Leslie B. Rout, Jr., "Reflections on the Evolution of Post-War Jazz," *Negro Digest,* February 1969, 96.

3. See Thomas Aldridge Newsome, "It's After the End of the World! Don't You Know That Yet? Black Creative Musicians in Chicago, 1946–1976" (PhD dissertation, University of North Carolina at Chapel Hill, 2001). A similar law governing New York City entertainment venues was struck down as unconstitutional in the 1980s; see Paul Chevigny, *Gigs: Jazz and the Cabaret Laws in New York City* (London and New York: Routledge, 2005).

4. Drake, *Black Metropolis.*

5. Bontemps and Conroy, *Anyplace but Here,* 329.

6. Ibid., 322.

7. Ibid., 331.

8. Schatzberg and Kelly, *African-American Organized Crime,* 201.

9. Association for the Advancement of Creative Musicians, program, Twenty-fifth Anniversary Festival, 1990.

10. Terry Martin, "Chicago: The Avant Garde," *Coda,* December-January 1966–67.

11. Pete Welding, "Caught in the Act: Charlie Parker Memorial Concert," *Down Beat,* May 23, 1963.

12. Figi, "Chicago/Wild Onions," 21.

13. Ibid.

14. For accounts of the Clef Club's activities and goals, see Reid Badger, *A Life in Ragtime: A Biography of James Reese Europe* (New York: Oxford University Press, 1995); Ted Vincent, *Keep Cool: The Black Activists Who Built the Jazz Age* (London: Pluto Press, 1995).

15. Raoul Abdul, *Blacks in Classical Music: A Personal History* (New York: Dodd, Mead, 1977), 217–19; Samuel A. Floyd, Jr., "Music in the Harlem Renaissance: An Overview," in *Black Music in the Harlem Renaissance: A Collection of Essays,* ed. Samuel A. Floyd, Jr. (Knoxville: University of Tennessee Press, 1990), 17.

16. Paula Marie Seniors, "Beyond Lift Every Voice and Sing: The Culture of Uplift, Identity, and Politics in Black Musical Theater" (PhD dissertation, University of California, San Diego, 2003), 43.

17. Ibid., 17.

18. Quoted in ibid., 20.

19. Jost, *Sozialgeschichte des Jazz in den USA,* 221.

20. Quoted in Noal Cohen and Michael Fitzgerald, *Rat Race Blues: The Musical Life of Gigi Gryce* (Berkeley: Berkeley Hills Books, 2002), 166.

21. Quoted in ibid., 169.

22. Quoted in ibid., 167. Also see Bruce Wright's autobiography, *Black Justice in a White World* (New York: Barricade Books, 1996).

23. Quoted in Cohen, *Rat Race Blues,* 167.

24. Kofsky, *Black Nationalism and the Revolution in Music,* 228.

25. Ibid., 229.

26. Nat Hentoff, *The Jazz Life* (New York: Dial Press, 1961). For another journalistic

account of the "Newport Rebels," see John S. Wilson, "2 Jazz Festivals Open in Newport," *New York Times,* July 1, 1960. Mingus's recording documenting the initiative and its intergenerational component can be heard on Charles Mingus, *Newport Rebels* (Candid CCD 79022, 1960), compact disc.

27. Gene Lees, "Newport Jazz Festival: The Trouble," *Down Beat,* August 18, 1960, 44.

28. Ibid. A historical account is provided in Frank Kofsky, "Black Nationalism in Jazz: The Forerunners Resist Establishment Repression, 1958–1963," *Journal of Ethnic Studies* 10, no. 2 (1982).

29. Quoted in Rob Backus, *Fire Music: A Political History of Jazz* (Chicago: Vanguard Books, 1976), 71. For Olatunji's own account of the partnership, see Olatunji, *The Beat of My Drum.*

30. Backus, *Fire Music,* 72.

31. Ibid. A recording of a Coltrane concert at the Center of African Culture, produced by the Triumvirate, was released. See John Coltrane, *The Olatunji Concert: The Last Live Recording* (Impulse 314 589 120-2: [1967] 2001), compact disc.

32. Rout, Jr., "Reflections on the Evolution of Post-War Jazz," 96.

33. Frank Kofsky, "Horace Tapscott," *Jazz & Pop,* December 1969, 16. Horace Tapscott's book-length account of the UGMAA was published as Horace Tapscott, *Songs of the Unsung: The Musical and Social Journey of Horace Tapscott,* ed. Steven Isoardi (Durham: Duke University Press, 2001).

34. Robert Levin, "The Jazz Composers Guild: An Assertion of Dignity," *Down Beat,* May 6, 1965, 17.

35. Ibid., 18.

36. Attali, *Noise,* 138.

37. Dan Morgenstern and Martin Williams, "The October Revolution: Two Views of the Avant-Garde in Action," *Down Beat,* November 19, 1964.

38. The *Down Beat* review of a second major guild concert in December 1964, written by a critic who was often presented as both sympathetic to new music and, through his own activities as a musician, an authoritative voice, was nonetheless generally dismissive, placing the new musicians in what Milton Babbitt once called "competition with the historically certified products of the past": "With the exceptions of Taylor, Bley, and possibly Shepp and Sun-Ra, rarely did a voice in this series approach the artistic level of players from the '40s—Charlie Parker, Dizzy Gillespie, J. J. Johnson, Bud Powell, Kenny Clarke, etc. So far as the development of 'free' playing is concerned, I didn't hear more than one or two choruses that derived any benefit from harmonic or rhythmic 'liberation.'" Don Heckman, "Caught in the Act: The Jazz Composers Guild," *Down Beat,* February 11, 1965, 37.

39. Jean Levin, "Au profit des Panthères: Concert au profit des Black Panthers," *Jazz* 181, September 1970, 11.

40. Jost, *Sozialgeschichte des Jazz in den USA,* 212.

41. Paul Bley, with David Lee, *Stopping Time: Paul Bley and the Transformation of Jazz* (Montreal: Vehicule Press, 1999), 91.

42. Will Menter, "The Making of Jazz and Improvised Music: Four Musicians' Collectives in England and the USA" (PhD dissertation, University of Bristol, 1981), 190.

43. Bley, *Stopping Time,* 92.

44. Menter, "'The Making of Jazz and Improvised Music'," 191.

45. Levin, "The Jazz Composers Guild," 17.

46. Ibid.

47. Ibid.

48. Menter, "'The Making of Jazz and Improvised Music'," 193.

49. Ibid., 183.

50. Levin, "The Jazz Composers Guild," 18.

51. Bley, *Stopping Time*, 92.

52. Ibid., 97.

53. Quoted in Jost, *Sozialgeschichte des Jazz in den USA*, 214. "Die Musiker haben es in der Gesellschaft nicht nur mit der Kunst zu tun. Sie sind selbst die Gesellschaft, auch wenn sie sich nur an ihrer Peripherie befinden. Entweder aktiv oder unbewußt lehnen sie sich gegen eine bizarre Gesellschaft auf. Ich glaube, die Guild hat nicht überlebt, weil die Leute, die sich damit befaßt haben, nicht genügend soziales Bewußtsein aufbrachten; sie haben all das vernachlässigt, was für den Menschen, der heute in New York lebt und der nicht nur seinen Lebensunterhalt verdienen, sondern sich dabei auch noch ehrlich ausdrücken will, zum Alltag gehört."

54. Quoted in ibid. "Wir haben eine Möglichkeit verpatzt. Aber wir haben wenigstens etwas unternommen. . . . Aber all dies war trotzdem nicht vergebens. Wir sind da ein bißchen schlauer draus hervorgegangen."

55. Kofsky, *Black Nationalism and the Revolution in Music*, 229.

56. For a critique of this and other standard explanatory tropes surrounding the Great Migration, see Griffin, *Who Set You Flowin'*.

57. Attali, *Noise*, 139–40.

58. Association for the Advancement of Creative Musicians, program, Twenty-fifth Anniversary Festival, 1990.

59. Apparently no copy of the original postcard has been found, but the discussion as it ensued continually referred to its contents. The discussions were heard in AACM General Body Meeting, audiotape, May 8, 1965, Chicago, Illinois, Collection of Muhal Richard Abrams; AACM General Body Meeting, audiotape, May 15, 1965, Chicago, Illinois, Collection of Muhal Richard Abrams. Transcriptions are by the author and have been slightly edited for clarity and narrative flow.

60. Those whose voices were heard on the tapes of the May 8 and May 15 meetings included bassists Charles Clark, Betty Dupree, Melvin Jackson, Malachi Favors (later Maghostut) and Reggie Willis; drummers Jerol Donavon (later Ajaramu) and Steve McCall; singers Floradine Geemes, Sandra Lashley and Conchita Brooks; trumpeter Fred Berry; saxophonists Troy Robinson, Eugene Easton, Ruben Cooper, Jimmy Ellis, Maurice McIntyre (later Kalaparusha), Joseph Jarman (later Shaku), Roscoe Mitchell and Gene Dinwiddie; trombonists Julian Priester and Lester Lashley; and pianists Jodie Christian, Willie Pickens, Claudine Myers (later Amina), Bob Dogan, Ken Chaney and Richard Abrams (later Muhal). AACM General Body Meeting, May 8; AACM General Body Meeting, May 15.

61. Except as noted, quotes and narratives in this section come from the audiotape AACM General Body Meeting, May 8.

62. Floyd, *The Power of Black Music*.

63. Belgrad, *The Culture of Spontaneity,* 191.

64. Quoted in Robert P. Morgan, *Twentieth-Century Music: A History of Musical Style in Modern Europe and America* (New York: W. W. Norton, 1991), 197.

65. Ibid., 197–98.

66. Bill Quinn, "The AACM: A Promise," *Down Beat Music '68,* 1968, 46.

67. Except as noted, quotes and narratives from the May 15 meeting come from AACM General Body Meeting, May 15, Chicago, Illinois.

68. Sandra Lashley was a singer, and the spouse of trombonist and bassist Lester Lashley.

69. Except as noted, quotes and narratives in this section come from: AACM Board Meeting, audiotape, May 20, 1965, Chicago, Illinois, Collection of Muhal Richard Abrams.

70. Those familiar with AACM events may have noticed that the musicians often "face the East," observing a moment of silence before performing. When I came to the collective in 1971, facing the East had become a given; no explanation was offered.

71. Incidentally, AACM dues were still one dollar per week as of 2004.

72. S. B. Fuller was a Chicago businessman who, in developing a variety of successful ventures, including a cosmetics firm and a newspaper chain, became something of a national icon for black business.

73. This was an ongoing dream of the AACM—to elicit and/or encourage philanthropic impulses, to foster support for the experimental arts among the businesspeople in the African American community. It must be said that, for a variety of reasons, the nature and purpose of black philanthropy has yet to be fully explored in terms of the arts. This may be an artifact of the generally poorly developed notion of a noncommercial space for black cultural production.

74. Except as noted, quotes and narratives in this section come from: AACM Executive Board Meeting, audiotape, May 27, 1965, Chicago, Illinois, Collection of Muhal Richard Abrams.

75. Attali, *Noise,* 138.

76. Muhal Richard Abrams, Personal communication, February 11, 2006.

77. Except as noted, quotes and narratives in this section come from: AACM General Body Meeting, audiotape, May 29, 1965, Chicago, Illinois, Collection of Muhal Richard Abrams.

78. Answering the roll call were Betty Dupree, Gene Easton, Philip Cohran, Arthur Reed, Jerol Donavon, Bob Dogan, Steve McCall, Ken Chaney, Sandra Lashley, Henry Gibson (later "Master Henry"), Floradine Geemes, Richard Abrams, Jodie Christian, Martin Alexander, Peggy Abrams (spouse of Richard Abrams), Roscoe Mitchell, Malachi Favors, John Koger, and Thurman Barker. Arriving after the roll call were Joseph Jarman and Charles Clark.

79. Except as noted, quotes and narratives in this section come from the audiotape of the May 29 general body meeting: AACM General Body Meeting, May 29, Chicago, Illinois.

80. Stokely Carmichael and Charles V. Hamilton, *Black Power: The Politics of Liberation in America* (New York: Vintage Books, 1967), 40. Emphasis in the original.

81. Ibid., 46.

82. See Student Non-Violent Coordinating Committee, "Position Paper on Black Power [1966]," in *Modern Black Nationalism*, ed. William Van Deburg (New York: New York University Press, 1997).

83. Menter, "The Making of Jazz and Improvised Music'," 185.

84. Ibid.

85. Levin, "The Jazz Composers Guild."

86. By the beginning of the twenty-first century, with political strategies articulated by constructed and imagined communities of ethnicity, race, gender, and sexual orientation having become commonplace, this notion of political and economic solidarity among marginalized and subordinated groups was far less controversial than it was in 1965. In fact, many of these newer communities of advocacy appeared in the wake of the Black Power and civil rights movements, and drew directly from the examples of all-black organizations in the 1960s.

CHAPTER 5

1. "State of Illinois Charter, Association for the Advancement of Creative Musicians, Chicago, Illinois," August 5, 1965, copy in Collection of George E. Lewis.

2. Porter, *What Is This Thing Called Jazz?*, 70–71.

3. Alan Merriam and Raymond Mack, "The Jazz Community," *Social Forces* 38 (1960): 215.

4. Ibid.

5. Ibid., 216.

6. "State of Illinois Charter, Association for the Advancement of Creative Musicians, Chicago, Illinois"; "Creative Musicians Sponsor Artists Concert Showcase," *Chicago Defender*, August 7, 1965.

7. AACM internal memo, undated, probably 1966.

8. Richard Abrams and Ken Chaney, press release for first AACM event, 1965, Archives of the AACM, Chicago, Illinois. In the copy of this manuscript in my possession, the words "new music" are partially crossed out, with "contemporary music" written in the margin as the intended replacement. The text of the original is essentially reproduced in the published version, "Creative Musicians Sponsor Artists Concert Showcase."

9. "Creative Musicians Sponsor Artists Concert Showcase."

10. Concert program, Joseph Jarman Quintet, August 16, 1965, in the Jamil B. Figi Donation, Chicago Jazz Archive, University of Chicago.

11. Concert program, Joseph Jarman Quintet, August 25, 1965, in the Jamil B. Figi Donation, Chicago Jazz Archive, University of Chicago; "Creative Musicians Present Artistic Heritage Ensemble," *Chicago Defender*, August 11–17, 1965. According to Cohran, no less a personage than Captain Walter Dyett was in attendance, "because so many of his students were in it. He came up because of the trumpet, and he said he liked my compositions."

12. Porter, *What Is This Thing Called Jazz?* 71.

13. "Strictly Ad Lib [announcement of AACM formation]," *Down Beat*, September 9, 1965.

14. "Strictly Ad Lib [announcement of AACM concert series]," *Down Beat,* October 7, 1965.

15. A 2006 interview with Muhal Richard Abrams and me, conducted by writer Howard Mandel, provided a glimpse into the process by which information about unusual music enters the media flow. Mandel began his professional career as a writer in mid-1970s Chicago, with pieces on AACM concerts and many other music events that appeared in *Down Beat* and the *Reader,* a free paper, as well as the mainstream newspaper, the *Chicago Daily News.* "There was all this music coming out that I thought was very significant," Mandel recalled about his particular interest in the AACM during his period at the now-defunct daily. "The only person writing about it was John Litweiler, and he wasn't in the daily newspapers. I thought if I can be very careful about what I say, not say anything more than I can back up, then there's a niche here I can fill. . . . I was a copy clerk there and editorial assistant, and they knew I liked music, and asked if I'd like to do that, and that was exactly what I wanted to do. . . . I had to cover Chicago [the jazz-rock band originally known as the "Chicago Transit Authority"], Cat Stevens, and then Braxton. I was the third string music writer, trying to cover everything their main guys weren't interested in."

I asked Mandel, "Did you have to convince them this music was worth writing about, or did they say to you, be free, write about what you want?"

"It's a little of both," he replied. "I had to interest them in the topic to begin with. Then they'd say, if you think this is interesting enough, OK. But I had to always offer them stuff they had a reference point for."

"But what reference point did they have for Braxton?" I wondered.

"Very little. But that was because they trusted me, they thought I was doing relevant material." Howard Mandel, interview with Muhal Richard Abrams and George Lewis, New York City, August 3, 2006.

16. AACM General Body Meeting, audiotape, October 2, 1965, Chicago, Illinois, Collection of Muhal Richard Abrams.

17. Cromwell, "Jazz Mecca'."

18. Meeting quotes in this section, unless otherwise noted, come from AACM General Body Meeting, October 2.

19. Cohran interview.

20. Quinn, "The AACM," 48.

21. Shapiro, "Blues and the Abstract Truth," 30.

22. Concert program, Artistic Heritage Ensemble. The performers included Easton, tenor sax, flute; Sue Denmon, vocalist; composer; Charles J. Williams, alto sax and clarinet; Master Henry Gibson, congas, bongos, and timbales; Betty Dupree, bass; and Cohran, cornet, zither, harp, frankiphone, composer. Also performing was the dancer and choreographer Darlene Blackburn, the cousin of Clifton Blackburn, later known as Kahil El'Zabar.

23. Quinn, "The AACM," 48.

24. Cromwell, "Jazz Mecca'," 111.

25. Quinn, "The AACM," 48.

26. Unless otherwise noted, quotes and narratives from Amina Claudine Myers

hereafter come from Amina Claudine Myers, interview with the author, New York City, June 25, 1998.

27. John Litweiler, "Altoists and Other Chicagoans," *Coda,* March 1967, 29.

28. Jarman interview.

29. Ibid.

30. Pete Welding, review of Joseph Jarman/John Cage event, *Down Beat,* January 13, 1966, 35.

31. Richard Kostelanetz, *Conversing with Cage* (New York: Routledge, [1987] 2003), 225. As the interview proceeds, the black musicians are enlisted as grist for a renewed instantiation of the standard "critique of jazz" trope. I have already commented at length in another essay on the ways in which such critiques draw upon tropes of whiteness as authority, and nothing in Cage's account of his Chicago experience undercuts that thesis in the slightest. See Lewis, "Afterword to 'Improvised Music after 1950'"; Lewis, "Improvised Music after 1950."

32. The DVD of Haskell Wexler's *Medium Cool,* a cinema verité documentary about the 1968 Democratic Convention, includes commentaries for each scene by the director and his associates that (however inadvertently) evince a similar sense of the incredulous. In one scene, apparently shot in an apartment somewhere in Chicago's black community, the filmmaker tells us that some of the actors are "real black militants" to whom they were introduced by the Chicago writer and broadcaster Studs Terkel. In fact, among the "militants" are Muhal Richard Abrams, AACM trumpeter John Shenoy Jackson, and Jeff Donaldson, one of the founders of the Africobra art movement, as well as several other people who were associated with the more progressive African American art scene of mid-1960s Chicago. Wexler and the others, speaking many years later, still had no idea who these people were, but were astonished at their amazing ability to improvise their speaking parts. The reality was that these were people who may have had more experience in the performance and visual worlds than the filmmakers themselves. One could say that Terkel, whom I've never met, seems to be quite a kidder. See Haskell Wexler, *Medium Cool* (DVD-Video, Paramount 06907, 2001).

33. Rebecca Y. Kim, "Sound Experiments in Chicago: John Cage and Improvisation" (paper delivered at the 32nd Annual Conference of the Society for American Music, Chicago, Illinois, March 16, 2006).

34. Welding, review of Joseph Jarman/John Cage event, 35.

35. Ibid.

36. Welding, review of Joseph Jarman/John Cage event, 35–36.

37. For information on the ONCE Festival, widely considered as one of the signal activities of the post-Cage avant-garde, see Richard S. James, "ONCE: Microcosm of the 1960s Musical and Multimedia Avant-Garde," *American Music* 5, no. 4 (1987). A compilation of recordings of the music of the period by ONCE composers Robert Ashley, David Behrman, George Cacioppo, Gordon Mumma, Pauline Oliveros, Roger Reynolds, Donald Scavarda, Robert Sheff, and others is contained in *Music from the ONCE Festival, 1961–1966* (New World Records 80567).

38. Roscoe Mitchell, *Congliptious* (Nessa N-2, 1968), compact disc; Art Ensemble of Chicago, *People in Sorrow* (Nessa N-3, 1969), vinyl disc.

39. Pete Welding, review of Roscoe Mitchell concert, *Down Beat,* May 19, 1966, 44.

40. Ibid., 45

41. This information is taken from AACM-produced flyers in the Jamil B. Figi Collection, Chicago Jazz Archive, University of Chicago.

42. "Strictly Ad Lib [announcement of Amina Claudine Myers/Jerol Donavon club bookings]," *Down Beat*, October 6, 1966.

43. "Jazz Musicians Group in Chicago Growing," *Down Beat*, July 28, 1966.

44. Menter, "The Making of Jazz and Improvised Music'," 110.

45. Ibid.

46. Ibid., 112.

47. Ibid., 110.

48. Ibid., 109.

49. John Litweiler, "Chicago's AACM," *Sounds and Fury*, June 1966.

50. "Strictly Ad Lib [AACM concerts at Lincoln Center]," *Down Beat*, August 11, 1966. Information on participating artists was also gleaned from AACM-produced flyers in the Jamil B. Figi Collection, Chicago Jazz Archive, University of Chicago.

51. "Strictly Ad Lib [Jam session with Lester Bowie and Leroy Jenkins]," *Down Beat*, August 25, 1966.

52. The term "conduction" was coined in the late 1980s by trumpeter-composer Lawrence "Butch" Morris to refer to his developed system of practicum as an improvising conductor of ensembles of improvisors. Hear Lawrence D. "Butch" Morris, *Testament: AConduction Collection* (New World Records 80478, 1995), set of 10 compact discs.

53. Beauchamp, *Art Ensemble of Chicago*, 35.

54. Lester Bowie, interview with the author, Brooklyn, New York, July 22, 1999.

55. Ibid.

56. Kelley, "Dig They Freedom," 18.

57. Bowie interview.

58. Ibid.

59. Beauchamp, *Art Ensemble of Chicago*, 38.

60. Bowie interview.

61. Beauchamp, *Art Ensemble of Chicago*, 38.

62. Ibid. Recalling his Lincoln University experience in 1999, Bowie felt strongly that major black postsecondary institutions had completely missed the cultural boat: "These fucking black colleges should be meccas for art. I mean all the arts, photography, painting. People would be coming from all over the fucking world to study at a Fisk or a Tuskegee if they had the bad motherfuckers teaching the fucking music and shit. That's our contribution to society, our art."

63. Bowie interview.

64. A substantial biography of Bass, including an interview spanning the course of her career, can be found in Cheryl Andryco, "Fontella Bass: Coming Full Circle" (MA Thesis, Michigan State University, 1996).

65. Bowie.

66. Beauchamp, *Art Ensemble of Chicago*, 40.

67. Bowie interview.

68. Beauchamp, *Art Ensemble of Chicago,* 40.

69. Bowie interview.

70. Except as notes, hereafter quotes and narratives from Maurice McIntyre and Kalaparusha come from Kalaparusha Ahrah Difda, Bronx, New York, July 22, 1999.

71. Roscoe Mitchell, *Sound* (Delmark DD-408, 1966), compact disc.

72. Chuck Nessa, "New Music Report," *Coda,* October/November 1966.

73. "Strictly Ad Lib [Announcement of Roscoe Mitchell recording session]," *Down Beat,* September 22, 1966.

74. Martin, "Chicago."

75. Joseph Jarman, *Song For* (Delmark DD-410, 1967), compact disc.

76. Steve Silverstein, "Recording History: The AACM and the Chicago Avant-Garde Jazz Scene of the Mid-Sixties," *Tape Op,* Winter 1998/99, 56.

77. Ibid.

78. Ibid., 57.

79. Ibid.

80. Fielder interview.

81. Silverstein, "Recording History," 57.

82. Ibid.

83. Fielder interview.

84. Silverstein, "Recording History," 58.

85. "Pay Last Tribute to Gaddy, 74," *Chicago Defender* (Big Weekend Edition), September 4, 1971.

86. "Final Bar [passing of Christopher Gaddy]," *Down Beat,* April 18, 1968.

87. Bud Spangler, "The Home Front," *Change* 2 (Spring/Summer 1966). Ted Panken, interview with George Lewis and Leo Smith (WKCR-FM, New York City, September 12, 1995 [accessed November 22, 2005]), transcript, available from http://www.jazzhouse.org/library/.

88. Litweiler, "The Chicago Scene."

89. Joseph Jarman, "New York," *Change* 2 (Spring/Summer 1966): 10.

90. Martin, "Blowing Out in Chicago," 48; Nessa, "New Music Report."

91. Litweiler, "Altoists and Other Chicagoans," 28.

92. Braxton has been written about more extensively than any other AACM member or group, and the several Braxton biographies are varied in their approaches to their subject. For an unsurpassed account of the AACM and its effect on Braxton, see Radano, *New Musical Figurations.* In his series of interviews, Graham Lock delves extensively into Braxton's philosophies of culture; see Graham Lock, *Forces in Motion: The Music and Thoughts of Anthony Braxton* (New York: Da Capo Press, 1988). Extensive musical analysis, combined with an in-depth view of Braxton's aesthetics and symbolisms, appears in Mike Heffley, *The Music of Anthony Braxton* (Westport, Connecticut: Greenwood Press, 1996). The late Swiss musicologist Peter Niklas Wilson's useful German-language overview of Braxton's career and work is contained in Peter Niklas Wilson, *Anthony Braxton: Sein Leben, seine Musik, seine Schallplatten* (Waakirchen, Switzerland: Oreos Verlag, 1993). For a narrative linking Braxton with canonical European and Euro-American composers, such

as Arnold Schoenberg, John Cage and Karlheinz Stockhausen, see Alun Ford, *Anthony Braxton: Creative Music Continuum* (Exeter, Great Britain: Stride Publications, 1997).

93. For accounts of the rioting, which amounted to a pogrom against Tulsa's African American community, see Scott Ellsworth, with a foreword by John Hope Franklin, *Death in a Promised Land: The Tulsa Race Riot of 1921* (Baton Rouge: Louisiana State University Press, 1982). Also see James S. Hirsch, *Riot and Remembrance: America's Worst Race Riot and Its Legacy* (New York: Houghton Mifflin, 2002).

94. Unless otherwise noted, quotes and narratives from Anthony Braxton hereafter come from Anthony Braxton, interview with the author, Middletown, Connecticut, June 27, 1998, and October 23, 1998.

95. The Reverend Clay Evans was the well-known pastor of one of the South Side's largest religious institutions, the Fellowship Missionary Baptist Church. Evans was also a local celebrity as a gospel performer, notably with a cover of Stuart Hamblen's 1951 hit song, "It Is No Secret (What God Can Do)."

96. For an account of the interethnic and economic tensions that accompanied the transformation of the neighborhood surrounding CVS, see Louis Rosen, *The South Side: The Racial Transformation of an American Neighborhood* (Chicago: I. R. Dee, 1998).

97. Richard Abrams, *Levels and Degrees of Light* (Delmark DS-413, 1967), vinyl; (Delmark DD-413, 1967), compact disc.

98. Hear Eddie Harris, *The Electrifying Eddie Harris* (Atlantic 1495, 1967), vinyl disc; Eddie Harris, *Plug Me In* (Atlantic 1506, 1968), vinyl disc; Eddie Harris, *The Tender Storm* (Atlantic 1478, 1966), vinyl disc.

99. Ron Welburn, "The Black Aesthetic Imperative," in *The Black Aesthetic*, ed. Addison Gayle, Jr. (New York: Doubleday, 1971), 149.

100. Black, "For the Record."

101. Welburn, "The Black Aesthetic Imperative," 148.

102. Miles Davis, *Bitches Brew* (Sony 65744, 1970), two compact discs.

103. Welburn, "The Black Aesthetic Imperative," 149.

104. Aimé Césaire, *Notebook of a Return to the Native Land*, trans. and ed. Clayton Eshleman and Annette Smith (Middletown, Conn.: Wesleyan University Press, 2001), 34. In the original:

> *ô fraiche source de la lumiere*
> *ceux qui n'ont inventé ni la poudre ni la boussole*
> *ceux qui n'ont jamais su dompter la vapeur ni l'electricité*
> *ceux qui n'ont exploré ni les mers ni le ciel*
> *mais ceux sans qui la terre ne serait pas la terre*

Aimé Césaire, *Cahier d'un retour au pays natal* (Paris: Présence Africaine, 1971), 115.

105. Aimé Césaire, *Cahier d'un retour au pays natal*, 2nd ed., ed. Abiola Irele (Columbus: Ohio State University Press, 2000), 117.

106. Norman Mailer, quoted in Michele Wallace, *Black Macho and the Myth of the Superwoman* (London and New York: Verso, 1978), 46. See Norman Mailer, *Existential Errands* (New York: New American Library, 1973). More recently, ripostes to this framing of black engagement with technology can be found in the growing body of Afrofuturist

literature. See the work of Mark Dery, generally credited with introducing the concept of Afrofuturism in *Flame Wars: The Discourse of Cyberculture* (Durham: Duke University Press, 1995). Also see Alondra Nelson, "Introduction: Future Texts," *Social Text 71*, vol. 20, no. 2 (2002).

107. Silverstein, "Recording History," 58.

108. John Litweiler, "The New Music," *Coda*, July 1968; Jack Cooke, review of Lester Bowie recording, *Numbers 1&2, Jazz Monthly* 162, August 1968.

109. Lawrence Kart, review of Richard Abrams recording, *Levels and Degrees of Light, Down Beat*, November 14, 1968; A. B. Spellman, "Revolution in Sound: Black Genius Creates a New Music in Western World," *Ebony*, August 1969, 89. The reverb issue apparently stuck in the craws of some for many years. A later compact disc release of the album managed to remove the reverberation, seriously damaging the recording's musical integrity. Particularly on "The Bird Song," the reverberation effect had been integral to the form of the piece itself. The wash of sound was emotionally telling and dramatic, as the words of the poetry are obscured in a wave of collectivity, with bird calls blending with harmonics from arco bass and violin. The fact that CD listeners can now finally hear the words to "The Bird Song" did not mitigate the bowdlerization of the piece; without the reverb, the drama of the work is largely lost. See Abrams, *Levels and Degrees of Light*.

110. Martin, "Blowing Out in Chicago," 20.

111. Ibid., 21.

112. Ibid., 47.

113. Ibid.

114. Ibid., 21–22.

115. Jarman interview.

116. Litweiler, "Altoists and Other Chicagoans," 29.

117. Leslie B. Rout, Jr., "AACM: New Music (!) New Ideas (?)," *Journal of Popular Culture* 1 (1967): 129.

118. Jarman, "AACM History: Interview with Leo Smith."

119. Litweiler, "The New Music," 34.

120. Jarman, "AACM History: Interview with Leo Smith."

121. Ibid.

122. Litweiler, "The New Music," 34.

123. Bill Quinn, "Caught in the Act: Joseph Jarman," *Down Beat*, March 9, 1967, 28.

124. Ibid.

125. Ibid.

126. Quinn, "The AACM," 48.

127. John Litweiler, "Chicago's Richard Abrams: A Man with an Idea," *Down Beat*, October 5, 1967, 23.

128. Ibid., 26.

129. Ibid.

130. Ibid.

131. Litweiler, "The Chicago Scene," 36.

132. Marcia J. Citron, *Gender and the Musical Canon* (Cambridge: Cambridge University Press, 1993), 39.

133. Jost, *Sozialgeschichte des Jazz in den USA,* 216. "Daß jedoch diese für den vom Star-Syndrom bestimmten amerikanischen Jazz ganz und gar untypische Organisationsform gerade im Chicago der 60er Jahre und gerade im Rahmen der AACM besondere Geltung erfuhr, war natürlich kein Zufall, sondern Ausdruck des gesellschaftlichen Bewußtseins der AACM-Leute."

134. Litweiler, "The Chicago Scene," 37.

135. Quinn, "The AACM," 47.

136. Allan Chase, *Sun Ra and the AACM* (1992 [accessed November 23, 2005]), available from http://www.dpo.uab.edu/~moudry/articles/ra&aacm.htm.

137. Szwed, *Space Is the Place.*

138. Terry Martin, "The Chicago Avant-Garde," *Jazz Monthly* 157, March 1968, 13.

139. Lock, *Forces in Motion,* 154.

140. John Corbett, liner notes, Sun Ra recording, *Angels and Demons at Play/The Nubians of Plutonia* (Evidence ECD-22066-2, 1993).

141. Martin, "The Chicago Avant-Garde," 13.

142. Chase, *Sun Ra and the AACM.*

143. Corbett, Liner notes, Sun Ra recording, *Angels and Demons.*

144. Martin, "The Chicago Avant-Garde," 13.

145. Martin, "Blowing Out in Chicago."

146. Bert Vuisje, *De nieuwe jazz: Twintig interviews door Bert Vuisje* (Baarn: Bosch & Keuning, 1978), 196.

147. Litweiler, "Chicago's Richard Abrams," 23. Anecdote warning: In 1975 I played a concert on the near North Side of Chicago led and produced by tenor saxophonist John Neely, playing his sprightly bebop-based music with Bill Brimfield on trumpet, Steve McCall on drums, Thomas "Tiaz" Palmer on bass, and a pianist whose name I don't quite remember. At the intermission, Muhal came in, and as we were all talking, Sun Ra came in, dressed as those who were familiar with him might expect, in a fashion that we were all used to, highly congruent as his wardrobe was with the more Afrocentrically oriented residents of Chicago's South Side. I don't remember whether they talked about music or not, but with so much in common history between Ra, Steve, Muhal, and Neely, there were certainly no lapses in the discussion. I do remember that I didn't say anything at all.

148. Abrams.

149. Harold Bloom, *The Anxiety of Influence: A Theory of Poetry* (New York: Oxford University Press, 1973).

150. Ted Panken, interview with Lester Bowie and Don Moye (WKCR-FM, New York City, November 22, 1994 [accessed November 22, 2005]), transcript, available from http://www.jazzhouse.org/library/.

151. Ibid.

152. Szwed, *Space Is the Place,* 179.

153. Moondog, *Jazztime U.S.A.: Rimshot; Improvisation in 4/4; Improvisation in 7/4* (Brunswick BL54001, 1953).

154. Chase, *Sun Ra and the AACM.*

155. Ibid.

156. Ibid.

157. Vijay Iyer, *Sun Ra: A Music Full of Africa* (accessed November 25, 2005); available from http://www.cnmat.berkeley.edu/~vijay/mbase2.html.

CHAPTER 6

1. John Litweiler, "Caught in the Act: Various Artists," *Down Beat,* October 19, 1967, 47.

2. Martin, "The Chicago Avant-Garde," 18.

3. Figi, "Jazz: A Family for the New Music," 21.

4. Concert program, Artistic Heritage Ensemble.

5. Semmes, "The Dialectics of Cultural Survival," 455–56.

6. Semmes, "The Dialectics of Cultural Survival," 456.

7. Ibid., 457.

8. Ibid., 449.

9. Ibid., 457.

10. Ibid., 458.

11. Ibid. Also see Shapiro, "Blues and the Abstract Truth."

12. Jeff Donaldson, "The Rise, Fall, and Legacy of the Wall of Respect Movement," *International Review of African American Art* 15, no. 1 (1998): 22.

13. Ibid.

14. Ibid.

15. For an account of the artistic relationship between Abrams, Donaldson, OBAC, and the AACM, as well as a color reproduction of the Donaldson painting, see George Lewis, "Purposive Patterning: Jeff Donaldson, Muhal Richard Abrams, and the Multi-dominance of Consciousness," *Lenox Avenue* 5 (1999).

16. Donaldson, "The Rise, Fall, and Legacy of the Wall of Respect Movement," 22.

17. Ibid., 25.

18. Ibid., 23.

19. Ibid.

20. J. Edgar Hoover, "Memorandum to Special Agent in Charge, Albany, New York," in *Modem Black Nationalism,* ed. William Van Deburg (New York: New York University Press, [1967] 1997).

21. Donaldson, "The Rise, Fall, and Legacy of the Wall of Respect Movement," 23.

22. Semmes, "The Dialectics of Cultural Survival," 458. According to a 1980 *New York Times* article, the Chicago Police Department's "Red Squad," one of a number of similar municipal units around the country devoted to covert surveillance, "infiltrated and used electronic surveillance against more than 800 organizations," including the League of Women Voters, the World Council of Churches, and black-run activist organizations such as the Kenwood-Oakland Community Organization, the National Association for the Advancement of Colored People, and Rev. Jesse Jackson's Operation PUSH. See Nathaniel Sheppard, Jr., "How Chicago Red Squad Sabotaged 60's Dissidents," *New York Times,* December 2, 1980, sec. B, p. 12, col. 1.

23. The originally self-produced 1971 album by the Pharaohs has recently been reissued. See the Pharaohs, *The Awakening* (Ubiquity/Luv N' Haight, 1972).

24. Semmes, "The Dialectics of Cultural Survival," 458.

25. See Jerry DeMuth, "Chicago Jazz Kicks Open Coffin and Goes 'Creative,'" *Chicago Sun-Times,* October , 1967.

26. "Down Beat Critics Poll," *Down Beat,* August 24, 1967, 17.

27. Except as noted, quotes and narratives from Wadada Leo Smith in this chapter come from Wadada Leo Smith, interview with the author, Sespe, California, December 21, 1997.

28. The Civilian Conservation Corps was a Depression-era program.

29. Unless otherwise noted, hereafter quotes and narrative from John Stubblefield come from John Stubblefield, interview with the author, New York City, October 22, 1998.

30. The school is now the University of Arkansas at Pine Bluff.

31. Pharoah Sanders, just five years older than Stubblefield, was also a native of Little Rock.

32. For an account of black Greek-letter sororities and fraternities, see Lawrence Otis Graham, *Our Kind of People: Inside America's Black Upper Class* (New York: HarperCollins, 1999), 89–100.

33. Unless otherwise noted, hereafter, quotes and narrative around Wallace LaRoy McMillan come from Wallace LaRoy McMillan, interview with the author, Chicago, Illinois, June 18, 1999.

34. Ibid.

35. Philip Cohran and the Artistic Heritage Ensemble, *On the Beach* (Chicago: Zulu Records, 1967).

36. For an ethnographically based account of the discourse of the "outside" among free jazz musicians of the 1990s, see David Such, *Avant-Garde Jazz Musicians Performing Out There* (Iowa City: University of Iowa Press, 1993).

37. Ted Panken, radio interview with Von Freeman (WKCR-FM, New York City, June 7, 1987 [accessed November 30, 2005]), transcript, available from http://www.jazzhouse.org/library/.

38. Quinn, "The AACM," 49.

39. Creative Construction Company, *Creative Construction Company,* vol. 1 (Muse Records MR 5071, 1975), vinyl disc.

40. AACM meeting, October 2.

41. Douglas Ewart, E-mail communication, December 29, 2005. Abrams recalls that although he taught classes at Lincoln Center in 1967, the school was not formally organized until 1968. Abrams.

42. Quinn, "The AACM."

43. Something that may well come as a surprise to many is Mitchell's recollection that "I don't believe there were classes in improvising."

44. Menter, "The Making of Jazz and Improvised Music,'" 113.

45. Ibid., 112.

46. Ibid.

47. Dominique-Rene De Lerma, ed., "The Impact of the AACM in the Twentieth Century: A Panel Discussion" (transcript, Center for Black Music Research, Chicago, Illinois, 1990), 13.

48. Rout, Jr., "AACM," 138.

49. Ibid., 129.

50. Ibid., 136.

51. Ibid., 131.

52. Ibid., 129.

53. Ibid., 134.

54. Ibid., 136.

55. Ibid.

56. Ibid., 137–38.

57. Ibid., 137.

58. Ibid.

59. Amina Claudine Myers, "A Day in the Life . . . . By Ariae," manuscript, unpaged, collection of Amina Claudine Myers, 1967[?].

60. Joseph Jarman, *Black Case,* vols. 1 and 2, *Return from Exile* (Chicago: Art Ensemble of Chicago Publishing Company, 1977), 76.

61. Muhal Richard Abrams, *The Dream,* audiotape, 1968, collection of Muhal Richard Abrams.

62. Ibid. Transcribed by the author.

63. Joseph Jarman, *As if It Were the Seasons* (Delmark DD-417, 1968), compact disc.

64. One such session featured McCall, Lester Bowie, Roscoe Mitchell, and bassist Scotty Holt: Nick Gravenites, *Whole Lotta Soul/Drunken Boat* (Out of Sight Records, 1965), vinyl disc. See Dan Plonsey, *Roscoe Mitchell Discography (Preliminary)* (2003 [accessed July 4, 2006]); available from http://www.plonsey.com/beanbenders/Roscoedisco.html. According to Plonsey, this recording was Mitchell's first.

65. John Litweiler, "Caught in the Act: Roscoe Mitchell," *Down Beat,* July 25, 1968, 30.

66. Ted Panken, radio interview with Roscoe Mitchell (WKCR-FM, New York City, December 5, 1995 [accessed November 30, 2005]), transcript, available from http://www.jazzhouse.org/library/. For an account of the Asian American improvisation movement, see Wong, *Speak It Louder.*

67. Litweiler, "The New Music," 35.

68. "Potpourri [Announcement of Steve McCall in Germany]," *Down Beat,* November 14, 1968.

69. Maurice McIntyre, "The A.A.C.M.," *New Regime* 1, no. 1 (1968): 2.

70. McIntyre, "The A.A.C.M.," 1.

71. Lester Bowie, "A Word from the Desk," *New Regime* 1, no. 1 (1968): 5.

72. Ibid.

73. Ibid.

74. Ibid.

75. Henry Threadgill, "Where Are Our Critics?" *New Regime* 1, no. 1 (1968): 11.

76. Ibid., 12.

77. Anthony Braxton, "24–70°," *New Regime* 1, no. 1 (1968).

78. Ibid.

79. Joseph Jarman, "On Questions Asked of Me by Jerry Figi on Our Music," *New Regime* 2 (1968): 18.

80. Cooke, review of Lester Bowie recording, *Numbers 1&2,* 12.

81. Martin, "The Chicago Avant-Garde," 12.

82. Ibid., 17.

83. Ibid., 14.

84. Radano, *New Musical Figurations,* 25.

85. Lawrence Kart, review of Roscoe Mitchell recording, *Congliptious, Down Beat,* February 6, 1969, 26.

86. Max Harrison, review of Roscoe Mitchell recording, *Congliptious, Jazz Monthly* 171, June 1969, 28.

87. Ibid., 29.

88. Ibid., 28.

89. Will Smith, review of Roscoe Mitchell recording, *Congliptious, Jazz & Pop,* August 1969, 26.

90. Lester Bowie, *Numbers 1&2* (Nessa N-1, 1967), compact disc. Transcription by the author.

91. Ibid.

92. Despite being released under Bowie's name, the album presented two compositions by Roscoe Mitchell, according to Mitchell.

93. Michael James, review of Lester Bowie recording, *Numbers 1&2, Jazz Monthly* 160, June 1968, 16.

94. Ibid. Susanne K. Langer's well-known aesthetic theory of "significant form" is worked out in her 1942 opus, *Philosophy in a New Key: A Study in the Symbolism of Reason, Rite, and Art* (Cambridge: Harvard University Press, 1942). The theory was further developed in Susanne K. Langer, *Feeling and Form: A Theory of Art . . .* (New York: Scribner, 1953).

95. Cooke, review of Lester Bowie recording, *Numbers 1&2.*

96. Ibid.

97. Jack Cooke, review of Richard Abrams recording, *Levels and Degrees of Light;* and Joseph Jarman recording, *Song For, Jazz Monthly* 166, December 1968, 12.

98. Michael Robinson, "The Association: The 'New Thing' Is Their Thing," *Chicago Tribune,* Sunday Magazine, November 24, 1968.

99. Quinn, "The AACM," 46.

100. Ibid.

101. Ibid., 48.

102. Ibid., 46. The diversity mentioned in the article included women only to a limited extent. The article mentions vocalists Sandra Lashley and Sherri Scott, and a cellist, Caroline Revis. Curiously, Claudine Myers, who was active at this time, is not mentioned.

103. Ibid.

104. Richard Abrams, program, Concert by the Richard Abrams Septet, May 24, 1967, Northwestern University, in the Jamil B. Figi Donation, Chicago Jazz Archive, Joseph Regenstein Library, University of Chicago.

105. Quinn, "The AACM," 46.

106. Rout, Jr., "AACM," 132–33.

107. Ibid., 135.

108. In our interview, Cranshaw regarded with amused detachment some of the more heated rhetoric that emanated from the AACM in its early years: "Joseph Jarman, they used that quote a million times about, I used to be a hip ghetto nigger and all that. I said, wait a minute, Joseph Jarman was never a hip ghetto man, nooo."

109. Rout, Jr., "AACM," 138.

110. Ibid.

111. Muhal Richard Abrams, *Things to Come from Those Now Gone* (Delmark DE-430, 1972), compact disc.

112. Marilyn Lashley, interview with the author, San Diego, California, August 16, 2003.

113. Wallace, *Black Macho and the Myth of the Superwoman*, 10.

114. Farah Jasmine Griffin, *If You Can't Be Free, Be a Mystery: In Search of Billie Holiday* (New York: Free Press, 2001), 179.

115. Ibid.

116. Ibid.

117. Quoted in ibid.

118. Wallace, *Black Macho and the Myth of the Superwoman*, 172.

119. Haki R. Madhubuti, *From Plan to Planet: Life-Studies; The Need for Afrikan Minds and Institutions* (Chicago: Third World Press, 1973), 77.

120. Wallace, *Black Macho and the Myth of the Superwoman*, 14.

121. Myers.

122. Taylor, *Notes and Tones*, 184.

123. Madhubuti, *From Plan to Planet*, 78.

124. Patricia Hill Collins, *Fighting Words: Black Women and the Search for Justice* (Minneapolis: University of Minnesota Press, 1998), 168.

125. "Final Bar [passing of Charles Clark]," *Down Beat*, May 29, 1969. Fred Hopkins, the important Chicago experimentalist bassist, was one of the first recipients of the scholarship in the early 1970s.

126. Ted Panken, radio interview with Joseph Jarman, transcript, February 15, 1987, WKCR-FM, New York City, collection of Ted Panken.

127. Beauchamp, *Art Ensemble of Chicago*, 73.

128. Litweiler, *The Freedom Principle*, 183.

129. McCoy Tyner, *Asante* (Blue Note 7243 4 93384 2 5, 1970), compact disc.

130. For a statement of purpose and philosophy from the group's founder, see Ben Ammi, *God, the Black Man, and Truth* (Chicago: Communicators Press, 1982). Also see *The African Hebrew Israelites of Jerusalem: A Village of Peace* (accessed December 1, 2005); available from http://www.kingdomofyah.com/ourstory.htm. For an journalist's account of their early arrival and issues of acceptance in Israel, see Danielle Haas, "Black Hebrews Fight for Citizenship in Israel," *San Francisco Chronicle*, November 15, 2002.

131. Barry Gifford, "Chicago: The 'New' Music," *Jazz & Pop*, January 1969, 40.

132. Andrew Ross, *No Respect: Intellectuals and Popular Culture* (London: Routledge, 1989), 93.

133. Amiri [Leroi Jones] Baraka, *Black Music* (New York: William Morrow and Company, 1968), 125.

134. Ibid., 126.

135. Ibid., 127.

136. Ibid., 118.

137. Ibid., 125.

138. Abram Kardiner and Lionel Ovesey, *The Mark of Oppression: Explorations in the Personality of the American Negro* (Cleveland: World Publishing Company, [1951] 1962).

139. Howard S. Becker, *Outsiders: Studies in the Sociology of Deviance* (New York: Free Press, [1963] 1973); Merriam and Mack, "The Jazz Community." In an environment in which black poverty was represented as "soulful" and "authentic," perhaps the mere fact of being middle-class may well have been enough for an African American to be classified as "deviant."

140. Frazier, *Black Bourgeoisie*, 187.

141. See Scott DeVeaux, *Jazz in America: Who's Listening?* (Carson, Calif.: Seven Locks Press, 1995).

142. Paul DiMaggio and Francie Ostrower, "Participation in the Arts by Black and White Americans," *Social Forces* 68, no. 3 (1990).

143. Ibid.

144. Kobena Mercer, *Welcome to the Jungle: New Positions in Black Cultural Studies* (New York: Routledge, 1994), 62.

145. Ibid., 65.

146. DiMaggio, "Participation in the Arts by Black and White Americans," 774.

147. Ibid.

148. Baraka, *Black Music*, 130.

149. Ibid., 125.

150. Ron Karenga, "Black Cultural Nationalism," in *The Black Aesthetic*, ed. Addison Gayle, Jr. (New York: Doubleday, 1971), 33.

151. Ibid., 33–34.

152. bell hooks, "An Aesthetic of Blackness: Strange and Oppositional," in *Yearning: Race, Gender, and Cultural Politics* (Boston: South End Press, 1990), 107–8. Such a lack of recognition, for example, leads Karenga to the dubious declaration concerning the blues that "today they are not functional because they do not commit us to the struggle of today and tomorrow, but keep us in the past." Karenga, "Black Cultural Nationalism," 38.

153. hooks, "An Aesthetic of Blackness."

154. Ibid., p. 108.

155. Ibid., 110.

156. Ibid., 108–9.

157. hooks, "An Aesthetic of Blackness," 109.

158. Other Jarman performances were equally provocative. A 1968 performance with

dancer Kim An Wong at the Francis Parker School, based on the Tibetan Book of the Dead, was sponsored by long-time AACM supporter and former dancer Larayne Black and her husband, the Chicago architect John Black. As *Down Beat* noted matter-of-factly, the performance "was halted by school officials when the dancers disrobed." "Strictly Ad Lib [performance of Joseph Jarman and Kim An Wong]," *Down Beat,* December 13, 1968.

159. Lock, *Forces in Motion,* 47.

160. Radano, *New Musical Figurations,* 97–99.

161. Menter, "The Making of Jazz and Improvised Music'," 115.

162. Kalaparusha Ahrah Difda, interview with the author, New York City, July 22, 1999.

163. Cromwell, "Jazz Mecca'," 109.

164. Vuisje, *De nieuwe jazz,* 199.

CHAPTER 7

1. Semmes, "The Dialectics of Cultural Survival," 447.

2. Ibid., 448.

3. Ibid., 449.

4. Ibid.

5. Beauchamp, *Art Ensemble of Chicago,* 45.

6. Ibid.

7. Martin, "Blowing Out in Chicago," 48.

8. Beauchamp, *Art Ensemble of Chicago,* 47. Emphasis in the original.

9. Quotes from Steve McCall's mother and sister Rochelle Toyozumi are from Toyozumi.

10. Claude Delcloo, "Letter to the AACM," in *New Regime* (Chicago: Association for the Advancement of Creative Musicians, 1968).

11. Beauchamp, *Art Ensemble of Chicago,* 28.

12. Ibid.

13. Anthony Braxton, *Three Compositions of New Jazz* (Delmark DD-415, 1968), compact disc.

14. "Chicago Exodus."

15. For instance, one of the best-known books, Tyler Stovall's "Paris Noir," virtually erases this presence. See Tyler Stovall, *Paris Noir: African Americans in the City of Light* (Boston: Houghton Mifflin, 1996). One of the few histories that mentions working-class African American experimentalists who were highly prominent in Paris during the 1960s, 1970s, and 1980s is Michel Fabre and John A. Williams, *A Street Guide to African Americans in Paris* (Paris: Cercle d'Études Afro-Americaines, 1996).

16. Bennetta Jules-Rosette, "Black Paris: Touristic Simulation," *Annals of Tourism Research* 21, no. 4 (1994): 689.

17. Ibid., 680.

18. One is further tempted to speculate that the same issue may be active among a number of historians of black Americans in Paris.

19. Jules-Rosette, "Black Paris," 679.

20. Beauchamp, *Art Ensemble of Chicago,* 81.

21. "Flashes (announcement of AACM Nessa and Delmark recordings)," *Jazz Hot* 250, May 1969, 12.

22. Beauchamp, *Art Ensemble of Chicago,* 73.

23. Moye interview.

24. Daniel Caux, "Le délire et la rigueur de l'Art Ensemble de Chicago," *Jazz Hot* 252, July-August 1969, 8.

25. Ibid.

26. "Ils sont noirs. Lorsqu'on s'aventure dans leur antre, au Lucernaire, rue d'Odessa, on croit assister à un rite magique: Avec recueillement et sérieux, quatre hommes explorent une jungle d'instruments baroques: des cuivres, cordes et percussions de toutes sortes. Tour à tour austère, et violent, religieux, et déchaîné, tel est l'AACM de Chicago, lequel depuis juillet présente un des spectacles de free-jazz parmi les plus fantastiques qu'on puisse imaginer." David Nijinski, "La musique à bout de bras: Program note, Concert of the Art Ensemble of Chicago, Théâtre du Lucernaire," in *Larayne Black Collection, Chicago Historical Society* (1969).

27. "On dirait bien du Xénakis—tiens, voilà Stockhausen pulsation en plus—ici un passage pop—là on s'ennuie un peu—mélodie de timbres—etc., etc. L'AACM s'sen tout. . . . En entrant au Lucernaire, attendez-vous à ce que l'on vous fasse les poches: vous y serez roué de coups, détroussé, puis insulté, et renvoyé tout nu et pleurnichant à votre mère. Mais surtout ne retourner pas chez vous. . . . Si vous avez su écouter l'AACM de Chicago, vous deviendrez tout-à-coup un terroriste subversif. . . . Vous verrez combien il est enivrant de rapter Boulez, de faire la peau à Bério ou de passer à tabac Xénakis." Ibid.

28. Quoted in David Harvey, *The Condition of Postmodernity: An Enquiry into the Origins of Cultural Change* (Cambridge, Mass: Blackwell, 1993), 51.

29. Program, Concert of the Art Ensemble of Chicago, Association-Maison de la Culture d'Angers, France, 1970, Larayne Black Collection, Chicago Historical Society.

30. Beauchamp, *Art Ensemble of Chicago,* 74.

31. Ibid.

32. "Ils travaillent au moins pendant cinq heures par jour, cinq heures passées à rechercher des sonorités nouvelles, à faire dire aux instruments ce qu'ils n'ont pas vraiment l'habitude de dire." Nijinski, "La musique à bout de bras."

33. "Flashes (announcement of arrival of AACM musicians in Paris)," *Jazz* 168, July-August 1969, 14.

34. For Braxton's part, "The so-called rivalry between me and Roscoe Mitchell is nonexistent."

35. "Ils créèrent un hallucinant climat onirique: confettis, serpentins et surtout fumigènes (on ne se voyait plus à un mètre), musiciens se déplaçant dans la salle, émergeant brusquement de la fumée." Daniel Caux, "L'été au Lucernaire," *Jazz Hot* 253, September 1969, 15.

36. Except as noted, quotes and narratives from Wadada Leo Smith in this chapter come from Wadada Leo Smith, interview with the author, La Jolla, California, March 7, 1999.

37. Smith interview.

38. Beauchamp, *Art Ensemble of Chicago,* 42.

39. Ted Panken, radio interview with Leroy Jenkins (WKCR-FM, New York City, October 12, 1993 [accessed December 1, 2005]), transcript, available from http://www.jazzhouse.org/library/.

40. Program, Concert of the Art Ensemble of Chicago, Association-Maison de la Culture d'Angers, France.

41. Joseph Jarman, "Gens en peine: L'Art Ensemble de Chicago vous offre cette musique pour Noël," *Le monde*, December 24, 1969.

42. Program notes, Concerts of the Art Ensemble of Chicago in Lille and Arras, France, November 3–4, 1969, Larayne Black Collection, Chicago Historical Society, unpaged.

43. Philippe Carles, "Les nouvelles têtes de la nouvelle musique," *Jazz* 171, October 1969, 23–25.

44. "Free jazz sur Seine," *Jazz* 169–70, September 1969, 19.

45. Ibid., 21.

46. Ibid., 21–22. Other recordings made during this marathon recording paroxysm include Art Ensemble of Chicago, *Live in Paris* (Fuel 2000 302 061 383 2, [1969] 2004), compact disc; Art Ensemble of Chicago, *A Jackson in Your House* (Affinity AFF 752, [1969] 1989), compact disc; Art Ensemble of Chicago, *A.A.C.M. Great Black Music/Message to Our Folks* (Spot 549, [1969] 2004), compact disc; Art Ensemble of Chicago, *A.A.C.M. Great Black Music: Reese and the Smooth Ones* (BYG-Actuel GET 329, 1969), vinyl; Anthony Braxton, *B-Xo/N-O-1–47A* (Get Back GET 315, 1969), compact disc; Anthony Braxton, *This Time* (Get Back GET 347, 1970), compact disc. For more detailed information, see Plonsey, *Roscoe Mitchell Discography;* and Jason Guthartz, *Anthony Braxton Discography* (accessed March 8, 2007); available from http://restructures.net/BraxDisco/BraxDisco.htm.

47. Archie Shepp, *Yasmina, A Black Woman* (BYG-Actuel 529304, 1969).

48. "Que ce soit dans leur musique ou dans la vie, on trouvera chez les membres de l'AACM une nette défiance de tout culte de la personnalité au profit de l'esprit collectif." Daniel Caux, "A.A.C.M. Chicago," *Jazz Hot* 254, October 1969, 16.

49. Beauchamp, *Art Ensemble of Chicago,* 28.

50. Caux, "A.A.C.M. Chicago," 17.

51. "Si, en employant le mot "populaire," vous pensez à l'argent, alors là non, l'AACM ne rapporte pas énormément d'argent . . . mais l'association est bien connue des milieux musicaux, tous les musiciens en ont entendu parler." Ibid.

52. Nous avons bien essayé de joindre les gens de New York mais, apparemment, il y a des difficultés. . . . Cependant, ils sont conscients de l'existence de l'AACM; un mouvement a été fait vers eux. Nous ne voulons pas agresser les gens ni leur dicter ce qu'ils doivent faire. Nous attendons toujours . . . peut-être un jour se manifesteront—ils et pourrons-nous établir un programme en commun." Ibid.

53. "Votre démarche nous parait radicalement différente." Ibid., 18.

54. "Lorsque j'étais militaire, [Sun Ra] était effectivement à Chicago mais quand je suis rentré, il était à New York."Ibid.

55. "Si nous sommes influencés par Sun Ra, nous le sommes, autant par tout ce que nous vivons, ce que nous regardons, ce que nous écoutons, ce que nous sentons. Aucune force, aucune influence n'est prédominante. Dans le cours de ma vie, Johnny Griffin a pu avoir tout autant d'importance pour moi que Sun Ra." Ibid.

56. "Il faut dire que lorsqu'il quitta Chicago, il n'était pas encore le Sun Ra que nous connaissons dans Heliocentric Worlds, le Sun Ra new-yorkais. Son évolution et la nôtre se sont faites ensuite sans se recouper." Ibid.

57. "À nos yeux, les héros, idoles, y maîtres, n'existent pas. Nous aimons et respectons chaque musicien, qu'il soit du passé, de l'avenir ou . . . qu'il n'existe pas encore . . . comme nous intéresse tout autant le chant des oiseaux. . . . Être ici en train de boire du coca-cola peut influencer le processus de création musicale aussi bien que n'importe quoi." Ibid.

58. ". . . se rattache malgré tout à ce qu'on appelle a New Thing ou le Free Jazz. . . . Que signifie pour vous la tradition, le blues, par exemple?" Ibid.

59. "Nous jouons le blues, nous jouons le jazz, le rock, la musique espagnole, gitane, africaine, la musique classique, la musique européenne contemporaine, vaudou . . . tout ce que vous voudrez . . . parce que, finalement, c'est 'la musique' que nous jouons: nous créons des sons, un point c'est tout." Ibid., 18.

60. "Étranger aux desseins de l'AACM." Ibid., 17.

61. "La musique est une réponse à ces problèmes: c'est-à-dire que lorsque les gens l'entendent, ils peuvent percevoir un écho de ces problèmes. Grâce à la musique, ils peuvent devenir à leur tour plus actifs et plus responsables." Ibid.

62. "Il est dangereux d'enfermer un musicien dans une définition, d'affirmer qu'il joue de telle manière et que cette manière sera surtout appréciée par telle ou telle couche du public. Nous condamnons ce genre d'attitude. Le public est partout. . . . Nous utilisons tout ce qui peut servir nos objectifs, nos désirs. Il ne doit pas y avoir de limite." Ibid., 18.

63. "Il faut, en effet, que la presse spécialisée dans le jazz réévalue ce qui se passe actuellement dans la musique. . . . Nous souhaitons que des gens comme vous approfondissent leur manière de rendre compte de la musique. Il faut, maintenant, inventer une nouvelle façon de parler des choses, découvrir toute cette vie dans sa nouveauté. . . . Pour vous aussi, cela sera profitable parce que c'est de la vie qu'il s'agit." Ibid., 19.

64. "Nous visons à installer l'AACM partout, à tous les coins de l'univers. Une telle ambition nécessite un sérieux travail d'information." Ibid., 17.

65. Beauchamp, *Art Ensemble of Chicago*, 29.

66. *How They Took the Stars and Stripes from the American Center in Paris: The Bohen and Mellon Foundations and the Death of a Cultural Institution* (accessed 1996); available from http://www.capitalresearch.org/crc/fw/fw-0396.html.

67. Ibid.

68. To this point, the account of the American Center is drawn from ibid.

69. Beauchamp, *Art Ensemble of Chicago*, 73.

70. Ibid., 29.

71. These included trombonist Grachan Moncur III; organist Shirley Scott; pianists Bobby Few, Mal Waldron, Dave Burrell, Burton Greene, and Cecil Taylor; trumpeters Clifford Thornton and Jacques Coursil; saxophonists Archie Shepp, Jimmy Lyons, Dewey Redman, Kenneth Terroade, Don Byas, Arthur Jones, Steve Lacy, Robin Kenyatta, Byard Lancaster, Noah Howard, and Reverend Frank Wright; drummers Muhammad Ali, Andrew Cyrille, and Sunny Murray; and bassists Alan Silva and Earl Freeman.

72. Beauchamp, *Art Ensemble of Chicago*, 74.

73. Radano, *New Musical Figurations*, 140.

74. Art Ensemble of Chicago, *Les stances à Sophie* (Emi Pathe CO62 11365, 1970), compact disc.

75. Moshe Mizrahi, "Les stances à Sophie ('Sophie's Ways')" (1970).

76. R. Szyfmanowicz, "Brigitte Fontaine, Areski et l'Art Ensemble de Chicago à La Fac Dauphine," *Jazz Hot* 262, June 1970, 6.

77. One of the pieces even appeared as a 45 rpm record. See ibid. According to Smith, the record company replaced his name with that of Lester Bowie for commercial purposes. "The Art Ensemble was at the height of their popularity then," Smith recalled, "and they wanted to package the deal as a Brigitte Fontaine–Art Ensemble record." Nonetheless, as Smith points out, "Brigitte did a piece for me called Leo's Tune, which was quite a tribute." See Brigitte Fontaine, *Comme à la Radio* (Saravah SHL1018, 1970).

78. "C'est le mec avec qui je vivais à ce moment-là, un caméraman américain qui habitait en France. Nous jouions, Areski et moi, dans un théâtre où l'Art Ensemble of Chicago était programmé à une autre heure. Comme c'était un genre de spectacle improvisé, ils passaient de temps en temps jouer un petit truc, à deux ou trois à la fois. Et donc le mec a eu cette idée que l'on fasse un spectacle et un disque ensemble, avec l'Ensemble." Philippe Katerine, interview with Brigitte Fontaine (2003 [accessed November 23, 2005]); available from http://katerine.free.fr/katint10.htm.

79. "Areski et elle n'ont d'autre ambition que d'animer un spectacle où le jazz est seulement convié, element de mise en scène au même titre que les mimes, les attitudes, la cape noire ou le chapeau melon de la chanteuse." Gabriel Dumetz, "Brigitte et l'Art Ensemble," *Jazz* 177, April 1970, 13.

80. "Attention, pour moi l'Art Ensemble of Chicago, ce ne sont pas des musiciens de jazz, juste des musiciens. Je n'aime pas le jazz, je déteste le jazz, j'exècre le jazz, je vomis le jazz. À part bien entendu les grands, ceux de quand le jazz était vivant, c'est-à-dire quand j'étais très petite: Thelonious Monk, Charlie Parker, Coltrane. . . . Mais pour moi, maintenant, le jazz ça ne veut plus rien dire." Katerine, interview with Brigitte Fontaine.

81. Office de Radiodiffusion Télévision Française (ORTF) was the French public monopoly charged with coordinating television and radio between 1964 and 1974.

82. See the entry for Baraka in Carles, et al., *Dictionnaire du jazz, nouvelle édition augmentée.*

83. For an excellent addition to the literature on French reception of black experimental music, see Lehman, *I Love You with an Asterisk.*

84. "Musique inventée et jouée par les Noirs mais culturellement et économiquement colonisée par les Blancs." Philippe Carles and Jean-Louis Comolli, *Free Jazz/Black Power* (Paris: Gallimard, [1971] 2000), 48.

85. "Avec le free jazz, on assiste à une véritable *mise en place politique* de la musique, par la convergence des préoccupations directement militantes, et de leur influence, directe aussi, sur la conception même de la musique et sur les recherches esthétiques." Ibid., 71.

86. "Un certain univers lexical sans cesse sollicité ('collages,' 'mélanges,' 'emprunts' . . .) que les inventaires scrupuleux de 'citations' ou 'références' dont les chroniques de disques ou concerts free sont tissées. Francis Marmande, "Travail de la citation: Espace rupture," *Jazz* 194, November 1971, 16.

87. Carles and Comolli, *Free Jazz/Black Power*, 83. "La critique européenne a joué—au

plan culturel sinon directement au plan commercial—un rôle relativement plus important que la critique américaine." Translation by Chadwick Jenkins.

88. "Car la colonisation économique du jazz par le capitalisme américain n'est que l'un des aspects de la colonisation, de l'exploitation économique des Noirs par le même système: la prise de conscience du caractère intolérable de cette exploitation amène les musiciens comme les masses à la nécessité de la révolution. Ce n'est donc pas un hasard si l'ensemble de la critique de jazz (à l'exception des critiques noirs A. B. Spellman et LeRoi Jones) a—pudiquement—passé sous silence ou minimisé au nom du purisme esthétique, dans ses histoires et commentaires, la gravité de l'exploitation capitaliste du jazz." Ibid., 84.

89. "La critique de jazz, qui se constitue à la même époque en Amérique et en Europe, relève ces caractéristiques dominantes et, avec une belle inconscience, les élit comme *valeurs* transhistoriques du jazz: s'aveuglant sur leurs déterminations et leur contingence historiques, sociales, idéologiques, elle les propose comme références et modèles aux musicians." Ibid., 88.

90. "The aim of jazz is the mechanical reproduction of a regressive moment, a castration symbolism. 'Give up your masculinity, let yourself be castrated,' the eunuchlike sound of the jazz band both mocks and proclaims, 'and you will be rewarded, accepted into a fraternity which shares the mystery of impotence with you, a mystery revealed at the moment of the initiation rite." Theodor Adorno, "Perennial Fashion—Jazz," in *Prisms*, ed. Samuel Weber and Sherry Weber (Cambridge: MIT Press, [1953] 1981), 129.

91. "Le jazz n'est pas une musique œcuménique, mais une musique de divisions, de tensions non résolues et de blessures non refermées." Carles and Comolli, *Free Jazz/Black Power*, 109.

92. "Affirmations explicites de la nouvelle conscience noire, qui prolongent l'action 'négrifiante' du *hard bop*." Ibid., 339.

93. Ibid., 81, note 2.

94. See Vinko Globokar, "Reflexionen über Improvisation," in *Improvisation und neue Musik: Acht Kongressreferate*, ed. Reinhold Brinkmann (Mainz: Schott, 1979).

95. Alfred Willener, *The Action-Image of Society: On Cultural Politicization*, trans. A. M. Sheridan Smith (London: Tavistock Publications, 1970), 256.

96. Ibid., xiii–xiv.

97. Ibid., 230.

98. Ibid.

99. Ibid., 236.

100. Ibid., 258.

101. Ibid., 259. Later theorists with roots in the events of May 1968, such as Jacques Attali, also cite the importance of free jazz and improvisation as creating the conditions for the emergence of a new social order. Attali cites a statement by Malcolm X as foreshadowing the kind of organization that was fervently desired by these artists. The quote, which valorizes improvisation as the key to creating the conditions for change, points up something of the mindset that was emerging in the black community at mid-decade, shortly before Malcolm's murder in 1965: "The white musician can jam if he's got some sheet music in front of him. He can jam on something he's heard jammed before. But that black musician, he picks up his horn and starts blowing some sounds

that he never thought of before. He improvises, he creates, it comes from within. It's his soul; it's that soul music . . . he will improvise; he'll bring it from within himself. And this is what you and I want. You and I want to create an organization that will give us so much power we can sit and do as we please." Quoted in Attali, *Noise*, 139–40.

102. Willener, *The Action-Image of Society*, 234.

103. Ibid., 230.

104. Program notes, Concerts of the Art Ensemble of Chicago in Lille and Arras, France.

105. Willener, *The Action-Image of Society*, 246.

106. The citation is from a 1966 Comolli article, quoted in ibid., 244.

107. Beauchamp, *Art Ensemble of Chicago*, 75.

108. Levin, "Au profit des Panthères."

109. In 1971, Thornton was arrested by French police after entering the country on his way to perform. According to an account in *Down Beat* magazine, "He was shown a letter from the Minister of the Interior, dated Dec. 8, 1970, which proscribed his entry because of his "suspected membership in the Black Panther Party." He was denied the right to make phone calls, and six hours later, was put on a plane to New York. See "France Bars Thornton as Panther 'Suspect,'" *Down Beat*, April 29, 1971, 8.

110. Valerie Wilmer, "Caught in the Act: Art Ensemble of Chicago," *Down Beat*, June 25, 1970, 26.

111. Ibid. For an example of the work of Bass with the Art Ensemble, hear Art Ensemble of Chicago, *The Art Ensemble of Chicago with Fontella Bass* (Verve 067865, 1971), compact disc.

112. "Prennent souvent leurs distances vis-à-vis du swing." Caux, "L'ete au Lucernaire."

113. "Ayant complètement déstructuré le jazz, ils le reconstruisent suivant des lois peu orthodoxes faisant la part belle à une concentration des sons et surtout à une disconti-nuité, un découpage du temps tout à fait inhabituel. . . . On aurait tort de rejeter cette musique à la fois désinvolte et obstinée qui, refusant tout lyrisme, démystifie en même temps la musique sérieuse occidentale—secteur tabou—et un 'vrai jazz' aux limites arbi-trairement définies." Ibid.

114. Hentoff, "The New Jazz."

115. Arrigo Polillo, "Adesso c'è la "new thing": Discordante, aspra, furibonda," *Epoca* 1969.

116. "Dai giovani contestatori di mezza Europa." Ibid.

117. "Paradossalmente, infatti, la loro musica non è compresa dalla maggior parte dei negri, che ad essa preferiscono il più facile e divertente *rhythm and blues* . . . e non è natu-ralmente amata dai bianchi, che ne avvertono l'ostilità." Ibid.

118. "Dove la loro predicazione in musica, molte volte accompagnata da dichiarazioni programmatiche, ha trovato ardenti proseliti fra i giovani, e in particolare fra quelli con-vinti che il mondo debba essere buttato all'aria al più presto." Ibid.

119. Beauchamp, *Art Ensemble of Chicago*, 29.

120. While much has been written about the displaced-persons camps set up by the Allied occupation forces in Germany after the end of World War II hostilities, the Inter-net has become a site for the exchange of less-accessed remembrances from the dwin-

dling number of people still alive with firsthand experience of the camps. Here is one such reminiscence concerning the Ludwigsburg riots, which the correspondent dates to October and November 1945: "Food was desperately short—the food riots I mentioned above were sparked off by lousy food in the camp, when our complaints were finally investigated, it was found that the Camp Commandant, an U.S. Army officer, and several mates had been flogging the food on the Black Market. I believe he was sent back to the States in disgrace—probably for being caught." See George Carrington, *Displaced Persons: DP Camps in Germany* (accessed September 24, 2006); available from http://www .dpcamps.org/dpcampsGermanyF.html.

121. Except as noted, quotes from Famoudou Don Moye in this section come from Moye.

122. Lester Bowie, Amina Claudine Myers, and Leroy Jenkins, among others, all had similar experiences.

123. Beauchamp, *Art Ensemble of Chicago,* 59.

124. Ibid.

125. Ibid., 29.

126. "Eine exotische Pflanze auf kargem Boden . . . die ebenso bizarre erscheinen mußte wie britischer Flamenco." Jost, *Europas Jazz, 1960–80,* 11.

127. Wolfram Knauer, "Emanzipation wovon? Zum Verhältnis des amerikanischen und des deutschen Jazz in den 50er und 60er Jahren," in *Jazz in Deutschland: Darmstädter Beiträge zur Jazzforschung,* vol. 4, ed. Wolfram Knauer (Hofheim: Wolke Verlag Hofheim, 1996), 156.

128. See Christian Broecking, "Adorno versus Berendt Revisited: Was bleibt von der Kontroverse im Merkur 1953?" in *Jazz und Gesellschaft: Sozialgeschichtliche Aspekte des Jazz,* ed. Wolfram Knauer (Hofheim: Wolke Verlag, 2002).

129. See Max Harrison, "Donaueschingen 1957: One of the 'Dead Sea Scrolls' of Jazz," *Jazz Journal International,* December 1977.

130. "Der Kritiker K. H. Ruppel meinte, dieses Konzert sei 'für den Durchbruch des Jazz auf den Konzertpodien Europas so wichtig wie Benny Goodman's Carnegie Hall Concert 1938 für das Konzertleben der USA.'" Joachim-Ernst Berendt, "Jazz in Donaueschingen 1954–1994: Versuch eines Rückblicks," in *Spiegel der Neuen Musik: Donau-eschingen, Chronik—Tendenzen—Werkbesprechungen, mit Essays von Joachim-Ernst Berendt und Hermann Naber,* ed. Josef Häusler (Kassel: Bärenreiter-Verlag, 1996), 409.

131. "König Jazz entthront König Zwölfton." Quoted in ibid.

132. "Wir müssen aufpassen, daß das, worauf es uns eigentlich ankommt, nicht in den Hintergrund gedrängt wird durch Dinge, die wir zwar auch lieben, die aber nicht im Mit-telpunkt dessen stehen, was wir in Donaueschingen wollen." Quoted in ibid.

133. Ibid.

134. "Den ersten Versuch, die Erfahrungen des Freien Jazz auf die Komposition eines modernen Orchesterstückes anzuwenden." Ibid., 411.

135. Joachim-Ernst Berendt, *Ein Fenster aus Jazz: Essays, Portraits, Reflexionen* (Frankfurt am Main: S. Fischer Verlag, 1977), 222. Perhaps the most thorough historical account of European free jazz activity can be found in Jost, *Europas Jazz, 1960–80.* For a set of influ-ential critical essays on European improvised music, see Bert Noglik, *Klangspuren: Wege improvisierter Musik* (Frankfurt am Main: Fischer Taschenbuch Verlag, 1990). Noglik's

interviews with European improvisors, originally published in the German Democratic Republic before reunification, are contained in an earlier volume, Bert Noglik, *Jazz-Werkstatt International* (Berlin and Hamburg: Verlag Neue Musik and Rowohlt Taschenbuch Verlag, 1982). In recent years, several well-researched extended treatments of European free jazz and free improvisation have emerged. For a pan-European summary (from a U.S. scholar's perspective) of recent ideas in European free music, see Heffley, *Northern Sun, Southern Moon*. British guitarist Derek Bailey, a leading exponent of free improvisation, is the biographical subject of Ben Watson, *Derek Bailey and the Story of Free Improvisation* (London and New York: Verso, 2004). An important book on the connection between free jazz and high-culture composition in the Netherlands is to be found in Kevin Whitehead, *New Dutch Swing* (New York: Billboard Books, 1998). An extended treatment of the British scene is found in John Wickes, *Innovations in British Jazz*, vol. 1, *1960–1980* (London: Soundworld, 1999). For more on "Emanzipation" discourse, see Knauer, "Emanzipation wovon?" Also see Ekkehard Jost, "Die europäische Jazz-Emanzipation," in *That's Jazz: Der Sound des 20. Jahrhunderts*, ed. Klaus Wolbert (Darmstadt: Verlag Jürgen Häusser, 1997).

136. Gunter Hampel, *The 8th of July 1969* (Birth 001, 1969).

137. "Je suis désolé, mais tout ça c'est de la merde. La musique se suffit à elle-même. On n'a pas besoin de voir Coltrane ou Ornette. Ces gens se servent de l'esthétique avec la musique: ce n'est pas intéressant et c'est pourquoi je n'aime pas l'A.A.C.M. S'ils ne brûlaient pas d'encens et ne se peignaient pas la figure, leur musique serait triste. . . . Il n'est pas nécessaire de faire le clown pour faire accepter une musique, sinon c'est qu'on sait qu'elle ne se suffit pas à elle-même. Et alors, il vaut mieux faire carrément la putain et gagner de l'argent!" Gérard Badini, Georges Locatelli, Jacques Thollot, and René Thomas, "Les musiciens ont la parole," *Jazz Hot* 259, March 1970, 14.

138. For a fuller account of this event, as well as the connections between the AACM and the European movement, see Lewis, "'Gittin' to Know Y'All.'" The English-language version is George E. Lewis, *Gittin' to Know Y'All: Improvised Music, Interculturalism, and the Racial Imagination* (2004 [accessed November 22, 2005]); available from http://repository .lib.uoguelph.ca/ojs/viewarticle.php?id=28&layout=html, 2005, 1–33.

139. Lester Bowie, *Gittin' to Know Y'All* (MPS 15269,15038, 1970), vinyl disc.

140. "Das bietet Baden-Baden im Winter: Das Free Jazz Treffen des SWF," *Jazz Podium* 19, no. 2, February 1970.

141. "Sonderten sich ab, bildeten eine Clique, deren Unzugänglichkeit in Kontrast zu Bowies sicher ehrlich gemeintem Kontaktstück stand und den sonst so erfrischend familiären Charakter, der diese Treffen auszeichnet, etwas störte. . . . Das Schwarz-Weiß Problem breitete sich wie ein Schatten über das Geschehen." "Das bietet Baden-Baden im Winter," 56.

142. "Strictly Ad Lib. Report on Newport Jazz Festival performance by Misha Mengelberg," *Down Beat*, September 8, 1966.

143. Wolfgang Dauner, "Mit Jazz in Südamerika (Fortsetzung von Heft 12/68)," *Jazz Podium* 1969; Wolfgang Dauner, "Mit Jazz in Südamerika: Eindrücke und Erlebnisse von der vom Goethe-Institut durchgeführten Tournee der deutschen All Star Band," *Jazz Podium*, December 1968.

144. For an account of U.S. military support for American and European experimental music in Germany, see Amy C. Beal, *New Music, New Allies: American Experimental*

Music in West Germany from the Zero Hour to Reunification (Berkeley: University of California Press, 2006). For an account of State Department–supported jazz performances in Europe during the 1960s, see Penny M. Von Eschen, *Satchmo Blows Up the World: Jazz Ambassadors Play the Cold War* (Cambridge: Harvard University Press, 2004).

145. See Saunders, *The Cultural Cold War.*

146. See Lewis, "Afterword to 'Improvised Music after 1950'"; Lewis, "Improvised Music after 1950."

147. "Die Betonung des Sound eine Flucht vor solistischer Virtuosität ist, die sie noch nicht besitzen." Gudrun Endress, "AACM: Die dritte Generation des Free Jazz," *Jazz Podium* 19, no. 3, March 1970, 97.

148. One AACM composer (me) was included in Endress's 1980 book of interviews. See Gudrun Endress, *Jazz Podium: Musiker über sich selbst* (Stuttgart: Deutsche Verlags-Anstalt, 1980).

149. Beauchamp, *Art Ensemble of Chicago,* 43.

150. Ibid., 60.

151. Ibid., 42.

152. Val Wilmer, *Mama Said There'd Be Days Like This: My Life in the Jazz World.* London: Women's Press, 1980), 192.

153. Ibid., 60.

154. Program, Concert of the Art Ensemble of Chicago, Association-Maison de la Culture d'Angers, France.

155. Cromwell, "Jazz Mecca."

CHAPTER 8

1. Jones interview.

2. Beauchamp, *Art Ensemble of Chicago,* 60.

3. Quotes from Emilio Cruz in this section come from Emilio Cruz, interview with the author, New York City, July 24, 1999. Julian Beck and Judith Malina founded the important experimental theater troupe, the Living Theatre, in 1947; for an early account, see Renfreu Neff, *The Living Theatre: U.S.A* (Indianapolis: Bobbs-Merrill, 1970). During the late 1960s, the Judson Church in New York's Greenwich Village became a center for new dance, including the emerging practice of contact improvisation as promulgated by Steve Paxton, Nancy Stark Smith, and others; see Sally Banes, *Democracy's Body: Judson Dance Theater, 1962–1964* (Durham: Duke University Press, 1993). For a recent account, one of the first that places these movements in context with African American experimentalisms of the period, see Sells, *Avant-Garde Performance and the Limits of Criticism.*

4. George Lipsitz, interview with Julius Hemphill, July 31, 1994.

5. For an account detailing the rise and fall of Laclede Town, see John M. McGuire, "Farewell to Utopia: Laclede Town," *Everyday Magazine, St. Louis Post-Dispatch,* February 12, 1995.

6. The list of Sumner alumni comes from Bowie.

7. Quotes from Oliver Lake in this section are taken from Oliver Lake, interview with the author, Montclair, New Jersey, October 21, 1998.

8. George Lipsitz, "Like a Weed in a Vacant Lot: The Black Artists Group in St. Louis,"

in *Decomposition: Post-Disciplinary Performance,* ed. Sue-Ellen Case, Philip Brett, and Susan Foster (Bloomington and Indianapolis: Indiana University Press, 2000), 55.

9. Ibid.

10. Lipsitz interview with Julius Hemphill.

11. Quotes from Julius Hemphill in this section are from ibid.

12. In my interview with Lake, he maintained that there was originally no "s" or apostrophe in the "Artist" part of the name.

13. See Andryco, "Fontella Bass." Quotes from Baikida E. J. Carroll in this section come from Baikida E. J. Carroll, interview with the author, La Jolla, California, April 8, 2000.

14. Members included Cathy Allen, Liz Carpentier, Roswell Darby, Robert Edwards (a trombonist known as "Happy Tooth"), Carl Flowers, Stanley Hanks, Darryl Harris, Ricky Curtis, Portia Hunt, Pat Mountjoy, Muthal Naidoo, Victor Reef, Carl Richardson, LeRoi Shelton, Joseph Steward, Valerie Williams, and Vincent Terrell. "At large" members included Hamiet Bluiett, John Hicks, Danny Trice, David Hine, Richard Martin, Joseph Bowie, Leonard Smith (then also known as Abdellah Yacub); Jerome "Scrooge" Harris, Manuel Hughes, K. Curtis Lyle, Lester Bowie, and Phillip Wilson. Black Artists Group, *A Black Theater for St. Louis: A Building Proposal for the Black Artists' Group* (St. Louis: Black Artists Group, 1970).

15. Ibid.

16. Bluiett moved to New York in 1969, and joined the Mingus ensemble in 1972, according to Looker, *BAG: "Point from Which Creation Begins."*

17. Black Artists Group, "A Black Theater for St. Louis'."

18. Lipsitz, "Like a Weed in a Vacant Lot," 56.

19. John B. Litweiler, "Caught in the Act: Oliver Lake/Julius Hemphill," *Down Beat,* June 12, 1969, 35.

20. Lipsitz, "Like a Weed in a Vacant Lot," 57.

21. Ibid.

22. In 1972, Pruitt-Igoe was dynamited, recalling the old Vietnam-era conundrum: "We had to destroy the city in order to save it."

23. Lipsitz, "Like a Weed in a Vacant Lot," 57.

24. Ibid., 57–58.

25. Quoted in Ben Looker, "'Poets of Action': The St. Louis Black Artists' Group, 1968–1972," *Gateway-Heritage, The Quarterly Magazine of the Missouri Historical Society* 22, no. 1, Summer (2001): 25.

26. Looker, *BAG: "Point from Which Creation Begins,"* 206.

27. Carroll interview.

28. Baikida E. J. Carroll, *Orange Fish Tears* (Palm, 1975), vinyl disc.

29. Looker, *BAG: "Point from Which Creation Begins,"* 194.

30. Radano, *New Musical Figurations,* 142. It is probable that Braxton himself was Radano's primary informant in this regard. In a 1971 article in *Jazz Hot,* Braxton was publicly critical of what he saw as a tendency of the AACM musicians in Paris toward unhealthy competition with each other: "We had lots of trouble—though the A.A.C.M. could have become a tremendous help in getting contemporary music accepted on the

planet, there was also a lot of dissension, even between the member musicians, and even if everything didn't end up as a complete failure, the result is still rather disappointing, it's really a shame." ("Nous avons eu des tas d'ennuis—pourtant l'A.A.C.M. aurait pu devenir un soutien formidable pour faire accepter la musique contemporaine sur la planète, mais il y a eu aussi un tas de dissensions même entre les musiciens membres, et si le tout ne s'est pas soldé par un complet échec, le résultat est néanmoins assez décevant, c'est bien dommage.) François Postif, "KFQ-4/6F," *Jazz Hot*, April 1971, 15.

31. Barker interview.

32. Difda, Donavon, and Myers interviews.

33. "Ad Lib: Chicago Announcement, performance by the Pharaohs," *Down Beat*, March 2, 1972, 36; Mike Bourne, review of Pharaohs LP, *Awakening*, *Down Beat*, August 17, 1972.

34. Quotes in this section come from Douglas Ewart, interviews with the author, Chicago, Illinois, December 26, 1997; and Mills College, Oakland, California, February 7, 1999.

35. In 1983, Derek Bailey reconnected Douglas with Rodriguez, when we all met at Bailey's home in Hackney, London.

36. Bontemps and Conroy, *Anyplace but Here*, 322.

37. Now pianist and composer Carolyn Wilkins Ritt.

38. The AACM Big Band had been performing there since at least the end of 1970. See "Ad Lib: Chicago," *Down Beat*, January 7, 1971.

39. "Musician's Group Here Gives Avant Garde Recital," *Chicago Defender* (daily edition), October 19, 1971.

40. "*Down Beat* Critics Poll," *Down Beat*, August 20, 1970.

41. "35th Annual *Down Beat* Readers Poll," *Down Beat*, December 24, 1970.

42. Threadgill interview. Posters advertising these events are on view in the J. B. Figi Collection, Chicago Jazz Archive, Regenstein Library, University of Chicago.

43. "Ad Lib: Chicago. Announcement of performance by Eddie Harris and Richard Abrams," *Down Beat*, June 8, 1972.

44. "Ad Lib: Chicago. Announcement, performance by the Gallery Ensemble," *Down Beat*, March 2, 1972.

45. Jarman interview. Also see Menter, "The Making of Jazz and Improvised Music'." While the ethics of Jackson's activities might be seen as questionable by some, on another view, this kind of steady income was largely unavailable to black experimentalists, while white experimentalists benefited from a variety of sources of largesse, including access to private foundation grants, university residencies, private donors, academic posts, and family connections. See, for example, Catherine M. Cameron, *Dialectics in the Arts: The Rise of Experimentalism in American Music* (Westport, Conn.: Praeger, 1996).

46. Quotes from Chico Freeman in this section are from Chico Freeman, interview with the author, New York City, July 24, 1999.

47. For a recent account providing historical corroboration and theoretical context for the experiences of Northwestern-educated AACM members, see Sarah Susannah Willie, *Acting Black: College, Identity, and the Performance of Race* (New York and London: Routledge, 2003). Chapter 5 is of particular relevance.

48. "Negroes Protest at Northwestern," *New York Times*, May 4, 1968.

49. "Negro Protest Ends at Northwestern U.," *New York Times*, May 5, 1968.

50. For a contemporaneous essay by the black students on their issues, see John H. Bracey, Jr., August Meier, and Elliott Rudwick, eds., "Northwestern University Black Students: If Our Demands Are Impossible, Then Peace between Us Is Impossible Too," in *Black Nationalism in America* (Indianapolis and New York: Bobbs-Merrill, 1970).

51. See Fred M. Hechinger, "The Demand Grows for 'Black Studies,'" *New York Times*, June 23, 1968; Darlene Clark Hine, "The Black Studies Movement: Afrocentric-Traditionalist-Feminist Paradigms for the Next Stage," *Black Scholar* 22 (1992).

52. Quotes from Iqua Colson and Adegoke Steve in this section are from Iqua Colson and Adegoke Steve Colson, interview with the author, Montclair, New Jersey, October 21, 1998.

53. Robert B. Stepto, *Blue as the Lake: A Personal Geography* (Boston: Beacon Press, 1998).

54. Frazier, *Black Bourgeoisie*.

55. The Links Cotillion has been an annual black society debutante event since the mid-1950s.

56. For a first-person account of the Von Freeman sessions, see George Lewis, "Teaching Improvised Music: An Ethnographic Memoir," in *Arcana: Musicians on Music*, ed. John Zorn (New York: Granary Books, 2000).

57. Panken, radio interview with Von Freeman.

58. *"Reader's* Heavy Sixty," *Chicago Reader*, September 29, 1972.

59. J. B. Figi, "Still Too Much a Stranger: Fred Anderson Quartet's Metallic Cocaine Bebop," *Chicago Reader*, October 20, 1972.

60. Jerry DeMuth, "Caught in the Act: The Ann Arbor Blues and Jazz Festival," *Down Beat*, November 9, 1972.

61. Jane Welch, "Europe's Answer to Woodstock: The First Actuel Festival Paris Music Festival," *Down Beat*, January 22, 1970, 16.

62. Lawrence Kart, "Maurice McIntyre," *Down Beat*, April 16, 1970. Hear Kalaparusha Maurice McIntyre, *Humility in the Light of the Creator* (Delmark DD-419, 1969), compact disc.

63. John B. Litweiler, "Caught in the Act: Kalaparusha and the Light," *Down Beat*, July 18, 1974.

64. Herb Nolan and Ray Townley, "Ann Arbor Blues and Jazz Festival," *Down Beat*, October 25, 1973, 30.

65. Steve Metalitz, "The Status of a Non-existent Market," *Chicago Reader*, May 26, 1972.

66. Ibid.

67. Ray Townley, "Heard and Seen: Richard Abrams," *Coda*, January 1973.

68. *Down Beat* News, "McCall Waxes Two New Discs; Reports Sextet a Hit in Berlin," *Down Beat*, January 31, 1974.

69. "Zwischen den Chaoskollektiven, Pastoralteilen und afrikanischen Percussionsklängen gab es allerdings von den Saxophonisten zu viele Solis, deren nun schon konventionelles Genudel durch die Undynamik und die Beibehaltung des gleichen Rasters

nahezu gestaltlos wurde." Ulrich Olshausen, "Von Blues Bis Free-Jazz: Alles Dran: Berliner Jazztage 1973 war ein voller Erfolg," *Jazz Podium,* December 1973, 22.

70. The reference to rock, a musical form noted for engaging electric sound, perhaps accounted for this reviewer's willingness to at least entertain the possibility that the extreme reverberation was, in fact, an essential part of the impact of the work. "La première intuition sensorielle que provoque l'audition de *Bird Song* est, irrésistiblement, l'image puissante d'une immense et haute volière." Here, the reverberation represented a situation in which "l'impression de bourdonnement, de bruissement est longtemps maintenue." See Marc Bernard, "Richard Abrams et l'A.A.C.M.," *Jazz* 209, March 1973, 21. For this French author, the electronics did not render David Moore's words "unintelligible"; in fact, the writer carefully translated the poem into French.

71. "Pour une large part à l'origine des travaux de Roscoe Mitchell, Lester Bowie, Anthony Braxton, individualités remarquables dont les success européens pourraient faire oublier qu'ils ne sont pas tout l'A.a.c.m." Ibid., 20.

72. "Les activités et divertissements des Chicagoans soient limités à des locaux bien chauffés. . . . Le froid serait même un facteur decisive: l'importance des phénomènes 'thermodynamiques' dans le blues de Chicago correspondrait . . . au besoin des prolétaires noirs de pallier l'absence de chauffage central." Philippe Carles and Daniel Soutif, "Chicago," *Jazz* 212, June 1973.

73. "Malgré les tentatives intégrationistes de quelques-uns," Carles observed, "les barriéres socials/raciales qui divisent la ville semblent n'avoir rien perdu leur efficacité." Ibid.

74. "Pour une dizaine de clients, et nous sommes les seuls Blancs." Ibid.

75. "Le seul lieu où, véritablement, Noirs et Blancs semblent avoir quelque chance de se rencontrer." Carles, "Chicago."

76. "Dans la salle: la famille et les amis des musiciens. Droit d'entrée: une participation facultative aux frais." Ibid.

77. "Avant de jouer, les musiciens, dos au public, restent immobiles pendant quelques minutes. Puis ils se tournent et s'approchent de leurs instruments: tous portent un masque de caoutchouc digne d'un film 'd'horreur.' Gong (Abrams), sonorities électroniques, une danseuse commence de dessiner des mouvements très lente. Peu à peu, à force de petites percussions, de sifflets et d'instruments-jouets, l'espace devient une sorte d'immense volière. Les 'oiseaux' disparus, une masse de percussions se developpe sur fond de gong. Durée de premier morceau: une demi-heure." Ibid.

78. "Le silence est valorisé, les moindres modifications du son deviennent décisives." Ibid.

79. "L'investigation et la transcription de toutes les musiques font aussi partie de notre programme . . . mais si l'on veut se donner les moyens de réussir, dans n'importe quel domaine, il est essentiel de venir de là où on est . . . nous sommes embarquées sur le même bateau." Philippe Carles, "La terre promise selon Abrams," *Jazz* 212, June 1973, 10.

80. "L'Afrique . . . est un mélange de tas de choses, surtout après avoir traverse la periode coloniale. . . . L'importante n'est pas un retour physique mais mental." Ibid., 11.

81. "L'Art Ensemble a toujours essayé de changer les rapports avec les organisateurs, les agents, etc. Nous refusons certains choses, nous exigeons certaines conditions de travail. . . . Si les gens refusent nos principes, nous refusons les leurs. Nos vies sont plus

importantes. À Paris, nous devrions jouer dans des endroits comme l'Opéra, là où ont lieu les concerts de grand musique. Les clubs, le Quartier latin, c'est très marrant, mais ce n'est plus là que ça doit se passer. . . . Je pense que l'Art Ensemble of Chicago existera aussi longtemps que nous vivrons." Philippe Carles, "Joseph Jarman," *Jazz* 215, September 1973, 39.

82. Potpourri, "Announcement about the Art Ensemble," *Down Beat,* December 19, 1974.

83. Ray Townley, "Lester . . . Who?" *Down Beat,* January 31, 1974, 11.

84. City Scene: Chicago, "Announcement of Event by Fred Anderson, Chico Freeman, and George Lewis," *Down Beat,* October 10, 1974; City Scene: Chicago, "Announcement of Event by Muhal Richard Abrams," *Down Beat,* April 25, 1974.

85. "Heavy 75: Who's Who in the Chicago Alternative Culture," *Chicago Reader,* September 27, 1974, "*Reader's* Pop Poll 1973," *Chicago Reader,* March 1, 1974.

86. Ray Townley, "Profile: Muhal Richard Abrams," *Down Beat,* August 15, 1974.

87. Philippe Carles and Francis Marmande, "Montreux," *Jazz* 225, September 1974.

88. *Down Beat* News, "Ellington Fellowship Program Set for Yale," *Down Beat,* October 12, 1972. Also see Dan Morgenstern, "Yale's Conservatory without Walls," *Down Beat,* December 7, 1972. For a fuller account of the philosophy behind Professor Ruff's program, see his autobiography, Willie Ruff, *A Call to Assembly: The Autobiography of a Musical Storyteller* (New York: Viking, 1991).

89. Panken radio interview with George Lewis and Leo Smith.

90. Leo Smith, *Rhythm* (Self-published, 1976).

91. Smith, *Notes (8 pieces) source a new world music.*

92. Smith, "(M1) American Music." For an extended analysis of Smith's writings, see Porter, *What Is This Thing Called Jazz?*

93. Bill Smith, "Leo Smith," *Coda,* November 1975, 6.

94. Derek Bailey, *Improvisation: Its Nature and Practice in Music* (Ashbourne: Moorland Publishing, 1980).

95. Robert Farris Thompson, "Mambo Minkisi: The Mind and Music of Leo Smith," *Coda,* November 1975, 11.

96. Quotes from Edward Wilkerson throughout this book are taken from Edward Wilkerson, interview with the author, Chicago, Illinois, February 11, 1999.

97. At the time of this writing, Williams is chair of the Department of Film and Television at Howard University.

98. Art Ensemble of Chicago, *Live at Mandel Hall* (Delmark DE-432, 1972), compact disc.

99. Quotes from Rasul Siddik in this section are taken from Rasul Siddik, interview with the author, Los Angeles, California, October 8, 1998.

100. This was an accurate ground-level assessment, since in 1966 the *New York Times* reported that black soldiers were 22 percent of all Vietnam combat deaths. At this time, African Americans comprised approximately 10 percent of the U.S. population. See "Excerpts from a Report to the President by the National Advisory Panel on Selective Service," *New York Times,* March 5, 1967. Siddik, like other young black men of the period, had already received powerful corroboration for his view from Martin Luther King, Jr., who in 1967 had recommended avoidance of military service by blacks who

were against the war, and by Muhammad Ali, who had refused induction that same year. King observed that the draft was taking African Americans "in extraordinarily high proportions relative to the rest of the population. We were taking the black young men who had been crippled by our society and sending them eight thousand miles away to guarantee liberties in Southeast Asia which they had not found in southwest Georgia and East Harlem." Martin Luther King, "Beyond Vietnam," in *Voices of a People's History of the United States,* ed. Howard Zinn, and Anthony Amove (New York: Seven Stories Press, 2004), 424.

101. In my interview with Gordon Emanuel Cranshaw, the question of his lack of military service came up. "How did you escape that one?" I asked. "Same way Muhal did, by acting a fool," laughed Cranshaw. "They'd ask you a question like, do you use drugs, and we'd say, *awwwohhh* [moans incoherently]. They'd say, well, Mr. Cranshaw, we don't think you'd be the right influence around our boys, fighting for our country. I said, *Aww* [mock disappointment]. I'll just have to live with it [laughs]." Interview with Emanuel Cranshaw, Chicago, Illinois, February 11, 1999.

102. An online discussion group yielded this testimony from journalist and activist Ken Lawrence: "White draft resisters were treated fairly gently, often being given Conscientious Objector status and alternative service, although quite a few members of Chicago Area Draft Resisters went to prison. Black draft resisters were denied the CO option, ostensibly because they could not legitimately claim religious opposition to war, and were routinely sentenced to long prison terms." Ken Lawrence, *Noam Chomsky on Kosovo (FWD)* (1999 [accessed November 22, 2005]); available from http://mailman .lbo-talk.org/1999/1999-March/005970.html. March 30, 1999. Also see Ken Lawrence, *Thirty Years of Selective Service Racism* (Chicago: National Black Draft Counselors, 1971). For a report of a Selective Service plan to herd these "new" nonreligious conscientious objectors, who were mainly black and/or poor, into work camps, see Ken Lawrence, "The C.O. 'Camps,'" *Nation,* June 28, 1980.

103. *The University of Iowa Electronic Music Studios: Alumni* (accessed November 22, 2005]); available from http://theremin.music.uiowa.edu/Alumni.html. McCreary's fellow alumni included electronic music composer Charles Dodge.

104. The Awakening, *Hear, Sense, and Feel* (Black Jazz BJQD-9, 1972).

105. Dick Washburn, "Frank Gordon's 'Kera's Dance' Solo," *Down Beat,* April 26, 1973, 33.

106. Art T. Burton, *Black, Buckskin, and Blue: African-American Scouts and Soldiers on the Western Frontier* (Austin: Eakin Press, 1999); Art T. Burton, *Black, Red, and Deadly: Black and Indian Gunfighters of the Indian Territories, 1870–1907* (Austin: Eakin Press, 1991).

107. Quotes from Art Turk Burton in this section come from Art Turk Burton, interview with the author, Chicago, Illinois, June 28, 1999.

108. An exponent of this tradition was Otha Turner (1907–2003), the leader of the Rising Star Fife and Drum Band.

109. MacDonald, *Blacks and White TV,* 70.

110. City Scene: Chicago, "Announcement of Event at NAME Gallery, Chicago," *Down Beat* (1974).

111. Roberto Terlizzi, "Steve McCall," *Coda,* December 1974, 7.

112. Douglas Ewart, telephone interview of George Lewis, March 3, 2004.

113. Quotes throughout the book from Rita Warford come from Rita Warford, interview with the author, New York City, November 1, 1999.

114. hooks, "Performance Practice as a Site of Opposition," 211.

115. Ibid.

116. Ibid.

117. Later, Murray became Atu Harold Murray. A reference to his association with Sun Ra appears in Szwed, *Space Is the Place,* 205. As it happens, Murray, like the former Herman Blount, hailed from Birmingham, Alabama.

118. AACM Tenth Anniversary program book, 1975, Collection of George E. Lewis.

119. John B. Litweiler, "AACM's 10th Anniversary: An Interview with Muhal Richard Abrams, Founder and Father Figure," *Chicago Reader,* May 9, 1975; John B. Litweiler, "AACM's 10th Anniversary: New Voices in the Wilderness," *Chicago Reader,* May 9, 1975.

120. Neil Tesser, "AACM's 10th Anniversary: A Symbol of Committed Excellence," *Chicago Reader,* May 9, 1975, 14.

121. Litweiler, "AACM's 10th Anniversary," 13.

122. Washington, "'All the Things You Could Be by Now.'"

123. Neil Tesser, "Whither the Avant-Garde?" *Chicago Reader,* February 7, 1975, x1.

124. Ibid.

125. Ibid., x2.

126. Neil Tesser, "*Reader's* Guide to Jazz," *Chicago Reader,* September 26, 1975, 36.

127. John B. Litweiler, "Roscoe Mitchell: A Funny Thing Happened on the Way to Perfection," *Chicago Reader,* September 31, 1975, 36.

128. AACM Tenth Anniversary program book.

129. Litweiler, "Roscoe Mitchell." The "lower-case" foreshadowing is most evident on the work "SII Examples" from Roscoe Mitchell, *L-R-G; The Maze; SII Examples* (Nessa NCD-14, 1978), compact disc.

130. Hear the recorded version of the piece on Mitchell, *Nonaah.*

131. Litweiler, "Roscoe Mitchell."

132. Roscoe Mitchell, *The Roscoe Mitchell Solo Saxophone Concerts* (Sackville 2006, 1974). George Lewis, *The George Lewis Solo Trombone Record* (Sackville 3012, 1976), compact disc. Anthony Braxton, *Trio and Duet* (Sackville 3007, 1974), vinyl disc.

133. Mitchell, *The Roscoe Mitchell Solo Saxophone Concerts.*

134. John Shenoy Jackson, AACM administrator, had compiled a breakdown of expenses, listed in John Shenoy Jackson, "Intra-Office Memorandum to all AACM Members: Festival Income and Current Expenses," 1975, Archives of Evod Magek. According to Jackson's accounts, various members had lent the AACM small (if personally significant) sums of ten to twenty dollars, which Jackson described as "bona fide debts" owed by the association. The implication was that a phone bill for $46.86, submitted by one member and duly noted by Jackson, counted as a "non-bonafide debt."

CHAPTER 9

1. Bret Primack, "Leroy Jenkins: Gut-Plucking Revolutionary," *Down Beat,* November 16, 1978, 24, 50.

2. Robert Palmer, liner notes to recording, *Creative Construction Company,* vol. 1, Muse

Records MR 5071 (1975), vinyl disc (the concert recording included a second volume: Creative Construction Company, *Creative Construction Company*, vol. 2 [Muse Records MR 5097, 1976], vinyl disc); Primack, "Leroy Jenkins." For more background on Kunle M'wanga, see Wilmer, *Mama Said There'd Be Days Like This*, 191.

3. Donal Henahan, "The New and Newer Music Fails to Impress at Tully," *New York Times*, January 27, 1973, 20.

4. Carla Bley, *Escalator over the Hill: A Chronotransduction* (JCOA Records JCOA/EOTH 839 310-2, 1971), compact disc.

5. "Potpourri: Announcement of Concerts by Jazz Composers Orchestra Association," *Down Beat*, May 11, 1972, 11.

6. Joe H. Klee, "Caught in the Act: Don Cherry and the Jazz Composers Orchestra," *Down Beat*, May 10, 1973, 33.

7. Roger Riggins, "Caught in the Act: The Revolutionary Ensemble," *Down Beat*, October 26, 1972, 34.

8. "Ad Lib: New York. Announcement of Performance by the Revolutionary Ensemble," *Down Beat*, March 30, 1972, 36.

9. Anthony Braxton, *For Alto* (Delmark DE-420, 1969), compact disc.

10. Leonard Feather, "The Blindfold Test: Phil Woods," *Down Beat*, October 14, 1971, 33.

11. Braxton, *Tri-Axium Writings*, vols. 1–3.

12. Circle, *Paris-Concert* (ECM 1018, 1971), compact disc.

13. "Vous remarquerez que je n'emploie pas le mot 'jazz' pour parler de ma musique. Pourtant, j'aime le mot 'jazz,' Il a une bonne consonance, c'est une magnifique trouvaille en tant que terme, mais je ne me considère comme un musicien de jazz—et même je suis en train de me demander se je suis seulement un musicien." Postif, "KFQ-4/6F."

14. "*Down Beat* News: New York Musicians Stage Own Festival," *Down Beat*, September 14, 1972, 9.

15. Diane Weathers, "The Collective Black Artists," *Black World* 23, no. 1 (1973): 72–74.

16. "Potpourri: Announcement of symposium by the Collective Black Artists," *Down Beat*, May 11, 1972, 11.

17. Robert D. Rusch, "*Down Beat* News: CBA Conference Seeks Unity of Black Artists," *Down Beat*, July 20, 1972, 11.

18. Ibid.

19. Ibid.

20. Robert Palmer, "Pop: Newport Newcomers," *New York Times*, June 10, 1973, 30.

21. Scott Albin, "Caught in the Act: Art Ensemble of Chicago," *Down Beat*, December 4, 1975, 34.

22. Ibid.

23. Samuel Gilmore, "Coordination and Convention: The Organization of the Concert World," *Symbolic Interaction* 10, no. 2 (1987): 213.

24. The terms "Downtown I" and "Downtown II" were created by Michael Dessen and myself. For a recent collection of the writings of artists associated with Downtown II, see John Zorn, ed., *Arcana: Musicians on Music* (New York: Granary Books, 2000).

25. John Rockwell, "Face of Jazz Is Changing Visibly," *New York Times*, June 4, 1974, 33.

26. Ibid.

27. "Guggenheim to Mingus; Protest at Foundation," *Down Beat*, May 27, 1971, 8.

28. "Jazz Grants," *Down Beat*, October 25, 1973, 46.

29. "$407,276 in Grants to Go to Composers," *New York Times*, February 11, 1974, 75. According to a 1978 *Village Voice* article, the NEA disbursed $6,650,000 for symphony orchestras, $3,400,000 for opera, $310,000 for "contemporary performance of new music," $475,000 for "composers and librettists" (excluding "jazz" composers), and $640,000 for all forms classified as jazz, of which $80,000 went for "jazz composition" and $100,000 for "jazz performance." See Gary Giddins, "Weather Bird: American Money for American Music," *Village Voice*, January 2, 1978, 68. Not surprisingly, NEA "classical" music composition grants and music panel assignments tended to rotate among a small coterie of white academics. See Jann Pasler, "Musique et institution aux États-Unis," *Inharmoniques* 2, May 1987, 104–34. Moreover, in 1987, "minorities"—African Americans, Native Americans, Asian Americans, and Latino Americans combined—received 6.3 percent of all grants for music. See Samuel Gilmore, "Minorities and Distributional Equity at the National Endowment for the Arts," *Journal of Arts Management, Law and Society* 23, no. 2 (Summer 1993): 137–73. Many black musicians in New York, such as the important bassist Reggie Workman of the Collective Black Artists, saw these discrepancies as a form of racial discrimination. See Weathers, "The Collective Black Artists," 72–74.

30. Rockwell, "Face of Jazz Is Changing Visibly."

31. For an extensive collection of *Voice* articles on Downtown I, see Tom Johnson, *The Voice of New Music: New York City 1972–1982* (Paris: Editions 75, 1989 [accessed November 8, 2005]), available at http://homepage.mac.com/javiruiz/English/booksenglish .html. This collection of articles was originally available in book form (Eindhoven: Het Apollohuis, 1989).

32. For the most thorough account of the Creative Music Studio, see Robert E. Sweet, *Music Universe, Music Mind: Revisiting the Creative Music Studio, Woodstock, New York* (Ann Arbor: Arborville Publishing, 1996).

33. Kalaparusha Ahrah Difda. As it happens, I was also part of this tour.

34. Griffin, *Who Set You Flowin'*.

35. Section 8 is a housing subsidy program administered by the U.S. Department of Housing and Urban Development (HUD). Though there have undoubtedly been some changes in the relationship of the building to the program, as of 2002, the agreement between the Manhattan Plaza developers, the city of New York, and HUD, was that 10 percent of the tenants would pay full-market rents for their apartments, while the rest would receive a rent subsidy pegged to their income. Of these remaining tenants, 30 percent were eligible for the subsidy if they were originally Hell's Kitchen residents living in substandard housing, or were elderly or disabled. The others, including the AACM and other musicians, were eligible for the subsidy if they were able to show that at least half their income was derived from employment or self-employment in the performing arts. In my recollection, the tenants included Dexter Gordon, Tennessee Williams, and Charles Mingus. See Nahma Sandrow, "Center-Stage Living, at Balcony Rents," *New York Times*, June 9, 2002.

36. Undoubtedly, the convergence of the AACM musicians with Manhattan Plaza was highly fortuitous. In 2002, one of the building's developers recalled that just one year after the apartment complex opened, it had become "harder to get into than Harvard." See Sandrow, "Center-Stage Living, at Balcony Rents."

37. See Tapscott, *Songs of the Unsung.*

38. Palmer, "Pop."

39. Gary Giddins, "Inside Free Jazz: The AACM in New York," *Village Voice,* May 30, 1977, 46.

40. Ibid., 48.

41. Litweiler, "Air: Impossible to Pigeonhole"; Charles Mitchell, "Caught in the Act: The Fred Anderson Sextet," *Down Beat,* June 3, 1976; Bob Ness, "Profile: Leo Smith," *Down Beat,* October 7, 1976; Arnold Jay Smith, "Profile: John Stubblefield," *Down Beat,* January 29, 1976.

42. Chuck Berg, review of recording by the Creative Construction Company, *Down Beat,* May 20, 1976; Creative Construction Company, *Creative Construction Company,* vols. 1 and 2; Jenkins, *For Players Only.*

43. John B. Litweiler, "Von Freeman: Underrated but Undaunted," *Down Beat,* November 4, 1976. Neil Tesser, "Von and Chico Freeman: Tenor Dynasty," *Down Beat,* July 1980.

44. Fred Bouchard, "Arista's Steve Backer Maneuvers in the Front Line," *Down Beat,* March 1980.

45. Lock, *Forces in Motion,* 131.

46. See Anthony Braxton, *The Montreux/Berlin Concerts* (Arista AL 5002, 1976), 2 vinyl discs.

47. William Grant Still, "A Negro Symphony Orchestra," *Opportunity,* September 1939, 267, 286–287.

48. Anthony Braxton, *New York, Fall 1974* (Arista AL 4032, 1975), vinyl disc.

49. "Après George Lewis, on ne pourra plus jouer du trombone comme avant." Laurent Goddet, "La fête de la biere," *Jazz Hot,* July-August 1976, 41.

50. "Une compréhension diabolique entre les deux hommes." Ibid. The concert Goddet reviewed was released as Anthony Braxton, and George Lewis, *Elements of Surprise* (Moers Music 01036, 1977), vinyl disc.

51. Scott Albin, review of Anthony Braxton Quartet and Tashi, *Down Beat,* March 25, 1976, 41.

52. Chuck Berg, "Newport '76," *Down Beat,* February 12, 1976, 25. For an excellent analysis of U.S. media discourses on Braxton's version of black experimentalism, see Radano, *New Musical Figurations.* For a detailed analysis of French reception, see Lehman, *I Love You with an Asterisk.*

53. Anthony Braxton, *For Four Orchestras* (Arista A3L 8900, 1978), Three vinyl discs; Braxton, *The Montreux/Berlin Concerts.*

54. Lock, *Forces in Motion,* 134.

55. Ibid., 132.

56. Art Lange, review of Anthony Braxton recording, *For Four Orchestras, Down Beat,* June 7, 1979.

57. Lock, *Forces in Motion,* 131.

58. Ibid.

59. Jean-Loup Bourget, "Muhal Richard Abrams: Entretien avec l'un des principaux inventeurs des nouveaux sons venus de Chicago," *Jazz,* July-August 1977, 22.

60. Francis Marmande, "Kalaparusha, alias Maurice McIntyre," *Jazz,* December 1977, 33.

61. Valerie Wilmer, "Amina Claudine Myers," *Coda* 169, 1979, 6.

62. Ibid., 5.

63. Robert Palmer, "WKCR Will Start 90 Straight Hours of Jazz Tonight," *New York Times,* May 14, 1977, 34.

64. These included percussionists Ajaramu, Thurman Barker, and Kahil El'Zabar; saxophonists Douglas Ewart, Edward Wilkerson, Mwata Bowden, and Wallace McMillan; pianist Adegoke Steve Colson; bassists Felix Blackmon, Leonard Jones, and Brian Smith; singers Iqua Colson and Bernard Mixon; bassoonist James Johnson; trumpeters Frank Gordon and John Shenoy Jackson; and myself and Martin "Sparx" Alexander as trombonists. Among the members who had become established in New York, there was the trio Air (Henry Threadgill, Fred Hopkins, and Steve McCall), as well as the trio of Anthony Braxton, Leo Smith, and Leroy Jenkins.

65. Balliett, "Jazz," 96.

66. Ibid., 92.

67. Jerry DeMuth, "AACM Bands in Europe Make Fests, LPs, Clubs," *Down Beat,* September 1979, 14.

68. See Franco Bolelli, *Musica creativa: Forme espressioni e problematiche del "nuovo jazz."* (Milan: Squilibri Edizioni, 1978).

69. The Charing Cross performance was recorded privately, and a subsequent studio session was released as Company, *Fables* (Incus 36, 1980).

70. I took part in several Company Weeks and recordings over succeeding years, but perhaps the most interesting in terms of the sheer mix of personalities was the tour that took us to Wales in 1981. The event included Misha Mengelberg, another musician with whom, as a result of this tour, I developed a long-standing, almost familial relationship, as well as John Zorn and Steve Lacy. Derek was asking us to create combinations of musicians for each evening, and once it was realized that Steve, for all his openness, was having a hard time figuring out why John was taking his saxophone apart, people started placing them together for performances, hoping that they would kiss and make up—which they never did. This misguided attempt by the rest of us at music-as-interpersonal-diplomacy probably accounted in part for the comment attributed to Zorn that he "was hating the tour so much." See Watson, *Derek Bailey and the Story of Free Improvisation,* 231.

71. "Ils ont débarqué! Si l'an passé le festival de Moers témoigna des musiques improvisées européennes, cette année il fut incontestablement le théâtre d'une offensive en règle de la part de la nouvelle génération américaine. Issus pour la plupart de l'A.A.C.M., tous ces musiciens résident à New York. Ils ont superbement démontré à quel point la musique qui est en train de se faire là-bas, est tout à la fois vivante, accomplie et multi-forme." Alex Dutilh, "Ils ont débarqué," *Jazz Hot* 339–340, Summer 1977, 16.

72. "Il en existe maintenant de taille raisonnable qui m'ont fait l'impression d'être très rapides. Je suis convaincu qu'il est possible de met en pied un programme permettant à l'ordinateur de dialoguer avec le ou les improvisateurrs. . . . Je n'ai pas l'impression qu'il soit si difficile que l'on pense de dominer cet instrument nouveau. . . . En réalité, nous savons bien que derrière l'ordinateur se trouve un homme. . . . Pourquoi ne pas être cet homme et ne pas se servir de cet instrument à des fins musicales." Laurent Goddet, "Le Grand George," *Jazz Hot* 351–352, Summer 1978, 22–23. Translation by the author.

73. "A Moers, tuttavia, la sua *performance*, in duo ha lasciato perplessi: Lewis ha utilizzato in concerto una strumentazione elettronica piuttostocomplessa, che consisteva specialmente in una base preregistrata su nastro ed in alcune apparecchiature che modificavano il timbro naturale del trombone." Luca Cerchiari, "A quattri'occhi con George Lewis," *Musica Jazz* 34, Nos. 8–9, August -September 1978, 17. A quartet version of the work appeared in 1980 as George Lewis, *Homage to Charles Parker* (Black Saint 120029, 1980), compact disc.

74. "L'idée était en gestation depuis longtemps. C'est au retour du Festival de Moers, cette année, qu'elle nous est apparue comme une nécessité. Il fallait absolument consacrer un numéro spécial à l'A.A.C.M. . . . Les formes les plus avancées de la musique improvisée sont toutes, sur un ou plusieurs aspects, redevables à l'A.A.C.M. Tout comme l'est la sauvegarde de la tradition culturelle négro-américaine, à laquelle contribue activement l'Association de Chicago. Par ailleurs, si New York est redevenue depuis deux ou trois ans le lieu d'une activité musicale débordante de créativité, un champ d'expérience sans doute aussi dense qu'à 'l'époque du be bop, elle le doit également en grande partie à son invasion par les musiciens de l'A.A.C.M." Alex Dutilh, editorial, *Jazz Hot*, December 1978–January 1979, 11.

75. ". . . apporter aux jeunes noirs une musique qui est la leur et que ne leur délivrent pas les média ni les institutions culturelles officielles. La démarche est riche de potentialities, car elle s'adresse à des jeunes dépourvus de références chez lesquels les notions d' 'avant-garde' ou de 'musique expérimentale' ou 'créative' perdent leur sens." Alex Dutilh, "L'AACM ou L'ardeur collective," *Jazz Hot*, December 1978–January 1979, 14.

76. ". . . à la différence de la 'Guild' fondée par Cecil Taylor et rongée par des problèmes de personnes, ou de l'Arkestra de Sun Ra qui fonctionne de manière introvertie et centralisée, l'A.A.C.M. a su se préserver de ces écueils. En pratiquant systématiquement le brassage entre tous ses membres, elle a évité le premier, posant en principe le respect mutuel des musiciens. Tous ses membres ont ainsi, à un moment ou à un autre, ponctuellement ou régulièrement, joué la (les) musique(s) des autres." Ibid.

77. "En dernière analyse, la seule constante de l'A.A.C.M. c'est son refus catégorique d'une constance. . . . Les influences, les instruments, les formules orchestrales, les approches harmoniques, rythmiques ou compositionnelles, les rapports aux autres arts, aux autres musiques, aux autres musiciens, à ceux qui font partie de l'association . . . tout cela (et d'autres éléments) se veut résolument pluriel'."Ibid., 15.

78. "Il concerto che ci è stato donato (è il caso di dirlo) in quella occasione è stato sicuramente uno dei più straordinari avvenimenti musicali a cui negli ultimi anni ci sia accaduto di assistere in Italia." Valerio Tura, "Muhal, Il Primo," *Musica Jazz* 34, no. 4, April 1978, 14.

79. "Non ho inventato niente. Non avrebbe potuto nascere l'A.A.C.M. senza la collaborazione ed anche a volte il sacrificio di tutti ed in ogni caso senza una grande volontà e determinazione. Solo, ecco, se le cose che abbiamo fatto vanno avanti, allora vuoi dire che erano giuste, buone; ci sono decine di giovani musicisti di grande valore che voi nemmeno conoscete di nome qui in Europa, che sono cresciuti, fin da ragazzini, si può dire, con noi, ed ora sono degli ottimi musicisti da ogni punto di vista." Ibid.

80. For a standard account of this interdisciplinary movement away from traditional spaces, see RoseLee Goldberg, *Performance Art: From Futurism to the Present* (New York: Harry N. Abrams, 1988).

81. Scott DeVeaux, "The Emergence of the Jazz Concert, 1935–1945," *American Music* 7, no. 1 (1989): 25.

82. Jones, "New York Loft and Coffee Shop Jazz," 13, 42. The article also appears in a number of later editions of Baraka, *Black Music,* 92–98.

83. Gary Giddins, "Weather Bird: Up from the Saloon: Lofts Celebrate Alternate Jazz," *Village Voice,* June 7, 1976, 82.

84. A useful account of the loft period appears in Jost, *Sozialgeschichte des Jazz in den USA,* 224–25.

85. See *Wildflowers: The New York Loft Jazz Sessions,* vols. 1–5 (Casablanca/Douglas NBLP 7045, 7046, 7047, 7048, 7049, 1977), vinyl discs; *Wildflowers: The New York Loft Jazz Sessions,* vols. 1–5 (KnitClassics 3037, 2000), compact discs. Other new performers included pianist Anthony Davis, guitarist Michael Gregory Jackson, drummer Paul Maddox (now Pheeroan ak Laff), and saxophonist David Murray. Those newcomers were augmented by members of the existing New York experimental improvisation scene, such as pianist Dave Burrell; trombonists Grachan Moncur III and Roswell Rudd; drummers Jerome Cooper, Andrew Cyrille, Barry Altschul, and Sunny Murray; saxophonists Sam Rivers, Byard Lancaster, Ken McIntyre, Marion Brown, Frank Lowe, Jimmy Lyons, and David S. Ware; trumpeters Olu Dara, Ahmed Abdullah, and Ted Daniel; guitarist Bern Nix; and vibraphonist Khan Jamal.

86. Stanley Crouch, "New York Jazz Notes," *Players,* July 1977, 6.

87. Hubert Saal and Abigail Kuflik, "Jazz Comes Back!" *Newsweek,* United States edition, August 8, 1977, 51.

88. These included pianists Michelle Rosewoman and Marilyn Crispell; saxophonists Jemeel Moondoc, Daniel Carter, Marty Ehrlich, and Charles Tyler; trombonists Craig Harris and Ray Anderson; drummers John Betsch and Ronald Shannon Jackson; guitarists James "Blood" Ulmer, Jean-Paul Bourelly, and James Emery; bassists Mark Dresser, Jerome Harris, John Lindberg, Wilber Morris, William Parker, and Mark Helias; clarinetist John Carter; cellist Diedre Murray; violinists Jason Hwang and Billy Bang; and vibraphonist Khan Jamal.

89. Tesser, "Von and Chico Freeman," 28.

90. Kevin Whitehead, "Fred Hopkins," *Coda* 196, 1984, 24.

91. Gary Giddins, "Weather Bird: Goings On about Town," *Village Voice,* August 29, 1977, 76.

92. Ibid.

93. See Peter Keepnews, "Public Domain," *Soho Weekly News,* September 27, 1979, 23–24, 50.

94. Gary Giddins, "Weather Bird: Riffing about Music," *Village Voice,* February 3, 1975, 106.

95. Air, *Air Lore* (Arista Novus AN3014, 1980), vinyl disc; Air, *Air Time* (Nessa N-12, 1978), vinyl disc; Air, *Air Time* (Nessa NCD-12, 1996), compact disc.

96. Fred Anderson, *Another Place* (Moers Music 01058, 1978), vinyl disc; Anthony Braxton, *Creative Orchestra Music 1976* (Arista AL4080, 1976), vinyl disc; Sharon Friedman and Larry Birnbaum, "Fred Anderson: AACM's Biggest Secret," *Down Beat,* March 8, 1979, 20–21, 48.

97. Valerie Wilmer, "Lester Bowie: Extending the Tradition," *Down Beat,* April 29, 1971, 30.

98. Bob Rusch and Hillary J. Ryan, "William Parker," *Cadence,* December 1990, 6.

99. Ibid., 6–7.

100. Jimmy Stewart, "Introduction to Black Aesthetics in Music," in *The Black Aesthetic,* ed. Addison Gayle, Jr. (New York: Doubleday, 1971), 94.

101. Linda Prince, "Betty Carter: Bebopper Breathes Fire," *Down Beat,* May 3, 1979, 14.

102. Stewart, "Introduction to Black Aesthetics in Music," 94.

103. Such, *Avant-Garde Jazz Musicians Performing Out There,* 75–92.

104. Rusch, "William Parker," 7.

105. Peter Occhiogrosso, "Anthony Braxton Explains Himself," *Down Beat,* August 12, 1976, 49.

106. Gary Giddins, "Leroy Jenkins's Territorial Imperative," *Village Voice,* April 24, 1978, 68.

107. Rafi Zabor, "Funny, You Look Like a Jazz Musician," *Village Voice,* July 2, 1979, 73.

108. Ludwig Van Trikt, "Leroy Jenkins," *Cadence,* November 1997, 6.

109. Pete LaScala, "Chords and Discords: Letter to the Editor," *Down Beat* (1979); Chip Stern, review of Muhal Richard Abrams recording, *Lifea Blinec, Down Beat,* October 5, 1978, 9.

110. Gary Giddins, "The ABCs of Muhal's Life Line," *Village Voice,* June 19, 1978, 63; Peter Occhiogrosso, "Don't Stop the Carnival, Just Keep It out of the Classroom," *Soho Weekly News,* September 21, 1978, 111.

111. Attali, *Noise,* 138.

112. Vuisje, *De nieuwe jazz,* 196.

113. Gunther Schuller, "Third Stream," in *Musings: The Musical Worlds of Gunther Schuller* (New York and Oxford: Oxford University Press, 1986), 115.

114. Kofsky, *Black Nationalism and the Revolution in Music,* 240.

115. Hal Foster, *Recodings: Art, Spectacle, Cultural Politics* (Seattle: Bay Press, 1985), 13.

116. Rockwell, "Face of Jazz Is Changing Visibly," 33.

117. Ben Ratliff, "A Pleasant Swim with Gunther Schuller, The Man Who Named the Third Stream," *New York Times,* March 20, 2001, E1.

118. For an account of the "crisis of the listener" and proposed solutions relating to jazz, see Henry Pleasants, *The Agony of Modern Music* (New York: Simon and Schuster, 1955). Also see Henry Pleasants, *Death of a Music? The Decline of the European Tradition and the Rise of Jazz* (London: Jazz Book Club, 1962). As it happens, Pleasants, whose books championed jazz as the American music of the future, had served as the CIA station chief in Bonn in the 1950s. See Douglas Martin, "Henry Pleasants, 89, Spy Who Knew His Music," *New York Times,* January 14, 2000.

119. AACM General Body Meeting, May 15.

120. For example, while John Hammond recognized that Ellington, with his extended work, *Black, Brown, and Beige,* was "trying to achieve something of greater significance," the producer clearly felt that something more was needed from the composer: "No one can justly criticize him for this if he keeps up the quality of his music for dancing."

See Mark Tucker, ed., *The Duke Ellington Reader* (New York: Oxford University Press, 1993), 173.

121. The African American composer William Banfield has published an insightful set of dialogues with a diverse array of composers concerning these and many other issues. See William C. Banfield, *Musical Landscapes in Color: Conversations with Black American Composers* (Lanham, MD: Scarecrow Press, 2003). For an internationally oriented compendium of the works of Afrodiasporic composers, see Samuel A. Floyd, Jr., ed., *International Dictionary of Black Composers* (Chicago and London: Fitzroy Dearborn, 1999).

122. In a 1979 essay contrasting composition with improvisation, musicologist Carl Dahlhaus summarizes the former as an autonomous, internally consistent structure, fully worked out and written out, and designed to be realized by a performer in a process separate from that of the work itself. See Carl Dahlhaus, "Was heisst improvisation?" in *Improvisation und neue Musik: Acht Kongressreferate,* ed. Reinhold Brinkmann (Mainz: Schott, 1979), 9.

123. Sidney Bechet, *An Introduction to Sidney Bechet: His Best Recordings* (Best of Jazz 4017, 1994), compact disc.

124. Jarman, *Black Case,* 75.

125. Hardja Susilo, "Changing Strategies for the Cross-Cultural Karawitan Experience: A Quarter-Century Perspective." (essay: 1986), 9.

126. Kostelanetz, *Conversing with Cage,* 222.

127. Hear Anthony Braxton, *This Time* (BYG-Actuel 529 347, 1970), vinyl disc.

128. Muhal Richard Abrams, *1-OQA+19* (Black Saint 120017-2, 1978), compact disc; Muhal Richard Abrams, *Lifea Blinec* (Arista Novus AN3000, 1978), vinyl disc; Anthony Braxton, *For Trio* (Arista AB 4181, 1978), vinyl disc.

129. Air, *Air Lore;* Chico Freeman, *Chico* (India Navigation IN 1031, 1977), vinyl disc; George Lewis, *Chicago Slow Dance* (Lovely Music LP 1101, 1977), vinyl disc; Lewis, *Homage to Charles Parker;* Mitchell, *L-R-G; The Maze; SII Examples;* Leo Smith, *Spirit Catcher* (Nessa N-19, 1979), vinyl disc.

130. Smith is referring to a Berlin performance of a Braxton double concerto, in which Braxton and I performed as soloists. A recording of the performance was released on Braxton, *The Montreux/Berlin Concerts.*

131. Joachim-Ernst Berendt, translated by Barbara and Helmut Bredigkeit, "Albert Mangelsdorff: Big Noise from Frankfurt," *Down Beat,* February 10, 1977, 34. A later review of the recording saw the orchestration of the work as exhibiting "gratifying color and complexity." See Neil Tesser, review of the Montreux/Berlin Concerts, *Down Beat,* October 20, 1977, 23.

132. Tucker, ed., *The Duke Ellington Reader,* 326.

133. Amiri Baraka and Amina Baraka, *The Music: Reflections on Jazz and Blues* (New York: William Morrow, 1987), 260.

134. Southern, "Music Research and the Black Aesthetic," 6.

135. Ross, *No Respect,* 97.

136. Baraka, *The Music,* 177.

137. Baraka, *Black Music,* 180–211.

138. Vuisje, *De nieuwe jazz,* 199.

139. Beauchamp, *Art Ensemble of Chicago*, 43.

140. Ekkehard Jost, *Jazzmusiker: Materialen zur Soziologie der afro-amerikanischen Musik* (Frankfurt am Main: Ullstein Materialen, 1982), 122: "Etwas, was mich an vielen Leuten irritiert, die hier über Jazz schreiben, ist die Tatsache, daß sie glauben, wenn man eine Musik lobt dann muß man die andere runtermachen. Das mag ich gar nicht! Denn das ist völlig unnötig."

141. George Coppens, "Lester Bowie," *Coda* 164–65, 1979, 14.

142. Baraka, *The Music*, 260.

143. Coppens, "Lester Bowie," 14.

144. Baraka, *Blues People*, 177.

145. Oja, *Making Music Modern*, 295.

146. Ibid., 296.

147. Ibid., 295–96.

148. Alain Locke, *The Negro and His Music* (New York: Arno Press and the *New York Times*, 1969), 2.

149. Ibid., 95.

150. Ibid., 89.

151. Oja, *Making Music Modern*, 304.

152. Henry Cowell, ed., *American Composers on American Music: A Symposium* (New York: Frederic Ungar Publishing, 1933), 128.

153. Henry Cowell, concert program, 1931, Town Hall, New York City, in the Henry Cowell Collection, Box 54, New York Public Library.

154. Henry Cowell, "Letter from Henry Cowell to Charles Ives" (undated), in the Henry Cowell Collection, Box 17, Folder 516, New York Public Library.

155. Floyd, "Music in the Harlem Renaissance," 3.

156. Locke, *The Negro and His Music*, 130.

157. Paul Burgett, "Vindication as a Thematic Principle in the Writings of Alain Locke on the Music of Black Americans," in *Black Music in the Harlem Renaissance: A Collection of Essays*, ed. Samuel A. Floyd, Jr. (Knoxville: University of Tennessee Press, 1990), 36.

158. Locke, *The Negro and His Music*, 99.

159. Oja, *Making Music Modern*, 305.

160. Ibid., 314.

161. Quoted in ibid.

162. Quoted in Levy, "'The White Hope of American Music,'" 152.

163. Baraka, *Blues People*, 193–94.

164. Ted Gioia, *The Imperfect Art: Reflections on Jazz and Modern Culture* (New York: Oxford University Press, 1988), 71–72.

165. Parker and McClellan, interview with Charlie Parker.

166. DeVeaux, "Constructing the Jazz Tradition," 500.

167. See Verna Arvey, *In One Lifetime* (Fayetteville: University of Arkansas Press, 1984), 65–73. Arvey, Still's widow, provides an account of the composer's struggle to escape Varese's influence. For an excellent essay addressing this topic, see Murchison, "'Dean of Afro-American Composers.'"

168. Gioia, *The Imperfect Art*, 71–72, Porter, *What Is This Thing Called Jazz?*, 75.

169. Parker and McClellan, interview with Charlie Parker.

170. Oja, *Making Music Modern*, 331–32.

171. Porter, *What Is This Thing Called Jazz?*, 77.

172. Baraka, *Blues People*, 137.

173. Ibid., 38.

174. DeVeaux, "Constructing the Jazz Tradition," 345.

175. Baraka, *The Music*, 177.

176. Ellison, "On Bird, Bird-Watching, and Jazz," 69.

177. DeVeaux, "The Emergence of the Jazz Concert, 1935–1945," 26.

178. Quoted in ibid., 26n5.

179. See Pleasants, *The Agony of Modern Music*.

180. Catherine M. Cameron, "Fighting with Words: American Composers' Commentary on Their Work," *Comparative Studies in Society and History* 27, no. 3 (1985): 436–40.

181. See Cameron, *Dialectics in the Arts;* Johnson, *The Voice of New Music;* Richard Kostelanetz, ed., *Dictionary of the Avant-Gardes* (Chicago: A cappella books, 1993); Michael Nyman, *Experimental Music: Cage and Beyond*, 2nd ed. (New York: Schirmer Books, 1999). Somewhat more inclusive accounts are found in Kyle Gann, *American Music in the Twentieth Century* (New York: Schirmer Books, 1997); Nathan Rubin, *John Cage and the Twenty-six Pianos: Forces in American Music from 1940–1990* (Moraga, Calif.: Sarah's Books, 1994).

182. Cage, *Silence*, 67–75.

183. Locke, *The Negro and His Music*, 97.

184. See, for instance, the important interviews with African American improvisors published as Taylor, *Notes and Tones*.

185. Oja, *Making Music Modern*, 362.

186. William Appleman Williams, *The Contours of American History* (New York: W. W. Norton, 1988).

187. Locke, *The Negro and His Music*, 95–96.

188. Cage, *Silence*, 73.

189. This thesis is developed in detail in Lewis, "Improvised Music after 1950," 131–62.

190. David W. Noble, *Death of a Nation: American Culture and the End of Exceptionalism* (Minneapolis: University of Minnesota Press, 2002), 199. Noble's discussion of twentieth-century American classical music in the context of racially coded constructions of subjectivity in American culture has few counterparts in the music-historical literature on the subject, which tends to avoid discussing connections between race and power. Besides the work of Carol Oja, for other salutary exceptions, see Lisa Barg, "Black Voices/White Sounds: Race and Representation in Virgil Thomson's Four Saints in Three Acts," *American Music* 18, no. 2 (Summer 2000); John Corbett, "Experimental Oriental," in *Western Music and Its Others: Difference, Representation, and Appropriation in Music*, ed. Georgina Born and David Hesmondhalgh (Berkeley: University of California Press, 2000); Levy, "'The White Hope of American Music'"; Lloyd Whitesell, "White Noise: Race and Erasure in the Cultural Avant-Garde," *American Music* 19, no. 2 (Summer 2001).

191. Cage, *Silence*, 72.

192. Ron Welburn and Ralph Ellison, "Ralph Ellison's Territorial Vantage," in *Living with Music: Ralph Ellison's Jazz Writings,* ed. Robert G. O'Meally (New York: Modern Library, [1976] 2001), 30.

193. An important exception to the rule of nonengagement with African American forms was composer and "former jazz trumpeter" Conlon Nancarrow, whose idiosyncratic use of player pianos as a performance medium, articulated from the relative safety of Mexico City, dovetailed with his prescient, proto-postmodern incorporation of elements of the blues and Mexican *corridos.* One should note here that the trope of the "former jazz musician," a common one in the literature on white composers of this generation, often asserts a double reflection: the engagement itself wards off charges of elitism, while the discourse frames involvement with jazz as a form of youthful indiscretion.

194. Quoted in Belgrad, *The Culture of Spontaneity,* 253.

195. John Holzaepfel, *David Tudor and the Performance of American Experimental Music, 1950–1959* (PhD dissertation, City University of New York, 1993), 196. According to composer Sean Griffin, the performance of at least one such secondary score has been issued as Tudor's recorded version of Morton Feldman's "Intersection 3" from 1953. See Morton Feldman, *New Directions in Music 2: Morton Feldman* (Columbia/Odyssey MS 6090, 1969), vinyl disc., for the recorded version of the work. For an analysis comparing the recorded work with Tudor's private score, see Sean Griffin (PhD qualifying examination, University of California, San Diego, 2001).

196. Frank O'Hara, "New Directions in Music: Morton Feldman," in *Give My Regards to Eighth Street: Collected Writings of Morton Feldman, with an afterword by Frank O'Hara,* ed. B. H. Friedman (Cambridge, Mass.: Exact Change Press, 2000), 213.

197. George Lipsitz, "Listening to Learn and Learning to Listen: Popular Culture, Cultural Theory and American Studies," *American Quarterly* 42, no. 4 (1990): 621.

198. Howard Becker, *Art Worlds* (Berkeley: University of California Press, 1982), 132–33.

199. ". . . außerhalb der offiziell anerkannten und daher durch Subventionen und Stipendien geförderten *Kultur.* Es bedurfte noch vieler Jahre und erheblicher Anstrengungen von seiten dieser neuen Generation von Jazzmusikern, den verengten Kulturbegriff des etablierten Bildungssystems so aufzubrechen, daß nicht nur John Cage, sondern auch Cecil Taylor davon profitieren konnte—in geringerem Maße, versteht sich." Jost, *Sozialgeschichte des Jazz in den USA,* 183.

200. Cage, *Silence,* 73.

201. See Cameron, *Dialectics in the Arts.*

202. Cameron, "Fighting with Words'," 432–33. According to Cameron's rather celebratory scenario, this new patronage was "open, in the sense that no restrictions were put on the direction that artists might choose to take. . . . Experimentalism flourished in the free and unrestricted environment of the university (432). At the same time, her representative sample of forty-two experimental composers, representing three generations, is all white (435). Additionally, those who are pleased to believe that jazz is an especially masculinist art world relative to many others might want to note that all but one of the forty-two composers listed by this female researcher is male.

203. Rout, Jr., "Reflections on the Evolution of Post-War Jazz," 96–97.

204. See Hentoff, "The New Jazz," 38–39.

205. Leonard Feather, "Feather's Nest: The New Esthetic," *Down Beat,* June 15, 1967, 15.

206. See Rhys Chatham, "5 Generations of Composers at the Kitchen," in *The Kitchen Turns Twenty: A Retrospective Anthology,* ed. Lee Morrissey (New York: Kitchen Center, 1992). In the second edition of his canonical history of experimental music, Michael Nyman is particularly defensive, even defiant, about the fact that the second edition made no effort whatsoever to redress the lack of cultural and ethnic diversity in the first edition. While admitting that a sequel to his book "would have to be less ethnocentric," Nyman maintains that were he writing the first edition today he "would *not* do it any differently." Nyman, *Experimental Music,* 2nd ed., xviii.

207. Attali, *Noise,* 140.

208. John Rockwell, "New Music in America," *Journal of American Culture* 4, no. 4 (1981): 136.

209. John Rockwell, "A New Music Director Comes to the Avant-Garde Kitchen," *New York Times,* September 14, 1980.

210. Tom Johnson, "The Kitchen Improvises," *Village Voice,* September 24–30, 1980.

211. Ibid. For similar estimates of the Kitchen's 1980 budget, see Rockwell, "A New Music Director Comes to the Avant-Garde Kitchen."

212. Information compiled from Kitchen concert announcement mailers printed during my term as music curator (between September 1980 and June 1982) shows that the Kitchen's music program presented, among others, Tom Hamilton, John Zorn, Bertram Turetzky, Rae Imamura, Carles Santos, Derek Bailey, Evan Parker, Takehisa Kosugi, Stuart Dempster, William Hellermann, Eliane Radigue, Julius Hemphill, Anthony Davis, Julius Eastman, Michael Byron, William Hawley, Amina Claudine Myers, Arnold Dreyblatt, Gerry Hemingway, Robert Moran, Glenn Branca, Dick Higgins, Jackson MacLow, Ned Sublette, John Morton, Arlene Dunlap/Daniel Lentz, Jamaican Music Festival, John Morton, Carl Stone, Trans Museq (Davey Williams and LaDonna Smith), Roscoe Mitchell, Peg Ahrens, Defunkt, Tona Scherchen-Hsiao, the Ethnic Heritage Ensemble (Kahil El'Zabar, Edward Wilkerson, and Joseph Bowie), Frederic Rzewski, Rhys Chatham, Ingram Marshall, Douglas Ewart, Muhal Richard Abrams, Robert Ashley, Diamanda Galas, Anthony Braxton, Gerald Oshita, and Joan LaBarbara.

213. Gregory Sandow, "But Is It Art?," *Village Voice,* March 4–10, 1981.

214. For example, the *Voice* tradition of a regular, composer-written column on new music was founded in the early 1960s by the African American composer Carman Moore.

215. Sweet, *Music Universe, Music Mind.*

216. Susan McClary, *Conventional Wisdom* (Berkeley: University of California Press, 2000), 148.

217. Richard Teitelbaum, "World Band," in *Soundings* 1, ed. Peter Garland (Self-published, 1972).

218. Iris Brooks, *New Music America History: A Caterpillar or a Butterfly?* (Valencia and Santa Monica: California Institute of the Arts/High Performance Books, 1992), 10.

219. Advertisement for New Music America Festival, *EAR,* February -March 1981.

220. Tom Johnson, "New Music, New York, New Institution," *Village Voice,* July 2, 1979.

221. Ibid.

CHAPTER 10

1. Quotes from Mwata Bowden throughout this book come from Mwata Bowden, interview with the author, Chicago, Illinois, June 18, 1999.

2. Wilkerson interview.

3. The list of meeting participants is culled from an AACM internal memo describing the meeting and an audiotape of the meeting itself. Quotes from the meeting in this chapter come from the audiotape and were transcribed by me: AACM Conference, audiotape, August 1977 (exact date unknown), collection of Joseph Jarman; "Caucus Results," 1977 (date unknown), Archives of the AACM.

4. Laurent Goddet, "Kahil El'Zabar: The Preacher," *Jazz Hot*, October 1978, 26.

5. See Lipsitz, "Like a Weed in a Vacant Lot"; Looker, *BAG*.

6. "Und der einzige Grund, weshalb wir es Schwarze Musik nennen, ist, um es von all den musikalischen Scheusslichkeiten abzugrenzen, die es hier gibt. Andersfalls würden wir es gar nicht Schwarze Musik nennen, wir würden es einfach nur *Musik* nennen. Denn das ist es ja schliesslich. Es ist Musik, die vom Universum ausgeht. Genau das ist es! Wir können ebenso all die anderen Namen nehmen, mit denen irgend jemand diese Musik bezeichnet; wir können all diese Namen nennen und sie auf den Mist werfen und sie dort liegen lassen." Jost, *Jazzmusiker*, 192.

7. Jimmy Carter, interview, *Playboy*, November 1976.

8. "NEA Grants to Jazz for '80," *Down Beat*, July 1980.

9. AACM Conference, August 1977.

10. "Caucus Results."

11. Ibid.

12. Abrams interview.

13. Quotes from Dushun Mosley throughout this book are from Dushun Mosley, interview with the author, AACM School, Chicago, Illinois, February 13, 1999.

14. "3 X 4 Eye" was the title of a Mitchell composition of the period. For a later interpretation, see Roscoe Mitchell, and the Sound Ensemble, *3 X 4 Eye* (Black Saint 120050, 1994), compact disc.

15. See Colson Unity Troupe, *Triumph!* (Silver Sphinx, 1978), vinyl disc.

16. Of the many Fromm Foundation awards for music given between 1952 and 1987, just four were presented to black composers—T. J. Anderson, Ornette Coleman, Primous Fountain, and Olly Wilson. See David Gable and Christoph Wolff, eds., *A Life for New Music: The Fromm Music Foundation 1952–1987; Selected Papers of Paul Fromm* (Cambridge: Department of Music, Harvard University, 1988).

17. "Guggenheim to Mingus."

18. Paul J. DiMaggio, "Support for the Arts from Independent Foundations," in *Nonprofit Enterprise in the Arts*, ed. Paul DiMaggio (New York: Oxford University Press, 1986), 129.

19. See Pasler, "Musique et institution aux États-Unis."

20. Stanley Crouch, "Jazz at the Crossroads: Startling, Organized, Earworthy," *Down Beat*, June 1980, 15.

21. Ken Oda, *A. B. Spellman of the Arts Endowment, on the NEA's Impact on the Arts* (accessed November 19, 2001); available from http://www.koanart.com/nea.html.

22. See A. B. Spellman, *Four Lives in the Bebop Business* (New York: Pantheon Books, 1966); Spellman, "Revolution in Sound."

23. Gilmore, "Minorities and Distributional Equity at the National Endowment for the Arts," 170.

24. DiMaggio, "Support for the Arts from Independent Foundations," 129. The NEA model of patronage was undoubtedly influenced by the European social democratic example, with the striking exception of the U.S. emphasis on arts funding as a species of social work. U.S. musicians of all races and genres who have visited Europe usually return bearing anecdotal evidence contrasting the meager and grudging support for the arts at home with what they find overseas: large, well-equipped, state-funded radio studios, relatively new performance facilities, and not least, artists' fees that tend to be higher in many cases. For a comparative overview of arts funding in the United States and Europe, see John Michael Montias, "Public Support for the Performing Arts in Europe and the United States," in *Nonprofit Enterprise in the Arts,* ed. Paul DiMaggio (New York: Oxford University Press, 1986). For an account of the Dutch system of funding for musical composition, which was striking to this U.S. reader for its complete absence of social-work discourse, see the 200-plus page description of the history and goals of the Fonds voor de Scheppende Toonkunst (Funds for Creative Sonic Art), in B. Van der Lelij, B. G. M. Völker, H. Steketee, and F. M. H. M. Driessen, *Componeren in Nederland* (Utrecht: Bureau Driessen, 1996).

25. Gilmore, "Minorities and Distributional Equity at the National Endowment for the Arts," 159.

26. See Ellen Weller, "Making Diversity in Urban America: The Intersections of Cultural Tourism, Public Arts Funding, and Multicultural Performance in San Diego, California" (PhD dissertation, University of California, San Diego, 2002).

27. Quotes from Ameen Muhammad and Ernest Dawkins throughout this book are taken from Ernest Dawkins, interview with the author, Chicago, Illinois, June 24, 1999; Ameen Muhammad, interview with the author, Chicago, Illinois, February 10, 1999. For more on Wade Walton, see Paul Oliver, *Savannah Syncopators: African Retentions in the Blues* (New York: Stein and Day, 1970).

28. Charles W. Cochran, Jr., Obituary, Greater Union Baptist Church, Chicago, Illinois, September, 1978.

29. See Jean-Loup Bourget, "Delmark Story," *Jazz* 261, January 1978; and Jean-Loup Bourget, "Nessa Story," *Jazz* 264, May 1978.

30. Renzo Pognant Gros, review of AACM Summer Festival in Chicago, *Musica Jazz,* December 1978.

31. Brent Staples, "Festival AACM à Chicago," *Jazz Hot,* October 1978. "La majeure partie de la musique de cette célébration du treizième anniversaire de l'AACM fut produite par la seconde génération des membres de l'AACM." Staples's witty account of his Chicago period is found in his memoir, Brent A. Staples, *Parallel Time: Growing Up in Black and White* (New York: Pantheon Books, 1994).

32. A recording of the concert was released as Anderson, *Another Place.*

33. Quotes and narratives from Reggie Nicholson hereafter come from Reggie Nicholson, interview with the author, New York City, October 19, 1998.

34. Despite a lasting impact on a generation of Chicago improvisors (in particular, on younger white artists) information on percussionist Hal Russell, who is of the same

generation as the first-generation AACM members and passed away in 1992, is difficult to find in traditional sources. Russell's best-known musical project, the NRG Ensemble, began around 1978, around the same time that Nicholson was studying with him. Recordings of the ensemble are easier to obtain; Chuck Nessa released the group's first recording in 1981. See Hal Russell, *Hal Russell NRG Ensemble* (Nessa ncd-21, 1981), compact disc. For more detailed information, see entry on Hal Russell in *MusicWeb Encyclopaedia of Popular Music,* available from http://www.musicweb.uk.net/encyclopaedia/r/R173 .htm, accessed March 13, 2007).

35. "New York Chapter Roster," January 1, 1981, Archives of the AACM.

36. Edward L. Wilkerson, Internal Memo, Exact date unknown, probably February 1978, Archives of the AACM.

37. Ibid.

38. Ibid.

39. Ibid.

40. "Employment Agreement for Administrator," April 1981; "Job Announcement for Administrator," September 14, 1981; and "Technical Assistance Project Memo," August 10, 1980; all from the Archives of Evod Magek.

41. "State of New York Certificate of Incorporation, National Council of the Association for the Advancement of Creative Musicians," November 18, 1982, copy in Collection of Muhal Richard Abrams.

42. "Internal Revenue Service Foundation Status Classification, National Council of the Association for the Advancement of Creative Musicians," January 18, 1985, copy in Collection of Muhal Richard Abrams.

43. "AACM Performance Evaluation Sheet," 1983[?], Archives of Evod Magek.

44. "AACM Technical Assistance Project," July 21–24, 1980, Archives of Evod Magek.

45. Except as noted, quotes and narratives from Kahil El'Zabar hereafter come from Kahil El'Zabar, interview with the author, Chicago, Illinois, February 4, 1999.

46. For a review of a representative FEPA event, see Jim DeJong, "After Hours Addendum," *Down Beat,* December 1981.

47. Program booklet, AACM Sixteenth Anniversary Festival, December 1981, Archives of Evod Magek.

48. See Serge Loupien, "Les aleas de la Haye, helas!" *Jazz* 289, September 1980.

49. Adegoke Steve Colson, E-mail communication, June 5, 2006. See Colson Unity Troupe, *No Reservation* (Black Saint 120043, 1980), vinyl disc.

50. Joachim-Ernst Berendt, "Caught! Ninth Moers International New Jazz Festival," translated by Reni and Joe Weisel, *Down Beat,* September 1980, 57.

51. Ethnic Heritage Ensemble, *Three Gentlemen from Chicago* (Moers Music 1076, 1981).

52. "L'A.a.c.m. de Chicago à laquelle ils appartiennent (Kahil El-Zabar et Edward Wilkerson en ont été présidents) a déjà fait ses preuves et cette 'étiquette' est maintenant gage de qualité." Jean-Louis Libois, "Kahil el Zabar (concert review)," *Jazz* 282, January 1980, 17.

53. ". . . une musique évidente, comme née du fond des âges mais frémissante et profondément originale. . . . Rien d'étonnant à cela: les trois musiciens viennent de Chicago, deux étant issus de la troisième génération de l'AACM." Philippe Lesage, "Kahil Le Prophete," *Jazz Hot* 370, February 1980, 40.

54. "Si e cominciato malissimo, con l'Ethnic Heritage Ensemble, che deve al fatto di essere uscito dalla AACM, e alia dabbenaggine di certi operatori culturali che sappiamo, una immeritatissima fama intemazionale. In realtà i tre dell'E.H.E. sono dei poveri sprovveduti che si illudono di proporre una raffinata operazione culturale travestendosi da africani (il leader si fa chiamare Kahil El Zabar) e suonancio un po' di musica esotica mescolata a pessimo *free jazz*. Musicisti da stazione di metropolitana, li ha definiti un collega: sottoscrivo. Il fatto che certa gente possa essere scritturata qua e la in Europa (anche al Festival del 'nuovo jazz' di Moers) e davvero un brutto segno." Polillo, "Adesso c'è la "new thing," 11.

55. "Delusione atroce, la sera dopo, con Muhal Richard Abrams, santone de Il'AACM, conferma che questa associazione ha fabbricato—nel campo della musica afro-americana—piu miti di qualunque cosa vi possa venire in mente. Muhal ha infatti suonato, per un'ora filata, diniostrando una poverta tecnica e un'indigenza di idee inimmaginabili." Ibid., 12.

56. When I met Muhammad in the early 1990s, I remarked with no sense of irony, "You must be one of the new guys." Ameen replied with his usual grace, "I suppose you could say that. I've been a member for about ten years."

57. Abrams interview.

58. Except as noted, quotes and narratives from Janis Lane-Ewart hereafter come from Janis Lane-Ewart, interview with the author, Chicago, Illinois, June 21, 1999.

59. Douglas Ewart, Dismissal letter from AACM Chair to Consultant, November 27, 1982.

60. Douglas R. Ewart, Letter to AACM from Yokohama, Japan, 1987, Lane-Ewart.

61. "AACM internal memo, History of Jazz Programming, 1982–1983," Archives of Evod Magek.

62. R. Bruce Dold, "School for Kids of Note: Musicians Create an Academy in Inner City," *Chicago Tribune,* March 25, 1983.

CHAPTER 11

1. For an account of the Chicago-based AACM after the split, see Nanette T. DeJong, "Chosen Identities and Musical Symbols: The Curaçaoan Jazz Community and the Association for the Advancement of Creative Musicians" (PhD dissertation, University of Michigan, 1997).

2. Douglas Ewart, *Bamboo Meditations at Banff* (Aarawak 003, 1994), compact disc; Douglas Ewart, *Red Hills* (Aarawak 001, 1983), Audiocassette.

3. 8 Bold Souls, *8 Bold Souls* (Sessoms, 1987). 8 Bold Souls, *Ant Farm* (Arabesque Recordings, 1994), compact disc; Edward Wilkerson and Shadow Vignettes, *Birth of a Notion* (Sessoms, 1985).

4. This information was taken from concert flyers in the collection of Muhal Richard Abrams. The New York Chapter also presented flutist Nicole Mitchell and pianist-vocalist Ann Ward, who are introduced later in this chapter.

5. Porter, *What Is This Thing Called Jazz?*, 311–12. Porter's thoughtful account of Marsalis is complemented by the trumpeter's own forthright declaration of the purposes and strategies envisioned at the time regarding the promulgation of a revised canon for jazz. See Wynton Marsalis, "What Jazz Is—And Isn't," *New York Times,* July 31, 1988.

Herman Gray has advanced the notion that Marsalis's advocacy of a highly selective version of a jazz canon recapitulates a neoconservative version of the strategies of both prescription and resistance promulgated by the Black Aesthetic movement of the 1970s. See Herman S. Gray, "Jazz Tradition, Institutional Formation, and Cultural Practice," in *Cultural Moves: African Americans and the Politics of Representation* (Berkeley: University of California Press, 2005).

6. Jon Pareles, "Pop View: Classical and Jazz Artists Meet Halfway," *New York Times*, March 15, 1987.

7. Stanley Crouch, "Bringing Atlantis Up to the Top," *Village Voice*, April 16, 1979.

8. Quoted in Porter, *What Is This Thing Called Jazz?*, 304.

9. Dan Morgenstern, "Jazz in the '70s: No Energy Crisis," *Down Beat*, January 1980, 19.

10. AACM General Body Meeting, May 8.

11. Frank Conroy, "Stop Nitpicking a Genius," *New York Times Magazine*, June 25, 1995. For further elaboration on these issues from a similar viewpoint, see also Tom Piazza, *Blues Up and Down: Jazz in Our Time* (New York: St. Martin's Press, 1997). An important ethnographic study of young jazz musicians of the 1990s who take Marsalis's musical and cultural work as a touchstone for their own is Travis Arnell Jackson, "Performance and Musical Meaning: Analyzing 'Jazz' on the New York Scene." (PhD dissertation, Columbia University, 1998).

12. Griffin, *If You Can't Be Free, Be a Mystery* 143–44.

13. As the saxophonist Jimmy Heath remarked, on the eve of a "Classical Jazz" concert featuring his music, "There were grants before, from the government, but nothing like this. The budget, which, I might add, is probably minuscule compared to the classical budget, is still bigger than anything I'm used to, and Lincoln Center itself has an aura of prestige. It's all very helpful to musicians and to the music." Quoted in Peter Watrous, "Jazz, Classical, Art, Business: A Series Wraps All into One," *New York Times*, August 2, 1994, C15.

14. West names Marsalis, Louis Armstrong, Ella Baker, W. E. B. DuBois, and Martin Luther King, Jr., among others, as part of a new breed of "intellectual freedom fighters, that is, cultural workers who simultaneously position themselves within (or alongside) the mainstream while clearly aligned with groups who vow to keep alive potent traditions of critique and resistance." Going further, West exhorts cultural workers to "take clues from the great musicians or preachers of color who are open to the best of what other traditions offer yet are rooted in nourishing subcultures that build on the grand achievements of a vital heritage." See Cornel West, *Keeping Faith: Philosophy and Race in America* (New York: Routledge, 1993), 27.

15. Christian Broecking, *Der Marsalis-Faktor: Gespräche über afroamerikanische Kultur in der neunziger Jahre* (Waakirchen-Schaftlach [Switzerland]: Oreos Verlag, 1995), 111. "Ich will da ganz ehrlich sein: Ich möchte lieber Wynton Marsalis mit einem Ellington-Konzert hören als das, was Bowie oder Threadgill machen. Auch wenn ich sie für einige Dinge schätze, die sie zustande gebracht haben. Ja, auch sie sollten eine reguläre Bühne haben, und ich wünschte, daß Sonny Rollins eine hätte. Aber das Problem stellt sich, solange wir keine eigenen unabhängigen Institutionen haben. Bis dahin kann ich nur sagen: Es ist zu begrüßen, daß die afroamerikanische Tradition von Wynton Marsalis bewahrt wird. Ich würde seine Arbeit in diesen Zeiten sogar als progressiv bezeichnen."

16. Conroy, "Stop Nitpicking a Genius."

17. Ludwig Van Trikt, "Anthony Davis X," *Cadence*, November 1985, 5.

18. Paul Baker, "Roscoe Mitchell: The Next Step," *Coda* 228, October/November 1989, 19.

19. Van Trikt, "Leroy Jenkins," 5.

20. Film and music scholar Krin Gabbard acidly comments that "some of my more cynical friends in jazz circles have pointed out that the only musicians we see in Burns's finale are the ones with major-label recording contracts." See Krin Gabbard, "Ken Burns's 'Jazz': Beautiful Music, But Missing a Beat," *Chronicle of Higher Education* 47, no. 16 (2000), B18. However, the extensive sponsorship for jazz events at Lincoln Center has by no means been limited to media corporations.

21. Watrous, "Jazz, Classical, Art, Business."

22. Burton Hersh, "The Secret Life of Lincoln Center," *Town and Country*, January 1980.

23. Attali, *Noise*, 140.

24. Suzanne McElfresh, "Julius Hemphill," *Bomb*, Fall 1994, 49.

25. Fred Anderson, telephone communication, January 10, 2005. Also see Friedman and Birnbaum, "Fred Anderson," 20. In addition to the problems revealed in the article, there could be little question of the impact of race on Anderson's situation. Later, Anderson founded the successful Velvet Lounge, which is still in operation as a center for Chicago's new generation of improvisors, as well as musicians from around the world.

26. Lewis, "Improvised Music after 1950"

27. "Cette Grande Musique Noire n'appartient pas au seul Art Ensemble. . . . Mahalia, Aretha, Woody Herman, Stan Kenton, Duke Ellington, Louis Armstrong, Bessie Smith, tous font de la Grande Musique Noire, tous ont leurs racines dans la Grande Musique Noire." Ibid., 15.

28. "Ce qu'on appelle 'rock and roll,' par exemple, vient des églises noires. . . . Ensuite ils ont appelé leur musique 'rock music.' C'était de la Grande Musique Noire, mais personne ne reconnaît." Philippe Carles, Francis Marmande, and Daniel Soutif, "Ensemble sur l'art de Chicago," *Jazz*, April 1974, 15.

29. Mahon, *Right to Rock*, 27. The book is a fine account of the Black Rock Coalition and the identity politics of rock as these impact both discourses and economics in the music business.

30. Jason Berry, "Declamations on Great Black Music," *Lenox Avenue: A Journal of Interartistic Inquiry* 3 (1997): 51.

31. Quoted in George E. Lewis, "Singing Omar's Song: A (Re)construction of Great Black Music," *Lenox Avenue: A Journal of Interartistic Inquiry* 4 (1998).

32. Paul Gilroy, "Sounds Authentic: Black Music, Ethnicity, and the Challenge of a 'Changing' Same," *Black Music Research Journal* 11, no. 2 (1991): 134.

33. Jost, *Jazzmusiker*, 198: "Die Musik ist für jeden da, Und wenn man sie einmal erklingen läßt, dann geht sie in den Besitz der Öffentlichkeit über. Man kann also nicht sagen: Der und der sollte die und die Musik nicht spielen."

34. AACM General Body Meeting, May 15, Chicago, Illinois.

35. Attali, *Noise*.

36. "Beaucoup de jeunes musiciens européens ont été influencés par votre travail. . . .

Pensez-vous que ces musiciens devraient chercher leurs propres 'racines'?" Carles, "Ensemble sur l'art de Chicago," 15.

37. "Non, 'leurs propres racines' ça n'existe pas. Nous n'avons pas de racines particulières. Ce qui est determinant, c'est l'environnement, les sentiments, la façon de vivre, de voir. . . . Vous pouvez trouver des idées n'importe où dans la vie." Ibid.

38. Attali, *Noise*, 132.

39. Ibid., 139.

40. "Mais il n'y a qu'une *A.a.c.m.*, elle a deux aspects différents. Un aspect international, avec les musiciens que vous connaissez—moi-même, l'Art Ensemble, et ainsi de suite—et puis, il y a l'aspect local. Certains de ces musiciens sont tout à fait éminents. Mais ils n'ont pas été lancés sur la scène nationale ou internationale. On peut dire, d'une certain façon, qu'il y a ces deux parties qui ensemble n'en forment qu'une. L'un des buts originaux de l'A.a.c.m. était d'encourager renseignement de la musique . . . et de diffuser cette musique dans le monde entier." Jean-Loup Bourget, "Muhal Richard Abrams: Vers la musique," *Jazz*, July-August 1977, 22.

41. "AACM Board of Directors & Respective Job Descriptions," 1987, Archives of Evod Magek; "Minutes, AACM Board of Directors Meeting," April 30, 1986, Archives of Evod Magek.

42. "So etwas wie ein Gütezeichen für eine kreative Musik ersten Ranges machte." Jost, *Sozialgeschichte des Jazz in den USA*, 215.

43. ". . . ne manquèrent pas de lasser. Une lassitude provoquée par une trop grande similitude d'inspiration, ce côté 'un pied dans la tradition-un pied dans l'avant-garde' un peu agaçant, des compositions souvent peu attrayantes et des solistes certes rompus à toutes les disciplines mais manquant souvent de *groove* et de personnalité affirmée." Gérard Rouy, "Moers," *Jazz*, July-August 1986, 24.

44. "Une musique sensiblement différente de celle de ses confrères de Chicago; débarrassé de tous les africanismes (vestimentaires et instrumentaux) de pacotille." Ibid.

45. Steve Lake, "Moers Festival," *Wire*, August 1986, 14.

46. See Art Ensemble of Chicago, *Art Ensemble of Soweto* (DIW 52954, 1992), compact disc; Art Ensemble of Chicago, *Chi-Congo* (Varese Sarabande (USA) VSD 3020615282, [1970] 2005); Ernest Dawkins and the New Horizons Ensemble, *Jo'Burg Jump* (Delmark DE-524, 2000), compact disc.

47. Bill Shoemaker, review of recordings by Muhal Richard Abrams, George Lewis and Douglas Ewart, Ari Brown, and Ernest Dawkins, *Jazz Times*, July/August 1996, 95.

48. Muhal Richard Abrams, advertising poster for concert, "A Salute to FMP (Free Music Productions)," 1995, Archives of the AACM.

49. Willard Jenkins, "Midwest Musings," *Jazz Times*, November 1987, 20.

50. Lloyd Sachs, "Jazz Festival Plays as Concert or Ambience for Lawn Party," *Chicago Sun-Times*, September 10, 1987, 66.

51. Lloyd Sachs, "Quality Fest Falls Short of Greatness," *Chicago Sun-Times*, September 7, 1987, 23.

52. Seth Tisue, *Chicago Now: Old Listings* (1995 [accessed November 20, 2005]); available from http://tisue.net/chicagonow/old1995.html.

53. Lewis, *Gittin' to Know Y'all*.

54. Tisue, *Chicago Now*.

55. Abrams, advertising poster for concert, "A Salute to FMP (Free Music Productions)."

56. Tisue, *Chicago Now.*

57. Except as noted, quotes and narratives from Rita Warford hereafter come from Rita Warford, interview with the author, New York City, November 1, 1999.

58. Quotes and narratives from Ann Ward in this section come from Ann Ward, interview with the author, Chicago, Illinois, February 15, 1999.

59. For an account of classical music in Chicago that includes the Umbrian Glee Club and other African American initiatives, see Mark Clague and J. Kimo Williams, (*Encyclopedia of Chicago*, s.v. "Classical Music," 2005 [accessed November 20, 2005]); available from http://www.encyclopedia.chicagohistory.org/pages/295.html.

60. The reference is to a fictional conspiracy for the extermination of African Americans that appears as a climactic conceit in the classic spy novel, John A. Williams, *The Man Who Cried I Am* (Boston: Little, Brown, 1967). As writer Herb Boyd explains, Williams promoted the book by leaving photocopies of the portion detailing the "Plan" on subway seats around Manhattan. Both the racial atmosphere of the 1960s and the samizdat-like appearance of the physical medium contributed to the apparent plausibility of the narrative. "The ploy worked so well," Boyd noted, "that soon after, black folks all over New York City were talking about 'the plan,' a fictitious plot that many thought was true." See Herb Boyd, "The Man and the Plan: Conspiracy Theories and Paranoia in Our Culture," *Black Issues Book Review* 4, no. 2 (2002). Indeed, for many, such a plan was assumed to be in the works. For example, consider Charles Mingus's pointed remarks to a live audience in 1964 about his piece, *Meditations:* "Eric Dolphy once explained to me that there was something similar to the concentration camps once in Germany now down South, where they separate the picketers, the green from the red or something like that. And the only difference between the electric barbed wire is that they don't have gas chambers and hot stoves to cook us in yet. Quoted in Robert K. McMichael, "'We Insist—Freedom Now!': Black Moral Authority, Jazz, and the Changeable Shape of Whiteness," *American Music* 16, no. 4 (1998): 386. Also see Charles Mingus, *The Great Concert of Charles Mingus* (Verve B0000AKNJL, [1964] 2004). Finally, as Williams told writer Robert Fleming, "The King Alfred Plan came from my reading of Hitler's 'Final Solution.' When you read the particulars of the FBI's COINTELPRO program of the 1960s and 1970s, it reads just like the plan in my book, although I made it up." See Robert Fleming, "John A. Williams: A Writer beyond 'Isms," *Black Issues Book Review* 4, no. 4 (2002).

61. Quotes and narratives from Nicole Mitchell in this section come from Nicole Mitchell, interview with the author, Chicago, Illinois, September 9, 1999.

62. In 1991, I became the third African American hired at UCSD as full-time, tenure-track music faculty.

63. Before Jimmy Cheatham passed away in 2007, his wife and longtime collaborator, the pianist Jeannie Cheatham, published an autobiography with extensive discussion of their lives on the road and at UCSD. See Jeannie Cheatham, *Meet Me with Your Black Drawers On: My Life in Music* (Austin: University of Texas Press, 2006).

64. Nicole Mitchell, e-mail communication, May 4, 2006.

65. Quotes from Maia in this section come from Maia, interview with the author, Chicago, Illinois, June 25, 1999.

66. For accounts of the early history of the Hubert family, see Georgia Historical

Society, *Camilla and Zack Hubert Homesite* (accessed November 22, 2005]); available from http://www.georgiahistory.com/Markers/Markers04/camillaz.htm. Also see "Member Leola Hubbard and Family Honored with Centennial Heritage Farm Award," *Carson Valley Views,* Available from https://www.carsonvalley.org/newsletters/VIEWSSpring04.pdf, accessed November 20, 2005, Spring 2004.

67. *Muhammad Speaks,* the Nation of Islam's newspaper, was created by the movement's founder, the Honorable Elijah Muhammad.

68. For an account of Cohran's work that references Maia's son, trumpeter Gabriel Hubert, see Peter Margasak, "Brass in the Blood." (*Chicago Reader,* July 25, 2003 [accessed November 22, 2005]); available from http://www.chicagoreader.com/hitsville/030725.html.

69. Quotes from Shanta Nurullah in this section come from Shanta Nurullah, interview with the author, Chicago, Illinois, February 14, 1999.

70. Samana, *Samana* (Storywiz, 1996), compact disc.

71. See Hirsch, *Riot and Remembrance.* Also see R. Halliburton, Jr., *The Tulsa Race War of 1921* (San Francisco: R and E Research Associates, 1975); *Tulsa Race Riot: A Report by the Oklahoma Commission to Study the Tulsa Race Riot of 1921* (accessed November 22, 2005]); available from http://www.tulsareparations.org/TRR.htm.

72. For an account of this particular neighborhood's instantiation of neighborhood change, see Rosen, *The South Side.*

73. See Mayfair Academy, *Tommy Sutton* (accessed November 22, 2005]); available from http://www.mayfairacademy.net/ma/mrsutton.html.

74. Lester Lashley, interview with the author, Chicago, Illinois, 2005.

75. Nurullah's experience, according to historian Patricia Hill Collins, was all too common. Collins writes that "although Black cultural nationalism staunchly opposed racial oppression, it ironically incorporated dominant ideologies about White and Black gender roles into its domain assumptions." The drive to create "nuclear families in which benevolent male authority ruled, with women assuming their proper, natural roles as wives and mothers, reproduced appropriate gender roles for men and women. Within this interpretive framework, strong African American women in black families and in black civil society were labeled deviant." See Collins, *Fighting Words,* 168–69.

76. According to Nicole Mitchell, Elysses joined the AACM in 2007.

CHAPTER 12

1. Charles McWhinnie, "'Light' Henry Huff, Jazz Musician," *Chicago Sun-Times,* April 2, 1993.

2. Lloyd Sachs, "Fred Hopkins, Jazz Bassist, dies," *Chicago Sun-Times,* January 9, 1999.

3. Kate N. Grossman, "Joel Alexander Brandon, 56, Master Whistler, Composer," *Chicago Sun-Times,* July 19, 2003.

4. John Corbett, "Fanfare for a Warrior: Remembering Lester Bowie," *Down Beat,* March 2000. In fact, Ameen Muhammad, who was at the service, told me that Lester had pulled the same trick on him.

5. See Seton Hawkins, "Sathima Bea Benjamin: Jazz, Community, and Gender" (BA thesis, Columbia University, 2005). Also see Sathima Bea Benjamin, *Southern Touch* (Enja ENJ-7015, 1992).

6. Michael Brecker passed away in 2007.

7. Abrams, press release for first AACM event. Part of that atmosphere involved the presence of artists, both AACM members and not, as part of the production team. Joan Logue, video artist extraordinaire, and the experienced on-location engineer Jon Rosenberg supervised the video and audio documentation of the event, as they have for several years. Amina and Peggy took tickets at the door and handled CD and vinyl record sales; Kalaparush, Jarman, and Adegoke served as ushers; Threadgill and I advised Muhal on sound balance; Reggie Nicholson handled the financials.

8. Amiri Baraka, "The Changing Same (R&B and New Black Music)," in Baraka, *Black Music,* 129.

9. Ibid.

10. For recent information on COGIC membership figures, see Allen H. Anderson, *An Introduction to Pentecostalism: Global Charismatic Christianity* (Cambridge: Cambridge University Press, 2004), 52. The account of COGIC's origins comes from Lawrence H. Mamiya and C. Eric Lincoln, *The Black Church in the African-American Experience* (Durham: Duke University Press, 1990).

11. See Cheryl J. Sanders, *African-American Worship in the Pentecostal and Holiness Movements,* available from http:// wesley.nnu.edu/ wesleyan_theology / theojrnl / 31–35 / 32-2-6.htm; accessed March 15, 2007. The Web site summarizes themes in Sanders's more extended book on the subject. See Cheryl J. Sanders, *Saints in Exile: The Holiness-Pentecostal Experience in African American Religion and Culture* (New York: Oxford University Press, 1996).

12. Howard Reich, "Malachi Favors, 76; Bass Player's Style Was Distinctive, Influential," *Chicago Tribune,* February 3, 2004.

13. "Obituary for Vandy Harris," Trinity United Church of Christ, Chicago, Illinois, August 5, 2005.

14. Ibid.

15. See Albert B. Cleage, Jr., *The Black Messiah* (New York: Sheed and Ward, 1968).

16. "Obituary for Vandy Harris."

17. Ibid. See also John Litweiler, "Sax Player, Bandleader Vandy Harris Dies at 63; Thrived in AACM Movement," *Chicago Sun-Times,* July 29, 2005.

18. "Obituary for Ameen Muhammad," Gatling's Chapel, Chicago, Illinois, March 5, 2003 (accessed December 1, 2005); available from http:// www.jazzhope.com / review _2003_03_05.htm. Howard Reich, "Ameen Muhammad, 48 [obituary]," *Chicago Tribune,* March 4, 2003.

19. Evod Magek, *Through Love to Freedom,* vol. 1 (Black Pot Records, 1998), compact disc.

20. "Obituary for Evod Magek," Carter Funeral Chapel, Chicago, Illinois, October 14, 2005.

21. Joseph A. Shelton, Jr., Obituary, Stinson Funeral Home, Detroit, Michigan, December 8, 2006.

AFTERWORD

1. Clifford, "On Ethnographic Authority," 139.

2. Jost, *Jazzmusiker,* 184.

3. Richard Abrams, David N. Baker, and Charles Ellison, "The Social Role of Jazz," in *Reflections on Afro-American Music,* ed. Dominique-René De Lerma (Kent State University Press, 1973), 105.

4. Lily Koppel, "For These Street Players, Brass Runs in the Family," *New York Times,* September 4, 2006.

5. Lawrence W. Levine, "Jazz and American Culture," in *The Jazz Cadence of American Culture,* ed. Robert G. O'Meally (New York: Columbia University Press, 1998), 444.

6. Quoted in Radano, *New Musical Figurations,* 266.

7. Abrams, "The Social Role of Jazz," 106.

8. Giddins, "Inside Free Jazz," 48.

9. For a description of "totalism," see Gann, *American Music in the Twentieth Century.*

10. Cole Gagne, *Soundpieces 2: Interviews with American Composers* (Metuchen, N.J.: Scarecrow Press, 1993), 511.

11. Peter Watrous, "John Zorn Takes Over the Town," *New York Times,* February 24, 1989.

12. John Rockwell, "As Important as Anyone in His Generation," *New York Times,* February 21, 1988.

13. John Rockwell, "Jazz: Two Braxton Programs," *New York Times,* April 23, 1982.

14. Watrous, "John Zorn Takes Over the Town."

15. Larry Nai, "Interview with Greg Osby," *Cadence,* May 2001, 16.

16. Bill Shoemaker, "Avant-Garde," *Jazz Times,* September 2000, 60.

17. Ibid.

18. Ibid., 62, 64. The Beroepsvereniging voor Improviserende Musici (Association of Improvising Musicians) was founded in 1971 by saxophonist Hans Dulfer, pianist Misha Mengelberg, and other Dutch musicians. The London Musicians Collective was founded between 1975 and 1976, but its original members, including Evan Parker, Derek Bailey, Paul Lytton, John Stevens, Tony Oxley, Howard Riley, Paul Rutherford, Barry Guy and Trevor Watts, felt themselves to constitute a collective entity as early as 1971. For a succinct history of the LMC, see Clive Bell, *A Brief History of the LMC* (1999 [accessed December 10, 2005]); available from http://www.l-m-c.org.uk/archive/history.html.

19. *European Free Improvisation Pages* (accessed December 10, 2005); available from http://www.shef.ac.uk/misc/rec/ps/efi/index.html.

20. Attali, *Noise,* 140.

21. Lewis, *Gittin' to Know Y'all.*

22. Craft, "Towards a New Consciousness," 8.

23. Ibid.

24. Shoemaker, "Avant-Garde," 60. Since Shoemaker's writing, the work of Japanese "noise" artists such as Toshimaru Nakamura and Sachiko M has become internationally influential.

25. Ibid.

26. Michael Hardt and Antonio Negri, "What the Protesters in Genoa Want," *New York Times,* July 20, 2001.

27. Jost, *Jazzmusiker,* 194.

bibliography

8 Bold Souls. *8 Bold Souls*. Sessoms, 1987.

———. *Ant Farm*. Arabesque Recordings, 1994. Compact disc.

———. *Last Option*. Thrill Jockey Records 071, 1999. Compact disc.

"35th Annual *Down Beat* Readers Poll." *Down Beat,* December 24, 1970, 15–19.

"$407,276 in Grants to Go to Composers." *New York Times,* February 11, 1974, 75.

Association for the Advancement of Creative Musicians. "AACM Board of Directors & Respective Job Descriptions." Archives of Evod Magek, 1987.

———. AACM Board Meeting, May 20, Chicago, Illinois. Audiotape. Collection of Muhal Richard Abrams, 1965.

———. AACM Conference, August . Exact date unknown. Audiotape. Collection of Joseph Jarman, 1977.

———. AACM Executive Board Meeting, May 27, Chicago, Illinois. Audiotape. Collection of Muhal Richard Abrams, 1965.

———. AACM General Body Meeting, May 8, Chicago, Illinois. Audiotape. Collection of Muhal Richard Abrams, 1965.

———. AACM General Body Meeting, May 15, Chicago, Illinois. Audiotape. Collection of Muhal Richard Abrams, 1965.

———. AACM General Body Meeting, May 29, Chicago, Illinois. Audiotape. Collection of Muhal Richard Abrams, 1965.

———. AACM General Body Meeting, October 2, Chicago, Illinois. Audiotape. Collection of Muhal Richard Abrams, 1965.

———. "AACM internal memo, History of Jazz Programming, 1982–1983." Archives of Evod Magek, 1983.

———. "AACM Performance Evaluation Sheet." Archives of Evod Magek, 1983[?].

———. "AACM Technical Assistance Project." Archives of Evod Magek, July 21–24, 1980.

———. AACM Tenth Anniversary Program Book. Collection of George E. Lewis, 1975.

———. Advertising Poster for concert, "A Salute to FMP (Free Music Productions)." Archives of the AACM, 1995.

———. First AACM Board Meeting, Thursday, May 20, 740 E. 75th St., Chicago, Illinois. Audiotape. Collection of Muhal Richard Abrams, 1965.

———. "Minutes, AACM Board of Directors Meeting." Archives of Evod Magek, April 30, 1986.

———. "New York Chapter Roster." Archives of the AACM. January 1, 1981.

———. Program. Twenty-fifth Anniversary Festival. 1990.

———. Program booklet, AACM 16th Anniversary Festival. Archives of Evod Magek, December 1981.

Abdul, Raoul. *Blacks in Classical Music: A Personal History.* New York: Dodd, Mead, 1977.

Abrams, Muhal Richard. *1-OQA+19.* Black Saint 120017-2, 1978. Compact disc.

———. *The Dream.* Audiotape. Collection of Muhal Richard Abrams, 1968.

———. *Levels and Degrees of Light.* Delmark DS-413, 1967. Vinyl disc. Delmark DD-413, 1967. Compact disc.

———. *Lifea Blinec.* Arista Novus AN3000, 1978. Vinyl disc.

———. *One Line, Two Views.* New World Records 80469-2, 1995. Compact disc.

———. Program. Concert by the Richard Abrams Septet, Northwestern University, May 24, 1967. Jamil B. Figi Donation, Chicago Jazz Archive, Joseph Regenstein Library, University of Chicago, 1967.

———. *Spihumonesty.* Black Saint 120032, 1980. Compact disc.

———. *Things to Come from Those Now Gone.* Delmark DE-430, 1972. Compact disc.

———. *The UMO Jazz Orchestra Plays the Music of Muhal Richard Abrams.* Slam CD 506, 1999. Compact disc.

———. *The Visibility of Thought.* Mutable Music MM17502-2, 2001. Compact disc.

Abrams, Richard, and Ken Chaney. "Press Release for first AACM event." Archives of the AACM, Chicago, Illinois, 1965.

Abrams, Muhal Richard, and Amina Claudine Myers. *Duet.* Black Saint 120051, 1993. Compact disc.

Abrams, Muhal Richard, and John Shenoy Jackson. "Association for the Advancement of Creative Musicians." *Black World,* November 1973, 72–74.

Abrams, Muhal Richard, George Lewis, and Roscoe Mitchell. *Streaming.* PI Recordings PI 22, 2006. Compact disc.

Abrams, Richard, David N. Baker, and Charles Ellison. "The Social Role of Jazz." In *Reflections on Afro-American Music,* ed. Dominique-René De Lerma, 101–10. Kent State University Press, 1973.

Abu Bakr, Rashidah Ismaeli. "Slightly Autobiographical: The 1960s on the Lower East Side." *African American Review* 27, no. 4 (1993): 585–92.

"Ad Lib: Chicago." *Down Beat,* January 7, 1971, 40.

"Ad Lib: Chicago Announcement, performance by the Pharaohs." *Down Beat,* March 2, 1972, 36.

"Ad Lib: Chicago [Experimental Band announcement]." *Down Beat,* May 9, 1963, 45.

"Ad Lib: Chicago [Report on the Richard Abrams Trio]." *Down Beat,* July 21, 1960, 71.

"Ad Lib: Chicago. Announcement of performance by Eddie Harris and Richard Abrams." *Down Beat,* June 8, 1972, 43.

"Ad Lib: Chicago. Announcement, performance by the Gallery Ensemble." *Down Beat,* March 2, 1972, 36.

"Ad Lib: New York. Announcement of Performance by the Revolutionary Ensemble." *Down Beat,* March 30, 1972, 36.

Adorno, Theodor. "Perennial Fashion—Jazz." In *Prisms,* translated by Samuel Weber and Sherry Weber, 119–32. Cambridge: MIT Press, [1953] 1981.

Advertisement for New Music America Festival. *EAR,* February-March 1981, 29.

The African Hebrew Israelites of Jerusalem: A Village of Peace. [Accessed December 1, 2005.] Available from http://www.kingdomofyah.com/ourstory.htm.

Air. *Air Lore.* Arista Novus AN3014, 1980. Vinyl disc.

———. *Air Raid.* Trio Records PA-7156, 1979. Compact disc.

———. *Air Song.* Trio PA-7120, 1975. Compact disc.

———. *Air Time.* Nessa N-12, 1978. Vinyl disc.

———. *Air Time.* Nessa NCD-12, 1996. Compact disc.

Albin, Scott. "Caught in the Act: Art Ensemble of Chicago." *Down Beat,* December 4, 1975, 34.

———. Review of Anthony Braxton Quartet and Tashi. *Down Beat,* March 25, 1976, 41, 48.

Ammi, Ben. *God, the Black Man, and Truth.* Chicago: Communicators Press, 1982.

Anderson, Allen H. *An Introduction to Pentecostalism: Global Charismatic Christianity.* Cambridge: Cambridge University Press, 2004.

Anderson, Fred. *Another Place.* Moers Music 01058, 1978. Vinyl disc.

———. *Fred Anderson Quartet Live at the Velvet Lounge.* Vol. 2. Asian Improv AIR 0054, 2000. Compact disc.

———. *Live at the Velvet Lounge.* OkkaDisk OD12023, 1998. Compact disc.

———. *Timeless: Live at the Velvet Lounge.* Delmark DVD 1568, 2006. DVD-Video disc.

Anderson, Fred, Marilyn Crispell, and Hamid Drake. *Destiny* OkkaDisk OD12003, 1994. Compact disc.

Andryco, Cheryl. "Fontella Bass: Coming Full Circle." MA Thesis, Michigan State University, 1996.

Art Ensemble of Chicago. *A.A.C.M. Great Black Music/Message to Our Folks.* Spot 549, [1969] 2004. Compact disc.

———. *The Art Ensemble: 1967/68.* Nessa NCD-2500 A/B/C, 1993. Three compact discs.

———. *The Art Ensemble of Chicago in Concert.* EFOR Films 2869005, [1981] 2004. DVD-Video disc.

———. *Art Ensemble of Soweto.* DIW 52954, 1992. Compact disc.

———. *Chi-Congo.* Varese Sarabande (USA) VSD 3020615282, [1970] 2005.

———. *Coming Home Jamaica.* Atlantic/WEA, 1998. Compact disc.

———. *A Jackson in Your House.* Affinity AFF 752, [1969] 1989. Compact disc.

———. *Les stances a Sophie.* Emi Pathe CO62 11365, 1970. Compact disc.

————. *Live at Mandel Hall.* Delmark DE-432, 1972. Compact disc.

————. *Live in Paris.* Fuel 2000 302 061 383 2, [1969] 2004. Compact disc.

————. *People in Sorrow.* Nessa N-3, 1969. Vinyl disc.

————. Program, Concert of the Art Ensemble of Chicago, Association-Maison de la Culture d'Angers, France. Larayne Black Collection, Chicago Historical Society, 1970.

————. Program notes, Concerts of the Art Ensemble of Chicago in Lille and Arras, France. Unpaged, Larayne Black Collection, Chicago Historical Society, November 3–4, 1969.

————. *Swim: A Musical Adventure.* Kultur Video D4009, 2005. DVD-Video disc.

Artistic Heritage Ensemble. Concert program. Jamil B. Figi Donation, Chicago Jazz Archive, University of Chicago, August 25, 1965.

Arvey, Verna. *In One Lifetime.* Fayetteville: University of Arkansas Press, 1984.

Attali, Jacques, translated by Brian Massumi. *Noise: The Political Economy of Music.* Minneapolis: University of Minnesota Press, 1989.

The Awakening. *Hear, Sense, and Feel.* Black Jazz BJQD-9, 1972.

Backus, Rob. *Fire Music: A Political History of Jazz.* Chicago: Vanguard Books, 1976.

Badger, Reid. *A Life in Ragtime: A Biography of James Reese Europe.* New York: Oxford University Press, 1995.

Badini, Gérard, Georges Locatelli, Jacques Thollot, and René Thomas. "Les musiciens ont la parole." *Jazz Hot* 259, March 1970, 12–14.

Bailey, Derek. *Improvisation: Its Nature and Practice in Music.* Ashbourne: Moorland Publishing, 1980.

Baker, Paul. "Roscoe Mitchell: The Next Step." *Coda* 228, October /November 1989, 18–21.

Balliett, Whitney. "Jazz: New York Notes." *New Yorker,* June 20, 1977, 92–97.

Banes, Sally. *Democracy's Body: Judson Dance Theater, 1962–1964.* Durham: Duke University Press, 1993.

————. *Greenwich Village 1963: Avant-Garde Performance and the Effervescent Body.* Durham: Duke University Press, 1993.

Banfield, William C. *Musical Landscapes in Color: Conversations with Black American Composers.* Lanham, MD: Scarecrow Press, 2003.

Baraka, Amiri [Leroi Jones]. *The Autobiography of Leroi Jones.* Chicago: Lawrence Hill Books, 1984.

————. *Black Music.* New York: William Morrow and Company, 1968.

————. *Blues People: The Negro Experience in White America and the Music That Developed from It.* New York: Morrow Quill Paperbacks, 1963.

————. "Jazz and the White Critic." In *The Jazz Cadence of American Culture,* ed. Robert G. O'Meally, 137–42. New York: Columbia University Press, 1998.

Baraka, Amiri, and Amina Baraka. *The Music: Reflections on Jazz and Blues.* New York: William Morrow, 1987.

Barclay, Dolores, Todd Lewan, and Allan G. Breed. "Prosperity Made Blacks a Target for Land Grabs; History: Specter of lynching boosted impact of lesser threats." *Los Angeles Times,* December 9, 2001, A1.

Barg, Lisa. "Black Voices/White Sounds: Race and Representation in Virgil Thomson's Four Saints in Three Acts." *American Music* 18, no. 2 (Summer 2000): 121–61.

Barker, Thurman. *Strike Force: The Thurman Barker Percussion Quintet.* Uptee Productions, 2004. Compact disc.

Baugher, Carl E. *Turning Corners: The Life and Music of Leroy Jenkins.* Redwood, N.Y.: Cadence Jazz Books, 2000.

Beal, Amy C. *New Music, New Allies: American Experimental Music in West Germany from the Zero Hour to Reunification.* Berkeley: University of California Press, 2006.

Beauchamp, Lincoln T., Jr., ed. *Art Ensemble of Chicago: Great Black Music; Ancient to the Future.* Chicago: Art Ensemble of Chicago, 1998.

Bechet, Sidney. *An Introduction to Sidney Bechet: His Best Recordings.* Best of Jazz 4017, 1994. Compact disc.

Becker, Howard S. *Art Worlds.* Berkeley: University of California Press, 1982.

———. *Outsiders: Studies in the Sociology of Deviance.* New York: Free Press, [1963] 1973.

Belgrad, Daniel. *The Culture of Spontaneity: Improvisation and the Arts in Postwar America.* Chicago: University of Chicago Press, 1998.

Bell, Clive. *A Brief History of the LMC.* 1999. [Accessed December 10, 2005.] Available from http://www.l-m-c.org.uk/archive/history.html.

Benjamin, Sathima Bea. *Southern Touch.* Enja ENJ-7015, 1992.

Berendt, Joachim-Ernst. "Albert Mangelsdorff: Big Noise from Frankfurt." Translated by Barbara and Helmut Bredigkeit. *Down Beat*, February 10, 1977, 34–35.

———. "Caught! Ninth Moers International New Jazz Festival." Translated by Reni and Joe Weisel. *Down Beat*, September 1980, 54, 57–58.

———. *Ein Fenster aus Jazz: Essays, Portraits, Reflexionen.* Frankfurt am Main: S. Fischer Verlag, 1977.

———. "Jazz in Donaueschingen 1954–1994: Versuch eines Rückblicks." In *Spiegel der Neuen Musik: Donaueschingen, Chronik—Tendenzen—Werkbesprechungen, mit Essays von Joachim-Ernst Berendt und Hermann Naber*, ed. Josef Häusler, 408–16. Kassel: Bärenreiter-Verlag, 1996.

Berg, Chuck. "Newport '76." *Down Beat*, February 12, 1976, 25–26, 40, 42.

———. Review of recording by the Creative Construction Company. *Down Beat*, May 20, 1976, 29.

Berliner, Paul. *Thinking in Jazz: The Infinite Art of Improvisation.* Chicago: University of Chicago Press, 1994.

Bernard, Marc. "Richard Abrams et l'A.A.C.M." *Jazz* 209, March 1973, 20–21.

Berry, Jason. "Declamations on Great Black Music." *Lenox Avenue: A Journal of Interartistic Inquiry* 3 (1997): 41–54.

Bisceglia, Jacques. Biography. 2004. [Accessed July 3, 2006.] Available from http://www.positifs.org/jazz-passion/4-dequelqueslivres/Bio_Bisceglia.htm. In French.

Black Artists Group. *A Black Theater for St. Louis: A Building Proposal for the Black Artists' Group.* St. Louis: Black Artists Group, 1970.

Black, Edwin. "For the Record: Charles Stepney." *Down Beat*, November 26, 1970, 12, 32.

Bley, Carla. *Escalator over the Hill: A Chronotransduction.* JCOA Records JCOA/EOTH 839 310-2, 1971. Compact disc.

Bley, Paul, with David Lee. *Stopping Time: Paul Bley and the Transformation of Jazz.* Montreal: Vehicule Press, 1999.

Bloom, Harold. *The Anxiety of Influence: A Theory of Poetry.* New York: Oxford University Press, 1973.

Bolelli, Franco. *Musica creativa: Forme espressioni e problematiche del "nuovo jazz."* Milan: Squilibri Edizioni, 1978.

Bontemps, Arna, and Jack Conroy. *Anyplace but Here.* New York: Hill and Wang, 1966.

Bouchard, Fred. "Arista's Steve Backer Maneuvers in the Front Line." *Down Beat,* March 1980, 31–32, 65.

Bourget, Jean-Loup. "Delmark Story." *Jazz* 261, January 1978, 38–39.

———. "Muhal Richard Abrams: Entretien avec l'un des principaux inventeurs des nouveaux sons venus de Chicago." *Jazz,* July -August 1977, 22–25.

———. "Muhal Richard Abrams: Vers la musique." *Jazz,* July -August 1977, 22–25, 42.

———. "Nessa Story." *Jazz* 264, May 1978, 30–31, 46.

Bourne, Mike. Review of Pharaohs LP, *Awakening. Down Beat,* August 17, 1972, 23–24.

Bowie, Lester. *Avant Pop.* ECM 13326, 1986. Compact disc.

———. *Gittin' to Know Y'all.* MPS 15269,15038, 1970. Vinyl disc.

———. *Numbers 1&2.* Nessa N-1, 1967. Compact disc.

———. "A Word from the Desk." *New Regime* 1, no. 1 (1968): 5–6.

Boyd, Herb. "The Man and the Plan: Conspiracy Theories and Paranoia in Our Culture." *Black Issues Book Review* 4, no. 2 (2002): 39–40.

Bracey, John H., Jr., August Meier, and Elliott Rudwick, eds. "Northwestern University Black Students: If Our Demands Are Impossible, Then Peace between Us Is Impossible Too." In *Black Nationalism in America.* Indianapolis and New York: Bobbs-Merrill, 1970.

Braxton, Anthony. "24–70°." *New Regime* 1, no. 1 (1968): 38–39.

———. *Composition no. 247.* Leo Records LR 306, 2001. Compact disc.

———. *Creative Orchestra Music 1976.* Arista AL4080, 1976. Vinyl disc.

———. *For Alto.* Delmark DE-420, 1969. Compact disc.

———. *For Four Orchestras.* Arista A3L 8900, 1978. Three vinyl discs.

———. *For Trio.* Arista AB 4181, 1978. Vinyl disc.

———. *The Montreux/Berlin Concerts.* Arista AL 5002, 1976. 2 vinyl discs.

———. *New York, Fall 1974.* Arista AL 4032, 1975. Vinyl disc.

———. *This Time.* BYG-Actuel 529 347, 1970. Vinyl disc.

———. *Three Compositions of New Jazz.* Delmark DD-415, 1968. Compact disc.

———. *Town Hall (Trio & Quintet) 1972.* hatART 6119, 1972. Compact disc.

———. *Tri-Axium Writings.* Vols. 1–3. Dartmouth: Synthesis/Frog Peak, 1985.

———. *Trillium R, Composition no. 162 (Opera in Four Acts): Shala Fears for the Poor.* Braxton House BH-008, 1999. Four compact discs.

———. *Trio and Duet.* Sackville 3007, 1974. Vinyl disc.

Braxton, Anthony, and George Lewis. *Elements of Surprise.* Moers Music 01036, 1977. Vinyl disc.

"Biography of William Brimfield." (No author.) Collection of Muhal Richard Abrams, dated April 15, 1975.

Broecking, Christian. "Adorno versus Berendt Revisited: Was bleibt von der Kontroverse im Merkur 1953?" In *Jazz und Gesellschaft: Sozialgeschichtliche Aspekte des Jazz*, ed. Wolfram Knauer, 41–53. Hofheim: Wolke Verlag, 2002.

———. *Der Marsalis-Faktor: Gespräche über afroamerikanische Kultur in der neunziger Jahre.* Waakirchen-Schaftlach (Switzerland): Oreos Verlag, 1995.

Brooks, Iris. *New Music America History: A Caterpillar or a Butterfly?*. Valencia and Santa Monica: California Institute of the Arts/High Performance Books, 1992.

Brown, Ari. *Venus*. Delmark DE-504, 1998. Compact disc.

Broyles, Michael. *Mavericks and Other Traditions in American Music*. New Haven: Yale University Press, 2004.

Budds, Michael J. *Jazz in the Sixties: The Expansion of Musical Resources and Techniques: An Expanded Edition*. Iowa City: University of Iowa Press, 1990.

Burgett, Paul. "Vindication as a Thematic Principle in the Writings of Alain Locke on the Music of Black Americans." In *Black Music in the Harlem Renaissance: A Collection of Essays*, ed. Samuel A. Floyd, Jr., 29–40. Knoxville: University of Tennessee Press, 1990.

Burns, Ken. *Jazz: A History of America's Music*, episode 10. DVD-Video, PBS Paramount, [2000] 2004.

Burton, Art T. *Black, Buckskin, and Blue: African-American Scouts and Soldiers on the Western Frontier*. Austin: Eakin Press, 1999.

———. *Black, Red, and Deadly: Black and Indian Gunfighters of the Indian Territories, 1870–1907*. Austin: Eakin Press, 1991.

Cage, John. *Silence*. Middletown: Wesleyan University Press, 1961.

Cameron, Catherine M. *Dialectics in the Arts: The Rise of Experimentalism in American Music*. Westport, Conn.: Praeger, 1996.

———. "Fighting with Words: American Composers' Commentary on Their Work." *Comparative Studies in Society and History* 27, no. 3 (1985): 430–60.

Campbell, Robert L., Robert Pruter, and Armin Büttner. *The King Fleming Discography*. [Accessed November 25, 2005.] Available from http://hubcap.clemson.edu/~campber/fleming.html.

Carles, Philippe. "Joseph Jarman." *Jazz* 215, September 1973, 38–39.

———. "La terre promise selon Abrams." *Jazz* 212, June 1973, 10–12.

———. "Les nouvelles têtes de la nouvelle musique." *Jazz* 171, October 1969, 22–25.

Carles, Philippe, Andre Clergeat, and Jean-Louis Comolli, eds. *Dictionnaire du jazz, nouvelle édition augmentée*. Paris: Robert Laffont, 1994.

Carles, Philippe, and Jean-Louis Comolli. *Free Jazz/Black Power*. Paris: Gallimard, [1971] 2000.

Carles, Philippe, and Francis Marmande. "Montreux." *Jazz* 225, September 1974, 4–12.

Carles, Philippe, Francis Marmande, and Daniel Soutif. "Ensemble sur l'art de Chicago." *Jazz*, April 1974, 20–24.

Carles, Philippe, and Daniel Soutif. "Chicago." *Jazz* 212, June 1973, 8.

Carmichael, Stokely, and Charles V. Hamilton. *Black Power: The Politics of Liberation in America*. New York: Vintage Books, 1967.

Carrington, George. *Displaced Persons: DP Camps in Germany.* [Accessed September 24, 2006.] Available from http://www.dpcamps.org/dpcampsGermanyF.html.

Carroll, Baikida E. J. *Orange Fish Tears.* Palm, 1975. Vinyl disc.

Carter, Jimmy. Interview. *Playboy,* November 1976.

"Caucus Results." Archives of the AACM, 1977 (date unknown).

Caux, Daniel. "A.A.C.M. Chicago." *Jazz Hot* 254, October 1969, 16–19.

———. "Le délire et la rigueur de l'Art Ensemble de Chicago." *Jazz Hot* 252, July -August 1969, 8.

———. "L'été au Lucernaire." *Jazz Hot* 253, September 1969, 15.

Cerchiari, Luca. "A quattri'occhi con George Lewis." *Musica Jazz* 34, nos. 8–9, August -September 1978, 17–18.

Césaire, Aimé. *Cahier d'un retour au pays natal.* Paris: Présence Africaine, 1971.

———. *Cahier d'un retour au pays natal.* 2nd ed. Edited by Abiola Irele. Columbus: Ohio State University Press, 2000.

———. *Notebook of a Return to the Native Land.* Translated and edited by Clayton Eshleman and Annette Smith. Middletown, Conn.: Wesleyan University Press, 2001.

Charry, Eric. "Freedom and Form in Ornette Coleman's Early Atlantic Recordings." *Annual Review of Jazz Studies* 9 (1997–1998): 261–94.

Chase, Allan. *Sun Ra and the AACM.* 1992. [Accessed November 23, 2005.] Available from http://www.dpo.uab.edu/~moudry/articles/ra&aacm.htm.

Chatham, Rhys. "5 Generations of Composers at the Kitchen." In *The Kitchen Turns Twenty: A Retrospective Anthology,* ed. Lee Morrissey, 7–22. New York: Kitchen Center, 1992.

Cheatham, Jeannie. *Meet Me with Your Black Drawers On: My Life in Music.* Austin: University of Texas Press, 2006.

Chevigny, Paul. *Gigs: Jazz and the Cabaret Laws in New York City.* London and New York: Routledge, 2005.

"Chicago Exodus: AACM Members Off to Paris." *Down Beat,* June 26, 1969, 14.

Christian, Jodie. *Soul Fountain.* Delmark DE-498, 1997. Compact disc.

Circle. *Paris-Concert.* ECM 1018, 1971. Compact disc.

Citron, Marcia J. *Gender and the Musical Canon.* Cambridge: Cambridge University Press, 1993.

City Scene: Chicago. "Announcement of Event by Fred Anderson, Chico Freeman, and George Lewis." *Down Beat,* October 10, 1974, 45.

———. "Announcement of Event at NAME Gallery, Chicago." *Down Beat* (1974): 38.

———. "Announcement of Event by Muhal Richard Abrams." *Down Beat,* April 25, 1974, 45.

Clague, Mark, and J. Kimo Williams. *Encyclopedia of Chicago,* s.v. "Classical Music," 2005. [Accessed November 20, 2005.] Available from http://www.encyclopedia .chicagohistory.org/pages/295.html.

Cleage, Albert B., Jr. *The Black Messiah.* New York: Sheed and Ward, 1968.

Clifford, James. "On Ethnographic Authority." *Representations* 2 (1983): 118–46.

Cochran Jr., Charles W. Obituary. Greater Union Baptist Church, Chicago, Illinois, September 1978.

Cohen, Noal, and Michael Fitzgerald. *Rat Race Blues: The Musical Life of Gigi Gryce.* Berkeley: Berkeley Hills Books, 2002.

Cohodas, Nadine. *Spinning Blues into Gold: The Chess Brothers and the Legendary Chess Records.* New York: St. Martin's Press, 2001.

Cohran, Philip, and the Artistic Heritage Ensemble. *On The Beach.* Chicago: Zulu Records, 1967. Vinyl disc.

Collins, Patricia Hill. *Fighting Words: Black Women and the Search for Justice.* Minneapolis: University of Minnesota Press, 1998.

Colson, Steve and Iqua. *Hope for Love.* Silver Sphinx, 2003. Compact disc.

Colson Unity Troupe. *No Reservation.* Black Saint 120043, 1980. Vinyl disc.

———. *Triumph!* Silver Sphinx, 1978. Vinyl disc.

Coltrane, John. *A Love Supreme: Deluxe Edition.* Impulse 314 589 945-2, [1964] 2002. Two compact discs.

———. *The Olatunji Concert: The Last Live Recording.* Impulse 314 589 120-2, [1967] 2001. Compact disc.

Company. *Fables.* Incus 36, 1980.

Conroy, Frank. "Stop Nitpicking a Genius." *New York Times Magazine,* June 25, 1995, 28–31, 48, 54, 70.

Cooke, Jack. Review of Lester Bowie recording, *Numbers 1&2. Jazz Monthly* 162, August 1968, 24.

———. Review of Richard Abrams recording, *Levels and Degrees of Light*; and Joseph Jarman recording, *Song For. Jazz Monthly* 166, December 1968, 11–12.

Coppens, George. "Lester Bowie." *Coda* 164–65, 1979, 12–15.

Corbett, John. "Experimental Oriental." In *Western Music and Its Others: Difference, Representation, and Appropriation in Music,* ed. Georgina Born and David Hesmondhalgh, 163–86. Berkeley: University of California Press, 2000.

———. "Fanfare for a Warrior: Remembering Lester Bowie." *Down Beat,* March 2000, 22–27.

———. Liner notes, Sun Ra recording, *Angels and Demons at Play/The Nubians of Plutonia.* Evidence ECD-22066-2, 1993.

Coss, Bill. "Cecil Taylor's Struggle for Existence." *Down Beat,* October 26, 1961, 19–21.

Cowell, Henry. Concert program, Town Hall, New York City, 1931. Henry Cowell Collection, Box 54, New York Public Library.

———. "Letter from Henry Cowell to Charles Ives." Undated. Henry Cowell Collection, Box 17, Folder 516, New York Public Library.

———. *New Musical Resources.* Cambridge and New York: Cambridge University Press, [1930] 1996.

———, ed. *American Composers on American Music: A Symposium.* New York: Frederic Ungar Publishing, 1933.

Craft, Morgan. "Towards a New Consciousness." *Wire* 260, October 2005, 8.

Creative Construction Company. *Creative Construction Company,* vol. 1, Muse Records MR 5071, 1975. Vinyl disc.

———. *Creative Construction Company.* Vol. 2. Muse Records MR 5097, 1976. Vinyl disc.

"Creative Musicians Present Artistic Heritage Ensemble." *Chicago Defender,* August 11–17, 1965, n.p.

"Creative Musicians Sponsor Artists Concert Showcase." *Chicago Defender,* August 7, 1965, n.p.

Cromwell, Arthur C. "Jazz Mecca: An Ethnographic Study of Chicago's South Side Jazz Community." PhD dissertation, Ohio University, 1998.

Crouch, Stanley. "Bringing Atlantis Up to the Top." *Village Voice,* April 16, 1979, 65–67.

———. "Jazz at the Crossroads: Startling, Organized, Earworthy." *Down Beat,* June 1980, 15.

———. "New York Jazz Notes." *Players,* July 1977, 5–7.

Cruz, Jon. *Culture on the Margins: The Black Diaspora and the Rise of American Cultural Interpretation.* Princeton: Princeton University Press, 1999.

Dahlhaus, Carl. "Was heisst improvisation?" In *Improvisation und neue Musik: Acht Kongressreferate,* ed. Reinhold Brinkmann, 9–23. Mainz: Schott, 1979.

Dance, Stanley. Review of Krin Gabbard, *Representing Jazz* and *Jazz among the Discourses. Jazz Times,* November 1995, 75.

"Das bietet Baden-Baden im Winter: Das Free Jazz Treffen des SWF." *Jazz Podium* 19, no. 2, February 1970, 56.

Dauner, Wolfgang. "Mit Jazz in Südamerika: Eindrücke und Erlebnisse von der vom Goethe-Institut durchgeführten Tournee der deutschen All Star Band." *Jazz Podium,* December 1968, 383–85.

———. "Mit Jazz in Südamerika (Fortsetzung von Heft 12/68)." *Jazz Podium* 1969, 16–17.

Davis, Charles T., and Henry Louis Gates, Jr. *The Slave's Narrative.* Oxford and New York: Oxford University Press, 1985.

Davis, Miles. *Bitches Brew.* Sony 65744, 1970. Two compact discs.

Dawkins, Ernest, and the New Horizons Ensemble. *30 Years of Great Black Music: Chicago Now.* Vol. 1. Silkheart SHCD140, 1995. Compact disc.

———. *30 Years of Great Black Music: Chicago Now.* Vol. 2. Silkheart SHCD141, 1997. Compact disc.

———. *After the Dawn Has Risen: Live at Leverkusener Jazztage.* Open Minds/Sound Aspects, 1992. Compact disc.

———. *Cape Town Shuffle: Live at Hothouse.* Delmark DG-545, 2003. Compact disc.

———. *Jo'Burg Jump.* Delmark DE-524, 2000. Compact disc.

De Lerma, Dominique-Rene, ed. "The Impact of the AACM in the Twentieth Century: A Panel Discussion." Transcript. Center for Black Music Research, Chicago, Illinois 1990.

Dean, Roger. *New Structures in Jazz and Improvised Music since 1960.* Milton Keynes and Philadelphia: Open University Press, 1992.

DeJong, Jim. "After Hours Addendum." *Down Beat,* December 1981, 13.

DeJong, Nanette T. "Chosen Identities and Musical Symbols: The Curaçaoan Jazz Community and the Association for the Advancement of Creative Musicians." PhD dissertation, University of Michigan, 1997.

Delany, Sarah Louise, and A. Elizabeth Delany, with Amy Hill Hearth. *Having Our Say: The Delany Sisters' First 100 Years.* New York: Kodansha International, 1993.

Delcloo, Claude. "Letter to the AACM." In *New Regime* 1, no. 1, dated December 16, 1968, unpaged. Chicago: Association for the Advancement of Creative Musicians, 1968.

DeMicheal, Don. "Ira Sullivan: Legend in the Making." *Down Beat*, September 15, 1960, 18–19.

———. "John Coltrane and Eric Dolphy Answer the Jazz Critics." *Down Beat*, April 12, 1962, 20–23.

———. Review of Ornette Coleman recording, *This Is Our Music*, *Down Beat*, May 11, 1961, 25.

DeMuth, Jerry. "AACM Bands in Europe Make Fests, LPs, Clubs." *Down Beat*, September 1979, 14.

———. "Caught in the Act: The Ann Arbor Blues and Jazz Festival." *Down Beat*, November 9, 1972, 30–33.

———. "Chicago Jazz Kicks Open Coffin and Goes 'Creative.'" *Chicago Sun-Times*, October 1967.

Dery, Mark. *Flame Wars: The Discourse of Cyberculture.* Durham: Duke University Press, 1995.

DeVeaux, Scott. *The Birth of Bebop: A Social and Musical History.* Berkeley: University of California Press, 1997.

———. "Constructing the Jazz Tradition." In *The Jazz Cadence of American Culture,* ed. Robert G. O'Meally, 483–512. New York: Columbia University Press, 1998.

———. "The Emergence of the Jazz Concert, 1935–1945." *American Music* 7, no. 1 (1989): 6–29.

———. *Jazz in America: Who's Listening?* Carson, Calif.: Seven Locks Press, 1995.

DiMaggio, Paul J. "Support for the Arts from Independent Foundations." In *Nonprofit Enterprise in the Arts,* ed. Paul DiMaggio, 113–39. New York: Oxford University Press, 1986.

DiMaggio, Paul, and Francie Ostrower. "Participation in the Arts by Black and White Americans." *Social Forces* 68, no. 3 (1990): 753–78.

Dold, R. Bruce. "School for Kids of Note: Musicians Create an Academy in Inner City." *Chicago Tribune,* March 25, 1983, sec. 5, 1, 14.

Donaldson, Jeff. "The Rise, Fall, and Legacy of the Wall of Respect Movement." *International Review of African American Art* 15, no. 1 (1998): 22–26.

"*Down Beat* Critics Poll." *Down Beat*, August 24, 1967, 15–18.

"*Down Beat* Critics Poll." *Down Beat*, August 20, 1970, 18–20.

"*Down Beat* News: Ellington Fellowship Program Set for Yale." *Down Beat*, October 12, 1972, 10.

"*Down Beat* News: McCall Waxes Two New Discs; Reports Sextet a Hit in Berlin." *Down Beat,* January 31, 1974, 8.

"*Down Beat* News: New York Musicians Stage Own Festival." *Down Beat*, September 14, 1972, 9.

Drake, Hamid, and Peter Brötzmann. *The Dried Rat-Dog.* Okka Disk OD 120004, 1994. Compact disc.

Drake, St. Clair, and Horace R. Cayton. *Black Metropolis: A Study of Negro Life in a Northern City.* Chicago: University of Chicago Press, [1945] 1970.

Dumetz, Gabriel. "Brigitte et l'Art Ensemble." *Jazz* 177, April 1970, 13.

Dutilh, Alex. Editorial. *Jazz Hot,* December 1978–January 1979, 11.

———. "Ils ont débarqué." *Jazz Hot* 339–340, Summer 1977, 16–18.

———. "L'AACM ou L'ardeur collective." *Jazz Hot,* December 1978–January 1979, 12–16.

Ellison, Ralph. "The Golden Age, Time Past." In *The Jazz Cadence of American Culture,* ed. Robert G. O'Meally, 448–56. New York: Columbia University Press, 1998.

———. "On Bird, Bird-Watching, and Jazz." In *Living with Music: Ralph Ellison's Jazz Writings,* ed. Robert G. O'Meally, 65–76. New York: Modern Library, [1962] 2001.

Ellsworth, Scott. *Death in a Promised Land: The Tulsa Race Riot of 1921.* Foreword by John Hope Franklin. Baton Rouge: Louisiana State University Press, 1982.

"Employment Agreement for Administrator." Archives of Evod Magek, April 1981.

Endress, Gudrun. "AACM: Die dritte Generation des Free Jazz." *Jazz Podium* 19, no. 3, March 1970, 96–99.

———. *Jazz Podium: Musiker über sich selbst.* Stuttgart: Deutsche Verlags-Anstalt, 1980.

Equal Interest. *Equal Interest.* OmniTone 12001, 1999. Compact disc.

Ethnic Heritage Ensemble. *Ka-Real.* Silkheart SHCD150, 2000. Compact disc.

———. *Three Gentlemen from Chicago.* Moers Music 1076, 1981.

European Free Improvisation Pages. [Accessed December 10, 2005.] Available from http://www.shef.ac.uk/misc/rec/ps/efi/index.html.

"Events/Comments: Is New Music Being Used for Political or Social Ends?" *Source: Music of the Avant Garde 3,* no. 2(6) (1969): 7–9, 90–91.

Ewart, Douglas. *Bamboo Meditations at Banff.* Aarawak 003, 1994. Compact disc.

———. Dismissal letter from AACM Chair to Consultant. November 27, 1982.

———. Letter to AACM from Yokohama, Japan. 1987.

———. *Red Hills.* Aarawak 001, 1983. Audiocassette.

———. *Songs of Sunlife: Inside The Didjeridu.* Innova 594, 2003. Compact disc.

Ewart, Douglas, and Inventions (Clarinet Choir). *Angles of Entrance.* AArawak 004, 1996. Compact disc.

"Excerpts from a Report to the President by the National Advisory Panel on Selective Service." *New York Times,* March 5, 1967, 82.

Fabre, Michel, and John A. Williams. *A Street Guide to African Americans in Paris.* Paris: Cercle d'Études Afro-Americaines, 1996.

Facts about Berklee. [Accessed July 3, 2006.] Available from http://www.berklee.edu/about/facts.html.

Feather, Leonard. "The Blindfold Test: Benny Carter." *Down Beat,* November 23, 1961, 39.

———. "The Blindfold Test: Miles Davis." *Down Beat,* June 18, 1964, 31.

———. "The Blindfold Test: Phil Woods." *Down Beat,* October 14, 1971, 33.

———. "The Blindfold Test: Ruby Braff." *Down Beat,* January 21, 1960, 37.

———. "Feather's Nest." *Down Beat,* February 15, 1962, 40.

———. "Feather's Nest: The New Esthetic." *Down Beat,* June 15, 1967, 15.

———. *Inside Jazz.* New York: Da Capo Press, [1949] 1976.

———. "Sonny Rollins: Blindfold Test, Part Two." *Down Beat,* August 16, 1962.

Feldman, Morton. *New Directions in Music 2: Morton Feldman.* Columbia/Odyssey MS 6090, 1969. Vinyl disc.

Figi, J. B. "Chicago/Wild Onions." *Change* 2 (Spring/Summer 1966): 21–23.

———. "Jazz: A Family for the New Music." *Chicagoland and FM Guide,* November 1968, 19–21.

———. "Still Too Much a Stranger: Fred Anderson Quartet's Metallic Cocaine Bebop." *Chicago Reader,* October 20, 1972, 1.

"Final Bar [passing of Charles Clark]." *Down Beat,* May 29, 1969, 10, 13.

"Final Bar [passing of Christopher Gaddy]." *Down Beat,* April 18, 1968, 14.

Fischlin, Daniel and Ajay Heble, eds. *The Other Side of Nowhere: Jazz, Improvisation, and Communities in Dialogue.* Middletown: Wesleyan University Press, 2004.

"Flashes (announcement of AACM Nessa and Delmark recordings)." *Jazz Hot* 250, May 1969, 12.

"Flashes (announcement of arrival of AACM musicians in Paris)." *Jazz* 168, July -August 1969, 14.

Fleming, King. *King! The King Fleming Songbook.* Southport Records S-SSD 0041, 1995. Compact disc.

Fleming, Robert. "John A. Williams: A Writer beyond 'Isms." *Black Issues Book Review* 4, no. 4 (2002): 46–48.

Floyd, Samuel A., Jr. "Music in the Harlem Renaissance: An Overview." In *Black Music in the Harlem Renaissance: A Collection of Essays,* ed. Samuel A. Floyd Jr., 1–27. Knoxville: University of Tennessee Press, 1990.

———. *The Power of Black Music: Interpreting Its History from Africa to the United States.* New York: Oxford University Press, 1995.

———, ed. *International Dictionary of Black Composers.* Chicago and London: Fitzroy Dearborn, 1999.

Ford, Alun. *Anthony Braxton: Creative Music Continuum.* Exeter, Great Britain: Stride Publications, 1997.

Foster, Hal. *Recodings: Art, Spectacle, Cultural Politics.* Seattle: Bay Press, 1985.

"France Bars Thornton as Panther 'Suspect.'" *Down Beat,* April 29, 1971, 8–9.

Fraser, Wilmot Alfred. "Jazzology: A Study of the Tradition in Which Jazz Musicians Learn to Improvise." PhD dissertation, University of Pennsylvania, 1983.

Frazier, E. Franklin. *Black Bourgeoisie: The Rise of a New Middle Class in the United States.* New York: Collier Books, [1957] 1969.

"Free Jazz sur Seine." *Jazz* 169–70, September 1969, 19–22.

Freeman, Chico. *Chico.* India Navigation IN 1031, 1977. Vinyl disc.

———. *Live at Ronnie Scott's.* DRG Records S1425, 1986. Compact disc.

———. *You'll Know When You Get There.* Black Saint 120128, 1988. Compact disc.

Freeman, Chico, and Von Freeman. *Freeman and Freeman.* India Navigation IN 1070, [1981] 1989. Compact disc.

Freeman, Chico, featuring Arthur Blythe. *Focus.* Contemporary, 1995. Compact disc.

Friedman, Sharon, and Larry Birnbaum. "Fred Anderson: AACM's Biggest Secret." *Down Beat,* March 8, 1979, 20–21, 48.

Gabbard, Krin. *Jazz among the Discourses.* Durham: Duke University Press, 1995.

———. "Ken Burns's 'Jazz': Beautiful Music, But Missing a Beat." *Chronicle of Higher Education* 47, no. 16 (2000): B18.

———. *Representing Jazz.* Durham: Duke University Press, 1995.

Gable, David, and Christoph Wolff, eds. *A Life for New Music: The Fromm Music Foundation 1952–1987; Selected Papers of Paul Fromm.* Cambridge: Department of Music, Harvard University, 1988.

Gagne, Cole. *Soundpieces 2: Interviews with American Composers.* Metuchen, N.J.: Scarecrow Press, 1993.

Gann, Kyle. *American Music in the Twentieth Century.* New York: Schirmer Books, 1997.

Georgia Historical Society. *Camilla and Zack Hubert Homesite.* [Accessed November 20, 2005.] Available from http://www.georgiahistory.com/Markers/Markers04/camillaz.htm.

Giddins, Gary. "The ABCs of Muhal's Life Line." *Village Voice,* June 19, 1978, 63–64.

———. "Inside Free Jazz: The AACM in New York." *Village Voice,* May 30, 1977, 46–48.

———. "Leroy Jenkins's Territorial Imperative." *Village Voice,* April 24, 1978, 68.

———. "Weather Bird: American Money for American Music." *Village Voice,* January 2, 1978, 68.

———. "Weather Bird: Goings On about Town." *Village Voice,* August 29, 1977, 76.

———. "Weather Bird: Riffing about Music." *Village Voice,* February 3, 1975, 106–7.

———. "Weather Bird: Up from the Saloon: Lofts Celebrate Alternate Jazz." *Village Voice,* June 7, 1976, 82.

Gifford, Barry. "Chicago: The 'New' Music." *Jazz & Pop,* January 1969, 40–41.

Gilmore, Samuel. "Coordination and Convention: The Organization of the Concert World." *Symbolic Interaction* 10, no. 2 (1987): 209–27.

———. "Minorities and Distributional Equity at the National Endowment for the Arts." *Journal of Arts Management, Law and Society* 23, no. 2 (Summer 1993): 137–73.

Gilroy, Paul. "Sounds Authentic: Black Music, Ethnicity, and the Challenge of a 'Changing' Same." *Black Music Research Journal* 11, no. 2 (1991): 111–36.

Gioia, Ted. *The Imperfect Art: Reflections on Jazz and Modern Culture.* New York: Oxford University Press, 1988.

Globokar, Vinko. "Reflexionen über Improvisation." In *Improvisation und neue Musik: Acht Kongressreferate,* ed. Reinhold Brinkmann, 24–41. Mainz: Schott, 1979.

Goddet, Laurent. "Kahil El'Zabar: The Preacher." *Jazz Hot,* October 1978, 26–28.

———. "La fête de la biere." *Jazz Hot,* July-August 1976, 40–42.

———. "Le Grand George." *Jazz Hot* 351–352, Summer 1978, 17–23.

Goehr, Lydia. *The Imaginary Museum of Musical Works: An Essay in the Philosophy of Music.* Oxford: Oxford University Press, 1992.

Goldberg, RoseLee. *Performance Art: From Futurism to the Present.* New York: Harry N. Abrams, 1988.

Gordon, Frank. *Clarion Echoes.* Soul Note 121096, [1985] 1993. Compact disc.

Graham, Lawrence Otis. *Our Kind of People: Inside America's Black Upper Class.* New York: HarperCollins, 1999.

Gravenites, Nick. *Whole Lotta Soul/Drunken Boat.* Out of Sight Records, 1965. Vinyl disc.

Gray, Herman S. *Cultural Moves: African Americans and the Politics of Representation.* Berkeley: University of California Press, 2005.

————. "Jazz Tradition, Institutional Formation, and Cultural Practice." In *Cultural Moves: African Americans and the Politics of Representation.* Berkeley: University of California Press, 2005.

Griffin, Farah Jasmine. *If You Can't be Free, Be a Mystery: In Search of Billie Holiday.* New York: Free Press, 2001.

————. *"Who Set You Flowin'?": The African-American Migration Narrative.* New York: Oxford University Press, 1995.

Griffin, Sean. PhD qualifying examination, University of California, San Diego, 2001.

Gros, Renzo Pognant. Review of AACM Summer Festival in Chicago. *Musica Jazz,* December 1978, 38–39.

Grossman, James R. *Land of Hope: Chicago, Black Southerners, and the Great Migration.* Chicago: University of Chicago Press, 1989.

Grossman, Kate N. "Joel Alexander Brandon, 56, Master Whistler, Composer." *Chicago Sun-Times,* July 19, 2003, 38.

"Guggenheim to Mingus; Protest at Foundation." *Down Beat,* May 27, 1971, 8.

Guthartz, Jason. *Anthony Braxton Discography.* [Accessed March 8, 2007.] Available from http://restructures.net/BraxDisco/BraxDisco.htm

Haas, Danielle. "Black Hebrews Fight for Citizenship in Israel." *San Francisco Chronicle,* November 15, 2002.

Haley, Alex. *Roots.* Garden City, N.Y.: Doubleday, 1976.

Halliburton Jr., R. *The Tulsa Race War of 1921.* San Francisco: R and E Research Associates, 1975.

Hampel, Gunter. *The 8th of July 1969.* Birth 001, 1969.

Hardt, Michael, and Antonio Negri. "What the Protesters in Genoa Want." *New York Times,* July 20, 2001, A21.

Harriott, Joe. *Abstract.* Polygram/Redial 538183, 1962. Compact disc.

————. *Free Form.* Polygram/Redial 538184, 1961. Compact disc.

Harris, Eddie. *The Electrifying Eddie Harris.* Atlantic 1495, 1967. Vinyl disc.

————. *Exodus to Jazz.* Collectables 7145, 1960. Compact disc.

————. *Plug Me In.* Atlantic 1506, 1968. Vinyl disc.

————. *The Tender Storm.* Atlantic 1478, 1966. Vinyl disc.

Harris, Vandy. *Pure Fire.* Self-published, 1996. Compact disc.

Harrison, Max. "Donaueschingen 1957: One of the 'Dead Sea Scrolls' of Jazz." *Jazz Journal International,* December 1977, 32–33.

————. Review of Roscoe Mitchell recording, *Congliptious. Jazz Monthly* 171, June 1969, 28–29.

Harvey, David. *The Condition of Postmodernity: An Enquiry into the Origins of Cultural Change.* Cambridge, Mass: Blackwell, 1993.

Hawkins, Seton. "Sathima Bea Benjamin: Jazz, Community, and Gender." BA thesis, Columbia University, 2005.

"Heavy 75: Who's Who in the Chicago Alternative Culture." *Chicago Reader,* September 27, 1974.

Heble, Ajay. *Landing on the Wrong Note: Jazz, Dissonance, and Critical Practice.* New York: Routledge, 2000.

Hechinger, Fred M. "The Demand Grows for 'Black Studies.'" *New York Times,* June 23, 1968, E9.

Heckman, Don. "Caught in the Act: The Jazz Composers Guild." *Down Beat,* February 11, 1965, 37–38.

Heffley, Mike. *The Music of Anthony Braxton.* Westport, Connecticut: Greenwood Press, 1996.

———. *Northern Sun, Southern Moon: Europe's Reinvention of Jazz.* New Haven: Yale University Press, 2005.

Henahan, Donal. "The New and Newer Music Fails to Impress at Tully." *New York Times,* January 27, 1973, 20.

Hentoff, Nat. *The Jazz Life.* New York: Dial Press, 1961.

———. "The New Jazz: Black, Angry, and Hard to Understand." *New York Times Magazine,* December 23, 1966, 34–39.

Hernton, Calvin. "Umbra: A Personal Recounting." *African American Review* 27, no. 4 (1993): 579–84.

Hersh, Burton. "The Secret Life of Lincoln Center." *Town and Country,* January 1980, 71–72, 109–13.

Hine, Darlene Clark. "Black Migration to the Urban Midwest: The Gender Dimension, 1915–1945." In *The Great Migration in Historical Perspective,* ed. Joe William Trotter. Bloomington: Indiana University Press, 1991.

———. "The Black Studies Movement: Afrocentric-Traditionalist-Feminist Paradigms for the Next Stage." *Black Scholar* 22 (1992): 11–18.

Hirsch, Arnold R. *Making the Second Ghetto: Race and Housing in Chicago, 1940–1960.* Chicago: University of Chicago Press, [1983] 1998.

Hirsch, James S. *Riot and Remembrance: America's Worst Race Riot and Its Legacy.* New York: Houghton Mifflin, 2002.

Holzaepfel, John. *David Tudor and the Performance of American Experimental Music, 1950–1959.* PhD dissertation, City University of New York, 1993.

hooks, bell. "An Aesthetic of Blackness: Strange and Oppositional." In *Yearning: Race, Gender, and Cultural Politics,* 103–13. Boston: South End Press, 1990.

———. "Performance Practice as a Site of Opposition." In *Let's Get It On: The Politics of Black Performance,* ed. Catherine Ugwu, 210–21. Seattle: Bay Press, 1995.

Hoover, J. Edgar. "Memorandum to Special Agent in Charge, Albany, New York." In *Modern Black Nationalism,* ed. William Van Deburg, 122–23. New York: New York University Press, [1967] 1997.

How They Took the Stars and Stripes from the American Center in Paris: The Bohen and Mellon Foundations and the Death of a Cultural Institution, 1996. Available from http://www.capitalresearch.org/crc/fw/fw-0396.html.

"Internal Revenue Service Foundation Status Classification, National Council of the Association for the Advancement of Creative Musicians." Copy in collection of Muhal Richard Abrams, January 18, 1985.

Isotope 217. *Utonian_Automatic.* Thrill Jockey 063, 1999. Compact disc.

Ives, Charles. *Ives Plays Ives*. CRI CD 837 DDD, 1999. Compact disc.

Iyer, Vijay. *Sun Ra: A Music Full of Africa*. [Accessed November 25, 2005.] Available from http://www.cnmat.berkeley.edu/~vijay/mbase2.html.

Jackson, John Shenoy. "Intra-Office Memorandum to all AACM Members: Festival Income and Current Expenses." Archives of Evod Magek, 1975.

Jackson, Travis Arnell. "Performance and Musical Meaning: Analyzing 'Jazz' on the New York Scene." PhD dissertation, Columbia University, 1998.

James, Michael. Review of Lester Bowie recording, *Numbers 1&2*. *Jazz Monthly* 160, June 1968, 16.

James, Richard S. "ONCE: Microcosm of the 1960s Musical and Multimedia Avant-Garde." *American Music* 5, no. 4 (1987): 359–90.

Jamin, Jean, and Patrick Williams. "Glossaire et index des musiciens de jazz." *L'homme* 158–59 (2001): 301–38.

Jarman, Joseph. "AACM History: Interview with Leo Smith." Collection of Shaku Joseph Jarman. Tape recording, New York City, January 2, 1981.

———. *As If It Were the Seasons*. Delmark DD-417, 1968. Compact disc.

———. *Black Case*. Vols. 1 and 2. *Return from Exile*. Chicago: Art Ensemble of Chicago Publishing Company, 1977.

———. "Gens en peine: L'Art Ensemble de Chicago vous offre cette musique pour Noël." *Le Monde,* December 24, 1969, 14.

———. "New York." *Change* 2 (Spring/Summer 1966): 10.

———. "On Questions Asked of Me by Jerry Figi on Our Music." *New Regime* 2 (1968): 18–19.

———. *Pachinko Dream Track 10*. Music & Arts 1040, 1999. Compact disc.

———. *Song For*. Delmark DD-410, 1967. Compact disc.

Jarman, Joseph, and Famoudou Don Moye. *Egwu-Anwu (Sun Song)*. India Navigation, 1978. Vinyl disc.

Jarman, Joseph, Quintet. Concert program. Jamil B. Figi Donation, Chicago Jazz Archive, University of Chicago, August 16, 1965.

"Jazz Grants." *Down Beat,* October 25, 1973, 46.

"Jazz Musicians Group in Chicago Growing." *Down Beat,* July 28, 1966, 11.

"Jazzy Beat Poet Known for 'Bird Lives' Graffiti, Dies." *New York Times,* May 18, 2003, sec. 1, p. 43.

Jenkins, Leroy. *For Players Only*. JCOA LP 1010, 1975.

———. *Leroy Jenkins' Driftwood: The Art of Improvisation*. Mutable Music 17523-2, 2005. Compact disc.

———. *Leroy Jenkins' Sting: Urban Blues*. Black Saint 120083, 1984. Compact disc.

———. *Mixed Quintet*. Black Saint 120060, 1979. Compact disc.

———. *Space Minds, New Worlds, Survival of America*. Tomato TOM-2032, [1978] 2003. Compact disc.

———. *Themes and Improvisations on the Blues*. CRI CR663, 1994. Compact disc.

Jenkins, Willard. "Midwest Musings." *Jazz Times,* November 1987, 20.

"Job Announcement for Administrator." Archives of Evod Magek, September 14, 1981.

Johnson, James Weldon, edited with an introduction by William L. Andrews. *The Autobiography of an Ex-Colored Man.* New York: Penguin Books, [1912] 1990.

Johnson, Tom. "The Kitchen Improvises." *Village Voice,* September 24–30, 1980, 72.

———. "New Music, New York, New Institution." *Village Voice,* July 2, 1979, 88–89.

———. *The Voice of New Music: New York City 1972–1982.* Eindhoven: Het Apollohuis; and Paris: Editions 75, 1989. [Accessed November 8, 2005.] Available at http://homepage.mac.com/javiruiz/English/booksenglish.html.

Jones, Hettie. *How I Became Hettie Jones.* New York: E. P. Dutton, 1990.

Jones, LeRoi. *Dutchman.* In *Political Stages: Plays That Shaped a Century,* ed. Emily Mann and David Roessel, 131–59. New York: Applause Theater and Cinema Books, [1964] 2002.

———. "Jazz and the White Critic: A Provocative Essay on the Situation of Jazz Criticism." *Down Beat,* August 15, 1963, 16–17, 34.

———. "New York Loft and Coffee Shop Jazz." *Down Beat,* May 9, 1963, 13, 42.

———. "Tokenism: 300 Years for Five Cents." In *Home: Social Essays,* 68–81. New York: William Morrow, 1966.

Jost, Ekkehard. "Die europäische Jazz-Emanzipation." In *That's Jazz: Der Sound des 20. Jahrhunderts,* ed. Klaus Wolbert, 501–12. Darmstadt: Verlag Jürgen Häusser, 1997.

———. *Europas Jazz, 1960–80.* Frankfurt am Main: Fischer Taschenbuch Verlag, 1987.

———. *Free Jazz.* New York: Da Capo Press, [1975] 1994.

———. *Jazzmusiker: Materialen zur Soziologie der afro-amerikanischen Musik.* Frankfurt am Main: Ullstein Materialen, 1982.

———. *Sozialgeschichte des Jazz in den USA.* Frankfurt am Main: Wolke-Verlag, 1991.

Jules-Rosette, Bennetta. "Black Paris: Touristic Simulation." *Annals of Tourism Research* 21, no. 4 (1994): 679–700.

Kardiner, Abram, and Lionel Ovesey. *The Mark of Oppression: Explorations in the Personality of the American Negro.* Cleveland: World Publishing Company, [1951] 1962.

Karenga, Ron. "Black Cultural Nationalism." In *The Black Aesthetic,* ed. Addison Gayle Jr., 32–38. New York: Doubleday, 1971.

Kart, Lawrence. "Maurice McIntyre." *Down Beat,* April 16, 1970, 22–23.

———. Review of Richard Abrams recording, *Levels and Degrees of Light. Down Beat,* November 14, 1968, 20.

———. Review of Roscoe Mitchell recording, *Congliptious. Down Beat,* February 6, 1969, 26–27.

Katerine, Philippe. Interview with Brigitte Fontaine, 2003. [Accessed November 23, 2005.] Available from http://katerine.free.fr/katint10.htm.

Keepnews, Peter. "Public Domain." *Soho Weekly News,* September 27, 1979, 23–24, 50.

Kelley, Robin D. G. "Dig They Freedom: Meditations on History and the Black Avant-Garde." *Lenox Avenue: A Journal of Interartistic Inquiry* 3 (1997): 13–27.

Kim, Rebecca Y. "Sound Experiments in Chicago: John Cage and Improvisation." Paper delivered at the 32nd Annual Conference of the Society for American Music, Chicago, Illinois, March 16, 2006.

Kimmelman, Michael. "The Dia Generation." *New York Times,* April 6, 2003, sec. 6, p. 30.

King, Martin Luther. "Beyond Vietnam." In *Voices of a People's History of the United States*, ed. Howard Zinn and Anthony Amove, 423–427. New York: Seven Stories Press, 2004.

Klee, Joe H. "Caught in the Act: Don Cherry and the Jazz Composers Orchestra." *Down Beat*, May 10, 1973, 33.

Knauer, Wolfram. "Emanzipation wovon? Zum Verhältnis des amerikanischen und des deutschen Jazz in den 50er und 60er Jahren." In *Jazz in Deutschland: Darmstädter Beiträge zur Jazzforschung*, vol. 4, ed. Wolfram Knauer. Hofheim: Wolke Verlag Hofheim, 1996.

Kofsky, Frank. *Black Nationalism and the Revolution in Music.* New York: Pathfinder, 1970.

———. "Black Nationalism in Jazz: The Forerunners Resist Establishment Repression, 1958–1963." *Journal of Ethnic Studies* 10, no. 2 (1982): 1–27.

———. "Horace Tapscott." *Jazz & Pop*, December 1969, 16–18.

Koppel, Lily. "For These Street Players, Brass Runs in the Family." *New York Times*, September 4, 2006, sec. E; col. 1; Arts/Cultural Desk, 1.

Kostelanetz, Richard. *Conversing with Cage.* New York: Routledge, [1987] 2003.

———, ed. *Dictionary of the Avant-Gardes.* Chicago: A cappella books, 1993.

Lake, Steve. "Moers Festival." *Wire*, August 1986, 14–15.

Lange, Art. Review of Anthony Braxton recording, *For Four Orchestras. Down Beat*, June 7, 1979, 18.

Langer, Susanne K. *Feeling and Form: A Theory of Art . . .* New York: Scribner, 1953.

———. *Philosophy in a New Key: A Study in the Symbolism of Reason, Rite, and Art.* Cambridge: Harvard University Press, 1942.

LaScala, Pete. "Chords and Discords: Letter to the Editor." *Down Beat* (1979): 9, 46.

Lashley, Yorel. "Walking into the Sun after Many Rainy Seasons: The Association for the Advancement of Creative Musicians and the Mississippi Freedom Schools and Their Redefinition of African-American Identity." MA Thesis, University of Wisconsin-Madison, 1998.

Lawrence, Ken. "The C.O. 'Camps.'" *Nation*, June 28, 1980, 773–74.

———. *Noam Chomsky on Kosovo (FWD).* 1999. [Accessed November 22, 2005.] Available from http://mailman.lbo-talk.org/1999/1999-March/005970.html. March 30, 1999.

———. *Thirty Years of Selective Service Racism.* Chicago: National Black Draft Counselors, 1971.

Lees, Gene. *Cats of Any Color: Jazz Black and White.* New York: Oxford University Press, 1994.

———. "Newport Jazz Festival: The Trouble." *Down Beat*, August 18, 1960, 20–23, 44.

———. "Report on Chicago." *Down Beat*, February 18, 1960, 18–22.

———. *You Can't Steal a Gift: Dizzy, Clark, Milt, and Nat.* Lincoln and London: University of Nebraska Press, 2001.

Lehman, Stephen H. *I Love You with an Asterisk: African-American Experimental Composers and the French Jazz Press, 1970–1980.* 2004. [Accessed November 22, 2005.] Available from http://repository.lib.uoguelph.ca/ojs/index.php, 2005, 38–53.

Lesage, Philippe. "Kahil Le Prophète." *Jazz Hot* 370, February 1980, 40.

Levin, Jean. "Au profit des Panthères: Concert au profit des Black Panthers." *Jazz* 181, September 1970, 11.

Levin, Robert. "The Emergence of Jimmy Lyons." In *Music and Politics,* ed. John Sinclair and Robert Levin. New York and Cleveland: World Publishing, 1971.

———. "The Jazz Composers Guild: An Assertion of Dignity." *Down Beat,* May 6, 1965, 17–18.

Levine, Lawrence W. "Jazz and American Culture." In *The Jazz Cadence of American Culture,* ed. Robert G. O'Meally, 431–47. New York: Columbia University Press, 1998.

Levy, Beth E. "'The White Hope of American Music'; or, How Roy Harris Became Western." *American Music* 19, no. 2 (Summer 2001): 131–67.

Lewan, Todd, and Dolores Barclay. "'When They Steal Your Land, They Steal Your Future'; History: Study details black landowners' losses, now worth millions." *Los Angeles Times,* December 2, 2001, A1.

Lewis, George E. "Afterword to 'Improvised Music after 1950': The Changing Same." In *The Other Side of Nowhere: Jazz, Improvisation, and Communities in Dialogue,* ed. Daniel Fischlin and Ajay Heble. Middletown, Conn.: Wesleyan University Press, 2004.

———. *Changing with the Times.* New World Records 80434-2, 1993. Compact disc.

———. *Chicago Slow Dance.* Lovely Music LP 1101, 1977. Vinyl disc.

———. *Endless Shout.* Tzadik 7054, 2000. Compact disc.

———. *The George Lewis Solo Trombone Record.* Sackville 3012, 1976. Compact disc.

———. "'Gittin' to Know Y'All': Von improvisierter Musik, vom Treffen der Kulturen und von der 'racial imagination.'" In *Jazz und Gesellschaft: Sozialgeschichtliche Aspekte des Jazz,* ed. Wolfram Knauer, 213–47. Hofheim: Wolke-Verlag, 2002.

———. *Gittin' to Know Y'All: Improvised Music, Interculturalism and the Racial Imagination.* 2004. [Accessed November 22, 2005.] Available from http://repository.lib.uoguelph .ca/ojs/viewarticle.php?id=28&layout=html, 2005, 1–33.

———. *Homage to Charles Parker.* Black Saint 120029, 1980. Compact disc.

———. "Improvised Music after 1950: Afrological and Eurological Perspectives." In *The Other Side of Nowhere: Jazz, Improvisation, and Communities in Dialogue,* ed. Daniel Fischlin and Ajay Heble, 131–62. Middletown, Conn.: Wesleyan University Press, 2004.

———. Interview by Mary Lui, Chicago Historical Society, Chicago, Illinois, June 23, 1999.

———. Interview by telephone by Douglas Ewart, March 3, 2004.

———. "Purposive Patterning: Jeff Donaldson, Muhal Richard Abrams, and the Multidominance of Consciousness." *Lenox Avenue* 5 (1999): 63–69.

———. *Sequel (For Lester Bowie): A Composition for Cybernetic Improvisors.* Intakt CD 111, 2006. Compact disc.

———. *The Shadowgraph Series: Compositions for Creative Orchestra.* Spool Line 13, 2001. Compact disc.

———. "Singing Omar's Song: A (Re)construction of Great Black Music." *Lenox Avenue: A Journal of Interartistic Inquiry* 4 (1998): 69–92.

———. "Teaching Improvised Music: An Ethnographic Memoir." In *Arcana: Musicians on Music,* ed. John Zorn. New York: Granary Books, 2000.

Lewis, George, and Douglas Ewart. *George Lewis/Douglas Ewart.* Black Saint 120026, 1979. Compact disc.

Libois, Jean-Louis. "Kahil el Zabar (concert review)." *Jazz* 282, January 1980, 17.

Lipsitz, George. Interview with Julius Hemphill. July 31, 1994.

———. "Like a Weed in a Vacant Lot: The Black Artists Group in St. Louis." In *Decomposition: Post-Disciplinary Performance,* ed. Sue-Ellen Case, Philip Brett, and Susan Foster, 50–61. Bloomington and Indianapolis: Indiana University Press, 2000.

———. "Listening to Learn and Learning to Listen: Popular Culture, Cultural Theory, and American Studies." *American Quarterly* 42, no. 4 (1990): 621–36.

Litwack, Leon F. *Trouble in Mind: Black Southerners in the Age of Jim Crow.* New York: Alfred A. Knopf, 1998.

Litweiler, John B. "AACM's 10th Anniversary: An Interview with Muhal Richard Abrams, Founder and Father Figure." *Chicago Reader,* May 9, 1975, 13.

———. "AACM's 10th Anniversary: New Voices in the Wilderness." *Chicago Reader,* May 9, 1975, 12.

———. "Air: Impossible to Pigeonhole." *Down Beat,* December 16, 1976, 22, 50–51.

———. "Air: Uncommon Ensemble Excitement from the Streets of Chicago." *Chicago Reader,* December 17, 1976, 28–31.

———. "Altoists and Other Chicagoans." *Coda,* March 1967, 28–29.

———. "Caught in the Act: Kalaparusha and the Light." *Down Beat,* July 18, 1974, 38.

———. "Caught in the Act: Oliver Lake / Julius Hemphill." *Down Beat,* June 12, 1969, 34–35.

———. "Caught in the Act: Roscoe Mitchell." *Down Beat,* July 25, 1968, 29–32.

———. "Caught in the Act: Various Artists." *Down Beat,* October 19, 1967, 44, 47.

———. "The Chicago Scene." *Coda,* May 1967, 36–38.

———. "Chicago's AACM." *Sounds and Fury,* June 1966, 45.

———. "Chicago's Richard Abrams: A Man with an Idea." *Down Beat,* October 5, 1967, 23, 26, 41.

———. *The Freedom Principle: Jazz after 1958.* New York: Da Capo, 1984.

———. "The New Music." *Coda,* March 1968, 33–34.

———. "The New Music." *Coda,* July 1968, 35.

———. "Roscoe Mitchell: A Funny Thing Happened on the Way to Perfection." *Chicago Reader,* September 31, 1975, 36–37.

———. "Sax Player, Bandleader Vandy Harris Dies at 63; Thrived in AACM Movement." *Chicago Sun-Times,* July 29, 2005, 68.

———. "Von Freeman: Underrated but Undaunted." *Down Beat,* November 4, 1976, 16–17, 36.

Lock, Graham. *Forces in Motion: The Music and Thoughts of Anthony Braxton.* New York: Da Capo Press, 1988.

Locke, Alain. *The Negro and His Music.* New York: Arno Press and the *New York Times,* 1969.

Loewen, James W. *The Mississippi Chinese: Between Black and White.* Prospect Heights: Waveland Press, 1988.

Looker, Benjamin. *BAG: "Point from Which Creation Begins": The Black Artists Group of St. Louis.* St. Louis: Missouri Historical Society Press, 2004.

————. "'Poets of Action': The St. Louis Black Artists' Group, 1968–1972." *Gateway-Heritage, The Quarterly Magazine of the Missouri Historical Society* 22, no. 1, Summer (2001): 16–27.

Lott, Eric. "Double V, Double-Time: Bebop's Politics of Style." In *The Jazz Cadence of American Culture,* ed. Robert G. O'Meally, 457–68. New York: Columbia University Press, 1998.

Loupien, Serge. "Les aleas de la Haye, helas!" *Jazz* 289, September 1980, 36–37.

Lui, Mary. Interview with Jamil B. Figi. Transcript. Chicago Historical Society, Chicago, Illinois, October 29 and November 6, 1998.

Lutz, H. B. "Varese at the Gate: Brief but Potent." *Village Voice,* November 19, 1958, 9.

MacDonald, J. Fred. *Blacks and White TV: African Americans in Television since 1948,* 2nd ed. Chicago: Nelson-Hall Publishers, 1992.

Madhubuti, Haki R. *From Plan to Planet: Life-Studies; The Need for Afrikan Minds and Institutions.* Chicago: Third World Press, 1973.

Magek, Evod. *Through Love to Freedom.* Vol. 1. Black Pot Records, 1998. Compact disc.

Mahon, Maureen. *Right to Rock: The Black Rock Coalition and the Cultural Politics of Race.* Durham: Duke University Press, 2004.

Maia. *Introducing . . . Maia.* M'Ladiah Productions MBM 105, 2000. Compact disc.

Mailer, Norman. *Existential Errands.* New York: New American Library, 1973.

Mamiya, Lawrence H., and C. Eric Lincoln. *The Black Church in the African-American Experience.* Durham: Duke University Press, 1990.

Mandel, Howard. Interview with Muhal Richard Abrams and George Lewis, New York City. August 3, 2006.

Margasak, Peter. "Brass in the Blood." *Chicago Reader,* July 25, 2003. [Accessed November 20, 2005.] Available from http:// www.chicagoreader.com / hitsville / 030725.html.

Marmande, Francis. "Kalaparusha, alias Maurice McIntyre." *Jazz,* December 1977, 32–33.

————. "Travail de la citation: Espace rupture." *Jazz* 194, November 1971, 16–19.

Marsalis, Wynton. "What Jazz Is—And Isn't." *New York Times,* July 31, 1988, 21, 24.

Martin, Douglas. "Henry Pleasants, 89, Spy Who Knew His Music." *New York Times,* January 14, 2000, B11.

Martin, Terry. "Blowing Out in Chicago: Roscoe Mitchell." *Down Beat,* April 6, 1967, 20–21, 47–48.

————. "Chicago: The Avant Garde." *Coda,* December -January 1966–67, 21.

————. "The Chicago Avant-Garde." *Jazz Monthly* 157, March 1968, 12–18.

Mayfair Academy. *Tommy Sutton.* [Accessed November 20, 2005.] Available from http:// www.May fairacademy.net / ma / mrsutton.html.

McClary, Susan. *Conventional Wisdom.* Berkeley: University of California Press, 2000.

McElfresh, Suzanne. "Julius Hemphill." *Bomb,* Fall 1994, 46–49.

McGuire, John M. "Farewell to Utopia: Laclede Town." *Everyday Magazine, St. Louis Post-Dispatch,* February 12, 1995, 1D.

McIntyre, Kalaparusha Maurice. "The A.A.C.M." *New Regime* 1, no. 1 (1968): 1–2.

————. *Humility in the Light of the Creator.* Delmark DD-419, 1969. Compact disc.

———. *Morning Song.* Delmark DG-553, 2004. Compact disc.

———. *Peace and Blessings.* Black Saint 120037, 1979. Compact disc.

———. *Ram's Run.* Cadence CJR1009, 1982. Vinyl disc.

McIntyre, Kalaparusha Maurice, and the Light. *South Eastern.* CIMP 247, 2002. Compact disc.

McMichael, Robert K. "'We Insist—Freedom Now!': Black Moral Authority, Jazz, and the Changeable Shape of Whiteness." *American Music* 16, no. 4 (1998): 375–416.

McWhinnie, Charles. "'Light' Henry Huff, Jazz Musician." *Chicago Sun-Times,* April 2, 1993, 58.

"Member Leola Hubbard and Family Honored with Centennial Heritage Farm Award." *Carson Valley Views,* Spring 2004. [Accessed November 20, 2005.] Available from https://www.carsonvalley.org/newsletters/VIEWSSpring04.pdf.

Menter, Will. "The Making of Jazz and Improvised Music: Four Musicians' Collectives in England and the USA." PhD dissertation, University of Bristol, 1981.

Mercer, Kobena. *Welcome to the Jungle: New Positions in Black Cultural Studies.* New York: Routledge, 1994.

Merriam, Alan, and Raymond Mack. "The Jazz Community." *Social Forces* 38 (1960): 211–22.

Messiaen, Olivier. *Technique de mon langage musical.* Paris: A. Leduc, 1944.

———. *The Technique of My Musical Language.* Trans. John Satterfield. Paris: A. Leduc, 1956.

Metalitz, Steve. "The Status of a Non-existent Market." *Chicago Reader,* May 26, 1972.

Mingus, Charles. "Another View of Coleman." *Down Beat,* May 26, 1960, 21.

———. *The Great Concert of Charles Mingus.* Verve B0000AKNJL, [1964] 2004.

———. *Newport Rebels.* Candid CCD 79022, 1960. Compact disc.

Mintz, Sidney W., and Richard Price. *The Birth of African-American Culture: An Anthropological Perspective.* Boston: Beacon Press, 1992.

Mitchell, Charles. "Caught in the Act: The Fred Anderson Sextet." *Down Beat,* June 3, 1976, 35–36.

Mitchell, Nicole. *Nicole Mitchell/Black Earth Ensemble: Afrika Rising.* Dreamtime 004, 2002. Compact disc.

———. *Nicole Mitchell/Black Earth Ensemble: Vision Quest.* Dreamtime Records, 2001. Compact disc.

Mitchell, Roscoe. *Congliptious.* Nessa N-2, 1968. Compact disc.

———. *L-R-G; The Maze; SII Examples.* Nessa NCD-14, 1978. Compact disc.

———. *Nonaah.* Nessa 9/10, 1977. Vinyl disc.

———. *Quartet Featuring Muhal Richard Abrams.* Sackville 2009, 1975. Compact disc.

———. Quartet recording: Unreleased tape. Collection of Roscoe Mitchell, 1962.

———. *The Roscoe Mitchell Solo Saxophone Concerts.* Sackville 2006, 1974.

———. *Solo [3].* Mutable Music 17515, 2004. Three compact discs.

———. *Sound.* Delmark DD-408, 1966. Compact disc.

Mitchell, Roscoe, and Muhal Richard Abrams. *Duets and Solos.* Black Saint 120133, 1993. Compact disc.

Mitchell, Roscoe, and the Sound Ensemble. *3 X 4 Eye*. Black Saint 120050, 1994. Compact disc.

Mizrahi, Moshe. "Les stances à Sophie ("Sophie's Ways")." 1970.

MJT+3. *Daddy-O Presents MJT+3*. Cadet LP 621, 1957. Vinyl disc.

Monson, Ingrid. *Saying Something: Jazz Improvisation and Interaction*. Chicago: University of Chicago Press, 1996.

Montias, John Michael. "Public Support for the Performing Arts in Europe and the United States." In *Nonprofit Enterprise in the Arts,* ed. Paul DiMaggio, 287–319. New York: Oxford University Press, 1986.

Moondog. *Jazztime U.S.A.: Rimshot; Improvisation in 4/4; Improvisation in 7/4*. Brunswick BL54001, 1953.

Moore, F. Richard. *Elements of Computer Music*. Englewood Cliffs, N.J.: Prentice-Hall, 1990.

Morgan, Robert P. *Twentieth-Century Music: A History of Musical Style in Modern Europe and America*. New York: W. W. Norton, 1991.

Morgenstern, Dan. "Caught in the Act: Titans of the Tenor Sax." *Down Beat,* April 7, 1966, 35–37.

———. "Jazz in the '70s: No Energy Crisis." *Down Beat,* January 1980, 19–20, 71.

———. "Yale's Conservatory without Walls." *Down Beat,* December 7, 1972, 11, 38.

Morgenstern, Dan, and Martin Williams. "The October Revolution: Two Views of the Avant-Garde in Action." *Down Beat,* November 19, 1964, 15, 33.

Morris, Lawrence D. "Butch." *Testament: A Conduction Collection*. New World Records 80478, 1995. Set of 10 compact discs.

Moten, Fred. *In the Break: The Aesthetics of the Black Radical Tradition*. Minneapolis: University of Minnesota, 2003.

Moye, Famoudou Don, and Enoch Williamson. *Afrikan Song*. AECO/Southport 3009, 1998. Compact disc.

Murchison, Gayle. "'Dean of Afro-American Composers' or 'Harlem Renaissance Man': The New Negro and the Musical Poetics of William Grant Still." In *William Grant Still: A Study in Contradictions,* ed. Catherine Parsons Smith, 39–65. Berkeley: University of California Press, 2000.

Murray, Diedre, and Fred Hopkins. *Stringology*. Black Saint 120143, 1993. Compact disc.

Music from the ONCE Festival, 1961–1966. New World Records 80567.

"Musician's Group Here Gives Avant Garde Recital." *Chicago Defender* (daily edition), October 19, 1971, 14–15.

Myers, Amina Claudine. "A Day in the Life . . . . By Ariae." Manuscript. Unpaged. Collection of Amina Claudine Myers, 1967[?].

———. *Amina Claudine Myers Salutes Bessie Smith*. Leo Records, 1980. Compact disc.

———. *Jumping in the Sugar Bowl*. Minor Music, 1984. Compact disc.

———. *Women in (E)motion*. Tradition und Moderne T&M 102, 1993. Compact disc.

Nai, Larry. "Interview with Greg Osby." *Cadence,* May 2001, 5–16.

"NEA Grants to Jazz for '80." *Down Beat,* July 1980, 11, 14, 72.

Neff, Renfreu. *The Living Theatre: U.S.A.* Indianapolis: Bobbs-Merrill, 1970.

"Negro Protest Ends at Northwestern U." *New York Times,* May 5, 1968, 31.

"Negroes Protest at Northwestern." *New York Times,* May 4, 1968, 27.

Nelson, Alondra. "Introduction: Future Texts." *Social Text 71,* vol. 20, no. 2 (2002): 1–15.

Ness, Bob. "Profile: Leo Smith." *Down Beat,* October 7, 1976, 36–37.

Nessa, Chuck. "New Music Report." *Coda,* October / November 1966, 20.

New York Art Quartet. *New York Art Quartet.* ESP Records, 1964.

Newsome, Thomas Aldridge. "It's After the End of the World! Don't You Know That Yet? Black Creative Musicians in Chicago, 1946–1976." PhD dissertation, University of North Carolina at Chapel Hill, 2001.

Nicholson, Reggie. *Solo Concept.* Abstract Recordings 02, 2005. Compact disc.

Nijinski, David. "La musique à bout de bras: Program note, Concert of the Art Ensemble of Chicago, Théâtre du Lucernaire." In *Larayne Black Collection, Chicago Historical Society,* 1969.

Noble, David W. *Death of a Nation: American Culture and the End of Exceptionalism.* Minneapolis: University of Minnesota Press, 2002.

Noglik, Bert. *Jazz-Werkstatt International.* Berlin and Hamburg: Verlag Neue Musik and Rowohlt Taschenbuch Verlag, 1982.

———. *Klangspuren: Wege improvisierter Musik.* Frankfurt am Main: Fischer Taschenbuch Verlag, 1990.

Nolan, Herb, and Ray Townley. "Ann Arbor Blues and Jazz Festival." *Down Beat,* October 25, 1973.

Nyman, Michael. *Experimental Music: Cage and Beyond,* 2nd ed. New York: Schirmer Books, 1999.

O'Hara, Frank. "New Directions in Music: Morton Feldman." In *Give My Regards to Eighth Street: Collected Writings of Morton Feldman, with an afterword by Frank O'Hara,* ed. B. H. Friedman, 211–17. Cambridge, Mass.: Exact Change Press, 2000.

O'Meally, Robert G., Brent Hayes Edwards, and Farah Jasmine Griffin, ed. *Uptown Conversation: The New Jazz Studies.* New York: Columbia University Press, 2004.

"Obituary for Ameen Muhammad." Gatling's Chapel, Chicago, Illinois, March 5, 2003. [Accessed December 1, 2005.] Available from http:// www.jazzhope.com/ review _2003_03_05.htm.

"Obituary for Evod Magek." Carter Funeral Chapel, Chicago, Illinois, October 14, 2005.

"Obituary for Vandy Harris." Trinity United Church of Christ, Chicago, Illinois, August 5, 2005.

Occhiogrosso, Peter. "Anthony Braxton Explains Himself." *Down Beat,* August 12, 1976, 15–16, 49.

———. "Don't Stop the Carnival, Just Keep It out of the Classroom." *Soho Weekly News,* September 21, 1978, 84, 111.

Oda, Ken. *A. B. Spellman of the Arts Endowment, on the NEA's Impact on the Arts.* [Accessed November 19, 2001.] Available from http:// www.koanart.com/ nea.html.

Oja, Carol. *Making Music Modern: New York in the 1920s.* New York: Oxford University Press, 2000.

Olatunji, Babatunde, with Robert Atkinson, assisted by Akinsola Akiwowo. *The Beat of My Drum: An Autobiography.* Philadelphia: Temple University Press, 2005.

Oliver, Paul. *Savannah Syncopators: African Retentions in the Blues.* New York: Stein and Day, 1970.

Olshausen, Ulrich. "Von Blues Bis Free-Jazz: Alles Dran: Berliner Jazztage 1973 war ein voller Erfolg." *Jazz Podium,* December 1973, 20–22.

Palmer, Robert. Liner notes to recording, *Creative Construction Company,* vol. 1. Muse Records MR 5071, 1975.

———. "Pop: Newport Newcomers." *New York Times,* June 10, 1973, 30.

———. "WKCR Will Start 90 Straight Hours of Jazz Tonight." *New York Times,* May 14, 1977, 34.

Panish, Jon. *The Color of Jazz: Race and Representation in Postwar American Culture.* Jackson: University of Mississippi Press, 1997.

Panken, Ted. Radio interview with Alvin Fielder. WKCR-FM, New York City. Transcript. Collection of Ted Panken, July 1, 2002.

———. Radio interview with Eddie Harris. WKCR-FM, New York City, June 24, 1994. [Accessed December 1, 2005.] Transcript. Available from http://www.jazzhouse.org/library/index.php3?sel=Interviews.

———. Radio interview with George Lewis and Leo Smith. WKCR-FM, New York City, September 12, 1995. [Accessed November 22, 2005.] Transcript. Available from http://www.jazzhouse.org/library/index.php3?sel=Interviews.

———. Radio interview with Johnny Griffin. WKCR-FM, New York City, April 18, 1990. Transcript. Collection of Ted Panken.

———. Radio interview with Joseph Jarman. WKCR-FM, New York City, February 15, 1987. Transcript. Collection of Ted Panken.

———. Radio interview with Joseph Jarman. WKCR-FM, New York City, June 17, 1987. [Accessed November 29, 2005.] Transcript. Available from http://www.jazzhouse.org/library/index.php3?sel=Interviews.

———. Radio interview with Leroy Jenkins. WKCR-FM, New York City, October 12, 1993. [Accessed December 1, 2005.] Transcript. Available from http://www.jazzhouse.org/library/index.php3?sel=Interviews.

———. Radio interview with Lester Bowie and Don Moye. WKCR-FM, New York City, November 22, 1994. [Accessed November 22, 2005.] Transcript. Available from http://www.jazzhouse.org/library/index.php3?sel=Interviews.

———. Radio interview with Richard Davis. WKCR-FM, New York City, August 18, 1993. Transcript. Available from http://www.jazzhouse.org/library/index.php3?sel=Interviews.

———. Radio interview with Roscoe Mitchell. WKCR-FM, New York City, December 5, 1995. [Accessed November 30, 2005.] Transcript. Available from http://www.jazzhouse.org/library/index.php3?sel=Interviews.

———. Radio interview with Thurman Barker. WKCR-FM, New York City, February 15, 1995. [Accessed December 1, 2005.] Transcript. Available from http://www.jazzhouse.org/library/index.php3?sel=Interviews

———. Radio interview with Von Freeman. WKCR-FM, New York City, June 7, 1987. [Accessed November 30, 2005.] Transcript. Available from http://www.jazzhouse.org/library/index.php3?sel=Interviews.

Pareles, Jon. "Pop View: Classical and Jazz Artists Meet Halfway." *New York Times,* March 15, 1987, sec. 2, 27.

Parker, Charlie, and John McLellan. Interview with Charlie Parker, June 13, 1953. [Accessed November 17, 2005.] Available from http://www.plosin.com/milesAhead/BirdInterviews.html#530600.

Pasler, Jann. "Musique et institution aux États-Unis." *Inharmoniques* 2, May 1987, 104–34.

"Pay Last Tribute to Gaddy, 74." *Chicago Defender* (Big Weekend Edition), September 4, 1971, 24.

Pease, Ted. *The Schillinger/Berklee Connection.* [Accessed July 3 2006.] Available from http://www.berklee.edu/bt/122/connection.html.

Peretti, Burton W. "Oral Histories of Jazz Musicians: The NEA Transcripts as Texts in Context." In *Jazz among the Discourses,* ed. Krin Gabbard, 117–33. Durham: Duke University Press, 1995.

Pharaohs, The. *The Awakening.* Ubiquity/Luv N' Haight, 1972.

Piazza, Tom. *Blues Up and Down: Jazz in Our Time.* New York: St. Martin's Press, 1997.

Pleasants, Henry. *The Agony of Modern Music.* New York: Simon and Schuster, 1955.

———. *Death of a Music? The Decline of the European Tradition and the Rise of Jazz.* London: Jazz Book Club, 1962.

Plonsey, Dan. *Roscoe Mitchell Discography (Preliminary).* 2003. [Accessed July 4, 2006. Available from http://www.plonsey.com/beanbenders/Roscoedisco.html.

Poggioli, Renato. *The Theory of the Avant-Garde.* Translated from the Italian by Gerald Fitzgerald. Cambridge: Belknap Press of Harvard University Press, 1968.

Polillo, Arrigo. "Adesso c'è la "new thing": Discordante, aspra, furibonda." *Epoca* 1969.

Porter, Eric. *What Is This Thing Called Jazz? African American Musicians as Artists, Critics, and Activists.* Berkeley: University of California Press, 2002.

Postif, François. "KFQ-4/6F." *Jazz Hot,* April 1971, 14–17.

"Potpourri. [Announcement about the Art Ensemble.]" *Down Beat,* December 19, 1974, 11.

"Potpourri. [Announcement of concerts by Jazz Composers Orchestra Association.]" *Down Beat,* May 11, 1972, 11.

"Potpourri. [Announcement of Steve McCall in Germany.]" *Down Beat,* November 14, 1968, 13.

"Potpourri. [Announcement of symposium by the Collective Black Artists.]" *Down Beat,* May 11, 1972, 11.

Primack, Bret. "Leroy Jenkins: Gut-Plucking Revolutionary." *Down Beat,* November 16, 1978, 23–24, 50–51.

Prince, Linda. "Betty Carter: Bebopper Breathes Fire." *Down Beat,* May 3, 1979, 12–14, 43.

Quinn, Bill. "The AACM: A Promise." *Down Beat Music '68,* 1968, 46–50.

———. "Caught in the Act: Joseph Jarman." *Down Beat,* March 9, 1967, 27–28.

Radano, Ronald M. "The Jazz Avant-Garde and the Jazz Community: Action and Reaction." In *Annual Review of Jazz Studies* 3, ed. Dan Morgenstern, Charles Nanry, and David A. Cayer, 71–79. New Brunswick: Transaction Books, 1985.

———. *New Musical Figurations: Anthony Braxton's Cultural Critique.* Chicago: University of Chicago Press, 1993.

Ratliff, Ben. "A Pleasant Swim with Gunther Schuller, The Man Who Named the Third Stream." *New York Times,* March 20, 2001, E1.

"*Reader*'s Heavy Sixty." *Chicago Reader,* September 29, 1972.

"*Reader*'s Pop Poll 1973." *Chicago Reader,* March 1, 1974, 1–2.

Reich, Howard. "Ameen Muhammad, 48 [obituary]." *Chicago Tribune,* March 4, 2003, 9.

———. "Malachi Favors, 76; Bass Player's Style Was Distinctive, Influential." *Chicago Tribune,* February 3, 2004, 6.

Revolutionary Ensemble. *The Psyche.* Mutable Music 17514-2, [1975] 2002. Compact disc.

Riggins, Roger. "Caught in the Act: The Revolutionary Ensemble." *Down Beat,* October 26, 1972, 34.

Robinson, Michael. "The Association: The 'New Thing' Is Their Thing." *Chicago Tribune,* Sunday Magazine, November 24, 1968.

Rockwell, John. "As Important as Anyone in His Generation." *New York Times,* February 21, 1988, sec. 2, p. 27.

———. "Face of Jazz Is Changing Visibly." *New York Times,* June 4, 1974, 33.

———. "Jazz: Two Braxton Programs." *New York Times,* April 23, 1982, C32.

———. "A New Music Director Comes to the Avant-Garde Kitchen." *New York Times,* September 14, 1980, sec. 2, p. 23.

———. "New Music in America." *Journal of American Culture* 4, no. 4 (1981): 132–38.

Rollins, Sonny. *Our Man in Jazz.* BMG 7 4321 19256-2, 1962.

Rosen, Louis. *The South Side: The Racial Transformation of an American Neighborhood.* Chicago: I. R. Dee, 1998.

Ross, Andrew. *No Respect: Intellectuals and Popular Culture.* London: Routledge, 1989.

Rout, Leslie B., Jr. "AACM: New Music (!) New Ideas (?)." *Journal of Popular Culture* 1 (1967): 128–10.

———. "Reflections on the Evolution of Post-War Jazz." *Negro Digest,* February 1969, 32–34, 92–97.

Rouy, Gérard. "Moers." *Jazz,* July -August 1986, 23–24.

Rubin, Nathan. *John Cage and the Twenty-six Pianos: Forces in American Music from 1940–1990.* Moraga, Calif.: Sarah's Books, 1994.

Ruff, Willie. *A Call to Assembly: The Autobiography of a Musical Storyteller.* New York: Viking, 1991.

Rusch, Bob, and Hillary J. Ryan. "William Parker." *Cadence,* December 1990, 5–16, 77.

Rusch, Robert D. "*Down Beat* News: CBA Conference Seeks Unity of Black Artists." *Down Beat,* July 20, 1972, 10–11.

Russell, Hal. *MusicWeb Encyclopaedia of Popular Music.* [Accessed March 13, 2007.] Available from http://www.musicweb.uk.net/encyclopaedia/r/R173.HTM.

Saal, Hubert, and Abigail Kuflik. "Jazz Comes Back!" *Newsweek,* United States edition, August 8, 1977, 51–57.

Sachs, Lloyd. "Fred Hopkins, Jazz Bassist, Dies." *Chicago Sun-Times,* January 9, 1999.

———. "Jazz Festival Plays as Concert or Ambience for Lawn Party." *Chicago Sun-Times,* September 10, 1987, 66.

———. "Quality Fest Falls Short of Greatness." *Chicago Sun-Times,* September 7, 1987, 23.

Samana. *Samana.* Storywiz, 1996. Compact disc.

Sanders, Cheryl J. *African-American Worship in the Pentecostal and Holiness Movements.* [Accessed March 15, 2007.] Available from http://wesley.nnu.edu/wesleyan_theology/theojrnl/31–35/32-2-6.htm.

———. *Saints in Exile: The Holiness-Pentecostal Experience in African American Religion and Culture.* New York: Oxford University Press, 1996.

Sandow, Gregory. "But Is It Art?" *Village Voice,* March 4–10, 1981, 63.

Sandrow, Nahma. "Center-Stage Living, at Balcony Rents." *New York Times,* June 9, 2002, sec. 11, col. 5, Real Estate Desk, 1.

Saunders, Frances Stonor. *The Cultural Cold War: The CIA and the World of Arts and Letters.* New York: New Press, 1999.

Schatzberg, Rufus, and Robert J. Kelly. *African-American Organized Crime: A Social History.* New Brunswick: Rutgers University Press, 1996.

Schillinger, Joseph. *The Mathematical Basis of the Arts.* New York: Philosophical Library, [1948] 1966.

———. *The Schillinger System of Musical Composition.* New York: Da Capo Press, [1941] 1978.

Schuller, Gunther. "Sonny Rollins and the Challenge of Thematic Improvisation." In *Musings: The Musical Worlds of Gunther Schuller,* 86–97. Oxford: Oxford University Press, [1958] 1986.

———. "Third Stream." In *Musings: The Musical Worlds of Gunther Schuller,* 114–18. New York and Oxford: Oxford University Press, 1986.

Sells, Mike. *Avant-Garde Performance and the Limits of Criticism: Approaching the Living Theatre, Happenings/Fluxus, and the Black Arts Movement.* Ann Arbor: University of Michigan Press, 2005.

Semmes, Clovis E. "The Dialectics of Cultural Survival and the Community Artist: Phil Cohran and the Affro-Arts Theater." *Journal of Black Studies* 24, no. 4 (1994): 447–61.

Seniors, Paula Marie. "Beyond Lift Every Voice and Sing: The Culture of Uplift, Identity, and Politics in Black Musical Theater." PhD dissertation, University of California, San Diego, 2003.

Shapiro, Peter. "Blues and the Abstract Truth: Phil Cohran." *Wire,* May 2001, 28–31.

Shelton, Joseph A., Jr. Obituary. Stinson Funeral Home, Detroit, Michigan, December 8, 2006.

Shepp, Archie. *Yasmina, A Black Woman.* BYG-Actuel 529304, 1969.

Shoemaker, Bill. "Avant-Garde." *Jazz Times,* September 2000, 60, 62, 64.

———. Review of recordings by Muhal Richard Abrams, George Lewis and Douglas Ewart, Ari Brown, and Ernest Dawkins. *Jazz Times,* July/August 1996, 94–95.

Silverstein, Steve. "Recording History: The AACM and the Chicago Avant-Garde Jazz Scene of the Mid-Sixties." *Tape Op,* Winter 1998/99, 56–58.

Smith, Arnold Jay. "Profile: John Stubblefield." *Down Beat,* January 29, 1976, 30.

Smith, Bill. "Leo Smith." *Coda,* November 1975, 2–9.

Smith, Wadada Leo. *Golden Quartet: The Year of the Elephant.* PI Recordings PI 04, 2002. Compact disc.

———. *Kabell Years 1971–1979.* Tzadik TZ 7610-4, 2004. Four compact discs.

———. "(M1) American Music." *Black Perspective in Music* 2, no. 2 (Autumn 1974): 111–16.

———. *Notes (8 pieces) source a new world music: creative music.* Self-published, 1973.

———. *Rhythm.* Self-published, 1976.

———. *Spirit Catcher.* Nessa N-19, 1979. Vinyl disc.

———. *Tao-Njia.* Tzadik 7017, 1996. Compact disc.

Smith, Will. Review of Roscoe Mitchell recording, *Congliptious. Jazz & Pop,* August 1969, 26.

Southern, Eileen. "Music Research and the Black Aesthetic." *Black World,* November 1973, 4–13.

Spangler, Bud. "The Home Front." *Change* 2 (Spring/Summer 1966): n.p.

Spellman, A. B. *Four Lives in the Bebop Business.* New York: Pantheon Books, 1966.

———. "Revolution in Sound: Black Genius Creates a New Music in Western World." *Ebony,* August 1969, 84–89.

Spencer, Jon Michael. *The New Negroes and Their Music: The Success of the Harlem Renaissance.* Knoxville: University of Tennessee Press, 1997.

Spivey, Donald. *Union and the Black Musician: The Narrative of William Everett Samuels and Chicago Local 208.* Lanham: University Press of America, 1984.

Stanyek, Jason. "Transmissions of an Interculture: Pan-African Jazz and Intercultural Improvisation." In *The Other Side of Nowhere: Jazz, Improvisation, and Communities in Dialogue,* ed. Daniel Fischlin and Ajay Heble, 87–130. Middletown: Wesleyan University Press, 2004.

Staples, Brent A. "Festival AACM à Chicago." *Jazz Hot,* October 1978, 30–31.

———. *Parallel Time: Growing Up in Black and White.* New York: Pantheon Books, 1994.

"State of Illinois Charter, Association for the Advancement of Creative Musicians, Chicago, Illinois." Copy in collection of George E. Lewis, August 5, 1965.

"State of New York Certificate of Incorporation, National Council of the Association for the Advancement of Creative Musicians." Copy in collection of Muhal Richard Abrams, November 18, 1982.

Stepto, Robert B. *Blue as the Lake: A Personal Geography.* Boston: Beacon Press, 1998.

Stern, Chip. Review of Muhal Richard Abrams recording, *Lifea Blinec. Down Beat,* October 5, 1978, 26–27.

Stewart, Jimmy. "Introduction to Black Aesthetics in Music." In *The Black Aesthetic,* ed. Addison Gayle, Jr., 81–96. New York: Doubleday, 1971.

Sticks and Stones. *Sticks and Stones.* 482 Music, 482-1012, 2002. Compact disc.

Still, William Grant. "A Negro Symphony Orchestra." *Opportunity,* September 1939, 267, 286–287.

Stockhausen, Karlheinz. *Texte zur Musik.* Köln: M.D. Schauberg, 1963.

Stovall, Tyler. *Paris Noir: African Americans in the City of Light.* Boston: Houghton Mifflin, 1996.

"Strictly Ad Lib [AACM concerts at Lincoln Center]." *Down Beat,* August 11, 1966, 13.

"Strictly Ad Lib [AACM concerts at Lincoln Center]." *Down Beat,* July 28, 1966, 12.

"Strictly Ad Lib [Announcement of AACM concert series]." *Down Beat,* October 7, 1965, 41.

"Strictly Ad Lib [Announcement of AACM formation]." *Down Beat,* September 9, 1965, 41.

"Strictly Ad Lib [Announcement of Amina Claudine Myers/Jerol Donavon club bookings]." *Down Beat,* October 6, 1966, 12.

"Strictly Ad Lib [Announcement of Roscoe Mitchell recording session]." *Down Beat,* September 22, 1966, 48.

"Strictly Ad Lib [Announcement of Sonny Rollins performance]." *Down Beat,* June 6, 1963, 10.

"Strictly Ad Lib [Jam session with Lester Bowie and Leroy Jenkins]." *Down Beat,* August 25, 1966, 14.

"Strictly Ad Lib [Performance of Joseph Jarman and Kim An Wong]." *Down Beat,* December 13, 1968, 54.

"Strictly Ad Lib. [Report on Newport Jazz Festival performance by Misha Mengelberg]." *Down Beat,* September 8, 1966, 43.

"Strictly Ad Lib: Chicago [Report on Ira Sullivan–Roland Kirk Quintet]." *Down Beat,* September 29, 1960, 65.

"Strictly Ad Lib: Chicago [Announcement of the passing of Nicky Hill]." *Down Beat,* August 1, 1963, 45.

Stubblefield, John. *Morning Song.* Enja ENJ-8036-2, 1993. Compact disc.

Student Non-Violent Coordinating Committee. "Position Paper on Black Power [1966]." In *Modern Black Nationalism,* ed. William Van Deburg, 112–23. New York: New York University Press, 1997.

Such, David. *Avant-Garde Jazz Musicians Performing Out There.* Iowa City: University of Iowa Press, 1993.

Sukenick, Ronald. *Down and In: Life in the Underground.* New York: William Morrow, 1987.

"The Sun Also Rises." *Down Beat,* March 29, 1962, 15.

Susilo, Hardja. "Changing Strategies for the Cross-Cultural Karawitan Experience: A Quarter-Century Perspective." Essay, 1986.

Sweet, Robert E. *Music Universe, Music Mind: Revisiting the Creative Music Studio, Woodstock, New York.* Ann Arbor: Arborville Publishing, 1996.

Szwed, John F. "Josef Skvorecky and the Tradition of Jazz Literature." *World Literature Today* 54, no. 4 (1980): 586–90.

———. *Space Is the Place: The Lives and Times of Sun Ra.* New York: Pantheon Books, 1997.

Szyfmanowicz, R. "Brigitte Fontaine, Areski et l'Art Ensemble de Chicago à La Fac Dauphine." *Jazz Hot* 262, June 1970, 6.

Talalay, Kathryn. *Composition in Black and White: The Life of Philippa Schuyler.* New York: Oxford University Press, 1995.

Tapscott, Horace. *Songs of the Unsung: The Musical and Social Journey of Horace Tapscott.* Edited by Steven Isoardi. Durham: Duke University Press, 2001.

Taylor, Arthur. *Notes and Tones: Musician-to-Musician Interviews.* New York: Da Capo Press, [1977] 1993.

"Technical Assistance Project Memo." Archives of Evod Magek, August 10, 1980.

Teitelbaum, Richard. "World Band." In *Soundings* 1, ed. Peter Garland. Self-published, 1972.

Terlizzi, Roberto. "Steve McCall." *Coda,* December 1974, 6–7.

Tesser, Neil. "AACM's 10th Anniversary: A Symbol of Committed Excellence." *Chicago Reader,* May 9, 1975, 14.

———. "*Reader's* Guide to Jazz." *Chicago Reader,* September 26, 1975, 35–36.

———. Review of the Montreux/Berlin Concerts. *Down Beat,* October 20, 1977, 22–24.

———. "Von and Chico Freeman: Tenor Dynasty." *Down Beat,* July 1980, 24–28.

———. "Whither the Avant-Garde?" *Chicago Reader,* February 7, 1975, x1–x2.

Thomas, Lorenzo. "Alea's Children: The Avant-Garde on the Lower East Side, 1960–1970." *African American Review* 27, no. 4 (1993): 573–78.

Thompson, Malachi. *Buddy Bolden's Rag.* Delmark DE-481, 1995. Compact disc.

Thompson, Robert Farris. "Mambo Minkisi: The Mind and Music of Leo Smith." *Coda,* November 1975, 10–12.

Threadgill, Henry. *Henry Threadgill's Zooid: Up Popped the Two Lips.* PI Recordings PI 02, 2001. Compact disc.

———. "Where Are Our Critics?" *New Regime* 1, no. 1 (1968): 11–12.

Threadgill, Henry, and Make a Move. *Everybody's Mouth's a Book.* PI Recordings PI 01, 2001. Compact disc.

———. *Where's Your Cup?* Columbia 67617, 1996. Compact disc.

Tisue, Seth. *Chicago Now: Old Listings.* 1995. [Accessed November 20, 2005.] Available from http://tisue.net/chicagonow/old1995.html.

Townley, Ray. "Heard and Seen: Richard Abrams." *Coda,* January 1973, 40–42.

———. "Lester . . . Who?" *Down Beat,* January 31, 1974, 11–12.

———. "Profile: Muhal Richard Abrams." *Down Beat,* August 15, 1974, 34.

Travis, Dempsey J. *An Autobiography of Black Chicago.* Chicago: Urban Research Press, 1981.

———. *An Autobiography of Black Jazz.* Chicago: Urban Research Press, 1983.

Tristano, Lennie. *Intuition.* Capitol Jazz CDP 7243 8 52771 2 2, 1949. Compact disc.

Tucker, Mark, ed. *The Duke Ellington Reader.* New York: Oxford University Press, 1993.

Tulsa Race Riot: A Report by the Oklahoma Commission to Study the Tulsa Race Riot of 1921. [Accessed November 20, 2005.] Available from htt://www.tulsareparations.org/TRR.htm.

Tura, Valerio. "Muhal, Il Primo." *Musica Jazz* 34, no. 4, April 1978, 14–15.

Tynan, John. Review of Ornette Coleman recording, *Free Jazz, Down Beat,* January 18, 1962, 28.

———. "Take 5." *Down Beat,* November 23, 1961, 40.

Tyner, McCoy. *Asante.* Blue Note 7243 4 93384 2 5, 1970. Compact disc.

The University of Iowa Electronic Music Studios: Alumni. [Accessed November 22, 2005.] Available from http://theremin.music.uiowa.edu/Alumni.html.

Van der Lelij, B., B. G. M. Völker, H. Steketee, and F. M. H. M. Driessen. *Componeren in Nederland.* Utrecht: Bureau Driessen, 1996.

Van Trikt, Ludwig. "Anthony Davis X." *Cadence,* November 1985, 5.

———. "Leroy Jenkins." *Cadence,* November 1997, 5–9.

Vincent, Ted. *Keep Cool: The Black Activists Who Built the Jazz Age.* London: Pluto Press, 1995.

Von Eschen, Penny M. *Satchmo Blows Up the World: Jazz Ambassadors Play the Cold War.* Cambridge: Harvard University Press, 2004.

Vuisje, Bert. *De nieuwe jazz: Twintig interviews door Bert Vuisje.* Baarn: Bosch & Keuning, 1978.

Wallace, Michele. *Black Macho and the Myth of the Superwoman.* London and New York: Verso, 1978.

Walton, Charles. *Dr. William "Bill" Fielder: Trumpeter and Jazz Improvisor.* 2004. [Accessed November 25, 2005. Available from http://www.jazzinchicago.org/Internal/Articles/tabid/43/ctl/ArticleView/mid/522/articleId/115/DrWilliamBillFieldertrumpeterandjazzimprovisor.aspx.

Wang, Richard. "Lecture by Dr. Richard Wang." Paper presented at the Trading Fours: Jazz and Its Milieu, University of Chicago, May 11, 2001.

Ware, Wilbur. *The Chicago Sound.* Riverside OJCCD-1737-2, 1957. Compact disc.

Washburn, Dick. "Frank Gordon's 'Kera's Dance' Solo." *Down Beat,* April 26, 1973, 33–34.

Washington, Salim. "'All the Things You Could Be by Now': Charles Mingus Presents Charles Mingus and the Limits of Avant-Garde Jazz." In *Uptown Conversation: The New Jazz Studies,* ed. Robert G. O'Meally, Brent Hayes Edwards, and Farah Jasmine Griffin. New York: Columbia University Press, 2004.

Watrous, Peter. "Jazz, Classical, Art, Business: A Series Wraps All into One." *New York Times,* August 2, 1994, C15.

———. "John Zorn Takes Over the Town." *New York Times,* February 24, 1989, C23.

Watson, Ben. *Derek Bailey and the Story of Free Improvisation.* London and New York: Verso, 2004.

Weathers, Diane. "The Collective Black Artists." *Black World* 23, no. 1 (1973): 72–74.

Welburn, Ron. "The Black Aesthetic Imperative." In *The Black Aesthetic,* ed. Addison Gayle, Jr., 132–49. New York: Doubleday, 1971.

Welburn, Ron, and Ralph Ellison. "Ralph Ellison's Territorial Vantage." In *Living with Music: Ralph Ellison's Jazz Writings,* ed. Robert G. O'Meally, 15–33. New York: Modern Library, [1976] 2001.

Welch, Jane. "Europe's Answer to Woodstock: The First Actuel Festival Paris Music Festival." *Down Beat,* January 22, 1970, 16–17, 31.

Welding, Pete. "Caught in the Act: Charlie Parker Memorial Concert." *Down Beat,* May 23, 1963, 36.

———. Review of Joseph Jarman/John Cage event. *Down Beat,* January 13, 1966, 35–36.

———. Review of Roscoe Mitchell concert. *Down Beat,* May 19, 1966, 44, 48.

Weller, Ellen. "Making Diversity in Urban America: The Intersections of Cultural Tourism, Public Arts Funding, and Multicultural Performance in San Diego, California." PhD dissertation, University of California, San Diego, 2002.

West, Cornel. *Keeping Faith: Philosophy and Race in America.* New York: Routledge, 1993.

Wexler, Haskell. *Medium Cool.* DVD-Video, Paramount 06907, 2001.

Whitehead, Kevin. "Fred Hopkins." *Coda* 196, 1984, 23–26.

———. *New Dutch Swing.* New York: Billboard Books, 1998.

Whitesell, Lloyd. "White Noise: Race and Erasure in the Cultural Avant-Garde." *American Music* 19, no. 2 (Summer 2001): 168–89.

Wickes, John. *Innovations in British Jazz*. Vol. 1, *1960–1980*. London: Soundworld, 1999.

Wildflowers: The New York Loft Jazz Sessions. Vols. 1–5. Casablanca / Douglas NBLP 7045, 7046, 7047, 7048, 7049, 1977. Vinyl discs.

Wildflowers: The New York Loft Jazz Sessions. Vols. 1–5. KnitClassics 3037, 2000. Compact discs.

Wilkerson, Edward L. Internal Memo. Exact date unknown, probably February. Archives of the AACM. 1978.

Wilkerson, Edward, and Shadow Vignettes. *Birth of a Notion*. Sessoms, 1985.

Willener, Alfred. *The Action-Image of Society: On Cultural Politicization*. Translated by A. M. Sheridan Smith. London: Tavistock Publications, 1970.

Williams, John A. *The Man Who Cried I Am*. Boston: Little, Brown, 1967.

Williams, Martin. "The Bystander." *Down Beat*, May 10, 1962, 39.

Williams, William Appleman. *The Contours of American History*. New York: W. W. Norton, 1988.

Willie, Sarah Susannah. *Acting Black: College, Identity, and the Performance of Race*. New York and London: Routledge, 2003.

Wilmer, Valerie. "Amina Claudine Myers." *Coda* 169, 1979, 4–6.

———. *As Serious As Your Life: The Story of the New Jazz*. London and New York: Serpent's Tail, [1977] 1992.

———. "Caught in the Act: Art Ensemble of Chicago." *Down Beat*, June 25, 1970, 26.

———. "Lester Bowie: Extending the Tradition." *Down Beat*, April 29, 1971, 13, 30.

———. *Mama Said There'd Be Days Like This: My Life in the Jazz World*. London: Women's Press, 1980.

Wilson, John S. "2 Jazz Festivals Open in Newport." *New York Times*, July 1, 1960, 13.

———. "Jazz Played on a Plastic Sax." *New York Times*, July 31, 1960, X9.

———. "Space Age Jazz Lacks Boosters: Cosmic Group Fails to Orbit with Rhythmic Propulsion." *New York Times*, February 19, 1962, 23.

———. " 'Village' Becomes Focal Point for Modern Jazz: Five Spot Café and the Half Note Spur the Move Downtown." *New York Times*, October 27, 1960, 43.

Wilson, Peter Niklas. *Anthony Braxton: Sein Leben, seine Musik, seine Schallplatten*. Waakirchen, Switzerland: Oreos Verlag, 1993.

Wong, Deborah Anne. *Speak It Louder: Asian Americans Making Music*. New York: Routledge, 2004.

Wright, Bruce. *Black Justice in a White World*. New York: Barricade Books, 1996.

Wright, Richard. *12 Million Black Voices*. New York: Thunder's Mouth Press, [1941] 1988.

X, Malcolm, with the assistance of Alex Haley. *The Autobiography of Malcolm X*. New York: Ballantine Books, 1973.

Xenakis, Iannis. *Formalized Music: Thought and Mathematics in Composition*. Bloomington: Indiana University Press, 1972.

———. "Musiques formelles." *La Revue Musicale* 253–54 (1963).

Yogananda, Paramahansa. *Autobiography of a Yogi*. Los Angeles: Self-Realization Fellowship, [1946] 1981.

Zabor, Rafi. "Funny, You Look Like a Jazz Musician." *Village Voice*, July 2, 1979, 72–73.

Zinn, Howard, and Anthony Amove, eds. *Voices of a People's History of the United States*. New York: Seven Stories Press, 2004

Zorn, John, ed. *Arcana: Musicians on Music*. New York: Granary Books, 2000.

ARCHIVES AND PRIVATE COLLECTIONS

AACM. Archives. Chicago, Illinois.

Abrams, Muhal Richard. Collection.

Black, Larayne. Collection. Chicago Historical Society.

Chicago Jazz Archive. Joseph Regenstein Library, University of Chicago.

Cowell, Henry. Collection. New York Public Library.

Jarman, Shaku Joseph. Collection.

Lewis, George E. Collection.

Magek, Evod. Archives.

Mitchell, Roscoe. Collection.

Myers, Amina Claudine. Collection.

Panken, Ted. Collection.

Index